THE NORTHROP FRYE QUOTE BOOK

THE NORTHROP FRYE QUOTE BOOK

Compiled by John Robert Colombo
WITH A BIOGRAPHICAL APPRECIATION BY JEAN O'GRADY

DUNDURN
TORONTO

Copyright © John Robert Colombo, 2014
Northrop Frye quotations copyright © Victoria University (in the University of Toronto), 2014
Introduction and Selection copyright © John Robert Colombo, 2014
Biographical appreciation copyright © Jean O'Grady, 2014

All rights reserved. No part of this publication may be reproduced, stored in a retrieval system, or transmitted in any form or by any means, electronic, mechanical, photocopying, recording, or otherwise (except for brief passages for purposes of review) without the prior permission of Dundurn Press. Permission to photocopy should be requested from Access Copyright.

Editor: Dominic Farrell
Design: Jesse Hooper
Printer: Webcom

Library and Archives Canada Cataloguing in Publication

Frye, Northrop, 1912-1991, author
    The Northrop Frye quote book / edited by John Robert Colombo ; foreword by Jean O'Grady.

Includes bibliographical references.
Issued in print and electronic formats.
ISBN 978-1-4597-1958-3 (pbk.) ISBN 978-1-4597-1947-7 (pdf).--
ISBN 978-1-4597-1948-4 (epub)

    1. Frye, Northrop, 1912-1991--Quotations. 2. Criticism--Quotations. I. Colombo, John Robert, 1936-, editor of compilation II. Title. III. Title: Quote book.

PN75.F7A25 2014   801'.95092   C2013-907425-2
                                            C2013-907426-0

1   2   3   4   5   18 17 16 15 14

We acknowledge the support of the **Canada Council for the Arts** and the **Ontario Arts Council** for our publishing program. We also acknowledge the financial support of the **Government of Canada** through the **Canada Book Fund** and **Livres Canada Books**, and the **Government of Ontario** through the **Ontario Book Publishing Tax Credit** and the **Ontario Media Development Corporation**.

Care has been taken to trace the ownership of copyright material used in this book. The author and the publisher welcome any information enabling them to rectify any references or credits in subsequent editions.

J. Kirk Howard, President

The publisher is not responsible for websites or their content unless they are owned by the publisher.

VISIT US AT
Dundurn.com | @dundurnpress | Facebook.com/dundurnpress | Pinterest.com/dundurnpress

Dundurn	Gazelle Book Services Limited	Dundurn
3 Church Street, Suite 500	White Cross Mills	2250 Military Road
Toronto, Ontario, Canada	High Town, Lancaster, England	Tonawanda, NY
M5E 1M2	L41 4XS	U.S.A. 14150

Contents

INTRODUCTION / JOHN ROBERT COLOMBO 7

BIOGRAPHICAL APPRECIATION / JEAN O'GRADY 11

QUOTATIONS 21

ACKNOWLEDGEMENTS 353

BIBLIOGRAPHY 355

Introduction

There is no Canadian writer of whom we can say what we can say of the world's major writers, that their readers can grow up inside their work without ever being aware of a circumference.

Northrop Frye came to that conclusion after a detailed study of the imaginative achievements of Canada's writers from the earliest period to 1965 when that sentence from his study first appeared in print. Over the decades since then, the statement has come to be regarded as a benchmark of individual and national literary achievement. It might or might not have been true at the time; it may or may not be true today. Its singular deficiency is that it fails to take into account the phenomenal cultural achievement of Northrop Frye himself.

When we think of the world's major writers, we tend to think of creative writers of poetry and fiction, and only then of the writers of dramas, essays, biographies, and memoirs. Only as an afterthought does it occur to us to include writers of criticism — literary, philosophical, social, cultural. Even with the admission of theoreticians and critics to the ranks of "creative writers," they are seen to be there "on sufferance," as lurkers rather than as full participants. Yet our understanding of the world and our appreciation of its literary heritage would be greatly diminished if we relegated theory and criticism to "also-ran" status. Robertson Davies, himself a novelist, essayist, and dramatist, was also a trenchant critic; he once observed that no one had ever erected a statue to a critic. For reasons of sentiment and patriotism, statues are regularly raised to honour popular (or once-popular) artists. Indeed, it has been claimed that there are more memorials to "the immortal memory" of Robert Burns in Canadian cities than there are in his native Scotland. But has any author of criticism ever been honoured with a single statue or public memorial in Scotland or Canada?

There is, however, no need to raise another monument to recall the achievement of Northrop Frye. His thirty-volume *Collected Works*, the effort of a lifetime and the twenty-year labour of dozens of scholars, is itself a considerable achievement, and a suitable memorial in keeping with the seriousness of a man of exceptional modesty (though there was nothing modest at all about his aims and objectives as a critic!). His presence is recalled in the naming of Northrop Frye Hall, which rises close by the E.J. Pratt Library on the campus of Victoria College, University of Toronto. Well it marks his association with that venerable educational institution from the year 1929, when at the age of seventeen he enrolled as an undergraduate, to the year of his death at the age of seventy-nine in 1991, when he served still as chancellor emeritus and university professor.

His courses on the symbolism of the Bible and on modern poetry, as well as those on Milton, Spenser, and the Renaissance, not to mention Blake, were hugely popular. It used to be said that students entered first year at Vic as believers in the existence of God; they lost their religious faith in second year; but they regained their faith in third year, when they realized that Northrop Frye was God! As well, for a heady period in the 1970s, Frye achieved renown as the world's most widely quoted contemporary scholar in the field of the humanities. In sum, he may well be the single Canadian author who offers his readers the opportunity to "grow up inside their work without being aware of a circumference."

The present book is a compilation of more than 3,600 quotations taken from the writings of Northrop Frye, writings both published and unpublished during his lifetime, selected to illuminate topics that were of special concern to him and are subjects of general interest to the reader today, whether scholar, student, or browser. The quotations appear under alphabetically arranged headings — approximately 1,140 of them, from A to Z — so that the reader may easily have at his or her fingertips the insights of one of the world's leading literary critics. The present work might be described as both encyclopaedic and episodic; Frye, in his own terms, would characterize it as both diachronic and synchronic.

To give some instances, included are entries on specific subjects — Accountants, Advertising, Atlantic Seaboard, Americanization — as well as on general subjects — Abstract Expressionism, Absurdity, Allegory, Art — to limit the inquiry to the first letter of the alphabet. Attempts have been made to select passages for inclusion that are short, self-contained, and significant. In describing a passage as "significant," what is meant is that the quoted matter is interesting in its own right or important in the eyes of the world.

The purpose of this dictionary of quotations is "to delight and instruct," to recall a touchstone remark: delight the specialist user with unexpected insights and instruct the novice reader with variations on received opinions. Both the specialist and the browser alike might express surprise at the author's erudition — particularly the immense range of works that Frye makes reference to in his studies, a range that displays his familiarity with both the serious literature of the past and the popular writing of the day (not that he would endorse those terms). In compiling these passages, I was always surprised at how much he had read and had noted. I was struck by the truth of David Staines's observation: "In whatever direction you happen to be going, you always meet Frye on his way back."

Frye took pains to employ a prose style that is plain and unadorned, seemingly artless. The word "seemingly" is important, because the adverb disguises the fact that the prose is versatile and enduring. Although some of these passages were written almost eighty years ago, it seems they have hardly aged at all.

This quoted matter is taken from a great range of sources over the decades: convocation and commencement addresses, scholarly presentations and speeches, interviews and reviews, essays and chapters of books. With a handful of exceptions, all of the passages are reproduced from the volumes of the *Collected Works*. (The temptation to include descriptions *of* Frye, often quite insightful and amusing ones, was resisted.) There are no quotations from his correspondence (except for some passages from the two volumes of the letters that he wrote to his wife Helen); no bon mots of the *obiter dicta* variety; and no marginalia from the 2,053 books from his own library that form part of the Frye Collection at the E.J. Pratt Library. (Scholars will find these sources to be worth exploring.) Yet there is "god's plenty" in what is included.

Gifted both as theoretician and as aphorist, Frye evolved grand schemes (one thinks of the Five Fictional Modes or the Four Forms of Prose Fiction, et cetera), and at the same time, he coined vivid expressions with droll wit and odd humour to "bring home" his schemes. (A favourite aphorism is irresistible: "Literature is conscious mythology.") As Alberto Manguel has noted, his writings are "rich with tempting asides." It seems his essays grew out of such "kernels" of thought. Indeed, he once explained, "The way I begin a book is to write detached aphorisms in a notebook, and 95 percent of the work I do in completing a book is to fit these detached aphorisms together into a continuous narrative line." Later, he added, "Most of my writings consist of an attempt to translate aphorisms into continuous prose."

The author returned time and again to the theme of the Order of Words, and pains have been taken here to follow the order of Frye's own words. Full sentences have been favoured, so there are few quotations with internal deletions. The ellipses that do sometimes intrude signify that the self-contained quotation does appear in the context of a longer passage that is simply too detailed or digressive to reprint.

As a popular speaker and commentator, with an exceptionally active academic, administrative, and writing career, Frye was called upon to deliver hundreds of addresses, presentations, talks, commentaries, and interviews. He completed over three hundred articles and reviews, published twenty-three books, and over the decades accepted thirty-one honourary degrees. It is not surprising that in addressing so many audiences and such a range of listeners and readers he availed himself of such opportunities to repeat many of his principal notions and fundamental formulations — Order of Words, Primary and Secondary Concerns, the veto over Value Judgments, the importance of Imagination, the autonomy of Literature, et cetera. So, repetition is characteristic of his *oeuvre*. It is not "vain repetition" but "elegant variation" — or, indeed, "theme and variation" — not unlike the thirteen ways of looking at a blackbird, or the thirty-two ways of looking at Glenn Gould. or the thirty-six ways to paint Mount Fuji.

In all of this, one finds that Frye's approach seemed fully realized from the outset. He knew his own mind all along; hence there is no Early Frye or Late Frye, only Middle Frye. While many of these pages feature themes and some of the innumerable variations upon them, preference has been given to earlier formulations over later ones, to basic statements over detailed ones, and to popular expressions over academic ones. No special attempt has been made to "date" his utterances other than to identify the years of their earliest appearances in print.

It was ten years ago that I set myself the task of reading all of Frye's writings, both published and unpublished, a feat made possible by the appearance over the last decade of the successive volumes of the *Collected Works*. I wish I could say I understood everything that I read — the Ogdoads *are* complicated! — but after a while I began to focus on the pattern behind the particulars. I came to the conclusion that Frye was no "absent-minded professor"; indeed, it is probably true that he had a memory that was eidetic. He could seemingly draw on recollections of everything that he had ever read and of everything that he had ever written. He was simply one of the great readers of our time. Harold Bloom called him "the foremost living student of Western literature," but he was also widely read in non-Western literature and philosophy. He had the ability to discern structures, not Platonic (based on visions) but Aristotelian (based on observations). The sociologist Edmund Carpenter, a one-time colleague on campus and sometime debating partner, once told me that Frye was "a genius of some kind." I have come to the conclusion that Carpenter was right.

The standard dictionary of quotations is a work of collective expression, a mosaic of the ideas, impressions, and opinions contributed by hundreds or thousands of thoughtful people over great periods of time. This is not such a book. The present work is a specialized dictionary of quotations, for it is based on the thoughts and writings of a single person; it is the handiwork of one contributor, albeit a remarkable one. It is evidence that there *is* a Canadian writer of whom it may be said that we as his readers can grow up inside his work "without ever being aware of a circumference."

Biographical Appreciation

JEAN O'GRADY

> *Northrop Frye*
> *What a guy*
> *Read more books than*
> *You or I*

So begins a ditty about Frye popular at one time among undergraduates at Victoria College. It captures the local view of Frye — affectionate, proprietorial, somewhat in awe of the great man but by no means overwhelmed.

There is a curious dichotomy between this picture of Frye and that of the eminent man-of-letters celebrated by the world at large. Frye became an international phenomenon, the literary critic who opened up criticism as a discipline in its own right, and adumbrated a vast structure for the whole of literature. His books have been translated into twenty languages, including Serbo-Croatian, Korean, and Portuguese; his theories have been used to elucidate works from Old English to Russian. Scholars have held conferences on his work in Canada, the United States, Australia, Italy, China, Korea, and Inner Mongolia. The Northrop Frye papers in the Victoria University Library contain letters from twenty-six different colleges and universities offering Frye a job — and this is just in the eighteen years between 1959 and 1977. The offers range from a permanent appointment as Mackenzie King Professor at Harvard to a position in the English Department at Arizona State University.

In spite of this worldwide fame, and his thirty-eight honorary degrees, Frye spent most of his working life at the (with all due respect) comparatively obscure Victoria College in the University of Toronto. He enrolled there as an undergraduate in the college in 1929, studying philosophy and English; then, after his graduation, he studied theology at Emmanuel, the theological college of Victoria University, while doing some part-time lecturing in the college English department. As it became apparent that teaching was his vocation, the college authorities helped to send him to England for two years, to round out his English studies at Merton College, Oxford University. He persevered there, in spite of finding Oxford "dismally cold, wet, clammy, muggy, damp, and moist, like a morgue." Upon finishing his studies at Oxford, he was relieved to be taken on permanently in the English Department at Victoria in 1939. There he remained, except for spells as a visiting professor, until his retirement. For years he rode the subway to work like any beginning lecturer, expounded his pass course in Biblical symbolism to undergraduates of every degree of sophistication, and often spent Saturday afternoons grading essays.

I first met him in this guise myself in 1960. I was going to study English Language and Literature and had been advised by my high-school guidance counsellor to enrol at Victoria so that I would, as they said, "get Frye." I did get him, for several courses, and an amazing figure he was: dumpy and pasty-coloured, with an almost shifty air, as if he didn't quite belong inside this mortal envelope. He would open his mouth and, in a quiet and unemphatic voice, give expression to the most searching analyses, the most suggestive generalizations, the most piercing insights, all in sentences and whole paragraphs perfectly controlled and modulated. Even his witty remarks were delivered deadpan, with just the occasional quick upturn at the side of his mouth if you seemed to get the joke.

Going back into the past, here's a reminiscence of Frye as a lecturer by one of his students in 1946, political columnist Douglas Fisher, who had just arrived at college under the veterans' preference with many other former soldiers:

> Our class, perhaps forty [people], was stiff. The general tone was serious, almost apprehensive. It reeked of both earnestness and doubt.... At 9:05, a slight chap walked in, his suit too large, a dour Russian quality about its hang and texture. He was blond, his hair heavy, but haloed with wisps and snarls. (In his younger days, this blond mop had earned him the nickname "Buttercup.") On first look, he seemed prissy, uncomfortable, yet curiously like a robot. Stiff — and we were stiffer.
>
> He began while staring out the window.... "My subject today is George Bernard Shaw...." and he was away. A tape recorder would have picked up little but the teacher's voice. Except for an occasional titter, the class didn't loosen up. When the bell rang, the man stopped talking, bobbed his head, and left.
>
> He was no sooner gone from the room when an uproar of comments made the place noisy.
>
> "This can't be university, it's too entertaining."
>
> "What's this man's name?"
>
> A girl beside me looked at me for seconds but her mind wasn't there. When her beatific smile finally broke, she said, "That was better than any movie I've ever seen."

> What I knew was — if this was university, I wanted a lot more of it, and the teacher.... What a break! Northrop Frye as first voice heard at university.

Frye was always the opposite of grandstanding or charismatic, the conduit of a force that came purely from the mind and owed nothing to physical stature. In 1950, when he spent a year as a visiting professor at Harvard, he went to a store where the proprietors took a friendly interest in the students. As Frye relates it, "The clerk asked me what I was studying, and I said, with only a touch of shrillness, that I was teaching. Just for the summer, of course. He wrapped my parcel, handed it to me, and said, 'I hope your permanent appointment comes through all right.'"

Working on *The Collected Writings of Northrop Frye*, I encountered another form of this contrast between appearance and reality. The edition includes not only the published works, but also letters written to his future wife Helen, diaries, and seventy-six densely packed notebooks, in which Frye wrestled with trains of thought, worked and re-worked the shapes of his books, and reflected on his own strengths and weaknesses. At the end of his life, instead of burning these notebooks, he allowed them to pass to the Northrop Frye Fonds at Victoria's E.J. Pratt Library, and thus implicitly gave us our liberty to publish them. It is not too much to say that they reveal an entirely new Frye, unsuspected by the general public and even by most of his associates: one given to waspish comments on his colleagues, or to politically incorrect remarks like "Probably one has to lie to men — certainly to women."

The letters written during his courtship of his wife have aroused much interest, a typical reaction being, "Who would have believed that Northrop Frye could be so amorous?" And who would believe, before the notebooks were published, that Frye longed to write a novel — indeed, to write eight novels, each in a different mode, covering between them all types of fiction from the comedy of manners to the war novel.

He is sometimes accused of being exclusively concerned with Western literature, yet these notebooks and diaries reveal that he was reading about Eastern philosophy in the 1940s, long before it became fashionable, and that he hoped to write what he called a "Bardo" novel based on inter-life existence as described in the *Tibetan Book of the Dead*.

His published works seem complicated enough, but it now appears that they were just the tip of the iceberg. His ambition was to write a series of eight books that he called the "ogdoad," which would survey the whole of human speculation, providing a guide to the symbolic universe, or what he once described as "the architecture of the spiritual world." Hayden White spoke more truly than he knew when he remarked that he sensed a subterranean Frye — that when talking to Frye he "had the feeling that he was always in that shop in the back of the mind of which Montaigne spoke, working on some intellectual issue."

In suggesting this series of contrasts, between inner man and public persona, awkward figure and eloquent speaker, Toronto teacher and international icon, I'm working with categories that are not exactly parallel. But I feel I have a warrant in the practice of Frye himself, that inveterate manipulator of equivalents, correspondences, and categories. The particular binary oppositions I've been suggesting seem to me important because they lead in to something very central to Frye's thought, which might best be described as the relation between the individual and his society. In Frye's case, the question involves his own Canadianness and his Protestant inheritance. How is the individual absolutely himself yet the committed member of a corporate entity? The question is parallel to one encountered in his literary criticism, where Frye maintained that he recognized the uniqueness of the work of art, while his critics complained that he was obliterating it by relating the work to generic and archetypal patterns.

As background to these matters, I'd like to look briefly at the outlines of Frye's thought as a whole. Though Frye first gained recognition with his book on Blake, *Fearful Symmetry*, in 1947, it was *Anatomy of Criticism*, published in 1957, that brought him worldwide attention. Written with verve and wit, this Canadian classic not only ushered in that explosion of serious critical thought that made "theory" the dominant genre in the last half of the twentieth century, but it also constituted a readable, civilized contribution to literary discourse in the tradition of Johnson, Arnold, and Eliot.

When it was written in the 1950s, literary criticism was a mixture of appreciation, explication of themes, study of sources and influences, biographies of authors, historical background, and the "New Criticism" that studied lyrical poems line-by-line. The *Anatomy*'s revolutionary proposal was that criticism was a science, of which all these practices were constituent parts, and it was so in virtue of the fact that literature itself forms its own universe with its own laws. Authors shape their works according to these laws or conventions, however much they may seem to be capturing life or expressing their emotions. Poems are made from other poems; or, in the words of Yeats,

> *There is no singing school but studying*
> *Monuments of its own magnificence.*

Thus, instead of a collection of individual works, organized mainly chronologically, you had a body of work that could be anatomized just as a human body could; and this is what Frye proceeded to do.

Criticism may look at literature from several different perspectives, expounded in the four main chapters of the book. In "First Essay: Historical Criticism," Frye sees the history of literature as the increasing displacement of a mythic core toward realism. As we move through the various modes — mythic in earliest time, romantic in the Middle Ages, high mimetic in the Renaissance, low mimetic in the nineteenth century, and ironic today — so the status and power of the hero decline from the god or godlike man of myth, through the ordinary man, to the victim or powerless man in irony. (Frye said that he used the term "man" for "man or woman" on Sydney

Smith's principle that "man generally embraces woman.") Non-narrative or thematic literature, such as most poetry, goes through a parallel sequence of five modes based on the relation between poet and audience.

The "Second Essay" approaches literature not as developing through time but as an organism spread out simultaneously in space. Here Frye introduces his notion of "polysemous meaning," that a text can be looked at on different levels; he suggests five such types of criticism, based largely on the approaches their practitioners take to symbolism — the literal, the descriptive, the formal, and then the archetypal and the anagogic, which are his particular province. On the archetypal level, we relate the poem to literature as a whole, studying genres, conventions, and images that are repeated from poem to poem. Seen as a whole, in its archetypal phase, literature visualizes the goal of human work, or of Paradise regained. The final phase, the anagogic, is difficult to grasp: in it, universal archetypal symbols such as the city, garden, quest, and marriage define a literature that has "swallowed" nature: the distinction between man as perceiving subject and nature as object has disappeared, and "nature is now inside the mind of an infinite man who constructs his cities out of the milky way." Sometimes I think of this as the ecologist's nightmare.

The details of archetypal criticism, studied in the "Third Essay," are organized into two areas, the static and the dynamic. Statically, Frye discerns two groups of archetypal symbols, corresponding to the two extremes of wish and nightmare: the apocalyptic imagery of gardens, sheepfolds, bread and wine, and so on, which are the metaphors of human desire, and the demonic imagery of monsters, waste lands, and fiery furnaces, which define all that man rejects. For the dynamic movement of plot, Frye invokes one of the most basic patterns, the cycle, as in the changing of the year from spring, to summer, to fall, to winter, and back to spring. He distinguishes four basic, pre-generic plot types — comedy, romance, tragedy, and irony, which he positions on this circle.

Finally, the "Fourth Essay" discusses rhetorical criticism, in which literature is looked at according to the genres such as epic, lyric, and satire.

This approach to literature was so novel and so suggestive that within a few years Frye had become the darling of North American graduate-school English departments; carrying a copy of his book was the very hallmark of the serious and up-to-date student. He was the first individual critic to have a conference of the English Institute dedicated to his work, in 1965, at which time Murray Krieger made his oft-quoted remark that "he has had an influence — indeed an absolute hold — on a generation of developing critics greater and more exclusive than that of any one theorist in recent critical history." Of course, this influence was subject to historical fluctuation: during the heyday of Deconstruction some years later, any attempt to see a grand structure was suspect, and Frye became for a while a past number.

But even at the time of its publication, there was considerable resistance to *The Anatomy of Criticism*. Some critics, appalled at the *Anatomy*'s encyclopaedic subdivisions, balked at the thought that swallowing such an enormous pill was necessary for its salutary effects. Frye always denied the accusation that he was trying to make everyone accept his whole "system," or that his project was like a straitjacket; he remarked to an interviewer that perhaps he would ultimately be found less useful as a systematizer than as a quarry for later thinkers, "a kind of lumber-room ... a resource person for anyone to explore and get ideas from." He also declared his own indifference to his future reputation: "If posterity doesn't like me, the hell with posterity — I won't be living in it anyway."

Perhaps the major contemporary criticism of the *Anatomy* was that the book minimized the writer's immediate involvement in and meaning for his society. To Frye's annoyance, the literary establishment associated him particularly with two specific ideas, that criticism should be a science, and that the role of the critic was not to evaluate individual works. For some objectors, this turned literature into an autonomous verbal structure to be studied in and for itself, cut off from social history, from its authors' concerns, and from the realistic representation of the world. The Fryegian critic seemed a dry anatomist, utterly uninvolved in the needs of his readers for guidance and wisdom, and of his society for literary discourse.

Even on a personal and biographical level, the notion that Frye as a critic was removed from society and its concerns was radically unjust, as he was always deeply involved in Canadian culture. He may have worked out his critical principles from his study of William Blake, but he honed them on Canadian poetry: for ten years, from 1951 to 1960, he wrote the "Poetry in English" section of the *University of Toronto Quarterly*'s annual survey of Canadian literature, for which he had to read virtually all the poetry published during the preceding twelve months. This, in the days before the full flowering of Canadian literature, must have been tedious at times, but wit and wordplay abound in Frye's reviews, whatever may be said of the poems themselves.

Although, as a "reviewing" rather than a strictly "academic" critic, he had to relax his stand against value judgments and offer some guidance about what was worthwhile reading, he never attempted to tell the poets how to write. Margaret Atwood described Frye's usefulness to the writer in terms of his recognition of genre: "We all know the doggerel poem about critics: 'Seeing an elephant, he exclaimed with a laugh, / What a wondrous thing is this giraffe.' Perhaps one of his greatest gifts to writers was his lifelong work to ensure that if you created an elephant, it would never again be mistaken for a giraffe." In these reviews, he concentrated on encouraging conversation about Canadian poetry and in developing an informed reading public that would allow that poetry to flourish — which it did in part thanks to his efforts.

On a theoretical level, Frye turned to probing the backbone of the *Anatomy*, the existence of a literary universe that provides an imaginative vision for society. While continuing to produce a stream of practical criticism — books on Shakespeare, Milton, and T.S. Eliot, articles on the Renaissance, Yeats, Joyce, Samuel Butler, and numerous others — he also wrote works of general theory such as *The Well-Tempered Critic* (1963) and *The Critical Path* (1971) that explore the relation between critic, poet, and society. In *The Critical Path*, subtitled "An Essay on the Social Context of Literary Criticism," he put forth some important new conceptions of social development. According to his analysis, there is a constant dialectic in human history between the myth of concern and the myth of freedom. The myth of concern is society's central mythology, the body of what it believes as a society and what holds it together. (Later Frye split this into the primary concerns essential for survival, and the secondary concerns of religion, politics, and ideology.)

Authors, Frye says, tend to be children of concern, in that they address mankind's enduring hopes and fears through their images of wish and nightmare, and their depiction of the business of loving, gaining a living, and facing death. Against this concern stands the myth of freedom, a sort of liberal opposition which criticizes the myth of concern from an individualistic, often scientific, point of view. Included in the myth of freedom are all the academic disciplines, which must be conducted as scientifically as their subject matter allows, and must not have any ideological bias or outside loyalties. Literary criticism is one of these disciplines, indeed a central one: its subject matter may be concerned, but it must itself remain in the myth of freedom.

In the background of this defence of the critic or teacher's freedom from ideological and social constraints — indeed, part of the reason for undertaking it — was the student revolution of the late 1960s and 1970s, with its demand for immediate "relevance" and moral engagement in university studies, along with individual choice of a congenial curriculum. Frye was actually spending a term as visiting lecturer at Berkeley when the first violent student unrest broke out in the spring of 1969, leading him to say that the student radicals reminded him of a sentence in an old cookbook: "Brains are very perishable, and unless frozen or pre-cooked, should be used as soon as possible." His response was consistently to defend the values of a traditional, disinterested liberal education. "An arts degree is useless," he would say, "if it isn't, it isn't worth a damn."

Frye saw that the student came to university stuffed with the clichés and received ideas of society, which were essentially unreal and phantasmagoric. Fads come and go, endless consumer goods are consumed or thrown away, politicians are assassinated, millions mourn a Diana they never knew. For four years, the student could withdraw himself from this society, and concentrate on the more stable forms proffered by mankind's achievements in the arts and sciences: on the authority of the logical argument, the repeatable experiment, the compelling imagination. In the light of this vision provided by culture, the student will become a radical critic of what is — not a "well-rounded individual," with its comfortable overtones of contentment and softness, but maladjusted and crotchety, "a critical and carping intellectual," "probably one of that miserable band who read the *Canadian Forum*."

But sometimes Frye wondered if it was too late, worrying that by the time a student reached university it would be impossible to influence his mind, since it was already pre-programmed by television and advertisements. He became involved in schemes for earlier education, helping to found a curriculum institute in which university professors joined with elementary and high-school teachers to suggest improvements in the school curriculum, and later overseeing the production of a series of English readers for grades seven to thirteen. His concern was to keep the imagination in play, for only through imagination could the individual think metaphorically and engage in the play of mind through language that constructed reality in human form.

The most striking of the shorter essays that continue to discuss this theme, "The Responsibilities of the Critic," given as a speech at Johns Hopkins University in 1976, marks a vital transition in Frye's approach and is almost a manifesto for the second half of his career. In this talk, he is less concerned with the articulation of the literary universe as a whole than with the transformative potential of individual works. Concentrating on the reader and the act of reading, Frye contends that literary works may become a focus of consciousness and open up new worlds of perception. "It seems strange," he says in the essay "Expanding Eyes" (1975), "to overlook the possibility that arts, including literature, might just conceivably be what they have always been taken to be, possible techniques of meditation ... ways of cultivating, focusing, and ordering one's mental processes." He talks of Blake's offering his works in this spirit, not as icons but as mandalas, things for the reader to contemplate to the point at which he or she might reflect, "yes, we too could see things that way." The critic has a role in unlocking the power of such prophetic writers, helping to turn literature from an object to be admired to a power to be possessed. He does so not by judgment but by an act of recognition: "What the critic tries to do is to lead us from what poets and prophets meant, or thought they meant, to the inner structure of what they said," thereby opening a window into the created world.

Increasingly, Frye turned to the powers of language in all its aspects, literary and non-literary, to convey vision; latterly, he tended to define himself as a "cultural critic" rather than a "literary critic." In *Words with Power*, Frye studies this kerygmatic or prophetic authority in both the Bible and literature. He invokes Longinus's treatise *On the Sublime* in describing those dazzling moments in our response to art when the ego is dispossessed and "all the doors of perception in the psyche, the doors of dream and fantasy as well as of waking consciousness, are thrown open."

The Great Code in 1981, and *Words with Power* in 1990, both begin with expositions of the theory of language that respond to the growth of linguistics and semiotics in the previous decades. Language is seen to go through three phases, later expanded to four — the metaphorical, the dialectical, the rhetorical, and the descriptive — each in turn being dominant. Literature, however, keeps alive the earliest, metaphoric phase of language; and in these last major works, Frye delves into the basic source for those metaphors in the Bible. The Bible itself is written in the language of myth and metaphor, and thus it is a mistake to read it "literally" (as that phrase is commonly understood): its literal meaning is metaphorical. But the Bible's myths and metaphors are not hypothetical, like those of literature, since they are offered as myths to live by and metaphors to live in: they attempt to influence the reader in his way of life. Unwilling to call biblical language merely rhetorical, Frye suggests a fifth type of language, the kerygmatic, which is a rhetoric of proclamation on the "other side" of myth and metaphor.

In *Words with Power*, Frye studies this kerygmatic or prophetic authority in both the Bible and literature. *The Great Code*, whose title comes from Blake's assertion that "The Old and New Testaments are the Great Code of Art," lays the groundwork with a study of the Bible itself. As in the "Third Essay" of *Anatomy*, there are two aspects, the cyclical and the dialectical. Looked at as a plot, or *mythos*, the Bible is a comedy: it gives the history of mankind, under the name of Israel, from Creation in Paradise, through a fall into time and encroaching darkness, to Apocalypse and the regaining of Paradise, with a series of falls and recoveries in between.

Seen dialectically, the Bible's imagery falls into the two categories, mentioned before, of apocalyptic and demonic imagery. Its images of desire — shepherd, lamb, bridegroom, tree of life and so on — are ultimately all identified with a single figure, which is Christ. This human figure is both the fulfilled individual and the giant form of his society. In Paul's words, "So we, being many, are one body in Christ"; in Frye's interpretation, "the community with which the individual is identical is no longer a whole of which he is a part, but another aspect of himself."

Frye's *Return of Eden*, a study of Milton, ends with "the realization that there is only one man, one mind, and one world, and that all walls of partition have been broken down forever." Frye is not inculcating religious doctrine here, since, from a literary point of view, "belief" in Christ is not in question. Rather, he is pointing out that mankind's imagination culminates in a single human figure, who is both one and many, the individual glorified as his social body.

Those familiar with Blake will recognize that Frye has come full circle back to *Fearful Symmetry*. Blake's universe is populated by mighty individual figures, such as the human imagination, embodied as the chained Los; or a vengeful God, represented as Noboddady. For Blake, it is the local that becomes the universal, not some construct abstracted from many locals and resembling none. He believed in the radiance of the particular: a world in a grain of sand, eternity in an hour. In so stating, I too hope to have come full circle, by a long route recalling my earlier question of the relation of the individual to his society. Society — that is, a real society — is the fulfillment of the individual, not an obliteration of him.

What of Frye himself and his relation to his society? The particular milieu he was born into was middle-class, white, Canadian, and Methodist. Methodists are supposed to undergo a "conversion," the defining experience of their lives, when they are convinced of their utter sinfulness and of God's ability to forgive them. It's typical of Frye that he underwent an anti-conversion: he had been brought up by a church-going mother, but one morning, at the age of about fifteen, walking to school, he discovered, as he put it, that "the whole shitty, smelly garment of fundamentalism dropped off into the sewer and stayed there," and he realized that he had never really believed in the vengeful God who threw some into hell and rewarded others with a permanent appointment in the heavenly choir. Nevertheless, he remained within the Protestant tradition, imbued with its Bible culture, its radical individualism, its emphasis on the spirit. However, he sought all his life to define a religion that did justice to man's spirituality without falling into what he saw as superstitious idolatry.

The religion he defined was radical to say the least. By the time of his last book, *The Double Vision* (1991), he had virtually jettisoned the ideas of God the father, of the historical Jesus as an atoning figure, of the afterlife, of the Creation as a historical event, and of the Apocalypse as something that was likely to happen. As we might guess, they're all metaphors. What remains is the figure of Jesus, who is the creative principle linking mankind with the divine, and through whose vision man sees the eternal here and now.

Often enough, in his early years, Frye felt a deficiency of the eternal at Victoria College, with its endless fuss over locking the girls into residence by 11:00 p.m. and its insistence on never serving a glass of wine; but, particularly as the multiversity developed, he stressed the vital importance of colleges with specific traditions. He felt a loyalty to his community and enjoyed being part of it, even to serving as its principal for nine years.

As for his Canadian identity, that was also something he cherished. He could no more be an American than he could be a Catholic, and he was true to his roots in not forsaking Canada for the more lucrative field of the United States. According to his reading, Canadians differed from the Americans both geographically and historically. In its history, Canada had skipped over, intellectually speaking, the rational eighteenth century, and was always the home of a more Tory, less revolutionary attitude than the American. Hence, "Americans like to make money: Canadians like to audit it." Geographically, Canada lacked an eastern seaboard where settlement was concentrated, and the immense distances stretching out between isolated towns led to a garrison mentality in regard to nature. Such speculations on the nature of Canadianness feature largely in his celebrated "Conclusions" to the two editions of *Literary History of Canada*, which have become an honoured part of the literature they discuss.

Frye once defined the Canadian genius as the ability to produce strange hybrids, such as the University of Toronto in education, the United Church in religion, and Confederation in politics. He himself has some of this Canadian characteristic of contrasting entities strangely combined: the local teacher and the world celebrity; the committed Christian and the man who didn't know whether Christ ever existed and didn't think it much mattered; the believer in community and the shy introvert; the eloquent speaker and the tongue-tied conversationalist. On this showing, he himself was one of our most characteristic as well as our most honoured and widely quoted products.

A

A'S
I've spoken of the three A's of irony, Anxiety, Alienation & Absurdity: to these one should add a fourth, Aggression.
> Entry, Notebook 12 (1968–70), 490, *The "Third Book" Notebooks of Northrop Frye, 1964–1972: The Critical Comedy* (2002), CW, 9.

ABORTION
I think that having an abortion might be a traumatic shock to a woman, and she ought to consider carefully all the factors before going into it. But I'm not prepared to say whether it is right or wrong.
> "*Chatelaine's* Celebrity I.D." (1982), asked to comment on the subject of abortion, *Interviews with Northrop Frye* (2008), CW, 24.

ABSTRACT EXPRESSIONISM
To bring my own prejudice into the open, abstract expressionism is a genre I have always distrusted, mainly because so much of it seems to me to express a violent reactionary anarchism, a repudiating not so much of the traditions as of the community of painting.
> "Introduction to *Arthur Lismer*" (1979), *Northrop Frye on Canada* (2003), CW, 12.

The difference between nonobjective and abstract painting may be suggested by the difference between mathematics and music.
> "The Pursuit of Form" (1948), *Northrop Frye on Canada* (2003), CW, 12.

I remember some Clyfford Stills I saw in Buffalo: wonderful pictures, but they wouldn't endure anything else in the same room except another Clyfford Still. (I was told later that Still was personally almost a psychotic, and of course I disapprove of putting that fact into a casual relation to the pictures, but the effect of the picture is unmistakable.)
> Entry, Notebook 12 (1968–70), 279, *The "Third Book" Notebooks of Northrop Frye, 1964–1972: The Critical Comedy* (2002), CW, 9.

ABSURDITY
Whatever gives form and pattern to fiction, whatever technical skill keeps us turning the pages to get to the end, is absurd, and contradicts our sense of reality.
> "Dickens and the Comedy of Humours" (1967), *Northrop Frye's Writings on the Eighteenth and Nineteenth Centuries* (2005), CW, 17.

The word "absurd" refers primarily to the disappearance of the sense of continuity in our day.... The sense of absurdity comes from time, not space; from the feeling that life is not a continuous absorption of experiences into a steadily growing individuality, but a discontinuous series of encounters between moods and situations which keep bringing us back to the same point.
> "The University and Personal Life: Student Anarchism and the Educational Contract" (1968), *Northrop Frye's Writings on Education* (2001), CW, 7.

Just as the poetic metaphor is always a logical absurdity, so every inherited convention of plot in literature is more or less mad.
> "Myth, Fiction, and Displacement" (1961), *The Educated Imagination* (1963), "*The Educated Imagination*" *and Other Writings on Critical Theory, 1933–1963* (2006), CW, 21.

ACADIA
The notion of a distinguished Canadian novelist coming from such a place as Bouctouche would have struck us as queer indeed.

"Autobiographical Reflections: Speech at Moncton's Centennial Celebration" (1990), *Northrop Frye's Fiction and Miscellaneous Writings* (2007), CW, 25. The reference is to Acadian novelist and playwright Antonine Maillet.

ACCOUNTANTS

Perhaps we have used honesty and balance sheets as a substitute for brilliance and riches. Americans like to make money; Canadians like to audit it. I don't know of any other country where the accountant enjoys a higher social and moral status.
"View of Canada" (1976), *Northrop Frye on Canada* (2003), CW, 12.

ACHIEVEMENT

Every creative achievement is an invention, and to invent something is, subjectively, to construct it, and, objectively, to find it.
"The Symbol as a Medium of Exchange" (1984), *"The Secular Scripture" and Other Writings on Critical Theory, 1976–1991* (2006), CW, 18.

ACID RAIN

But the new response to the patterns of history seems to have made itself felt, along with a growing sense that we can no longer afford leaders who think that acid rain is something one gets by eating grapefruit.
"Speech at the New Canadian Embassy, Washington" (1989), *Northrop Frye on Canada* (2003), CW, 12. This remark is an indirect reference to the ecological views of U.S. President Ronald Reagan, *Northrop Frye on Canada* (2003), CW, 12.

ACTIONS

Inconsistency of action, being a coward one day & a hero the next, can never be patched up, though again on a verbal plane it may be "accounted for."
Entry, Notebook 24 (1970–72), 74, *The "Third Book" Notebooks of Northrop Frye, 1964–1972: The Critical Comedy* (2002), CW, 9.

I have often noticed that a man's beliefs are not revealed by any profession of faith, however sincere, but by what his actions show that he believes.
"The Dialectic of Belief and Vision" (1985), *Northrop Frye on Religion* (2000), CW, 4.

In a temptation somebody is being persuaded to do something that looks like an act, but which is really the loss of the power to act. Consequently, the abstaining from this kind of pseudo-activity is often the sign that one possesses a genuine power of action.
The Return of Eden (1965), *Northrop Frye on Milton and Blake* (2005), CW, 16.

ACTIVISM

Social concern does have its own case: environmental pollution, the energy crisis, the atom bomb, all show that a purely laissez-faire attitude to the development of science is pernicious.
"Introduction to *Art and Reality*" (1986), *Northrop Frye on Modern Culture* (2003), CW, 11.

As I used to tell my American friends at the time, Canadian activists have an outlet that your students don't have, namely the American Embassy. If all else fails they can go down and demonstrate there.
"Towards an Oral History of the University of Toronto" (1982), referring to student activism in the 1960s, *Interviews with Northrop Frye* (2008), CW, 24.

ADOLESCENCE

In the 1920s the cult of adolescence extended into the university, where the typical undergraduate was supposed to be a case of arrested development in a coonskin coat.
"The View from Here" (1980), *Northrop Frye's Writings on Education* (2001), CW, 7.

This conception of the adolescent can hardly have any basis in biology: it is a deliberate creation of industrial society, and one wonders why such a creation was made.... I would like to make it clear that when I use the word "adolescent," I do not refer primarily to young people, but to a social neurosis which has been projected on young people.
"The Definition of a University" (1970), *Northrop Frye's Writings on Education* (2001), CW, 7.

I say creation because I think the adolescent is a deliberate creation of an adult society, and that we have done with young people what

Victorian society did with women: on the pretext of coddling and protecting them, we have subordinated them and kept them out of any real social role or influence, and we have done this because they represent a kind of projection of our own anxiety.

"Education and the Rejection of Reality" (1971), *Northrop Frye's Writings on Education* (2001), CW, 7.

I always thought of adolescence as something to grow away from.

"Beginnings" (1981), interview by Susan Gabori, *Northrop Frye on Canada* (2003), CW, 12.

ADONIS
Jesus and Adonis are both dying gods; they have very similar imagery and very similar rituals attached to them; but Jesus is a person and Adonis is not.

"The Meaning of Recreation: Humanism in Society" (1979), *Northrop Frye on Religion* (2000), CW, 4.

ADULTS
Or we may even find ourselves reading the opposite meaning into what is said: if we pass a theatre advertising "adult entertainment," we know that "adult" in such contexts generally means "infantile."

"Language as the Home of Human Life" (1985), *Northrop Frye's Writings on Education* (2001), CW, 7.

ADVERTISING
Advertising as a socially approved form of drug culture: imaginary world, promises us magical powers within that world.

"On Education II" (1972), 18, *Northrop Frye's Fiction and Miscellaneous Writings* (2007), CW, 25.

Advertisers are very well aware that man participates in society through his imagination, and consequently advertising is addressed entirely to what you might call a passive imagination: that is, its statements are so outrageous that they stun and numb the reason.

"Breakthrough" (1967), *Interviews with Northrop Frye* (2008), CW, 24.

Advertising implies a competitive market and an absence of monopoly; propaganda implies a centralizing of power. If advertising is selling soap we know that it is only a soap, not the exclusive way of cleanliness. Hence the statements of advertising contain a residual irony.

The Critical Path: An Essay on the Social Context of Literary Criticism (1971), "The Critical Path" *and Other Writings on Critical Theory, 1963–1975* (2009), CW, 27.

Democracies seem to depend on advertising, and dictatorships on propaganda. The difference is not so much in the rhetoric, as in the fact that advertising is more open to the spirit of criticism.

"Criticism in Society" (1985), *Interviews with Northrop Frye* (2008), CW, 24.

We have here a type of irony which exactly corresponds to that of two other major arts of the ironic age, advertising and propaganda. These arts pretend to address themselves seriously to a subliminal audience of cretins, an audience that may not even exist, but which is assumed to be simple-minded enough to accept at their face value the statements made about the purity of a soap or a government's motives.

"First Essay: Historical Criticism: Theory of Modes" (1957), *Anatomy of Criticism: Four Essays* (2006), CW, 22.

One cannot read far in advertising without encountering over-writing, a too earnestly didactic tone, an uncritical acceptance of snobbish standards, and obtrusive sexual symbolism. These are precisely the qualities of inferior literature.

"Humanities in a New World" (1958), *Northrop Frye's Writings on Education* (2001), CW, 7.

Advertising implies an economy which has some independence from the political structure, and as long as this independence exists, advertising can be taken as a kind of ironic game.

The Modern Century (1967), *Northrop Frye on Modern Culture* (2003), CW, 11.

Our reaction to advertising is really a form of literary criticism. We don't take it literally, and we aren't supposed to: anyone who believed

literally what every advertiser said would hardly be capable of managing his own affairs.
"The Vocation of Eloquence," *The Educated Imagination* (1963), *"The Educated Imagination" and Other Writings on Critical Theory, 1933–1963* (2006), CW, 21.

Television advertising is entirely a monologue relying on the power of a visual medium to hold the body motionless and, if possible, spellbound.
"Reviews of Television Programs for the Canadian Radio-Television Commission: Reflections on November 5th" (1970), *Northrop Frye on Literature and Society, 1936–1989: Unpublished Papers* (2002), CW, 10.

The fiction need not be his own creation: anyone who believes advertising literally, for example, would be for all practical purposes a lunatic.
"On Teaching Literature" (1972), *Northrop Frye's Writings on Education* (2001), CW, 7.

Advertising is halfway between: its conventions may be accepted by a ten-year-old but must be greatly weakened by twenty if one is to retain any self-control at all in a consumerist society. (That's why it's so important to break the hold of the rhetoric of advertising as soon as possible.)
Entry, Notebook 50 (1987–90), 600, *Northrop Frye's Late Notebooks, 1982–1990: Architecture of the Spiritual World* (2000), CW, 5.

The two words practical and useful do not of course mean quite the same thing: some forms of verbal technology, like preaching, may be useful without always being practical; others, like advertising, may be practical without always being useful.
"Humanities in a New World" (1958), *Northrop Frye's Writings on Education* (2001), CW, 7.

Advertising, propaganda, the speeches of politicians, popular books and magazines, the clichés of rumour, all have their own kind of pastoral myths, quest myths, hero myths, sacrificial myths, and nothing will drive these shoddy constructs out of the mind except the genuine forms of the same thing.

"Elementary Teaching and Elementary Scholarship" (1963), *Northrop Frye's Writings on Education* (2001), CW, 7.

For the deeply disaffected in our society, advertising *is* propaganda, and one's response should be that of an enemy of "the system" and not of any player of games.
"Reviews of Television Programs for the Canadian Radio-Television Commission: Reflections on November 5th" (1970), *Northrop Frye on Literature and Society, 1936–1989: Unpublished Papers* (2002), CW, 10.

AESTHETICS

Every art, however, needs its own critical organization, and poetics will form a part of aesthetics as soon as aesthetics becomes the unified criticism of all the arts instead of whatever it is now.
"Polemical Introduction" (1957), *Anatomy of Criticism: Four Essays* (2006), CW, 22.

AFRICA

The revolt of Africa hasn't yet come, but is certainly coming.
Entry, 23 Jan. 1949, 116, *The Diaries of Northrop Frye: 1942–1955* (2001), CW, 8.

AFTERLIFE

So many people are repelled by the idea of a life after death that if there *is* a life after death a lot of people are going to be damn mad. But then a lot of people are damn mad about having been born into this world, though few of them, and those mostly suicides, get to the point of formulating it in those terms.
Entry, Notebook 21 (1969–76), 293, *Northrop Frye's Notebooks and Lectures on the Bible and Other Religious Texts* (2003), CW, 13.

There even used to be a version, or perversion, of Christianity which asserted that real life began after death. This is not much in fashion now, but in its day it doubtless encouraged some people to die without ever having come alive.
"Baccalaureate Sermon" (1967), *Northrop Frye on Religion* (2000), CW, 4.

AGING

The only thing that keeps me reconciled to life in my seventies is my realization that everything goes in cycles.

"Criticism in Society" (1985), *Interviews with Northrop Frye* (2008), CW, 24.

The body must go helplessly from youth to age: the imagination, though of course it is influenced by this, may be contemplative at ten or youthful at eighty.

"Part Two: The Development of the Symbolism," *Fearful Symmetry: A Study of William Blake* (1947, 2004), CW, 14.

At seventy-five the sense of perspective becomes more important than the sense of discovery. And yet the perspective includes a recapturing of discovery: the sun has been told often enough that it shines on nothing new, but it knows better, and keeps rising as placidly as ever.

"Preface to *On Education*" (1988), *Northrop Frye's Writings on Education* (2001), CW, 7.

But as our personal future narrows, we become more aware of another dimension of time entirely, and may even catch glimpses of the powers and forces of a far greater creative design. Perhaps when we think we are working for the future we are really being contained in the present, though an infinite present, eternity in an hour, as Blake calls it. Perhaps too that present is also a presence, not an impersonal cause in which to lose ourselves, but a person in whom to find ourselves again.

"Address on Receiving the Royal Bank Award" (1978), *Northrop Frye's Writings on Education* (2001), CW, 7.

As life goes on, the future becomes steadily more predictable, & the life consequently less interesting. Children fascinate us; old men bore us because they conceal no surprises.

Entry, Notebook 3 (1946–48), 146, *Northrop Frye's Notebooks and Lectures on the Bible and Other Religious Texts* (2003), CW, 13.

AGNOSTICISM

It is curious but significant that "gnostic" and "agnostic" are both dirty words in the Christian tradition: wisdom is not identified either with knowledge or with the denial of knowledge.

"Metaphor I," *The Great Code* (1982), *The Great Code: The Bible and Literature* (2006), CW, 19.

The advantages of being an agnostic are obvious: one does not have to pretend that one knows things that in fact one does not know.

"Baccalaureate Sermon" (1967), *Northrop Frye on Religion* (2000), CW, 4.

AIR

Air is the invisible medium by which things become visible, hence the spiritual is the power of making things visible, the medium of creative energy.

"*Pistis* and *Mythos*" (1972), *Northrop Frye on Religion* (2000), CW, 4.

But as the function of air is to be invisible, in order to make the physical world visible, so the spiritual world is invisible in order to make spiritual experience possible and visible to the participant.

"On the Bible" (1989), *Northrop Frye on Religion* (2000), CW, 4.

Now imagine a world where you could see the air: what you'd have is the image of fog, mist or vapour.

Entry, Notebook 21 (1969–76), 503, *Northrop Frye's Notebooks and Lectures on the Bible and Other Religious Texts* (2003), CW, 13.

The Spirit of the Bible is to the conscious world what the air is to the physical world. In the physical world, the things we see are visible only because the air is invisible. For the corresponding reason, the Spirit has to be invisible to consciousness, but is none the less a personal presence, personal as we are, present as everything around us is.

"To Come to Light" (1986), *Northrop Frye on Religion* (2000), CW, 4.

ALCOHOL

I find myself unusually sensitive to alcohol: I feel perceptibly more stupid after a single drink.

Entry, Notebook 3 (1946–48), 6, *Northrop Frye's Notebooks and Lectures on the Bible and Other Religious Texts* (2003), CW, 13.

ALGEBRA

Algebra is neither difficult nor easy to the keen student, but to, say, the girl who has already decided on a life of bridge and Saturday shopping it is impenetrably obscure. She "can't do" algebra because it has no place in her vision of life. Nevertheless the educational system mildly compels her at least to try a little algebra, because this is a democracy, and it is her right to be exposed to quadratic equations however little she wants them.

"Academy without Walls" (1961), *Northrop Frye on Modern Culture* (2003), CW, 11.

ALICE IN WONDERLAND

If I hadn't had the Alice books at an early age, it would have been like a couple of front teeth missing!

"Literature in Education" (1979), *Interviews with Northrop Frye* (2008), CW, 24.

The principle is, if looking-glass reality is Alice's dream why isn't our reality the red king's dream?

"New Fictional Formulas: Notebook 30o" (after 1965), 2, *Northrop Frye's Fiction and Miscellaneous Writings* (2007), CW, 25.

In a slightly different but related area, one feels that Alice could hardly have held her Wonderland together if she had even reached the Menarche, much less become an adult.

"Second Variation: The Garden," *Words with Power: Being a Second Study of "The Bible and Literature"* (1990), CW, 26.

I suppose the fascination with Alice is not that she's a child in the state of innocence, but that she's a *preternatural* child: what seven-year-old girls would have been like without the Fall.

Entry, Notebook 21 (1969–76), 558, *Northrop Frye's Notebooks and Lectures on the Bible and Other Religious Texts* (2003), CW, 13.

I've often said that if I understood the two Alice books I'd have very little left to understand about literature. Actually I think the Alice books, while they carry over, begin rather than sum up — a new twist to fiction that has to do with intellectual paradox & the disintegrating of the ego.

Entry, Notebook 24 (1970–72), 226, *The "Third Book" Notebooks of Northrop Frye, 1964–1972: The Critical Comedy* (2002), CW, 9.

ALIEN BEINGS

I think we have a feeling of being alienated and isolated by all that empty space and a need to populate it somehow with something which is humanly intelligible. Just as you have movies like *Star Wars* that talk about distant galaxies as being united by beings that look remarkably like Hollywood actors, so you have myths about unidentified flying objects that, again, tend to indicate that there is something way out there which is like ourselves.

"Between Paradise and Apocalypse" (1978), *Interviews with Northrop Frye* (2008), CW, 24.

The sheer bumptiousness of Carl Sagan & others who want to communicate with beings in other worlds amazes me. They should be saying: look, there are several billion Yahoos here robbing, murdering, torturing, exploiting, abusing & enslaving each other: they're stupid, malicious, superstitious and obstinate. Would you like to look at the .0001 per cent of them who are roughly presentable?

Entry, Notebook 44 (1986–91), 425, *Northrop Frye's Late Notebooks, 1982–1990: Architecture of the Spiritual World* (2000), CW, 5.

ALIENATION

We live in a world that got along without us for billions of years, and could still get along without us, in fact still may. When this fact penetrates the public consciousness, a kind of alienation develops.

"Criticism as Education" (1979), *Northrop Frye's Writings on Education* (2001), CW, 7.

Alienation is minimal identity, a classical atom against the external world.

Entry, Notebook 54-8 (late 1972–77), 68, *Northrop Frye's Notebooks on Romance* (2004), CW, 15.

ALLEGORY

Allegorical interpretation, as a method of criticism, begins with the fact that allegory is a structural element in narrative: it has to be there, and is not added by critical interpretation alone. In fact, all commentary, or the relating of the events of a narrative to conceptual terminology, is in one sense allegorical interpretation.

"Allegory" (1965), *"The Critical Path" and Other Writings on Critical Theory, 1963–1975* (2009), CW, 27.

We have allegory when one literary work is joined to another, or to a myth, by a certain interpretation of meaning rather than by structure.

"Myth, Fiction, and Displacement" (1961), *"The Educated Imagination" and Other Writings on Critical Theory, 1933–1963* (2006), CW, 21.

ALUMNI

There are now only two groups of people who have any really long-term and continuous relationship to the university: the alumni and the graduate students in the humanities working on their Ph.D.'s.

"Convocation Address, York University" (1969), *Northrop Frye's Writings on Education* (2001), CW, 7.

AMATEURISM

… practically everybody confuses the merits of practising an art as a yoga with the objective merits of its products, sooner or later. That is, they want to give up their amateur standing as soon as possible. The irony of the situation is that if most writers of poetry & other dabblers would think entirely of the benefit to them & not at all of publication, the publishable merit of what they produce would be greatly & constantly increased.

Entry, Notebook 3 (1946–48), 57, *Northrop Frye's Notebooks and Lectures on the Bible and Other Religious Texts* (2003), CW, 13.

… he stands for a spirit no professional can do without: the spirit of painting for fun.

"Water-Colour Annual" (1944), *Northrop Frye on Canada* (2003), CW, 12.

AMBIGUITY

So the term *ambiguous*, which is pejorative when applied to descriptive verbal structures, is an essential concept of literature.

"The Transferability of Literary Concepts" (1955), *"The Educated Imagination" and Other Writings on Critical Theory, 1933–1963* (2006), CW, 21.

AMERICANISM

I do not see how America can find its identity, much less avoid chaos, unless a massive citizens' resistance develops which is opposed to exploitation and impersonality on the one hand, and to jack-booted radicalism on the other. It would not be a new movement, but simply the will of the people, the people as a genuine society strong enough to contain and dissolve all mobs. It would be based on a conception of freedom as the social expression of tolerance, and on the understanding that violence and lying cannot produce anything except more violence and more lies. It would be politically active, because democracy has to do with majority rule and not merely with enduring the tyranny of organized minorities. It would not be conservative or radical in its direction, but both at once.

"America: True or False?" (1969), *Northrop Frye on Canada* (2003), CW, 12.

It is a peculiarity of American social mythology that its mythology of the past largely contradicts its mythology of the present.

"Report on the 'Adventures' Readers" (1965), *Northrop Frye's Writings on Education* (2001), CW, 7.

AMERICANIZATION

I'm not greatly worried about what is called the Americanization of Canada. What people mean when they speak of Americanization has been just as lethal to American culture as it has been to Canadian culture. It's a kind of levelling down which I think every concerned citizen of democracy should fight, whether he is a Canadian or an American.

"From Nationalism to Regionalism: The Maturing of Canadian Culture" (1980), *Interviews with Northrop Frye* (2008), CW, 24.

… when Canada was, in the stock phrase, "flooded with American programmes," it was clear that the majority of Canadians preferred the flood to any Canadian ark that would float above it.

"Across the River and Out of the Trees" (1980), *Northrop Frye on Canada* (2003), CW, 12.

But of course America itself is becoming Americanized in this sense, and the uniformity imposed on New Delhi and Singapore, or on Toronto and Vancouver, is no greater than that imposed on New Orleans or Baltimore.

"Conclusion to *Literary History of Canada*" (1965), *Northrop Frye on Canada* (2003), CW, 12.

AMERICANS & CANADIANS

I remember that practically every American I met began the conversation by producing a Canadian relative or ancestor. So, if asked to name the chief products of Canada, I'd begin with "Americans."

"Education and the Humanities" (1947), referring to a year spent at Harvard University, *Northrop Frye's Writings on Education* (2001), CW, 7.

ANAGNORISIS

Much of my critical thinking has turned on the double meaning of Aristotle's term *anagnorisis*, which can mean "discovery" or "recognition," depending on whether the emphasis falls on the newness of the appearance or on its reappearance.

"Introduction" (1990), *Words with Power: Being a Second Study of "The Bible and Literature"* (2008), CW, 26.

Epiphany is not a new experience: it is the knowledge that one has the experience: it's recognition or anagnorisis.

Entry, Notebook 19 (1964–67), 152, *The "Third Book" Notebooks of Northrop Frye, 1964–1972: The Critical Comedy* (2002), CW, 9.

ANAGOGY

When we pass into anagogy, nature becomes, not the container, but the thing contained, and the archetypal universal symbols — the city, the garden, the quest, the marriage — are no longer the desirable forms that man constructs inside nature, but are themselves the forms of nature. Nature is now inside the mind of an infinite man who builds his cities out of the Milky Way. This is not reality, but it is the conceivable or imaginative limit of desire, which is infinite, eternal, and hence apocalyptic.

"Second Essay: Ethical Criticism: Theory of Symbols" (1957), *Anatomy of Criticism: Four Essays* (2006), CW, 22.

ANALOGY

Analogy establishes the parallels between human life and natural phenomena, and identity conceives of a "sun-god" or a "tree-god."

"Myth, Fiction, and Displacement" (1961), *"The Educated Imagination" and Other Writings on Critical Theory, 1933–1963* (2006), CW, 21.

ANARCHISM

The anarchism of today seem[s] almost as indifferent to the future as to the past: one protest will be followed by another, because even if one issue is resolved society will still be "sick," but there appears to be no clear programme of taking control or assuming permanent responsibility in society.

"The University and Personal Life: Student Anarchism and the Educational Contract" (1968), *Northrop Frye's Writings on Education* (2001), CW, 7.

But now I really begin to feel that I'm living in a post-Marxist age. I think we're moving into something like an age of anarchism: the kind of violence and unrest going on now in China, in the city riots (which are not really race riots: race hatred is an effect but not a cause of them) in America, in Nigeria, in Canadian separatism — none of all this can satisfactorily be explained in Marxist terms. Something else is happening.

Entry, Notebook 19 (1964–67), 427, *The "Third Book" Notebooks of Northrop Frye, 1964–1972: The Critical Comedy* (2002), CW, 9.

ANATOMY OF CRITICISM

I began the *Anatomy of Criticism* long ago by remarking that every serious subject, including criticism, seems to go through a kind of inductive metamorphosis, in which what has previously been assumed without discussion turns into the central problem to be discussed.

"Varieties of Eighteenth-Century Sensibility" (1990), *Northrop Frye's Writings on the Eighteenth and Nineteenth Centuries* (2005), CW, 17.

Anatomy of Criticism presents a vision of literature as forming a total schematic order, interconnected by recurring or conventional myths and metaphors, which I call archetypes. The vision has an objective pole: it is based on a study of literary genres and conventions, and on certain elements in Western cultural history. The order of words is there, and it is no good trying to write it off as a hallucination of my own. The fact that literature is based on unifying principles as schematic as those of music is concealed by many things, most of them psychological blocks, but the unity exists, and can be shown and taught to others, including children. But, of course, my version of that vision also has a subjective pole: it is a model only, coloured by my preferences and limited by my ignorance.

"Expanding Eyes" (1975), *"The Critical Path" and Other Writings on Critical Theory, 1963–1975* (2009), CW, 27.

ANCESTRY

If we are interested in our ancestry, it is natural to trace our direct ancestry first, but we all know that we eventually come to a point at which everyone alive was an ancestral relative.

"Framework and Assumption" (1985), *"The Secular Scripture" and Other Writings on Critical Theory, 1976–1991* (2006), CW, 18.

... we all belong to something before we are anything....

The Double Vision (1991), *Northrop Frye on Religion* (2000), CW, 4.

ANGELS

If I had been on the hills of Bethlehem in the year one, I do not think I should have heard angels singing because I do not hear them now, & there is no reason to suppose that they have stopped.

Entry, Notebook 11f (1969–70), 5, *Northrop Frye's Notebooks and Lectures on the Bible and Other Religious Texts* (2003), CW, 13.

The bird is not a higher form of imagination than we are, but its ability to fly symbolizes one, and men usually assign wings to what they visualize as superior forms of human existence.

"Part Three: The Final Synthesis," *Fearful Symmetry: A Study of William Blake* (1947, 2004), CW, 14.

Angels are *spiritual* beings because they don't travel but just epiphanize (when they do) in an interpenetrating space, and all angels by the royal metaphor are One Spirit, a little higher (Ps. 8) than we are.

Entry, Notebook 11e (*ca.* 1978), 59, *Northrop Frye's Notebooks and Lectures on the Bible and Other Religious Texts* (2003), CW, 13.

ANGLICANISM

Incidentally, I hate to seem intolerant, but I do not approve of Anglicanism. There are two possible approaches to Christianity, or any religion — the Protestant or individual approach, and the Catholic or collective one. Anglicanism never made up its mind which it was going to be, and did not much want to, as it is based on the useful but muddle-headed English idea of pleasing everybody.

"NF to HK," 25 Aug. 1932, *The Correspondence of Northrop Frye and Helen Kemp, 1932–1939* (1996), CW, 1.

ANGST

Fear without an object, as a condition of mind prior to being afraid *of* anything, is called *Angst* or anxiety, a somewhat narrow term for what may be almost anything between pleasure and pain.

"Towards Defining an Age of Sensibility" (1956), *Northrop Frye's Writings on the Eighteenth and Nineteenth Centuries* (2005), CW, 17.

ANIMALS

The deaths of animals seem to have an extraordinary resonance in Canadian literature, as though the screams of all the trapped and tortured creatures who built up the Canadian fur trade were still echoing in our minds.

"Canadian Culture Today" (1977), *Northrop Frye on Canada* (2003), CW, 12.

I don't know why I have such a horror of animals. A recurrent nightmare is badly hurting an animal and then stomping it furiously into a battered wreck in a paroxysm of cowardly mercy. And that is to some extent what I'm like. Any intimate contact with any animal I

dislike, & their convulsive movements give me panic. If I go to hell, Satan will probably give me a wet bird to hold.
> Entry, 24 Jul. 1942, *The Diaries of Northrop Frye: 1942–1955* (2001), CW, 8.

ANNIVERSARIES

The value of centenaries and similar observations is that they call attention, not simply to great men, but to what we do with our great men.
> "Blake after Two Centuries" (1957), *Northrop Frye on Milton and Blake* (2005), CW, 16.

We choose an anniversary like this to get free of time for a moment, when we can remember without being trapped in the past, and expect, plan, or hope without being trapped in the future.
> "To Come to Light" (1988), *Northrop Frye on Religion* (1999), CW, 4.

ANSWERS

I don't think there are any answers. I think that the answer cheats you out of the right to ask the question and that the function of the answer is to make you formulate a better question.
> "The Great Teacher" (1988), *Interviews with Northrop Frye* (2008), CW, 24.

When it comes to meeting the threat to identity, a myth of freedom seems very ineffective in comparison with the narcotic charm of a closed myth of concern, with its instant, convinced, and final answers. It takes time to realize that these answers are not only not genuine answers, but that only the questions can be genuine, and all such answers cheat us out of our real birthright, which is the right to ask questions.
> *The Critical Path: An Essay on the Social Context of Literary Criticism* (1971), *"The Critical Path" and Other Writings on Critical Theory, 1963–1975* (2009), CW, 27.

I think there are all questions and there aren't any answers.
> "The Great Teacher" (1988), *Interviews with Northrop Frye* (2008), CW, 24.

ANTHEM, NATIONAL

I'm thinking of the national anthem, where the French version is doing all sorts of interesting things like *"ton histoire est une épopée des plus brillants exploits,"* while the poor English can only repeat "we stand on guard," like the sentry in Pompeii about to be covered up with lava. I understand that the repetitions of this phrase have recently been cut from five to three, but it's still pretty fatuous.
> "Reviews of Television Programs for the Canadian Radio-Television Commission: Reflections on Television ... November 1971–March 1972" (1972), *Northrop Frye on Literature and Society, 1936–1989: Unpublished Papers* (2002), CW, 10.

ANTHOLOGIES

In any case anthologies ought to have blank pages at the end on which the reader may copy his own neglected favourites.
> "Canada and Its Poetry" (1943), *Northrop Frye on Canada* (2003), CW, 12.

ANTHROPOLOGY

... anthropologists in particular are fond of reminding us that some societies will believe anything, including no doubt some societies of anthropologists.
> *Creation and Recreation* (1980), *Northrop Frye on Religion* (2000), CW, 4.

The Golden Bough purports to be a work of anthropology, but it has had more influence on literary criticism than in its own alleged field, and it may yet prove to be really a work of literary criticism.
> "Second Essay: Ethical Criticism: Theory of Symbols" (1957), *Anatomy of Criticism: Four Essays* (2006), CW, 22.

Anthropology is the history of law, as law is the articulated form of custom.
> Entry, 4 Jun. 1950, 394, *The Diaries of Northrop Frye: 1942–1955* (2001), CW, 8.

ANTHROPOMORPHISM

Nowhere does the Bible seem to be afraid of the word "anthropomorphic."
> *The Double Vision* (1991), *Northrop Frye on Religion* (2000), CW, 4.

Man can only make things in his own image. He's stuck with that. There's nothing else he has material for.
> "Between Paradise and Apocalypse" (1978), *Interviews with Northrop Frye* (2008), CW, 24.

ANTI-INTELLECTUALISM
Dictatorships try to suppress the critical intelligence wherever they can; our own society is profoundly and perversely anti-intellectual; some religious groups think that only blind faith can see clearly. All such attitudes are dangerous to civilized life and abhorrent to the gospel.
> "To Come to Light" (1986), *Northrop Frye on Religion* (2000), CW, 4.

ANTI-SEMITISM
The sources of anti-Semitism are very complex. I myself think that anti-Semitism among Christians is always, sooner or later, a disguised form of anti-Christianity. It's your own religion you hate, and you project it on something else.
> "Between Paradise and Apocalypse" (1978), *Interviews with Northrop Frye* (2008), CW, 24.

The fact that every tribal group is or appears to be potentially conspiratorial accounts for certain aspects of anti-Semitism, the Jews being scapegoats for the Nazis who could project their own tribalism on them.
> Entry, Notebook 27 (1986), 520, *Northrop Frye's Late Notebooks, 1982–1990: Architecture of the Spiritual World* (2000), CW, 5.

ANTICHRIST
Thus from the point of view of any one of the three great Biblical religions, our age seems to be an age of a consolidating Antichrist.
> "The Church and Modern Culture" (1950), *Northrop Frye on Modern Culture* (2003), CW, 11.

There is no alternative to Christ except Antichrist, and the form of Antichrist is the form of the society of power incarnate in a divine king, an inspired dictator, or an infallible counsellor.
> "The Church: Its Relation to Society" (1949), *Northrop Frye on Religion* (2000), CW, 4.

The Jesus about whom a biography can be written is dead and gone, and survives only as Antichrist.
> "Part Three: The Final Synthesis," interpreting Blake's insight, *Fearful Symmetry: A Study of William Blake* (1947, 2004), CW, 14.

ANTIQUES
Nowadays, the expanding of the antique market and the growing sense of the possible commercial value of whatever is no longer being produced has considerably shortened this process. The sojourn in a period of unfashionable limbo has to be very brief when an "antique" can be an object twenty years old.
> "Canada: New World Without Revolution" (1975), *Northrop Frye on Canada* (2003), CW, 12.

ANTITHESES
Antitheses are usually resolved, not by picking one side and refuting the other, or by making eclectic choices between them, but by trying to get past the antithetical way of stating the problem.
> "The Archetypes of Literature" (1951), *"The Educated Imagination" and Other Writings on Critical Theory, 1933–1963* (2006), CW, 21.

ANTONY AND CLEOPATRA
I don't know what the central Shakespeare play will be in the twenty-first century, assuming we reach it, but I'd place a small bet on *Antony and Cleopatra*.
> "The Stage Is All the World" (1985), *Northrop Frye's Writings on Shakespeare and the Renaissance* (2010), CW, 28. Frye argues that *Hamlet* made possible the Romantic movement, and in the twentieth century *King Lear* came into the foreground.

ANXIETY
Those who are not capable of faith have to settle for anxieties instead.
> "The Knowledge of Good and Evil" (1966), *Northrop Frye's Writings on Education* (2001), CW, 7.

As long as man is capable of anxiety he is capable of passing through it to a genuine human destiny.

The Modern Century (1967), *Northrop Frye on Modern Culture* (2003), CW, 11.

... in fact all our really urgent, mysterious and frightening questions have to do with the burden of the past and the meaning of tradition.
"Address on Receiving the Royal Bank Award" (1978), *Northrop Frye's Writings on Education* (2001), CW, 7.

After the three R's, the three A's: anxiety, alienation, absurdity.
"The University and Personal Life: Student Anarchism and the Educational Contract" (1968), *Northrop Frye's Writings on Education* (2001), CW, 7.

APARTHEID

Amiable apartheid, not a word I'd use for anything I approved of, but there are degrees.
Entry, Notebook 42b: Notes III (1980s), 4, referring to attitudes in his youth in Moncton, N.B., *Northrop Frye's Fiction and Miscellaneous Writings* (2007), CW, 25.

APATHY

But apathy, on the part of a majority, means that democracy is no longer a matter of majority rule, but is simply a state of enduring the tyranny of organized minorities.
"Convocation Address: Acadia University" (1969), *Northrop Frye on Literature and Society, 1936–1989: Unpublished Papers* (2002), CW, 10.

APHORISMS

The aphorism works on the principle of the Bloody Mary: it has to be swallowed at a gulp and allowed to explode from within.
"Poetry of the Tout Ensemble" (1957), *Northrop Frye on Twentieth-Century Literature* (2010), CW, 29.

The aphorism is a verbal *perception*: that is, it's a verbal analogy of a *Gestalt* perception.
Entry, Notebook 19 (1964–67), 110, *The "Third Book" Notebooks of Northrop Frye, 1964–1972: The Critical Comedy* (2002), CW, 9.

If the writer wants to suggest a kind of aloofness, if he wants to suggest that it is your business to come to him and not his business to come to you; if he wants to suggest that there are riches or reserves in his mind which what he is writing gives you only an occasional hint of, then he will naturally turn to a more discontinuous form, and he'll write in a series of aphorisms.
"Literature as Possession" (1959), *"The Educated Imagination" and Other Writings on Critical Theory, 1933–1963* (2006), CW, 21.

An aphorism is not a cliché: it penetrates & bites. It has wit, and consequently an affinity with satire. It appeals to the instinct in us to say "I don't care if a man's right or wrong; all I care about is whether his mind is alive or dead." Naturally this will not do as a guide to thought, but it's normal & healthy as an occasional reaction.
Entry, Notebook 11f (1969–70), 154, *Northrop Frye's Notebooks and Lectures on the Bible and Other Religious Texts* (2003), CW, 13.

My own writing is developed out of a number of discontinuous aphorisms. When I'm in the routine of teaching I find my writing becomes extremely furtive; I scribble notes; that's where the aphoristic side of my writing develops. When I have to settle down to a sustained piece of narrative writing, I pull in on myself, sometimes to a frightening degree, in order to pull the aphorisms together in the right sequence, to produce the right sort of connective tissue. I've said quite frequently and meant it very intensely that I don't run my writing operation, my writing operation runs me.
"Canadian Energies: Dialogues on Creativity" (1980), *Interviews with Northrop Frye* (2008), CW, 24.

The obvious is the opposite of the commonplace. The aphorism represents most clearly the stage at which the idea is able to pass into a power.
Entry, Notebook 3-12 (1946–48), 7, sec. 12, *Northrop Frye's Notebooks and Lectures on the Bible and Other Religious Texts* (2003), CW, 13.

Christ speaks in aphorisms, not because they are alive, but because he is.
Entry, Notebook 11f (1969–70), 154, *Northrop Frye's Notebooks and Lectures on the Bible and Other Religious Texts* (2003), CW, 13.

Further on the aloofness of the aphoristic sequence: in some respects it's a dialogue with the void: what one says is surrounded by silence. It has affinities with the lyric, for instance the echo-song.

Entry, Notebook 33 (1946–50), 61, *Northrop Frye's Notebooks on Romance* (2004), CW, 15.

We notice that discontinuous prose carries an authority and a sense of aloofness which suggests to the reader that he must come to it and be instructed, and that great reserves of wisdom are implied in the spaces between the sentences.

"*Rencontre:* The General Editor's Introduction" (1960s), *Northrop Frye on Literature and Society, 1936–1989: Unpublished Papers* (2002), CW, 10.

The way I begin a book is to write detached aphorisms in a notebook, and ninety-five per cent of the work I do in completing a book is to fit these detached aphorisms together into a continuous narrative.

"Response to Papers on 'Northrop Frye and Eighteenth-Century Literature'" (1990), *"The Secular Scripture" and Other Writings on Critical Theory, 1976–1991* (2006), CW, 18.

Oracular writers, from Heraclitus to Marshall McLuhan, have always written prose of that kind, that is, in separated sentences, where every sentence is surrounded by a big packet of silence.

"The Limits of Dialogue" (1969), *Interviews with Northrop Frye* (2008), CW, 24.

God, it would be wonderful to write a whole book in the discontinuous aphoristic form in which things actually come to me: I'd still have the sequence problem, but not the crippling angel of continuity to wrestle with. The hell with it, at least for now.

Entry, Notebook 44 (1986–91), 671, *Northrop Frye's Late Notebooks, 1982–1990: Architecture of the Spiritual World* (2000), CW, 5.

APOCALYPSE

Well, it can mean that, although I prefer not to think of the apocalypse as a big show of fireworks starting next Tuesday. I'd prefer to think of it as the ultimate expanding of human consciousness, which, as I see it, is what is meant by the term "revelation" as applied to the Bible.

"On *The Great Code* (I)" (1982), setting aside the notion of the apocalypse as "the end," *Interviews with Northrop Frye* (2008), CW, 24.

Literature is a human apocalypse, man's revelation to man, and criticism is not a body of adjudications, but the awareness of that revelation, the last judgment of mankind.

"The Keys of Dreamland," *The Educated Imagination* (1963), *"The Educated Imagination" and Other Writings on Critical Theory, 1933–1963* (2006), CW, 21. This sentence caught the eye of A.C. Hamilton in *Northrop Frye: Anatomy of His Criticism* (1990): "This one gnomic sentence encapsulates his entire vision of literature and the function of literary criticism. I realized that if it alone of all his writings had survived, like an anthropologist shaping Neanderthal man from one bone sliver, I could reconstruct the *Anatomy*."

Our own age is an extremely apocalyptic one, and there are always two aspects to an apocalypse: the vision we finally get when it clears away, and the sun and moon turning to blood before that happens.

"Literature as a Critique of Pure Reason" (1982), *"The Secular Scripture" and Other Writings on Critical Theory, 1976–1991* (2006), CW, 18.

In the New Testament Christ descends to the lower world in his death and burial, returns to the surface of the earth at the Resurrection, ascends the higher ladder to the sky in the Ascension, and descends from there at the Apocalypse. The entire *axis mundi* is traversed in this quest, and any second coming after that can be only an enlarged version in ourselves of what is there now.

"Third Variation: The Cave," *Words with Power: Being a Second Study of "The Bible and Literature"* (1990), CW, 26.

Why is the apocalypse a world of total metaphor as well as a world of desire?

Entry, Notebook 12 (1968–70), 202, *The "Third Book" Notebooks of Northrop Frye, 1964–1972: The Critical Comedy* (2002), CW, 9.

... the Biblical Apocalypse is our grammar of apocalyptic imagery.
> "Third Essay: Archetypal Criticism: Theory of Myths" (1957), *Anatomy of Criticism: Four Essays* (2006), CW, 22.

The apocalypse is the way the world looks after the ego has disappeared.
> "Typology II," *The Great Code* (1982), *The Great Code: The Bible and Literature* (2006), CW, 19.

The idea of manifestation & disappearance seems to belong to hell; the idea of concealment and realization seems to belong to heaven: one is creation, the other apocalypse.
> Entry, 25 Feb. 1950, 146, *The Diaries of Northrop Frye: 1942–1955* (2001), CW, 8.

Our age likes to imagine itself as the victim of an apocalypse, with all the furies of the four horsemen tearing it to pieces with calamities that no previous age has ever had to endure. This of course is mere self-pity, and the Old Testament prophets who saw Nineveh and Babylon buried under the sands would see nothing unprecedented in the ruins of Berlin.
> "Education and the Humanities" (1947), *Northrop Frye's Writings on Education* (2001), CW, 7.

APOSTLES

The apostles developed into bishops, not into gurus or teachers of illumination.
> Entry, Notebook 24 (1970–72), 40, *The "Third Book" Notebooks of Northrop Frye, 1964–1972: The Critical Comedy* (2002), CW, 9.

APPLAUSE

Applause, it has been said, is the echo of a platitude, but the applause itself indicates that the response comes from the entire personality and is therefore an organic part of it.
> "Part One: The Argument," *Fearful Symmetry: A Study of William Blake* (1947, 2004), CW, 14.

ARCHAEOLOGY

Nevertheless, an archaeologist who is looking for buried treasure instead of studying the past belongs, not in the tradition of the scholars, but in the tradition of the grave-robbers.
> "Research and Graduate Education in the Humanities" (1968), *Northrop Frye's Writings on Education* (2001), CW, 7.

Archaeology is a science in which we dig underground, using steps and descending ladders as we go, to find what remains of civilizations that at one time towered high in the air.
> "Repetitions of Jacob's Dream" (1983), *Northrop Frye on Religion* (2000), CW, 4.

Our attitude to the past needs more of the impartiality of the archaeologist who excavates all layers and cultural periods of his site with equal care.
> "Canada: New World Without Revolution" (1975), *Northrop Frye on Canada* (2003), CW, 12.

ARCHETYPE

I used the word "archetype" because it was a traditional term in criticism, though not many people had ever run across it. But I didn't realize at the time that Jung had monopolized the term and that everybody would think I was a Jungian critic because I used it.
> "Northrop Frye in Conversation" (1989), *Interviews with Northrop Frye* (2008), CW, 24.

I mean by an archetype a symbol which connects one poem with another and thereby helps to unify and integrate our literary experience.
> "Second Essay: Ethical Criticism: Theory of Symbols" (1957), *Anatomy of Criticism: Four Essays* (2006), CW, 22.

I don't object to a feeling that there is something about the archetype which is not removed to another world but at any rate inexhaustible in this one; something which can't ever be completely analysed or understood. There's a residual mystery about it.
> "Archetype and History" (1986), *Interviews with Northrop Frye* (2008), CW, 24.

... for example, I took the word "archetype" not from Jung, as is so often said, but from a footnote in Beattie's *Minstrel*.
> "Varieties of Eighteenth-Century Sensibility" (1990), *Northrop Frye's Writings on the Eighteenth and Nineteenth Centuries* (2005), CW, 17. The source is *The Poetical Works of James Beattie* (1870).

The archetype is thus primarily the *communicable* symbol, and archetypal criticism is particularly concerned with literature as a social fact and as a technique of communication.
> "The Literary Meaning of 'Archetype'" (1936), *Northrop Frye on Literature and Society, 1936–1989: Unpublished Papers* (2002), CW, 10.

ARCHITECTURE

I am not a historian: I'm an architect of the spiritual world.
> Entry, Notebook 50 (1987–90), 799, *Northrop Frye's Late Notebooks, 1982–1990: Architecture of the Spiritual World* (2000), CW, 5.

Even if fifty new cathedrals were built this year, the cathedral would still be as dead as the step pyramid, at least as an imaginative power in our culture.
> "Introduction," "A History of Communications," by Harold Innis (1982), *Northrop Frye on Canada* (2003), CW, 12.

The turning point between fine & useful arts is architecture, which is fine when conspicuous (cathedral & castle) & useful when essentially a matter of housing.
> Entry, 29 Jan. 1949, 137, *The Diaries of Northrop Frye: 1942–1955* (2001), CW, 8.

The surrounding streets keep steadily turning into anonymous masses of buildings that look eyeless in spite of being practically all windows. Many of them seem to have had no architect, but appear to have sprung out of their excavations like vast toadstools.
> "Canada: New World Without Revolution" (1975), *Northrop Frye on Canada* (2003), CW, 12.

Architecture: wonder why there always has to be a prick and a cunt: I wondered this when sitting in the Skydome with the CN tower beside me. Islam had a mosque and a minaret; Christianity a basilica and a bell-tower; even the New York fair had a trylon and a perisphere. Something points to the sky and something contained on earth.
> Entry, Notes 54.1 (May 1990), 41, *Northrop Frye's Late Notebooks, 1982–1990: Architecture of the Spiritual World* (2000), CW, 6.

ARGUMENTS

As I've often said, the irrefutable philosopher is not the person who cannot be refuted but the philosopher who's still there after he's been refuted.
> "Northrop Frye in Conversation" (1989), *Interviews with Northrop Frye* (2008), CW, 24.

They that take the argument will perish by the argument; any statement that can be argued about at all can be refuted. The natural response to indoctrination is resistance, and nothing will make it successful except a well-organized secret police.
> "Humanities in a New World" (1958), *Northrop Frye's Writings on Education* (2001), CW, 7.

… nothing is more remarkable in the Bible than the elimination of anything like an argument.
> Entry, Notebook 21 (1969–76), 360, *Northrop Frye's Notebooks and Lectures on the Bible and Other Religious Texts* (2003), CW, 13.

At a certain point the bad argument will become the bad man, and what will be demanded from you and your education will not be objectivity of mind, but the courage to fight.
> "To the Class of '62 at Queen's" (1962), *Northrop Frye's Writings on Education* (2001), CW, 7.

ARISTOCRACY

When we discover that we do not need an aristocracy we shall discover who our real aristocracy are. Our real aristocracy, of course, are the children.
> "Preserving Human Values" (1961), *Northrop Frye on Modern Culture* (2003), CW, 11.

Hence our dream of the complete or workless man, whom our aristocracies try to produce. The versatile man, who can do anything, and the entertainer or actor, who can pretend to be anything, are proximate dreams of the same kind.
> Entry, Notebook 19 (1964–67), 269, *The "Third Book" Notebooks of Northrop Frye, 1964–1972: The Critical Comedy* (2002), CW, 9.

ARISTOTLE

Aristotle is interested in poetry; Plato in the poet.

"The Myth of Deliverance: II, The Reversal of Energy" (1981), *Northrop Frye's Writings on Shakespeare and the Renaissance* (2010), CW, 28.

ART

But great art comes from harnessing a conscious intention to the creative powers beneath consciousness, and we do not get closer to the author's meaning by getting closer to the book's meaning. The greater the book, the more obvious it is that the author's consciousness merely held the nozzle of the hose, so to speak.
"*Don Quixote*" (1949), *Northrop Frye's Writings on Shakespeare and the Renaissance* (2010), CW, 28.

The formal principles of the arts are concealed inside us somewhere.
Entry, Notebook 20 (after 1965), 15, *Northrop Frye's Fiction and Miscellaneous Writings* (2007), CW, 25.

It is important that the limits of art seem to lie somewhere between pure dream & pure reality.
Entry, Notebook 38 (1952–55), 56, *Notebooks for "Anatomy of Criticism"* (2007), CW, 23.

Through such an analysis we may come to realize that the two essential facts about a work of art, that it is contemporary with its own time and that it is contemporary with ours, are not opposed but complementary facts.
"First Essay: Historical Criticism: Theory of Modes" (1957), *Anatomy of Criticism: Four Essays* (2006), CW, 22.

It speaks with authority, but not the familiar authority of parental or social conditioning: there will always be, I expect, some mystery about the real source of its authority.
"The View from Here" (1980), *Northrop Frye's Writings on Education* (2001), CW, 7.

Art proves the inadequacy of abstract and rational ideas by the rule that examples and illustrations are more powerful than doctrines or precepts.
"Part One: The Argument," *Fearful Symmetry: A Study of William Blake* (1947, 2004), CW, 14.

The function of art is to awaken faith by making us aware of the imaginative world concealed within us.
Entry, Notebook 21 (1969–76), 572, *Northrop Frye's Notebooks and Lectures on the Bible and Other Religious Texts* (2003), CW, 13.

And the greater the work of art, the more completely it reveals the gigantic myth which is the vision of this world as God sees it, the outlines of that vision being creation, fall, redemption, and apocalypse.
"Part One: The Argument," *Fearful Symmetry: A Study of William Blake* (1947, 2004), CW, 14.

In short, works of art constituted for him what they have always been since Palaeolithic times, a focus of meditation, a means of concentrating consciousness.
"The View from Here" (1980), referring to William Blake, *Northrop Frye's Writings on Education* (2001), CW, 7.

All art, even the greatest, is flawed, and our total response to it is bound to include a certain critical detachment.
"Part One: The Argument," *Fearful Symmetry: A Study of William Blake* (1947, 2004), CW, 14.

The total form of art, so to speak, is a world whose content is nature but whose form is human; hence when it "imitates" nature it assimilates nature to human forms.
"Myth, Fiction, and Displacement" (1961), *"The Educated Imagination" and Other Writings on Critical Theory, 1933–1963* (2006), CW, 21.

The sources of art are enthusiasm and inspiration: if society mocks and derides these, it is society that is mad, not the artist, no matter what excesses the latter may commit....
"Part One: The Argument," *Fearful Symmetry: A Study of William Blake* (1947, 2004), CW, 14.

Art is not simply an identity of illusion and reality, but a counter-illusion: its world is a material world, but the material of an intelligible spiritual world.
Entry, Notebook 27 (1986), 399, *Northrop Frye's Late Notebooks, 1982–1990: Architecture of the Spiritual World* (2000), CW, 5.

Art, according to Plato, is a dream for awakened minds, a work of imagination withdrawn from ordinary life, dominated by the same forces that dominate the dream, and yet giving us a perspective and dimension on reality that we don't get from any other approach to reality.
"The Keys to Dreamland," *The Educated Imagination* (1963), *"The Educated Imagination" and Other Writings on Critical Theory, 1933–1963* (2006), CW, 21.

We have as great art as humanity can ever produce with us now.
"Humanities in a New World" (1958), *Northrop Frye's Writings on Education* (2001), CW, 7.

In art we learn as the child learns, through the concrete illustration of stories and pictures, and without that childlike desire to listen to stories and see pictures art could not exist.
"Part One: The Argument," *Fearful Symmetry: A Study of William Blake* (1947, 2004), CW, 14.

It is difficult to see things that move quickly and are far away: in the world of time and space, therefore, all things are more or less blurred. Art sees its images as permanent living forms outside time and space.
"Part One: The Argument," *Fearful Symmetry: A Study of William Blake* (1947, 2004), CW, 14.

You can't "substitute art for religion" without making art include religion, & so recovering it from the individual or ego-centric sphere. That's really what I'm trying to do.
Entry, Notebook 3 (1946–48), 128, *Northrop Frye's Notebooks and Lectures on the Bible and Other Religious Texts* (2003), CW, 13.

Commercial art is not only monotonous but also prudish, ready to give way to any kind of pressure in order to please every kind of superstition and immaturity.
"The Church and Modern Culture" (1950), *Northrop Frye on Modern Culture* (2003), CW, 11.

... the idea I got from Pynchon: that art is a form of creative paranoia, which counteracts the real paranoia that starts wars and buggers nature.
Entry, Notebook 44 (1986–91), 114, referring to the novelist Thomas Pynchon, *Northrop Frye's Late Notebooks, 1982–1990: Architecture of the Spiritual World* (2000), CW, 5.

I've been saying that art drives a wedge between being & not-being. Wonder if it also drives a wedge between life & death. By death I mean not simple extinction, but shadow-life, Hades, the world we perhaps enter in dreams.
Entry, Notebook 19 (1964–67), 2, *The "Third Book" Notebooks of Northrop Frye, 1964–1972: The Critical Comedy* (2002), CW, 9.

Art, then, owes its existence to man's dissatisfaction with nature and his desire to transform the physical world into a human one.
"Humanities in a New World" (1958), *Northrop Frye's Writings on Education* (2001), CW, 7.

What does improve in the arts is the comprehension of them, and the refining of society which results from it.
"Tentative Conclusion" (1957), *Anatomy of Criticism: Four Essays* (2006), CW, 22.

Art is not an escape from reality but a vision of the world in its human form.
"The Primary Necessities of Existence" (1985), *Interviews with Northrop Frye* (2008), CW, 24.

A work of art is an effort at imaginative communication: if it succeeds in being that, it becomes the focus of a community. The critic is there, not so much to explain the poet, as to translate literature into a continuous dialogue with society.
"The Responsibilities of the Critic" (1976), *"The Secular Scripture" and Other Writings on Critical Theory, 1976–1991* (2006), CW, 18.

ART, CANADIAN

I am a Canadian intellectual, and therefore (in Canada it is a therefore) I am a cultural regionalist, but the extent to which Canadian culture can grow out of the Canadian soil I realize in advance to be an exceedingly limited one.
"Design as a Creative Principle in the Arts" (1966), *"The Critical Path" and Other Writings on Critical Theory, 1963–1975* (2009), CW, 27.

Still, it is good to see some abstract painting in Canada: the only really modern art in Toronto is in the Museum, where it is labelled ancient.

"Gordon Webber and Canadian Abstract Art" (1941), *Northrop Frye on Canada* (2003), CW, 12.

ART, MOSLEM

In Moslem art I notice that the effect of a great mosque is overall, in contrast to the cathedral where you move from point to point.

Entry, Notebook 21 (1969–76), 340, *Northrop Frye's Notebooks and Lectures on the Bible and Other Religious Texts* (2003), CW, 13.

ARTHURIAN LEGENDS

The Arthurian legends might well have become, in a different cultural setting, the starting point of great apocalyptic visions of Celtic triumph and Teutonic or Latin disaster, paralleling the Biblical dreams of a fallen Babylon and an eternal Jerusalem.

"History and Myth in the Bible" (1975), *Northrop Frye on Religion* (2000), CW, 4.

ARTICULATION

Articulateness is the only freedom, and relates only to the individual. All society can do is to arrange for conditions of this freedom.

Entry, Notebook 54-8 (late 1972–77), 61, *Northrop Frye's Notebooks on Romance* (2004), CW, 15

The better the poem, the more precisely and inevitably it expresses the inarticulate need for articulation.

"Interior Monologue of M. Teste" (1959), *"The Educated Imagination" and Other Writings on Critical Theory, 1933–1963* (2006), CW, 21.

ARTISTS

Art flourishes when the artist is regarded, not as a long-haired wild-eyed shaman, but as a skilled labourer who gets properly paid for his work — whether he is famous or anonymous does not matter.

"The Jooss Ballet" (1936), *Northrop Frye on Modern Culture* (2003), CW, 11.

The "artist" too, of course, is an intermediate figure between aristocrat & beat, with the same satyrical display of balls.

Entry, Notebook 12 (1968–70), 44, *The "Third Book" Notebooks of Northrop Frye, 1964–1972: The Critical Comedy* (2002), CW, 9.

Most of the world's best art has been produced by men who had genius but were otherwise no better, to say the least, than ourselves. (That, incidentally, is why no artist can become a classic until he dies, for his death separates his genius from his life, and so releases and purifies the former.

"Education and the Humanities" (1947), *Northrop Frye's Writings on Education* (2001), CW, 7.

The creative artists are important because their works are the only visible and audible models of what is going on. The rest of it is a mysterious process in which the activity of God takes place through human beings, both the living and the dead.

Entry, Notebook 50 (1987–1990), 459, *Northrop Frye's Late Notebooks, 1982–1990: Architecture of the Spiritual World* (2000), CW, 5.

ARTS

Literature is unique among the arts in being able to reflect the world escaped from, in its conventions of tragedy and irony and satire, along with the world escaped to, in its conventions of pastoral and romance and comedy.

The Critical Path: An Essay on the Social Context of Literary Criticism (1971), *"The Critical Path" and Other Writings on Critical Theory, 1963–1975* (2009), CW, 27.

I merely stress the possibility, importance, and genuineness of a response to the arts in which we can no longer separate that response from our social context and personal commitments. As for the danger of poetry becoming a "substitute" for religion, that again is merely bad metaphor: if both poetry and religion are functioning properly, their interpenetration will take care of itself.

"Expanding Eyes" (1975), *"The Critical Path" and Other Writings on Critical Theory, 1963–1975* (2009), CW, 27.

The arts in their turn cannot help releasing the powerful acids of satire, realism, ribaldry,

and fantasy in their attempt to dissolve all the existential concretions that get in their way.
> "Second Essay: Ethical Criticism: Theory of Symbols" (1957), *Anatomy of Criticism: Four Essays* (2006), CW, 22.

For the arts reflect the world that produces them, and everything the detractors of modern art say about it is true, except that what they are objecting to is not so much something in our art as something in our lives.
> "Academy without Walls" (1961), *Northrop Frye on Modern Culture* (2003), CW, 11.

In other words, the arts belong to a conception of reality in which reality is something that man makes, something that man constructs himself, so that when the issue is raised about the rights and wrongs of such reality, we have to raise the question of what our vision of society is in the largest sense.
> "The Social Importance of Literature" (1968), *Northrop Frye's Writings on Education* (2001), CW, 7.

Everything worth doing and done well is an art, whether love, conversation, religion, education, sport, cookery or commerce.
> "Part One: The Argument," *Fearful Symmetry: A Study of William Blake* (1947, 2004), CW, 14.

ARTS & SCIENCES

The individual artist is a representative of human imagination, just as the individual scientist is a representative of human reason.
> "Speculation and Concern" (1966), *Northrop Frye's Writings on Education* (2001), CW, 7.

The natural direction of science, then, is onward: it moves toward still greater achievements in the future. The arts have this in common with religion, that their direction is not onward into the future but upward from where we stand.
> "Humanities in a New World" (1958), *Northrop Frye's Writings on Education* (2001), CW, 7.

But subjective art is as impossible a conception as subjective science. The arts are techniques of communication....
> "Speculation and Concern" (1966), *Northrop Frye's Writings on Education* (2001), CW, 7.

For the arts, including the liberal arts, do not, like the sciences, improve: they revolve around certain classics, or models, which will remain models as long as the art endures.
> "Comment" (1961), *Northrop Frye on Twentieth-Century Literature* (2010), CW, 29.

The sciences are primarily concerned with the world as it is, and the arts are primarily concerned with the world man wants to live in. What is not readily recognized is the fact that both require the same mental processes.
> "The Primary Necessities of Existence" (1985), *Interviews with Northrop Frye* (2008), CW, 24.

The polarizing of creative power between vision and sense is the basis of the distinction between the arts and the sciences. The sciences begin with sense, and work towards a mental construct founded on it. The arts begin with vision, and work towards a mental construct founded on it.
> "The Imaginative and the Imaginary" (1962), *"The Educated Imagination" and Other Writings on Critical Theory, 1933–1963* (2006), CW, 21.

The sciences demand intellect, the arts demand good taste, or disciplined imagination and emotions.
> "By Liberal Things" (1959), *Northrop Frye's Writings on Education* (2001), CW, 7.

... fifty years of teaching have only confirmed my conviction that only the arts and sciences are stable social realities: everything else simply dissolves and re-forms. The world of 1989 is no more like the world I was born into in 1912 than it is like the Stone Age, but nothing has improved since then except scientific and scholarly knowledge, and nothing has remained steady except human creative power.
> "Speech at the New Canadian Embassy, Washington" (1989), *Northrop Frye on Canada* (2003), CW, 12.

ASSASSINATION

It seems almost as though the Hitlers and Stalins of the world do not get shot because the people who hate them are the kind of people to whom murder, for however good a cause, is repugnant. But the Lincolns and

40 Assassination

Gandhis of the world are hated by the kind of people to whom murder comes naturally and agreeably.

"Gandhi" (1948), *Northrop Frye on Modern Culture* (2003), CW, 11.

ASTROLOGY

I have been studying astrology recently and found that I was born under the sign of Cancer, the Crab. This interested me at once, of course, as I saw there must be *something* in the science after all, so I read on and learned quite a bit about it.

"NF to HK," 25 Aug. 1932, *The Correspondence of Northrop Frye and Helen Kemp, 1932–1939* (1996), CW, 1.

There are many who "believe in" astrology, i.e., would like to feel that there is "something in it," but I should imagine that relatively few of them are astronomers.

"The Times of the Signs" (1973), *"The Critical Path" and Other Writings on Critical Theory, 1963–1975* (2009), CW, 27.

Even at that I'm suspicious of astrology: it's too close to the view that creation was made for man, a notion not only wrong but ultimately sick.

Entry, Notebook 11e (1978), 38, *Northrop Frye's Notebooks and Lectures on the Bible and Other Religious Texts* (2003), CW, 13.

ASTRONOMY

In my childhood I dreamed of becoming a great astronomer & discovering a new planet beyond Neptune that I was going to call Pluto.

Entry, Notebook 3 (1946–48), 172, *Northrop Frye's Notebooks and Lectures on the Bible and Other Religious Texts* (2003), CW, 13.

But then I like astronomy to be spectacular & obvious. I'll take the galaxies millions of light years away on faith, or rather trust, and as for seeing, if I can see mountains on the moon I'm perfectly happy.

Entry, 18 Aug. 1950, 555, after attending a lecture by astronomer Harlow Shapley and viewing through a telescope a galaxy and then the moons of Jupiter, Harvard University, *The Diaries of Northrop Frye: 1942–1955* (2001), CW, 8.

ATHEISM

If we say, "There is a God," we have suggested the possibility of saying, "There is no God," and so in a sense have already said it. The most effective ideologies today, as said earlier, are those that have developed enough flexibility and tolerance to take account of this fact.

"Concern and Myth," *Words with Power: Being a Second Study of "The Bible and Literature"* (2008), CW, 26.

ATLANTIS

What's under the Atlantic is what's inside us: if we uncover it we either find a spring of living water or we get drowned in a new flood just for us.

Entry, Notes 53 (1989–90), 27, *Northrop Frye's Late Notebooks, 1982–1990: Architecture of the Spiritual World* (2000), CW, 6.

Why does Atlantis have to be in the *past*? If it's a myth, of course, it's present, an example or warning.

Entry, Notebook 24 (1970–72), 197, *The "Third Book" Notebooks of Northrop Frye, 1964–1972: The Critical Comedy* (2002), CW, 9.

I'm no nearer understanding Atlantis or reincarnation symbolism, but I do understand more clearly that it polarizes the Bible in some way.

Entry, Notebook 24 (1970–72), 224, *The "Third Book" Notebooks of Northrop Frye, 1964–1972: The Critical Comedy* (2002), CW, 9.

The myth of Atlantis, as I've known from the beginning, is another version of the myth of the fall, except that those who deal with it usually try to place it in history, whereas it doesn't really belong in history necessarily.

Entry, Notes 53 (1989–90), 41, *Northrop Frye's Late Notebooks, 1982–1990: Architecture of the Spiritual World* (2000), CW, 6.

Plato dreams up an ideal state, with future overtones, then says it corresponds exactly to an anti-diluvian state that fell from grace.

Entry, Notebook 21 (1969–76), 313, *Northrop Frye's Notebooks and Lectures on the Bible and Other Religious Texts* (2003), CW, 13.

ATOM BOMBS

Man is a very frivolous animal, with a short memory and a limited imagination, and he can tie himself up in words to the point of persuading himself that dropping atom bombs on people he's never seen is a kind of shrewd move in an exciting chess game.

"Laurence Hyde, 'Southern Cross,' and 'The Oxford Dictionary of Nursery Rhymes'" (1952), *Northrop Frye on Literature and Society, 1936–1989: Unpublished Papers* (2002), CW, 10.

I said I felt distressed at the thought of a city going up in smoke, but the thought of a chain-reaction blowing the whole world to pieces filled me with profound peace.

Entry, 20 Feb. 1950, 130, an informal discussion with colleagues on "the H-bomb," *The Diaries of Northrop Frye: 1942–1955* (2001), CW, 8.

When Russian and American spokesmen both tell us that nobody would start an atomic war because there would be no sense in such a thing and nobody could gain anything at all from it, we are not reassured. We simply do not believe that human society is as sane as that any more.

"The View from Here" (1980), *Northrop Frye's Writings on Education* (2001), CW, 7.

ATWOOD, MARGARET

Margaret Atwood, like the CN Tower, is a free-standing structure, and needs no patronizing props of reference to her sex or her nationality.

"Margaret Eleanor Atwood" (1983), *Northrop Frye on Canada* (2003), CW, 12.

AUDIENCES

The writer has two centres of gravity: one in his own time and audience; the other in our time and in us. It is a mysterious but primary fact of literature that a poet remote from us in space and time and culture can still communicate his central vision to us, though we may admire him for reasons quite unintelligible to him or his age.

"Tradition and Change in the Theory of Criticism" (1969), *Northrop Frye on Literature and Society, 1936–1989: Unpublished Papers* (2002), CW, 10.

Any dramatist who knew his audience as well as Shakespeare would know that the important difference in it is not the difference between intelligent and stupid people, but the difference between intelligent and stupid responses to the play, both of which may exist in the same mind.

"A Natural Perspective: The Development of Shakespearean Comedy and Romance; II, Making Nature Afraid" (1963), *Northrop Frye's Writings on Shakespeare and the Renaissance* (2010), CW, 28.

... to say that society should be tolerant is as fallacious as saying that the artist should be a good man. Both these things are true, but on different grounds. The role of the artist & the quality of art depends primarily on the quality of the audience's imaginative response.

Entry, Notebook 8 (1946–58), *Northrop Frye's Notebooks on Renaissance Literature* (2006), CW, 20.

AUSTEN, JANE

Jane is a blind spot to me: I enjoy reading her for relaxation and I admire her skill and ingenuity, but I never feel much sense of cultural infusion, of the kind I require from a great writer.

Entry, 23 Aug. 1942, 75, *The Diaries of Northrop Frye: 1942–1955* (2001), CW, 8.

AUTHORITY

I believe that one of the intellectual activities of our time consists in trying to see what is behind the social and political façade of authority.

"The Wisdom of the Reader" (1979), *Interviews with Northrop Frye* (2008), CW, 24.

Every writer, past or present, big or little, is, by the act of writing, making a bid for authority, for filling a place in our imaginative experience that no one else can fill in quite the same way.

"Literary Criticism" (1963), *"The Critical Path" and Other Writings on Critical Theory, 1963–1975* (2009), CW, 27.

Authority is of the subject: this is what equalizes teacher & student.

"On Education II" (post-1972), 26, *Northrop Frye's Fiction and Miscellaneous Writings* (2007), CW, 25.

All personal authority comes from teachers who want to stop being teachers.
>   Entry, Notebook 50 (1987–90), 493, *Northrop Frye's Late Notebooks, 1982–1990: Architecture of the Spiritual World* (2000), CW, 5.

The source of actual or "temporal" authority in society is seldom hard to locate. It is always in the near vicinity of whatever one pays one's taxes to.
>   "The Problem of Spiritual Authority in the Nineteenth Century" (1964), *Northrop Frye's Writings on the Eighteenth and Nineteenth Centuries* (2005), CW, 17.

The authority of the logical argument, the repeatable experiment, the established fact, the compelling work of art, is the only authority that exacts no bows or salutes. It is not sacrosanct, for what is true today may be inadequately true tomorrow, but it is what holds society together for today.
>   "The Ethics of Change: The Role of the University" (1968), *Northrop Frye's Writings on Education* (2001), CW, 7.

We have seen that spiritual authority begins in the recognition of truth, and truth usually has about it some quality of the objective, something presented to us.
>   "The Problem of Spiritual Authority in the Nineteenth Century" (1964), *Northrop Frye's Writings on the Eighteenth and Nineteenth Centuries* (2005), CW, 17.

There is only one real authority in society, and that is the authority of the arts and sciences, the authority of logical reasoning, uncooked evidence, repeatable experiments, verifiable scholarship, precise and disciplined creative imagination.
>   "Universities and the Deluge of Cant" (1972), *Northrop Frye's Writings on Education* (2001), CW, 7.

No human being or human institution is fit to be trusted with any temporal authority that is not subject to cancellation by some other authority.
>   *The Double Vision* (1991), *Northrop Frye on Religion* (2000), CW, 4.

... authority in the sciences is thus impersonal, and comes from the subject itself; authority in the arts is personal, and derives from individual genius. We still need loyalty to something with enough authority to form a community, but it must be a *free* authority, something that fulfils and does not diminish the individual. Such an authority can ultimately only be the kind of authority that education embodies.
>   "The Ethics of Change: The Role of the University" (1968), *Northrop Frye's Writings on Education* (2001), CW, 7.

The authority of the logical argument, the repeatable experiment, the compelling imagination, is the final authority in society, and it is an authority that demands no submission, no subordinating, no lessening of dignity. As this authority is the same thing as freedom, the university is also the only place in society where freedom is defined.
>   "A Revolution Betrayed: Freedom and Necessity in Education" (1970), *Northrop Frye's Writings on Education* (2001), CW, 7.

AUTHORSHIP

A few novelists, most of them bad ones, may eke out a small living by writing, or even hit a best-seller jackpot; but a poet would have to be spectacularly bad before he could live on his poetry.
>   "Culture and the National Will" (1957), *Northrop Frye on Canada* (2003), CW, 12.

AUTOBIOGRAPHY

Autobiography is, like blank verse, very easy to write and very hard to write well.
>   "Herbert Read's *The Innocent Eye*" (1947), *Northrop Frye on Modern Culture* (2003), CW, 11.

Thus an autobiography coming into a library would be classified as nonfiction if the librarian believed the author, and as fiction if she thought he was lying. It is difficult to see what use such a distinction can be to a literary critic.
>   "Fourth Essay: Rhetorical Criticism: Theory of Genres" (1957), *Anatomy of Criticism: Four Essays* (2006), CW, 22.

AUTOMOBILE

Washington was a city designed for automobiles rather than pedestrians long before there were any automobiles: Los Angeles, a city never designed at all, seems to have broken through the control even of the automobile. It was, after all, named after angels, who traditionally do not travel through space but simply manifest themselves elsewhere.

"Canada: New World Without Revolution" (1975), *Northrop Frye on Canada* (2003), CW, 12.

AVIATION

Technology is the most dramatic aspect of this development: one cannot take off in a jet plane and expect a radically different way of life in the place where the plane lands.

"Canadian Culture Today" (1977), *Northrop Frye on Canada* (2003), CW, 12.

Technology can improve the efficiency of aeroplanes to a degree that outstrips the wildest dreams with which it began. But no sooner has it done so than the airline companies go broke, airports get clogged up, citizens complain about sonic-boom noise, and terrorists develop a taste for free rides to Cuba.

"The Quality of Life in the '70s" (1971), *Northrop Frye on Modern Culture* (2003), CW, 11.

What's produced the aeroplane is not so much a desire to fly as a rebellion against the tyranny of time and space. And that's a process that can never stop, no matter how high our Titovs and Glenns may go.

"The Motive for Metaphor," *The Educated Imagination* (1963), *"The Educated Imagination" and Other Writings on Critical Theory, 1933–1963* (2006), CW, 21.

Elsewhere the plane may mean a loosening of bonds, a way of escape; in Canada it is a means of tightening the country into a recognizable shape.

"View of Canada" (1976), *Northrop Frye on Canada* (2003), CW, 12.

... it's the airplane, I think, that has made one crucial difference to the Canadian consciousness. The airplane supplied a perspective that began to pull the country together....

"View of Canada" (1976), *Northrop Frye on Canada* (2003), CW, 12.

The airplane is a recent invention, but the vision that produced it was already ancient in the arts when Daedalus flew out of the labyrinth and Jehovah rode the sky on the wings of a seraph.

"The Imaginative and the Imaginary" (1962), *"The Educated Imagination" and Other Writings on Critical Theory, 1933–1963* (2006), CW, 21.

AWARDS

Our real judgments, therefore, are positive, not comparative or superlative.

"Governor General's Awards (I)" (1963), on being a judge, *Northrop Frye on Canada* (2003), CW, 12.

But the real importance of the awards, and the justification for associating them with so distinguished an office, is not that they pick the "best" books, but that they indicate a specific interest on the part of the nation in the production of good ones.

"Speech on Acceptance of the Governor General's Award for *Northrop Frye on Shakespeare*" (1987), *Northrop Frye's Writings on Shakespeare and the Renaissance* (2010), CW, 28.

Lobbying for a writer to get a prize which, if she won it, would become worthless because she won it doesn't strike me as a very dignified occupation.

Entry, 23 Jan. 1952, 58, on refusing to join a recommendation that Mazo de la Roche be considered for a Nobel Prize, *The Diaries of Northrop Frye: 1942–1955* (2001), CW, 8.

We are not conferring a distinction on them; we are merely pointing out the distinction they themselves have achieved.

"Governor General's Awards (I)" (1963), speaking as a judge, *Northrop Frye on Canada* (2003), CW, 12.

AXIS MUNDI

About the *axis mundi*, we can say two things, first, that it is not there, and second, that it won't go away.

"The *Koiné* of Myth: Myth as a Universally Intelligible Language" (1984), *"The Secular Scripture" and Other Writings on Critical Theory, 1976–1991* (2006), CW, 18.

AYATOLLAH

God doesn't create post-mortem hells even for people devoting their lives to cruelty and tyranny, but if he did the Ayatollah would certainly be howling in one of them forever.

Entry, Notes 53 (1989–90), 162, *Northrop Frye's Late Notebooks, 1982–1990: Architecture of the Spiritual World* (2000), CW, 6.

B

BABEL
The society of power always tends to resemble the pyramid or tower of Babel: the society of love tends to resemble the communion table.
"The Church: Its Relation to Society" (1949), *Northrop Frye on Religion* (2000), CW, 4.

Babel is action with confused words.
Entry, Notebook 44 (1986–91), 599, *Northrop Frye's Late Notebooks, 1982–1990: Architecture of the Spiritual World* (2000), CW, 5.

BABIES
The parents of a new baby are proud of its novelty; they may even speak of it as unique; but the source of their pride is the fact that it is a recognizable human being, and conforms to a prescribed convention.
"Nature and Homer" (1958), *"The Educated Imagination" and Other Writings on Critical Theory, 1933–1963* (2006), CW, 21.

BACH, J.S.
I'm probably just nutty, but the 1st movement of the 6th Brandenburg Suite has something sinister about it to me, as though a race of superhuman Robots, cultivated but ruthless, were marching along at a terrific speed to wipe us out.
Entry, Notebook 5 (1935–42), 17, *Northrop Frye's Fiction and Miscellaneous Writings* (2007), CW, 25.

I think Bach is the great Protestant poet of the Pathos: not only two Passions, but even the B minor centres on the Kyrie and the Crucifixion.
Entry, Notebook 5 (1935–42), 22, *Northrop Frye's Fiction and Miscellaneous Writings* (2007), CW, 25.

If we are listening to music, let us say, on the level of Bach or Mozart, the response keeps shifting from the personal to the impersonal. On the one hand we feel that this is Bach, that it couldn't possibly be anyone else. On the other hand, there are moments when Bach disappears, and what we feel is: this is the voice of music itself; this is what music was created to say. At that level, we are not hearing the music so much as recognizing it.
"The Teacher's Source of Authority" (1978), *Northrop Frye's Writings on Education* (2001), CW, 7.

BACK TO BASICS
I distrust all slogans of the "back to basics" type because I distrust anything that stars with "back to." That is, I know that what is called a pastoral myth is operating — that at one time people were much better taught than they are now. I simply don't believe that.
"The Scholar in Society" (1983), *Interviews with Northrop Frye* (2008), CW, 24.

BALLET
The ballet cannot remain permanently in fairyland — the satiric attitude is too important and essential to contemporary art for that.
"Ballet Russe" (1935), *Northrop Frye on Modern Culture* (2003), CW, 11.

BAPTISM
Just as the Eucharist in Christianity is founded on the metaphorical basis of food and drink, so baptism becomes the physical image of spiritual cleanliness, the separating of the true individual from the excreta of original sin.
"Third Variation: The Cave," *Words with Power: Being a Second Study of "The Bible and Literature"* (1990), CW, 26.

BASEBALL
There is certainly no evidence that baseball has descended from a ritual of human

sacrifice, but the umpire is quite as much of a *pharmakos* as if it had: he is an abandoned scoundrel, a greater robber than Barabbas; he has the evil eye; the supporters of the losing team scream for his death.

"First Essay: Historical Criticism: Theory of Modes" (1957), *Anatomy of Criticism: Four Essays* (2006), CW, 22.

BEAT MOVEMENT

The beat philosophy may be wrong — that is, it may be crazy itself instead of merely making use of craziness — but its symbolism is a contemporary cultural force to be reckoned with.

"World Enough Without Time" (1959), *"The Educated Imagination" and Other Writings on Critical Theory, 1933–1963* (2006), CW, 21.

BEAUTY

The beautiful has the same relation to the diminutive that the sublime has to bigness, and is closely related to the sense of the intricate and exquisite.

"First Essay: Historical Criticism: Theory of Modes" (1957), *Anatomy of Criticism: Four Essays* (2006), CW, 22.

The pursuit of beauty is much more dangerous nonsense than the pursuit of truth or goodness, because it affords a stronger temptation to the ego.

"Second Essay: Ethical Criticism: Theory of Symbols" (1957), *Anatomy of Criticism: Four Essays* (2006), CW, 22.

The progress of criticism has a good deal to do with recognizing beauty in a greater and greater variety of phenomena and situations and works of art. The ugly, in proportion, tends to become whatever violates primary concern.

"Second Variation: The Garden," *Words with Power: Being a Second Study of "The Bible and Literature"* (2008), CW, 26.

The cult of beauty, then, is reactionary: it is continually setting up barriers to the conquest of experience by art, and limits the variety of expression in art wherever it can.

"Yeats and the Language of Symbolism" (1947), *"The Critical Path" and Other Writings on Critical Theory, 1963–1975* (2009), CW, 27.

Identity is love; difference beauty.

Entry, Notebook 50 (1987–90), 77, *Northrop Frye's Late Notebooks, 1982–1990: Architecture of the Spiritual World* (2000), CW, 5.

When we speak of the human body as beautiful we mean a body of someone in good physical condition between about eighteen and thirty, and when Dégas expresses interest in thick-bottomed matrons squatting in hip-baths, we confuse the shock to our sense of propriety with a shock to our sense of beauty.

"Yeats and the Language of Symbolism" (1947), *"The Critical Path" and Other Writings on Critical Theory, 1963–1975* (2009), CW, 27.

The notion that thinking the world is beautiful has actual survival value may have nothing in it, but it's worth thinking about. Otherwise, why do we call both art and nature beautiful? It seems absurd on the face of it to apply the same term to a Mozart divertimento and some cutie in a bathing suit.

Entry, Notes 53 (1989–90), 50, *Northrop Frye's Late Notebooks, 1982–1990: Architecture of the Spiritual World* (2000), CW, 6.

BEAUTY CONTESTS

A beauty contest is a narcissistic middle-class ritual: the contestants have the immobility, the fixed smiles, the mechanical responses, the sense of remoteness, of wax mannequins in a shop window, which have much the same social function.

"Reviews of Television Programs for the Canadian Radio-Television Commission: Reflections on Television ... November 1971–March 1972" (1972), *Northrop Frye on Literature and Society, 1936–1989: Unpublished Papers* (2002), CW, 10.

BECAUSE

... as I have tried to show elsewhere, nothing can follow "because" except some kind of pseudo-critical moral anxiety.

"Criticism, Visible and Invisible" (1964), *"The Critical Path" and Other Writings on Critical Theory, 1963–1975* (2009), CW, 27.

BECKETT, SAMUEL

The dramatic convention parodied in *Waiting for Godot* is clearly the act that killed vaudeville, the weary dialogue of two faceless figures who will say anything to put off leaving the stage.

"The Nightmare Life in Death" (1960), *Northrop Frye on Twentieth-Century Literature* (2010), CW, 29.

BEETHOVEN, LUDWIG VAN
I would like to hear the 9th as the only thing on the programme, with the Ode sung in some language I don't understand.

"NF to HK," 18 Apr. 1934, describing a performance of Beethoven's *Ninth Symphony*, *The Correspondence of Northrop Frye and Helen Kemp, 1932–1939* (1996), CW, 1.

The master of comedy gets little reward for not being sententious. Because what was a profound truth to Beethoven was only a platitude to Mozart, Beethoven is listened to with awestruck reverence and Mozart indulgently smiled at as charmingly superficial.

"Chaucer's *Canterbury Tales*" (1936), *Northrop Frye on Literature and Society, 1936–1989: Unpublished Papers* (2002), CW, 10.

BEHAVIOUR
Behaviorism is senility. When an organism has reached its adjustment, it stops evolving, & a man who has stopped evolving in this world is still only an ape.

Entry, 2 Mar. 1953, 8, *The Diaries of Northrop Frye: 1942–1955* (2001), CW, 8.

Most of our behaviour is mechanical; that of some people wholly so. I think there is a point at which one breaks through this & forms a kernel of autonomy or free will. Total liberation completes what this starts.

Entry, Notebook 21 (1969–76), 213, *Northrop Frye's Notebooks and Lectures on the Bible and Other Religious Texts* (2003), CW, 13.

BEING
Now, how is Being related to God? Theologians say Being is an analogy of God, philosophers say that God is an analogy of Being.

Entry, Notebook 12 (1968–70), 436, *The "Third Book" Notebooks of Northrop Frye, 1964–1972: The Critical Comedy* (2002), CW, 9.

BELIEF
To say "this really happened, and history doesn't really happen" is walking a tightrope over Niagara gorge, but something like that must be what's being asked of us.

"Notes for 'The Dialectic of Belief and Vision'" (1983), 30, *Northrop Frye's Fiction and Miscellaneous Writings* (2007), CW, 25.

Belief without vision is always hysterical. Because vision is itself the confirmation of belief: the hypostasis of the hoped for and the *elenchos* of the unseen is not and never can be the acceptance of something without evidence.

"Notes for 'The Dialectic of Belief and Vision'" (1983), 7, *Northrop Frye's Fiction and Miscellaneous Writings* (2007), CW, 25.

Belief is rather the creative energy that turns the illusory into the real. Such belief is neither rational nor ideological, but belongs on the other side of the imaginative.

"Spirit and Symbol," *Words with Power: Being a Second Study of "The Bible and Literature"* (2008), CW, 26.

Just as we have a principle of economy of means in the arts, and of economy of hypotheses in the sciences, so we need a principle of economy of belief.

"The Times of the Signs" (1973), *"The Critical Path" and Other Writings on Critical Theory, 1963–1975* (2009), CW, 27.

I think a genuine belief is an axiom of behaviour. If you want to know what a man believes you watch him, you see what he does. What he really believes will be what his actions show that he believes.

"Between Paradise and Apocalypse" (1978), *Interviews with Northrop Frye* (2008), CW, 24.

I don't believe in anything that is to be believed: that is, I don't trust anything that remains in the dark as an object of belief.

Entry, Notebook 11f (1969–70), 162, *Northrop Frye's Notebooks and Lectures on the Bible and Other Religious Texts* (2003), CW, 13.

Only what may not have happened at all is a fit subject for belief.

Entry, Notebook 46 (1980s–90), 34, *Northrop Frye's Late Notebooks, 1982–1990: Architecture of the Spiritual World* (2000), CW, 6.

A belief can only be replaced by another belief, even when a godless religion is substituted for a godly one.
"The Well-Tempered Critic (II)" (1961), *"The Educated Imagination" and Other Writings on Critical Theory, 1933–1963* (2006), CW, 21.

Everything possible to be believed is an image of truth is the motto of my present job.
Entry, Notebook 19 (1964–67), 203, *The "Third Book" Notebooks of Northrop Frye, 1964–1972: The Critical Comedy* (2002), CW, 9.

As long as both imagination and belief are working properly, we can avoid the neurotic extremes of the dilettante who is so bemused by imaginative possibilities that he has no convictions, and the bigot who is so bemused by his convictions that he cannot see them as also possibilities.
"The Well-Tempered Critic (II)" (1961), *"The Educated Imagination" and Other Writings on Critical Theory, 1933–1963* (2006), CW, 21.

A metaphor will be "believed," that is, assumed as part of the framework of one's thinking, as long as it seems emotionally convincing, and is irrefutable until it ceases to be so.
"Blake's Bible" (2 Jun. 1987), *Northrop Frye on Milton and Blake* (2005), CW, 16.

The willing suspension of *belief*, not disbelief, is what matters.
Entry, Notebook 19 (1964–67), 421, recalling Coleridge's words about the "willing suspension of disbelief," *The "Third Book" Notebooks of Northrop Frye, 1964–1972: The Critical Comedy* (2002), CW, 9.

The world of the imagination is a world of unborn or embryonic beliefs: if you believe what you read in literature, you can, quite literally, believe anything.
"Giants in Time," *The Educated Imagination* (1963), *"The Educated Imagination" and Other Writings on Critical Theory, 1933–1963* (2006), CW, 21.

A belief is a course of action inspired by a shaping vision. This shaping vision is the opposite of idolatry. In both cases you become what you behold.
Entry, Notebook 24 (1970–72), 195, *The "Third Book" Notebooks of Northrop Frye, 1964–1972: The Critical Comedy* (2002), CW, 9.

When something is certain it ceases to be believed, even though we continue to use the word.
Entry, Notebook 54-8 (late 1972–77), 24, *Northrop Frye's Notebooks on Romance* (2004), CW, 15.

A better way of putting the question is "If I had been there is this what I should have experienced?" It is only in these terms that belief or doubt arises, & what does rise is nearly all doubt. The doubt is of oneself rather than of the event, which, as just said, eludes the categories of doubt & belief.
Entry, Notebook 11f (1969–70), 5, *Northrop Frye's Notebooks and Lectures on the Bible and Other Religious Texts* (2003), CW, 13.

In belief as ordinarily understood, experience is divided between the involuntarily credible, or what we can't help believing (*e.g.*, the data of sense experience, or some of them), and the voluntarily credible, which is accepted without confirming or supporting evidence.
"*Pistis* and *Mythos*" (1972), *Northrop Frye on Religion* (2000), CW, 4.

Problems of belief are still with me: for all practical purposes "I don't believe in God" and "I believe in no God" are interchangeable. They seem to me to be very different statements, and the agnostic-atheist distinction doesn't exhaust the difference.
Entry, Notebook 27 (1986), 38, *Northrop Frye's Late Notebooks, 1982–1990: Architecture of the Spiritual World* (2000), CW, 5.

I'm a Xn [Christian] partly faute de mieux: I see no better faith, & certainly couldn't invent one of my own except out of Xn assumptions. But some of my other principles are: a) the less we believe the better b) nothing should be believed that has to be believed in.

Entry, Notebook 21 (1969–76), 499, *Northrop Frye's Notebooks and Lectures on the Bible and Other Religious Texts* (2003), CW, 13.

Belief has to be redefined as the process of existential choice, which involves selecting a community.
Entry, Notebook 54-8 (late 1972–77), 42, *Northrop Frye's Notebooks on Romance* (2004), CW, 15.

If there is a creative force in the world which is greater than the purely human one, we shall not find it on the level of professed belief, but only on the level of common action and social vision.
Creation and Recreation (1980), *Northrop Frye on Religion* (2000), CW, 4.

When we consider beliefs that others hold and that we do not, our feelings are increasingly those of a sense of freedom delivered from obsession. In short, the less we "believe" in the ordinary sense the better, and one comes to distrust believing in anything that has to be believed in.
"Pistis and Mythos" (1972), *Northrop Frye on Religion* (2000), CW, 4.

Thus the artist may keep his life continuous by a belief in creativity, the businessman by a belief in productivity, the religious man by a belief in God, the politician by a belief in policy. But the more intense the immediate experience, the more obviously its context in past and future time drops away from it.
"The University and Personal Life: Student Anarchism and the Educational Contract" (1968), *Northrop Frye's Writings on Education* (2001), CW, 7.

A man may go to church on Sunday morning and find himself repeating an extremely impressive statement of what he believes in, but by Monday evening he may have demonstrated that his real conception of human society is a very different one.
"Preserving Human Values" (1961), *Northrop Frye on Modern Culture* (2003), CW, 11.

BELONGING
To participate in anything in human society means entering into a common bond of guilt, of guilt and of inevitable compromise. I am not saying that we accept the evils of what we join: I am saying that whatever we join contains evils, and that what we accept is the guilt of belonging to it.
"The Ethics of Change: The Role of the University" (1968), *Northrop Frye's Writings on Education* (2001), CW, 7.

BEREAVEMENT
In moments of despair or bereavement or horror, we find ourselves staring blankly into an unresponding emptiness, utterly frustrated by its indifference. We come from the unknown at birth, and we rejoin it at death with all our questions about it unanswered.
"To Come to Light" (1988), *Northrop Frye on Religion* (1999), CW, 4.

BESTSELLERS
A modern bestseller has only a temporary incarnation as a book between its initial appearance as a magazine serial and its ultimate appearance as a movie.
"The Church and Modern Culture" (1950), *Northrop Frye on Modern Culture* (2003), CW, 11.

BIBLE
The Bible is the world's greatest work of art and therefore has primary claim to the title of God's word.
"Part One: The Argument," *Fearful Symmetry: A Study of William Blake* (1947, 2004), CW, 14.

... the Bible (which would still be a popular book if it were not a sacred one)....
"Second Essay: Ethical Criticism: Theory of Symbols" (1957), *Anatomy of Criticism: Four Essays* (2006), CW, 22.

The Bible never calls itself the Bible nor does the phrase Word of God ever mean the Bible.
Entry, Notebook 11e (1978), 79, *Northrop Frye's Notebooks and Lectures on the Bible and Other Religious Texts* (2003), CW, 13.

The Bible is a structure of fiction and a structure of syntax, I think, rather than of meanings.
"Symbolism in the Bible" (1981–82), *Northrop Frye's Notebooks and Lectures on the Bible and Other Religious Texts* (2003), CW, 13.

If the Bible did not exist, at least as a form, it would be necessary for literary critics to invent the same kind of total and definitive verbal structure out of the fragmentary myths and legends and folk tales we have outside it.

"The Road of Excess" (1970), *Northrop Frye on Milton and Blake* (2005), CW, 16.

I can only point out the inner coherence of the book and the way in which if you look for guidance in life you get a great deal more than you actually bargain for.

"The Hypnotic Gaze of the Bible" (1982), *Interviews with Northrop Frye* (2008), CW, 24.

The Bible begins by showing on its first page that the reality of God manifests itself in creation, and on its last page that the same reality is manifested in a new creation in which man is a participant. He becomes a participant by being redeemed, or separated from the predatory and destructive elements acquired from his origin in nature. In between these visions of creation comes the Incarnation, which presents God and man as indissolubly locked together in a common enterprise.

"Spirit and Symbol," *Words with Power: Being a Second Study of "The Bible and Literature"* (1990), CW, 26.

If a book is believed to originate from a source beyond the limitations of the human mind, and a benevolent source at that, one would expect it to speak the language of breakthrough, a language that would smash these structures beyond repair, and let some genuine air and light in. But that, of course, is not how anxiety operates.

"History and Myth in the Bible" (1975), *Northrop Frye on Religion* (2000), CW, 4.

The Bible is to me the body of words through which I can see the world as a cosmos, as an order, and where I can see human nature as something redeemable, as something with a right to survive.

"Northrop Frye in Conversation" (1989), *Interviews with Northrop Frye* (2008), CW, 24.

In the Bible there are references to a prophecy which has to be sealed up and hidden away until its time has come. That time comes when in the age of the people the gods become names for human powers that belong to us, and that we can in part recover.

"The Responsibilities of the Critic" (1976), *"The Secular Scripture" and Other Writings on Critical Theory, 1976–1991* (2006), CW, 18.

Yet the suggestion in it of infinite mysteries connected with *logos* or articulate speech is as fascinating to the literary critic in me as a flame to a moth, even if in the end it proves equally destructive.

"Teaching the Humanities Today" (1977), *Northrop Frye's Writings on Education* (2001), CW, 7.

Even the Bible must be shaken upside-down before it will yield all its secrets.

"Part One: The Argument," *Fearful Symmetry: A Study of William Blake* (1947, 2004), CW, 14.

BIBLE AS LITERATURE PLUS

The real reason why the Bible fascinates me as a literary critic is that its language comes out of direct experience. It's not secondhand language.

"The Primary Necessities of Existence" (1985), *Interviews with Northrop Frye* (2008), CW, 24.

Fact is objective, and fiction is a human construct. The Bible is neither. It's something beyond both.

"The Great Teacher" (1988), *Interviews with Northrop Frye* (2008), CW, 24.

In the Bible I think you have uniquely a book which has no outside.... In the Bible what is inside the book and what it points to outside the book have become identified. The Bible is not confined by what we usually call the imaginative, which I sometimes call the hypothetical.

"Maintaining Freedom in Paradise" (1982), *Interviews with Northrop Frye* (2008), CW 24.

The Bible to me is not a structure of doctrine, not a structure of propositions, but a collection of stories making up one single story, and that's the interrelationship of God and man. You can understand the importance

of that interpenetration without necessarily believing in God.
"Canadian and American Values" (1988), *Interviews with Northrop Frye* (2008), CW, 24.

... it is, in short, a work of literature plus. The present book attempts to explain once more what that "plus" is, why the beginning of the response to the Bible must be a literary response, and why, within the Bible itself, all the values connected with the term "truth" can be reached only by passing through myth and metaphor.
"Introduction" (1990), *Words with Power: Being a Second Study of "The Bible and Literature"* (2008), CW, 26.

I'm trying to distinguish the sacred book, the Bible, from secular literature. That literature is written in the imaginative language of myth and metaphor, but it doesn't provide a model to adopt as a way of life, whereas the object of the writers of the Gospels writing about Jesus was the imitation of Christ, in the sense that they were telling a story just as the writers of literature tell a story. But the particular story they told was the one that they wanted to make a model of the life of the person reading it.
"Cultural Identity in Canada" (1990), *Interviews with Northrop Frye* (2008), CW, 24.

Works of literature aren't on a par with the Bible: they form models for the central understanding of the Bible. One has to see the Bible *as though* it were literary before one can pass beyond the literary.
"Notes for 'The Dialectic of Belief and Vision'" (1983), 22, *Northrop Frye's Fiction and Miscellaneous Writings* (2007), CW, 25.

It's just nonsense to apply evaluation to the Bible, and that's because it keeps continually breaking out of the category of literature.
"Getting the Order Right" (1978), *Interviews with Northrop Frye* (2008), CW, 24.

Nothing happens in the Bible except verbal events, but it's the interplay among those verbal events in which the truth emerges. Afterwards it is inexhaustible.

"Archetype and History" (1986), *Interviews with Northrop Frye* (2008), CW, 24.

The Bible is the only place in our tradition I know where one can get a view of literature that goes beyond literature, and so establishes its relative finiteness, and yet includes all the elements of literature. In this age of posts and metas, I can find nothing in our cultural tradition except the Bible that really illustrates the metaliterary.
"Auguries of Experience" (1987), *"The Secular Scripture" and Other Writings on Critical Theory, 1976–1991* (2006), CW, 18.

One thinks more particularly of the Bible, which is one long folk tale from beginning to end, and the most primitive and popular book in the world.
"Blake after Two Centuries" (1957), *Northrop Frye on Milton and Blake* (2005), CW, 16.

Perhaps our conclusion will be that the Bible is the only work of literature that ever succeeded in getting beyond literature. I am not at this point discussing the Bible's truth or reality, only the language in which that truth or reality is being presented to us. That that language is mythical seems to me unanswerable.
Entry, Notebook 11f (1969–70), 61, *Northrop Frye's Notebooks and Lectures on the Bible and Other Religious Texts* (2003), CW, 13.

If the Word is the beginning, it is the end too, and the Omega as well as the Alpha, and what this principle indicates is that to receive the revelation of the Bible we must examine the total verbal structure of the Bible.
"The Mythical Approach to Creation" (1985), *Northrop Frye on Religion* (2000), CW, 4.

The Bible suggests that there is a structure beyond the hypothetical.
Entry, Notebook 27 (1986), 68, *Northrop Frye's Late Notebooks, 1982–1990: Architecture of the Spiritual World* (2000), CW, 5.

With such a book as the Bible, which has had so tremendous a role to play in our cultural tradition, all value judgments are palpably absurd and futile.

"Reconsidering Levels of Meaning" (1979), *Northrop Frye's Fiction and Miscellaneous Writings* (2007), CW, 25.

The Bible *is* a colossal literary tour de force, whatever "more" it is, and the canonical instinct is so sure, in the large view, as to suggest a direct intervention by God. I don't see this in the Koran, & I don't see how anybody could see it in the Koran. But what does this lead to? Apparently to the reflection that God is exactly like me: in a world howling with tyranny and misery all he cares about is getting his damn book finished.
   Entry, Notebook 44 (1986–91), 661, *Northrop Frye's Late Notebooks, 1982–1990: Architecture of the Spiritual World* (2000), CW, 5.

The function of the Bible is to give us knowledge of myth (and metaphor). Not experience: that's the reader's response. The Bible guides and girds the experience: unorganized mythical experience is hysteria or insanity.
   Entry, Notebook 11b (late 1980), 22, *Northrop Frye's Notebooks and Lectures on the Bible and Other Religious Texts* (2003), CW, 13.

If we insist that the Bible is "more" than a work of literature, we ought at least to stick to the word "more," and try to see what it means.
   "Language II," *The Great Code* (1982), *The Great Code: The Bible and Literature* (2006), CW, 19.

To say that the Bible is "more" than a work of literature is merely to say that other methods of approaching it are possible.
   "Fourth Essay: Rhetorical Criticism: Theory of Genres" (1957), *Anatomy of Criticism: Four Essays* (2006), CW, 22.

BIBLE AS MYTHOLOGY

To me the Bible is a single and definitive myth.
   "Breakthrough" (1967), *Interviews with Northrop Frye* (2008), CW, 24.

The Bible teaches the knowledge of myth: the poets teach the experience of it.
   Entry, Notebook 11b (late 1980), 26, *Northrop Frye's Notebooks and Lectures on the Bible and Other Religious Texts* (2003), CW, 13.

To me the Bible, though not a work of literature, is none the less written in the literary language of myth and metaphor throughout, and therefore its "literal" meaning is its poetic and imaginative meaning, whatever other kinds of meaning may be found in it.
   "Preface to Essays Translated into Russian" (1988), *Northrop Frye's Fiction and Miscellaneous Writings* (2007), CW, 25.

If we take the Bible as a key to mythology, instead of taking mythology in general as a key to the Bible, we should at least have a definite starting point, wherever we end.
   "Typology I," *The Great Code* (1982), *The Great Code: The Bible and Literature* (2006), CW, 19.

When we do look into it, we find that the sense of unified continuity is what the Bible has as a work of fiction, as a definitive myth extending over time and space, over invisible and visible orders of reality, and with a parabolic dramatic structure of which the five acts are creation, fall, exile, redemption, and restoration.
   "Fourth Essay: Rhetorical Criticism: Theory of Genres" (1957), *Anatomy of Criticism: Four Essays* (2006), CW, 22.

… and for me the two statements, The Bible tells a story, and, The Bible is a myth, are essentially the same statement.
   "Myth I," *The Great Code* (1982), *The Great Code: The Bible and Literature* (2006), CW, 19.

The Bible is for the literary critic the best place to study the mythological framework that Western culture has inherited.
   "Literature and Society" (1968), *"The Critical Path" and Other Writings on Critical Theory, 1963–1975* (2009), CW, 27.

At this point the word *mythos* begins to turn into the word "myth," and we have to face the possibility that the entire Bible has to be read in the same way that most of us now read the story of Noah's ark.
   "History and Myth in the Bible" (1975), *Northrop Frye on Religion* (2000), CW, 4.

As there is no boundary line, it follows that nothing in the Bible which may be historically accurate is there because it is historically accurate.

"Pistis and Mythos" (1972), *Northrop Frye on Religion* (2000), CW, 4.

A genuine higher criticism of the Bible, therefore, would be a synthesizing process which would start with the assumption that the Bible is a definitive myth, a single archetypal structure extending from creation to apocalypse.

"Fourth Essay: Rhetorical Criticism: Theory of Genres" (1957), *Anatomy of Criticism: Four Essays* (2006), CW, 22.

… *The Great Code* tried to show, by realizing that the Bible's roots are not in doctrine, which is a structure of secondary concern, nor in history, which is the record of it, but in the creative imagination, which from palaeolithic times has been the central force driving humanity from mere survival into life more abundantly.

"*Words with Power*: Draft Introduction" (before 1990), 6, *Northrop Frye's Fiction and Miscellaneous Writings* (2007), CW, 25.

BIBLE AS SOURCE OF SYMBOLISM

The Bible to Blake was really the Magna Carta of the human imagination.

"William Blake: Prophet of the New Age" (1987), *Interviews with Northrop Frye* (2008), CW, 24.

In our culture, the Bible is the work which provides the fundamental mythical context for the metaphorical functions of language, for the stories which we tell ourselves. The Bible helps us to rediscover ourselves, to quest for and discover our individual and collective identities.

"Identity and Myth" (1979), *Interviews with Northrop Frye* (2008), CW, 24.

The Bible is therefore the archetype of Western culture, and the Bible, with its derivatives, provides the basis for most of our major art: for Dante, Milton, Michelangelo, Raphael, Bach, the great cathedrals, and so on.

"Part One: The Argument," *Fearful Symmetry: A Study of William Blake* (1947, 2004), CW, 14.

In other words, it's the *myth* of the Bible that should be the basis of literary training, its imaginative survey of the human situation which is so broad and comprehensive that everything else finds its place inside it.

"Verticals of Adam," *The Educated Imagination* (1963), *"The Educated Imagination" and Other Writings on Critical Theory, 1933–1963* (2006), CW, 21.

To grow up in ignorance of what is in the Bible or Homer is as crippling to the imagination as being deprived of the multiplication table.

"The Developing Imagination" (1962), *Northrop Frye's Writings on Education* (2001), CW, 7.

A student of English literature who doesn't know the Bible doesn't know what is going on in English literature.

"Reconsidering Levels of Meaning" (1979), *Northrop Frye's Fiction and Miscellaneous Writings* (2007), CW, 25.

My chairman said the only thing to do was to draft a course in the English Bible and teach it. He said, "How do you expect to teach Milton to students who don't know a Philistine from a Pharisee?"

I said, "Perhaps in the kind of society they are going into, that particular distinction won't be important to them." But I didn't often talk like that to my chairman, except in moments of stress, so I drafted the course and I'm still teaching it.

"The Meaning of Recreation: Humanism in Society" (1979), on teaching Milton to undergraduates under department chairman John Robins in the late 1930s, *Northrop Frye on Religion* (2000), CW, 4.

… the Bible forms the lowest stratum in the teaching of literature. It should be taught so early and so thoroughly that it sinks straight to the bottom of the mind, where everything that comes along later can settle on it.

"Verticals of Adam," *The Educated Imagination* (1963), *"The Educated Imagination" and Other Writings on Critical Theory, 1933–1963* (2006), CW, 21.

BIBLE AS UNITY

In our culture the central sacred book is the Christian Bible, which is also probably the most systematically constructed sacred book in the world.

"Fourth Essay: Rhetorical Criticism: Theory of Genres" (1957), *Anatomy of Criticism: Four Essays* (2006), CW, 22.

Everything that could possibly go wrong with a book has gone wrong with the Bible at some stage or other in its history. So the Bible, therefore, is a unity which has passed beyond unity.

"Symbolism in the Bible" (1981–82), *Northrop Frye's Notebooks and Lectures on the Bible and Other Religious Texts* (2003), CW, 13.

This poetic unity is there: how it got there will doubtless always be something of a mystery. It is not a product of history, or authorship, or editing, or of any such conception as "inspiration," a word which may assert something but explains nothing. We can only call it a mystery of canonicity, and let it go for the time being, holding in the meantime to our central principle: the Bible is not a work of literature, but its literal meaning is its mythical and metaphorical meaning.

"Spirit and Symbol," *Words with Power: Being a Second Study of "The Bible and Literature"* (2008), CW, 26.

The curious paradox in the construction of the Bible. It's all bits & pieces, a mosaic of discontinuous concerned prose; yet it's a unity too. Inspiration seems to apply to the greatest unity & the greatest editorial diversity. There's one spirit, obviously, but a vast number of minds. So while the shape & unity of the whole canon is important, we shouldn't *reduce* the variety to unity, but see them both as interpenetrating.

Entry, Notebook 21 (1969–76), 259, *Northrop Frye's Notebooks and Lectures on the Bible and Other Religious Texts* (2003), CW, 13.

The New Testament has the same paradoxical relation to the Old that a preface has to a book: it's written later, but belongs logically earlier ("before Abraham was, I am").

Entry, Notes 54-5 (1976), 41, *Northrop Frye's Notebooks and Lectures on the Bible and Other Religious Texts* (2003), CW, 13.

There isn't a page of the Bible where the editing process is not utterly obvious.

"Symbolism in the Bible" (1981–82), *Northrop Frye's Notebooks and Lectures on the Bible and Other Religious Texts* (2003), CW, 13.

The Bible is, first of all — to use a word no less accurate for being a fashionable term — a mosaic: a pattern of commandments, aphorisms, epigrams, proverbs, parables, riddles, pericopes, parallel couplets, formulaic phrases, folk tales, oracles, epiphanies, *Gattungen*, *Loggia*, bits of occasional verse, marginal glosses, legends, snippets from historical documents, laws, letters, sermons, hymns, ecstatic visions, rituals, fables, genealogical lists, and so on almost indefinitely.

"Language II," *The Great Code* (1982), *The Great Code: The Bible and Literature* (2006), CW, 19.

... if the Bible is to be regarded as "inspired" in any sense, sacred or secular, the editing and conflating and redacting and splicing and glossing and expurgating processes all have to be taken as inspired too.

"Language II," *The Great Code* (1982), *The Great Code: The Bible and Literature* (2006), CW, 19.

It is historically impossible that the Bible could have achieved such a unity of structure and imagery, over such a variety of periods and authors. But as the unity is there, so much the worse for history.

Entry, Notebook 44 (1986–91), 512, *Northrop Frye's Late Notebooks, 1982–1990: Architecture of the Spiritual World* (2000), CW, 5.

Yes, it's utterly impossible to understand a word of the New Testament without having the Old.

"The Great Teacher" (1988), *Interviews with Northrop Frye* (2008), CW, 24.

BILINGUALISM

I suppose no reasonable Canadian denies the extraordinary advantages of a bilingual culture, despite all the complaints one may hear in

English Canada about "shoving all that French down our throats," though those who use such phrases are unlikely to have much French in their throats.

"Speech at the New Canadian Embassy, Washington" (1989), *Northrop Frye on Canada* (2003), CW, 12.

BIOGRAPHY

The first and most striking unit of poetry larger than the individual poem is the total work of the man who wrote the poem.

"Second Essay: Ethical Criticism: Theory of Symbols" (1957), *Anatomy of Criticism: Four Essays* (2006), CW, 22.

There are poets — and they include Shakespeare — who seem to have pursued a policy of keeping their lives away from their readers. Human nature being what it is, it is precisely such poets who are most eagerly read for biographical allusions.

"Emily Dickinson" (1962), *Northrop Frye's Writings on the Eighteenth and Nineteenth Centuries* (2005), CW, 17.

BIRNEY, EARLE

This is a book for those interested in Canadian poetry to buy and for those interested in complaining that we haven't got any to ignore.

"Canadian Poets: Earle Birney" (1942), reviewing Birney's volume *David*, *Northrop Frye on Canada* (2003), CW, 12.

He has a very simple & honest mind, & tends to be attracted by the simplified clarity of extreme positions. Helps him as a poet, maybe.

Entry, 20 Jul. 1942, 26, *The Diaries of Northrop Frye: 1942–1955* (2001), CW, 8.

BIRTH

We all belong to something long before we are anything. We were predestined to be mid-twentieth-century middle-class North Americans before we escaped from the womb.

"Criticism as Education" (1979), *Northrop Frye's Writings on Education* (2001), CW, 7.

Death is not the opposite of life; death is the opposite of birth.

Entry, Notebook 11f (1969–70), 144, *Northrop Frye's Notebooks and Lectures on the Bible and Other Religious Texts* (2003), CW, 13.

For death, the Gospel tells us, is the last of our new beginnings: it is not the opposite of life, but only the opposite of birth, until we reach it, when it becomes birth, and in our last and greatest act of renunciation we find that all things have been made anew.

"Sermon in Merton College Chapel" (1970), *Northrop Frye on Religion* (2000), CW, 4.

… every new birth provokes the return of an avenging death.

"Third Essay: Archetypal Criticism: Theory of Myths" (1957), *Anatomy of Criticism: Four Essays* (2006), CW, 22.

BISHOP, ELIZABETH

She spent half her time in Nova Scotia, so much so that one or two Americans suggested Canadians really ought to make her Canada's national poet. I think it was a bit of a problem for her too to decide whether she was Canadian or American, and she finally solved the problem by going to live in Brazil.

"Autobiographical Reflections: Speech at Moncton's Centennial Celebration" (1990), referring to the American poet who was raised in the Maritimes, *Northrop Frye's Fiction and Miscellaneous Writings* (2007), CW, 25.

BLACK CULTURE

If the viewer is black and sees a white society gorging itself on luxuries and privileges, the results can be explosive.

"Communications" (1970), *Northrop Frye on Modern Culture* (2003), CW, 11.

BLACK MASS

But the black mass seems to me an extremely literary notion and a rather second-rate literary notion. Aleister Crowley is a good example of the level it operates on.

"Between Paradise and Apocalypse" (1978), *Interviews with Northrop Frye* (2008), CW, 24.

BLAKE, WILLIAM

I think I've learned everything I know from Blake. Blake was practically the only man of

his time who realized that we all live inside a big mythical and metaphorical framework of images, and that unless we become aware of that we can never change anything of the social condition — we just keep on responding to the same conditioning. That was where I derived the notion that literature, as a whole, made sense.
  "The Great Teacher" (1988), *Interviews with Northrop Frye* (2008), CW, 24.

What Blake demonstrates is the sanity of genius and the madness of the commonplace mind, and it is here that he has something very apposite to say to the twentieth century, with its interest in the arts of neurosis and the politics of paranoia.
  "Part One: The Argument," *Fearful Symmetry: A Study of William Blake* (1947, 2004), CW, 14.

Blake does not exactly say that the Bible is a work of art: he says "The Old & New Testaments are the Great Code of Art." The Bible tells the artist what the function of art is and what his creative powers are trying to accomplish.
  "Blake's Treatment of the Archetype" (1950), *Northrop Frye on Milton and Blake* (2005), CW, 16.

If the Prophecies are normal poems, or at least a normal expression of poetic genius, and if Blake nevertheless meant to teach some system by them, that system could only be something connected with the principles of poetic thought. Blake's "message," then, is not simply *his* message, nor is it an extraliterary message. What he is trying to say is what he thinks poetry is trying to say: the imaginative content implied by the existence of an imaginative form of language. I finished my book in the full conviction that learning to read Blake was a step, and for me a necessary step, in learning to read poetry, and to write criticism.
  "The Keys to the Gates" (1966), *Northrop Frye on Milton and Blake* (2005), CW, 16.

… the titles of the sets of aphorisms which introduce Blake's canon, "There is No Natural Religion" and "All Religions are One," contain the whole of his thought if they are understood simultaneously.

"Part Three: The Final Synthesis," *Fearful Symmetry: A Study of William Blake* (1947, 2004), CW, 14.

Only the Blake — I know Blake as no man has ever known him — of that I'm quite sure. But I lack so woefully in the way of subtlety.
  "NF to HK," 3 May 1935, *The Correspondence of Northrop Frye and Helen Kemp, 1932–1939* (1996), CW, 1.

Blake was the first poet in English literature, and so far as I know the first person in the modern world, to realize that the traditional authoritarian cosmos had had it, that it no longer appealed to the intelligence or the imagination, and would have to be replaced by another model.
  "Blake's Biblical Illustrations" (1983), *Northrop Frye on Milton and Blake* (2005), CW, 16.

I was originally attracted to him because he was, so far as I knew and still know, the first person in the modern world to see the events of his day in their mythical and imaginative context.
  "Third Variation: The Cave," *Words with Power: Being a Second Study of "The Bible and Literature"* (1990), CW, 26.

The conclusion for Blake, and the key to much of his symbolism, is that the fall of man and the creation of the physical world were the same event.
  "Part One: The Argument," *Fearful Symmetry: A Study of William Blake* (1947, 2004), CW, 14.

Blake's Prophetic Books represent one of the few successful efforts to tackle conversational rhythm in verse — so successful that many critics are still wondering if they are "real poetry."
  "Fourth Essay: Rhetorical Criticism: Theory of Genres" (1957), *Anatomy of Criticism: Four Essays* (2006), CW, 22.

The question in Blake's Tyger means: can we actually think of the world of the tiger as a created order?
  Entry, Notes 54-5 (1976), 87, *Northrop Frye's Notebooks and Lectures on the Bible and Other Religious Texts* (2003), CW, 13.

Whatever other qualities Blake may have had or lacked, he certainly had courage and simplicity. Whatever other qualities our own age may have or lack, it is certainly an age of fearfulness and complexity. And every age learns most from those who most directly confront it.

"Blake after Two Centuries" (1957), *Northrop Frye on Milton and Blake* (2005), CW, 16.

The only way to crack his code was to take him away from all the mystical and occult traditions that people had associated him with and put him squarely in English literature, which is where he belonged. That was really what took me so long to do — to see what he was driving at and to begin to realize that what he meant was fundamentally what he kept saying he meant.

"Getting the Order Right" (1978), *Interviews with Northrop Frye* (2008), CW, 24.

Read Blake or go to hell: that's my message to the modern world.

"NF to HK," 23 Apr. 1935, *The Correspondence of Northrop Frye and Helen Kemp, 1932–1939* (1996), CW, 1.

BLAVATSKY, H.P.

Yet *The Secret Doctrine*, whatever else it is, is a very remarkable essay on the morphology of symbols, and the charlatanism of its author is less a reflection on her than on the age that compelled her to express herself in such devious ways.

"Yeats and the Language of Symbolism" (1947), *"The Critical Path" and Other Writings on Critical Theory, 1963–1975* (2009), CW, 27.

Works based on an interconnection of oracular poetry and prose commentary are usually found in or near the area of religion (even Madame Blavatsky's *Secret Doctrine* takes this form).

"The Well-Tempered Critic (II)" (1961), *"The Educated Imagination" and Other Writings on Critical Theory, 1933–1963* (2006), CW, 21.

... no reputable scientist has had the influence on the poetry of the last century that Swedenborg or Blavatsky has had.

"New Directions from Old" (1960), *"The Educated Imagination" and Other Writings on Critical Theory, 1933–1963* (2006), CW, 21.

If Blake had told us that he had gone to visit the wise men of the East and had learned from them the doctrines which he has set down in his poems, we should know what he meant, or ought to by now. When Madame Blavatsky tells us the same thing we are not sure what she means.

"Part Three: The Final Synthesis," *Fearful Symmetry: A Study of William Blake* (1947, 2004), CW, 14.

BODY

It also leaves the human mind as a function of the body, for man has received his body from nature, and his mind is his unique instrument for achieving a harmonious and comfortable adjustment to nature.

"Trends in Modern Culture" (1952), *Northrop Frye on Modern Culture* (2003), CW, 11.

I think as long as the human body has a top and a bottom it's likely to be read into the symbolism of the mythological universe that man lives in.

"Symbolism in the Bible" (1981–82), *Northrop Frye's Notebooks and Lectures on the Bible and Other Religious Texts* (2003), CW, 13.

BOEHME, JAKOB

It has been said of Boehme that his books are like a picnic to which the author brings the words and the reader the meaning. The remark may have been intended as a sneer at Boehme, but it is an exact description of all works of literary art without exception.

"Part Three: The Final Synthesis," *Fearful Symmetry: A Study of William Blake* (1947, 2004), CW, 14.

BOOKS

The book *qua* book is not linear: we follow a line while we are reading it, but the book itself is a stationary visual focus of a community.

"The Search for Acceptable Words" (1973), *"The Critical Path" and Other Writings on Critical Theory, 1963–1975* (2009), CW, 27.

It seems to me that the printed book, with its established text and its mechanically accurate reproduction, is the inevitable form of the verbal classic or model, in whatever age it is produced.
"Comment" (1961), *Northrop Frye on Twentieth-Century Literature* (2010), CW, 29.

It is a common academic failing to dream of writing the perfect book, and then, because no achievement can reach perfection, not writing it.
"Humanities in a New World" (1958), *Northrop Frye's Writings on Education* (2001), CW, 7.

... the book individualizes its audience....
"Communications" (1970), *Northrop Frye on Modern Culture* (2003), CW, 11.

The book happens to be the most efficient technological instrument that the human mind has ever devised, and consequently it will always be here, at the centre of our technology, no matter what else we do.
"Back to the Garden" (1982), *Interviews with Northrop Frye* (2008), CW, 24.

The tremendous efficiency and economy of the book has once again demonstrated itself. It's the world's most patient medium, for one thing. It doesn't go away. It comes back with exactly the same message no matter how often you consult it.
"The Scholar in Society" (1983), *Interviews with Northrop Frye* (2008), CW, 24.

... nobody believes that a book is an object: it's a focus of verbal energy.
Entry, Notes 53 (1989–90), 176, *Northrop Frye's Late Notebooks, 1982–1990: Architecture of the Spiritual World* (2000), CW, 6.

The psychological effect of studying such a work as Hegel's *Phenomenology of Mind* in paperback seems to me to be quite different from studying the same book in a hard cover. And by dramatizing the book as intellectual tool, the paperback also dramatized the extraordinary effectiveness of the book, the fact that, familiar and unobtrusive as it is, the book is one of the most efficient technological instruments ever developed in human history.
"The Renaissance of Books" (1973), *Northrop Frye on Modern Culture* (2003), CW, 11.

Now that society, after some years of reeling from the impact of television, is beginning to bring it under control, we can see more clearly that the book is the chief technological device that makes democracy and the open society continuously possible.
"The Renaissance of Books" (1973), *Northrop Frye on Modern Culture* (2001), CW, 11.

But the book is actually a companion in dialogue: it helps to structure and make sense of the flood of automatic gabble that keeps rolling through the mind. This interior monologue, as it is called, never relates to other people, however often it is poured over them. Further, a book stays where it is, and does not vanish into ether or the garbage bin like the mass media.
"Preface to *On Education*" (1988), *Northrop Frye's Writings on Education* (2001), CW, 7.

So the book becomes the focus of a community, as more and more people read it and are affected by it. It moves in the opposite direction from the introversion of what has been well called "the lonely crowd," where no one can communicate with his neighbour because he is too close to him mentally to have anything to say.
"Preface to *On Education*" (1988), *Northrop Frye's Writings on Education* (2001), CW, 7.

Good books may instruct, but bad ones are more likely to inspire.
"Auguries of Experience" (1987), *"The Secular Scripture" and Other Writings on Critical Theory, 1976–1991* (2006), CW, 18.

What we'd never see except in a book is often what we go to books to find.
"The Keys to Dreamland," *The Educated Imagination* (1963), *"The Educated Imagination" and Other Writings on Critical Theory, 1933–1963* (2006), CW, 21.

The document is also the focus of a community, the community of readers, and while this community may be restricted to one group for centuries, its natural tendency is to expand over the community as a whole. Thus it is only writing that makes democracy technically possible.

"Communications" (1970), *Northrop Frye on Modern Culture* (2003), CW, 11.

It is necessary for one deeply interested in books to acquire the detachment from one's reading that ordinary people have who are not much interested in them: to have something of their massive indifference which is not blown about by every wind of doctrine.

Entry, Notebook 3 (1946–48), *Northrop Frye Newsletter*, Fall 2000.

The success of a book that takes no risks is not worth achieving.

Entry, Notebook 47 (1989–90), 17, *Northrop Frye's Late Notebooks, 1982–1990: Architecture of the Spiritual World* (2000), CW, 6.

The second-hand bookshop however represents something irreplaceable in one's literary experience, and it is bound to revive sooner or later, if only as an aspect of the junk-antique business.

"The Renaissance of Books" (1973), *Northrop Frye on Modern Culture* (2001), CW, 11.

There are signs that in America and Britain, as in France, the paperbound book will become the salvation of the impoverished intellectual.

"The Church and Modern Culture" (1950), *Northrop Frye on Modern Culture* (2003), CW, 11.

I have finished eleven books so far, but I have never finished any of them with the sense that I had succeeded or that I had achieved anything. I always finish them with a sense that they were simply being abandoned....

"The Question of 'Success'" (1967), *Northrop Frye's Writings on Education* (2001), CW, 7.

A good book must delight and it must instruct. Anyone who desires to quarrel with or qualify that statement should take up some other occupation.

"On Book Reviewing" (1949), *Northrop Frye on Modern Culture* (2003), CW, 11.

BORDUAS, PAUL-ÉMILE

For Borduas, the human mind contained an it as well as an I or ego, and this It was what he felt needed expression.

"Canadian Culture Today" (1977), *Northrop Frye on Canada* (2003), CW, 12.

BOREDOM

I know it's a difficult thing, but the great test of maturity is knowing when one is bored. I think that people are really bored out of their minds by what they get from the news media.

"The Great Test of Maturity" (1986), *Interviews with Northrop Frye* (2008), CW, 24.

A man is bored because he bores himself.

"Leisure and Boredom" (1963), *Northrop Frye on Literature and Society, 1936–1989: Unpublished Papers* (2002), CW, 10.

BORGES, JORGE LUIS

One of the wisest and shrewdest men of our time, the Argentine writer Borges, has remarked that literature not only begins in a mythology but also ends in one.

"Tradition and Change in the Theory of Criticism" (1969), *Northrop Frye on Literature and Society, 1936–1989: Unpublished Papers* (2002), CW, 10.

BOSTON

When I was growing up in the Maritime Provinces during the [1920s], there was a strong political loyalty to Confederation, but an even stronger sense that Boston was our real capital, and that the Maritimes formed the periphery of New England, or what was often called "the Boston states."

"Canadian Culture Today" (1977), *Northrop Frye on Canada* (2003), CW, 12.

BOURGEOIS

The word "bourgeois" is practically synonymous with creative man: the middle class has produced culture and civilization alike.

Entry, Notebook 31 (late 1946–50), 8, *Northrop Frye's Notebooks on Romance* (2004), CW, 15.

The implication, which I've always accepted, is that God's aim is to be a bourgeois, the middle class of the middle world, which means after upper & lower unrealities have vanished.

> Entry, Notebook 50 (1987–90), 578, *Northrop Frye's Late Notebooks, 1982–1990: Architecture of the Spiritual World* (2000), CW, 5.

What I am expounding may be called a bourgeois liberal view, which throughout my lifetime has never been regarded as an "advanced" view. But it may begin to look more central with the repudiation of Marxism in Marxist countries, the growing uneasiness with the anti-intellectualism in American life, and the steadily decreasing dividends of terrorism in Third World Countries.

> *The Double Vision* (1991), *Northrop Frye on Religion* (2000), CW, 4.

General attitude toward life: That of a liberal bourgeois intellectual, which I consider the flower of humanity.

> "*Chatelaine*'s Celebrity I.D." (1982), *Interviews with Northrop Frye*, CW, 24.

BREATH

Breathing is the most primary of all concerns, the act marking the transition from the embryo to the baby, and our most continuous activity thereafter. We can go for days without food, or for a lifetime without sex, but ten minutes without breathing and we "expire."

> "Spirit and Symbol," *Words with Power: Being a Second Study of "The Bible and Literature"* (2008), CW, 26.

BRITISH EMPIRE

There is a great deal to be said for the British Commonwealth, but everything connected with the British Empire, from the Indian question to the defence of Singapore & Hong Kong, is entirely vicious.

> Entry, Notebook 42a (1942–44), 5, *Northrop Frye's Notebooks on Romance* (2004), CW, 15.

BROADCASTING

I think the combination of what are called private broadcasters and of nationally subsidized broadcasting is a rather healthy thing for a country.

> "The Primary Necessities of Existence" (1985), *Interviews with Northrop Frye* (2008), CW, 24.

BROWNING, ROBERT

At the end, when English becomes a long-dead language, it is not difficult to imagine a professor in the remote future, who does not altogether understand the true genius of our tongue, saying: "This man was the greatest of all, for the qualities of the other great ones are combined and blended in him."

> "Robert Browning: An Abstract Study" (1932–33), *Northrop Frye's Student Essays, 1932–1938* (1997), CW, 3.

BUDDHISM

Xy [Christianity] stands for the triumph over death; Buddhism for the triumph over birth. The latter is a Thanatos vision because death is the only visible symbol of Nirvana, just as life after death, or rebirth, is the only visible symbol of heaven.

> Entry, Notebook 12 (1968–70), 420, *The "Third Book" Notebooks of Northrop Frye, 1964–1972: The Critical Comedy* (2002), CW, 9.

The Buddhists keep saying, with tremendous and unending prolixity, that the subject-object duality is horseshit. Okay, it's horseshit: what's so infernally difficult about it. The fact that it's so difficult to overcome derives from the fact that the metaphorical kernel of subject & object is the contrast of life & death. The person from whom *that's* disappeared really is a sage.

> Entry, Notebook 44 (1986–91), 109, *Northrop Frye's Late Notebooks, 1982–1990: Architecture of the Spiritual World* (2000), CW, 5.

Buddha promises an unborn world; Jesus a paradise or unfallen world.

> Entry, Notebook 6 (1967–68), 2, *The "Third Book" Notebooks of Northrop Frye, 1964–1972: The Critical Comedy* (2002), CW, 9.

BULTMANN, RUDOLF

I don't understand the twentieth-century attraction for these antiseptic sounding words beginning with "de." I don't know why Bultmann speaks of demythologizing the Bible when he means remythologizing it. And I don't understand in literary criticism why Derrida speaks of deconstruction when what he means is reconstruction. But that's just original sin.

"Symbolism in the Bible" (1981–82), *Northrop Frye's Notebooks and Lectures on the Bible and Other Religious Texts* (2003), CW, 13.

BUREAUCRACY

I think the only government of which the human race is capable is more or less efficient or corrupt bureaucracy. The degrees of efficiency and corruption are what make the difference.

"Towards an Oral History of the University of Toronto" (1982), *Interviews with Northrop Frye* (2008), CW, 24.

The work of most middle-class people today consists mainly in the polluting of paper, or what is known as filling out forms.

"The Responsibilities of the Critic" (1976), *"The Secular Scripture" and Other Writings on Critical Theory, 1976–1991* (2006), CW, 18.

BURTON, ROBERT

That is, having written one of the most delightful books in the language, he knows that reading that book would be a much better cure for melancholy than most of the remedies he prescribes.

"*Rencontre:* The General Editor's Introduction" (1960s), discussing the "ethical tradition of rhetorical prose" of *Anatomy of Melancholy*, *Northrop Frye on Literature and Society, 1936–1989: Unpublished Papers* (2002), CW, 10.

BYRON, LORD

The main appeal of Byron's poetry is in the fact that it is Byron's.

"Lord Byron" (1959), *Northrop Frye's Writings on the Eighteenth and Nineteenth Centuries* (2005), CW, 17.

BYZANTIUM

You have to sail to Byzantium as well as be there.

Entry, Notebook 50 (1987–90), 520, *Northrop Frye's Late Notebooks, 1982–1990: Architecture of the Spiritual World* (2000), CW, 5.

C

C.C.F.

I think with the C.C.F. that a co-operative state is necessary to preserve us from chaos. I think with Liberals that it is impossible to administer that state at present.

"NF to HK," 4 Sep. 1933, referring to the Canadian Co-operative Federation (forerunner of the New Democratic Party or NDP), *The Correspondence of Northrop Frye and Helen Kemp, 1932–1939* (1996), CW, 1.

CALLAGHAN, MORLEY

Morley Callaghan's books, I think I am right in saying, were sometimes banned by the public library in Toronto — I forget what the rationalization was, but the real reason could only have been that if a Canadian were to do anything so ethically dubious as write, he should at least write like a proper colonial and not like someone who had lived in the Paris of Joyce and Gertrude Stein.

"Across the River and Out of the Trees" (1980), *Northrop Frye on Canada* (2003), CW, 12.

CANADA

Our country is abstract to ourselves.

"CRTC Guru" (1968–69), *Interviews with Northrop Frye* (2008), CW, 24.

If one comes from a relatively small country culturally, that smallness provides a perspective difficult to explain. I should have been a totally different kind of critic as an American, just as, say, Kierkegaard would have been totally different as a German.

"The Critical Path" (1979), *Interviews with Northrop Frye* (2008), CW, 24.

The liveliest thing about Canada is its culture. It is the one thing that is really respected all over the world. Culture is a product of articulateness. And it is also indirectly a product of education.

"Love of Learning" (1987), *Interviews with Northrop Frye* (2008), CW, 24.

I keep finding that there are parallels between Biblical history and Canadian history, which would be of no importance if Canadian poets themselves were not aware of it.

"Introduction to Canadian Literature: Moscow Talk" (1988), 34, *Northrop Frye's Fiction and Miscellaneous Writings* (2007), CW, 25.

I cannot think of any society in history that has disintegrated simply through a lack of will to survive. Consequently I do not believe what I so often hear from the news media today, that Canada is about to blunder and bungle its way out of history into oblivion, leaving only a faint echo of ridicule behind it.

The Double Vision (1991), *Northrop Frye on Religion* (2000), CW, 4.

Canada, with four million square miles and only four centuries of documented history, has naturally been a country more preoccupied with space than with time, with environment rather than tradition.

"Canada: New World Without Revolution" (1975), *Northrop Frye on Canada* (2003), CW, 12.

Here we are: not an obstacle on the route to Cathay, not on the edge of the earth, not on the sidelines, but ringed by the world's great powers: Japan and China here; the USSR here; the European Common Market here, and the United States here. And here is Canada, in the middle.

"View of Canada" (1976), *Northrop Frye on Canada* (2003), CW, 12.

But now Canada has become a kind of global Switzerland, surrounded by the United States on the south, the European common market on the east, the Soviet Union on the north, China and Japan on the west.

"Conclusion to *Literary History of Canada*" (1965), *Northrop Frye on Canada* (2003), CW, 12.

One of the derivations proposed for the word Canada is a Portuguese phrase meaning "nobody here." The etymology of the word Utopia is very similar, and perhaps the real Canada is an ideal with nobody in it. The Canada to which we really do owe loyalty is the Canada that we have failed to create.... It is expressed in our culture, but not attained in our life, just as Blake's new Jerusalem to be built in England's green and pleasant land is no less a genuine ideal for not having been built there ... the uncreated identity of Canada may be after all not so bad a heritage to take with us.

The Modern Century (1967), *Northrop Frye on Modern Culture* (2003), CW, 11.

Canada seems to impress non-Canadians as a moderate and reasonable country, potentially as happy a country to live in as the world affords.

"The Cultural Development of Canada" (1990), *Northrop Frye on Canada* (2003), CW, 12.

It is only now emerging from its beginning as a shambling, awkward, absurd country, groping and thrusting its way through incredible distances into the West and North, plundered by profiteers, interrupted by European wars, divided by language, and bedevilled by climate, yet slowly and inexorably bringing a culture to life.

"Preface and Introduction to Pratt's Poetry" (1958), *Northrop Frye on Canada* (2003), CW, 12.

Canada, with its empty spaces, its largely unknown lakes and rivers and islands, its division of language, its dependence on immense railways to hold it physically together, has had this peculiar problem of an obliterated environment throughout most of its history. The effects of this are clear in the curiously abortive cultural developments of Canada.... They are shown even more clearly in its present lack of will to resist its own disintegration, in the fact that it is practically the only country left in the world which is a pure colony, colonial in psychology as well as in mercantile economics.

Preface, *The Bush Garden* (1971), *Northrop Frye on Canada* (2003), CW, 12.

A century ago Canada was a nation in the world, but not wholly of it: the major cultural and political developments of Western Europe, still the main centre of the historical stage, were little known or understood in Canada.... Today, Canada is too much a part of the world to be thought of as a nation in it.

The Modern Century (1967), *Northrop Frye on Modern Culture* (2003), CW, 11.

"Canada" is a political entity; the cultural counterpart that we call "Canada" is really a federation not of provinces but of regions and communities.

"From Nationalism to Regionalism: The Maturing of Canadian Culture" (1980), *Interviews with Northrop Frye* (2008), CW, 24.

Canada is not "new" or "young": it is exactly the same age as any other country under a system of industrial capitalism; and even if it were, a reluctance to write poetry is not a sign of youth but of decadence.

"Canada and Its Poetry" (1943), *Northrop Frye on Canada* (2003), CW, 12.

The essential element in the national sense of unity is the east-west feeling, developed historically along the St. Lawrence-Great Lakes axis, and expressed in the national motto, *a mare usque ad mare*. The tension between this political sense of unity and the imaginative sense of locality is the essence of whatever the word "Canadian" means.

Preface, *The Bush Garden* (1971), *Northrop Frye on Canada* (2003), CW, 12.

Some years ago I first saw Herbert Marcuse's *One Dimensional Man* in a bookshop, and what came into my mind was a quite irrelevant reflection: "I wonder what he'd say if he had to live in a one-dimensional country?" For Canada, through most of its history, has been a strip of territory as narrow as Chile, besides being longer and more broken up.

"Canadian Culture Today" (1977), *Northrop Frye on Canada* (2003), CW, 12.

CANADA & THE UNITED STATES

But Canada has, for all practical purposes, no Atlantic seaboard.... To enter the United States is a matter of crossing an ocean; to enter Canada is a matter of being silently swallowed by an alien continent.

"Conclusion to *Literary History of Canada*" (1965), *Northrop Frye on Canada* (2003), CW, 12.

Similarly, our undefended border is very effectively defended on one side, the United States being a highly protectionist country in culture as in other aspects of life, and the Canadian instinct for compromise has to make the best of it.

"National Consciousness in Canadian Culture" (1976), *Northrop Frye on Canada* (2003), CW, 12.

There is an aged and now somewhat infirm joke to the effect that the United States has passed from barbarism to decadence without an intervening period of civilization. A parallel and possibly more accurate statement might be made of Canada: that it has passed from a pre-national to a post–national phase without ever having become a nation.

"Culture as Interpenetration" (1982), *Northrop Frye on Canada* (2003), CW, 12.

An independent Canada would be much more useful to the United States itself than a dependent or annexed one would be, and it is of great importance to the United States to have a critical view of it centred in Canada, a view which is not hostile but is simply another view.

"Conclusion to *Literary History of Canada*" (1965), *Northrop Frye on Canada* (2003), CW, 12.

Canada may be an American colony, as is often said, by me among others, but Canadians have never thought of the United States as a parental figure, like Britain, and analogies of youthful revolt and the like would be absurd.

"Conclusion to *Literary History of Canada*" (1965), *Northrop Frye on Canada* (2003), CW, 12.

I was recently reading the letters of Wallace Stevens, and came across his remark that the imagination transforms reality, giving as his example the fact that people living in the United States become Americans. It struck me that no Canadian poet could have said this. People living in Canada may become Canadians up to a point, but up to a far more limited point.

"Canadian Identity and Cultural Regionalism" (1970), *Northrop Frye on Literature and Society, 1936–1989: Unpublished Papers* (2002), CW, 10.

A Canadian going to the United States to teach in a university there is often asked by his American students if he notices any difference. They expect the answer to be no, and nine-tenths of the time it is no, but the tenth time there is some point of discussion that suddenly makes him feel like a Finn in Russia or a Dane in Germany. His students have been conditioned from infancy to be citizens of a vast imperial power; he has been conditioned to watch, to take sides in decisions made elsewhere.

"America: True or False?" (1969), *Northrop Frye on Canada* (2003), CW, 12.

What is resented in Canada about annexation to the United States is not annexation itself, but the feeling that Canada would disappear into a larger entity without having anything of any real distinctiveness to contribute to that entity: that, in short, if the United States did annex Canada it would notice nothing except an increase in natural resources.

Preface, *The Bush Garden* (1971), *Northrop Frye on Canada* (2003), CW, 12.

In looking at two countries as closely related as Canada and the United States, no difference is unique or exclusive: we can point to nothing in Canada that does not have a counterpart, or many counterparts, south of the border. What is different is a matter of emphasis and of degree.

"Canadian Culture Today" (1977), *Northrop Frye on Canada* (2003), CW, 12.

What else is "distinctively Canadian"? Well, historically, a Canadian is an American who rejects the Revolution.

"Letters in Canada: Poetry" (1953), *Northrop Frye on Canada* (2003), CW, 12.

It is an insult to Canada to have American authorities in charge of Canadian immigration who do not know the elementary facts of Canadian political life, and who cannot distinguish a Communist from a social-democrat.
"Nothing to Fear but Fear" (1949), *Northrop Frye on Modern Culture* (2003), CW, 11.

American students have been conditioned from infancy to think of themselves as citizens of one of the world's great powers. Canadians are conditioned from infancy to think of themselves as citizens of a country of uncertain identity, a confusing past, and a hazardous future.
"Canadian Culture Today" (1977), *Northrop Frye on Canada* (2003), CW, 12.

Canadians are so closely identified with Americans in their political fortunes that to make the identification complete actually improves the perspective.
"The Present Condition of the World" (1943), *Northrop Frye on Literature and Society, 1936–1989: Unpublished Papers* (2002), CW, 10.

CANADIAN BROADCASTING CORPORATION
Every aspect of Canadian culture has been affected by the enormously beneficent influence of the Canadian Broadcasting Corporation.
"English Canadian Literature, 1929–1954" (1955), *Northrop Frye on Canada* (2003), CW, 12.

CANADIAN CONTENT
What I would like to see is ninety-five per cent Canadian attitude.
"CRTC Guru" (1968–69), referring to CRTC's rules regulating the balance between Canadian and foreign (*i.e.*, American) content, *Interviews with Northrop Frye* (2008), CW, 24.

The CRTC has constantly been reminded, first by broadcasters and later by cable operators, that the majority of Canadians prefer American programs, including the brutal ones.
"National Consciousness in Canadian Culture" (1976), *Northrop Frye on Canada* (2003), CW, 12.

CANADIAN FORUM, THE
In short, the man with a liberal education will not have an integrated personality or be educated for living: he will be a chronically irritated man, probably one of that miserable band who read the *Canadian Forum*, which is always finding fault and viewing with alarm.
"A Liberal Education" (1945), *Northrop Frye's Writings on Education* (2001), CW, 7.

CANADIAN IDENTITY
I tend to think more and more as I get older that the only social identity that's really worth preserving is a cultural identity. And Canada seems to me to have achieved that, so I don't join with other people in lamenting the loss of a political identity.
"Richard Cartwright and the Roots of Canadian Conservatism" (1984), *Interviews with Northrop Frye* (2008), CW, 24.

All identity has a boundary, whether we call it Canada or the individual, and our social mythology keeps this walled and bound unit as its central structure.
"Foreword to *The Prospect of Change*" (1965), *Northrop Frye on Canada* (2003), CW, 12.

Canada is the Switzerland of the twentieth century, surrounded by the great powers of the world and preserving its identity by having many identities.
"Speech at the New Canadian Embassy, Washington" (1989), *Northrop Frye on Canada* (2003), CW, 12.

One disadvantage of living in Canada is that one is continually called upon to make statements about the Canadian identity, and Canadian identity is an eminently exhaustible subject.
"National Consciousness in Canadian Culture" (1976), *Northrop Frye on Canada* (2003), CW, 12.

There have been many fables about people who made long journeys to find some precious object. The moral is often that the pot of gold at the end of the rainbow is in their own backyard. But this is not the Canadian moral. The Canadian identity is bound up

with the feeling that the end of the rainbow never falls on Canada.
> "View of Canada" (1976), *Northrop Frye on Canada* (2003), CW, 12.

It seems to me that the Canadian sensibility has been profoundly disturbed not so much by our famous problem of identity — "Who are we?" — as by some such riddle as "Where is here?"
> "View of Canada" (1976), *Northrop Frye on Canada* (2003), CW, 12.

... the Canadian problem of identity seemed to me primarily connected with locale, less a matter of "Who am I?" than of "Where is here?" Another friend, commenting on this, told me a story about a doctor from the south (that is, from one of the Canadian cities) travelling in the Arctic tundra with an Eskimo guide. A blizzard blew up, and they had to bivouac for the night. What with the cold, the storm, and the loneliness, the doctor panicked and began shouting, "We are lost!" The Eskimo looked at him thoughtfully and said, "We are not lost. We are here."
> "Haunted by Lack of Ghosts" (1976), *Northrop Frye on Canada* (2000), CW, 12.

In a year bound to be full of discussions of our identity, I should like to suggest that our identity, like the real identity of all nations, is the one that we have failed to achieve.
> *The Modern Century* (1967), *Northrop Frye on Modern Culture* (2003), CW, 11.

CANADIAN LITERATURE

Canada is now producing a literature which has an imaginative integrity equal to that of other countries.
> "From Nationalism to Regionalism: The Maturing of Canadian Culture" (1980), *Interviews with Northrop Frye* (2008), CW, 24.

To study Canadian literature one has to stand on its own level: to stand above it and sneer at it, or to stand below it and exaggerate it, are equally unscholarly procedures.
> "Roy Daniells" (1979), *Northrop Frye on Canada* (2003), CW, 12.

The literary, in Canada, is often only an incidental quality of writings which, like those of many of the early explorers, are as innocent of literary intention as a mating loon.
> "Conclusion to *Literary History of Canada*" (1965), *Northrop Frye on Canada* (2003), CW, 12.

The constructs of the imagination tell us things about human life that we don't get in any other way. That's why it's important for Canadians to pay particular attention to Canadian literature, even when the imported brands are better seasoned.
> "Verticals of Adam," *The Educated Imagination* (1963), *"The Educated Imagination" and Other Writings on Critical Theory, 1933–1963* (2006), CW, 21.

Articles proclaiming the imminent advent of literary greatness had been appearing for a long time, giving to Canadian literature, or its history, the quality that Milton Wilson has described, in a practically definitive phrase, as "one half-baked phoenix after another."
> "Across the River and Out of the Trees" (1980), *Northrop Frye on Canada* (2003), CW, 12. The English professor Milton Wilson was quoted in the anthology *Recent Canadian Verse* (1959).

The study of Canadian literature is not a painful patriotic duty like voting, but a simple necessity of getting one's bearings.
> "Culture and the National Will" (1957), *Northrop Frye on Canada* (2003), CW, 12.

However important Canadian literature may be or become in a university, it is not any university's primary duty to foster a national literature. Its primary duty is to build up a public receptive to it, a public that will not be panicked by plain speaking, not put off by crankiness, not bewildered by unexpected ways of thinking and feeling.
> "Language as the Home of Human Life" (1985), *Northrop Frye's Writings on Education* (2001), CW, 7.

I first heard about the Group of Seven in a lecture by John Robins on the ballad, and about contemporary Canadian poets and novelists in Pelham Edgar's course on Shakespeare. Fortunately, Pelham rather disliked Shakespeare, so I

learned a good deal about Canadian literature while reading Shakespeare on my own.
"The View from Here" (1980), describing his student years in the early 1930s, *Northrop Frye's Writings on Education* (2001), CW, 7.

Most Canadian literature is and always will be tripe for the simple reason that most literature of all countries in all ages is and always will be tripe. Any national group of authors will form a pyramid with a few serious writers on top and a broad base of pulp-scribblers at the bottom.
"Canadian Authors Meet" (1946), *Northrop Frye on Canada* (2003), CW, 12.

By 1904 he was discussing the perennial Canadian question, "Have we a National Literature?" The answer, as it always is, is in effect no, but wait a while.
"Pelham Edgar" (1952), *Northrop Frye on Canada* (2003), CW, 12.

I imagine that in another ten years there will be very little difference in tone between Canadian and American literature; but what there is now in Canada is a literature of extraordinary vigor and historical significance.
"National Consciousness in Canadian Culture" (1976), *Northrop Frye on Canada* (2003), CW, 12.

Similarly, I think Canadian literature will become more and more a literature of regions. It seems to be a cultural law that the more specific the setting of literature is, the more universal its communicating power.
"Address on Receiving the Royal Bank Award" (1978), *Northrop Frye's Writings on Education* (2001), CW, 7.

There's no such thing as "Canadianism," but there are a number of poets working within a specific environment with a specific kind of historical background and that, I think, will influence and give a distinctive quality to their work if they don't pay too much attention to it.
"Canadian Energies: Dialogues on Creativity" (1980), *Interviews with Northrop Frye* (2008), CW, 24.

Stephen Leacock's famous hero who rode off rapidly in all directions was unmistakably a Canadian.
"Conclusion to *Literary History of Canada*" (1965), *Northrop Frye on Canada* (2003), CW, 12.

Well, I have said in another speech that if a sculptor were to make a statue of a patriotic Canadian, he would depict somebody holding his breath and crossing his fingers. In other words, there has never been a time when Canada has not thought in terms of disintegration.
"Cultural Identity in Canada" (1990), *Interviews with Northrop Frye* (2008), CW, 24.

In surveying Canadian poetry and fiction, we feel constantly that all the energy has been absorbed in meeting a standard, a self-defeating enterprise because real standards can only be established, not met.
"Conclusion to *Literary History of Canada*" (1965), *Northrop Frye on Canada* (2003), CW, 12.

… everything that is central in Canadian writing seems to be marked by the imminence of the natural world.
"Conclusion to *Literary History of Canada*" (1965), *Northrop Frye on Canada* (2003), CW, 12.

CANCER

Even the individual body is a community of billions of cells and bacteria, with specialized functions and yet, presumably, with no "knowledge," whatever knowledge may be in such a context, that they are forming a larger body. But they too can make mistakes about their relation to that body, as we see in the intolerant anarchist revolution we call cancer. I myself have allergic ailments that, I am told, are caused by a panic-stricken xenophobia among the blood cells, their inability to distinguish a harmless from a dangerous intruder. Good health, in both bodies, depends on a sense of unity that also rejects a hysterical insistence on uniformity.
"Natural and Revealed Communities" (1987), comparing social bodies and human bodies, including his own, *Northrop Frye's Writings on Shakespeare and the Renaissance* (2010), CW, 28.

CAPITAL PUNISHMENT

It is not that one feels sorry for the criminal, but that one feels sorry for the society which is stuck with the utterly beastly business of putting people to death.

"Reviews of Television Programs for the Canadian Radio-Television Commission: Reflections on November 5th" (1970), *Northrop Frye on Literature and Society, 1936–1989: Unpublished Papers* (2002), CW, 10.

CAPITALISM

By the mid-1930s the climate of opinion had totally reversed, at least in the student circles I was attached to. Then it was a generally accepted dogma that capitalism had had its day and was certain to evolve very soon, with or without a revolution, into socialism, socialism being assumed to be both a more efficient and a morally superior system.

The Double Vision (1991), *Northrop Frye on Religion* (2000), CW, 4.

I think, with the C.C.F., that capitalism is crashing around our ears, and that any attempt to build it up again will bring it down with a bigger crash.

"NF to HK," 4 Sep. 1933, *The Correspondence of Northrop Frye and Helen Kemp, 1932–1939* (1996), CW, 1.

Only capitalism exists, and that can go in one of two directions: towards increasingly decentralized democracy or towards increasingly centralized state capitalism administered by a bureaucratic dictatorship.

Entry, Notebook 11e (1978), 39, *Northrop Frye's Notebooks and Lectures on the Bible and Other Religious Texts* (2003), CW, 13.

Communism in my youth (the depression period) was widely assumed to be both efficient and morally superior to capitalism. But capitalism didn't evolve into communism; the two systems settled down into an adversary relation in which they could improve themselves only by borrowing features from each other.

Entry, Notebook 44 (1986–91), 10, *Northrop Frye's Late Notebooks, 1982–1990: Architecture of the Spiritual World* (2000), CW, 5.

I think Americans are hardly aware of living under capitalism: what they want is democracy, whatever the economic basis for it is.

Entry, Note 53 (1989–90), 52, *Northrop Frye's Late Notebooks, 1982–1990: Architecture of the Spiritual World* (2000), CW, 6.

CASTANEDA, CARLOS

I glanced at a row of books by Carlos Castaneda recently, and saw that the earlier books were labelled "nonfiction" by the publisher and the later ones "fiction." I dare say an interesting story lies behind that, but as the earlier and the later books appeared to be generically identical, the distinction was of little critical use.

"Framework and Assumption" (1985), *"The Secular Scripture" and Other Writings on Critical Theory, 1976–1991* (2006), CW, 18.

CATHARSIS

The attitude of detached concern is what is meant in literature by catharsis.

"Violence and Television" (1975), *Northrop Frye on Modern Culture* (2003), CW, 11.

There must be at least fifty theories on the market about the meaning of *catharsis*. I can perhaps save time by giving you the correct one, which by coincidence happens to be mine. I think that by "pity and fear" is meant the moral feelings that draw you either toward or away from certain characters.

"Literature as Therapy" (1989), *"The Secular Scripture" and Other Writings on Critical Theory, 1976–1991* (2006), CW, 18.

CATHOLICISM

There is no such thing as a Holy Catholic Church, but a church that knows it isn't catholic and is sincerely trying to become so is certainly worthy of respect.

Entry, Notes 53 (1989–90), 93, *Northrop Frye's Late Notebooks, 1982–1990: Architecture of the Spiritual World* (2000), CW, 6.

Once you accept some high-flown fable about the dissociation of sensibility & grab the Catholic Church, you get stuck with the Legion of Decency & all the meddlesome rule of priests.

Entry, Notebook 21 (1969–76), 312, *Northrop Frye's Notebooks and Lectures on the Bible and Other Religious Texts* (2003), CW, 13.

By the way, I must get rid of my fear of Catholicism long enough to distinguish the kinds of it that are purely Fascist & therefore factional (the paronomasia of national & natural religion as the Satanic analogy should be noted) from a cosmopolitan & liberal residue.

Entry, Notebook 34 (1946–50), 7, *Northrop Frye's Notebooks on Romance* (2004), CW, 15.

Whatever value Catholicism has today is due to the fact that it's confined, against its will, to spiritual authority. I'm beginning to wonder if the doctrine of the inseparability of theory and practice, which Christianity shares with Communism, isn't a pretty pernicious doctrine.

Entry, 5 Jan. 1952, 14, *The Diaries of Northrop Frye: 1942–1955* (2001), CW, 8.

Why is the religious satire exclusively Protestant: don't Canadian Catholics ever laugh at themselves? Is it editorial predilection or Canadian poetry that admits so little right-wing satire?

"Letters in Canada: Poetry" (1958), *Northrop Frye on Canada* (2003), CW, 12.

The educated Catholic laity doesn't believe in the autonomous infallible, non-contradictory church any more, and even the upper hierarchy only asserts that it does out of habit. Well, out of desire to maintain power.

Entry, Notes 53 (1989–90), 2, *Northrop Frye's Late Notebooks, 1982–1990: Architecture of the Spiritual World* (2000), CW, 6.

Catholics perhaps have less trouble — or used to, anyway — because for them faith is essentially what runs the sacramental machinery, and that provides a continuity of action that takes the heat off the speculative mind. But the *history* of the Catholic Church certainly reveals the hysteria there.

Entry, Notebook 27 (1986), 444, *Northrop Frye's Late Notebooks, 1982–1990: Architecture of the Spiritual World* (2000), CW, 5.

I'm afraid that Catholics show their broad-mindedness only in assuming that Protestants will have some interest in Catholicism, but it doesn't seem to reverse.

Entry, 20 Apr. 1952, 259, *The Diaries of Northrop Frye: 1942–1955* (2001), CW, 8.

CELTS

... we find the most soaring imaginations, as a rule, in defeated or oppressed nations, like the Hebrews and the Celts.

"The Imaginative and the Imaginary" (1962), *"The Educated Imagination" and Other Writings on Critical Theory, 1933–1963* (2006), CW, 21.

The principle is that defeated nations have the greatest imaginations. Many people, certainly many poets, have been far more possessed imaginatively by the sense of Arthur's historical existence than of, say, Alfred the Great's, whose historicity is not open to question.

Entry, Notebook 21 (1969–76), 244, *Northrop Frye's Notebooks and Lectures on the Bible and Other Religious Texts* (2003), CW, 13.

CENSORSHIP

And while I have no idea what censors think they are doing, what they really are doing is defending the tinsel world of the soap opera and the low-grade movie against the adult competition that continually threatens to shatter it.

"Dr. Kinsey and the Dream Censor" (1948), *Northrop Frye on Modern Culture* (2003), CW, 11.

I draw the line against what is usually called hate literature, that is, something which deliberately churns up an hysterical hatred of a minority group. I think that there is a case for censorship there. Otherwise, censorship is such a self-defeating thing and it is based on a contempt for other peoples' vision.

"Stevens and the Value of Literature" (1990), *Interviews with Northrop Frye* (2008), CW, 24.

The difficulty with topical allusions is that they have to be subtle enough to get past the censor and broad enough to get across to the audience — an almost impossible requirement.

"The Tragedies of Nature and Fortune" (1961), referring specifically to allusions in the play

Coriolanus, Northrop Frye's Writings on Shakespeare and the Renaissance (2010), CW, 28.

Censorship is practically always wrong, because it invariably fastens on the most serious writers as its chief object of attack, whereas the serious writer is the ally of social concern, not its enemy.
"An Address" (1984), *Northrop Frye's Writings on Education* (2001), CW, 7.

You will perhaps not be surprised to learn that I have no use for the lame-brained hysterics who go around snatching books by Margaret Laurence and Alice Munro out of school libraries. I also resent the mindless cliché that the best way to sell a book is to ban it, which means that all its extra readers will be attracted to it for silly reasons.
Creation and Recreation (1980), *Northrop Frye on Religion* (2000), CW, 4.

… however rationalized it may be censorship is always an attack on human intelligence and imagination and is always a sign of weakness, not strength, in those who enforce it.
"Introduction to Canadian Literature" (1988), *Northrop Frye's Fiction and Miscellaneous Writings* (2007), CW, 25.

Censorship is itself a violent, or counterviolent, solution: it assumes that you've caught the real villain and are justified in doing what you like to him, which is precisely the fallacy of violence itself.
"Violence and Television" (1975), *Northrop Frye on Modern Culture* (2003), CW, 11.

The authority of open science is recognized in theory in both democratic and totalitarian societies, but both still try to control openness in historical writing by hiding or destroying the relevant documents.
"Introduction," *Words with Power: Being a Second Study of "The Bible and Literature"* (1990), CW, 26.

Censorship and democracy don't mix, and there is no argument in favour of censorship that does not assume an antidemocratic social tendency.
"Dr. Kinsey and the Dream Censor" (1948), *Northrop Frye on Modern Culture* (2003), CW, 11.

Practically all movements of censorship are simply expressions of mob hysteria, and almost invariably focus on the very people whom genuine social concern should be regarding as allies instead of enemies.
"Introduction to *Art and Reality*" (1986), *Northrop Frye on Modern Culture* (2003), CW, 11.

CENTENNIALS

The value of centenaries and similar observances is that they call attention, not simply to great men, but to what we do with our great men.
"Blake after Two Centuries" (1957), *Northrop Frye on Milton and Blake* (2005), CW, 16.

For the majority of people in North America, the most important thing that happened in 1867 was the purchase of Alaska from Russia by the United States.
The Modern Century (1967), *Northrop Frye on Modern Culture* (2003), CW, 11.

CENTRE & CIRCUMFERENCE

The proverb says that God's centre is everywhere and his circumference nowhere, but in a human perspective the divine circumference would be everywhere too, as a centre has no identity without a circumference.
"First Variation: The Mountain," *Words with Power: Being a Second Study of "The Bible and Literature"* (1990), CW, 26.

CHAMPLAIN, SAMUEL DE

In Orillia there's a statue of Champlain, dressed like one of the three musketeers, with spurs (so useful for getting more speed out of a birchbark canoe).
"Reconciliation with Nature" (1976), *Northrop Frye's Fiction and Miscellaneous Writings* (2007), CW, 25.

CHANGE

Besides, if a radical reaction includes a good deal of hysteria, a conservative one is bound to include a good deal of inertia.
"Teaching the Humanities Today" (1977), *Northrop Frye's Writings on Education* (2001), CW, 7.

In a world where dynasties rise and fall at much the same rate as women's hemlines, the

dynasty and the hemline look much alike in importance, and get much the same amount of featuring in the news.
> *The Modern Century* (1967), *Northrop Frye on Modern Culture* (2003), CW, 11.

What is connected with the universities is what is really happening: the political and economic charades also going on are what are called pseudo-events, created for and blown up by the news media to give us the illusion of living in history. The human lives behind these charades, of people losing their jobs or finding that they can no longer live on their pensions, certainly do not consist of pseudo-events. But they are not hot news items either.
> "The Authority of Learning" (1984), *Northrop Frye's Writings on Education* (2001), CW, 7.

CHAOS

Chaos comes into the first verse of the Book of Genesis and keeps on going long past Melville.
> "The Scholar in Society" (1983), *Interviews with Northrop Frye* (2008), CW, 24.

God screwed chaos for six days and separated on the seventh, panting. Chaos thereby split into cosmos, the child, and Schekinah, the surviving companion. The light and the dark, plentitude and vacancy.
> Entry, Notebook 44 (1986–91), 721, *Northrop Frye's Late Notebooks, 1982–1990: Architecture of the Spiritual World* (2000), CW, 5.

CHAPLIN, CHARLIE

If films can survive indefinitely our grandchildren will probably ask some very awkward questions if we didn't see the great Chaplin masterpieces when they were new, or did see them and missed the point.
> "The Great Charlie" (1941), *Northrop Frye on Modern Culture* (2003), CW, 11.

CHARITY

Charity is not only the greatest of virtues, but the only virtue there is.
> "Canadian and American Values" (1988), explaining that "charity" in the New Testament means "love," *Interviews with Northrop Frye* (2008), CW, 24.

In a world like ours differences in faith are much less important than agreement in charity. Faith, or the rejection of faith, often revolves around the question, "Why would a good God permit so much evil and suffering?" Charity starts with the question, "Why do we permit so much evil and suffering?" and that is a question on which all men and women of good will can act instead of arguing in circles.
> "To Come to Light" (1986), *Northrop Frye on Religion* (2000), CW, 4.

CHARMS & RIDDLES

If we stayed with the oracular world of charm, everything would seem solemn, awful, portentous, and the least breath of humour or irreverence would destroy the mood. If we stayed with the world of riddle, we should be subjected to an endless stream of irresponsible wisecracks.
> "Cycle and Apocalypse in *Finnegans Wake*" (1987), *Northrop Frye on Twentieth-Century Literature* (2010), CW, 29.

CHAUCER, GEOFFREY

By looking at Chaucer's pieces we see an exceedingly clever versifier: by looking at his completed structures we see the greatness of his mind in something like its true perspective.
> "Chaucer's *Canterbury Tales*" (1936), *Northrop Frye on Literature and Society, 1936–1989: Unpublished Papers* (2002), CW, 10.

CHESS

A chess move is a decisive choice that may not abolish chance, but sets up a train of consequences that forces it to retreat into the shadows.
> Entry, Notebook 50 (1987–90), 313, *Northrop Frye's Late Notebooks, 1982–1990: Architecture of the Spiritual World* (2000), CW, 5.

CHICAGO

It is such a cheerful, hospitable, adolescent city. They tell me that the clothing advertisers urge Chicagoans to get a metropolitan cut to their clothes to impress the hick visitors. This is typical Chicago.
> "NF to HK," 17 Jun. 1933, *The Correspondence of Northrop Frye and Helen Kemp, 1932–1939* (1996), CW, 1.

CHICAGO WORLD'S FAIR

It's a World's Fair all right, and very like the world — huge, pretentious, artificial, mostly vulgar, partly beautiful, and, in spite of everything, magnificent.

"NF to HK," 18 Jun. 1933, *The Correspondence of Northrop Frye and Helen Kemp, 1932–1939* (1996), CW, 1.

CHILDREN

I was brought up in a middle-class, nonconformist environment. I have been more or less writing footnotes to the assumptions I acquired at the age of three or so ever since.

"Music in My Life" (1985), *Interviews with Northrop Frye* (2008), CW, 24.

The adult tends to think of the child's vision as ignorant and undeveloped, but actually it is a clearer and more civilized vision than his own.

"The Imaginative and the Imaginary" (1962), *"The Educated Imagination" and Other Writings on Critical Theory, 1933–1963* (2006), CW, 21.

Whatever literature we learn early, from pre-school nursery rhymes to high-school Shakespeare and beyond, provides us with the keys to nearly all the imaginative experience that it is possible for us to have in life. The central part of this training consists of the Bible, the Classics, and the great heritage of our mother tongue.

"Culture and the National Will" (1957), *Northrop Frye on Canada* (2003), CW, 12.

Again, if the child is an undeveloped human being, the parent, the complement of the child, is an imperfect one.

Entry, Notebook 3 (1946–48), 66, *Northrop Frye's Notebooks and Lectures on the Bible and Other Religious Texts* (2003), CW, 13.

The child is born civilized: he assumes that the world he is born into has a human shape and meaning, and was probably made for his own benefit.

"Introduction to *Selected Poetry and Prose of William Blake*" (1953), *Northrop Frye on Milton and Blake* (2005), CW, 16.

You drop out of poetry as soon as you drop out of the child's timeless world.

"Frye's Literary Theory in the Classroom" (1980), discussing the loss with age of the appreciation of poetry, *Interviews with Northrop Frye* (2008), CW, 24.

Living with children is recognized to be purgatorial, differing from hell only in having some sort of end.

Entry, Notebook 18 (1956–62), 148, *Notebooks for "Anatomy of Criticism"* (2007), CW, 23.

The sound of children playing is a cliché of innocent happiness. I have listened to it, and what I hear is mainly aggressiveness and hysteria.

Entry, Notebook 18 (1956–62), 148, *Notebooks for "Anatomy of Criticism"* (2007), CW, 23.

I once read a book on the language of children which remarked that children seem endlessly fascinated by the fact that a word can have more than one meaning. The authors should have added that they ought to keep this fascination all their lives: if they lose it when they grow up they're not maturing, just degenerating.

"Introduction," *Northrop Frye on Shakespeare* (1986), *Northrop Frye's Writings on Shakespeare and the Renaissance* (2010), CW, 28.

As the older aristocracies declined, it became clearer that the real natural aristocracy, the group of those who really have a right to be fed and sheltered and cosseted by the rest of society, are the children.

"Convocation Address, Franklin and Marshall" (1968), *Northrop Frye's Writings on Education* (2001), CW, 7.

CHINA

The creatures in China cannot "reform" anything, because to reform is to introduce the unpredictable, and they've proved they can't deal with that. They can only repress: that's all they know, and they will devote their entire energies to repression until their devils call for them.

Entry, Notebook 50 (1987–90), 757, *Northrop Frye's Late Notebooks, 1982–1990: Architecture of the Spiritual World* (2000), CW, 5.

China will probably have the next century pretty well to itself as far as culture, & perhaps even civilization, are concerned.
>Entry, 19 Aug. 1942, 63, *The Diaries of Northrop Frye: 1942–1955* (2001), CW, 8.

Chinese painting, for example, will influence Western painting purely through its merits as painting, not through any Western attempt to understand Chinese cultural traditions for political reasons.
>"F.S.C. Northrop's *The Meeting of East and West*" (1947), *Northrop Frye on Modern Culture* (2003), CW, 11.

I know this sounds like an obsession, but for anyone living in 1967, the thought of millions of Chinese yelling their guts loose & waving the little red books of Chairman Mao's thoughts in the air ought to be pretty central. Anything can happen, but one thing that certainly can happen is that China will unify itself around the "thought" of Mao, & become strong enough to wipe us out with the back of its hand in a very few years.
>Entry, Notebook 19 (1964–67), 408, *The "Third Book" Notebooks of Northrop Frye, 1964–1972: The Critical Comedy* (2002), CW, 9.

CHOSEN PEOPLE
Every people is *the* chosen people: that's what a translated Bible means.
>Entry, Notebook 50 (1987–90), 821, *Northrop Frye's Late Notebooks, 1982–1990: Architecture of the Spiritual World* (2000), CW, 5.

CHRIST
Christ *is* both the one God and the one Man, the Lamb of God, the tree of life, or vine of which we are the branches, the stone which the builders rejected, and the rebuilt temple which is identical with his risen body.
>"Third Essay: Archetypal Criticism: Theory of Myths" (1957), *Anatomy of Criticism: Four Essays* (2006), CW, 22.

Christ's life can only be told mythically, but as myth is so obviously a human invention the myth cannot be the *real form* of the revelation.
>Entry, Notebook 12 (1968–70), 177, *The "Third Book" Notebooks of Northrop Frye, 1964–1972: The Critical Comedy* (2002), CW, 9.

In this age Christ is no longer a peculiar society nor a historical individual, but the body of man.
>Entry, 6 Feb. 1950, 92, *The Diaries of Northrop Frye: 1942–1955* (2001), CW, 8.

The real or eternal Christ is the form of man, and the real body of art is that which art reveals.
>Entry, 9 Aug. 1950, 534, *The Diaries of Northrop Frye: 1942–1955* (2001), CW, 8.

CHRISTENDOM
Christian faith produced the civilization of Christendom, which reigned supreme in the Western world from the Atlantic to the Caucasus for many centuries, and is still one of the greatest forces of the contemporary world. But while Christendom is a colossal achievement, once we think of all its intolerance, its persecutions, its "religious" wars, its bigotry, it is clear that it too is still not the Kingdom of God that Jesus spoke of.
>"The Leap in the Dark" (1971), *Northrop Frye on Religion* (2000), CW, 4.

CHRISTIANITY
There is nothing that we get from Christianity except a body of words, and they become transmuted into experience. I wouldn't talk about the objectivity of God. I'd talk about the transcendence of God.
>"Northrop Frye in Conversation" (1989), *Interviews with Northrop Frye* (2008), CW, 24.

Christianity, similarly, had to outgrow the notion that the end of the world was going to come in the next week or so, and after it had outgrown it, it settled down to being a way of life, rather than a way of postponing life.
>"Style and Image in the Twentieth Century" (1967), comparing Christianity with Russian and Chinese Communism, *Interviews with Northrop Frye* (2008), CW, 24.

I think it is the conception of God as the power that recreates man rather than God as

the creator of the order of nature that is the really valid element in Christianity.
>"Into the Wilderness" (1969), *Interviews with Northrop Frye* (2008), CW, 24.

A genuinely tragic Christian attitude would see suffering as a participation in the passion of a hero who was both divine and human, and so would establish a place within Christianity for the tragic hero.
>*"Fools of Time*: III, Little World of Man: The Tragedy of Isolation" (1966), *Northrop Frye's Writings on Shakespeare and the Renaissance* (2010), CW, 28.

Hence being a Xn [Christian] is one way of being a Buddhist.
>Entry, Notebook 50 (1987–90), 34, *Northrop Frye's Late Notebooks, 1982–1990: Architecture of the Spiritual World* (2000), CW, 5.

In the official Christian myth, the Creator is pure and innocent and the creature is foul and vicious; in the fabulous counterpart, the creator, being man, is foul and vicious but his creature, the work of art, is pure and innocent.
>Entry, Notebook 54-4 (late 1970s), 193, *Northrop Frye's Notebooks on Romance* (2004), CW, 15.

For Christianity, like the humanities, is teachable only to a very limited extent: the rest consists in realizing anew for oneself what every Christian has always known, but can explain only to a receptive mind.
>"Education and the Humanities" (1947), *Northrop Frye's Writings on Education* (2001), CW, 7.

It's given us a very strong sense of a meaning emerging out of human history rather than history as a meaningless series of cycles from which you have to be liberated.
>"Between Paradise and Apocalypse" (1978), *Interviews with Northrop Frye* (2008), CW, 24.

It still seems to be true that Christianity has some affinity for stupidity. If I were to see a small church labelled "the foursquare gospel" I'd give it a wide berth, because I know I'd find nothing inside except what I'd call hysteria.
>Entry, Notes 54-5 (1976), 152, *Northrop Frye's Notebooks and Lectures on the Bible and Other Religious Texts* (2003), CW, 13.

The revolutionary core of Christianity is its identifying of God with a suffering, persecuted, and enduring man. It was in the sign of the cross, a ridiculous and shameful emblem, that an outcast religion conquered the world's greatest empire.
>"Silence in the Sea" (1968), *Northrop Frye on Canada* (2003), CW, 12.

However, early Christianity discovered that Christianity would be much more saleable if you perverted its good news into bad news, and in particular if you put at the centre of your teaching the doctrine that after death, unless you did what you were told at this moment, you would suffer tortures for eternity, meaning endlessly in time.
>"Symbolism in the Bible" (1981–82), *Northrop Frye's Notebooks and Lectures on the Bible and Other Religious Texts* (2003), CW, 13.

It may be possible to Christianity to have its God and eat Him too, but it is not yet possible for a Christian philosopher to choose either the committed religious or the disinterested intellectual path and still get all the benefits of both.
>"Josef Pieper, *Leisure: The Basis of Culture*" (1950s), *Northrop Frye on Literature and Society, 1936–1989: Unpublished Papers* (2002), CW, 10.

The central form of Christianity is its vision of the humanity of God and the divinity of risen Man, and this, in varying ways, is what all great Christian artists have attempted to recreate.
>"Part One: The Argument," *Fearful Symmetry: A Study of William Blake* (1947, 2004), CW, 14.

CHRISTMAS

It is the latter vision that turns the darkness of Advent into the festival of blazing lights, the lights which are the glory of a God who is also Man, who is continually born and continually dying, and yet remains unborn and beyond the reach of death.
>"The Leap in the Dark" (1971), referring specifically to Christmas, *Northrop Frye on Religion* (2000), CW, 4.

The present secular Christmas is, in any case, really a New Year festival, with Santa Claus representing the spirit of the Old Year and the New one hazily identified with the Christ child. The identification is not pressed, because that would lead to the unwelcome inference that the birth of Christ and the death of Santa Claus are the same event.

"The Leap in the Dark" (1971), *Northrop Frye on Religion* (2000), CW, 4.

The story of Christmas, from its primitive beginnings to the present, is in part a story of how men, by cowering together in a common fear of menace, discovered a new fellowship, in fellowship a new hope, and in hope a new vision of society.

"Merry Christmas (III)" (1949), *Northrop Frye on Religion* (2000), CW, 4.

Christmas is far, far older than Christianity, as even the pre-Christian Yule and Saturnalia were late developments of it, and it was never completely assimilated to the Christian faith.

"Merry Christmas (I)" (1946), *Northrop Frye on Religion* (2000), CW, 4.

Perhaps the answer is that people go through the bother of Christmas because Christmas helps them to understand why they go through the bother of living out their lives the rest of the year. For one brief instant, we see human society as it should and could be....

"Merry Christmas (II)" (1948), *Northrop Frye on Religion* (2000), CW, 4.

There is no New Testament evidence whatever about what time of year Jesus was born, and as far as we can see, the Church seems to have been content to take the winter solstice festival from other religions.

"Symbolism in the Bible" (1981–82), *Northrop Frye's Notebooks and Lectures on the Bible and Other Religious Texts* (2003), CW, 13.

Christmas season then is a deliberately induced period of chaos & hysteria designed to assume stability after the New Year.

Entry, Notebook 3 (1946–48), 182, *Northrop Frye's Notebooks and Lectures on the Bible and Other Religious Texts* (2003), CW, 13.

The world clings to Christmas with a kind of desperation: it is the only traditional festival, apart from a flurry of new hats at Easter, that retains any real hold on ordinary life.

"Merry Christmas (II)" (1948), *Northrop Frye on Religion* (2000), CW, 4.

CHURCH

If the Sabbath was made for man, the Church was too.

Entry, Notes 53 (1989–90), 212, *Northrop Frye's Late Notebooks, 1982–1990: Architecture of the Spiritual World* (2000), CW, 6.

Law is the expression of temporal authority; justice is law informed by the vision of freedom and equality; the vision of freedom and equality is a steady vision only within the Christian church. Outside the church it is only a vague hope or a fitful glimpse afforded by the lucky chance of a good ruler.

"The Analogy of Democracy" (1952), *Northrop Frye on Religion* (2000), CW, 4.

We can save ourselves only through an established co-operative church, and if the church ever wakes up to that fact, that will constitute enough of a miracle to get us the rest of the way.

"NF to HK," 4 Sep. 1933, *The Correspondence of Northrop Frye and Helen Kemp, 1932–1939* (1996), CW, 1.

The dilemma the Church put modern man into is this: the Catholic position is that the Church contains the Word: the Protestant is that the Word contains the Church.

Entry, Notebook 32 (late 1946–51), 102, *Northrop Frye's Notebooks on Romance* (2004), CW, 15.

The society produced by the gospel is the church, and the church is a community whose members have all been made free and equal by their faith.

"The Return of Eden: Five Essays on Milton's Epics" (1965), *Northrop Frye on Milton and Blake* (2005), CW, 16.

If Milton or Blake had joined or founded a church, therefore, they would have lost the

real Church, the total vision which is the city of God, and gained a sect.
"Part Three: The Final Synthesis," *Fearful Symmetry: A Study of William Blake* (1947, 2004), CW, 14.

The church has the power to save the world when it is itself saved, and the saving power will work largely outside it until it is.
"The Analogy of Democracy" (1952), *Northrop Frye on Religion* (2000), CW, 4.

As I don't believe in substantial real presence, I don't believe anything *happens* at a church service. I don't understand the "this do in remembrance of me" aspect of Christianity: it seems silly, & I must think about it.
Entry, 8 Jan. 1950, 25, *The Diaries of Northrop Frye: 1942–1955* (2001), CW, 8.

The religious bodies have enough problems of their own, but if they fail to meet the spiritual needs of society, the university will become the only source of free authority, and hence would be almost compelled to slip into the role of a lay church for intellectuals.
"The Ethics of Change: The Role of the University" (1968), *Northrop Frye's Writings on Education* (2001), CW, 7.

CHURCHILL, WINSTON
I had the usual childish fantasies, when very young, of wanting to be a "great man" — fantasies that in our day only Churchill has realized. But Churchill's greatness was archaic: his funeral really buried that whole conception of greatness as a social ambition.
Entry, Notebook 12 (1968–70), 66, *The "Third Book" Notebooks of Northrop Frye, 1964–1972: The Critical Comedy* (2002), CW, 9.

CINCINNATI
There are more people in Cincinnati than in Shakespeare's London; but Cincinnati *cannot* produce genius. It isn't the capital of anything: no organization of state or nation or anything else with a body comes to a head in it.
Entry, 24 Jan. 1949, 120, *The Diaries of Northrop Frye: 1942–1955* (2001), CW, 8.

CITIES
The map still shows us self-contained cities like Hamilton and Toronto, but experience presents us with an urban sprawl, which ignores national boundaries and buries a vast area of beautiful and fertile land in a tomb of concrete.
The Modern Century (1967), *Northrop Frye on Modern Culture* (2003), CW, 11.

Engineers, along with architects and town planners, are deeply involved with the physical appearance of society. And the briefest glance at our society shows a stupefying hideousness and squalor, with the great octopus sprawl of streets and highways and buildings swallowing all the fertility of the nature around us. When this process is applied to the natural environment, we call it pollution: when it is applied to the human environment, we call it development. But whatever we call it, something is badly wrong with the creative power of the society that has produced it.
"Universities and the Deluge of Cant" (1972), *Northrop Frye's Writings on Education* (2001), CW, 7.

The amount of mental distress caused by living in an environment which expresses indifference or contempt for the perspectives of the human body is very little studied: one might call it proportion pollution.
"Canada: New World Without Revolution" (1975), *Northrop Frye on Canada* (2003), CW, 12.

The city is the community become conscious: it is to the country what man is to animals. Animals live; man knows that he lives; people live in the country & often live very well, but in the city some additional consciousness comes to life.
Entry, 24 Jan. 1949, 120, *The Diaries of Northrop Frye: 1942–1955* (2001), CW, 8.

Washington became a capital because it was in the logical place for one, between the north and the south: Ottawa became a capital because it was not Montreal or Kingston.
"National Consciousness in Canadian Culture" (1976), *Northrop Frye on Canada* (2003), CW, 12.

CITIZENS

A citizen's primary duty, I should think, is to try to know what should be changed in his society and what conserved. The operative word here is "know."
"Universities and the Deluge of Cant" (1972), *Northrop Frye's Writings on Education* (2001), CW, 7.

It is essential for the teacher of literature, at every level, to remember that in a modern democracy a citizen participates in society mainly through his imagination.
"Elementary Teaching and Elemental Scholarship" (1963), *Northrop Frye's Writings on Education* (2001), CW, 7.

CIVILIZATION

But for better or worse, our civilization, if it survives at all, will be one in which criticism and literature, that is, the theory and practice of literature itself, will be two parts of one thing.
"Literary Criticism" (1963), *"The Critical Path" and Other Writings on Critical Theory, 1963–1975* (2009), CW, 27.

Civilization is not merely an imitation of nature, but the process of making a total human form out of nature, and it is impelled by the force that we have just called desire.
"Second Essay: Ethical Criticism: Theory of Symbols" (1957), *Anatomy of Criticism: Four Essays* (2006), CW, 22.

In the civilized state of humanity we love those who are close to us: for those farther away we feel the tolerance and good will which express love at a distance. In the pure state of nature we feel only possessive about those close to us, and hostile and mistrustful of those further away. The latter do all sorts of vaguely irritating things, like speaking different languages, eating different foods, and holding different beliefs.
The Double Vision (1991), *Northrop Frye on Religion* (2000), CW, 4.

The totality of imaginative power, of which the matrix is art, is what we ordinarily call culture or civilization.
"Part One: The Argument," *Fearful Symmetry: A Study of William Blake* (1947, 2004), CW, 14.

The oldest civilization in the modern world is the American one, which was established in its present form in 1776.
"The Church and Modern Culture" (1950), *Northrop Frye on Modern Culture* (2003), CW, 11.

CLARITY

No darkness can comprehend any light; no ignorance or indifference can ever see any *claritas* in literature itself or in the criticism that attempts to convey it, just as no saint in ordinary life wears a visible gold plate around his head.
"Criticism, Visible and Invisible" (1964), using *claritas* as a synonym for clarity or intensity, *"The Critical Path" and Other Writings on Critical Theory, 1963–1975* (2009), CW, 27.

CLASSES

The social energy which maintains the class structure produces perverted culture in its three chief forms: mere upper-class culture, or ostentation, mere middle-class culture, or vulgarity, and mere lower-class culture, or squalor.
"Tentative Conclusion" (1957), *Anatomy of Criticism: Four Essays* (2006), CW, 22.

But it would be wrong to forget that the average American does not think of the rich and poor as separate classes, but as lucky and unlucky branches of an undifferentiated society he does not even think of as middle-class.
"The Present Condition of the World" (1943), *Northrop Frye on Literature and Society, 1936–1989: Unpublished Papers* (2002), CW, 10.

We have already got to the point where the phrase "leisure class" makes no sense. Perhaps our grandchildren will be living in a world in which the phrase "working class" makes even less sense.
"The Teacher's Source of Authority" (1978), *Northrop Frye's Writings on Education* (2001), CW, 7.

CLASSIC, LITERARY

The word "classic" as applied to a work of literature means primarily a work that refuses to go away, that remains confronting us until we do something about it, which means also doing something about ourselves.

"The Double Mirror" (1981), *Northrop Frye on Religion* (2000), CW, 4.

Masterpiece and classic don't mean inherent formal qualities but a locus of social acceptance. Perhaps they emerge when acceptance becomes recognition, a vision of form irradiating it.
Entry, Notebook 54-8 (late 1972–77), 13, *Northrop Frye's Notebooks on Romance* (2004), CW, 15.

The classic, what's worth studying, is what has already established itself in experience, and won't go away.
"Critical Views" (1980s), 17, *Northrop Frye's Fiction and Miscellaneous Writings* (2007), CW, 25.

If I were to be asked what my definition of a classic was, I would say it was a work that won't go away. It just stands in front of you until you deal with it. It's the angel that every Jacob has to wrestle with.
"Canadian Energies: Dialogues on Creativity" (1980), *Interviews with Northrop Frye* (2008), CW, 24.

What we call classics are works of literature that show an ability to communicate with other ages over the widest barriers of time, space, and language.
"The Expanding World of Metaphor" (1984), *"The Secular Scripture" and Other Writings on Critical Theory, 1976–1991* (2006), CW, 18.

The original writer is the person who returns to origins. The man who produces the imperishable classic is not a man with a new story but a man who tells one of the world's great stories again and tells it better.
"Music in My Life" (1985), *Interviews with Northrop Frye* (2008), CW, 24.

What we call a "classic" in literature is often a literary work so complex that understanding the "structure" becomes an indefinite and tentative sequence of responses.
"The Mythical Approach to Creation" (1985), *Northrop Frye on Religion* (2000), CW, 4.

Literature revolves around certain classics or models because it is really revolving around certain structural principles which those classics embody.
"The Developing Imagination" (1962), *Northrop Frye's Writings on Education* (2001), CW, 7.

This coincides with a feeling we have all had: that the study of mediocre works of art remains a random and peripheral form of critical experience, whereas the profound masterpiece draws us to a point at which we seem to see an enormous number of converging patterns of significance.
"Polemical Introduction" (1957), *Anatomy of Criticism: Four Essays* (2006), CW, 22.

CLASSICS, GREEK & ROMAN

… Classical mythology became purely poetic after its oracles had ceased.
"Third Essay: Archetypal Criticism: Theory of Myths" (1957), *Anatomy of Criticism: Four Essays* (2006), CW, 22.

The first thing to be laid on top of a Biblical training, in my opinion, is Classical mythology, which gives us the same kind of imaginative framework, of a more fragmentary kind. Here again there are all sorts of incidental or secondary reasons for the study: the literatures of all modern Western languages are so full of Classical myths that one hardly knows what's going on without some training in them. But again, the primary reason is the shape of the mythology. The Classical myths give us, much more clearly than the Bible, the main episodes of the central myth of the hero whose mysterious birth, triumph and marriage, death and betrayal and eventual rebirth follow the rhythm of the sun and the seasons.
The Educated Imagination (1963), *"The Educated Imagination" and Other Writings on Critical Theory, 1933–1963* (2006), CW, 21.

CLICHÉS

Belief in clichés and catchwords and slogans is an automatic response which saves the time and trouble of thinking, and this kind of misplaced mechanism is sinister and dangerous. So is dealing with the news of the day in the categories of a bad movie, which is an automatic form of retreat from the world, like taking a tranquillizer pill.

"Push-Button Gadgets May Help — But the Teacher Seems Here to Stay" (1960), *Northrop Frye's Writings on Education* (2001), CW, 7.

CLOTHES

Glanced over a book on nudism. I don't see the point myself: I don't wear clothes out of modesty. I wear them because they have pockets.

Entry, 20 Jul. 1942, 26, *The Diaries of Northrop Frye: 1942–1955* (2001), CW, 8.

COINCIDENCE

In ordinary life a coincidence is a piece of design for which we can find no practical use.

The Secular Scripture: A Study of the Structure of Romance (1975), "*The Secular Scripture*" *and Other Writings on Critical Theory, 1976–1991* (2006), CW, 18.

COLD WAR

The influence of Canada on the United States is almost impossible to describe in words: it's subjective to the verge of being mystical. But simply to have so powerful an insulating force separating it from the Soviet Union had a good deal to do with the fact that the Cold War stayed cold.

"Notes for 'Levels of Cultural Identity'" (1989), 55, *Northrop Frye's Fiction and Miscellaneous Writings* (2007), CW, 25.

The language of American democracy and the language of Russian Marxism, for example, get so self-enclosed and so solipsistic that neither can really get outside itself to reach at the other. That seems to me to be perhaps the greatest central danger society faces today.

"The Only Genuine Revolution" (1969), *Interviews with Northrop Frye* (2008), CW, 24.

COLERIDGE, SAMUEL TAYLOR

I think that if I believed in anything like reincarnation I would feel that maybe I was commissioned to write Coleridge's book on the Logos which he kept hugging to his bosom in the form of fifty-seven notebooks that a colleague of mine has tried to edit.

"Archetype and History" (1986), responding to the suggestion that his approach was "probably best called Coleridgean" and referring to the scholar Kathleen Coburn, *Interviews with Northrop Frye* (2008), CW, 24.

In continuous prose, even at his best, he is, as Chesterton says of Shaw, long-winded because he is quick-witted: he thinks of all the qualifications of his idea at once, hence his contemporary reputation for murkiness.

"Long Sequacious Notes" (1953), *Northrop Frye's Writings on the Eighteenth and Nineteenth Centuries* (2005), CW, 17.

COLLABORATION

It has been proved all through the history of drama that the word "collaborator" does not have to be used in its wartime sense of traitor, and that collaboration often, in fact usually, creates a distinct and unified personality.

"A Natural Perspective: The Development of Shakespearean Comedy and Romance: II, Making Nature Afraid" (1963), *Northrop Frye's Writings on Shakespeare and the Renaissance* (2010), CW, 28.

COLLAGE

There is, perhaps, an element of stunt or even a put-on about a good many experimental developments in our time, and yet we are in an age of collage: an age where we're more or less committed to the unexpected juxtaposition.

"Poets of Canada: 1920 to the Present" (1971), *Interviews with Northrop Frye* (2008), CW, 24.

COLONIAL WILLIAMSBURG

The kind of preservation that we have in Williamsburg and similar large-scale open museums is in a sense almost antihistorical: it shows us, not life in time as a continuous process, but life arrested at a certain point, in a sort of semi-permanent drama. There is nothing wrong with this, but it gives us a cross-section of history, a world confronting us rather than preceding us.

"Canada: New World Without Revolution" (1975), *Northrop Frye on Canada* (2003), CW, 12.

COLONIALISM

In culture, as in religion and politics, the homeland is the source of authority, and the first duty of a colonial culture is to respond to it.

"Culture as Interpenetration" (1982), *Northrop Frye on Canada* (2003), CW, 12.

Canada may very well be the only genuine colony left in the world. The degree of economic and to some extent political penetration by the United States is of course very great, and the reasons for it are quite obvious.
"Canadian and American Values" (1988), *Interviews with Northrop Frye* (2008), CW, 24.

The imperial and the regional are both inherently anti-poetic environments, yet they go hand-in-hand; and together they make up what I call the colonial in Canadian life.
"Canada and Its Poetry" (1943), *Northrop Frye on Canada* (2003), CW, 12.

The colonial position of Canada is therefore a frostbite at the roots of the Canadian imagination, and it produces a disease for which I think the best name is prudery.
"Canada and Its Poetry" (1943), *Northrop Frye on Canada* (2003), CW, 12.

COLOUR

There is an annual birth and death of colour, out of the black and white, in Canada.
"CRTC Guru" (1968–69), noting, as well, "You'll never get a Monet in Canada," *Interviews with Northrop Frye* (2008), CW, 24.

COMEDY

The statement "all's well that ends well" is a statement about the structure of comedy, and is not intended to apply to actual life.
"A Natural Perspective: The Development of Shakespearean Comedy and Romance; II, Making Nature Afraid" (1963), *Northrop Frye's Writings on Shakespeare and the Renaissance* (2010), CW, 28.

The only modern master of ideal comedy to rank with Aristophanes & Shakespeare is Mozart....
Entry, 24 Feb. 1952, 136, *The Diaries of Northrop Frye: 1942–1955* (2001), CW, 8.

Comedy is a structure in which Eros smashes an irrational law.
Entry, Notebook 54-5 (1976), 1, *Northrop Frye's Notebooks and Lectures on the Bible and Other Religious Texts* (2003), CW, 13.

The indication of tragedy is one of the most powerful effects that comedy, particularly satiric comedy, can produce. But only the indication is possible: to go further would upset the balance of tone.
"Chaucer's *Canterbury Tales*" (1936), *Northrop Frye on Literature and Society, 1936–1989: Unpublished Papers* (2002), CW, 10.

A tragic or comic plot is not a straight line: it is a parabola following the shapes of the mouths on the conventional masks. Comedy has a U-shaped plot, with the action sinking into deep and often potentially tragic complications, and then suddenly turning upward into a happy ending. Tragedy has an inverted U, with the action rising in crisis to a *peripety* and then plunging downward to catastrophe through a series of recognitions, usually of the inevitable consequences of previous acts.
"Myth, Fiction, and Displacement" (1961), *"The Educated Imagination" and Other Writings on Critical Theory, 1933–1963* (2006), CW, 21.

Man is a creator as an individual; as a member of a society or species, he is a creature. The end of a comedy leaves him creaturely, invited to join a party to celebrate the creation of a new society, from the further fortunes of which he is of course excluded by the ending of the play. The end of a tragedy leaves him alone in a waste and void chaos of experience with a world to remake out of it.
"*Fools of Time*: III, Little World of Man: The Tragedy of Isolation" (1966), *Northrop Frye's Writings on Shakespeare and the Renaissance* (2010), CW, 28.

Forgiveness and reconciliation come at the end of a comedy because they belong at the end of a comedy, not because Shakespeare "believed" in them. And so the play ends: it doesn't discuss any issues, solve any problems, expound any theories, or illustrate any doctrines. What it does is show us why comedies exist and why Shakespeare wrote so many of them.

"Northrop Frye on Shakespeare: VII, *Measure for Measure*" (1986), *Northrop Frye's Writings on Shakespeare and the Renaissance* (2010), CW, 28.

The supreme masters of comedy have rather a hard time of it with critics: because they amuse, one is tempted to patronize them. Besides, the appeal of comedy might perhaps without overstatement be described as more intellectualized than that of tragedy, and comedy usually includes a considered refusal to explore the emotional possibilities which tragedy affords.

"Chaucer's *Canterbury Tales*" (1936), *Northrop Frye on Literature and Society, 1936–1989: Unpublished Papers* (2002), CW, 10.

There is a continuous dream in life, which is the slave's life that we live when we are driven by the necessities of money or security or the tactics of conflict. The awareness of the reality of life comes in detached moments of release from this, or in later memories of them.

"Hart House Rededicated" (1969), *Northrop Frye's Writings on Education* (2001), CW, 7.

COMIC ART

A good deal of the worry over the ten-year-old's comic books would be far better expended on making sure that the central educational structure is a sound one.

"Culture and the National Will" (1957), *Northrop Frye on Canada* (2003), CW, 12.

All humour demands agreement that certain things, such as a picture of a wife beating her husband in a comic strip, are conventionally funny. To introduce a comic strip in which a husband beats his wife would distress the reader, because it would mean learning a new convention.

"Third Essay: Archetypal Criticism: Theory of Myths" (1957), *Anatomy of Criticism: Four Essays* (2006), CW, 22.

At its most naive it is an endless form in which a central character who never develops or ages goes through one adventure after another until the author himself collapses. We see this form in comic strips, where the central characters persist for years in a state of refrigerated deathlessness.

"Third Essay: Archetypal Criticism: Theory of Myths" (1957), *Anatomy of Criticism: Four Essays* (2006), CW, 22.

Soap operas & comic strips are as close to endless art as we can get: their unreality has something to do with the intolerable realism of their form.

Entry, 24 Feb. 1949, 220, *The Diaries of Northrop Frye: 1942–1955* (2001), CW, 8.

COMMANDMENT

Commandment says: this do; aphorism says, this understand; parable says, this see; oracle says, this hear. If that's right, there *is* a movement from oracle to parable and from commandment to aphorism.

Entry, Notebook 11f (1969–70), 47, *Northrop Frye's Notebooks and Lectures on the Bible and Other Religious Texts* (2003), CW, 13.

COMMITMENT

If the end of commitment is the community, the end of detachment is the individual. This is not an antithesis: the mature individual is mature only because he has reached a kind of social adjustment.

"The Ethics of Change: The Role of the University" (1968), *Northrop Frye's Writings on Education* (2001), CW, 7.

COMMONWEALTH

The idea of a Commonwealth is a very attractive idea to me, now that it no longer has an imperialistic basis. I think the symbol of royalty as something that nobody can possibly earn but that you can only get by accident is still something that I would buy. Otherwise, the whole of society becomes open to competition.

"Making the Revolutionary Act Now" (1983), *Interviews with Northrop Frye* (2008), CW, 24.

COMMUNICATION

Communication is the force holding together a community; at the centre of community is communion — the icon or concept symbolizing unity.

Entry, Notebook 11f (1969–70), 109, *Northrop Frye's Notebooks and Lectures on the Bible and Other Religious Texts* (2003), CW, 13.

The same feeling for strained distance is in many Canadian poets and novelists — certainly in Grove — and can hardly be an accident that the two most important Canadian thinkers to date, Edward Sapir and Harold Innis, have both been largely concerned with problems of communication.
"Letters in Canada: Poetry" (1953), *Northrop Frye on Canada* (2003), CW, 12.

The triumph of communication is the death of communication: where communication forms a total environment, there is nothing to be communicated.
The Modern Century (1967), *Northrop Frye on Modern Culture* (2003), CW, 11.

Control of communications is one of the primary aims of an ascendant class: whatever tends toward democracy must have, as one of its primary aims, the openness and sharing of communications.
"The Renaissance of Books" (1973), *Northrop Frye on Modern Culture* (2003), CW, 11.

COMMUNISM

But, if the first half of the century saw the passing of Fascism, the second half may see the passing of Communism. I don't look for catastrophic war, but for restricted bleeding wars, threats, interdicts, and an attempt on the part of each side to wait for the enemy to blow up through internal contradictions.
Entry, 1 Jan. 1951, 1, *The Diaries of Northrop Frye: 1942–1955* (2001), CW, 8.

But if the entire Communist world were annihilated tomorrow all our enemies would still be with us, in many respects stronger than ever.
"By Liberal Things" (1959), *Northrop Frye's Writings on Education* (2001), CW, 7.

Communism has no God, but that does not prevent it from being a religion with prophets, revealed scriptures, a body of infallible doctrine, heresies, saints, martyrs, and shrines.
"The Changing Pace in Canadian Education" (1963), *Northrop Frye's Writings on Education* (2001), CW, 7.

COMMUNITIES

But if we place the works of the human imagination in the centre of the community and make sure they stay there, we shall be able eventually to see that community itself as the total form of what human beings can bring forth, their own larger life that continues to live and move and possess its inward being.
"Literature as a Critique of Pure Reason" (1982), *"The Secular Scripture" and Other Writings on Critical Theory, 1976–1991* (2006), CW, 18.

But while communities enrich themselves by what they include, they define themselves by what they exclude. The more intensely a community feels its identity as a community, the more intensely it feels its difference from what is across its boundary. In a strong sense of community there is thus always an element that may become hostile and aggressive.
"Hart House Rededicated" (1969), *Northrop Frye's Writings on Education* (2001), CW, 7.

Total communication threatens a community's identity by attacking it from without: it's what a community can absorb, not what it can reach that's important. There's no reason why exclusion should be hostile: whether or not good fences make good neighbours, the fence certainly creates the neighbour.
Entry, Notebook 11f (1969–70), 119, *Northrop Frye's Notebooks and Lectures on the Bible and Other Religious Texts* (2003), CW, 13.

In an interpenetrating world every community would be the centre of the world.
"Northrop Frye in Conversation" (1989), *Interviews with Northrop Frye* (2008), CW, 24.

The study of literature therefore is a means of making one a member of a community beyond death, a community of the human imagination which has survived thousands of years of empires that have come and gone and is still adding to and building up its central imaginative structures.
"Reconsidering Levels of Meaning" (1979), *Northrop Frye's Fiction and Miscellaneous Writings* (2007), CW, 25.

All religions are one, not alike; "that they may be one," not that they should all think alike: community means people thinking along similar lines & motivated by similar drives; communion means that all men are the same man.

> Entry, Notebook 12 (1968–70), 560, *The "Third Book" Notebooks of Northrop Frye, 1964–1972: The Critical Comedy* (2002), CW, 9.

I think that the human community is really something that is prior to the individual. The individual grows out of the community, not the other way around.

> "Between Paradise and Apocalypse" (1978), *Interviews with Northrop Frye* (2008), CW, 24.

The form of human community envisaged by democracy is not new: it is the real form of human community which has been with us since the beginning of history, obscured by human weakness, ignorance, passion, and greed.

> "The Analogy of Democracy" (1952), *Northrop Frye on Religion* (2000), CW, 4.

COMPROMISE

If Canada had not been able to compromise, it would never have been Canada.

> "Canadian Voices" (1975), *Interviews with Northrop Frye* (2008), CW, 24.

Compromise is not a betrayal when a refusal to compromise would be a greater betrayal.

> "The Ethics of Change: The Role of the University" (1968), *Northrop Frye's Writings on Education* (2001), CW, 7.

COMPULSIONS

We live in a world of threefold external compulsion: of compulsion on action, or law; of compulsion on thinking, or fact; of compulsion on feeling, which is the characteristic of all pleasure whether it is produced by the *Paradiso* or by an ice cream soda. But in the world of imagination a fourth power, which contains morality, beauty, and truth but is never subordinated to them, rises free of all their compulsions.

> "Second Essay: Ethical Criticism: Theory of Symbols" (1957), *Anatomy of Criticism: Four Essays* (2006), CW, 22.

COMPUTERS

The mechanical age stopped with the Selectric typewriter, as far as I'm concerned.

> "'Condominium Mentality' in CanLit" (1989), *Interviews with Northrop Frye* (2008), CW, 24.

Computers can think; they have intelligence and consciousness. What they don't have (so far) is *will*: they have to be plugged in or turned on like other machines. Perhaps electricity is will on the mechanical level....

> Entry, Notebook 47 (1989–90), 18, *Northrop Frye's Late Notebooks, 1982–1990: Architecture of the Spiritual World* (2000), CW, 6.

Eventually, no doubt, we shall have machines that stand in the same relation to ordinary human brains that jet planes do to ordinary human feet.

> "Introduction to the Second Volume of Harold Innis's 'A History of Communciations'" (1980s), *Northrop Frye on Literature and Society, 1936–1989: Unpublished Papers* (2002), CW, 10.

I suppose computers are the physical realization of magic, just as the television screen is the physical realization of ghosts.

> Entry, Notebook 44 (1986–91), 262, *Northrop Frye's Late Notebooks, 1982–1990: Architecture of the Spiritual World* (2000), CW, 5.

There's no reason why man should not develop machines that can reproduce every activity of the human brain on a vastly higher level of speed and efficiency. But nobody has yet come up with a computer that wanted to do these things on its own: as well, so far, every machine is an expression of the will of its makers.

> Entry, Notes 54.2 (1982–91), 2, *Northrop Frye's Late Notebooks, 1982–1990: Architecture of the Spiritual World* (2000), CW, 6.

CONCERN

Briefly, the language of concern is the language of myth. Myth is the structural principle of literature that enters into and gives form to the verbal disciplines where concern is relevant.

> "The Instruments of Mental Production" (1966), *Northrop Frye's Writings on Education* (2001), CW, 7.

And I speak of concern rather than belief, because a general public assent to certain formulas is more important to a society than actual belief in them. Belief may be in theory the essential thing, but private beliefs elude social vigilance, as the public expression of them does not.

"The Myth of Deliverance: I, The Reversal of Action" (1981), *Northrop Frye's Writings on Shakespeare and the Renaissance* (2010), CW, 28.

To liberate the language of concern is to ensure that the whole imaginative range of concern is being expressed in society, instead of being confined to a selected type of imagination which is hitched to the tactics of one social group, as propaganda for it, or what we have called a rhetorical analogue to it.

The Critical Path: An Essay on the Social Context of Literary Criticism (1971), *"The Critical Path" and Other Writings on Critical Theory, 1963–1975* (2009), CW, 27.

It is out of the tension between concern and freedom that glimpses of a third order of experience emerge, of a world that may not exist but completes existence, the world of the definitive experience that poetry urges us to have but which we never quite get.

The Critical Path: An Essay on the Social Context of Literary Criticism (1971), *"The Critical Path" and Other Writings on Critical Theory, 1963–1975* (2009), CW, 27.

Concern is the response of the adult citizen to genuine social problems. Anxiety is based on the desire to exclude or subordinate, to preserve the values or benefits of society for the group of right people who know the right answers.

"Address on Receiving the Royal Bank Award" (1978), *Northrop Frye's Writings on Education* (2001), CW, 7.

Once a myth of concern is recognized to be such, it becomes clear that you can't express its truth without lying. Because you're contradicting accepted truth with something which is going to be made true but isn't true now.

Entry, Notebook 12 (1968–70), 237, *The "Third Book" Notebooks of Northrop Frye, 1964–1972: The Critical Comedy* (2002), CW, 9.

There has always been a practical distinction between what is important, like cathedrals, and what is necessary, like privies: in our day the important seems, possibly for the first time in history, to be becoming necessary as well.

"The Instruments of Mental Production" (1966), *Northrop Frye's Writings on Education* (2001), CW, 7.

CONCERNS, PRIMARY AND SECONDARY

Human beings are concerned beings, and it seems to me that there are two kinds of concern: primary and secondary. Primary concerns are such things as food, sex, property, and freedom of movement: concerns that we share with animals on a physical level. Secondary concerns include our political, religious, and other ideological loyalties.

The Double Vision (1991), *Northrop Frye on Religion* (2000), CW, 4.

I think mythology expresses the primary human concerns, and ideology the secondary and derivative ones.

Entry, Notebook 44 (1986–91), 6, *Northrop Frye's Late Notebooks, 1982–1990: Architecture of the Spiritual World* (2000), CW, 5.

The *most* primary concern of all, breathing, is transformed into spirit, & the spiritual meaning of food & drink, of love, of security & shelter & the sense of home, all follow. The transition from material to spiritual, of course, is through the *verbal*: we don't go into a Platonic intelligible world.

Entry, Notebook 44 (1986–91), 293, *Northrop Frye's Late Notebooks, 1982–1990: Architecture of the Spiritual World* (2000), CW, 5.

Literature seems to me to revolve around what I call the primary concerns of humanity, those that have to do with freedom, love, and staying alive, along with the ironies of their frustration, as distinct from the secondary or ideological concerns of politics and religion, for which the direct verbal expression is expository rather than literary.

"Auguries of Experience" (1987), *"The Secular Scripture" and Other Writings on Critical Theory, 1976–1991* (2006), CW, 18.

The physical primary concerns of humanity, food, sex, possessions and freedom of movement, are elements in human life that we share with animals. It is the secondary concerns that are distinctly human, so if the twentieth century is an age in which primary concerns must again become primary, what this indicates is not an abolishing of secondary concerns but a renewed integration of humanity with nature.

"Fourth Variation: The Furnace," *Words with Power: Being a Second Study of "The Bible and Literature"* (1990), CW, 26.

Primary concerns rest on platitudes so bald and obvious that one hesitates to list them: it is better to be fed than starving, better to be happy than miserable, better to be free than a slave, better to be healthy than sick. Secondary concerns arise through the consciousness of a social contract: loyalty to one's religion or country or community, commitment to faith, sacrifice of cherished elements in life for the sake of what is regarded as a higher cause.

"Crime and Sin in the Bible" (1986), *Northrop Frye on Religion* (2000), CW, 4.

All through history primary concerns have had to give way to secondary ones. It is better to live than die; nevertheless we go to war. Freedom is better than bondage, but we accept an immense amount of exploitation, both of ourselves and of others. Perhaps, with our nuclear weapons and our pollution of air and water, we have reached the first stage in history in which primary concerns will have to become primary.

"Crime and Sin in the Bible" (1986), *Northrop Frye on Religion* (2000), CW, 4.

Secondary concern has to do with the structure and source of authority in society, with religious belief and political loyalties, with the desire of the privileged to keep their privileges and of the nonprivileged to get along as well as they can in that situation.

I think the present age, with its threats of nuclear warfare and environmental pollution, is an age in which secondary concerns are rapidly dissolving.

"The Survival of Eros in Poetry" (1983), *"The Secular Scripture" and Other Writings on Critical Theory, 1976–1991* (2006), CW, 18.

CONDENSATION

Condensation means the opposite movement [of displacement], where the similarities and associations of ordinary experience become metaphorical identities.

"First Variation: The Mountain," *Words with Power: Being a Second Study of "The Bible and Literature"* (2008), CW, 26.

CONDITIONING

People robotize themselves to adjust to society & save trouble for themselves. Automatic conditioned reflex makes up I suppose 98 % of any normal life: if someone said 100 %, how could you refute him?

Entry, Notebook 48 (1993), 17, *Northrop Frye's Late Notebooks, 1982–1990: Architecture of the Spiritual World* (2000), CW, 6.

Most of the members of this audience, even when they were embryos in the womb, were still middle-class twentieth-century Canadians. Religion calls that original sin. Political theory calls it, or used to call it, the social contract. But whatever it is called it has an element in it which is to some extent ironic, even tragic.

"The Ethics of Change: The Role of the University" (1968), addressing a symposium at Queen's University, Kingston, Ont., *Northrop Frye's Writings on Education* (2001), CW, 7.

CONFEDERATION

The main thing wrong with Confederation was its impoverished cultural basis. It was thought of, however unconsciously, as a British colony and a Tory counterpart of the United States, with French and indigenous groups forming picturesque variations in the background.

"The Cultural Development of Canada" (1990), *Northrop Frye on Canada* (2003), CW, 12.

I feel that directly in front of us lies a primary need for what I shall call Reconfederation, and which I think of essentially as providing a cultural skeleton for the country that fits its present conditions. Without a cultural Reconfederation there can be only continued political tinkering of the most futile kind.

"The Cultural Development of Canada" (1990), *Northrop Frye on Canada* (2003), CW, 12.

It is clearly time to start creating a second positive event in our history: Reconfederation.

"Italy in Canada" (1990), referring to Confederation of 1867 as "the most positive event in Canadian history," *Northrop Frye on Canada* (2003), CW, 12.

It is possible that what we think of as the centenary of Confederation may turn out to be our genuine Confederation, a period of spiritual rebirth in response to the central social fact of our time: that man must unite, not divide, because he simply will not survive in a state of radical disunity.

"Foreword to *The Prospect of Change*" (1965), *Northrop Frye on Canada* (2003), CW, 12.

CONFORMISM

The epithet "conformist" is a double-edged one, for no social groups show more rigid patterns of conformity than nonconformist groups.

"The Ethics of Change: The Role of the University" (1968), *Northrop Frye's Writings on Education* (2001), CW, 7.

CONFUSION

... it's simply a matter of numbers — that millions of people are more confused than thousands of people.

"Between Paradise and Apocalypse" (1978), *Interviews with Northrop Frye* (2008), CW, 24.

CONSCIENCE

Consciousness is released by *scientia*: conscience is released by imagination.

Entry, Notebook 21 (1969–76), 109, *Northrop Frye's Notebooks and Lectures on the Bible and Other Religious Texts* (2003), CW, 13.

By conscience I mean the informing power of moral experience.

Entry, Notebook 19 (1964–67), 138, *The "Third Book" Notebooks of Northrop Frye, 1964–1972: The Critical Comedy* (2002), CW, 9.

CONSCIOUSNESS

The revolution of consciousness against routine is the starting point of all mental activity, and the centre of mental activity is imagination, the power of transforming "reality" into awareness of reality. Man can have no freedom except what begins in his own awareness of his condition.

"The Realistic Oriole: A Study of Wallace Stevens" (1957), *Northrop Frye on Twentieth-Century Literature* (2010), CW, 29.

In our day the intensifying of consciousness, in the form of techniques of meditation and the like, has become a heavy industry. I have been somewhat puzzled by the extent to which this activity overlooks or evades the fact that all intensified language sooner or later turns metaphorical, and that literature is not only the obvious but the inescapable guide to higher journeys of consciousness.

"Sequence and Mode," *Words with Power: Being a Second Study of "The Bible and Literature"* (2008), CW, 26.

The idea that the human consciousness lives inside a universe of words, which is in turn inside the universe of nature, has always been very central to me. Of course the difficulty with the word "universe" is that it suggests something spatial, whereas the true verbal universe is a conflict of powers and, consequently, exists in time as well as space.

"Northrop Frye in Conversation" (1989), *Interviews with Northrop Frye* (2008), CW, 24.

It is the articulated worlds of consciousness, the intelligible and imaginative worlds, that are at once the reward of freedom and the guarantee of it.

The Critical Path: An Essay on the Social Context of Literary Criticism (1971), *"The Critical Path" and Other Writings on Critical Theory, 1963–1975* (2009), CW, 27.

Consciousness in a world which without consciousness is only a mechanism: damn uncomfortable situation.
> Entry, Notes 58-5 (c. 1985), discussing Shakespeare's play *Hamlet*, *Northrop Frye's Notebooks on Renaissance Literature* (2006), CW, 20.

Hence while the production of culture may be, like ritual, a half-involuntary imitation of organic rhythms or processes, the response to culture is, like myth, a revolutionary act of consciousness.
> "Tentative Conclusion" (1957), *Anatomy of Criticism: Four Essays* (2006), CW, 22.

Consciousness is to the unconscious as the earth's crust is to the earth, & it has taken exactly the same length of time to develop.
> Entry, Notebook 3 (1946–48), 94, *Northrop Frye's Notebooks and Lectures on the Bible and Other Religious Texts* (2003), CW, 13.

It is fascinating to become conscious of all one's unconscious processes in order to become unconscious of them again: it's a new birth, for though a very young baby can be trained to correct automatisms, they break up when the age of self-will begins, and a change of form or style is needed in life as in athletics.
> Entry, Notebook 3 (1946–48), 36, *Northrop Frye's Notebooks and Lectures on the Bible and Other Religious Texts* (2003), CW, 13.

The consciousness doesn't know what the hell goes on in the body: its function is to escape from the body, hence the cooperating essence notion. Or it can control its own version of the body, as in yoga.
> Entry, Notebook 21 (1969–76), 237, *Northrop Frye's Notebooks and Lectures on the Bible and Other Religious Texts* (2003), CW, 13.

Consciousness is the unreality which transforms reality; life is the unreality which transforms the inanimate; time is the unreality which transforms space....
> Entry, Notebook 21 (1969–76), 362, *Northrop Frye's Notebooks and Lectures on the Bible and Other Religious Texts* (2003), CW, 13.

The world of waking consciousness represents, for the creative imagination, a low level of reality.
> Entry, Notebook 54-8 (late 1972–77), 27, *Northrop Frye's Notebooks on Romance* (2004), CW, 15.

Our waking existence is a continuum: sleep and dreams have beginnings and ends, but when we wake up again we rejoin the continuum.
> "The Renaissance of Books" (1973), *Northrop Frye on Modern Culture* (2003), CW, 11.

There is one consciousness that subjects itself to the text and understands, and another that, so to speak, overstands. It is only the possession of the latter that makes the operation of reading worthwhile: without it a reader is a pedant who understands but does not comprehend.
> "Identity and Metaphor," *Words with Power: Being a Second Study of "The Bible and Literature"* (1990), CW, 26.

Creation wasn't necessarily made for the sake of human consciousness, but consciousness is the human response to creation.
> Entry, Notes 52 (1982–90), 31, *Northrop Frye's Late Notebooks, 1982–1990: Architecture of the Spiritual World* (2000), CW, 6.

... what's below consciousness, traditionally called the body, may suddenly fuse with what's above consciousness, or spirit. These are the moments of inspiration, insight, intuition, enlightenment, whatever: no matter what they're called or what their context is, they invariably by-pass ordinary consciousness.
> Entry, Notes 53 (1989–90), 260, *Northrop Frye's Late Notebooks, 1982–1990: Architecture of the Spiritual World* (2000), CW, 6.

If we know we are in hell we are no longer wholly there: it is our consciousness that tells us where we are, and consciousness is a function of language, not the other way round.
> "The Authority of Learning" (1984), *Northrop Frye's Writings on Education* (2001), CW, 7.

There can be no ascent of consciousness, however, without this preliminary sending of roots down into the unconscious by practice.
> "Fourth Variation: The Furnace," considering the development of creative skill, *Words with Power: Being a Second Study of "The Bible and Literature"* (1990), CW, 26.

Consciousness is a magician who controls the demon of will.
> Entry, Notebook 44 (1986–91), 296, *Northrop Frye's Late Notebooks, 1982–1990: Architecture of the Spiritual World* (2000), CW, 5.

To increase consciousness is to increase mobility by metaphor.
> Entry, Notebook 23 (early 1980s), 6, *Northrop Frye's Notebooks and Lectures on the Bible and Other Religious Texts* (2003), CW, 13.

Sometimes we wonder whether humanity is capable of living in any world at all where consciousness is really a function of life.
> "To Come to Light" (1988), *Northrop Frye on Religion* (1999), CW, 4.

Love is the consciousness of consciousness, the total awakening of which "self-consciousness" is the demonic parody.
> Entry, Notebook 50 (1987–90), 640, *Northrop Frye's Late Notebooks, 1982–1990: Architecture of the Spiritual World* (2000), CW, 5.

CONSERVATIVISM

I should think, for example, that the doctrines of Mr. Buckley or Senator Goldwater would have little appeal to a society in which the high school graduates knew something about the working of pastoral myth in the political imagination.
> "The Developing Imagination" (1962), referring to conservative columnist William F. Buckley and Republican statesman Barry F. Goldwater, *Northrop Frye's Writings on Education* (2000), CW, 7.

CONSPIRACY THEORIES

... the conspiratorial fallacy makes only the mistake of attributing to consciousness what is unconscious. Jews *do* want to bend the world to their will; so do Catholics & Masons. Certain phenomena in society appear in consequence, not of deliberate manipulation or planning, but simply as the natural & inevitable manifestation of certain attitudes.
> Entry, Notebook 3 (1946–48), 160, *Northrop Frye's Notebooks and Lectures on the Bible and Other Religious Texts* (2003), CW, 13.

CONSTITUTION

A written constitution is often the consequence of a successful revolution, and a country with a revolutionary tradition normally acquires a strongly deductive attitude to the social contract, or at least the more doctrinaire of its citizens do.
> "Crime and Sin in the Bible" (1986), *Northrop Frye on Religion* (2000), CW, 4.

The United States was fortunate in achieving this articulating process in the eighteenth century, perhaps the only time in Western history when reason looked reasonable.
> "National Consciousness in Canadian Culture" (1976), *Northrop Frye on Canada* (2003), CW, 12.

CONTEMPLATION

Intensity of vision delays the automatic apparatus of response: the pure contemplative can't respond at all.
> Entry, Notebook 3 (1946–48), 107, *Northrop Frye's Notebooks and Lectures on the Bible and Other Religious Texts* (2003), CW, 13.

And I suppose something of this feeling enters into all contemplation, even at the lowest stages, for if one only stares vaguely at something there is still something of God in the way that a piece of solid matter unwinkingly stares back.
> Entry, Notebook 3 (1946–48), 47, *Northrop Frye's Notebooks and Lectures on the Bible and Other Religious Texts* (2003), CW, 13.

CONTEMPORARIES

The better poets of every age seem all the same size to contemporaries: it takes many years before the comparative standards become clear, and contemporary critics may as well accept the myopia which their nearsighted perspective focuses on them.

"Letters in Canada: Poetry" (1960), *Northrop Frye on Canada* (2003), CW, 12.

CONTINENTALISM

It is of immense importance to the United States itself that there should be other views of the human occupation of this continent, rooted in different ideologies and different historical traditions. And it is of immense importance to the world that a country which used to be at the edge of the earth and is now a kind of global Switzerland, surrounded by all the world's great powers, should have achieved the repatriating of its culture.

"Canadian Culture Today" (1977), *Northrop Frye on Canada* (2003), CW, 12.

CONTRACT, SOCIAL

Wisdom as a continuity of institutions goes back to the fact of a social contract, to the fact that we belong to something at least nine months before we are anything.

"Symbolism in the Bible" (1981–82), *Northrop Frye's Notebooks and Lectures on the Bible and Other Religious Texts* (2003), CW, 13.

CONTRADICTIONS

In continuous prose, the general principle is that when you are confronted with an inconsistency in something that you have to treat with respect, if you just keep on writing enough sentences, any statement whatever can be reconciled with any other.

"The Meaning of Recreation: Humanism in Society" (1979), *Northrop Frye on Religion* (2000), CW, 4.

The way to overcome these apparent difficulties and contradictions in sacred stories was provided by the discovery of continuous prose. In continuous prose, if you only write enough sentences, any statement can be reconciled with any other statement whatever. You just have to put in enough intervening sentences, which will eventually connect A with Z.

"Symbolism in the Bible" (1981–82), concerning in particular the genealogical descent of Jesus, *Northrop Frye's Notebooks and Lectures on the Bible and Other Religious Texts* (2003), CW, 13.

CONVENTION, LITERARY

All writers are conventional, because all writers have the same problem of transferring their language from direct speech to the imagination.

"The Singing School," *The Educated Imagination* (1963), *"The Educated Imagination" and Other Writings on Critical Theory, 1933–1963* (2006), CW, 21.

A writer's desire to write can only have come from previous experience of literature, and he'll start by imitating whatever he's read, which usually means what the people around him are writing. This provides for him what is called a convention, a certain typical and socially accepted way of writing.

"The Singing School," *The Educated Imagination* (1963), *"The Educated Imagination" and Other Writings on Critical Theory, 1933–1963* (2006), CW, 21.

To read a comedy of Shakespeare is not a very serious critical activity in itself until one has read all the comedies of Shakespeare. But as soon as one has done this, one becomes aware of certain conventional laws underlying the comic structure, which apply to all other writers of comedy.

"Sign and Significance" (1969), *"The Critical Path" and Other Writings on Critical Theory, 1963–1975* (2009), CW, 27.

The lapse of time brings with it a decreasing attention to subject-matter and an increasing awareness of convention.

"Culture as Interpenetration" (1982), *Northrop Frye on Canada* (2003), CW, 12.

All art is equally conventional, but we do not notice that fact unless we are unaccustomed to the convention.

Entry, Notebook 35 (1952–53), 36, *Notebooks for "Anatomy of Criticism"* (2007), CW, 23.

We notice that when we read deliberately for relaxation, we turn to highly conventionalized stories where the general structure is known in advance, such as the detective story, the Western, or the even more predictable dramas of television.

"The Developing Imagination" (1962), *Northrop Frye's Writings on Education* (2001), CW, 7.

As long as we have Mozart or Verdi or Sullivan to listen to, we can tolerate identical twins and lost heirs and love potions and folk tales: we can even stand a fairy queen if she is under two hundred pounds.
"Shakespeare's Comedy of Humours" (1950), *Northrop Frye on Literature and Society, 1936–1989: Unpublished Papers* (2002), CW, 10.

Hence while every new poem is a new and unique creation, it is also a re-shaping of familiar conventions of literature, otherwise it would not be recognizable as literature at all.
"Literature as Context: Milton's *Lycidas*" (1959), *Northrop Frye on Milton and Blake* (2005), CW, 16.

There are no unconventional writers; convention is something that we can never break with: we can only build on it.
"Violence and Television" (1975), *Northrop Frye on Modern Culture* (2003), CW, 11.

CONVENTION, SOCIAL
The strength of the conventional person is not in the conventions but in his common-sense way of handling them.
"Third Essay: Archetypal Criticism: Theory of Myths" (1957), *Anatomy of Criticism: Four Essays* (2006), CW, 22.

CONVERSATION
I never found it easy to meet people and make small talk.
"Beginnings" (1981), *Northrop* referring to summers as a student preacher, *Northrop Frye on Canada* (2003), CW, 12.

CONVERSION
Conversion is the demonic parody of rebirth: plunging into the rapture of social acceptance. Or rather, it's the legal analogy of rebirth, the return to professed belief in order to ground one's individual actions in those of a group.
Entry, Notebook 11e (1978), 36, *Northrop Frye's Notebooks and Lectures on the Bible and Other Religious Texts* (2003), CW, 13.

It's *conversion*, a once-and-for-all event, that's traditionally been the analogue of resurrection. The trouble with that is the uniqueness, which creates a fixation on that event. One should have bigger & better conversions every day, like a mechanized phoenix.
Entry, Notebook 21 (1969–76), 495, *Northrop Frye's Notebooks and Lectures on the Bible and Other Religious Texts* (2003), CW, 13.

In other words a conversion is an individual revolution, & is subject to the fallacy of the once-for-all revolution. We need a Trotskyite Billy Graham.
Entry, Notebook 21 (1969–76), 496, *Northrop Frye's Notebooks and Lectures on the Bible and Other Religious Texts* (2003), CW, 13.

CONVOCATION
May I congratulate also those of you who are receiving your degrees, and who are leaving the real world of the university and going out to the confused illusions of the world outside.
"Culture and the National Will" (1957), *Northrop Frye on Canada* (2003), CW, 12.

In these days of continuous education, the first degree is not so crucial an event as it was, but it is still an important crisis, like the first child; and there is even a chance of its developing into a permanent attachment, like a first marriage.
"Convocation Address: Acadia University" (1969), *Northrop Frye on Literature and Society, 1936–1989: Unpublished Papers* (2002), CW, 10.

A convocation is rather a calling together, a summoning of a tocsin to those who care about the university, to tell them that society must renew itself if it is to survive, that the university is at the centre of society, that those of us who are professionally concerned with the university are doing what we can, but that for what we have to do every one of you must help.
"The Day of Intellectual Battle: Reflections on Student Unrest" (1969), Convocation address, University of Western Ontario, *Northrop Frye's Writings on Education* (2001), CW, 7.

I think this ceremony today symbolizes something of unique importance, something that nothing else in your life can match. For one thing, you cease to be an undergraduate, whose natural impulse is to change everything in sight, and become an alumnus, whose natural impulse is to keep the university the way he remembers it.

"The University and the Heroic Vision" (1968), Convocation address, University of Saskatchewan, *Northrop Frye's Writings on Education* (2001), CW, 7.

COPYRIGHT

Demonstrating the debt of A to B is merely scholarship if A is dead, but proof of moral delinquency if A is alive.

"Second Essay: Ethical Criticism: Theory of Symbols" (1957), *Anatomy of Criticism: Four Essays* (2006), CW, 22.

The right of an individual author to benefit from the marketing of his work is of course an unquestioned moral principle, and is likely to remain one. Still, copyright, or the private possession of literary work for the purposes of making a living from it, is not the primary moral principle connected with literature, or the verbal arts generally. That primary principle is rather the principle of public access to the work.

"The Renaissance of Books" (1973), *Northrop Frye on Modern Culture* (2003), CW, 11.

CORRUPTION

Corruption is an essential aspect to social living, because the people who take advantage of corruption are not invariably the criminals, but also those who find this kind of omniscient purity a trifle exacting to live under.

"Symbolism in the Bible" (1981–82), *Northrop Frye's Notebooks and Lectures on the Bible and Other Religious Texts* (2003), CW, 13.

COSMOLOGY

Every cosmology is a renewed effort to see the creation as an end rather than a beginning.

"The *Koiné* of Myth: Myth as a Universally Intelligible Language" (1984), *"The Secular Scripture" and Other Writings on Critical Theory, 1976–1991* (2006), CW, 18.

Not many people have clearly understood that cosmology is a literary form, not a religious or scientific one. It is true of course that religion and science have regularly been confused with, or more accurately confused by, cosmological structures.

"New Directions from Old" (1960), *"The Educated Imagination" and Other Writings on Critical Theory, 1933–1963* (2006), CW, 21.

Cosmology is a literary art, but there are two kinds of cosmology, the kind designed to understand the world as it is, and the kind designed to transform it into the form of human desire.

"Preface to the 1969 Edition" (1969), *Fearful Symmetry: A Study of William Blake* (2004), CW, 14.

Cosmology is the process of assimilating science into mythology. It's always temporary, because it's always wrong — that is, it's full of fictions.

Entry, Notebook 19 (1964–67), 313, *The "Third Book" Notebooks of Northrop Frye, 1964–1972: The Critical Comedy* (2002), CW, 9.

The imagination constructs its own cosmos, parallel to but different from the cosmos of description, argument & ideology.

Entry, Notebook 50 (1987–90), 725, *Northrop Frye's Late Notebooks, 1982–1990: Architecture of the Spiritual World* (2000), CW, 5.

COUNTER-CULTURE

Hence all genuine products of the creative imagination, in literature, in the other arts, in film or television, are forced by the dialectic of their social function into an adversary relationship to mass culture. In other words, in our day genuine culture has to take the form of a counter-culture.

"Criticism and Environment" (1981), *Northrop Frye on Canada* (2003), CW, 12.

CREATION, ACT OF

The creation is what man still has to accomplish: it's not something that's there.

"Blake's Cosmos" (1971), *Interviews with Northrop Frye* (2008), CW, 24.

The act of creation, in its turn, is not producing something out of nothing, but the act of setting free what we already possess.
> "The Road of Excess" (1970), *Northrop Frye on Milton and Blake* (2005), CW, 16.

Creation and consummation are the two specifically human acts, and should neither be projected on God nor regarded as natural.
> Entry, Notebook 54-8 (late 1972–77), 46, *Northrop Frye's Notebooks on Romance* (2004), CW, 15.

To unite the dream world with the waking world is to create.
> Entry, Notebook 10 (late 1964–72), 38, *Northrop Frye's Notebooks on Romance* (2004), CW, 15.

Now we find that if we apply the word "creative" to human activities, the humanly creative is whatever profoundly disturbs our sense of "the" creation, a reversing or neutralizing of it.
> *Creation and Recreation* (1980), *Northrop Frye on Religion* (2000), CW, 4.

I suspect that every critical or creative effort in words is a beginning, a reconstructed creation myth.
> "Preface to *On Education*" (1988), *Northrop Frye's Writings on Education* (2001), CW, 7.

To create is to transform consciousness, or identity as, into identity with. Creation is thus a raid into the world of the dark, part of a conquest, and its goal is total identity.
> Entry, Notebook 24 (1970–72), 8, *The "Third Book" Notebooks of Northrop Frye, 1964–1972: The Critical Comedy* (2002), CW, 9.

Works of literature are not created out of nothing: they are created out of literature itself, so far as the poet knows it.
> "Literary Criticism" (1963), *"The Critical Path" and Other Writings on Critical Theory, 1963–1975* (2009), CW, 27.

CREATION, THE

"In the beginning" is really, as there's no article, "in beginning" or "to begin with."
> Entry, Notebook 44 (1986–91), 722, *Northrop Frye's Late Notebooks, 1982–1990: Architecture of the Spiritual World* (2000), CW, 5.

Creation is not the story of the origin of nature: it's the vision of the world as the product of a divine mind.
> Entry, Notes 52 (1982–90), 596, *Northrop Frye's Late Notebooks, 1982–1990: Architecture of the Spiritual World* (2000), CW, 6.

Everything God has created possesses two impulses: an impulse to die or decay, which is inevitable in a fallen world, and an impulse to return to its Creator, something that only man can do consciously.
> "The Survival of Eros in Poetry" (1983), *"The Secular Scripture" and Other Writings on Critical Theory, 1976–1991* (2006), CW, 18.

What was God doing during before he created the world? Preparing a hell for those who ask such questions, said Augustine: genuine humility might have said rather: preparing a hell for the cretins who invent stories about a beginning of time, which so obviously has no beginning.
> Entry, Notes 54-5 (1976), 59, *Northrop Frye's Notebooks and Lectures on the Bible and Other Religious Texts* (2003), CW, 13.

Creation and fall, in the sense of separation or alienation from the community, are thus the same thing.
> Entry, Notebook 12 (1968–70), 566, *The "Third Book" Notebooks of Northrop Frye, 1964–1972: The Critical Comedy* (2002), CW, 9.

According to Western traditions, [G]od made the world from nothing; according to Eastern ones, nothingness is still its content.
> Entry, Notebook 44 (1986–91), 133, *Northrop Frye's Late Notebooks, 1982–1990: Architecture of the Spiritual World* (2000), CW, 5.

A creation myth is in a sense the only myth we need, all other myths being implied in it.
> "The Mythical Approach to Creation" (1985), *Northrop Frye on Religion* (2000), CW, 4.

In the beginning was the event, is the axiom of all false literalism. The opening verse of Genesis means something more like "to begin with, everything is a (divine) creation," the word divine being bracketed for tactical reasons only.

Entry, Notes 52 (1982–90), 24, *Northrop Frye's Late Notebooks, 1982–1990: Architecture of the Spiritual World* (2000), CW, 6.

The "im" ending is a regular Hebrew plural: and so it would be theoretically possible, though very bad scholarship, to translate the opening verse of Genesis as "In the beginning, the gods created heaven and the earth," a fact which greatly amused Voltaire when he learned it. But the fact had been known for many centuries before him, and St. Augustine had explained the plural form as referring to the Christian Trinity — which isn't very much better as scholarship.

"Symbolism in the Bible" (1981–82), *Northrop Frye's Notebooks and Lectures on the Bible and Other Religious Texts* (2003), CW, 13.

Creation can never be a conception digestible by science, for it is not an event or a datum, or still less a verifiable fact, and it has outlived whatever use it had as a hypothesis. It is a different way of looking at the order of nature, which the scientist sees only as an order.

Entry, 3 Feb. 1952, 89, *The Diaries of Northrop Frye: 1942–1955* (2001), CW, 8.

The astronauts reading Genesis were right, & the God-is-dead people are wrong: God didn't annihilate himself as Creator of the order of Nature at the Incarnation: he just went underground.

Entry, Notebook 12 (1968–70), 416, *The "Third Book" Notebooks of Northrop Frye, 1964–1972: The Critical Comedy* (2002), CW, 9.

And creation, whether of God, man, or nature, seems to be an activity whose only intention is to abolish intention, to eliminate final dependence on or relation to something else, to destroy the shadow that falls between itself and its conception.

"Second Essay: Ethical Criticism: Theory of Symbols" (1957), *Anatomy of Criticism: Four Essays* (2006), CW, 22.

CREATIVE WRITING

The forms of literature cannot exist outside literature, and a writer's technical ability, his power to construct a literary form, depends more on his literary scholarship than on any other factor — a point of some importance for universities that teach writing courses.

"Nature and Homer" (1958), *"The Educated Imagination" and Other Writings on Critical Theory, 1933–1963* (2006), CW, 21.

CREATIVITY

The word "creative" is one of the most elastic and elusive metaphors in the language, as befits its theological origin.

"The Developing Imagination" (1962), *Northrop Frye's Writings on Education* (2001), CW, 7.

If there is a creative force in the world which is greater than the purely human one, we shall not find it on the level of professed belief, but only on a level of common action and social vision.

Creation and Recreation (1980), *Northrop Frye on Religion* (2000), CW, 4.

If we could transcend the level of professed belief, and reach the level of a worldwide community of action and charity, we should discover a new creative power in man altogether.

Creation and Recreation (1980), *Northrop Frye on Religion* (2000), CW, 4.

"Creativeness" ought not to be applied to genres but to the people working in them.

"Sacred and Secular Scriptures" (1975), *Interviews with Northrop Frye* (2008), CW, 24.

The creative tendency is toward the prerevolutionary, back to a time when, so to speak, Socrates and Jesus are still alive, when ideas are still disturbing and unpredictable and when society is less vainglorious about the stolidity of its structure and the permanence of its historical situation.

"The Meeting of Past and Future in William Morris" (1982), *Northrop Frye's Writings on the Eighteenth and Nineteenth Centuries* (2005), CW, 17.

A creative act of response is essential to allow the creative work to exist. Until that, the greatest work of literature is still wrapped in eternal silence far from enemies.

Entry, Notes 58-1 (before 1977), 4, *Northrop Frye's Notebooks on Romance* (2004), CW, 15.

I have never felt that I was necessarily an uncreative writer merely because I have confined myself to works of criticism, and I have often attacked the fallacy which says that writers who produce poems and stories are creative, and critics and scholars noncreative. The fallacy, once more, consists in ascribing creativity to the genres used instead of to the people working in them.

"The Beginning of the Word" (1980), *Northrop Frye's Writings on Education* (2001), CW, 7.

It is a striking feature of our culture that so much creative activity in literature, as in music and painting, should be either explicitly academic or explicitly resistant to education, a culture either of Brahmins or of Dharma bums.

"Elementary Teaching and Elemental Scholarship" (1963), *Northrop Frye's Writings on Education* (2001), CW, 7.

Creators don't create something out of nothing — only God can do that — and what you create does conform to a certain convention and it is within a certain genre. But creators are magicians: they dislike that feeling about it, and unless they are highly professional people they have a sense of being hampered and confined by the notions of convention and genre.

"Getting the Order Right" (1978), *Interviews with Northrop Frye* (2008), CW, 24.

Creative abilities normally go with more delicate and mysterious nuances of awareness, hence they are often accompanied by some kind of physical or psychic weakness.

"Emily Dickinson" (1962), *Northrop Frye's Writings on the Eighteenth and Nineteenth Centuries* (2005), CW, 17.

CRISES

It seems clear that there is always a crisis, always something of temporary priority that we ought to be attending to instead. But this means that the real temporary hurdle to be got over first, before we have any right to enjoy life, is life itself. The rationalizing of distraction is really an aspect of the death-wish in the human mind, its constant impulse to throw life away under the chariot of some cause that gets a lot of headlines.

"Hart House Rededicated" (1969), *Northrop Frye's Writings on Education* (2001), CW, 7.

CRITICISM

The central activity of criticism, which is the understanding of literature, is essentially one of establishing a context for the works of literature being studied. This means relating them to other things: to their context in the writer's life, in the writer's time, in the history of literature, and above all in the total structure of literature itself, or what I call the order of words.

"Criticism, Visible and Invisible" (1964), *"The Critical Path" and Other Writings on Critical Theory, 1963–1975* (2009), CW, 27.

A public that tries to do without criticism, and asserts that it knows what it wants or likes, brutalizes the arts and loses its cultural memory. Art for art's sake is a retreat from criticism which ends in an impoverishment of civilized life itself. The only way to forestall the work of criticism is through censorship, which has the same relation to criticism that lynching has to justice.

"Polemical Introduction" (1957), *Anatomy of Criticism: Four Essays* (2006), CW, 22.

Criticism is the primary act of human awareness: it expresses detachment without separation.

Entry, Notes 53 (1989–90), 242, *Northrop Frye's Late Notebooks, 1982–1990: Architecture of the Spiritual World* (2000), CW, 6.

Milton was of course a learned poet, but there is no poet whose literary influences are entirely confined to his own language. Thus every problem in literary criticism is a problem in comparative literature, or simply of literature itself.

"Literature as Context: Milton's *Lycidas*" (1959), *Northrop Frye on Milton and Blake* (2005), CW, 16.

When criticism gets so far back in time that there is no longer any documentary evidence to support it, it has to turn psychological, as the scholar's own subconscious is all that is left which is sufficiently primitive to work on.

"Literature, History, and Language" (1979), *"The Secular Scripture" and Other Writings on Critical Theory, 1976–1991* (2006), CW, 18.

But, like Tantalus, we may always see what we may not reach, and what we see is that there is no real difference between criticism and creation, nor between education and vision; there is only our failure to abolish the difference.
"Criticism as Education" (1979), *Northrop Frye's Writings on Education* (2001), CW, 7.

The fundamental critical act, I have said elsewhere, is the act of recognition, seeing what is there, as distinct from merely seeing a Narcissus mirror of our own experience and social and moral prejudice.
"On Value Judgments" (1968), *"The Critical Path" and Other Writings on Critical Theory, 1963–1975* (2009), CW, 27.

Criticism can talk, and all the arts are dumb.
"Polemical Introduction" (1957), *Anatomy of Criticism: Four Essays* (2006), CW, 22.

If criticism could ever be conceived as a coherent and systematic study, the elementary principles of which could be explained to any intelligent nineteen-year-old, then, from the point of view of such a conception, no critic now knows the first thing about criticism.
"Polemical Introduction" (1957), *Anatomy of Criticism: Four Essays* (2006), CW, 22.

Criticism and literature are related as theory to practice, and the function of criticism is to explain the social function and relevance of literature.
"Frye, Literary Critic" (1987), *Interviews with Northrop Frye* (2008), CW, 24.

The progress from information to garbage is slower with criticism than with newspapers....
"Tribute to Balachandra Rajan" (1985), *Northrop Frye on Milton and Blake* (2005), CW, 16.

If criticism exists, it must be an examination of literature in terms of a conceptual framework derivable from an inductive survey of the literary field.

"Polemical Introduction" (1957), *Anatomy of Criticism: Four Essays* (2006), CW, 22.

As soon as anyone stops to think about what a poem means or sounds like, he has moved into the area of criticism.
"Articulate English" (1957), *Northrop Frye on Literature and Society, 1936–1989: Unpublished Papers* (2002), CW, 10.

We have criticism simply because the directed experience of literature is never adequate.
"Freedom and Concern" (1985), *Interviews with Northrop Frye* (2008), CW, 24.

Criticism is the science of literature: a systematic and progressive comprehension of it.
"On Book Reviewing" (1949), *Northrop Frye on Modern Culture* (2003), CW, 11.

Criticism, in order to point beyond itself, needs to be actively iconoclastic about itself.
"Criticism, Visible and Invisible" (1964), *"The Critical Path" and Other Writings on Critical Theory, 1963–1975* (2009), CW, 27.

But while the arts do not evolve or improve, the sciences do, and there is a scientific element in criticism that will keep it expanding its range and consolidating its findings.
"The Study of English in Canada" (1957), *Northrop Frye's Writings on Education* (2001), CW, 7.

Criticism deals with the arts and may well be something of an art itself, but it does not follow that it must be unsystematic. If it is to be related to the sciences too, it does not follow that it must be deprived of the graces of culture.
"The Archetypes of Literature" (1951), *"The Educated Imagination" and Other Writings on Critical Theory, 1933–1963* (2006), CW, 21.

It is the function of the poet, the novelist, the dramatist to express, in imaginative form, and in the form of images and symbols, the informing hopes and anxieties and ideals of mankind. It is the function of criticism to examine this myth-making power as it has thrown up one culture, or one civilization, after another.

"Criticism and Society" (1966–76), *Northrop Frye on Literature and Society, 1936–1989: Unpublished Papers* (2002), CW, 10.

The work I have done on critical theory has convinced me that literature is, like mathematics, mainly structure rather than content, and that the teaching of it, or criticism, can follow a deductive pattern.

"The Developing Imagination" (1962), *Northrop Frye's Writings on Education* (2001), CW, 7.

Once we think of a poem in relation to other poems, we begin to develop a criticism based on that aspect of symbolism which relates poems to one another, choosing, as its main field of operations, conventional or recurring images.

"The Language of Poetry" (1955), *"The Educated Imagination" and Other Writings on Critical Theory, 1933–1963* (2006), CW, 21.

The point of literary history is not to articulate the memory of mankind by putting a mass of documents into an ordered and coherent narrative. Its documents are far better worth reading than any history of them could ever be. Its task is to reawaken and refresh our imaginative experience by showing us what unexplored riches of it lie within a certain area.

"Nature Methodized" (1960), *Northrop Frye's Writings on the Eighteenth and Nineteenth Centuries* (2005), CW, 17.

In literature the creative structure is normally produced by an individual; criticism represents the forming of a social consensus around it.

"Sequence and Mode," *Words with Power: Being a Second Study of "The Bible and Literature"* (2008), CW, 26.

To defend the right of criticism to exist at all, therefore, is to assume that criticism is a structure of thought and knowledge existing in its own right, with some measure of independence from the art it deals with.

"Polemical Introduction" (1957), *Anatomy of Criticism: Four Essays* (2006), CW, 22.

The libraries reflect our confusion by cataloguing criticism as one of the subdivisions of literature. Criticism, rather, is to art what history is to action and philosophy to wisdom: a verbal imitation of a human productive power which in itself does not speak.

"Polemical Introduction" (1957), *Anatomy of Criticism: Four Essays* (2006), CW, 22.

So while no one expects literature itself to behave like a science, there is surely no reason why criticism, as a systematic and organized study, should not be, at least partly, a science. Not a "pure" or "exact" science, perhaps, but these phrases form part of a 19th century cosmology which is no longer with us.

"The Archetypes of Literature" (1951), *"The Educated Imagination" and Other Writings on Critical Theory, 1933–1963* (2006), CW, 21.

The vision inspires the act, and the act realizes the vision. This is the most thoroughgoing view of the partnership of creation and criticism in literature I know, but for me, though other views may seem more reasonable and more plausible for a time, it is in the long run the only one that will hold.

"The Road of Excess" (1963), *Northrop Frye on Milton and Blake* (2005), CW, 16.

I should have much more respect for twentieth-century criticism if it produced fewer articles on the conception of tradition in Eliot and gave more attention to the ways in which the literary imagination of contemporary man is actually being formed and nourished. It is particularly in verbal education that such criticism is important, for the critic is above all a teacher, not of the writers he studies, but of the younger writers who study him.

"Comment" (1961), *Northrop Frye on Twentieth-Century Literature* (2010), CW, 29.

The work of criticism as I see it is to understand the place of the creative imagination in society — to see what it's doing and why society can't get along without it.

"Literature as a Critique of Pure Reason" (1982), *"The Secular Scripture" and Other Writings on Critical Theory, 1976–1991* (2006), CW, 18.

CRITICISM, FRYE'S

My professional career has been concerned with the study and criticism of literature, and so I have been aware, from the beginning, of two contexts of the word literature. Literature is an art of words, hence one context emphasizes the "art," the other the "words."

> Entry, Notes 52 (1982–90), 384, *Northrop Frye's Late Notebooks, 1982–1990: Architecture of the Spiritual World* (2000), CW, 6.

My attitude to teaching has always been essentially an evangelical attitude, and probably my attitude to scholarship as well. At any rate, one critic rang a bell in my mind when he spoke of my passion for democratizing criticism, taking the mysterious and the esoteric out of it.

> Entry, Notebook 42b: Notes IV (1972), 3, *Northrop Frye's Fiction and Miscellaneous Writings* (2007), CW, 25.

I think of criticism as a structure of knowledge about literature. If it isn't that it's not anything worth pursuing.

> "Frye, Literary Critic" (1987), *Interviews with Northrop Frye* (2008), CW, 24.

I suppose "critic" comes closest to being what I am, although I am a critic who recognizes no boundaries between criticizing that particular novel and criticizing Meech Lake and the future of Canada.

> "Cultural Identity in Canada" (1990), *Interviews with Northrop Frye* (2008), CW, 24.

I am still bewildered by the betrayal of criticism that turns all literature into an alphabet soup in which one can never find the crucial letters Alpha & Omega.

> Entry, Notebook 27 (1986), 434, *Northrop Frye's Late Notebooks, 1982–1990: Architecture of the Spiritual World* (2000), CW, 5.

For some time I have been concerned with the question: what is the total subject of which literary criticism forms part?

> "Appendix: The Social Context of Literary Criticism" (1968), *Northrop Frye on Literature and Society, 1936–1989: Unpublished Papers* (2002), CW, 10.

My view that criticism is not a parasitic growth on literature but a special form of literary language is now generally accepted.

> "CriticalViews" (1980s), 4, *Northrop Frye's Fiction and Miscellaneous Writings* (2007), CW, 25.

The critical path I wanted was a theory of criticism which would, first, account for the major phenomena of literary experience, and, second, would lead to some view of the place of literature in civilization as a whole.

> *The Critical Path: An Essay on the Social Context of Literary Criticism* (1971), *"The Critical Path" and Other Writings on Critical Theory, 1963–1975* (2009), CW, 27.

What I'm working toward is a conception of criticism which makes it (a) a social science (b) will show that existing social sciences, besides being that, are also applied humanities (c) will be therapeutically effective in making people more aware of their own mythological conditioning.

> Entry, Notes 54-5 (1976), 177, *Northrop Frye's Notebooks and Lectures on the Bible and Other Religious Texts* (2003), CW, 13.

Criticism is therefore the fulfilment of poetry, its own goal of understanding.

> Entry, Notebook 33 (1946–50), 37, *Northrop Frye's Notebooks on Romance* (2004), CW, 15.

I am almost the only critic I know who can really see criticism, and, like the man in H.G. Wells's very profound story about the seeing man in the blind community, I find myself isolated with my superior power instead of being able to benefit others directly with it.

> Entry, 1 Aug. 1950, 515, referring to Wells's story "The Country of the Blind" (1911), *The Diaries of Northrop Frye: 1942–1955* (2001), CW, 8.

This act, as I have so often urged, is not an act of judgment but of recognition. If the critic is the judge, the community he represents is supreme in authority over the poet; all human creation must conform to the anxieties of human institutions. But if the critic abandons judgment for recognition, the act of recognition liberates something in human

creative energy, and thereby helps to give the community the power to judge itself.
> "The Responsibilities of the Critic" (1976), *"The Secular Scripture" and Other Writings on Critical Theory, 1976–1991* (2006), CW, 18.

If one only had the erudition to write the secret history of literature!
> Entry, Notebook 12 (1968–70), 388, *The "Third Book" Notebooks of Northrop Frye, 1964–1972: The Critical Comedy* (2002), CW, 9.

CRITICISM & CRITICS
But the critic, as distinct from the teacher, is most useful when what he writes comes to us as conversation about a play we know, rather than as an introduction to a play we do not know.
> "General Editor's Introduction," *Shakespeare Series* (1968), *Northrop Frye's Writings on Shakespeare and the Renaissance* (2010), CW, 28.

The critic's lot, like the policeman's, is not a happy one. He is perhaps the only person who feels the disadvantages of universal free education and a low rate of illiteracy.
> "Review of *Voices* and *Genesis*" (1943), *Northrop Frye on Twentieth-Century Literature* (2010), CW, 29.

Modern literature seems at times to be animated by a spirit of practical communism: those who cannot write read the works of those who can and write an additional book about them.
> "T.S. Eliot and Other Observations" (1937), *Northrop Frye's Student Essays, 1932–1938* (1997), CW, 3.

… Canada is full of critics who are like those bright blue recycling boxes: they diversify the scene even though there is never anything in them but junk.
> Entry, Notebook 44 (1986–91), 654, *Northrop Frye's Late Notebooks, 1982–1990: Architecture of the Spiritual World* (2000), CW, 5.

Blake has always seemed to me a touchstone of the seriousness of a critic's view of literature. Whether he agrees or disagrees with Blake is of little importance, but if he is a bogus critic, his comments on Blake will reveal the fact with disconcerting clarity.
> "Preface to the Beacon Press Edition" (1962), *Fearful Symmetry: A Study of William Blake* (1947, 2004), CW, 14.

The door to our Eden is still locked, but he has a key, and the key is the act of recognition.
> "The Responsibilities of the Critic" (1976), *"The Secular Scripture" and Other Writings on Critical Theory, 1976–1991*, CW, 18.

The critic has no relevance except what he creates himself, though I suspect that that is equally true of the rest of the human race.
> "The Responsibilities of the Critic" (1976), *"The Secular Scripture" and Other Writings on Critical Theory, 1976–1991* (2006), CW, 18.

A critic is to be judged as a critic primarily by the authors he has understood.
> "Literature as a Critique of Pure Reason" (1982), *"The Secular Scripture" and Other Writings on Critical Theory, 1976–1991* (2006), CW, 18.

What the critic tries to do is lead us from what poets and prophets meant, or thought they meant, to the inner structure of what they said.
> "The Responsibilities of the Critic" (1976), *"The Secular Scripture" and Other Writings on Critical Theory, 1976–1991* (2006), CW, 18.

Just as the teacher of a language is a grammarian, so one of the functions of the literary critic is to be a grammarian of imagery, interpreting the symbolic systems of religion and philosophy in terms of poetic language.
> "Yeats and the Language of Symbolism" (1947), *"The Critical Path" and Other Writings on Critical Theory, 1963–1975* (2009), CW, 27.

It distresses me that literary scholars still tease themselves with the notion of criticism as failed creation, and continue to explain to one another, in a kind of ecstasy of masochism, how vain, futile and parasitic the critical enterprise really is.
> "Teaching the Humanities Today" (1977), *Northrop Frye's Writings on Education* (2001), CW, 7.

It seems to me that a critic practically has to maintain that the Earl of Oxford wrote the plays of Shakespeare before he can be clearly recognized as making pseudocritical statements.

"Literature as Context: Milton's *Lycidas*" (1959), *Northrop Frye on Milton and Blake* (2005), CW, 16.

I began to notice that as soon as a critic confined himself to talking seriously about literature, his criticism tightened up and took on a systematic, even a schematic, form.

"The Keys to the Gates" (1966), *Northrop Frye on Milton and Blake* (2005), CW, 16.

I may express it, in the manner of Coleridge, by saying that all literary critics are either *Iliad* critics or *Odyssey* critics. That is, interest in literature tends to centre either in the area of tragedy, realism, and irony, or in the area of comedy and romance.

"A Natural Perspective: The Development of Shakespearean Comedy and Romance: I, Mouldy Tales" (1963), making a dichotomy "rhetorical rather than factual," as well as "to delight and to instruct," *Northrop Frye's Writings on Shakespeare and the Renaissance* (2010), CW, 28.

There are critics who can find things in the Public Records Office, and there are critics who, like myself, could not find the Public Records Office. Not all critical statements or procedures can be equally valid.

"Literature as Context: Milton's *Lycidas*" (1961), *Northrop Frye on Milton and Blake* (2005), CW, 16.

Anything that could destroy the human imagination would have to be infinitely more powerful and infinitely more evil than any of the critics with whom I am personally acquainted.

"Freedom and Concern" (1985), *Interviews with Northrop Frye* (2008), CW, 24.

CRITICISM & EVALUATION

If I had to make a statement about the literature of our own time, I should say that it was mainly a literature of closed perspectives, an ironic literature, concentrating upon the cruelty or absurdity or obscenity of life, strongly moralizing in tone.

"Shakespeare and the Modern World" (1964), *Northrop Frye's Writings on Shakespeare and the Renaissance* (2010), CW, 28.

I think of literature as a specific field of imaginative activity, but the metaphor of "field" I have in mind is something like a magnetic field, a focus of energy, not a farmer's field with a fence around it.

"Framework and Assumption" (1985), *"The Secular Scripture" and Other Writings on Critical Theory, 1976–1991* (2006), CW, 18.

Scholarship, or the knowledge of literature, constantly expands and increases; value judgments are produced by a skill based on the knowledge we already have. Thus scholarship has both priority over value judgments and the power of veto over them.

"Literature as Context: Milton's *Lycidas*" (1959), *Northrop Frye on Milton and Blake* (2005), CW, 16.

In other words, there is as yet no way of distinguishing what is genuine criticism, and therefore progresses toward making the whole of literature intelligible, from what belongs only to the history of taste, and therefore follows the vacillations of fashionable prejudice.

"Polemical Introduction" (1957), *Anatomy of Criticism: Four Essays* (2006), CW, 22.

The more subjective the criticism, the nearer it tends to aesthetic anarchy.

"Dr. Edgar's Book" (1933), *"The Educated Imagination" and Other Writings on Critical Theory, 1933–1963* (2006), CW, 21.

I think the sooner one forgets about this judicial aspect of criticism the better. I've never tried to judge authors. I've only tried to understand them.

"The Voice in the Crowd" (1966), *Interviews with Northrop Frye* (2008), CW, 24.

When a critic interprets, he is talking about his poet; when he evaluates, he is talking about himself, or, at most, about himself as representative of his age.

"On Value Judgments" (1968), *"The Critical Path" and Other Writings on Critical Theory, 1963–1975* (2009), CW, 27.

I still feel that in criticism everything positive stands, everything negative dates.
> Entry, Notebook 3 (1946–48), 43, *Northrop Frye's Notebooks and Lectures on the Bible and Other Religious Texts* (2003), CW, 13.

Evaluating criticism is mainly effective as criticism only when its valuations are favourable.
> "Criticism, Visible and Invisible" (1964), *"The Critical Path" and Other Writings on Critical Theory, 1963–1975* (2009), CW, 27.

I think criticism becomes more sensible when it realizes that it has nothing to do with rejection, only with recognition.
> "Letter to the English Institute, 1965" (1965), *"The Critical Path" and Other Writings on Critical Theory, 1963–1975* (2009), CW, 27.

CRITICISM & MYTH

Myth is the content of literature, and literary criticism is the *kerygma* of literature.
> Entry, Notebook 50 (1987–90), 397, *Northrop Frye's Late Notebooks, 1982–1990: Architecture of the Spiritual World* (2000), CW, 5.

Either archetypal criticism is a will-o'-the-wisp, an endless labyrinth without an outlet, or we have to assume that literature is a total form, and not simply the name given to the aggregate of existing literary works.
> "Second Essay: Ethical Criticism: Theory of Symbols" (1957), *Anatomy of Criticism: Four Essays* (2006), CW, 22.

… criticism has an end in the structure of literature as a total form, as well as a beginning in the text studied.
> "Tentative Conclusion" (1957), *Anatomy of Criticism: Four Essays* (2006), CW, 22.

What is called myth criticism in literature, then, is not the study of a certain kind or aspect of literature, much less a patented critical methodology, but the study of the structural principles of literature itself, more particularly its conventions, its genres, and its archetypes or recurring images.
> "Literature and Myth" (1967), *"The Critical Path" and Other Writings on Critical Theory, 1963–1975* (2009), CW, 27.

Archetypal criticism studies literature as a phase of civilization; civilization is the process of constructing, by social work, a human form of nature, and the universal symbols of literature are those which express the goals of work.
> "The Literary Meaning of 'Archetype'" (1936), *Northrop Frye on Literature and Society, 1936–1989: Unpublished Papers* (2002), CW, 10.

It is relatively easy to see the place of a myth in a mythology, and one of the main uses of myth criticism is to enable us to understand the corresponding place that a work of literature has in the context of literature as a whole.
> "Myth, Fiction, and Displacement" (1961), *"The Educated Imagination" and Other Writings on Critical Theory, 1933–1963* (2006), CW, 21.

I see it as the essential task of the literary critic to distinguish ideology from myth, to help reconstitute a myth as a language, and to put literature in its proper cultural place as the central link of communication between society and the vision of its primary concerns.
> "The Dialect of Belief and Vision" (1985), *Northrop Frye on Religion* (2000), CW, 4.

One of the practical functions of criticism, by which I mean the conscious organizing of a cultural tradition, is, I think, to make us more aware of our mythological conditioning.
> "Introduction," *The Great Code* (1982), *The Great Code: The Bible and Literature* (2006), CW, 19.

The role of the critical act, then, is that of tearing down the wall of false mythology to reach the structure of serious convictions that each of us must have in order to be a responsible member of society.
> "The Wisdom of the Reader" (1979), *Interviews with Northrop Frye* (2008), CW, 24.

The poet presents a vision of society: the critic, in trying to interpret the vision, is almost compelled to translate it into a conception or theory of society.
> "*Fools of Time*: I, My Father as He Slept: The Tragedy of Order" (1966), *Northrop Frye's Writings on Shakespeare and the Renaissance* (2010), CW, 28.

Thus literature is only a part, though a central part, of the total mythopoeic structure of concern which extends into religion, philosophy, political theory, and many aspects of history, the vision a society has of its situation, destiny, and ideals, and of reality in terms of those human factors. It expresses not so much the world that man lives in as the world that he builds.

> "Literature and Myth" (1967), *"The Critical Path" and Other Writings on Critical Theory, 1963–1975* (2009), CW, 27.

Literature is the art of inscribing verbal patterns within a mythological cosmos.

> Entry, Notes 53 (1989–90), 206, *Northrop Frye's Late Notebooks, 1982–1990: Architecture of the Spiritual World* (2000), CW, 6.

I see the work of literature as the centre of a cross like a plus sign. The horizontal bar is the ideological concerns of the poet's environment, which his work is bound to reflect. The vertical bar is his mythological concerns which give him his literary convention, his genres, and his essential place or tradition in literature.

> Entry, Notes 52 (1982–90), 908, *Northrop Frye's Late Notebooks, 1982–1990: Architecture of the Spiritual World* (2000), CW, 6.

CROSSWORD PUZZLES

My morale is so low that I've bought a book of crossword puzzles — the Elizabeth Kingsley double-crostic kind. It's a form of nervous doodling that preoccupies me and is probably less lethal than smoking — though I sometimes think I make a mistake by not smoking. For the most part the puzzles are very easy to do — in fact, if they don't break open in three or four minutes I go on to another puzzle.

> Entry, 2 Mar. 1952, 150, *The Diaries of Northrop Frye: 1942–1955* (2001), CW, 8.

CRUCIFIXION

The crucified Christ is a vision of irresistible fate, and illustrates what man has always done in the world, is doing now, and will always be fated to do as long as he remains in the state of existence in which fate is to be found.

> "Part Three: The Final Synthesis," *Fearful Symmetry: A Study of William Blake* (1947, 2004), CW, 14.

If you take, say, the Crucifixion of Christ, that was a historical event, because even if Jesus was not crucified, a lot of other people were. And as a historical event, it is simply part of the continuous psychosis that we know as human history; but as a myth, this particular Crucifixion confronts us — confronts us with our own moral bankruptcy.

> "The End of History" (1984), *"The Secular Scripture" and Other Writings on Critical Theory, 1976–1991* (2006), CW, 18.

The writers of the Gospels say that crucifying Christ was wrong: it did not occur to them that crucifixion was wrong in itself (Luke 23:41).

> Entry, Notebook 19 (1964–67), 42, *The "Third Book" Notebooks of Northrop Frye, 1964–1972: The Critical Comedy* (2002), CW, 9.

I once wrote in one of my books that the doctrine that Christ died is the most difficult of all Christian doctrines to disbelieve.

> "Between Paradise and Apocalypse" (1978), *Interviews with Northrop Frye* (2008), CW, 24.

But if you'd been present at the Crucifixion of Christ, you might not have seen what the Gospels portray at all, because what you would have seen might have missed the whole point of what was really going on. You and I would have seen only a mentally unstable political agitator getting what was coming to him.

> "Symbolism in the Bible" (1981–82), contrasting historical evidence with Biblical testimony, *Northrop Frye's Notebooks and Lectures on the Bible and Other Religious Texts* (2003), CW, 13.

The only thing we can take literally in the gospels is the Crucifixion.

> Entry, Notebook 44 (1986–91), 123, *Northrop Frye's Late Notebooks, 1982–1990: Architecture of the Spiritual World* (2000), CW, 5.

The Crucifixion of Christ is an historical event (because even if Jesus weren't crucified a lot of other people were); but as an historical event it's impotent: only as a myth does it have the power to confront us.

Entry, Notes 52 (1982–90), 409, *Northrop Frye's Late Notebooks, 1982–1990: Architecture of the Spiritual World* (2000), CW, 6.

CULTIVATION

Even here there is the possibility of pedantry: literature is an essential part of the cultivated life, but not the whole of it, nor is the form of the cultivated life itself a literary form.

"Criticism, Visible and Invisible" (1964), *"The Critical Path" and Other Writings on Critical Theory, 1963–1975* (2009), CW, 27.

People are always horrified when they find that the commandant of a Nazi concentration camp can have a cultivated taste in literature and music. But if he had a cultivated taste in organic chemistry, there wouldn't be any shock.

"The Scholar in Society" (1983), *Interviews with Northrop Frye* (2008), CW, 24.

CULTURE

If I look over the seventy-seven years I've lived in this ghastly century, I don't see anything politically or economically that has not been part of a dissolving phantasmagoria. I see only one thing that has improved in that time, and that's science. I see only one thing that has remained stable during that time, and that's the arts. I would include religion with the arts, by the way.

"Northrop Frye in Conversation" (1989), *Interviews with Northrop Frye* (2008), CW, 24.

The cutbacks which threaten our cultural life at the present time are the product of superstitious priorities. In the twenty-third century nobody, except a Ph.D. student desperately looking for a subject in Canadian history, will dig out the names of people who are promoting cutbacks today. Those amongst us who are producing the literature, the poetry, and other cultural artefacts are the people who will interest mankind in the twenty-third century. They will be the essence of Canada.

"The Primary Necessities of Existence" (1985), *Interviews with Northrop Frye* (2008), CW, 24.

I think culture always has to have a feeling of *cult* about it.

"From Nationalism to Regionalism: The Maturing of Canadian Culture" (1980), *Interviews with Northrop Frye* (2008), CW, 24.

I have first to return to my three levels of culture, a level of lifestyle, a level of ideology and historical process, and a level of creativity and of education in the arts and sciences.

"Speech at the New Canadian Embassy, Washington" (1989), distinguishing aspects of the notion of "culture," *Northrop Frye on Canada* (2003), CW, 12.

As I say, all culture originates in remembering the Sabbath.

Entry, Notebook 3 (1946–48), *Northrop Frye Newsletter*, Fall 2000.

I do not know what the social causes of a culture are, or if there are any causes apart from conditioning factors, but half a century of contemplating its development, in Canada as elsewhere, has convinced me that it is the force that underlies both real social change and real social stability.

"Across the River and Out of the Trees" (1980), *Northrop Frye on Canada* (2003), CW, 12.

All human societies without exception are enclosed in an envelope of culture, of certain social, religious, legal, and other practices, and most of this cultural envelope consists of words. Completely natural societies, if they could exist, would probably communicate by telepathy or some kind of body language or gesture.

"Language as the Home of Human Life" (1985), *Northrop Frye's Writings on Education* (2001), CW, 7.

We live, then, in both a social and a cultural environment, and only the cultural environment, the world we study in the arts and sciences, can provide the kind of standards and values we need if we're to do anything better than adjust.

"The Vocation of Eloquence," adopting Matthew Arnold's notion of culture, *The Educated Imagination* (1963), *"The Educated Imagination" and Other Writings on Critical Theory, 1933–1963* (2006), CW, 21.

A man can tell me all about his tastes in food, clothes & women & tell me nothing. One remark about, say, Beethoven and I've got him....
  Diary entry, 20 Aug. 1942, *Northrop Frye Newsletter*, Fall 1996.

Cultures enrich themselves by what they include; they define themselves by what they exclude.
  "Tradition and Change in the Theory of Criticism" (1969), *Northrop Frye on Literature and Society, 1936–1989: Unpublished Papers* (2002), CW, 10.

Every age presents a symbolically interlocking group of phenomena: I suppose that's what the word "culture" means.
  Entry, Notebook 50 (1987–90), 728, *Northrop Frye's Late Notebooks, 1982–1990: Architecture of the Spiritual World* (2000), CW, 5.

But culture has something vegetable about it, something that increasingly needs to grow from roots, something that demands a small region and a restricted locale.
  "Canadian Culture Today" (1977), *Northrop Frye on Canada* (2003), CW, 12.

Mass culture is a most misleading phrase for what it describes because it is something imposed on the so-called "masses" and is not produced by them. To call it "popular culture" is clearly still more misleading.
  "Criticism and Environment" (1981), *Northrop Frye on Canada* (2003), CW, 12.

A culture which is the expression of a specific community is in contrast to a mass culture, which tends towards uniformity rather than unity, and towards the obliterating of the specific and distinctive.
  "A Summary of the 'Options' Conference" (1977), *Northrop Frye on Canada* (2003), CW, 12.

The fight for cultural distinctiveness ... is a fight for human dignity itself, for the variety in life that nothing but genuine culture can ever produce, for the unity that is at the opposite pole from uniformity.
  "National Consciousness in Canadian Culture" (1976), *Northrop Frye on Canada* (2003), CW, 12.

... the magic word that explained everything that was then going on in this area was the word "sub-culture" ... these sub-cultures seemed to be really specialized forms of mass culture. Perhaps genuine culture is also a genuine form of sub-culture.
  "Across the River and Out of the Trees" (1980), *Northrop Frye on Canada* (2003), CW, 12.

It is a peculiarity of North America today that culture is absorbed into society mainly through the university classroom.
  The Modern Century (1967), *Northrop Frye on Modern Culture* (2003), CW, 11.

In an immature society culture is an import; for a mature one it is a native manufacture which eventually becomes an export.
  "Across the River and Out of the Trees" (1980), *Northrop Frye on Canada* (2003), CW, 12.

As a greater variety of people come to study the modern languages, it becomes clear that there is much in every past culture which is profoundly alienating.
  "Teaching the Humanities Today" (1977), *Northrop Frye's Writings on Education* (2001), CW, 7.

There is no cultural development in the past which did not have in its background all the cruelty and folly of which mankind is capable; yet the works of culture themselves seem to be in a perpetual state of innocence.
  Creation and Recreation (1980), *Northrop Frye on Religion* (2000), CW, 4.

CULTURE, CANADIAN

Canadian economic and political development today is that of a fully matured Western democracy, but its culture is that of an emergent nation. To put it another way, as the Canadian economy becomes increasingly chaotic and its political leadership increasingly schizoid, its cultural life becomes proportionately more varied and lively.
  "Criticism and Environment" (1981), *Northrop Frye on Canada* (2003), CW, 12.

I think a peculiar feature of Canadian cultural life is its dependence on government assistance.

"From Nationalism to Regionalism: The Maturing of Canadian Culture" (1980), *Interviews with Northrop Frye* (2008), CW, 24.

Culture is born in leisure and an awareness of standards, and pioneer conditions tend to make energetic and uncritical work an end in itself, to preach a gospel of social unconsciousness, which lingers long after the pioneer conditions have disappeared. The impressive achievements of such a society are likely to be technological. It is in the inarticulate part of communication, railways and bridges and canals and highways, that Canada, one of whose symbols is the taciturn beaver, has shown its real strength.

"Conclusion to *Literary History of Canada*" (1965), *Northrop Frye on Canada* (2003), CW, 12.

It seems clear that for Canadian culture the old imperialist phrase "going native" has come home to roost. We are no longer an army of occupation, and the natives are ourselves.

"Canadian Culture Today" (1977), *Northrop Frye on Canada* (2003), CW, 12.

... for Canadian culture, no less than Alberta, has always been "next year country."

"Conclusion to *Literary History of Canada*" (1965), *Northrop Frye on Canada* (2003), CW, 12.

CULTURE, FRENCH-CANADIAN

It is clear that the culture of French Canada is, in the North American context, simply the largest of these enclave cultures. Still, an enclave culture with its own language has at least no problem of identity, and French writers in Canada, however limited their markets or audiences, have always had the advantage of knowing that they had a social function in carrying on the fight to preserve a threatened and beleaguered language.

"Criticism and Environment" (1981), *Northrop Frye on Canada* (2003), CW, 12.

CURES

We can't perhaps cure a lifetime disease by a touch of the hand but how do we know what we could do if creative and critical faculties were both liberated?

Entry, Notes 53 (1989–90), 248, *Northrop Frye's Late Notebooks, 1982–1990: Architecture of the Spiritual World* (2000), CW, 6.

CURRICULA

I feel that *Pride and Prejudice* and *Great Expectations* are admirable novels, well worthy of sustained study, but the mere absence of bad words or explicit descriptions of the sexual act does not seem to me a valid reason for studying books even on that level.

"The Social Importance of Literature" (1968), *Northrop Frye's Writings on Education* (2001), CW, 7.

CYCLES

Well, I don't like cycles; I think the cycle is simply a failed spiral. I think that when we come to the end of a cycle we ought to move up to another level and proceed accordingly.

"The Meaning of Recreation: Humanism in Society" (1979), referring to Vico's notion of *ricorso, Northrop Frye on Religion* (2000), CW, 4.

The human cycle of waking and dreaming corresponds closely to the natural cycle of light and darkness, and it is perhaps in this correspondence that all imaginative life begins.

"The Archetypes of Literature" (1951), *"The Educated Imagination" and Other Writings on Critical Theory, 1933–1963* (2006), CW, 21.

D

DADA
I think people have a tendency to overrate the literary value of the non-literary: there's a late romantic dadaism that makes them like to feel a special thrill in the random or unintentional effect.
> Entry, Notebook 42a (1942–44), 46, *Northrop Frye's Notebooks on Romance* (2004), CW, 15.

Art is form and synthesis, but art in so incoherent a world as ours can only be an art stuck together out of odds and ends. So arose the movement called Dadaism....
> "Men As Trees Walking" (1938), *Northrop Frye on Modern Culture* (2003), CW, 11.

DANTE
That affinity between the structure of the Bible and the structure of comedy has been recognized for many centuries and is the reason why Dante called his vision of hell and purgatory and heaven a *commedia*.
> "Symbolism in the Bible" (1981–82), *Northrop Frye's Notebooks and Lectures on the Bible and Other Religious Texts* (2003), CW, 13.

Dante's own *Commedia* is not affected by the fact that the geology of its hell, the geography of its purgatory, the astronomy of its paradise, are all impossible, and the theology of the whole poem rejected in part or *in toto* by many readers.
> "Part One: The Argument," *Fearful Symmetry: A Study of William Blake* (1947, 2004), CW, 14.

DARWINISM
This is in contrast to the pseudo-Darwinian "rational" views of history, which want to make man as apelike as possible, as recently as possible. All gradualist, or sham evolutionary theories of progress, whether bourgeois or Marxist in their setting, are imperialistic theories.
> Entry, Notebook 11f (1969–70), 177, contrasting this view with the humanist view, *Northrop Frye's Notebooks and Lectures on the Bible and Other Religious Texts* (2003), CW, 13.

DEATH
The dead is the unalterable: whatever reshapes the past performs an act of resurrection.
> Entry, Notebook 19 (1964–67), 344, *The "Third Book" Notebooks of Northrop Frye, 1964–1972: The Critical Comedy* (2002), CW, 9.

As death happens to everyone, it often seems the only principle we know that is utterly fair and without respect of persons.
> "Third Variation: The Cave," *Words with Power: Being a Second Study of "The Bible and Literature"* (2008), CW, 26.

... there's a myth that one's life appears as a total vision at the moment of death or near-death: I have yet to confirm this in my own experience.
> Entry, Notebook 50 (1987–1990), 167, *Northrop Frye's Late Notebooks, 1982–1990: Architecture of the Spiritual World* (2000), CW, 5.

Death is a process, not a condition. A stone is not dead: when did it die?
> Entry, Notebook 11f (1969–70), 66, *Northrop Frye's Notebooks and Lectures on the Bible and Other Religious Texts* (2003), CW, 13.

The Spirit of creation who brought life out of chaos brought death out of it too, for death is all that makes sense of life in time.
> *The Double Vision* (1991), *Northrop Frye on Religion* (2000), CW, 4.

Death is the one point at which man and nature really become identified; it is also, in a sense, the only event in which the genuinely heroic aspect of human life emerges.
"Haunted by Lack of Ghosts" (1976), *Northrop Frye on Canada* (2003), CW, 12.

We are constantly dying, and our past lives enter heaven to be lived over again with pleasure, or into hell to be forgotten or remembered only for purgation — in fact purgatory would be better, as there's no hell in that sense. (It's not that hell is other people, but hell is certainly what other people do to you.)
Entry, Notebook 21 (1969–76), 28, referring to Jean-Paul Sartre's famous statement about hell, *Northrop Frye's Notebooks and Lectures on the Bible and Other Religious Texts* (2003), CW, 13.

Death entered the world, then, not with the fall of Adam or Satan, but with the creation of the *objective* world by the birth of consciousness.
Entry, Notebook 12 (1968–70), 391, *The "Third Book" Notebooks of Northrop Frye, 1964–1972: The Critical Comedy* (2002), CW, 9.

There is no end to numbers, but one can get tired of counting. There is no end of the universe, but one can die and annihilate it. Perhaps that's the reason for death: to shake off infinity.
Entry, Notebook 50 (1987–90), 700, *Northrop Frye's Late Notebooks, 1982–1990: Architecture of the Spiritual World* (2000), CW, 5.

Death is not reduction of form to matter: it's deincarnation. All incarnation creates *a* centre which is *the* centre: in death the subjective centre disappears, which means also that it disappears *into the* centre.
Entry, Notebook 19 (1964–67), 140, *The "Third Book" Notebooks of Northrop Frye, 1964–1972: The Critical Comedy* (2002), CW, 9.

But if the two possibilities, of nothingness and of something that makes sense, weren't equally present, the mind couldn't grow. If I *knew* that there was nothing, my motivation for going on by myself would drop to zero.

If there is something, and I *knew* what that something was, the next life would be essentially the same as this one. So the mystery in death guarantees the liveliness of life.
Entry, Notebook 3 (1946–48), *Northrop Frye's Notebooks and Lectures on the Bible and Other Religious Texts* (2003), CW, 13.

The one thing truly unseen, the world across death, may, according to my principle, be what enables us to see what is visible.
Entry, Notebook 44 (1986–91), 170, *Northrop Frye's Late Notebooks, 1982–1990: Architecture of the Spiritual World* (2000), CW, 5.

We must be free or die, says Wordsworth. We must love one another or die, says Auden. We must grow older or die, says Northrop Frye at the age of seventy-eight.
Entry, Notebook 55.1 (1991), 6, *Northrop Frye's Late Notebooks, 1982–1990: Architecture of the Spiritual World* (2000), CW, 6.

The world of death is not one that we have to die to explore: it is there all the time, the end and final cause of the vision of the centre, just as Awe is the end and final cause of the vision of circumference.
"Emily Dickinson" (1962), referring specifically to Dickinson's poems, *Northrop Frye's Writings on the Eighteenth and Nineteenth Centuries* (2005), CW, 17.

There is something in having lived that is real, and therefore something in death that is unreal. Nothing that is real can be wholly destroyed, and at every death that touches us we are touched also by the sense of a world of light that is all around us, even though we live in a darkness that cannot comprehend it.
"Funeral Service for Virginia Knight" (1969), *Northrop Frye on Religion* (2000), CW, 4.

If there were no death, life would be uniform, as in the monotonous visions of heaven.
Entry, Notebook 24 (1970–72), 90, *The "Third Book" Notebooks of Northrop Frye, 1964–1972: The Critical Comedy* (2002), CW, 9.

What is significant about such religion is not that its God is dead, but that its God is death.

It cannot mask the self-absorption which is really a death-wish....
> "Cold Green Element" (1974), referring to "the religion of self-justification," *Northrop Frye on Canada* (2003), CW, 12.

DEBATES

Debates have not fared so well: the first one, "Resolved that student apathy is the fault of the system rather than the individual," achieved an unmistakable decision when no one turned up and it had to be cancelled.
> "The Time of the Flood" (1965), reporting as Victoria College's Principal on student activities, *Northrop Frye's Writings on Education* (2001), CW, 7.

The prestige of debating implies a world in which ideas are important and in which different social attitudes, whether conservative or liberal, are shaping a progress towards some actualization of an idea.
> "Foreword to *The Living Name*" (1964), *Northrop Frye's Writings on Education* (2001), CW, 7.

DEBT

To write off the debt of the past doesn't annihilate the consequences of the past: it merely adjusts one to the position from which to meet the present.
> Entry, 9 Jul. 1950, 472, *The Diaries of Northrop Frye: 1942–1955* (2001), CW, 8.

DECENTRALIZATION

I think the next century may see a general slaughter of state leviathans, a breaking down of petrified bureaucracies, and the emergence of a more decentralized ideal of a full and creative human life.
> "A Summary of the 'Options' Conference" (1977), *Northrop Frye on Canada* (2003), CW, 12.

DECONSTRUCTION

My function as a critic right now is to reverse the whole "deconstruction" procedure, which leads eventually to the total extinction of both literature and criticism: people are naturally attracted, first and most, by the suicidal and destructive. One should turn around to a reconstruction, which is a matter of seeing a narrative in its undisplaced form as a single complex metaphor.
> Entry, Notes 54-13 (1980–81), *Northrop Frye's Notebooks on Renaissance Literature* (2006), CW, 20.

I suppose the vogue for deconstruction has to do with its Romanticism: it takes off from the Romantic conception of creation as something opposed to *the* creation.
> Entry, Notebook 44 (1986–1991), 142, *Northrop Frye's Late Notebooks, 1982–1990: Architecture of the Spiritual World* (2000), CW, 5.

Deconstruction promises the unbounded without mentioning the finite, hence it can make sense but obliterates the idea of *total* sense.
> Entry, Notebook 50 (1987–1990), 614, *Northrop Frye's Late Notebooks, 1982–1990: Architecture of the Spiritual World* (2000), CW, 5.

Deconstruction, however, is in itself, I think, a birdshot critical technique: it aims at a variety of targets and bags whatever it happens to hit accidentally.
> "The Mythical Approach to Creation" (1985), *Northrop Frye on Religion* (2000), CW, 4.

I am often described as somebody who is now in the past and whose reputation has collapsed. But I don't think I'm any further down skid row than the deconstructionists are.
> "Northrop Frye in Conversation" (1989), *Interviews with Northrop Frye* (2008), CW, 24.

DEDICATION

To dedicate is a commitment, but to rededicate is something much more than merely renewing a commitment. It is to recognize the hope which belongs only to the future, and for its sake to be ready for whatever may come in the way of revolutionary change.
> "Hart House Rededicated" (1969), *Northrop Frye's Writings on Education* (2001), CW, 7.

DEISM

Deism is psychologically the low water-mark of the religious life, with God sound asleep in the soul and the soul carrying on automatically.
> Entry, Notebook 3 (1946–48), 1, *Northrop Frye's Notebooks and Lectures on the Bible and Other Religious Texts* (2003), CW, 13.

It is quite wrong to say that there is no established church in America today: there is one, and one which we may call, as a name will be useful, the Church of Deism or Natural Religion.
"The Present Condition of the World" (1943), *Northrop Frye on Literature and Society, 1936–1989: Unpublished Papers* (2002), CW, 10.

DEMAGOGUE

The intellectual tends to be aware only of the higher level of culture, just as the demagogue is aware only of the lower one. Real political guidance, of course, is constantly aware of both.
"The View from Here" (1980), *Northrop Frye's Writings on Education* (2001), CW, 7.

DEMOCRACY

The maturity of a democracy, today, is not contained in its voting processes or its choice of leaders, but in the principle of openness in descriptive writing.
"Sequence and Mode," *Words with Power: Being a Second Study of "The Bible and Literature"* (2008), CW, 26.

Democracy is the will of the people, but an unconditioned will in the people is as bad as it is anywhere else.
"Notes for 'Levels of Cultural Identity'" (1989), 13, *Northrop Frye's Fiction and Miscellaneous Writings* (2007), CW, 25.

Meanwhile, the hope of democracy rests entirely on the earnest student and the dedicated teacher, and there are still too many of both of us to lose that hope.
"By Liberal Things" (1959), *Northrop Frye's Writings on Education* (2001), CW, 7.

A plurality of ideologies is a good thing if it prevents one from becoming tyrannical. Perhaps the most effective element in democracy is its conception of the co-existence of ideologies.
Entry, Notebook 27 (1986), 446, *Northrop Frye's Late Notebooks, 1982–1990: Architecture of the Spiritual World* (2000), CW, 5.

The dynamic of democracy, and the basis of its hope, is not that man is good, but that neither men nor their institutions are ever as good as they could and should be.

"The Analogy of Democracy" (1952), *Northrop Frye on Religion* (2000), CW, 4.

As such, therefore, democracy is not to be judged by what it does but by what it aims at in spite of what it does.
"Preserving Human Values" (1961), *Northrop Frye on Modern Culture* (2003), CW, 11.

In a coherent society what a man does is derived from what he knows, and that is really the principle towards which a modern democracy evolves.
"The Question of 'Success'" (1967), *Northrop Frye's Writings on Education* (2001), CW, 7.

But technology in itself does not distinguish unity from uniformity. This distinction is the great mental achievement that democracy has created for the modern world: the realization that identity cannot be preserved either by cutting oneself off from others or by dissolving oneself in others, but only by the flexibility of a larger group where there are great variations of character, and sharp differences of opinion and emphasis, yet all contained within the sense of a common heritage and a common destiny.
"Foreword to *The Prospect of Change*" (1965), *Northrop Frye on Canada* (2003), CW, 12.

The basis of democracy is an utterly unquestioning acceptance of original sin, the certainty that everyone will abuse power if he gets a chance. Also that every organization capable of exerting social pressure becomes over-organized and presses too hard.
Entry, Notebook 50 (1987–90), 602, *Northrop Frye's Late Notebooks, 1982–1990: Architecture of the Spiritual World* (2000), CW, 5.

Democracy was not founded on a maudlin enthusiasm for the common man, but on an inference from original sin: that men are not fit to be trusted with too much power.
"The Critical Discipline" (1960), *Northrop Frye's Writings on Education* (2001), CW, 7.

Democracy is in essence a cultural laissez-faire, an encouragement of private enterprise in art, scholarship, and science.

"War on the Cultural Front" (1940), *Northrop Frye on Modern Culture* (2003), CW, 11.

The principle of a democracy is the principle of a jury trial: the control of the expert by common sense.
"Dr. Kinsey and the Dream Censor" (1948), *Northrop Frye on Modern Culture* (2003), CW, 11.

DEMONIC STATE

The demonic is, like the divine, something within the human mind, not something out there, but it is peculiarly characteristic of the demonic to build itself an external prison in order to have the fun of crawling into it.
"The Times of the Signs" (1973), *"The Critical Path" and Other Writings on Critical Theory, 1963–1975* (2009), CW, 27.

I suppose if you chose the wrong way often enough, eventually the situation in which you could recognize that it was a choice would disappear. In other words, the penalty of losing a temptation is demonic possession.
"On Evil" (1971), *Interviews with Northrop Frye* (2008), CW, 24.

There is certainly a demonic state of being, but it appears to be really an intensification of the human one.
The Double Vision (1991), *Northrop Frye on Religion* (2000), CW, 4.

DEMYTHOLOGIZATION

In approaching the Bible, I stumbled over the word "demythologize," applied primarily to the Gospels, which, as I soon realized, actually meant "remythologize," establishing a new context for Biblical myth from creation to apocalpyse.
"*Words with Power*: Draft Introduction" (1990s), 4, *Northrop Frye's Fiction and Miscellaneous Writings* (2007), CW, 25.

... that myth is the linguistic vehicle of *kerygma*, and that to "demythologize" any part of the Bible would be the same thing as to obliterate it.
"Language I," *The Great Code* (1982), *The Great Code: The Bible and Literature* (2006), CW, 19.

Collisions with words like deconstruction and demythologizing evidence of superstition that "de" words are more clinical. Both de's mean re.
"Critical Views" (1980s), 29, gnomic observation about assumption, *Northrop Frye's Fiction and Miscellaneous Writings* (2007), CW, 25.

It was clear to me that if everything that was mythical was extracted from, say, the Gospels, about all that would be left would be the verse in John [11:35] which reads "Jesus wept."
"Literature and Society" (1968), *"The Critical Path" and Other Writings on Critical Theory, 1963–1975* (2009), CW, 27.

It is impossible to demythologize the Gospels because every syllable of the Gospels was written in myth.
"Symbolism in the Bible" (1981–82), *Northrop Frye's Notebooks and Lectures on the Bible and Other Religious Texts* (2003), CW, 13.

I simply can't believe (there's that word again) that the people talking about demythologizing are really as stupid as they sound. How can they be so damn cocksure about what the modern man can and can't believe?
Entry, Notes 54-5 (1976), 151, *Northrop Frye's Notebooks and Lectures on the Bible and Other Religious Texts* (2003), CW, 13.

DEPRESSION

If any literary work is emotionally "depressing," there is something wrong with either the writing or the reader's response.
"Second Essay: Ethical Criticism: Theory of Symbols" (1957), *Anatomy of Criticism: Four Essays* (2006), CW, 22.

DESCENT

The symbolism of descent into chaos is as prominent in *King Lear* as *The Waste Land*, and sea monsters were swallowing maidens for thousands of years before Dylan Thomas's long-legged bait.
"World Enough Without Time" (1959), *"The Educated Imagination" and Other Writings on Critical Theory, 1933–1963* (2006), CW, 21.

But in the twentieth century, on the whole, images of descent are, so to speak, in the ascendant.

"New Directions from Old" (1960), *"The Educated Imagination" and Other Writings on Critical Theory, 1933–1963* (2006), CW, 21.

DESIRE

In this life he took his place at the centre of society where the great myths are formed, the new myths where the hero is man the worker rather than man the conqueror, and where the poet who shapes those myths is shaping also a human reality which is greater than the whole objective world, with all its light-years of space, because it includes the infinity of human desire.

"Silence in the Sea" (1968), referring to E.J. Pratt, *Northrop Frye on Canada* (2003), CW, 12.

DESTRUCTION

Literature cannot by itself prevent the total destruction that is one of the many possible fates in store for the human race, but I think that that fate would be inevitable without it.

"Literature as a Critique of Pure Reason" (1982), *"The Secular Scripture" and Other Writings on Critical Theory, 1976–1991* (2006), CW, 18.

At least I hope there's a limit: there are movies like *Star Wars* which suggest that we can learn to visit distant galaxies and smash them up too; but I'd prefer not to think of that as our future.

"Address on Receiving the Royal Bank Award" (1978), *Northrop Frye's Writings on Education* (2001), CW, 7.

DETACHMENT

Detachment without sympathy is Philistinism; sympathy without detachment is accurately called uncritical.

"The Developing Imagination" (1962), *Northrop Frye's Writings on Education* (2001), CW, 7.

It is becoming apparent that concern is a normal dimension of everybody, including scholars, and that for scholars in particular it is the corrective to detachment, and prevents detachment from degenerating into indifference.

"The Knowledge of Good and Evil" (1966), *Northrop Frye's Writings on Education* (2001), CW, 7.

These two cultural impulses, a growing detachment from what we possess and a growing sympathy with what is alien, are equally essential in a world like ours.

"The Developing Imagination" (1962), *Northrop Frye's Writings on Education* (2001), CW, 7.

DETECTIVE FICTION

The fact that we are now in an ironic phase of literature largely accounts for the popularity of the detective story, the formula of how a man-hunter locates a *pharmakos* and gets rid of him.

"First Essay: Historical Criticism: Theory of Modes" (1957), *Anatomy of Criticism: Four Essays* (2006), CW, 22.

In literature, as in life, the only real justice is poetic justice, and the story of the triumph of law does not quite achieve this.

The Secular Scripture: A Study of the Structure of Romance (1975), *"The Secular Scripture" and Other Writings on Critical Theory, 1976–1991* (2006), CW, 18.

As I said to Jay, non omnis Moriarty.

Entry, Notebook 27 (1986), 495, *Northrop Frye's Late Notebooks, 1982–1990: Architecture of the Spiritual World* (2000), CW, 5. The pun shared with colleague Jay Macpherson conflates Horace's *non omnis moriar* (I shall not wholly die) and Dr. Moriarty of the Sherlock Holmes stories.

The novel is designed to reveal character, the detective story to conceal it, as the fact that one of the characters is capable of murder is the concealed clue. Hence there must be a general woodenness of character — in short, poker faces.

Entry, Notebook 33 (1946–50), 41, *Northrop Frye's Notebooks on Romance* (2004), CW, 15.

The detective story is the modern substitute for public execution. Here the lightness is connected not with the puzzle, but with the inevitability of the revelation of the

murderer: it's the movement toward discovery that keeps one turning the pages.
> Entry, Notebook 34 (1946–50), 14, *Northrop Frye's Notebooks on Romance* (2004), CW, 15.

The detective story is a sacrificial ritual in a moral context: no detective story about a robbery would sell as well as one with a corpse.
> Entry, Notebook 34 (1946–50), 14, *Northrop Frye's Notebooks on Romance* (2004), CW, 15.

In the detective story I live for a moment in the pure present: I'm passively pulled along from stimulus to stimulus, and, ignorant & idle as that doubtless is, I'm fascinated by it. Yet I seldom finish without disappointment.
> Entry, 25 Jul. 1945, 32, *The Diaries of Northrop Frye: 1942–1955* (2001), CW, 8.

If he has a passion for detective stories, he may study the way in which the readability of this genre is increased by the rigidity of its conventions: it is almost a literary development of an important genre of sub-literary experience, the word-puzzle.
> "Nature and Homer" (1958), *"The Educated Imagination" and Other Writings on Critical Theory, 1933–1963* (2006), CW, 21.

The reason why detectives in detective stories are so preternaturally intelligent is that they're angels. Guardian angels of society; avenging angels for the murder. Everyone is guilty of something, so all the major characters are suspects.
> Entry, Notebook 27 (1986), 517, *Northrop Frye's Late Notebooks, 1982–1990: Architecture of the Spiritual World* (2000), CW, 5.

Second-rate literature is whatever I can't *learn* from. At the same time I have a curious compulsion to read detective stories. I don't know why: it may have something to do with organizing my dreams.
> Entry, Notebook 24 (1970–72), 208, *The "Third Book" Notebooks of Northrop Frye, 1964–1972: The Critical Comedy* (2002), CW, 9.

In a murder story, for instance, it's against the rules to conceal clues, but all murder stories, at any rate full-length novels, conceal an essential clue: the murderous character of the murderer.
> "Autobiographical Reflections" (1942–44), 2, *Northrop Frye's Fiction and Miscellaneous Writings* (2007), CW, 25.

The mystery story is popular not because the end is unexpected but because it's inevitable: we know that eventually the right victim will be chosen and that Death will be carried out in his person.
> Entry, Notebook 42b: Notes I (1942–44), 10, *Northrop Frye's Fiction and Miscellaneous Writings* (2007), CW, 25.

DETERMINISMS

I have learned to distrust all determinisms, whether they are economic or religious or mediumistic: they seem to me essentially rhetorical devices, which help to make a doctrine more popular and easier to grasp.
> "Literature and Society" (1968), *"The Critical Path" and Other Writings on Critical Theory, 1963–1975* (2009), CW, 27.

DEVIL

Surely if religion says anything at all, it says that it's no fair blaming the Devil for your own evil actions.
> "On Evil" (1971), *Interviews with Northrop Frye* (2008), CW, 24.

… in short, man is his own devil.
> Entry, Notebook 44 (1986–91), 613, *Northrop Frye's Late Notebooks, 1982–1990: Architecture of the Spiritual World* (2000), CW, 5.

No, you can't get along without the conception of active perversity, the personal devil, even if evil is fundamentally nothingness.
> Entry, Notebook 3 (1946–48), 105, *Northrop Frye's Notebooks and Lectures on the Bible and Other Religious Texts* (2003), CW, 13.

DHARMA

The statement "the practice of the dharma releases one from the law of karma and leads to nirvana" does not differ greatly in substance from the statement "if you're good you'll stop being bad and will get into a better state of

mind," but it gives less of a feeling of being sent back to Sunday school.
> "World Enough Without Time" (1959), *"The Educated Imagination" and Other Writings on Critical Theory, 1933–1963* (2006), CW, 21.

DIAGRAMS
... a good deal of our thinking is elaborated from subconscious diagrams.
> "Yeats and the Language of Symbolism" (1947), *"The Critical Path" and Other Writings on Critical Theory, 1963–1975* (2009), CW, 27.

DIALOGUE
"Dialogue": an overworked buzzword referring to the interpenetrating of opposites in ideology.
> Entry, Notebook 44 (1986–91), 102, *Northrop Frye's Late Notebooks, 1982–1990: Architecture of the Spiritual World* (2000), CW, 5.

In an age when the word "dialogue" has acquired so potent a charge of verbal magic, it is worth reminding ourselves that in Plato, who seems to have invented the conception, dialogue exists solely for the purpose of destroying false knowledge.
> "The Instruments of Mental Production" (1966), *Northrop Frye's Writings on Education* (2001), CW, 7.

DIANOIA
The dianoia is synchronic, the mythos diachronic.
> Entry, Notebook 11f (1969–70), 81, *Northrop Frye's Notebooks and Lectures on the Bible and Other Religious Texts* (2003), CW, 13.

DIARIES
Our literary or book production is so conventionalized these days that a man has to die and leave a diary behind before what he has to say can be published at all, if he thinks in an unconventional form.
> Entry, 24 Mar. 1952, 203, *The Diaries of Northrop Frye: 1942–1955* (2001), CW, 8.

DICKENS, CHARLES
What he writes, if I may use my own terminology for once, are not realistic novels but fairy tales in the low mimetic displacement.
> "Dickens and the Comedy of Humours" (1967), *Northrop Frye's Writings on the Eighteenth and Nineteenth Centuries* (2005), CW, 17.

DICKINSON, EMILY
... Emily Dickinson (the Grandma Moses of poetry)....
> "Elementary Teaching and Elemental Scholarship" (1963), *Northrop Frye's Writings on Education* (2001), CW, 7.

One feels something Oriental in her manner of existence: the seclusion, the need for a "preceptor," the use of brief poems as a form of social communication, would have seemed normal enough in the high cultures of the Far East, however unusual in her own.
> "Emily Dickinson" (1962), *Northrop Frye's Writings on the Eighteenth and Nineteenth Centuries* (2005), CW, 17.

DICTATORS
It is significant that our symbolic term for a tyrant is "dictator," that is, an uninterrupted oral speaker.
> *The Critical Path: An Essay on the Social Context of Literary Criticism* (1971), *"The Critical Path" and Other Writings on Critical Theory, 1963–1975* (2009), CW, 27.

We also cherish an intense if sometimes grudging admiration for billionaires and dictators, because we spring from an environment in which the predators are the aristocracy.
> "Some Reflections on Life and Habit" (1988), *Northrop Frye's Writings on the Eighteenth and Nineteenth Centuries* (2005), CW, 17.

DIDACTICISM
If literature is didactic, it tends to injure its own integrity; if it ceases wholly to be didactic, it tends to injure its own seriousness.
> "The Road of Excess" (1970), *Northrop Frye on Milton and Blake* (2005), CW, 16.

DIEFENBAKER, JOHN G.
I understand that he is occasionally alluded to as Dief the Chief, and it would in fact be correct to address him, if one had a working knowledge of Cree, Sioux, or Kainai, as Chief

Eagle, Chief Walking Buffalo, or Chief Many Spotted Horses.
"John George Diefenbaker" (1961), introducing the prime minister, *Northrop Frye on Canada* (2003), CW, 12.

DISCOVERY
I don't believe it is possible to discover anything within oneself which is not a response to something within a structure of intelligence or imagination.
"The Limits of Dialogue" (1969), *Interviews with Northrop Frye* (2008), CW, 24.

Of course every true discovery must in some sense relate to what has always been true, and so all genuine knowledge includes recognition, however interpreted.
"Introduction," *Words with Power: Being a Second Study of "The Bible and Literature"* (1990), CW, 26.

DISEASE
… we find ourselves in the position of the Renaissance doctors who refused to treat syphilis because Galen said nothing about it.
"Polemical Introduction" (1957), *Anatomy of Criticism: Four Essays* (2006), CW, 22.

Diseases are the revenge of nature for getting born: a lifetime of the nervous irritability of my lifestyle was bound to produce these particular diseases.
Entry, Notebook 44 (1986–91), 746, *Northrop Frye's Late Notebooks, 1982–1990: Architecture of the Spiritual World* (2000), CW, 5.

DISILLUSIONMENT
It is a curious tendency in human nature to believe in disillusionment: that is, to think we are nearest the truth when we have established as much falsehood as possible.
"The Realistic Oriole: A Study of Wallace Stevens" (1957), *Northrop Frye on Twentieth-Century Literature* (2010), CW, 19.

We think of disillusionment as misery, but it is being shut up in illusion that is the real misery, and disillusionment ought to feel like a release from prison.
"Sermon in Merton College Chapel" (1970), *Northrop Frye on Religion* (2000), CW, 4.

DISNEY, WALT
I finally got around to seeing *Fantasia* and, as I expected, disliked it, though not in the way I had anticipated. I thought I should be bored, but not actively bored, bored with a dentist's drill, so to speak, & a jittery nervous wreck after the experience.
Entry, Notebook 42b: Notes I (1942–44), 45, *Northrop Frye's Fiction and Miscellaneous Writings* (2007), CW, 25.

Even the cinema, so stultified by routine technical competence, immediately develops toward pantomime and ballet techniques as soon as an authentic genius, such as Walt Disney or Charlie Chaplin, is given a free hand.
"T.S. Eliot and Other Observations" (1937), *Northrop Frye's Student Essays, 1932–1938* (1997), CW, 3.

DISPLACEMENT
Displacement in a literary context means the alteration of a mythical structure in the direction of greater plausibility and accommodation to ordinary experiences.
"First Variation: The Mountain," *Words with Power: Being a Second Study of "The Bible and Literature"* (2008), CW, 26.

By displacement I mean the techniques a writer uses to make his story credible, logically motivated, or morally acceptable — lifelike, in short.
"Myth, Fiction, and Displacement" (1961), *"The Educated Imagination" and Other Writings on Critical Theory, 1933–1963* (2006), CW, 21.

DISSATISFACTION
Being dissatisfied with society is the price we pay for being free men and women.
"Culture and the National Will" (1957), *Northrop Frye on Canada* (2003), CW, 12.

DIVINE
I think that in human terms it means that there is no limit toward the expansion of the mind or the freedom and liberty of mankind.
"Canadian and American Values" (1988), finding meaning in the word "divine," *Interviews with Northrop Frye* (2008), CW, 24.

I would differentiate between the divine and the human because the human contains many things that are not divine.
> "On Evil" (1985), *Interviews with Northrop Frye* (2008), CW, 24.

DOCTRINES

A secret doctrine is a seed-doctrine: a condensed intuition that grows and unfolds into first myth & then kerygma.
> Entry, Notebook 50 (1987–90), 393, *Northrop Frye's Late Notebooks, 1982–1990: Architecture of the Spiritual World* (2000), CW, 5.

In our time we have seen first China and then the Soviet Union discover, to their considerable benefit, that doctrinaire Marxism would not work, simply because no doctrinaire anything will work.
> "Preface to *On Education*" (1988), *Northrop Frye's Writings on Education* (2001), CW, 7.

DOCUMENTARIES

Yet it is still perhaps the absence of a revolutionary tradition in Canada, the tendency to move continuously rather than discontinuously through time, that has given Canadian culture one very important and distinctive characteristic. This is its respect for the documentary.
> "Canada: New World Without Revolution" (1975), *Northrop Frye on Canada* (2003), CW, 12.

DOGGEREL

Doggerel is not necessarily stupid poetry; it is poetry that begins in the conscious mind and has never gone through the associative process.
> "Fourth Essay: Rhetorical Criticism: Theory of Genres" (1957), *Anatomy of Criticism: Four Essays* (2006), CW, 22.

DOGMATISM

Dogma is a form of original sin, because it is necessarily founded on a theory of words that is necessarily wrong. That's the only kind of dogmatic statement that can be right.
> Entry, Notebook 27 (1986), 376, *Northrop Frye's Late Notebooks, 1982–1990: Architecture of the Spiritual World* (2000), CW, 5.

"There is a God" already contains the statement "there is no God." Dogma, accepting one and forbidding the other, creates hysteria, as it disturbs an imaginary social consensus to admit the opposite.
> Entry, Notebook 44 (1986–91), 9, *Northrop Frye's Late Notebooks, 1982–1990: Architecture of the Spiritual World* (2000), CW, 5.

Nobody wants religious dogmatism, but nobody wants either a dogmatism that would seal off the religious perspective from human life altogether.
> "Installation Address as Chancellor" (1978), *Northrop Frye's Writings on Education* (2001), CW, 7.

The hysteria of dogmatism results from asserting that the mind is unified when it's actually divided. The next stage is pathological, projecting the minority voice on someone else.
> Entry, Notebook 44 (1986–91), 11, *Northrop Frye's Late Notebooks, 1982–1990: Architecture of the Spiritual World* (2000), CW, 5.

DON QUIXOTE

Don Quixote is the world's first and perhaps still its greatest novel, yet the path it indicated was not the one that the novel followed.
> "Don Quixote" (1949), contrasting its "far deeper problem of private mythology" with "character study" concerned with social and psychological change, *Northrop Frye's Writings on Shakespeare and the Renaissance* (2010), CW, 28.

The world is still looking for that lost island, and it still asks for nothing better than to have Sancho Panza for its ruler and Don Quixote for his honoured counsellor.
> "The Imaginative and the Imaginary" (1962), *"The Educated Imagination" and Other Writings on Critical Theory, 1933–1963* (2006), CW, 21.

Don Quixote is a very subtle example of a man who has developed a mythology in order to reveal an infinitely deeper destructive impulse. He's the first of a line of lunatics who try to destroy the present under pretext of destroying the past.
> Entry, Notebook 4 (1939), 87, *Northrop Frye's Fiction and Miscellaneous Writings* (2007), CW, 25.

DOUBT

It seems to me that as long as faith uses the language of propositions, it has to employ doubt as the other half of itself. Doubt is not the enemy of faith; the enemy of faith is indifference or stupidity.

"On *The Great Code* (I)" (1982), *Interviews with Northrop Frye* (2008), CW, 24.

I don't think doubt is the enemy of faith: I think doubt is the fertilizing principle of faith. To doubt the value of everything we're doing is only common sense. The voice of doubt is the voice of common sense; if anything at all is true, the vision of doubt is true.

"Substance and Evidence" (1974), *Northrop Frye on Religion* (2000), CW, 4.

But the opposite of faith is not doubt. The opposite of faith is the attitude that says, "What's all the fuss about?"

"On Evil" (1985), *Interviews with Northrop Frye* (2008), CW, 24.

DRAGONS

The same is true of the dragon: the dragon must be the hero's predecessor and the hero in turn must become a dragon.

"Part Two: The Development of the Symbolism," *Fearful Symmetry: A Study of William Blake* (1947, 2004), CW, 14.

The dragon is a particularly useful demonic animal not just because of its antisocial habits of breathing fire and eating virgins, but also because it doesn't exist, and is consequently an admirable animal for illustrating the paradox of evil, which is a very powerful moral force in human life as we know it, but in the apocalyptic world becomes simply nothingness, simply cannot exist at all.

"Symbolism in the Bible" (1981–82), *Northrop Frye's Notebooks and Lectures on the Bible and Other Religious Texts* (2003), CW, 13.

DRAMA

The gladiatorial combat, in which the audience has the actual power of life and death over the people who are entertaining them, is perhaps the most concentrated of all the savage or demonic parodies of drama.

"First Essay: Historical Criticism: Theory of Modes" (1957), *Anatomy of Criticism: Four Essays* (2006), CW, 22.

In great drama there is something for all levels of society at once.

"T.S. Eliot" (1963), *Northrop Frye on Twentieth-Century Literature* (2010), CW, 29.

I said that the drama presented to us is an illusion which has no reality behind it. Its reality is within it.

"Something Rich and Strange: Shakespeare's Approach to Romance" (1982), with reference to *The Tempest*, *Northrop Frye's Writings on Shakespeare and the Renaissance* (2010), CW, 28.

An audience's wants move horizontally in time: what it wants is a new variant of what pleased it before. The dramatist's wants move vertically in depth: he wants to achieve a profounder and clearer statement of what he said before.

"Comic Myth in Shakespeare" (1952), *Northrop Frye's Writings on Shakespeare and the Renaissance* (2010), CW, 28.

It is the voice of drama itself that we hear in Shakespeare or Sophocles, and the sense of a totality of dramatic experience, of what drama exists to set forth, looms closely behind them.

"Language II," *The Great Code* (1982), *The Great Code: The Bible and Literature* (2006), CW, 19.

We may have dramatists in the future who will write plays as good as *King Lear*, though they'll be very different ones, but drama as a whole will never get better than *King Lear*. *King Lear* is it, as far as drama is concerned....

"The Motive for Metaphor," *The Educated Imagination* (1963), *"The Educated Imagination" and Other Writings on Critical Theory, 1933–1963* (2006), CW, 21.

We come back here to our original point that poetic symbolism is language and not truth, a means of expression and not a body of doctrine, not something to look at but something to look and speak through, a dramatic mask.

"Yeats and the Language of Symbolism" (1947), *"The Critical Path" and Other Writings on Critical Theory, 1963–1975* (2009), CW, 27.

Dramatists from Euripides to Pirandello have been fascinated by the paradox of reality and illusion in drama; the play is an illusion like the dream, and yet a focus of reality more intense than life affords.
"Introduction to *Shakespeare's Tempest*" (1959), *Northrop Frye's Writings on Shakespeare and the Renaissance* (2010), CW, 28.

DREAMS

There are superficial resemblances between the poem and the dream, but the poet and the dreamer are even more distinct for Valéry than for Keats: nobody is so wide awake or consciously alert as the person who has to *observe* a dream.
"Interior Monologue of M. Teste" (1959), *"The Educated Imagination" and Other Writings on Critical Theory, 1933–1963* (2006), CW, 21.

The twentieth century has suffered greatly from the fact that Freud never had an anxiety dream.
"The Social Uses of Literature" (1972), distinguishing between those dreams that reshape reality to express desire and those that reshape it to express dread, *Northrop Frye on Literature and Society, 1936–1989: Unpublished Papers* (2002), CW, 10.

In the dream, a blind, unreasoning, childish will is still at work revenging itself on experience and rearranging it in terms of desire.
"Blake's Treatment of the Archetype" (1950), *Northrop Frye on Milton and Blake* (2005), CW, 16.

The individual, when he falls asleep and dreams, joins the general dream of man, which is why dreams are archetypal.
Entry, Notebook 12 (1968–70), 430, *The "Third Book" Notebooks of Northrop Frye, 1964–1972: The Critical Comedy* (2002), CW, 9.

The dream, then, expresses desire, concern, warning, quite genuinely, but always in slightly oblique language. There is only one gate of dreams, horn on one side and ivory on the other.
Entry, Notebook 44 (1986–91), 150, *Northrop Frye's Late Notebooks, 1982–1990: Architecture of the Spiritual World* (2000), CW, 5.

The two factors affecting the content of the dream, the events of the previous day and repressions going back to early childhood, correspond to the ideological and the mythological perspectives.
Entry, Notebook 44 (1986–91), 150, *Northrop Frye's Late Notebooks, 1982–1990: Architecture of the Spiritual World* (2000), CW, 5.

In other respects a work of art is like a dream, but it does not introduce us to the ordinary dream world, where we retreat from reality into our withdrawn selves. It takes us into the world of social vision that informs our waking life, where we see that most of what we call "reality" is the rubbish of leftover human constructs.
"The View from Here" (1980), *Northrop Frye's Writings on Education* (2001), CW, 7.

The poet Yeats took as a motto for one of his books the phrase "in dreams begin responsibilities." It is also in man's dream of a humanized world that all learning, art, and science begin.
"Humanities in a New World" (1958), *Northrop Frye's Writings on Education* (2001), CW, 7.

We wake up in the morning in our bedrooms, and feel that we have abolished an unreal world, the world of the dream, and are now in the world of waking reality. But everything surrounding us in that bedroom is a human artefact.
The Double Vision (1991), *Northrop Frye on Religion* (2000), CW, 4.

Each dream is a personal episode of a universal comedy of the human collective unconscious, a drama broken off from the one great epic.
Entry, 4 Jan. 1949, 30, *The Diaries of Northrop Frye: 1942–1955* (2001), CW, 8.

... but the primary point is that dreaming is a kind of thinking that is necessary to consciousness yet cannot be done by consciousness.

Entry, Notebook 3 (1946–48), 143, *Northrop Frye's Notebooks and Lectures on the Bible and Other Religious Texts* (2003), CW, 13.

Ideally, then, a night's sleep may present a complete cycle of dreaming from a threshold fall through a mythological period into a rococo-erotic one, thence to a dictatorship-power one, & finally a waking apocalypse-parody.

Entry, Notebook 32 (late 1946–51), *Northrop Frye's Notebooks on Romance* (2004), CW, 15.

The thing that's unsatisfactory about the dream is, as I say, that it's unintelligible even to the dreamer himself, whereas a work of art is a mode of communication, and communication is a way of keeping the community articulate.

"Between Paradise and Apocalypse" (1978), *Interviews with Northrop Frye* (2008), CW, 24.

Private judgment is for dreams, where, as Heraclitus says, every man is his own Logos.

"Typology I," *The Great Code* (1982), *The Great Code: The Bible and Literature* (2006), CW, 19.

We have all had dreams in which we accepted mysterious and portentous imagery without question, and may have felt on waking that if we had only been sufficiently conscious to ask ourselves about the meaning of what we saw, we might have made a major breakthrough to another dimension of experience altogether.

"The World as Music and Idea in Wagner's *Parsifal*" (1982), *Northrop Frye's Writings on the Eighteenth and Nineteenth Centuries* (2005), CW, 17.

The dreams we don't remember are likely to be the important ones. Normally some experience will remind me, like the echo of a plucked string, of something I dreamt the night before & cannot otherwise remember.

Entry, Notebook 3 (1946–48), 141, *Northrop Frye's Notebooks and Lectures on the Bible and Other Religious Texts* (2003), CW, 13.

Dreams have a curious cipher-like quality. They don't seem to mean very much to the dreamer even. It's very difficult to interpret one's own dreams, yet they do have very strong analogies to works of art which do come partly out of the unconscious as well,

and that is probably why Plato spoke of art as the dream for awakened minds.

"Between Paradise and Apocalypse" (1978), *Interviews with Northrop Frye* (2008), CW, 24.

A dream is the process of taking a subreality to be real which is induced in us by bodily and mental inertia. But a complete understanding of a dream includes the knowledge that it is one, a knowledge which at once wakes us up.

"Part Three: The Final Synthesis," *Fearful Symmetry: A Study of William Blake* (1947, 2004), CW, 14.

The therapeutic role of dreams must ultimately be that of enlarging vision, & dreams should be interpreted on the same principles as works of art: observe faithfully (literal), note all references to external events (allegorical), place in relation to your own libidinous urges (moral) & then aim for anagogic completeness.

Entry, Notebook 3 (1946–48), 148, *Northrop Frye's Notebooks and Lectures on the Bible and Other Religious Texts* (2003), CW, 13.

It is a great comfort to know that that world, in which we are compelled to spend about a third of our time, is unreal, and can never displace the world of experience in which reason predominates over passion, order over chaos, Classical values over Romantic ones, the solid over the gaseous, and the cool over the hot.

"Blake's Treatment of the Archetype" (1950), referring ironically to the world of dream, *Northrop Frye on Milton and Blake* (2005), CW, 16.

The great difficulty in evaluating dreams is, I think, the difficulty of remembering the *narrative* sequence: one can remember episodes, but their interconnection, which must be an important part of their meaning, gets blurred. Thus dreams are easier to understand as comment than as content, just as literary criticism, which is very like the interpretation of dreams, finds it easier to explain works of art in terms of their sources than in terms of their integrated meaning.

Entry, 16 Jan. 1949, 91, *The Diaries of Northrop Frye: 1942–1955* (2001), CW, 8.

Dreams are subjective, but maybe a dream fully interpreted would become a vision. There must be a point at which it ceases to be true that it's a subjective experience.

Entry, Notebook 3 (1946–48), 139, *Northrop Frye's Notebooks and Lectures on the Bible and Other Religious Texts* (2003), CW, 13.

Literature, then, is not a dream-world: it's two dreams, a wish-fulfilment dream and an anxiety dream, that are focussed together, like a pair of glasses, and become a fully conscious vision.

"The Keys to Dreamland," *The Educated Imagination* (1963), *"The Educated Imagination" and Other Writings on Critical Theory, 1933–1963* (2006), CW, 21.

One tiny bit I have to hold on to is that dreams can be read & even if they can't, are continually translating themselves into action & further thought. Dreams are the digestive process of the mind. They rearrange the data (food) of experience into the libidinous form of either a cosmic resolution or an "anxiety" tragic one.

Entry, Notebook 3 (1946–48), 138, *Northrop Frye's Notebooks and Lectures on the Bible and Other Religious Texts* (2003), CW, 13.

DRUGS

I often wonder, too, how far the users of drugs have been affected by a feeling that they have been cheated out of genuinely new sensory impressions by the mass media.

"Communications" (1970), *Northrop Frye on Modern Culture* (2003), CW, 11.

DYLAN, BOB

A line from an early ballad of Bob Dylan's, "There are no truths outside the gates of Eden," may make the central thesis of this essay more intelligible to some of its readers: certainly it makes *Paradise Lost* easier to teach to students familiar with it.

The Critical Path: An Essay on the Social Context of Literary Criticism (1971), *"The Critical Path" and Other Writings on Critical Theory, 1963–1975* (2009), CW, 27.

E

EAST & WEST
As long as there are two lobes in the brain, there are going to be the two possibilities of Western and oriental thinking.
"Canadian Energies: Dialogues on Creativity" (1980), *Interviews with Northrop Frye* (2008), CW, 24.

EASTER
We celebrate the Resurrection every Easter, but Easter by itself does not suggest resurrection; it suggests only the renewing of the cycle of time, the euphoria with which we greet the end of winter and the coming of summer.
The Double Vision (1991), *Northrop Frye on Religion* (2000), CW, 4.

EASTER ISLAND
Why the inhabitants of Easter Island put up all those immense statues is a profound & inscrutable mystery. Almost as profound and inscrutable as why anybody would carve a gigantic head of Theodore Roosevelt on a mountain in South Dakota.
Entry, Notebook 44 (1986–91), 431, *Northrop Frye's Late Notebooks, 1982–1990: Architecture of the Spiritual World* (2000), CW, 5.

ECOLOGY
Ecology, the sense of the need for conserving natural resources, is not a matter of letting the environment go back to the wilderness, but of finding some kind of working balance between man and nature founded on a respect for nature and its inner economies.
"Canada: New World Without Revolution" (1975), *Northrop Frye on Canada* (2003), CW, 12.

ECONOMICS
Economics is the dynamic of law: without law there is no answer to the unconditioned will of dialectic materialism.
Entry, 4 Jun. 1950, 394, *The Diaries of Northrop Frye: 1942–1955* (2001), CW, 8.

ÉCRITURE
It seems to be ending today in a vast chaos of *écriture* where there are no boundary lines between literature and anything else in words. Of course there are no boundary lines; but I think that when the present plague of darkness has lifted we shall start making discriminations again.
"The Double Mirror" (1981), *Northrop Frye on Religion* (2000), CW, 4.

ECSTASY
The mimetic is associated with what we make; the ecstatic is what gets made through us.
Entry, Notes 53 (1989–90), 69, *Northrop Frye's Late Notebooks, 1982–1990: Architecture of the Spiritual World* (2000), CW, 6.

EDEN
Man's primary duty is to regain as much as he can of his original state: the garden of Eden is gone as a place, but can be regained as a state of mind.
"Repetitions of Jacob's Dream" (1983), *Northrop Frye on Religion* (2000), CW, 4.

EDGAR, PELHAM
When he was born, Canadian literature was nothing much; today it's not bad. He had a lot to do with making the difference.
"Dean of Critics" (1948), *Northrop Frye on Canada* (2003), CW, 12.

EDITORS
A conference of editors seems to me a central part of the conception of a community of scholars.
"Welcoming Remarks to Conference on Editorial Problems, 1967" (1967), *"The Critical Path"*

and *Other Writings on Critical Theory, 1963–1975* (2009), CW, 27.

EDUCATION

The aim of education is to be able to distinguish illusion from reality.
"The Only Genuine Revolution" (1968), *Interviews with Northrop Frye* (2008), CW, 24.

... more nonsense is written in literary criticism, especially on matters of theory, than in any other scholarly discipline, not excluding education.
"On Value Judgments" (1968), *"The Critical Path" and Other Writings on Critical Theory, 1963–1975* (2009), CW, 27.

I would think of education as the only genuine revolution that society is ever likely to accomplish.
"The Only Genuine Revolution" (1968), *Interviews with Northrop Frye* (2008), CW, 24.

Education makes a bad man more dangerous; it does not make him a better man. Naturally a good deal of disillusionment results from discovering this.
"Wisdom and Knowledge" (1973), *Northrop Frye on Religion* (2000), CW, 4.

It is the social function of education to make one dissatisfied with one's environment, to compare the bumbling and bungling of the world around us with the precision and profundity of what, in the arts and sciences, the human mind shows itself capable of doing.
"Convocation Address, Franklin and Marshall" (1968), *Northrop Frye's Writings on Education* (2001), CW, 7.

If we assume that the mind is naturally active, education becomes that activity of the mind and not an externally imposed and alien structure standing for what some anonymous authority wants it to be.
"The Meeting of Past and Future in William Morris" (1982), *Northrop Frye's Writings on the Eighteenth and Nineteenth Centuries* (2005), CW, 17.

By education I mean the structuring of experience that goes on every moment of our waking lives, not merely schooling, which is a very small, though certainly very central, part of education.
"Violence and Television" (1975), *Northrop Frye on Modern Culture* (2003), CW, 11.

... the whole process of distinguishing reality from illusion is also a process of disillusionment, and that consequently the educated person is the one who refuses to accept the illusions and clichés and the bromides of society.
"The Only Genuine Revolution" (1969), *Interviews with Northrop Frye* (2008), CW, 24.

In these days we're in a hare-and-tortoise race between mob rule and education: to avoid collapsing into mob rule we have to try to educate a minority that'll stand out against it. The fable says the tortoise won in the end, which is consoling, but the hare shows a good deal of speed and few signs of tiring.
"Verticals of Adam," *The Educated Imagination* (1963), *"The Educated Imagination" and Other Writings on Critical Theory, 1933–1963* (2006), CW, 21.

In that sense we may say that nothing is really happening in the world except the education of the people in it.
"The Quality of Life in the '70s" (1971), *Northrop Frye on Modern Culture* (2003), CW, 11.

Education is, or has something to do with, a process of transferring the continuum of identity from the ego and the memory to the individual and the imagination. In the process memory becomes practice memory or habit.
Entry, Notebook 19 (1964–67), 124, *The "Third Book" Notebooks of Northrop Frye, 1964–1972: The Critical Comedy* (2002), CW, 9.

As for the analogy from democracy, the essential democratic principle in education is the supremacy of the subject over both the teacher and the student, and the more supreme it is, the more the difference between the teacher and the student is minimized.
"The Definition of a University" (1970), *Northrop Frye's Writings on Education* (2001), CW, 7.

Education can only lead to maladjustment in the ordinary world: that is its end and its purpose. If one's view of society has been formed by the great philosophers, one cannot be satisfied with the view of it taken by luxury advertising; it is not easy to find the tragedy of life in soap operas if one has found it in the wrath of Achilles or the madness of Lear.

> "By Liberal Things" (1959), *Northrop Frye's Writings on Education* (2001), CW, 7.

Education is in the repetitive process — it is something that has to go on and on and on. Things *should* break into the continuum from time to time, but the continuum is the education.

> "Sacred and Secular Scriptures" (1975), *Interviews with Northrop Frye* (2008), CW, 24.

It seems to me that if there is a general social respect for education, any educational system will work. If there is not, no educational system will work.

> "The Critic and the Writer" (1972), *Northrop Frye's Writings on Education* (2001), CW, 7.

The ideal state, then, is a projection into the future of a source of spiritual authority, founded on the myth of freedom, that sits in the middle of society, and which I shall call the educational contract.

> *The Critical Path: An Essay on the Social Context of Literary Criticism* (1971), *"The Critical Path" and Other Writings on Critical Theory, 1963–1975* (2009), CW, 27.

Education is loaded with an apparatus of magical systems and methods which are supposed to inscribe significant patterns on the student's *tabula rasa*.

> "The Present Condition of the World" (1943), *Northrop Frye on Literature and Society, 1936–1989: Unpublished Papers* (2002), CW, 10.

Education is concerned with two worlds: the world that man lives in and the world he wants to live in. It would, of course, be nonsense to say that the former was the business of the sciences and the latter the business of the humanities and the arts.

> "The Instruments of Mental Production" (1966), *Northrop Frye's Writings on Education* (2001), CW, 7.

Modern theories of education assimilate it to the bridge table, where *learning*, or acquiring information, corresponds to waiting with bowed head while the hands are being dealt, so that you can pick up your information and start playing.

> Entry, Notebook 11f (1969–70), 110, *Northrop Frye's Notebooks and Lectures on the Bible and Other Religious Texts* (2003), CW, 13.

If I had to characterize the content of education in a phrase, I should say that what we are trying to teach is a vision of society. There are many perspectives on this vision, but the vision itself is one of community, and provides the context and the fulfilment for each approach.

> "We Are Trying to Teach a Vision of Society" (1963), *Northrop Frye's Writings on Education* (2001), CW, 7.

That leads me to make a very different definition of education from the usual one. I should say that life in the world is life in a continuous illusion, and that education is the encounter with life on the level of reality. That is the opposite of the usual notion which we accept in practice if not in theory.

> "Education and the Rejection of Reality" (1971), *Northrop Frye's Writings on Education* (2001), CW, 7.

The educated man is the man who tries to live in his social environment according to the standards of his cultural environment. This gives him some detachment about his own society, some understanding of the forces that make it change so rapidly, and some ability to distinguish its temporary expedients from its permanent values.

> "The Developing Imagination" (1962), *Northrop Frye's Writings on Education* (2001), CW, 7.

But in all education it is the power of what is studied, not the student's power, that brings freedom and life to light. It is in the great things that man has made and thought that man still lives, for one more day at least, and while he lives they give his life a radiance beyond his knowing.

"The University and the Heroic Vision" (1968), *Northrop Frye's Writings on Education* (2001), CW, 7.

EDUCATION, LIBERAL

Offhand, I should say that the purpose of liberal education today is to achieve a neurotic maladjustment in the student, to twist him into a critical and carping intellectual, very dissatisfied with the world, very finicky about accepting what it offers him, and yet unable to leave it alone.
"A Liberal Education" (1945), *Northrop Frye's Writings on Education* (2001), CW, 7.

The ethical purpose of a liberal education is to liberate, which can only mean to make one capable of conceiving society as free, classless, and urbane. No such society exists, which is one reason why a liberal education must be deeply concerned with works of imagination.
"Tentative Conclusion" (1957), *Anatomy of Criticism: Four Essays* (2006), CW, 22.

We can get a whole liberal education simply by picking up one conventional poem and following its archetypes as they stretch out into the rest of literature.
"The Literary Meaning of 'Archetype'" (1936), *Northrop Frye on Literature and Society, 1936–1989: Unpublished Papers* (2002), CW, 10.

What is called a liberal education is the gaining of a vision of what human society could be like if these specifically humane factors, the intellect and the imagination, were always operating and always functional.
"Convocation Address: McGill University" (1983), *Northrop Frye on Literature and Society, 1936–1989: Unpublished Papers* (2002), CW, 10.

EDUCATION, LITERARY

Educators are now aware that any effective teaching of literature has to recapitulate its history and begin, in early childhood, with myths, folk tales, and legends.
"Myth, Fiction, and Displacement" (1961), *"The Educated Imagination" and Other Writings on Critical Theory, 1933–1963* (2006), CW, 21.

I see a literary training as a means of becoming aware of one's mythological conditioning.
"A Literate Person Is First and Foremost an Articulate Person" (1977), *Interviews with Northrop Frye* (2008), CW, 24.

In an ideal system of education the student would not be encouraged to accept social mythology rapturously as the fibre of his very being, but critically and with detachment, as something he may or may not believe but in either case has to live with. Nothing can provide this detachment except a study of literature that concentrates on the formal qualities of literature.
"Report on the 'Adventures' Readers" (1965), *Northrop Frye's Writings on Education* (2001), CW, 7.

Indeed, literature is perhaps our most immediately practical educator, from fairy tale and nursery rhyme onward, engaging our responses as it widens our vision and clarifies our perspectives.
"Extracts from *The Practical Imagination: Stories, Poems, Plays*" (1980), *"The Secular Scripture" and Other Writings on Critical Theory, 1976–1991* (2006), CW, 18.

The value of the study of literature is in part to compare the civilization around us with the civilization which the human imagination envisages, which extends from the heaven of human imagination to the hell of human imagination — which is much bigger than the actual world extends.
"The Only Genuine Revolution" (1968), *Interviews with Northrop Frye* (2008), CW, 24.

The primary function of education is to make one maladjusted to ordinary society; and literary education makes it more difficult to come to terms with the barbarizing of speech, or what *Finnegans Wake* calls the jinglish janglage.
"Elementary Teaching and Elemental Scholarship" (1963), *Northrop Frye's Writings on Education* (2001), CW, 7.

Literary education is not doing the whole of its proper work unless it marshals the verbal imagination against the assaults of advertising and propaganda that try to bludgeon it into passivity.

"Criticism, Visible and Invisible" (1964), *"The Critical Path" and Other Writings on Critical Theory, 1963–1975* (2009), CW, 27.

A literary training is a considerable handicap in trying to understand, for example, the releases of public relations counsels [sic]. I am not saying this just to be ironic: I am stating a fact.

"Elementary Teaching and Elemental Scholarship" (1963), *Northrop Frye's Writings on Education* (2001), CW, 7.

But one first-rate work of literature possessed is worth far more to one's literary education than any amount of casual familiarity with any number of books.

"General Editor's Introduction to *Shakespeare Series*" (1968), *Northrop Frye's Writings on Shakespeare and the Renaissance* (2010), CW, 28.

EDUCATION, PRIMARY

The thought of a citizenry unable to do these things fills us with such panic that we periodically hear complaints that the schools are not enabling children to grow up in a real world, and thus we get such slogans as a "back to basics" movement. The "basics," however, are not bodies of knowledge: they are skills, and the cultivating of a skill takes lifelong practice and repetition.

"The Authority of Learning" (1984), *Northrop Frye's Writings on Education* (2001), CW, 7.

Children in Canadian schools study Canadian geography, not because it is better than the geography of other nations, but because it is theirs; and similarly with Canadian history and politics. Canadian writing, too, has a value for Canadians independent of its international value.

"Culture and the National Will" (1957), *Northrop Frye on Canada* (2003), CW, 12.

That is, you read *in order* to read traffic signs and you count *in order* to make out your income tax. But if you are going to use these languages with any freedom or any responsibility or independence there's a long process ahead of you yet.

"Scientist and Artist" (1981), *Interviews with Northrop Frye* (2008), CW, 24.

EDUCATION, SECONDARY

The chief aim of secondary education is to make the student as far as possibly intellectually self-employed.

"The Critical Discipline" (1960), *Northrop Frye's Writings on Education* (2001), CW, 7.

No doubt about it, the progress from secondary to tertiary education is a mistake: if there's no break in between, there's just no power of articulation.

Entry, 18 Feb. 1952, 1125, *The Diaries of Northrop Frye: 1942–1955* (2001), CW, 8.

EDUCATION, COLLEGE & UNIVERSITY

What you get from your college education, ultimately, is something that cannot be directly taught. It is really a vision of society, a vision derived from the record of the best that humanity has done: the concepts of philosophy, the imagination of the arts, the accuracy and the discoveries of the sciences. This vision is not itself knowledge but a practical wisdom, which you take with you into society, which you apply as a criterion to society, and which is the source of your own expertise and special abilities.

"Baccalaureate Sermon" (1967), *Northrop Frye on Religion* (2000), CW, 4.

This principle applies also to the ritual act of going to college, in which so many young people engage every autumn. Finding out why they went is something that comes much later, if it comes at all. An inscrutable Providence has decreed that they should be at university during the mating season, and for some students, going to college is partly a sexual ritual, like the ceremonial dances of the whooping crane.

"By Liberal Things" (1959), *Northrop Frye's Writings on Education* (2001), CW, 7.

More thoughtful students are fond of asking themselves and each other why they came to college, and their reasons are generally given in terms of usefulness. But the thoughtful student soon realizes that the university is not there to be useful to him; he is there to be useful to it. It does not help him to prepare for life: life will not stay around to be prepared for.

"By Liberal Things" (1959), *Northrop Frye's Writings on Education* (2001), CW, 7.

What one "does" with a university education in the modern world is to return to one's community and devote one's life to trying to build up a real society out of it and to fight the mob spirit wherever it is. Creating such a society is the main meaning and purpose of human life, and your specialized preparation for it begins here.

"Speech at a Freshman Welcome" (1966), *Northrop Frye's Writings on Education* (2001), CW, 7.

EGYPT

Egyptian mythology begins with a god who creates the world by masturbation — a logical enough way of symbolizing the process of creation *de Deo*, but not one that we would expect to find in Homer, to say nothing of the Old Testament.

"Third Essay: Archetypal Criticism: Theory of Myths" (1957), *Anatomy of Criticism: Four Essays* (2006), CW, 22.

EICHMANN, ADOLF

It is clear that the Eichmann plea, that we must do what we are ordered to do, belongs only to the purely ironic vision: it is not an integral part of the tragic vision, where there must be some power of self-determination for the least heroic character.

"*Fools of Time*: II, The Tailors of the Earth: The Tragedy of Passion" (1966), discussing Shakespeare's history plays, *Northrop Frye's Writings on Shakespeare and the Renaissance* (2010), CW, 28.

ELECTIONS

It is true that not all illusion is a bad thing: elections, for example, would hardly arouse enough interest to keep a democracy functioning unless they were assimilated to sporting events, and unless the pseudo-issues were taken as real issues.

The Modern Century (1967), *Northrop Frye on Modern Culture* (2003), CW, 11.

Principles make voters nervous, and yet any departure from them towards expediency makes them suspicious.

"Speech at the New Canadian Embassy, Washington" (1989), *Northrop Frye on Canada* (2003), CW, 12.

This is how we select the governors of a democracy, when a number of well-meaning and confused Canadians gather at the polls in order to send some more well-meaning and equally confused Canadians to Ottawa. When they get there they haven't much idea what to do, and that is how democracy works, in its curious stumbling illogical fashion.

"The Question of 'Success'" (1967), *Northrop Frye's Writings on Education* (2001), CW, 7.

ELIOT, GEORGE

I think of myself as kind of another Casaubon in some respects, though I hope I have a better sense of perspective.

"Archetype and History" (1986), referring to the symbol-obsessed pedant Edward Casaubon in George Eliot's novel *Middlemarch*, *Interviews with Northrop Frye* (2008), CW, 24.

ELIOT, T.S.

In the plays we have an accentual line, close to prose in effect, which Eliot describes as a line of three main beats with a caesura. Naturally he must know, but this is my book, and what I hear is four beats.

"T.S. Eliot" (1963), sassily disagreeing with the playwright about the stress pattern of the lines of his poetic dramas, *Northrop Frye on Twentieth-Century Literature* (2010), CW, 29.

Mr. Eliot's version of this tradition was finally announced as Classical, royalist, and Anglo-Catholic, implying that whatever was Protestant, radical, and Romantic would have to go into the intellectual doghouse.

"Blake after Two Centuries" (1957), referring to T.S. Eliot's influential self-definition, *Northrop Frye on Milton and Blake* (2005), CW, 16.

The sense of outrage and betrayal that I felt when I first opened [T.S. Eliot's] *After Strange Gods* is something I hope never to feel again.

"Ned Pratt: The Personal Legend" (1964), *Northrop Frye on Canada* (2003), CW, 12.

Besides, he has a special claim on our attention as the first poet of English literature to study at Merton College who ever became more notable for anything else.
"T.S. Eliot and Other Observations" (1937), *Northrop Frye's Student Essays, 1932–1938* (1997), CW, 3.

T.S. Eliot, with his Order of Merit and his odour of sanctity, must look back with some nostalgia to the days when *The Waste Land* was a new poem and he could be described as a "drunken helot" and a "cultural Bolshevist."
"Academy without Walls" (1961), *Northrop Frye on Modern Culture* (2003), CW, 11.

The greatness of his achievement will finally be understood, not in the context of the tradition he chose, but in the context of the tradition that chose him.
"T.S. Eliot" (1963), *Northrop Frye on Twentieth-Century Literature* (2010), CW, 29.

ELITISM
There is no such thing as "*an* elite": democracy is a society of specific and decentralized elites, in other words skilled workers, people particularly good at certain jobs, and whenever anything is seriously taught it creates such an elite.
"Report on the 'Adventures' Readers" (1965), *Northrop Frye's Writings on Education* (2001), CW, 7.

The plurality of elites is the necessary complementary conception to democracy.
Entry, Notebook 11f (1969–70), 223, *Northrop Frye's Notebooks and Lectures on the Bible and Other Religious Texts* (2003), CW, 13.

It can hardly be said too often that "elitist" is a bogey word without content, with the same resemblance to reality that a child's Hallowe'en mask has to the child.
"The Beginning of the Word" (1980), *Northrop Frye's Writings on Education* (2001), CW, 7.

I'm not against the conception of elitism; I'd just like to see it universalized, to see it identified with social function. It's one of those semi-paranoid words like "establishment" that really refer to something that isn't there any more, but is still pretended to be a danger.
"Canadian Energies: Dialogues on Creativity" (1980), *Interviews with Northrop Frye* (2008), CW, 24.

Don't use words like "elitist": that's a cant word used by people who think democracy ought to be some kind of mob rule.
"Universities and the Deluge of Cant" (1972), *Northrop Frye's Writings on Education* (2001), CW, 7.

EMBLEMS

The language of emblems is as rational as the language of doctrine, but its logic is the poetic logic of metaphor, not the abstract logic of syllogism.
"Emily Dickinson" (1962), *Northrop Frye's Writings on the Eighteenth and Nineteenth Centuries* (2005), CW, 17.

EMOTION
The carburetor, so to speak, of religion is emotional motivation.
Entry, Notebook 11f (1969–70), 128, *Northrop Frye's Notebooks and Lectures on the Bible and Other Religious Texts* (2003), CW, 13.

EMPIRE
I know of no great literature written about an empire, with the very dubious exception of Virgil's *Aeneid*.
"Tradition and Change in the Theory of Criticism" (1969), *Northrop Frye on Literature and Society, 1936–1989: Unpublished Papers* (2002), CW, 10.

History has no record of any empire that did not, qua empire, decline and fall, and the process is still inevitable, even though the decline and fall of the Russian and Chinese empires has still to come.
"Speech at the New Canadian Embassy, Washington" (1989), *Northrop Frye on Canada* (2003), CW, 12.

ENEMIES
Our effective enemies are not foreign propagandists, but the hucksters and hidden

persuaders and segregators and censors and hysterical witch-hunters and all the rest of the black guard who can only live as parasites on a gullible and misinformed mob.

"Academy without Walls" (1961), *Northrop Frye on Modern Culture* (2003), CW, 11.

Groups of people in an insurgent or revolutionary situation *must* create a myth of the enemy.

Entry, Notebook 19 (1964–67), 299, *The "Third Book" Notebooks of Northrop Frye, 1964–1972: The Critical Comedy* (2002), CW, 9.

ENERGY

The body is "material," but matter is really energy, & the mind could well be a series of vibrations.

Entry, Notebook 24 (1970–72), 186, *The "Third Book" Notebooks of Northrop Frye, 1964–1972: The Critical Comedy* (2002), CW, 9.

Matter is energy congealed to the point at which we can live with it on a physical level: the spiritual world is an environment of released energy.

Entry, Notes 53 (1989–90), 178, *Northrop Frye's Late Notebooks, 1982–1990: Architecture of the Spiritual World* (2000), CW, 6.

ENGLAND

When the male limbs were exposed and the female ones covered, England was a great nation and produced Chippendale, but now that conditions have been reversed, everyone fusses because the country is not on sufficiently solid foundations.

"NF to HK," 21 Sep. 1936, *The Correspondence of Northrop Frye and Helen Kemp, 1932–1939* (1996), CW, 2.

England has to choose whether to turn its green and pleasant land into Jerusalem or a howling waste of Satanic mills, and Blake is practically the only Englishman who can express the fact that that choice is now before England, and is still a choice.

"Part Three: The Final Synthesis," *Fearful Symmetry: A Study of William Blake* (1947, 2004), CW, 14.

North England is very like Canada, except that all the houses are the same colour of brick and the trains are slower. The accent is different, too.

"NF to HK," 28 Mar. 1939, Liverpool, Lancs., *The Correspondence of Northrop Frye and Helen Kemp, 1932–1939* (1996), CW, 1.

ENGLISH LANGUAGE

English means, in the first place, the mother tongue. As that, it's the most practical subject in the world: you can't understand anything or take any part in your society without it.

"The Motive for Metaphor," *The Educated Imagination* (1963), *"The Educated Imagination" and Other Writings on Critical Theory, 1933–1963* (2006), CW, 21.

A student who learns only a few pages of Latin grammar will never see the point of having learned even that; and today he learns so little English in early life that the majority of our young people can hardly be said to possess even a native language.

"Humanities in a New World" (1958), *Northrop Frye's Writings on Education* (2001), CW, 7.

The twentieth century has seen the entire world condensing into a single communication unit, and this process has naturally gone further in English than in any other language, as English is now the most dominant language in the world.

"Draft Introduction to Twentieth-Century Literature" (1972), *Northrop Frye on Twentieth-Century Literature* (2010), CW, 29.

ENLIGHTENMENT

I fully sympathize with students of the late sixties who wanted something exciting and existential to happen in every lecture they attended. But the first characteristic of this kind of enlightenment of spirit is that it is totally unpredictable, and may never happen at all.

"Criticism as Education" (1979), *Northrop Frye's Writings on Education* (2001), CW, 7.

Thus, consciousness incarnated an individual, but is not confined to the individual. It's in the discovery of the realms of consciousness beyond the individual that all teachings of salvation and enlightenment in all the religions are directed towards.

"Symbolism in the Bible" (1981–82), *Northrop Frye's Notebooks and Lectures on the Bible and Other Religious Texts* (2003), CW, 13.

ENLIGHTENMENT, HISTORICAL

The English and the French in Canada spent the eighteenth century battering down each other's forts, so we missed out on the enlightenment.

"View of Canada" (1976), *Northrop Frye on Canada* (2003), CW, 12.

ENTERTAINMENT

I can imagine a Shakespearean comedy being mere entertainment just as I can imagine a television show being literature.

"The Only Genuine Revolution" (1968), *Interviews with Northrop Frye* (2008), CW, 24.

If literature ever lost its connection with entertainment, then it would have had it as literature.

"The Only Genuine Revolution" (1968), *Interviews with Northrop Frye* (2008), CW, 24.

ENVIRONMENT

Myth & metaphor confront the environment instead of trying to adapt to it or speak for it.

Entry, Notebook 44 (1986–91), 699, *Northrop Frye's Late Notebooks, 1982–1990: Architecture of the Spiritual World* (2000), CW, 5.

All organisms except human beings adapt to their environment: humanity alone has elected to go on to transform it as well.

"Unpublished Introduction to *Beyond Communication*" (1989), *Northrop Frye's Writings on Education* (2001), CW, 7.

The amount of mental distress caused by living in an environment which expresses indifference or contempt for the perspectives of the human body is very little studied: one might call it proportion pollution.

"Canada: New World Without Revolution" (1975), *Northrop Frye on Canada* (2003), CW, 12.

ENVIRONMENT, CANADIAN

In defiance of every geographical and economic law, Canada has made itself not simply a nation but an environment. It is only now emerging from its beginning as a shambling, awkward, absurd country, groping and thrusting its way through incredible distances into the west and north, plundered by profiteers, interrupted by European wars, divided by language, and bedevilled by climate, yet slowly and inexorably bringing a culture to life.

Editor's Introduction, *The Collected Poems of E.J. Pratt* (second edition (1958)).

EPICS

The epic teaches the nation its memories in a single form: the drama presents episodes of them.

Entry, Notebook 8 (1946–58), *Northrop Frye's Notebooks on Renaissance Literature* (2006), CW, 20.

EPIGRAMS

I'm not often impressed by epigrams, but here's one that is impressive: "to the living we owe understanding; to the dead only the truth."

Entry, Notebook 21 (1969–76), 12, quoting newspaper columnist Richard J. Needham, *Northrop Frye's Notebooks and Lectures on the Bible and Other Religious Texts* (2003), CW, 13.

EPIPHANY

The end of art is epiphany, perceiving the particular as universal, the grain of sand as the world.

Entry, Notebook 19 (1964–67), 159, *The "Third Book" Notebooks of Northrop Frye, 1964–1972: The Critical Comedy* (2002), CW, 9.

I use the term epiphany to mean the opposite of *sparagmos*.

Entry, Notebook 33 (1946–50), 33, making a reference to ritual dismemberment, *Northrop Frye's Notebooks on Romance* (2004), CW, 15.

EQUALITY

The democratic ideal is one of equality, where everyone has the same rights before the law, but not, except indirectly, one of freedom. It tries to provide the conditions of freedom, but freedom itself is an experience, not a condition, and only the individual can experience it.

"Address on Receiving the Royal Bank Award" (1978), *Northrop Frye's Writings on Education* (2001), CW, 7.

Once again, when we think in terms of service rather than possession, equality, along with freedom, becomes essential; in this context we must live in a world where everybody is on the same level, with the same rights and the same duties.
"Wisdom and Knowledge" (1973), *Northrop Frye on Religion* (2000), CW, 4.

EQUINOX
I can hardly imagine a gloomier donkey's carrot to pursue than the precession of the equinoxes, apart altogether from the fact that Virgil predicted a new Golden Age for the period of Pisces, and could hardly have been more wrong.
"The View from Here" (1980), *Northrop Frye's Writings on Education* (2001), CW, 7.

EROS
The culmination of Eros, I think, is the union of the red king & the white queen to produce the golden immortal child.
Entry, Notebook 48 (1993), 1, *Northrop Frye's Late Notebooks, 1982–1990: Architecture of the Spiritual World* (2000), CW, 6.

The fundamental idea of Eros is the reversal of the movement of time.
Entry, Notebook 6 (1967–68), 1, *The "Third Book" Notebooks of Northrop Frye, 1964–1972: The Critical Comedy* (2002), CW, 9.

ESTABLISHMENT
Don't use words like "establishment" as though they were concrete nouns, when they are the haziest of abstractions.
"Universities and the Deluge of Cant" (1972), *Northrop Frye's Writings on Education* (2001), CW, 7.

ETERNITY
The eternal and infinite are actually the now and the here made real, the real present and the real presence.
"T.S. Eliot's *Four Quartets*" (1979), 5, *Northrop Frye's Fiction and Miscellaneous Writings* (2007), CW, 25.

In this construct the eternal is described as a state of continuous peace, rest, and repose. One can understand the appeal of such metaphors after seventy years or so of human behaviour, but after all they are metaphors drawn from death, and seem hardly definitive for a conception of something genuinely beyond life.
"Metaphor I," *The Great Code* (1982), *The Great Code: The Bible and Literature* (2006), CW, 19.

EUPHUISM
Euphuism was only a temporary vogue which soon went out of fashion, but it keeps recurring in the history of prose. If you examine closely the prose style of someone like Walter Pater or James Branch Cabell, you will see that the tendency to euphuism is one of the permanent features of literature, and so is more important than its position in history seems to indicate.
"Literature as Possession" (1959), *"The Educated Imagination" and Other Writings on Critical Theory, 1933–1963* (2006), CW, 21.

EVALUATION
"Re-evaluation," I keep insisting, is leisure-class gossip, not the study of literature.
"Frye, Literary Critic" (1987), *Interviews with Northrop Frye* (2008), CW, 24.

Good taste in itself is inarticulate: it feels and knows, but cannot speak. Value judgments may be asserted, intuited, assumed, argued about, explained, attacked, or defended: what they never can be is demonstrated.
"Literary Criticism" (1963), *"The Critical Path" and Other Writings on Critical Theory, 1963–1975* (2009), CW, 27.

I realized early in my critical life that evaluation was a minor and subordinate function of the critical process, at best an incidental by-product, which should never be allowed to take priority over scholarship.
"Introduction," *The Great Code* (1982), *The Great Code: The Bible and Literature* (2006), CW, 19.

Of course evaluation has to go on: there are far more people engaged in teaching literature than can possibly have anything to say about it, and for them, evaluation is the only possible form of occupational therapy, giving them in the eyes of the dean's office the status of a "productive scholar."

> Entry, Notebook 19 (1964–67), 444, *The "Third Book" Notebooks of Northrop Frye, 1964–1972: The Critical Comedy* (2002), CW, 9.

EVANGELISTS

The Evangelists tell us not how Christ came, but how he comes: they are concerned not with a vanished past but with the imagination's "Eternal Now."

> "Part Three: The Final Synthesis," *Fearful Symmetry: A Study of William Blake* (1947, 2004), CW, 14.

EVENTS

Pseudo-events are such things as leadership conventions in political parties, which are blown up by the news media: it is the interlocking developments in technology, engineering, medicine, law, religion, the sciences, literature and other arts, along with their social consequences, that make up real history.

> "Convocation Address: McGill University" (1983), *Northrop Frye on Literature and Society, 1936–1989: Unpublished Papers* (2002), CW, 10.

EVIDENCE

Trustworthy evidence means a kind of authority that stops you from asking any more questions.

> "Symbolism in the Bible" (1981–82), *Northrop Frye's Notebooks and Lectures on the Bible and Other Religious Texts* (2003), CW, 13.

EVIL

Evil to me has something radically negative about it. It is something that really wants to tear down the whole structure of whatever it is that man is trying to build up.

> "On Evil" (1971), *Interviews with Northrop Frye* (2008), CW, 24.

Any discussion of evil has to start with the fact that most of our conceptions of good are really conceptions of moral good, and moral good is something that is founded on moral evil and is derived from it.

> "On Evil" (1971), *Interviews with Northrop Frye* (2008), CW, 24.

Man may be infinite if he is infinite only in his evil desires.

> "*Fools of Time*: I, My Father as He Slept: The Tragedy of Order" (1966), *Northrop Frye's Writings on Shakespeare and the Renaissance* (2010), CW, 28.

The knowledge of good and evil is something that results in a morality founded on sexual repression, but it is not a real knowledge.

> "The Bible and English Literature" (1985), *Northrop Frye on Religion* (2000), CW, 4.

… you wouldn't call the Duke of Wellington an evil man because he devotes himself to trying to defeat Napoleon. He is in that inextricable tangle of moral good and moral evil.

> "On Evil" (1985), *Interviews with Northrop Frye* (2008), CW, 24.

I am not saying that we accept the evils of what we join: I am saying that whatever we join contains evils, and that what we accept is the guilt of belonging to it.

> "The Ethics of Change: The Role of the University" (1968), *Northrop Frye's Writings on Education* (2001), CW, 7.

Well, I certainly think that man has to act as though he alone were responsible for evil. I don't think it would make sense in any other context.

> "On Evil" (1985), *Interviews with Northrop Frye* (2008), CW, 24.

We like to distinguish moral levels in evil: we feel that hurling defiance in the teeth of God is more admirable than, say, stealing pennies out of a blind beggar's cup.

> "Introduction to '*Paradise Lost*' and Selected Poetry and Prose" (1950), *Northrop Frye on Milton and Blake* (2005), CW, 16.

EVOCATION

Naming is the first act of dominating nature: it's quite different from evoking presences, which is creative.

Entry, Notes 52 (1982–90), 32, *Northrop Frye's Late Notebooks, 1982–1990: Architecture of the Spiritual World* (2000), CW, 6.

EVOLUTION

Some people who wanted to believe in progress thought that evolution had furnished a scientific proof of it. But of course evolution is a principle in biology, and cannot be directly applied to human history except as an analogy.

"Some Reflections on Life and Habit" (1988), *Northrop Frye's Writings on the Eighteenth and Nineteenth Centuries* (2005), CW, 17.

In our day there has been an invasion of teachers of yoga, Zen, kundalini, and other techniques of meditation, which often carry ideologies of evolution along with them, promising developments of consciousness that will usher in a new phase of human existence. Nobody can object to the teaching of these techniques, but the evolutionary metaphors seem, once again, to be merely analogies.

"Some Reflections on Life and Habit" (1988), *Northrop Frye's Writings on the Eighteenth and Nineteenth Centuries* (2005), CW, 17.

I do not mean that evolution is nonsense in its own sphere, which is biology, but when human institutions are assumed to develop from ape-like to something like what the writer approves of, we do get nonsense.

Entry, Notebook 21 (1969–76), 96, *Northrop Frye's Notebooks and Lectures on the Bible and Other Religious Texts* (2003), CW, 13.

As man has decided to transform his environment instead of adapting to it, it's probable that the word evolution, in its traditional sense, no longer applies to our future. The rules of the game have changed.

Entry, Notebook 50 (1987–90), 498, *Northrop Frye's Late Notebooks, 1982–1990: Architecture of the Spiritual World* (2000), CW, 5.

The doctrine of evolution breaks down completely in the arts: a form of art is not a species, and it does not evolve.

"Education and the Humanities" (1947), *Northrop Frye's Writings on Education* (2001), CW, 7.

EXCELSIOR

But in 1964 you may find this vision of human destiny a trifle simple-minded. It is perhaps not an accident that the word "excelsior," originally a motto for this upward climb, now means a form of stuffing designed to avoid direct contacts in experience.

"Education — Protection against Futility" (1964), referring to the Latin word for "ever upward," *Northrop Frye's Writings on Education* (2001), CW, 7.

EXISTENCE

Grammatically, logically, and syntactically, there is no difference between a lion and a unicorn: the question of actual existence does not enter the ordering of words as such.

"Language I," *The Great Code* (1982), *The Great Code: The Bible and Literature* (2006), CW, 19.

EXISTENTIAL

I am not fond of the word, but I know of no other that conveys the sense of anchoring an interest in the transcendental in the seabed of human concern.

"Language I," *The Great Code* (1982), *The Great Code: The Bible and Literature* (2006), CW, 19.

EXISTENTIALISM

The existential projection of irony is, perhaps, existentialism itself....

"First Essay: Historical Criticism: Theory of Modes" (1957), *Anatomy of Criticism: Four Essays* (2006), CW, 22.

Existentialists may be described as the people who have discovered that if A equals B, then A minus B equals nothing.

"Speculation and Concern" (1966), *Northrop Frye's Writings on Education* (2001), CW, 7.

EXODUS

It seems clear that the Egyptians knew nothing of an exodus, just as the Emperor Augustus knew nothing of the birth of Christ.

"Myth I," *The Great Code* (1982), *The Great Code: The Bible and Literature* (2006), CW, 19.

EXPERIENCE

Anyone born in 1912 has lived through more history than anyone dying in 1912 who had lived for seven or eight hundred years.

"Autobiographical Notes III: First Memories" (1980s), 24, *Northrop Frye's Fiction and Miscellaneous Writings* (2007), CW, 25.

That principle belongs to a still larger one: nothing that breaks through the barriers of ordinary experience can remain in the world of ordinary experience.

"Northrop Frye on Shakespeare: I, *Romeo and Juliet*" (1986), *Northrop Frye's Writings on Shakespeare and the Renaissance* (2010), CW, 28.

The presence of incommunicable experience in the centre of criticism will always keep criticism an art, as long as the critic recognizes that criticism comes out of it but cannot be built on it.

"Polemical Introduction" (1957), *Anatomy of Criticism: Four Essays* (2006), CW, 22.

Well, in the first place, I don't believe in either/or. I don't think that the aesthetic experience is in a separate category from the religious experience.

"Moncton, Mentors, and Memories" (1986), *Interviews with Northrop Frye* (2008), CW, 24.

But in the direct experience of literature, which is something distinct from criticism, we are aware of what we may call the persuasion of continuity, the power that keeps us turning the pages of a novel and that holds us in our seats at the theatre.

"Myth, Fiction, and Displacement" (1961), *"The Educated Imagination" and Other Writings on Critical Theory, 1933–1963* (2006), CW, 21.

Art is practical, not speculative; imaginative, not fantastic; it transforms experience, and does not merely interpret it.

"The Realistic Oriole: A Study of Wallace Stevens" (1957), *Northrop Frye on Twentieth-Century Literature* (2010), CW, 29.

Knowledge that tries to do without experience becomes paranoid; experience that tries to do without knowledge becomes schizophrenic.

"Some Reflections on Life and Habit" (1988), *Northrop Frye's Writings on the Eighteenth and Nineteenth Centuries* (2005), CW, 17.

Every writer is constantly on the lookout for experiences that seem to have a story or poem in them, but the story or poem is not in them; it is in the writer's grasp of the literary tradition and his power of assimilating experience to it.

"Nature and Homer" (1958), *"The Educated Imagination" and Other Writings on Critical Theory, 1933–1963* (2006), CW, 21.

History tells us of real events that we can assimilate to our ordinary experience because they are more or less what we should have experienced at the time. Poetry tells us of events that are real, not in the sense of having happened just like that, but in the sense of being the kind of thing that is always happening. There is a third category: the actual event which is probably nothing like what we should have experienced if we had been "there." The assumption here is that in some events, at least, our ordinary experience does not tell us what is really happening.

"History and Myth in the Bible" (1975), *Northrop Frye on Religion* (2000), CW, 4.

EXPERIMENTS

Humanity, alone of all organisms, has elected to transform its environment instead of simply adapting to it, and so only human beings have a lifelong commitment to experiment, trial and error, uncertainty, and all the other burdens of continuing knowledge.

"Some Reflections on Life and Habit" (1988), *Northrop Frye's Writings on the Eighteenth and Nineteenth Centuries* (2005), CW, 17.

EXPLORERS

We have never lost the feeling that Cathay is always over the horizon, a journey away. We have never been a culture that believed in happy endings. The real ending is ironic because it's here.

"Some Reflections on Life and Habit" (1988), *Northrop Frye's Writings on the Eighteenth and Nineteenth Centuries* (2005), CW, 17.

EXPO 67

The Montreal fair: what is the meaning of a billion-dollar fantasy world that is annihilated in six months? Civilization as a "happening."

Entry, Notebook 19 (1964–67), 384, *The "Third Book" Notebooks of Northrop Frye, 1964–1972: The Critical Comedy* (2002), CW, 9.

EXPRESSION

We can express ourselves only within the limits of a language that has been made articulate for us by our great writers. We can think only within the limits of ideas and concepts that have been worked out by our great writers. We can understand one another only within the limits of the social vision of our great writers.

"Toast to the Memory of Shakespeare" (1961), *Northrop Frye's Writings on Shakespeare and the Renaissance* (2010), CW, 28.

How well we can think depends on how much of it we have already done. Most students need to be taught, very carefully and patiently, that there is no such thing as an inarticulate idea waiting to have the right words wrapped around it. They have to learn that ideas do not exist until they have been incorporated into words. Until that point you don't know whether you are pregnant or just have gas on the stomach.

"The Primary Necessities of Existence" (1985), *Interviews with Northrop Frye* (2008), CW, 24.

EXTRA-SENSORY PERCEPTION

For example, there have been experiments in ESP and telepathy which may have established the fact that some human beings possess such powers. They certainly established the fact that the majority of people either do not possess them at all or possess them in an erratic, unreliable, and very largely useless form.

"Literary and Mechanical Models" (1989), *"The Secular Scripture" and Other Writings on Critical Theory, 1976–1991* (2006), CW, 18.

I've noticed a curious form of e.s.p. in me: whenever I dream of writing something in fiction somebody else who really does write gets the idea instead.

Entry, Notebook 3 (1946–48), 172, *Northrop Frye's Notebooks and Lectures on the Bible and Other Religious Texts* (2003), CW, 13.

EXTRATERRESTRIAL INTELLIGENCE

If planets on distant galaxies are inhabited by intelligent beings, that's so far something our technology doesn't permit us to do anything with. I would think that if they are more intelligent than we are, we probably couldn't see them.

"Between Paradise and Apocalypse" (1978), *Interviews with Northrop Frye* (2008), CW, 24.

EYE & EAR

The eye was satisfied in the garden of Eden, and will be again at the end of time, but throughout history we depend on the ear.

"History and Myth in the Bible" (1975), *Northrop Frye on Religion* (2000), CW, 4.

F

FABLE
The end of fable, as the total body of verbal imagination that man constructs, brings us back to the beginning of myth, the model world associated with divine creation in Genesis.
> *The Secular Scripture: A Study of the Structure of Romance* (1975), *"The Secular Scripture" and Other Writings on Critical Theory, 1976–1991* (2006), CW, 18.

FACTS
Anyone who says "the facts speak for themselves" is using another verbal figure of speech, technically known as prosopopoeia.
> "Myth I," *The Great Code* (1982), *The Great Code: The Bible and Literature* (2006), CW, 19.

FAIRIES
Fairies are the detritus of the oldest mythology in the world, the beings in nature that are close at hand, form the earliest stratum of the "supernatural," are present in rivers and trees and stones (they later become nymphs and satyrs and the like), and are closely related to the dream world.
> Entry, Notes 55-3 (before *c.* 1987), 8, *Northrop Frye's Notebooks on Romance* (2004), CW, 15.

FAIRY TALES
We often feel that certain types of literature, such as fairy tales, are somehow good for the imagination: the reason is that they restore the primitive perspective that mythology has. So does modern poetry, on the whole, as compared with fiction.
> "Verticals of Adam," *The Educated Imagination* (1963), *"The Educated Imagination" and Other Writings on Critical Theory, 1933–1963* (2006), CW, 21.

FAITH
Faith is the feeling that despair is not the whole answer.
> "Northrop Frye in Conversation" (1989), *Interviews with Northrop Frye* (2008), CW, 24.

My approach to faith turns it into *gaya scienza*, a joyful wisdom: most of the conventional approaches turn it into a burden of guilt feelings.
> Entry, Notebook 44 (1986–91), 649, *Northrop Frye's Late Notebooks, 1982–1990: Architecture of the Spiritual World* (2000), CW, 5.

Perhaps faith is not only existential but is always & necessarily projected, hence it must die to be reborn as imagination.
> Entry, Notebook 19 (1964–67), 286, *The "Third Book" Notebooks of Northrop Frye, 1964–1972: The Critical Comedy* (2002), CW, 9.

What is significant is not so much the losing of faith as the losing of guilt feelings about losing it.
> *The Modern Century* (1967), *Northrop Frye on Modern Culture* (2003), CW, 11.

Faith is the hypostasis of what is hoped for, the elenchus of the unseen. The only thing truly unseen, the world across death, may, according to my principle, be what enables us to see what is visible.
> Entry, Notebook 3 (1946–48), *Northrop Frye's Notebooks and Lectures on the Bible and Other Religious Texts* (2003), CW, 13.

… we have to live from one moment to the next by a combination of faith and self-hypnotism, like the people in the Far East who walk over hot coals, to the great bewilderment of tourists, most of whom are capable of self-hypnotism but not of faith.

"Address on Receiving the Royal Bank Award" (1978), *Northrop Frye's Writings on Education* (2001), CW, 7.

Faith, or the rejection of faith, often revolves around the question: "Why would a good God permit so much evil and suffering?" Charity starts with the question: "Why do we permit so much evil and suffering?", and that is a question on which all men and women of good will can act instead of arguing in circles.

"To Come to Light" (1988), *Northrop Frye on Religion* (1999), CW, 4.

I feel that the language of faith is not a complete language because it's a proposition language. And, as Hegel says, a proposition contains its own opposite.

"Maintaining Freedom in Paradise" (1982), *Interviews with Northrop Frye* (2008), CW, 24.

FALL OF MAN

The myth of the fall incorporates a fact which is non-mythically true: that with sex came death and individuality.

Entry, Notebook 12 (1968–70), 329, *The "Third Book" Notebooks of Northrop Frye, 1964–1972: The Critical Comedy* (2002), CW, 9.

FAMINE

A famine is a social problem, but only the individual starves.

"Concern and Myth," *Words with Power: Being a Second Study of "The Bible and Literature"* (1990), CW, 26.

FANTASY

Anyone recording, or reading about, reveries, daydreams, or conscious sexual fantasies must be struck by the total absence in such things of anything like real fantasy.

The Secular Scripture: A Study of the Structure of Romance (1975), *"The Secular Scripture" and Other Writings on Critical Theory, 1976–1991* (2006), CW, 18.

And of course there's James Branch Cabell & M.P. Shiel, two authors I've always had difficulty reading. I'm not as fond of this stuff as I used to think I was.

Entry, Notebook 24 (1970–72), 174, *The "Third Book" Notebooks of Northrop Frye, 1964–1972: The Critical Comedy* (2002), CW, 9.

The success of Tolkien's book, however, indicated a change of taste parallel to the post-Ginsberg change in poetry, towards the romantic, the fantastic, and the mythopoeic.... Romance, fantasy, and mythopeia are the inescapable forms for a society which no longer believes in its own permanence or continuity.

"The Renaissance of Books" (1973), referring to the popularity of *Lord of the Rings*, *Northrop Frye on Modern Culture* (2003), CW, 11.

Consciousness itself is a chosen point of view; there is no reason why the world of dream and fantasy should not be an equally valid choice.

"Academy without Walls" (1961), *Northrop Frye on Modern Culture* (2003), CW, 11.

FASCISM

The war against fascism is not over, but one phase of it is over — the phase in which dangerous enemies are those who explicitly call themselves Fascists.

"Ezra Pound" (1949), *Northrop Frye on Twentieth-Century Literature* (2010), CW, 29.

The Jesuits particularly I regard as the *fons et origo* of the Fascist spirit, and I believe that Fascism will last exactly as the Roman Catholic Church does, because the latter is the only institution that really believes in Fascism....

Entry, Notebook 42b: Notes I (1942–44), 64, *Northrop Frye's Fiction and Miscellaneous Writings* (2007), CW, 25.

Both Fascism and Communism claim to be the logical forms of true democracy, and both claim to be fighting, not democracy, but one another, for each maintains that democracy is merely the propaganda façade of its rival.

"The Church and Modern Culture" (1950), *Northrop Frye on Modern Culture* (2003), CW, 11.

In this neo-fascist age, there are many who dislike the kind of freedom which the university represents, and would like to kidnap the university by a pressure group of some kind, radical or established, according to their prejudices. But, if this happened, society's one light would go out.

"The Definition of a University" (1970), *Northrop Frye's Writings on Education* (2001), CW, 7.

One has to keep the contrast steadily in mind: if we hitch a political development to a cultural one, as in separatism, we get a kind of neo-fascism; if we hitch a cultural development to a political one, we get a pompous bureaucratic pseudo-culture.

Address, "The Authority of Learning" (1984), *Northrop Frye's Writings on Education* (2001), CW, 7.

FASHION

Well, as it happens, I am rather interested in people who are out of fashion, because they often indicate the limitations of the age that considers them so.

"Some Reflections on Life and Habit" (1988), *Northrop Frye's Writings on the Eighteenth and Nineteenth Centuries* (2005), CW, 17.

As art becomes increasingly fashionable, anything new in art becomes a new fashion. To encourage it is ever so revolutionary, and yet completely safe.

"Academy without Walls" (1961), *Northrop Frye on Modern Culture* (2003), CW, 11.

In a world where dynasties rise and fall at much the same rate as women's hemlines, the dynasty and the hemline look much alike in importance, and get much the same amount of featuring in the news.

The Modern Century (1967), *Northrop Frye on Modern Culture* (2003), CW, 11.

FATE

I wonder what those writers who talk about relentless and inexorable Fate would say to a man who had two Fates, pulling in opposite directions. The trouble is that I can't quite figure out which one is God.

"NF to HK," Jul. 1932, *The Correspondence of Northrop Frye and Helen Kemp, 1932–1939* (1996), CW, 1.

Fate specializes in practical jokes in bad taste: fate very seldom pulls out a card from the pack to help you.

"Symbolism in the Bible" (1981–82), contrasting tragic inevitability with comic intervention, *Northrop Frye's Notebooks and Lectures on the Bible and Other Religious Texts* (2003), CW, 13.

FATWAH

The twenty-first century will find *The Satanic Verses* a document of great interest to scholars and critics, but the Ayatollah will be of no interest to anybody except as one more nightmare of bigotry that history has produced in such profusion. One would hope that eventually the stupid human race would get the point.

Entry, Notes 53 (1989–90), 162, *Northrop Frye's Late Notebooks, 1982–1990: Architecture of the Spiritual World* (2000), CW, 6.

FEAR

Fear causes people to build walls against each other, and love knocks them down.

"To Come to Light" (1988), *Northrop Frye on Religion* (1999), CW, 4.

FEARFUL SYMMETRY

My very bad habit in those days was to start a paper the night before I was to read it. About half-past three in the morning some very funny things started happening in my mind, and I began to see dimensions of critical experience that I'd never dreamed existed before — a sudden expansion of the horizon. When I went out for breakfast — I remember it was a bitterly cold morning — I knew that I was to write a book on Blake. And fifteen years later I did.

"Music in My Life" (1985), *Interviews with Northrop Frye* (2008), CW, 24. Frye studied Blake's *Milton* under Herbert Davis at Oxford in 1932.

What a pity Joyce and Yeats couldn't have had my Blake book. All the time it would have saved them.

Attributed by former student and critic Hugh Kenner, letter to Irving Layton, 23 Sep. 1955, quoted by Elspeth Cameron in *Irving Layton: A Portrait* (1985).

My chief aim in my book was to remove the poet Blake from the mystical and occult quarantine that most commentators assigned him and put him in the middle of English literature, which is where he belongs and where he said he belonged.

> "Blake's Biblical Illustrations" (1983), *Northrop Frye on Milton and Blake* (2005), CW, 16.

I said I used to feel that perfect clarity of expression would automatically produce an adequate response from intelligent & cultivated people, but that after reading the reviews of FS I ... realized that people were just stupid.

> Entry, 21 Jan. 1949, 111, referring to the critical reception of *Fearful Symmetry*, *The Diaries of Northrop Frye: 1942–1955* (2001), CW, 8.

But what I have done is a masterpiece; finely written, well handled, and the best, clearest and most accurate exposition of Blake's thought yet written. If it's no good I'm no good.

> "NF to HK," 11 Mar. 1935, *The Correspondence of Northrop Frye and Helen Kemp, 1932–1939* (1996), CW, 1.

FEMINISM

Feminist *literary* criticism is mostly heifer-shit. Women frustrated by the lack of outlet for their abilities turn to pedantic nagging, and the nagging pedantry of most feminist writing is a reflection of frustration unaccompanied by any vision of transcending it.

> Entry, Notebook 44 (1986–91), 580, *Northrop Frye's Late Notebooks, 1982–1990: Architecture of the Spiritual World* (2000), CW, 5.

I think feminism is being very silly when it objects to words like "mankind" instead of just letting them fossilize. A kind of niggling pedantry is so deep in women that it seems almost a built-in characteristic. It isn't, of course, but it's a very deep social conditioning, and that's what I think the "animus" is.

> Entry, Notebook 50 (1987–90), 14, *Northrop Frye's Late Notebooks, 1982–1990: Architecture of the Spiritual World* (2000), CW, 5.

Feminists who refuse to accept that "man" means "men and women" have a very limited sense of metaphor.

> Entry, Notes 53 (1989–90), 211, *Northrop Frye's Late Notebooks, 1982–1990: Architecture of the Spiritual World* (2000), CW, 6.

FESTIVALS

Still, there'd be something to be said for three folklore festivals: a red & green one in the winter, a yellow & purple one in the spring & an orange and blue one in the fall, if the Halloween colour-scheme would change its black to blue.

> Entry, 16 Apr. 1949, 328, *The Diaries of Northrop Frye: 1942–1955* (2001), CW, 8.

FICTION

Romance is the structural core of all fiction: being directly descended from folktale, it brings us closer than any other aspect of literature to a sense of fiction, considered as a whole, as the epic of the creature, man's vision of his own life as a quest.

> *The Secular Scripture: A Study of the Structure of Romance* (1975), *"The Secular Scripture" and Other Writings on Critical Theory, 1976–1991* (2006), CW, 18.

If throughout this book I refer to popular fiction as frequently as to the greatest novels and epics, it is for the same reason that a musician attempting to explain the rudimentary facts about counterpoint would be more likely, at least at first, to illustrate from "Three Blind Mice" than from a complex Bach fugue.

> "Second Essay: Ethical Criticism: Theory of Symbols" (1957), *Anatomy of Criticism: Four Essays* (2006), CW, 22.

Fictions, therefore, may be classified, not morally, but by the hero's power of action, which may be greater than ours, less, or roughly the same.

> "First Essay: Historical Criticism: Theory of Modes" (1957), *Anatomy of Criticism: Four Essays* (2006), CW, 22.

Of all fictions, the marvellous journey is the one formula that is never exhausted....

> "First Essay: Historical Criticism: Theory of Modes" (1957), *Anatomy of Criticism: Four Essays* (2006), CW, 22.

If we were to call any form of prose outside of literature "non-fiction" and reserve the word "fiction" for prose which is literature, we should have a valuable and practicable critical term to work with.
"The Anatomy in Prose Fiction" (1942), *"The Educated Imagination" and Other Writings on Critical Theory, 1933–1963* (2006), CW, 21.

… when we examine fiction from the point of view of form, we can see four chief strands binding it together, novel, confession, anatomy, and romance.
"Four Forms of Prose Fiction" (1950), *"The Educated Imagination" and Other Writings on Critical Theory, 1933–1963* (2006), CW, 21.

One real handicap in my scholarship is the immense difficulty I find in finishing long works of fiction. I seem to get the point after about 100 pages.
Entry, Notebook 12 (1968–70), 314, *The "Third Book" Notebooks of Northrop Frye, 1964–1972: The Critical Comedy* (2002), CW, 9.

Metaphor, then, is a formal principle of poetry, and myth of fiction.
"Blake after Two Centuries" (1957), *Northrop Frye on Milton and Blake* (2005), CW, 16.

FILM
There is no better index to the general level of civilization in a country today than the quality of its cinemas. Hollywood has given a free hand to two authentic geniuses, Charlie Chaplin and Walt Disney, and it is obvious in their pictures how close we are to ballet and pantomime techniques, and how nearly the music comes to organizing every movement of the dramatic action.
"Music and the Savage Breast" (1938), *Northrop Frye on Modern Culture* (2003), CW, 11.

The film is the one real major art-form of our time: it has, with its greatest directors, solved the problem of the balance of eye and ear.
"Icons and Iconoclasm" (1970), *Northrop Frye on Literature and Society, 1936–1989: Unpublished Papers* (2002), CW, 10.

Canadian film has always been remarkable for its sensitive documentary feeling, applied to everything from Eskimo and Indian life to the urban cultures of Toronto and Montreal.
"Canada: New World Without Revolution" (1975), *Northrop Frye on Canada* (2003), CW, 12.

I recently went past two teen-age girls looking at the display in front of a movie which told them that inside was a thrill of a lifetime, on no account to be missed, and I heard one of them say, "Do you suppose it's any good?" That was the voice of sanity trying to get its bearings in a world of illusion. We may think of it as the voice of reason, but it's really the voice of the imagination doing its proper job.
"The Vocation of Eloquence," *The Educated Imagination* (1963), *"The Educated Imagination" and Other Writings on Critical Theory, 1933–1963* (2006), CW, 21.

This is partly because the movie is capable of the greatest concentration of any art form in human history. The possibilities of combining photographic, musical, and dramatic rhythms leave all preceding arts behind in their infinity.
"The Great Charlie" (1941), *Northrop Frye on Modern Culture* (2003), CW, 11.

That curious feeling of reincarnation, of Having Been Through All This Before, that assails one so frequently at movies, owes a great deal to the stereotyped music.
"Music at the Movies" (1942), *Northrop Frye on Modern Culture* (2003), CW, 11.

The average movie of today is a rigidly conventionalized New Comedy proceeding toward an act which, like death in Greek tragedy, takes place offstage, and is symbolized by the final embrace.
"The Argument of Comedy" (1948), *Northrop Frye's Writings on Shakespeare and the Renaissance* (2010), CW, 28.

In the movies, which provide the popular comedies of our own day, the triumph of youth is so relentless that the moviemakers are finding some difficulty in getting anyone over the age of seventeen into their audiences.

"Shakespeare's Comedy of Humours" (1950), *Northrop Frye on Literature and Society, 1936–1989: Unpublished Papers* (2002), CW, 10.

FINNEGANS WAKE

Finnegans Wake is not a book to read, but a book to decipher: as Joyce says, it's about a dreamer, but it's addressed to an ideal reader suffering from an ideal insomnia.

"The Keys to Dreamland," *The Educated Imagination* (1963), *"The Educated Imagination" and Other Writings on Critical Theory, 1933–1963* (2006), CW, 21.

Finnegans Wake, written in an associative language based on English but incorporating echoes and turns of speech from all over the world, is a prophecy, perhaps a rather ominous one, of what awaits us in future.

"*Rencontre*: The General Editor's Introduction" (1960s), *Northrop Frye on Literature and Society, 1936–1989: Unpublished Papers* (2002), CW, 10.

FLOWERS

The flowers burst into beauty: it was their idea.

Entry, Notebook 55.19 (1991), *Northrop Frye's Late Notebooks, 1982–1990: Architecture of the Spiritual World* (2000), CW, 6.

So far I've been dodging this point by saying that creation is the revelation of the cosmos to human consciousness, and didn't exist, at least as creation, before human consciousness did. But the flowers were just as lovely millions of years before Adam as they are now.

Entry, Notebook 55.1 (1991), 18, *Northrop Frye's Late Notebooks, 1982–1990: Architecture of the Spiritual World* (2000), CW, 6.

FOLK ART

Folk art is both popular and primitive, two words which mean much the same thing in the arts.

"Design as a Creative Principle in the Arts" (1966), *"The Critical Path" and Other Writings on Critical Theory, 1963–1975* (2009), CW, 27.

FOLK SONGS

There is a Newfoundland folk song with the original refrain, "I love my love but she'll love no more." Through a lucky short circuit in oral transmission, this turned into "I love my love and love is no more," a line that teases us out of thought like the Grecian urn.

"Approaching the Lyric" (1982), *"The Secular Scripture" and Other Writings on Critical Theory, 1976–1991* (2006), CW, 18.

Nationalism in so academic an art as music can never get very far away from a sentimental primitivism consisting largely of fine writing around a folk tune, which is by now a thoroughly sterile and irritating formula.

"Frederick Delius" (1936), *Northrop Frye on Modern Culture* (2003), CW, 11.

FOLK TALES

Folk tales are simply abstract story-patterns, uncomplicated and easy to remember, no more hampered by barriers of language and culture than migrating birds are by customs officers, and made up of interchangeable motifs that can be counted and indexed.

"Myth, Fiction, and Displacement" (1961), *"The Educated Imagination" and Other Writings on Critical Theory, 1933–1963* (2006), CW, 21.

Most of the stories about the accepted divine beings are myths rather than folk tales, but structurally this distinction is more one of content than of actual shape.

The Secular Scripture: A Study of the Structure of Romance (1975), *"The Secular Scripture" and Other Writings on Critical Theory, 1976–1991* (2006), CW, 18.

Myths, I have often said, stick together to form a mythology, unlike folk tales, which simply interchange themes and motifs so stereotyped that they can be counted and indexed.

"The Mythical Approach to Criticism" (1985), *Northrop Frye on Religion* (2000), CW, 4.

FOOD

One cannot live a day without being concerned about food, but one may live all one's life without being concerned about God.

"Framework and Assumption" (1985), *"The Secular Scripture" and Other Writings on Critical Theory, 1976–1991* (2006), CW, 18.

Even the most exalted flights of Platonic philosophy rise from banquets.
> "Third Variation: The Cave," *Words with Power: Being a Second Study of "The Bible and Literature"* (1990), CW, 26.

FOOLS
The fool is the man with the new idea that always turns out to be an old fallacy.
> "Typology II," *The Great Code* (1982), *The Great Code: The Bible and Literature* (2006), CW, 19.

FORESTS
I've said many times that man is born lost in a forest. If he is obsessed by the thereness of the forest, he stays lost and goes in circles; if he assumes the forest is not there, he keeps bumping into trees. The wise man looks for the invisible line between the is and the is not which is the way *through*.
> Entry, Notebook 44 (1986–91), 53, *Northrop Frye's Late Notebooks, 1982–1990: Architecture of the Spiritual World* (2000), CW, 5.

It's all very well in the abstract to be thrilled by moonlit dark forests, and nature's grand design. But the reality in Canada was all too often ... terrifying. No-man's land. Terra incognita....
> "View of Canada" (1976), *Northrop Frye on Canada* (2003), CW, 12.

FORM
Marshall says it's the form and not the content of the message that's important, which is why the nature of the medium is also important.... It seems to me that the form has this importance only as long as we're unconscious of it: to become aware of the form as a form is to separate the content. At that point the presentation goes into reverse & becomes a perception: the form comes from us then.
> Entry, Notebook 19 (1964–67), 58, reflecting on Marshall McLuhan's probe "the medium is the message," *The "Third Book" Notebooks of Northrop Frye, 1964–1972: The Critical Comedy* (2002), CW, 9.

It is only by a necessary economy of language that we can speak of *a* myth, *a* folk tale, or *a* legend at all: none of these things really exist except in specific verbal forms, and these verbal forms are literary forms.
> "Literature and Myth" (1967), *"The Critical Path" and Other Writings on Critical Theory, 1963–1975* (2009), CW, 27.

Poetry can only be made out of other poems; novels out of other novels. Literature shapes itself, and is not shaped externally: the *forms* of literature can no more exist outside literature than the forms of sonata and fugue and rondo can exist outside music.
> "Second Essay: Ethical Criticism: Theory of Symbols" (1957), *Anatomy of Criticism: Four Essays* (2006), CW, 22.

If one could only write the secret history of literary forms!
> Entry, Notebook 12 (1968–70), 385, *The "Third Book" Notebooks of Northrop Frye, 1964–1972: The Critical Comedy* (2002), CW, 9.

Content is often regarded, even by artists themselves, as dictating its own forms, but this is an elementary fallacy: the forms of every art are generated from within the art.
> "Culture as Interpenetration" (1982), *Northrop Frye on Canada* (2003), CW, 12.

FOWLES, JOHN
I read Fowles' *Magus* with the highest expectations, but finished it thinking he didn't know what the hell he was doing.
> Entry, Notebook 28 (after 1965), 6, *Northrop Frye's Fiction and Miscellaneous Writings* (2007), CW, 25.

FRANCE
If the French had held Canada they might well have sold it, as they did Louisiana. What is important is not nationality but cultural assumptions.
> "Canada: New World Without Revolution" (1975), *Northrop Frye on Canada* (2003), CW, 12.

As late as my own student days, I remember seeing in Paris an exhibition of a sculptor who lived in (I think) Dijon, advertised under the slogan "France is not Paris."
> "Culture as Interpenetration" (1982), *Northrop Frye on Canada* (2003), CW, 12.

FRATERNITY

A society of students, scholars, and artists is a society of neighbours, in the genuinely religious sense of that word.

The Modern Century (1967), *Northrop Frye on Modern Culture* (2003), CW, 11.

If we pursue either liberty or equality we lose both. The tertium quid of one thing needful is fraternity, or interpersonal relation, the kingdom of ends, the community of love, relaxing into tolerance and good will at a distance.

Entry, Notebook 54-8 (late 1972–77), 71, *Northrop Frye's Notebooks on Romance* (2004), CW, 15.

There's an illusory quality about both liberty and equality until they are solidly linked to fraternity: the interpenetrating of the Christ-nature within all of us.

Entry, Notebook 50 (1987–90), 827, *Northrop Frye's Late Notebooks, 1982–1990: Architecture of the Spiritual World* (2000), CW, 5.

FRAZER, SIR JAMES

But no matter what happens to the subjects he dealt with, Frazer will always be read, because he can be.

"Sir James Frazer" (1959), *"The Educated Imagination" and Other Writings on Critical Theory, 1933–1963* (2006), CW, 21.

But the fascination which *The Golden Bough* and Jung's book on libido symbols have for literary critics is not based on dilettantism, but on the fact that these books are primarily studies in literary criticism, and very important ones.

"The Archetypes of Literature" (1951), *"The Educated Imagination" and Other Writings on Critical Theory, 1933–1963* (2006), CW, 21.

The hypothetical ritual studied in Frazer's *Golden Bough* may be vulnerable enough in various anthropological contexts, but as a mythical structure it is as solid as the pyramids.

"Third Variation: The Cave," *Words with Power: Being a Second Study of "The Bible and Literature"* (1990), CW, 26.

… the big ideas don't always occur to the biggest people: imagine Frazer, undoubtedly one of the stupidest bastards who ever put pen to paper, getting the *Golden Bough* inspiration! And in this age of copyrights & private property we're stuck with him.

Entry, Notebook 3 (1946–48), 57, *Northrop Frye's Notebooks and Lectures on the Bible and Other Religious Texts* (2003), CW, 13.

When it first appeared, *The Golden Bough* was called an example of the Covent Garden school of anthropology, meaning that it was full of vegetation, Covent Garden being a market.

"Sir James Frazer" (1959), *"The Educated Imagination" and Other Writings on Critical Theory, 1933–1963* (2006), CW, 21.

FREE SPEECH

When newspapermen say that a democracy must have a free press, what they mean is "we want to run this paper ourselves." But behind that there may be a quite genuine belief that running the paper themselves would make for a freer society than external control would do, and the belief may well be right.

"Violence and Television" (1975), *Northrop Frye on Modern Culture* (2003), CW, 11.

Nobody is capable of free speech unless he knows how to use language, and such knowledge is not a gift: it has to be learned and worked at.

The Educated Imagination (1963), *"The Educated Imagination" and Other Writings on Critical Theory, 1933–1963* (2006), CW, 21.

The essential basis for the argument is simply that the more ignorant and superstitious a society is, the more insecure it is, and the more taboos it erects, while the amount of liberty of expression is regulated by the state of civilization then present; consequently it remains to be examined whether or not our society has advanced to the stage where it is sufficiently mature to throw off any kind of arbitrary restraint, that on free speech being largely arbitrary.

"That Trinity Debate" (1932), *Northrop Frye's Writings on Education* (2001), CW, 7.

FREEDOM

What was exploited in the American Revolution, and again in the Civil War, was a desire for democratic freedom, but what came to power was an oligarchy, and for many Americans the desire for freedom is as frustrated as ever.

"A Revolution Betrayed: Freedom and Necessity in Education" (1970), *Northrop Frye's Writings on Education* (2001), CW, 7.

The students crushed under tanks in Tiananmen Square may have been, in a way, as much in the grip of illusion as the thugs who crushed them. But they showed very clearly that all human beings want the same things, freedom and dignity and decent living conditions, that those are very simple and reasonable things to want, and that nothing but the release of the power to apply our knowledge and creative energies can get them.

"Speech at the New Canadian Embassy, Washington" (1989), *Northrop Frye on Canada* (2003), CW, 12.

If you want to smash human freedom, the first thing you have to do is smash language, because people will always be free as long as they have the words to form ideas freely.

"Frye's Literary Theory in the Classroom," *CEA Critic*, January 1980.

A state is free, then, in proportion to the amount of free life it permits, just as it is a slave-state in proportion to the amount of death or imaginative restraint for which it is organized.

"Part One: The Argument," *Fearful Symmetry: A Study of William Blake* (1947, 2004), CW, 14.

The only genuine freedom is a freedom of the will which is informed by a vision, and this vision can only come to us through the intellect and the imagination, and through the arts and sciences which embody them, the analogies of whatever truth and beauty we can reach. In this kind of freedom the opposition to necessity disappears: for scientists and artists and scholars, as such, what they want to do and what they have to do become the same thing.

The Critical Path: An Essay on the Social Context of Literary Criticism (1971), *"The Critical Path" and Other Writings on Critical Theory, 1963–1975* (2009), CW, 27.

There seems no escaping the inference that the real desire for freedom and equality is not only repressed too, but is in fact one of the most deeply repressed feelings we have.

Creation and Recreation (1980), *Northrop Frye on Religion* (2000), CW, 4.

History tells us that, ever since Adam's six hours in paradise, man has never known what to do with freedom except throw it away.

The Double Vision (1991), *Northrop Frye on Religion* (2000), CW, 4.

The difference between slavery & freedom is the difference between living other people's lives & living one's own. The former is alienation in the strict Marxist sense as well as automatism.

Entry, Notebook 21 (1969–76), 532, *Northrop Frye's Notebooks and Lectures on the Bible and Other Religious Texts* (2003), CW, 13.

What is freedom? Doing what one wants to do. But whatever "one" wants to do, whatever demands the coordinating of body and mind, must be learned. As Pope says, "Those move easiest who have learned to dance": only after repeated practice is one free to dance or think or even watch a football game with any comprehension.

"By Liberal Things" (1959), *Northrop Frye's Writings on Education* (2001), CW, 7.

I should define freedom as the power to do what one has learned to do. I do not see that the conception of freedom makes any sense at all without the learning of a discipline.

"Preserving Human Values" (1961), *Northrop Frye on Modern Culture* (2003), CW, 11.

Genuine freedom and discipline are the same thing; one cannot be set free to play the piano or speak German without a long period of directed attention and practice.

"Teaching the Humanities Today" (1977), *Northrop Frye's Writings on Education* (2001), CW, 7.

FREEDOM, ACADEMIC
I sometimes think there is no genuine freedom except academic freedom, where the resources of human knowledge are open for people to assimilate as they best can.
> "Literature as a Critique of Pure Reason" (1982), *"The Secular Scripture" and Other Writings on Critical Theory, 1976–1991* (2006), CW, 18.

Actually academic freedom is the only form of freedom, in the long run, of which humanity is capable, and it cannot be obtained unless the university itself is free.
> "The Definition of a University" (1970), *Northrop Frye's Writings on Education* (2001), CW, 7.

What academic freedom the university has so far been able to preserve has been preserved partly by a general lack of public interest: it may have to be preserved by more positive means in the future.
> "The Changing Pace in Canadian Education" (1963), *Northrop Frye's Writings on Education* (2001), CW, 7.

The conception of academic freedom does not mean merely freedom from interference by the world, though of course it means that too. It means that there must be a continuous current of mental energy flowing into the world from the university, which is the powerhouse of freedom.
> "By Liberal Things" (1959), *Northrop Frye's Writings on Education* (2001), CW, 7.

FREEDOM, INDIVIDUAL & SOCIAL
Individual & social freedom are the same thing, & just as the free man shows himself free by his rigid inner discipline, so the free society shows its freedom in its dependence on law & the complication of its institutions.
> Entry, 5 Apr. 1949, 312, *The Diaries of Northrop Frye: 1942–1955* (2001), CW, 8.

I think with Liberals that it is only by individual freedom and democratic development that any progress can be made.
> "NF to HK," 4 Sep. 1933, *The Correspondence of Northrop Frye and Helen Kemp, 1932–1939* (1996), CW, 1.

It is only when the individual is enabled to form an individual synthesis of ideas, beliefs, and tastes that a principle of freedom is established in society, and this alone distinguishes a people from a mob.
> "Trends in Modern Culture" (1952), *Northrop Frye on Modern Culture* (2003), CW, 11.

Once the scientist is allowed to pursue science without reference to political priorities; once the records of the past are thrown open to the historian; once the poet or novelist can write without the restrictions of ideology, I think the worst horrors of the police state will become relaxed and eventually impotent.
> "Preface to *On Education*" (1988), *Northrop Frye's Writings on Education* (2001), CW, 7.

FREEDOM & CONCERN
It is out of the tension between concern and freedom that glimpses of a third order of experience emerge, of a world that may not exist but completes existence, the world of the definitive experience that poetry urges us to have but which we never quite get.
> *The Critical Path: An Essay on the Social Context of Literary Criticism* (1971), *"The Critical Path" and Other Writings on Critical Theory, 1963–1975* (2009), CW, 27.

Certainly freedom is one of my primary concerns, but it always includes deliverance from everything society thinks is freedom.
> Entry, Notebook 44 (1986–91), 476, *Northrop Frye's Late Notebooks, 1982–1990: Architecture of the Spiritual World* (2000), CW, 5.

FRENCH CANADA
We speak of a British "conquest" of Canada, but the French Canadian was never really conquered.
> "Canadian Scene: Explorers and Observers" (1973), *Northrop Frye on Canada* (2003), CW, 12.

The fact that French Canada broke loose from a fairly rigorous cultural supervision in the 1950s made for a curious quality of rage and fury in French Canadian writing which it would be hard to match elsewhere, I think.

"Introduction to Canadian Literature: Moscow Talk" (1988), 21, *Northrop Frye's Fiction and Miscellaneous Writings* (2007), CW, 25.

Meanwhile the language and culture of French Canada is in flourishing shape, in no danger except when politicians refuse to leave it alone. Culture and language are an area — perhaps the only area — where privatization really does work.
"The Cultural Development of Canada" (1990), *Northrop Frye on Canada* (2003), CW, 12.

The French are on the whole the worse off by this arrangement, which has made Quebec into a cute tourist resort full of ye quainte junke made by real peasants, all of whom go to church and say their prayers like the children they are, and love their land and tell folk tales and sing ballads just as the fashionable novelists in the cities say they do.
"Canada and Its Poetry" (1943), contrasting stereotypical responses to colonialism, Quebec regionalism with English Canada's imperialism, *Northrop Frye on Canada* (2003), CW, 12.

A distinct society can be only a cultural unit where a language is spoken and a culture fostered by those genuinely interested in it for its own sake, and such societies are the only possible architects of a reconfederated Canada.
"The Cultural Development of Canada" (1990), *Northrop Frye on Canada* (2003), CW, 12.

FREUD, SIGMUND
Freud was quite right, however unconsciously, in talking about "the future of an illusion," because nothing can possibly have a future except an illusion.
"Auguries of Experience" (1987), *"The Secular Scripture" and Other Writings on Critical Theory, 1976–1991* (2006), CW, 18.

Freud was a conservative pessimist transformed by disciples into a revolutionary optimist; Marx was a Utopian transcender of history transformed into a determinist of "historicity."
Entry, Notebook 44 (1986–91), 558, *Northrop Frye's Late Notebooks, 1982–1990: Architecture of the Spiritual World* (2000), CW, 5.

Freud is the great Eros thinker of our time, of course, and he takes us on a journey backward in time to the birth trauma.
Entry, Notebook 6 (1967–68), 6, *The "Third Book" Notebooks of Northrop Frye, 1964–1972: The Critical Comedy* (2002), CW, 9.

Religion was a subject Freud had a Freudian block about, mainly because he wanted to be a lawgiving Moses in his own right, contemplating the back parts of his own God.
"Speculation and Concern" (1966), *Northrop Frye's Writings on Education* (2001), CW, 7.

I wonder if anyone of Freud's stature could emerge from psychology now: there might be a feeling that he was an armchair theorist who had not served enough time in laboratory routine to be a proper professional psychologist.
"The Instruments of Mental Production" (1966), *Northrop Frye's Writings on Education* (2001), CW, 7.

FREUDIANS
It isn't that Freudians are stupid, but that they're so easily satisfied with what they (think they) know. Similarly with Marxists and Christian fundamentalists. Discovery, for them, is not interesting.
Entry, Notebook 44 (1986–91), 402, *Northrop Frye's Late Notebooks, 1982–1990: Architecture of the Spiritual World* (2000), CW, 5.

FRONTIERS
What corresponded to the frontier in American life was never a border in Canada. It was a circumference: a frontier surrounded and enclosed all the tiny communities wherever they were.
"Criticism and Environment" (1981), *Northrop Frye on Canada* (2003), CW, 12.

In the United States, the frontier has been, imaginatively, an open-ended horizon in the West; in Canada, wherever one is, the frontier is a circumference.
"Canadian Culture Today" (1977), *Northrop Frye on Canada* (2003), CW, 12.

Every part of Canada is shut off by its geography, British Columbia from the prairies by the Rockies, the prairies from the Canadas by the immense hinterland of northern Ontario, Quebec from the Maritimes by the upthrust of Maine, the Maritimes from Newfoundland by the sea.

> "Canadian Culture Today" (1977), *Northrop Frye on Canada* (2003), CW, 12.

FRYE, HELEN
God bless, protect, and keep her among his own. I hope to see her again; but perhaps that is a weak hope. Faith is the hypostasis [substance] of what is hoped for, the elenchos [evidence] of the unseen.

> Entry, Notebook 44 (1986–91), 170, referring to the death of his wife, *Northrop Frye's Late Notebooks, 1982–1990: Architecture of the Spiritual World* (2000), CW, 5.

FRYE, NORTHROP
I myself am, for example, a Wasp: white and Anglo-Saxon by the accident of birth, and though born a Protestant too, I have remained one by conviction.

> "America: True or False?" (1969), *Northrop Frye on Canada* (2003), CW, 12.

I am, in cultural background, what is known as a WASP, and thus belong to the only group in society which it is entirely safe to ridicule. I expected that a good deal of contemporary literature would be devoted to attacking the alleged complacency of the values and standards I have been brought up in, and was not greatly disturbed when it did.

> "The Search for Acceptable Words" (1973), *"The Critical Path" and Other Writings on Critical Theory, 1963–1975* (2009), CW, 27.

FRYE AS AUTHOR
One of my less perceptive reviewers remarked recently that I seemed to be rewriting my central myth in every book I produced. I certainly do, and would never read or trust any writer who did not also do so.

> *The Critical Path: An Essay on the Social Context of Literary Criticism* (1971), *"The Critical Path" and Other Writings on Critical Theory, 1963–1975* (2009), CW, 27.

I myself have spent the greater part of seventy-eight years in writing out the implications of insights that occupied at most only a few seconds of all that time.

> Entry, Notes 53 (1989–90), 267, *Northrop Frye's Late Notebooks, 1982–1990: Architecture of the Spiritual World* (2000), CW, 6.

But my approach to my writing has always been evangelical. A good deal of my writing has grown out of a teaching interest rather than research or scholarly pressures, and I've always tried to keep in mind the fact that no idea is really any good unless it can be explained to a fairly young person.

> "A Literate Person Is First and Foremost an Articulate Person" (1977), *Interviews with Northrop Frye* (2008), CW, 24.

But then all my books have really been teachers' manuals, concerned more with establishing perspectives than with adding specifically to knowledge.

> "Introduction," *The Great Code* (1982), *The Great Code: The Bible and Literature* (2006), CW, 19.

I must pray for luminousness, the quality my work has at its best when I really know what I'm talking about....

> Entry, Notebook 12 (1968–70), 294, *The "Third Book" Notebooks of Northrop Frye, 1964–1972: The Critical Comedy* (2002), CW, 9.

The main difficulty in my writing, as I've often said, is in translating discontinuous aphorisms into continuous argument.

> Entry, Notebook 27 (1986), 112, *Northrop Frye's Late Notebooks, 1982–1990: Architecture of the Spiritual World* (2000), CW, 5.

It is true that I attempt overviews, and my style in consequence features what are called, in the sweeping cliché of tunnel vision, "sweeping generalizations."

> Entry, Notebook 44 (1986–91), 697, *Northrop Frye's Late Notebooks, 1982–1990: Architecture of the Spiritual World* (2000), CW, 5.

In particular, the notion that I belong to a school or have invented a school of mythical or archetypal criticism reflects nothing but confusion about me. I make this personal comment with some hesitation, in view of the great generosity with which my books have been received, but everyone who is understood by anybody is misunderstood by somebody.

"Criticism, Visible and Invisible" (1964), *"The Critical Path" and Other Writings on Critical Theory, 1963–1975* (2009), CW, 27.

FRYE AS CLERIC

While walking to school one day, that claustrophobic, evangelical, Christian environment that I was brought up in just lifted from my shoulders. It just vanished and has never come back. Ever since then I have been interested in religion solely as a means of expanding the mind, not contracting it.

"Beginnings" (1981), *Northrop Frye on Canada* (2003), CW, 12.

Any biography, including Ayre's, would say that I dropped preaching for academic life: that's the opposite of what my spiritual biography would say, that I fled into academia for refuge and have ever since tried to peek out into the congregation and make a preacher of myself.

Entry, Notes 53 (1989–90), 43, *Northrop Frye's Late Notebooks, 1982–1990: Architecture of the Spiritual World* (2000), CW, 6.

I used to describe myself as a United Church plainclothesman, meaning that I was in effect somebody who was attached to a church.

"Northrop Frye in Conversation" (1989), referring to his ordination as a man of the cloth, *Interviews with Northrop Frye* (2008), CW, 24.

The United Church of Canada, of which I am an ordained clergyman, would be surprised to hear that I am an ex-Christian. I think that the answer to the reviewer's puzzlement is simply that all my life I have learned my views of Christianity more or less from Blake, who would never split the efforts of man from the efforts of God.

"Freedom and Concern" (1985), rebutting the view expressed by the critic Herbert Levine in a review of *The Great Code* that it was written by "the ex-Christian Frye, who has apparently passed beyond good and evil," *Interviews with Northrop Frye* (2008), CW, 24.

I'm no evangelist or revivalist preacher, but I'd like to help out in a trend to make religion interesting and attractive to many people of good will who will have nothing to do with it now.

Entry, Notebook 27 (1986), 408, *Northrop Frye's Late Notebooks, 1982–1990: Architecture of the Spiritual World* (2000), CW, 5.

The one thing a religious service, or the reading of the Bible, does to me is to give — sometimes — the emotional intensity that a dream gives an experience, and for the same reason — that your conscious mind is asleep.

"NF to HK," 29 Sep. 1938, written about morning prayer aboard the ship the *Empress*, *The Correspondence of Northrop Frye and Helen Kemp, 1932–1939* (1996), CW, 1.

Oh, God, I'd like to say something new about religion & nobody really succeeds in doing so.

Entry, Notebook 11f (1969–70), 20, *Northrop Frye's Notebooks and Lectures on the Bible and Other Religious Texts* (2003), CW, 13.

It has a great deal of importance. Words like "infinite" and "eternal" are not fuzzy to me; they are words that prevent the human spirit from getting claustrophobia.

"*Chatelaine's* Celebrity I.D." (1982), *Interviews with Northrop Frye* (2008), CW, 24. From remarks made when Frye was asked to comment on "religion in my life."

I have never been a practising clergyman, but the fact that I was ordained has proved useful to many people: it enabled a Maoist, for instance, to describe me as the "high priest of clerical obscurantism."

"Autobiographical Notes IV: The Critic and the Writer" (1972), 3, *Northrop Frye's Fiction and Miscellaneous Writings* (2007), CW, 25.

FRYE AS CRITIC

So while my critical approach has been said to be deficient in rigor, this does not matter so much to me as long as it is also deficient in rigor mortis.

"Introduction," *Words with Power: Being a Second Study of "The Bible and Literature"* (1990), CW, 26.

In this connection, the reader will note a tendency in the present book, which has run through all my writing for the past twenty years or so, to address myself less to a purely academic audience than to undergraduates and a non-specialized public, including, of course, whatever academic critics are willing to take a more detached attitude. I know that this policy has confused even sympathetic academic reviewers, as well as driving others into all the hysterias of pedantry.

"Introduction," *Words with Power: Being a Second Study of "The Bible and Literature"* (1990).

Why am I so respected and yet so isolated? Is it only because I take criticism more seriously than any other living critic?

Entry, Notebook 44 (1986–91), 93, *Northrop Frye's Late Notebooks, 1982–1990: Architecture of the Spiritual World* (2000), CW, 5.

I don't know if there really is a word for the kind of thing I am.... I suppose "critic" comes closest to being what I am, although I am a critic who recognizes no boundaries between criticizing that specific novel and criticizing Meech Lake and the future of Canada.

"Cultural Identity in Canada" (1990), referring to no specific novel, *Northrop Frye's Fiction and Miscellaneous Writings* (2007), CW, 25.

I've been called a mystic as well as a myth critic, because some people think that's an even more contemptuous term. If myth is really mythos, story or plot, then mysticism is being initiated in the mysteries.

Entry, Notes 53 (1989–90), 153, *Northrop Frye's Late Notebooks, 1982–1990: Architecture of the Spiritual World* (2000), CW, 6.

It doesn't matter how often I'm mentioned by other critics: I form part of the subtext of every critic worth reading.

Entry, Notebook 44 (1988), 472, *Northrop Frye's Late Notebooks, 1982–1990: Architecture of the Spiritual World* (2000), CW, 5.

When one finds that very perceptive people are describing one as the exact opposite of what one is one may feel that one has hit a fairly central area of social resistance.

"Expanding Eyes" (1975), *"The Critical Path" and Other Writings on Critical Theory, 1963–1975* (2009), CW, 27.

I don't think my critical method is archetypal at all: I recognize the existence & importance of archetypes, but if I have a method, it would be better described as epiphanic. I look over a writer's work to see what shape its theme has, and then use the most revealing features of it to communicate that shape to the reader. As a method, it's a higher organization of commentary, because its basis is archetypal framework rather than allegory.

Entry, Notebook 19 (1964–67), 226, *The "Third Book" Notebooks of Northrop Frye, 1964–1972: The Critical Comedy* (2002), CW, 9.

I am providing a kind of resonance for literary experience, a third dimension, so to speak, in which the work we are experiencing draws strength and power from everything else we have read or may still read.

"Expanding Eyes" (1975), *"The Critical Path" and Other Writings on Critical Theory, 1963–1975* (2009), CW, 27.

I don't know the entire geography of the imaginative world; if I did criticism would stop with me. What I was investigating was one critical conception, the *axis mundi*, and looking at its aspects of ascent and descent, above and below.

"Cultural Identity in Canada" (1990), *Interviews with Northrop Frye* (2008), CW, 24.

FRYE AS INFLUENCE

However, if I am not the speaker of a prologue, I am not a member of an aging chorus either.

"Introduction," referring to his position between Bible-as-literature and Bible-as-scholarship, *Words with Power: Being a Second Study of "The Bible and Literature"* (1990), CW, 26.

I have had some influence, I know, but I neither want nor trust disciples, at least as that term is generally understood. I should be horrified to hear of anyone proposing to make his own work revolve around mine, unless I were sure that that meant a genuine freedom for him. And if I have no disciples I have no school. I think I have found a trail, and all I can do is to keep sniffing along it until either scent or nose fails me.

> "Expanding Eyes" (1975), *"The Critical Path" and Other Writings on Critical Theory, 1963–1975* (2009), CW, 27.

But as far as the general response to my work is concerned, I've seen it go through all the stages, from the what-nonsense stage through the brilliant-but-unsound stage, to the many-fine-insights-but stage, and finally to the of-course-we-knew-it-all-along stage. Everybody goes through that.

> "Getting the Order Right" (1978), *Interviews with Northrop Frye* (2008), CW, 24.

If posterity doesn't like me, the hell with posterity — I won't be living in it anyway.

> "Freedom and Concern" (1985), *Interviews with Northrop Frye* (2008), CW, 24.

FRYE AS PERSONALITY

That of a liberal bourgeois intellectual, which I consider the flower of humanity.

> "*Chatelaine's* Celebrity I.D." (1982), asked for his "general attitude toward life," *Interviews with Northrop Frye* (2008), CW, 24.

… I wonder where the hell all this business of confusing me with God began. I feel like signing myself up to write next year's Spring Thaw.

> Entry, 31 Mar. 1949, 305, referring to the annual satiric revue produced in Toronto between 1948 and 1971, *The Diaries of Northrop Frye: 1942–1955* (2001), CW, 8.

I notice that, at the age of sixty, I have unconsciously arranged my life so that nothing has ever happened to me, and no biographer could possibly take the smallest interest in me.

> "The Search for Acceptable Words" (1973), *"The Critical Path" and Other Writings on Critical Theory, 1963–1975* (2009), CW, 27.

I was predestined to be, for example, a middle-class mid-twentieth-century male white English-speaking Canadian in the instant of conception.

> "Typology I," *The Great Code* (1982), *The Great Code: The Bible and Literature* (2006), CW, 19.

And I suppose being a student of Blake and a Christian, I'm also a bourgeois liberal. I feel that anybody who isn't one, or at least doesn't want to be one, is still in the trees.

> "Northrop Frye in Conversation" (1989), *Interviews with Northrop Frye* (2008), CW, 24.

Question: I wonder if I would be prying if I said, Does Northrop Frye talk to God? *Frye (pause, semi-smile):* Yes.

> Intimate moment in conversation with interviewer and documentary film producer Harry Rasky, CBC-TV's *The Great Teacher: Northrop Frye*, 25 Dec. 1989, *Interviews with Northrop Frye* (2008), CW, 24.

I would think the utmost horror of being reborn as Northrop Frye; I would want to be someone else.

> "*Chatelaine's* Celebrity I.D." (1982), asked to respond to the proposition "if I could live my live over," *Interviews with Northrop Frye* (2008), CW, 24.

I have often been asked how I feel about being discussed in the third person, and I usually say that I meet it with a kind of controlled schizophrenia.

> "Epilogo" (1987), introducing a neologism, *"The Secular Scripture" and Other Writings on Critical Theory, 1976–1991* (2006), CW, 18.

… all of us belong to something before we are anything: I was conditioned to be a twentieth-century Canadian middle-class intellectual nine months before I appeared on earth.

> "Literature as a Critique of Pure Reason" (1982), *"The Secular Scripture" and Other Writings on Critical Theory, 1976–1991* (2006), CW, 18.

The sense of being something of a loner has always been in any case rather exceptionally true of me, with my introverted

temperament, indolent habits, and Canadian nationality.
> "Expanding Eyes" (1975), *"The Critical Path" and Other Writings on Critical Theory, 1963–1975* (2009), CW, 27.

They want to know about the after-life. It's true what Jessie said: they do think I'm in possession of secrets.
> Entry, 18 Mar. 2005, 230, referring to his students and to his colleague Jessie Macpherson, *The Diaries of Northrop Frye: 1942–1955* (2001), CW, 8.

FRYE AS SCHOLAR

For some years I have been in search of the co–ordinating principles that would make it possible for a student of literature to be trained in criticism as well as in scholarship: to specialize, say, in Chaucer and still be able to modulate to the key of Dostoevsky or Plato, to understand that literature is a coherent order of words and not what Pope calls a wild heap of wit.
> "The Well-Tempered Critic (I)" (1961), *"The Educated Imagination" and Other Writings on Critical Theory, 1933–1963* (2006), CW, 21.

Here my humanism essay, if that's what it's going to be, expands into my third book, where I'm beginning to feel that I really am the man who's found the lost chord, somebody who really can, on the basis of literature, put the Tarots & alchemy & kabalism & the rest of it together into a coherent speech & language.
> Entry, Notebook 11f (1969–70), 157, *Northrop Frye's Notebooks and Lectures on the Bible and Other Religious Texts* (2003), CW, 13.

There is no Frye school of mythopoeic poetry: criticism and poetry cannot possibly be related in that way; the myth of a poem is the structural principle of that poem, and consequently all poems that make any sense at all are equally mythopoeic, and so on and so on....
> "Conclusion to *Literary History of Canada*" (1965), *Northrop Frye on Canada* (2003), CW, 12.

Of course I was lucky to have found Blake, but the wise man transforms his luck into significance.
> Entry, Notebook 42a (1942–44), 26, *Northrop Frye's Notebooks on Romance* (2004), CW, 15.

I knew that my own interest in Blake had been sparked by the way he made imaginative sense out of the Nonconformist attitude that I had been brought up in myself.
> "Across the River and Out of the Trees" (1980), *Northrop Frye on Canada* (2003), CW, 12.

I'm not a very conventional scholar. I'm not a scholarly authority in any one thing. I'm more like the hero of Carlyle's *Sartor Resartus*: The Professor of Things in General.
> Remark quoted by Gillian Cosgrove, *Toronto Star*, 7 April 1980.

FUNDAMENTALISM

As it is, the religious bodies maintaining that revelation must be either literally true or else untrue are the ones that are most dramatically increasing their membership, appeal to the most devoted followers, and take in the most money, and we must either join or imitate them if we want that kind of success.
> "The Mythical Approach to Creation" (1985), *Northrop Frye on Religion* (2000), CW, 4.

If I see a sign advertising a four-square gospel church, I don't go in, because I know what I'll find: infantilism sustained by hysteria.
> Entry, Notebook 19 (1964–67), 392, *The "Third Book" Notebooks of Northrop Frye, 1964–1972: The Critical Comedy* (2002), CW, 9.

There are many who seem to think that the early study of the Bible in school would lead to obscurantism, racialism, imperialism, and the reactivating of the Inquisition: their mental processes are identical with those of the people who believe that detaching the science of geology from the Book of Genesis would inevitably destroy all moral values.
> "Elementary Teaching and Elemental Scholarship" (1963), *Northrop Frye's Writings on Education* (2001), CW, 7.

FUNERALS

As for the religion, all one can do at a funeral is proclaim the fact of resurrection: any funeral that doesn't do that is just variations on "Behold, he stinketh" [John 11:39].

> Entry, 6 Jan. 1949, 45, referring to officiating at a funeral of a friend, *The Diaries of Northrop Frye: 1942–1955* (2001), CW, 8.

FUTURE

The future that is technically possible is not necessarily the future that society wants or can accept.

> "The Times of the Signs" (1973), *"The Critical Path" and Other Writings on Critical Theory, 1963–1975* (2009), CW, 27.

To sacrifice the present, which exists, to a future which does not exist, and certainly will never exist in any presently recognizable form, is as perverse a notion as any in history.

> "Some Reflections on Life and Habit" (1988), *Northrop Frye's Writings on the Eighteenth and Nineteenth Centuries* (2005), CW, 17.

The legacy of the past is not, however, merely a tax-free inheritance added to our ordinary income. The best in the past, when liberated by the present, throws its shadow into the future, for whatever man has been capable of in imagination he can realize in life. In the future there is the possibility of an ideal society in which man's vision of his culture has liberated and equalized his social existence.

> "Presidential Address at the MLA," (1977), *Northrop Frye's Writings on Education* (2001), CW, 7.

But we don't like to think this way: we say to a young person: "you have a great future ahead of you," and forget what we mean is: "you will probably have a good deal more past to contemplate."

> "Address on Receiving the Royal Bank Award" (1978), *Northrop Frye's Writings on Education* (2001), CW, 7.

This loss of the sense of a future implicit in the present has naturally created a panic or latent hysteria, the future being feared in proportion to its meaninglessness.

> "The Ethics of Change: The Role of the University" (1968), *Northrop Frye's Writings on Education* (2001), CW, 7.

As centuries passed, the future kept retreating, and now after two thousand years we ought to be getting the point that there's never anything in the future except more future.

> Entry, Notes 53 (1989–90), 220, *Northrop Frye's Late Notebooks, 1982–1990: Architecture of the Spiritual World* (2000), CW, 6.

The future is the point at which "it is later than you think" becomes "too late."

> *The Modern Century* (1967), *Northrop Frye on Modern Culture* (2003), CW, 11.

The only certain thing about the past, apparently, is that it has gone; the only certain thing about the future is that it will cheat and disappoint those who try to grasp it.

> "Convocation Address, Franklin and Marshall" (1968), *Northrop Frye's Writings on Education* (2001), CW, 7.

Convocation addresses frequently refer to graduates as young people facing forward into the future, but of course nobody faces the future: we face the past and back into the future, and what knowledge of the future we may have, or think we have, we glean from a study of the past which is really a form of divination.

> "The View from Here" (1980), *Northrop Frye's Writings on Education* (2001), CW, 7.

There are two areas for which the future is the only metaphor: the predictable and the possible. The former is the basis of the vulgar, non-resonant, "foretelling" aspect of prophecy, & is now emancipated as scientific method. The latter is the apocalyptic hope, hope being a virtue greater than fate, but one relating to the future as faith does to the past.

> Entry, Notebook 15 (1970s), 2, *Northrop Frye's Notebooks and Lectures on the Bible and Other Religious Texts* (2003), CW, 13.

G

GALILEO
We think of modern science as beginning in the opposition of Galileo's view that the earth moves to that of the inquisitors that it stays put. But the opposition was not so clear-cut. Galileo only said that the earth moves: he never claimed that it was going anywhere in particular.
>"Education — Protection against Futility" (1964), *Northrop Frye's Writings on Education* (2001), CW, 7.

GARDENS
Planting a garden develops the conception "weed," a conception of vegetable value unintelligible except in the context of a garden.
>"The Imaginative and the Imaginary" (1962), *"The Educated Imagination" and Other Writings on Critical Theory, 1933–1963* (2006), CW, 21.

The virgin is the garden; the bride is the city.
>Entry, Notebook 50 (1987–90), 148, *Northrop Frye's Late Notebooks, 1982–1990: Architecture of the Spiritual World* (2000), CW, 5.

There is always something of the kindergarten about garden paradises.
>*The Double Vision* (1991), *Northrop Frye on Religion* (2000), CW, 4.

GARRISON MENTALITY
The physical forts of the seventeenth century had changed by the nineteenth into the cultural attitudes that I call the "garrison mentality." The garrison mentality is defensive and separatist. Each groups walls itself off and huddles inside, taking warmth and reassurance from numbers, but keeping its eyes fixed apprehensively on what's outside.
>"View of Canada" (1976), *Northrop Frye on Canada* (2003), CW, 12.

Canadians are now, however, one of the most highly urbanized people in the world, and the garrison mentality, which was social but not creative, has been replaced by the condominium mentality, which is neither social nor creative, and which forces the cultural energies of the country into forming a kind of counter-environment.
>"Speech at the New Canadian Embassy, Washington" (1989), *Northrop Frye on Canada* (2003), CW, 12.

It is significant that Canada's first work of fiction is about life in a garrison, for the garrison encapsulates a great deal of imaginative feeling in Canada, even down to the twentieth century.
>"Criticism and Environment" (1981), referring to Frances Brooke's *History of Emily Montague* (1769), *Northrop Frye on Canada* (2003), CW, 12.

And it means that the entire country is now a garrison, and there are signs that it is being organized to behave like one....
>"View of Canada" (1976), *Northrop Frye on Canada* (2003), CW, 12.

As I understood it, a garrison brings social activity into an intense if constricted focus, but its military and other priorities tend to obliterate the creative impulse.
>"Speech at the New Canadian Embassy, Washington" (1989), *Northrop Frye on Canada* (2003), CW, 12.

A garrison is a closely knit and beleaguered society, and its moral and social values are unquestionable. In a perilous enterprise one does not discuss causes or motives: one is either a fighter or a deserter.... I am concerned rather with a more creative side of the

garrison mentality, one that has had positive effects on our intellectual life.
> Preface, *The Bush Garden* (1971), *Northrop Frye on Canada* (2003), CW, 12.

I have spoken of what I call a garrison mentality and of the alternating moods of pastoral populism and imaginative terror (which has nothing to do with a poet's feeling terrified) in earlier Canadian writing.
> "Across the River and Out of the Trees" (1980), *Northrop Frye on Canada* (2003), CW, 12.

GAYS

The United Church, realizing that every religious body had a "gay" issue, brought the question into the open and got viciously slanged for doing so. Maybe they'll get some credit now for courage and foresight, but I doubt it.
> Entry, Notebook 50 (1987–90), 761, *Northrop Frye's Late Notebooks, 1982–1990: Architecture of the Spiritual World* (2000), CW, 5.

GENDER

I should say somewhere about here that when I say "he" I also mean "she": as the late President Smith used to say, man generally embraces woman.
> "By Liberal Things" (1959), alluding to former University of Toronto president Sidney Smith, *Northrop Frye's Writings on Education* (2001), CW, 7.

GENERATIONS

The conflict of generations is clearly projected from the self-conflicts of both generations. The aging have the fear of seeming to be no longer young in spirit which is one of the normal hazards of aging; the young the fear of the shadows of their own future selves, when they will inevitably be more committed to society.
> "The Ethics of Change: The Role of the University" (1968), *Northrop Frye's Writings on Education* (2001), CW, 7.

GENESIS

[To] read Genesis for biology is far sillier than to read *Macbeth* for Scottish history.
> "Part One: The Argument," *Fearful Symmetry: A Study of William Blake* (1947, 2004), CW, 14.

GENIUS

Perhaps I am a genius, in a sense, but when I think of my gawkiness and tactlessness and the mechanical barrenness of my infernally precocious brain, I shudder.
> "NF to HK," 16 Jan. 1935, *The Correspondence of Northrop Frye and Helen Kemp, 1932–1939* (1996), CW, 1.

By the standards of conventional scholarship, *The Great Code* was a silly and sloppy book. It was also a work of very great genius. The point is that genius is not enough.
> Entry, Notebook 44 (1986–91), 265, *Northrop Frye's Late Notebooks, 1982–1990: Architecture of the Spiritual World* (2000), CW, 5.

It's very lonely being a genius: you're just an arrogant crank who happens to be bright.
> Entry, 15 Feb. 1950, 116, irritated that a granting agency was questioning his scholarship, *The Diaries of Northrop Frye: 1942–1955* (2001), CW, 8.

Statement for the day of my death: The twentieth century saw an amazing development of scholarship and criticism in the humanities, carried out by people who were more intelligent, better trained, had more languages, had a better sense of proportion, and were infinitely more accurate scholars and competent professional men than I. I had genius. No one else is the field known to me had quite that.
> "Coda" (1999), *Northrop Frye's Late Notebooks, 1982–1990: Architecture of the Spiritual World* (2000), CW, 6. The editor notes that "Frye here links himself with the paradoxes of Socrates' apology ... and one can sense in the coda both the impishness of the Socratic ironist, jolting us with the unexpected, and the truth contained in the literal meaning of the word 'genius,' reminding us of what finally motivated this architect of the spiritual world."

GENOCIDE

What is particularly horrifying about the extinction of, say, the Beothuks in Newfoundland is the casualness with which it is done, the ability to murder people of a different ethnical group without losing five minutes' sleep over it. It is rather curious that the Eichmann trial of a few years ago should have come to so many people as a shocking discovery.

"Culture as Interpenetration" (1977), *Northrop Frye on Canada* (2003), CW, 12.

GENRE

The very word "genre" sticks out in an English sentence as the unpronounceable and alien thing it is.

"Polemical Introduction" (1957), *Anatomy of Criticism: Four Essays* (2006), CW, 22.

The reading of an individual romance, say a detective story or a Western, may be in itself a trivial enough imaginative experience. But a study of the whole convention of Westerns or detective stories would tell us a good deal about the shape of stories as a whole, and that, in its turn, would begin to give us some glimpse of still larger verbal structures, eventually of the mythological universe itself.

The Secular Scripture: A Study of the Structure of Romance (1975), *"The Secular Scripture" and Other Writings on Critical Theory, 1976–1991* (2006), CW, 18.

It is instructive to notice, too, how strong the popular demand is for such forms as detective stories, science fiction, comic strips, comic formulas like the P.G. Wodehouse stories, all of which are as rigorously conventional and stylized as the folk tale itself, works of pure "esemplastic" imagination, with the recognition turning up as predictably as the caesura in minor Augustan poetry.

"Myth, Fiction, and Displacement" (1961), *"The Educated Imagination" and Other Writings on Critical Theory, 1933–1963* (2006), CW, 21.

I should say rather that in fully realized writing there is no difference between structure and content, what is called content being the structure of the individual work, as distinct from the structure of the convention or genre to which it belongs.

"Conclusion to *Literary History of Canada*" (1965), *Northrop Frye on Canada* (2003), CW, 12.

A convention big enough to include an entire work of literature is called a genre. The genre invites, as any bookshop will show by its labels. Why do some conventions seem monotonous and others varied? No answer yet.

Entry, Notes 52 (1982–90), 962, *Northrop Frye's Late Notebooks, 1982–1990: Architecture of the Spiritual World* (2000), CW, 6.

Words may be acted in front of a spectator; they may be spoken in front of a listener; they may be sung or chanted; or they may be written for a reader.

"Fourth Essay: Rhetorical Criticism: Theory of Genres" (1957), *Anatomy of Criticism: Four Essays* (2006), CW, 22.

I should make more of the point that revaluation results from a confusion of genres.

Entry, Notebook 44 (1986–91), 716, *Northrop Frye's Late Notebooks, 1982–1990: Architecture of the Spiritual World* (2000), CW, 5.

GENTLEMAN

I teach English literature, a subject I conceive to be a necessary part of a gentleman's education. By a gentleman I mean, provisionally, a citizen who has an intelligent idea of how to occupy his leisure time.

"A Liberal Education" (1945), *Northrop Frye's Writings on Education* (2001), CW, 7.

GEOGRAPHY

The smallest details of the geography of two tiny chopped-up countries, Greece and Israel, have imposed themselves on our consciousness until they have become part of the map of our own imaginative world, whether we have ever seen these countries or not.

"Language II," *The Great Code* (1982), *The Great Code: The Bible and Literature* (2006), CW, 19.

GEOLOGY

Thus in the fifteenth century, for example, we had an elaborate classification of the nine orders of the angels, but no classification of rocks or geological strata.

"The Definition of a University" (1970), *Northrop Frye's Writings on Education* (2001), CW, 7.

GEOMETRY

The conception *pi* does not mean anything except another mathematical formulation of it. In ordinary experience the shortest distance between two points may not be a straight line, as the shortest way to get to the other side of a wall is around by the door, but geometry knows nothing of such existential untidiness.

> "Interior Monologue of M. Teste" (1959), *"The Educated Imagination" and Other Writings on Critical Theory, 1933–1963* (2006), CW, 21.

The child beginning geometry is presented with a dot and is told, first, that that is a point, and second, that it is not a point. He cannot advance until he accepts both statements at once.

> "Tentative Conclusion" (1957), *Anatomy of Criticism: Four Essays* (2006), CW, 22.

GERMAN THINKERS

The demons of the four quarters are Jung (N), Spengler (W), Heidegger (S) and Husserl (E): four clunk-headed Teutons.

> Entry, Notebook 12 (1968–70), 80, *The "Third Book" Notebooks of Northrop Frye, 1964–1972: The Critical Comedy* (2002), CW, 9.

GHOST STORIES

A ghostly world challenges us with the existence of a reality beyond realism which still may not be identifiable as real.

> "Henry James and the Comedy of the Occult" (1989), *Northrop Frye on Twentieth-Century Literature* (2010), CW, 29.

In a modern house, if we see a ghost or hear a ghostly voice, we know that we have left the television on.

> "Reviews of Television Programs for the Canadian Radio-Television Commission: Reflections on November 5th" (1970), *Northrop Frye on Literature and Society, 1936–1989: Unpublished Papers* (2002), CW, 10.

The detective story is the opposite of the ghost story; the former is all intellectual resolution and poetic justice, the latter all emotional response & brooding evil.

> Entry, 25 Jul. 1942, 32, *The Diaries of Northrop Frye: 1942–1955* (2001), CW, 8.

I've also been considering an article on ghost stories & the 19th c. occult (no other century produced ghost stories worth a damn). The main focus of interest, for reasons I've given elsewhere, would be Henry James. Curious that the only one who wrote better ghost stories was also named James.

> Entry, Notebook 44 (1986–91), 399, alluding to M.R. James, *Northrop Frye's Late Notebooks, 1982–1990: Architecture of the Spiritual World* (2000), CW, 5.

GHOSTS

There is nothing really more ghostly than an absence of ghosts. You notice in Europe that you're always in a place that has been lived in for many centuries, and that contributes some kind of inexplicable quality to the landscape.

> "Back to the Garden" (1982), *Interviews with Northrop Frye* (2008), CW, 24.

When I am asked if I "believe in" ghosts, I usually reply that ghosts, from all accounts, appear to be matters of experience rather than of belief, and that so far I have had no experience of them.

> *The Critical Path: An Essay on the Social Context of Literary Criticism* (1971), *"The Critical Path" and Other Writings on Critical Theory, 1963–1975* (2009), CW, 27.

If there is a ghost in *Hamlet*, that merely presents the postulate, "Let there be a ghost in *Hamlet*." It has nothing to do with whether ghosts exist or not, or whether Shakespeare or his audience thought they did.

> "The Transferability of Literary Concepts" (1955), *"The Educated Imagination" and Other Writings on Critical Theory, 1933–1963* (2006), CW, 21.

I suppose ghosts & haunting spirits are a product of evil design: I don't see any other postulate for associating ghosts with continuity in place.

> Entry, Notebook 34 (1946–50), 34, *Northrop Frye's Notebooks on Romance* (2004), CW, 15.

Any place where anything has really happened to us becomes part of our home, and for living people, as is said to be true of ghosts, it is natural to keep haunting the place where something that they cannot forget has occurred.

"Hart House Rededicated" (1969), *Northrop Frye's Writings on Education* (2001), CW, 7.

Ghosts are revenants, spirits trying to come home.
Entry, Notebook 50 (1987–90), 750, *Northrop Frye's Late Notebooks, 1982–1990: Architecture of the Spiritual World* (2000), CW, 5.

GIFT OF TONGUES

The so-called gift of tongues is the babble of chaos with the cerebral cortex turned off.
Entry, Notebook 12 (1968–70), 134, *The "Third Book" Notebooks of Northrop Frye, 1964–1972: The Critical Comedy* (2002), CW, 9.

GLOBAL VILLAGE

In the age of the global village the strongest political force is separatism.
"Rear-View Crystal Ball?" (1970), *Northrop Frye on Canada* (2003), CW, 12.

If the world is becoming a global village, it will also take on the features of real village life, including cliques, lifelong feuds, and impassable social barriers.
"Communications" (1970), *Northrop Frye on Modern Culture* (2003), CW, 11.

It is clear that the explosion of a nuclear bomb involves us personally, whether it is set off in Siberia or the mid-Pacific, and in the same way a massacre in Algeria is a personal outrage to us, and the segregation in South Africa is a personal humiliation to us.
"To the Class of '62 at Queen's" (1962), *Northrop Frye's Writings on Education* (2001), CW, 7.

GNOSTICISM

So are the Gnostic systems, which are intolerably dull and puzzling considered as abstract theologies, but might have more interest if read as epic poems.
"Part One: The Argument," *Fearful Symmetry: A Study of William Blake* (1947, 2004), CW, 14.

GOD

We all start from scratch: the immense differences in where we arrive are largely a matter of luck, plus conditioning of various kinds. That's one reason why one *has* to believe in a god who knows what people are and pays little attention to what they do.
Entry, Notebook 50 (1987–90), 212, *Northrop Frye's Late Notebooks, 1982–1990: Architecture of the Spiritual World* (2000), CW, 5.

It is the duty of humanity to kill whatever gods can die. The God that seems to me to be dead is the god "out there"; that is, the god of time and space, the first cause of the order of nature. That god is dead because he was never alive.
"Breakthrough" (1967), *Interviews with Northrop Frye* (2008), CW, 24.

The only thing that God can possibly mean is what he really does mean in Christianity, that is to say a suffering man.
"Into the Wilderness" (1969), *Interviews with Northrop Frye* (2008), CW, 24.

We project things we don't understand on God, and hope that he does.
"T.S. Eliot's *Four Quartets*" (1979), 4, *Northrop Frye's Fiction and Miscellaneous Writings* (2007), CW, 25.

God is a community, a kingdom of Heaven, & fellowship & the communion of saints precede all our experience.
Entry, 1 May 1949, 350, *The Diaries of Northrop Frye: 1942–1955* (2001), CW, 8.

The conception of "God," considered purely as a conception, need not & should not be taken seriously. If "God" doesn't mean a living presence who is not [sic] experienced as such, the word means nothing. That's what I feel, even if I haven't had the experience, or rather, haven't become aware of having had it.
Entry, Notebook 21 (1969–76), 569, *Northrop Frye's Notebooks and Lectures on the Bible and Other Religious Texts* (2003), CW, 13.

God made man. God was made man. God is man. Past, present, future. God's will is to be man.
Entry, Notebook 21 (1969–76), 344, *Northrop Frye's Notebooks and Lectures on the Bible and Other Religious Texts* (2003), CW, 13.

The worst thing we can say of God is that he knows all. The best thing we can say of him is that, on the whole, he tends to keep his knowledge to himself.
> Entry, Notes 52 (1982–90), 736, *Northrop Frye's Late Notebooks, 1982–1990: Architecture of the Spiritual World* (2000), CW, 6.

There's something to be said for the god of the gaps: when you're faced with the unknown you project in it, so "God" is the totality of nothingness first of all.
> Entry, Notebook 50 (1987–90), 598, *Northrop Frye's Late Notebooks, 1982–1990: Architecture of the Spiritual World* (2000), CW, 5.

Descartes' postulate is a restatement of the ontological proof: I can conceive a perfect being, but a perfect being must exist or he wouldn't be perfect: in short, I think, therefore God is.
> Entry, Notes 54-5 (1976), 96, *Northrop Frye's Notebooks and Lectures on the Bible and Other Religious Texts* (2003), CW, 13.

God's power works only with wisdom & love, not with folly & hatred. As 99.9 % of human life is folly & hatred, we don't see much of God's power. He must work deviously, a creative trickster, what Buddhists call the working of skilful means.
> Entry, Notebook 44 (1986–91), 511, *Northrop Frye's Late Notebooks, 1982–1990: Architecture of the Spiritual World* (2000), CW, 5.

Theoretically, god has no need of man: in practice, all gods are fed by human offerings & sacrifices, & starve & die when human imagination is withdrawn from them. If God owns us, he gets taken over by man.
> Entry, Notebook 21 (1969–76), 536, *Northrop Frye's Notebooks and Lectures on the Bible and Other Religious Texts* (2003), CW, 13.

The question "Is there, or is there not, a God?" is the ultimate in verbal unreality: hell itself cannot contain its utter futility and emptiness.
> Entry, Notebook 44 (1986–91), 455, *Northrop Frye's Late Notebooks, 1982–1990: Architecture of the Spiritual World* (2000), CW, 5.

God "exists," then, only as the will to love and unite: or rather, he's called into existence by that will.
> Entry, Notebook 11b (1980), 8, *Northrop Frye's Notebooks and Lectures on the Bible and Other Religious Texts* (2003), CW, 13.

As far as man is concerned, it seems to me there is no reality in the conception of God outside human consciousness. But man is not the whole of creation.
> "Maintaining Freedom in Paradise" (1982), *Interviews with Northrop Frye* (2008), CW, 24.

One cannot live a day without being concerned about food, but one may live all one's life without being concerned about God.
> "Framework and Assumption" (1985), *Myth and Metaphor* (1990), CW, 26.

A place of blood and terror is not the only place where God can be found, but it is the only kind of place where God can be born. For God can only be born in the context of God's wrath.
> "The Leap in the Dark" (1971), referring to the Feast of Advent, *Northrop Frye on Religion* (2000), CW, 4.

To me, God means the unlimited nature of the human heritage.
> Entry, Notebook 50 (1987–90), 165, *Northrop Frye's Late Notebooks, 1982–1990: Architecture of the Spiritual World* (2000), CW, 5.

Anyway, "God is dead" is a silly bloody remark; "God never was" would at least be intelligible.
> Entry, Notebook 50 (1987–90), 606, *Northrop Frye's Late Notebooks, 1982–1990: Architecture of the Spiritual World* (2000), CW, 5.

Well, God does not become God until he also becomes Man. Grace *is* incarnation. Its product is resurrection, or liberation.
> Entry, Notebook 50 (1987–90), 792, *Northrop Frye's Late Notebooks, 1982–1990: Architecture of the Spiritual World* (2000), CW, 5.

The *source* of God is the Poetic Genius or imaginative "unreal," & the true Creator is

the creating power, not a "secret doctrine" or anything constructed.
> Entry, Notebook 21 (1969–76), 358, *Northrop Frye's Notebooks and Lectures on the Bible and Other Religious Texts* (2003), CW, 13.

I feel I must have God on my own terms, because God on somebody else's terms is an idol.
> Entry, Notebook 19 (1964–67), 266, *The "Third Book" Notebooks of Northrop Frye, 1964–1972: The Critical Comedy* (2002), CW, 9.

It may well be that there is nothing to man except the experiences he has; consequently, what he responds to is something which includes himself or is essential in himself and infinitely more besides.
> "Into the Wilderness" (1969), *Interviews with Northrop Frye* (2008), CW, 24.

As soon as God speaks he condemns himself to death, for his consciousness withdraws from existence.
> Entry, Notebook 21 (1969–76), 7, *Northrop Frye's Notebooks and Lectures on the Bible and Other Religious Texts* (2003), CW, 13.

And so the presence of God comes to us not in the form of a history transmitted through a book, but in the form of a story in which the book itself is autonomous and definitive.
> "Symbolism in the Bible" (1981–82), *Northrop Frye's Notebooks and Lectures on the Bible and Other Religious Texts* (2003), CW, 13.

GODS

In the solar cycle of the day, the seasonal cycle of the year, and the organic cycle of human life, there is a single pattern of significance, out of which myth constructs a central narrative around a figure who is partly the sun, partly vegetative fertility, and partly a god or archetypal human being.
> "The Archetypes of Literature" (1951), *"The Educated Imagination" and Other Writings on Critical Theory, 1933–1963* (2006), CW, 21.

The god, whether traditional deity, glorified hero, or apotheosized poet, is the central image that poetry uses in trying to convey the sense of unlimited power in a humanized form.
> "Second Essay: Ethical Criticism: Theory of Symbols" (1957), *Anatomy of Criticism: Four Essays* (2006), CW, 22.

Gods that men no longer believe in become literary characters....
> "The Well-Tempered Critic (II)" (1961), *"The Educated Imagination" and Other Writings on Critical Theory, 1933–1963* (2006), CW, 21.

When myth starts to take form (I have some hesitation in working this out on a form-content basis, but it'll do for the moment) the first thing that crystallizes is gods.
> Entry, Notebook 50 (1987–90), 65, *Northrop Frye's Late Notebooks, 1982–1990: Architecture of the Spiritual World* (2000), CW, 5.

... the sacrificial *life* keeps the gods going: the gods live by the myths we live by. Woden and Mithra died of disbelief, not starvation.
> Entry, Notebook 50 (1987–90), 248, *Northrop Frye's Late Notebooks, 1982–1990: Architecture of the Spiritual World* (2000), CW, 5.

I think with the C.C.F. that man is unable, in a *laissez-faire* system, to avoid running after false gods and destroying himself.
> "NF to HK," 4 Sep. 1933, *The Correspondence of Northrop Frye and Helen Kemp, 1932–1939* (1996), CW, 1.

What was important about the Hebrews was not their belief that their god was the true god but that all other gods were false.
> "Icons and Iconoclasm" (1970), *Northrop Frye on Literature and Society, 1936–1989: Unpublished Papers* (2002), CW, 10.

For the student of English literature, the true gods are Jupiter and Venus; it's silly to insist that Zeus and Aphrodite have any existence.
> "The Classics and the Man of Letters" (1964), on the differences between the Greek and Latin pantheon, *Northrop Frye's Writings on Education* (2001), CW, 7.

The real "gods" are not forces within nature, but forces within the human transformation of nature. That is, the true gods are the gods of words, numbers, tones and colours that produce the arts.

> Entry, Notes 54.1 (May 1990), 20, *Northrop Frye's Late Notebooks, 1982–1990: Architecture of the Spiritual World* (2000), CW, 6.

GOLDEN AGE

Art belongs to human nature, and human nature is, properly speaking, the state that man lived in in Eden, or the golden age, before his fall into a lower world of physical nature to which he is not adapted. Man attempts to regain his original state through law, virtue, education, and such rational and conscious aids as art.

> "Recognition in *The Winter's Tale*" (1962), *Northrop Frye's Writings on Shakespeare and the Renaissance* (2010), CW, 28.

GOLDEN MEAN

During the 1930s and '40s, I was conscious too that many intellectual leaders whom I most admired were deserting wisdom for paradox, were falling in love with authoritarian standards and values, whether of the extreme right or the extreme left, and that the main danger of the intellectual in modern society is perhaps a fascination with the logical extreme instead of with the illogical golden mean.

> "Opening Ceremonies of the E.J. Pratt Memorial Room" (1964), *Northrop Frye on Canada* (2003), CW, 12.

GOODNESS

The social good is greater than the individual good, but it is only in the individual that any awareness of what the social good is can be achieved.

> Entry, Notebook 11f (1969–70), 144, *Northrop Frye's Notebooks and Lectures on the Bible and Other Religious Texts* (2003), CW, 13.

I said fifty years ago that the doctrine that man is by nature good does not lead to a very good-natured view of man.

> Entry, Notes 53 (1989–90), 245, *Northrop Frye's Late Notebooks, 1982–1990: Architecture of the Spiritual World* (2000), CW, 6.

GOSPELS

In the Christian Gospel, where a divine personality is presented, the only possible literary form would be that of a discontinuous sequence of epiphanies, which is the form that modern critics have discovered in it.

> "The Well-Tempered Critic (II)" (1961), *"The Educated Imagination" and Other Writings on Critical Theory, 1933–1963* (2006), CW, 21.

The gospel writers weren't interested in history, but in the power that stops history.

> Entry, Notebook 44 (1986–91), 365, *Northrop Frye's Late Notebooks, 1982–1990: Architecture of the Spiritual World* (2000), CW, 5.

To do anything with Christianity we have to separate the everlasting gospel from its institutional perversions, and that may be really a task for literary criticism.

> Entry, Notebook 12 (1968–70), 239, *The "Third Book" Notebooks of Northrop Frye, 1964–1972: The Critical Comedy* (2002), CW, 9.

To me the statement that the Gospel is a myth and the statement that the Gospel tells a story are exactly the same statement, and it's clear that the relationship between poetry and history is a midway one. It doesn't fall exactly into either camp.

> "The Meaning of Recreation: Humanism in Society" (1979), *Northrop Frye on Religion* (2000), CW, 4.

The gospel teaches us not to despise the letter of the law, but to read it as "letters," spiritually, with the full energy of an active and intelligent mind.

> "Part Three: The Final Synthesis," *Fearful Symmetry: A Study of William Blake* (1947, 2004), CW, 14.

If the Gospel writers had simply made up what they say out of their own imaginations or even out of their convictions, what they produced would still have been superb works of literature, though they would not have been the Gospels.

> *The Double Vision* (1991), *Northrop Frye on Religion* (2000), CW, 4.

The gospels are written mythical narratives, and for casual readers they remain that. But if anything in them strikes a reader with full kerygmatic force, there is, using the word advisedly, a *resurrection* of the original speaking presence in the reader.
"Spirit and Symbol," *Words with Power: Being a Second Study of "The Bible and Literature"* (1990), CW, 26.

The Gospels are myths, and any attempt to "demythologize" them will disintegrate them to nothing.
"*Pistis* and *Mythos*" (1972), *Northrop Frye on Religion* (2000), CW, 4.

That is the conception behind the gospel, the conception of a spiritual kingdom of which we are citizens and follow its laws, but which cannot be incorporated into actual society in the form of legislation.
"Symbolism in the Bible" (1981–82), *Northrop Frye's Notebooks and Lectures on the Bible and Other Religious Texts* (2003), CW, 13.

GOTHIC HORROR
I do realize, however, that my fondness (all right, weakness) for corny romanticism, facile supernaturalism, and Gothic horror generally is inspired by a nostalgia rather than the creative response, and as nostalgia longs for the vanished, there is a residue of indefiniteness about it that leads to some dissatisfaction & disillusionment with what one attains.
Entry, Notebook 34 (1946–50), 2, *Northrop Frye's Notebooks on Romance* (2004), CW, 15.

GOVERNMENTS
Government is based on majority rule; the universities are one of the most effective instruments of minority right. The university seeks truth at all cost; the government must seek compromise at all cost.
"John George Diefenbaker" (1961), *Northrop Frye on Canada* (2003), CW, 12.

Voltaire said that the Holy Roman Empire was not holy, not Roman, and not an empire; and some of our speakers seem to think that the time is fast approaching when the federal government at Ottawa will not be federal, not a government, and, considering the number of departments being exiled to Hull, not in Ottawa.
"A Summary of the 'Options' Conference" (1977), *Northrop Frye on Canada* (2003), CW, 12.

The worst governments are those with double ideologies, where a political doctrine is backed by a religious one, as in Iran. Israel is better, but I'd hate to live even there.
Entry, Notebook 27 (1986), 500, *Northrop Frye's Late Notebooks, 1982–1990: Architecture of the Spiritual World* (2000), CW, 5.

GOVERNOR GENERAL
Where there is no question of British rule any more, keeping this memento of the fact that we were once a British colony is one way of qualifying the extent to which we are now an American colony.
"Speech at the New Canadian Embassy, Washington" (1989), *Northrop Frye on Canada* (2003), CW, 12.

GRACE
The word "grace," with all its Renaissance overtones from the graceful courtier of Castiglione to the gracious God of Christianity, is the most important thematic word in Shakespearean comedy.
"Third Essay: Archetypal Criticism: Theory of Myths" (1957), *Anatomy of Criticism: Four Essays* (2006), CW, 22.

GRADUATE SCHOOL
A graduate school usually means, in practice, that the teaching staff has to do twice as much work for the same money: but teachers are curious people, and they seem to thrive on such arrangements.
"Culture and the National Will" (1957), *Northrop Frye on Canada* (2003), CW, 12.

GRADUATION, UNIVERSITY
When you came here you knew the answers: now you know that there are no answers, and that the advance of knowledge consists only in moving through a graded series of questions.
"Education — Protection against Futility" (1964), *Northrop Frye's Writings on Education* (2001), CW, 7.

When the student is graduated, he represents the university in the world: wherever he is, the university is; whatever his profession, he will always be a university teacher, teaching by his example and influence every moment of the day.
> "By Liberal Things" (1959), *Northrop Frye's Writings on Education* (2001), CW, 7.

The usual cliché of graduation oratory used to be that you have now completed your preparatory studies and are going out to deal with the world. I always resented this line when I was a student, and it seems even more incompetent to me today. In the first place, you are now fully participating in society, not preparing for something else more important. Nothing is going to happen to you which is more important than what has happened. In the second place, you are not going anywhere else: you are merely re-entering the world of education.
> "Baccalaureate Sermon" (1967), *Northrop Frye on Religion* (2000), CW, 4.

GRAIL

A great myth like that of the Grail means everything essential that it has ever been made to mean in the history of its development, and the complete story is the one that emerges gradually in the course of time, which in English literature takes us down through Mallory to Tennyson, Swinburne, Charles Williams, and many others still to come.
> "The World as Music and Idea in Wagner's *Parsifal*" (1982), *Northrop Frye's Writings on the Eighteenth and Nineteenth Centuries* (2005), CW, 17.

Here's the germ of an important critical principle: that the "real meaning" of a myth is often best grasped not by tracing it back to some hypothetical original, but by following its successive treatments by various writers.
> "Notes for 'The World as Music and Idea in Wagner's *Parsifal*'" (1982), 6, *Northrop Frye's Fiction and Miscellaneous Writings* (2007), CW, 25.

The only thing is that one does get very much aware of the passing of time when one gets into one's seventies. Besides, there must have been times when even the noble and pure-hearted Sir Galahad said, "Bugger the Grail."
> "Criticism in Society" (1985), *Interviews with Northrop Frye* (2008), CW, 24.

Similarly new formulations of myth recapture lost and neglected implications. The Grail stories are profounder than cauldrons-of-plenty myths, and my reading of them is profounder than they are.
> Entry, Notebook 27 (1986), 58, *Northrop Frye's Late Notebooks, 1982–1990: Architecture of the Spiritual World* (2000), CW, 5.

GRAMMAR

What did I learn in school? The most valuable thing by far was grammar. English should be analyzed by the structure of an inflected language, preferably Latin: philosophical as well as literary training. Linguists on this subject are talking nonsense.
> "Autobiographical Notes III: First Memories" (1980s), 13, *Northrop Frye's Fiction and Miscellaneous Writings* (2007), CW, 25.

Nine-tenths of "bad" grammar is a deliberate and conscious (or half-conscious or subconscious or unconscious, whatever your private psychological myth may be) variation of a known standard.
> "Reflections at a Movie" (1942), *Northrop Frye on Modern Culture* (2003), CW, 11.

Just as the teacher of a language is a grammarian, so one of the functions of the literary critic is to be a grammarian of imagery, interpreting the symbolic systems of religion and philosophy in terms of poetic language.
> "Yeats and the Language of Symbolism" (1947), *Northrop Frye on Twentieth-Century Literature* (2010), CW, 29.

GRAVES, ROBERT

Whatever one thinks of Mr. Graves as a poet, novelist, critic, translator, mythographer, editor, anthologist, collaborator, surveyor of modernist poetry, or restorer of the Nazarene gospel, there can be no reasonable doubt that Mr. Graves is big, and bigness is certainly one important attribute of greatness. He is not a minor poet; he is not a minor anything.

"Graves, Gods, and Scholars" (1956), *Northrop Frye on Twentieth-Century Literature* (2010), CW, 29.

GREATNESS

Strictly speaking, there is no such thing as a wise man, just as, strictly speaking, there is no such thing as a great man. There are only sources of wisdom, and they are extremely unpredictable. The implication is that your relation to others may be more truly yourself than anything that you may have squirrelled away inside you.

"Wisdom and Knowledge" (1973), *Northrop Frye on Religion* (2000), CW, 4.

It seems to me inevitable that any person who is at all objective and honest would not be a great man in his own eyes. To himself he would probably be a rather poor creature, and he would be most conscious of his deficiencies.

"The Question of 'Success'" (1967), *Northrop Frye's Writings on Education* (2001), CW, 7.

But something about greatness *ended* around 1940. We're doing different things now.

Entry, Notebook 12 (1968–70), 66, suggesting that the "great thinker" is no longer around, *The "Third Book" Notebooks of Northrop Frye, 1964–1972: The Critical Comedy* (2002), CW, 9.

GROUP OF SEVEN

The Group of Seven put on canvas the clear outlines of the Canadian landscape in the hard Canadian light, and provided a formula for a bright posterish painting, often with abstract tendencies. That much of this painting would be facile and insensitive is of course true; but there is a corresponding virtue, the virtue of good humour.

"Canadian Art in London" (1939), *Northrop Frye on Canada* (2003), CW, 12.

The romantic side of the movement is reflected in the name "Group of Seven" itself: there were never really more than six, in fact there were effectively only five, but seven is a sacred number, and the group had a strong theosophical bent.

"Canadian Scene: Explorers and Observers" (1973), *Northrop Frye on Canada* (2003), CW, 12.

The Group of Seven were really pre-Canadian in the sense that they were imaginative explorers. Their literary counterpart would not be our established writers so much as people like David Thompson and Samuel Hearne.

"From Nationalism to Regionalism: The Maturing of Canadian Culture" (1980), *Interviews with Northrop Frye* (2008), CW, 24.

Most of its characteristics reappear in the Group of Seven painters, in Tom Thomson and Emily Carr, with their odd mixture of *art nouveau* and cosmic consciousness.

"Poetry" (1958), discussing "emotional precision" vs. "woozy inspirationalism" in the Poets of Confederation, *Northrop Frye on Canada* (2003), CW, 12.

The room of Thomson, MacDonald, and Harris in the National Gallery gives the impression that all Canadian art has been inspired by *Finlandia*.

"Canadian Water-Colours" (1940), *Northrop Frye on Canada* (2003), CW, 12.

GROVE, FREDERICK PHILIP

Frederick Philip Grove was certainly the most serious of Canadian prose writers, and may well have been the most important one also.

"Canadian Dreiser" (1948), *Northrop Frye on Canada* (2003), CW, 12.

GULF OF ST. LAWRENCE

Yes, in the 1930s you had to go by ship. There weren't any transatlantic flights then. I suddenly realized when I was in the middle of the Gulf of St. Lawrence that I was surrounded by five Canadian provinces, all of them invisible. You don't get that kind of experience anywhere in the United States.

"Northrop Frye in Conversation" (1989), *Interviews with Northrop Frye* (2008), CW, 24.

GURDJIEFF, G.I.

Gurdjieff talks about objective art: as usual with him, I get the feeling that he doesn't know what he's talking about but has talked to somebody who does. I feel that this is the central mystery of art.

Entry, Notebook 24 (1970–72), 194, referring to the Armenian-Russian teacher, *The "Third*

Book" Notebooks of Northrop Frye, 1964–1972: The Critical Comedy (2002), CW, 9.

GYRE

The gyre is, of course, also a sexual symbol, male on the outside and female on the inside, and sex is closely connected with rising flames and the spiralling of smoke, fire being a traditional purgatorial image also.

"The Top of the Tower" (1969), *Northrop Frye on Twentieth-Century Literature* (2010), CW, 29.

HAL 9000

In the Clarke-Kubrick movie *2001*, the computer HAL suddenly develops an autonomous will, a power of using its intelligence for its own ends. That makes HAL a nightmare, of course, but it also makes him a fellow-creature: he's now a he and not an it, and the depiction of his gradual destruction had a genuine pathos.

Entry, Notes 54.2 (1982–1991), 2, *Northrop Frye's Late Notebooks, 1982–1990: Architecture of the Spiritual World* (2000), CW, 6.

HALIBURTON, THOMAS CHANDLER

... and it's more sensible to appreciate the good writer we have than to regret the great writer we might possibly have had.

"Haliburton: Mask and Ego" (1962), *Northrop Frye on Canada* (2003), CW, 12.

HALLUCINATIONS

It seems to me that at a certain point of intensity what literature conveys is a sense of a controlled hallucination. That is, in literature things are not really seen until they become not actual hallucinations, because that would merely substitute a subjective experience for an objective one, but a controlled hallucination, where things are seen with a kind of intensity with which they are not seen in ordinary experience.

"Literature as Therapy" (1989), *"The Secular Scripture" and Other Writings on Critical Theory, 1976–1991* (2006), CW, 18.

The poem or painting is in some respects a "hallucination": it is summoned up out of the artist's mind and imposed on us, and is allied to delirium tremens or pretending that one is Napoleon.

"The View from Here" (1980), *Northrop Frye's Writings on Education* (2001), CW, 7.

HAMLET

Hamlet is not about Hamlet at all, but about a situation into which Hamlet fits, and all attempts to treat the play as though it were primarily a character study of Hamlet destroy the symmetry of the play.

Entry, 31 Dec. 1948, 12, *The Diaries of Northrop Frye: 1942–1955* (2001), CW, 8.

HAPPINESS

The American Constitution talks about the pursuit of happiness, but that's bad grammar. You can't pursue happiness: you pursue the course of your life and if you're lucky it may produce happiness from time to time.

"Literature as a Critique of Pure Reason" (1982), *"The Secular Scripture" and Other Writings on Critical Theory, 1976–1991* (2006), CW, 18.

That's why the pursuit of happiness is, in itself, regressive. In thought it leads to the state of mind many theosophists are in, of confusing profound thoughts with pleasure at the idea of having profound thoughts.

Entry, 4 Jan. 1949, 30, *The Diaries of Northrop Frye: 1942–1955* (2001), CW, 8.

The basis of happiness is a sense of freedom or unimpeded movement in society, a detachment that does not withdraw; and the basis of that sense of independence is consciousness.

The Critical Path: An Essay on the Social Context of Literary Criticism (1971), *"The Critical Path" and Other Writings on Critical Theory, 1963–1975* (2009), CW, 27.

HARRIS, LAWREN

Nothing he paints ever seems to look at us.

"The Pursuit of Form" (1948), *Northrop Frye on Canada* (2003), CW, 12.

HARRON, DON
Maybe he's just too intelligent to be a good actor: that is, there's too solid a core of his own personality.
> Entry, 23 March 1952, 199, *The Diaries of Northrop Frye: 1942–1955* (2001), CW, 8.

HATRED
I don't share anti-Semitism, & feel that way about anti-Semites. But I do feel that way about Roman Catholics, and discover from that that a hatred is as objective as a headache: it's a disease one may not ever care to have but continues to be afflicted with.
> Entry, Notebook 42b: Notes I (1942–44), 29, *Northrop Frye's Fiction and Miscellaneous Writings* (2007), CW, 25.

HAYDN, FRANZ JOSEPH
If I had such a thing as a favourite composer, it would be Haydn. I think it's Haydn anyway.
> Entry, Notebook 5 (1935–42), 15, *Northrop Frye's Fiction and Miscellaneous Writings* (2007), CW, 25.

HEALING
All healing is casting out the devils of nature. *And* the psyche we acquire from nature.
> Entry, Notebook 44 (1986–1991), 746, *Northrop Frye's Late Notebooks, 1982–1990: Architecture of the Spiritual World* (2000), CW, 5.

HEALTH
It is easier to believe that a society which has been "sick" for thousands of years will get well immediately than to believe that we shall come to an immediate agreement on what constitutes health.
> "The Ethics of Change: The Role of the University" (1968), *Northrop Frye's Writings on Education* (2001), CW, 7.

HEART
Besides, the world, unlike nature, always betrays the heart that loves her.
> "The Critical Discipline" (1960), *Northrop Frye's Writings on Education* (2001), CW, 7.

His moral and social values are where those of most sensible people are, and where the heart usually is in the body, a little left of centre.
> "Preface and Introduction to Pratt's Poetry" (1958), referring to E.J. Pratt, *Northrop Frye on Canada* (2003), CW, 12.

HEAVEN
Heaven exists for me, but I always try to think of it as really the actualization of something present, rather than something to be prepared for in the future.
> "On *The Great Code* (II)" (1982), *Interviews with Northrop Frye* (2008), CW, 24.

Heaven *is* this world as it appears to the awakened imagination....
> "Part One: The Argument," *Fearful Symmetry: A Study of William Blake* (1947, 2004), CW, 14.

I suppose heaven could be defined as the gaining of the ability to explore the underground caverns of time at will.
> Entry, 24 Jan. 1949, 117, *The Diaries of Northrop Frye: 1942–1955* (2001), CW, 8.

Perhaps the myth of heaven as a place where harp playing is a compulsory cultural accomplishment will come true, and the theology and metaphysics of the future will be understood musically rather than verbally.
> "Speculation and Concern" (1966), *Northrop Frye's Writings on Education* (2001), CW, 7.

HEAVEN & HELL
Hell is the world created by man, and heaven, or at least the way to it, is the world created through man by God.
> *The Double Vision* (1991), *Northrop Frye on Religion* (2000), CW, 4.

When you have a myth like a paradise lost in the past or a hell threatening you in the future, you have myths which are distorted by the anxieties of time. The great strength of myth is that it really has no past or future, everything is in the present tense.
> "Nature and Civilization" (1989), *Interviews with Northrop Frye* (2008), CW, 24.

The reality of hell is the fact that we put it there, and the unreality of paradise is that we failed to put it there. If you transpose these past and future things into the present tense you have the genuine myth.

"Nature and Civilization" (1989), *Interviews with Northrop Frye* (2008), CW, 24.

HEBRAISM

I think that if Hellenism can come to symbolize a love of beauty, and Hebraism a moral energy, the cultural heritage of the English-speaking nations can also come to symbolize a sense of individual freedom which is one of the permanent achievements of human history, and will remain so however dark and troubled our future may become.

"The Developing Imagination" (1962), *Northrop Frye's Writings on Education* (2001), CW, 7.

HEBREW LANGUAGE

Hebrew and Greek are, to use a useful French distinction, only the *langue* of the Bible; the *langage* is something else again.

"The Meaning of Recreation: Humanism in Society" (1979), referring to the usage of French theorist Ferdinand de Saussure, *Northrop Frye on Religion* (2000), CW, 4.

HELL

Hell doesn't "exist," but it's the world we *have been* making and ought to stop making. It's the pure past, the bottom of God's revelation to Job.

Entry, Notebook 44 (1986–91), 695, *Northrop Frye's Late Notebooks, 1982–1990: Architecture of the Spiritual World* (2000), CW, 5.

Hell is ideological crap; nothingness is the true myth.

Entry, Notebook 27 (1986), 495, *Northrop Frye's Late Notebooks, 1982–1990: Architecture of the Spiritual World* (2000), CW, 5.

Hell is often supposed to be an after-death state created by God to which people are eternally tortured for finite offences. But this doctrine is merely one more example of the depravity of the human mind that thought it up. Man alone is responsible for hell, and much as he would like to pursue his cruelties beyond the grave, he is blocked from doing so.

The Double Vision (1991), *Northrop Frye on Religion* (2000), CW, 4.

The teaching of hell fire is undoubtedly bad, yet it has some psychological point: it brings one face to face with one of the limits of the human mind, & instils a fear which often acts as a spur to the imagination that without it might get nowhere.

Entry, 6 Feb. 1949, 162, *The Diaries of Northrop Frye: 1942–1955* (2001), CW, 8.

HERE & NOW

Nothing in Jesus' teaching seems to have been more difficult for his followers to grasp than his principle of the hereness of here.

"The Journey as Metaphor" (1985), *"The Secular Scripture" and Other Writings on Critical Theory, 1976–1991* (2006), CW, 18.

HERITAGE

Our cultural heritage, then, is our real and repressed social past, not the past of historical record but the great dreams of the arts, which keep recurring to haunt us with a sense of how little we know of the real dimensions of our own experiences.

Creation and Recreation (1980), *Northrop Frye on Religion* (2000), CW, 4.

HEROES

The true hero is the man who, whether as thinker, fighter, artist, martyr, or ordinary worker, helps in achieving the apocalyptic vision of art; and an act is anything that has a real relation to that achievement.

"Blake's Treatment of the Archetype" (1950), expressing Blake's view, *Northrop Frye on Milton and Blake* (2005), CW, 16.

The hero's act has thrown a switch in a larger machine than his own life, or even his own society.

"Third Essay: Archetypal Criticism: Theory of Myths" (1957), *Anatomy of Criticism: Four Essays* (2006), CW, 22.

The tragic hero is very great as compared with us, but there is something else, something on the side of him opposite the audience, compared to which he is small.

"Third Essay: Archetypal Criticism: Theory of Myths" (1957), *Anatomy of Criticism: Four Essays* (2006), CW, 22.

Myths of gods emerge into legends of heroes; legends of heroes merge into plots of tragedies and comedies; plots of tragedies and comedies merge into plots of more or less realistic fiction.

"First Essay: Historical Criticism: Theory of Modes" (1957), *Anatomy of Criticism: Four Essays* (2006), CW, 22.

… there is the association between the heroic and the demonic in that the demonic is the root of the heroic.

"On Evil" (1985), *Interviews with Northrop Frye* (2008), CW, 24.

HEROISM

The Christian teaching, as I understand it, is that the greatest form of heroism expresses itself in endurance and in resisting evil rather than in engaging oneself in a destructive activity.

"On Evil" (1985), *Interviews with Northrop Frye* (2008), CW, 24.

Man tends to admire that: Satan is usually man's model when man tries to be heroic, and it's this admiration for Satan that produces all our wars and all our destructive heroes.

"The Writer as Prophet: Milton, Blake, Swift, Shaw" (1950), *Northrop Frye on Literature and Society, 1936–1989: Unpublished Papers* (2002), CW, 10.

The conventional hero has always been ready to die if necessary; the heroism of today must be in the form of a readiness to survive.

"To the Class of '62 at Queen's" (1962), *Northrop Frye's Writings on Education* (2001), CW, 7.

HIERARCHY

Order without hierarchy, because hierarchy creates a limited order.

"Northrop Frye in Conversation" (1989), identifying "a principle of mine," *Interviews with Northrop Frye* (2008), CW, 24.

HIPPIE MOVEMENT

In adolescence particularly there are strong pressures toward introversion on the one hand, and rigid conformity to group action on the other. Both of these, as we saw in the hippie movement of a few years ago, tend to make a fetish of inarticulateness.

"Teaching the Humanities Today" (1977), *Northrop Frye's Writings on Education* (2001), CW, 7.

For many people the hippie movement is something to drop into and out of.

"Into the Wilderness" (1969), *Interviews with Northrop Frye* (2008), CW, 24.

A few years ago it was they who led the cult of doing one's own thing, but now they are turning increasingly to communes and social settlements, rather like the Utopian projects of the nineteenth century.

"The Quality of Life in the '70s" (1971), *Northrop Frye on Modern Culture* (2003), CW, 11.

HISTORIANS

The ideal historian, who has finally got rid of all passion, pride and prejudice, doesn't exist, and if he did exist he'd be the Recording Angel.

"Reinhold Niebuhr, 'The Irony of American History,' and Herbert Butterfield, 'History and Human Relations,'" (1952–53), *Northrop Frye on Literature and Society, 1936–1989: Unpublished Papers* (2002), CW, 10.

We notice that when a historian's scheme gets to a certain point of comprehensiveness it becomes mythical in shape, and so approaches the poetic in its structure.

"New Directions from Old" (1960), *"The Educated Imagination" and Other Writings on Critical Theory, 1933–1963* (2006), CW, 21.

I think it is obvious that anybody teaching history at a university here today is going to be a middle-class, twentieth-century Canadian. This gives him a position, a stance, a perspective on things which would not be that of somebody teaching in Indonesia or somebody teaching in the nineteenth century.

"The Only Genuine Revolution" (1969), *Interviews with Northrop Frye* (2008), CW, 24.

Here again what is of primary importance is the quality of our historical imagination, the ability, if I may try to express something very difficult to express, to see things, not merely as objects confronting us, but as growing in time, as having come out of our own past and moving towards our own future.

"Canada: New World Without Revolution" (1975), *Northrop Frye on Canada* (2003), CW, 12.

History is diachronic but history-*writing* is synchronic: it selects, rejects, censors, condenses & displaces just as the dream does.

Entry, Notebook 50 (1987–90), 303, *Northrop Frye's Late Notebooks, 1982–1990: Architecture of the Spiritual World* (2000), CW, 5.

HISTORY

The record of human history is so unutterably foul and never shows you a successful bid for freedom or dignity that isn't instantly smothered by a new kind of tyranny.

"Back to the Garden" (1982), *Interviews with Northrop Frye* (2008), CW, 24.

When I was young, George VI was the Emperor of India, and Hitler ruled an empire from Norway to Baghdad. All that has vanished into nothingness. That says to me that history is a process of continuing dissolution, and that the things that survive are the creative and the imaginative products.

"Canadian and American Values" (1988), *Interviews with Northrop Frye* (2008), CW, 24.

I think that probably every cycle is just a failed spiral, and that history and nature collapse into cycles because they are too lazy to start again at another level.

"Symbolism in the Bible" (1981–82), *Northrop Frye's Notebooks and Lectures on the Bible and Other Religious Texts* (2003), CW, 13.

The lesson of history, that there is nothing new under the sun and that we solve all problems simply by surviving them, might be rather discouraging to young people.

"Reviews of Television Programs for the Canadian Radio-Television Commission ... November 1971–March 1972" (1972), *Northrop Frye on Literature and Society, 1936–1989: Unpublished Papers* (2002), CW, 10.

... and history, which is essentially the actualizing of memory.

"The Primary Necessities of Existence" (1985), *Interviews with Northrop Frye* (2008), CW, 24.

... a linear chronicle is a wild fairy tale in which the fate of an empire hangs on the shape of a beauty's nose, or the murder of a noble moron touches off a world war.

"Part One: The Argument," *Fearful Symmetry: A Study of William Blake* (1947, 2004), CW, 14.

A strong and prosperous nation does not take kindly to a philosophy of history. It needs no great white hope in the future, nor promise in the past; it lives in the pure present as a causal agent, not as an actor in a larger drama.

"The Augustinian Interpretation of History" (1935–36), *Northrop Frye's Student Essays, 1932–1938* (1997), CW, 3.

Besides, history usually has to be arranged a good deal before it will fit the parable form, and, in general, historical parables are to history much what bestiaries are to zoology.

"History and Myth in the Bible" (1975), *Northrop Frye on Religion* (2000), CW, 4.

History begins as chronicle: history in the proper sense begins when chronicle is realized to be the content or raw material of history.

"*Pistis* and *Mythos*" (1972), *Northrop Frye on Religion* (2000), CW, 4.

HISTORY, CANADIAN

The central fact of Canadian history: the rejection of the American revolution.

"Address, Royal Society of Canada, 11 June 1956," *Studia Varia*, No. 24, 1957.

It has been said that those who do not learn history are condemned to repeat it: this means very little, because we are all in the position of voters in a Canadian election, condemned to repeat history anyway whether we learn it or not. But those who refuse to confront their own real past, in whatever form, are condemning themselves to die without having been born.

Creation and Recreation (1980), *Northrop Frye on Religion* (2000), CW, 4.

When we don't think of Canadian history as dull we think of it as theatrical. We think of it as a pageant of canoes and furs and tortures. And, when we think of it as a pageant, of course, we put it at a distance from us, and make it unreal.

"View of Canada" (1976), *Northrop Frye on Canada* (2003), CW, 12.

HISTORY, NATURAL

If you are studying natural history, no matter how fascinated you may be by anything that has eight legs, you can't just lump together an octopus and a spider and a string quartet.

"Sir James Frazer" (1959), *"The Educated Imagination" and Other Writings on Critical Theory, 1933–1963* (2006), CW, 21.

HISTORY & MYTH

Myth is the narrative shape of history, as in "Decline and Fall."

Entry, Notes 54-5 (1976), 63, *Northrop Frye's Notebooks and Lectures on the Bible and Other Religious Texts* (2003), CW, 13.

In a sense the historical is the opposite of the mythical, and to tell a historian that what gives shape to his book is a myth would sound to him vaguely insulting.

"New Directions from Old" (1960), *"The Educated Imagination" and Other Writings on Critical Theory, 1933–1963* (2006), CW, 21.

Man creates what he calls history as a screen to conceal the workings of the apocalypse from himself.

"Typology II," *The Great Code* (1982), *The Great Code: The Bible and Literature* (2006), CW, 19.

A more traditional language would say that myth *redeems* history: assigns it to its real place in the human panorama.

"Myth I," *The Great Code* (1982), *The Great Code: The Bible and Literature* (2006), CW, 19.

History itself is designed to record events, or, as we may say, to provide a primary verbal imitation of events. But it also, unconsciously perhaps, illustrates and provides examples for the poetic vision.

"The Road of Excess" (1970), *Northrop Frye on Milton and Blake* (2005), CW, 16.

The poet finds increasingly that he can deal with history only to the extent that history supplies him with, or affords a pretext for, the comic, tragic, romantic, or ironic myths that he actually uses.

"New Directions from Old" (1960), *"The Educated Imagination" and Other Writings on Critical Theory, 1933–1963* (2006), CW, 21.

The climb up the ladder from the surface of this earth is a climb out of history. The climb up from the subterranean world to the surface of this one is a climb *into* history: its type is the Exodus, the beginning of the history of Israel, and its antitype the Resurrection.

Entry, Notebook 50 (1987–90), 452, *Northrop Frye's Late Notebooks, 1982–1990: Architecture of the Spiritual World* (2000), CW, 5.

The point is not that myth falsifies history, but that history falsifies primary concern. The "overthought" is the ideological content, or what is, more or less, being "said." The "underthought" is the progression of metaphors that express the primary concerns.

Entry, Notebook 44 (1986–91), 511, employing G.M. Hopkins's terms for thought, *Northrop Frye's Late Notebooks, 1982–1990: Architecture of the Spiritual World* (2000), CW, 5.

Anyway, history has no shape except what it derives from myth.

Entry, Notes 53 (1989–90), 167, *Northrop Frye's Late Notebooks, 1982–1990: Architecture of the Spiritual World* (2000), CW, 6.

Similarly you never get history in literature: you get virtual history, history assimilated to myth.

Entry, Notebook 44 (1986–91), 286, *Northrop Frye's Late Notebooks, 1982–1990: Architecture of the Spiritual World* (2000), CW, 5.

For anything with a history that history is part of the context which determines meaning. Hence the descent of a literary work from a mythical structure is part of its critical interpretation. For anything with a *telos* or direction of development that *telos* is similarly part of the context and the meaning.

Entry, Notebook 24 (1970–72), 2, *The "Third Book" Notebooks of Northrop Frye, 1964–1972: The Critical Comedy* (2002), CW, 9.

The basis of myth is the repeating cycle of knowledge, with nothing new under the sun; the basis of history is the unique experience, which means there isn't any shape to history except what myth gives it. Nor is there any experience to myth except what it gets from history.

Entry, Notes 53 (1989–90), 172, *Northrop Frye's Late Notebooks, 1982–1990: Architecture of the Spiritual World* (2000), CW, 6.

History-experience-unique vs. Myth-insight-repetitive.

Entry, Notebook 46 (1980s–90), 28, *Northrop Frye's Late Notebooks, 1982–1990: Architecture of the Spiritual World* (2000), CW, 6.

As time goes on, and historical tradition becomes more tenuous, only the events with conventional poetic associations can carry the thrilling magic of a great name.

"Nature and Homer" (1958), *"The Educated Imagination" and Other Writings on Critical Theory, 1933–1963* (2006), CW, 21.

HITLER, ADOLF
Hearing Hitler's 1939 speeches was a terrifying & hideous experience: Churchill, too, gave a sense of archaic greatness. True, all the visual effects of movies and photography helped build up Hitler; but I wonder if he could have survived television. For in television you can turn the sound off, & that would reduce Hitler to Charlie Chaplin in no time.

Entry, Notebook 19 (1964–67), 166, *The "Third Book" Notebooks of Northrop Frye, 1964–1972: The Critical Comedy* (2002), CW, 9.

The only mark of real greatness in Hitler was the seriousness with which he accepted his Antichrist role, his pedantic insistence that even a child saying grace at meals should thank his Führer for his bread.

"The Eternal Tramp" (1947), *Northrop Frye on Modern Culture* (2003), CW, 11.

HOCKEY
Watching a hockey game is not directly a spectator sport, because anyone interested enough in hockey to watch a game knows how the game is played, & through that knowledge can see much *more* of what is going on, with or without a commentator, than the players.

Entry, Notebook 11f (1969–70), 110, *Northrop Frye's Notebooks and Lectures on the Bible and Other Religious Texts* (2003), CW, 13.

HOLIDAYS
Curious how much holidaying consists of running away from holy days.

Entry, Notebook 44 (1986–91), 675, *Northrop Frye's Late Notebooks, 1982–1990: Architecture of the Spiritual World* (2000), CW, 5.

HOLOMYTH
What I then started to look for was not a monomyth but a holomyth, a map of the verbal imagination that would provide a context for individual works. I think the Bible comes closer to indicating what such a holomyth would be like than any other work in our culture.

Entry, Notes 52 (1982–90), 620, *Northrop Frye's Late Notebooks, 1982–1990: Architecture of the Spiritual World* (2000), CW, 6.

HOMOSEXUALITY
I suppose Christianity belongs primarily to the onward and upward group. Its founder, apparently, was a homosexual with a beloved disciple and a mother fixation so intense that he even insisted his mother was a virgin. Or somebody did.

Entry, Notebook 19 (1964–67), 339, *The "Third Book" Notebooks of Northrop Frye, 1964–1972: The Critical Comedy* (2002), CW, 9.

HONESTY
The only person who is honest is the person who is consistently honest, and what is true of the moral life is true of the intellectual life as well.

"Education and the Rejection of Reality" (1971), *Northrop Frye's Writings on Education* (2001), CW, 7.

HOPE

Hope springs eternal: unfortunately it usually springs prematurely.
> *The Double Vision* (1991), *Northrop Frye on Religion* (2000), CW, 4.

If faith is the substance or hypostatis of hope, does that mean that literature as a whole is an expression of hope? Or that polytheism is?
> Entry, Notebook 50 (1987–90), 89, *Northrop Frye's Late Notebooks, 1982–1990: Architecture of the Spiritual World* (2000), CW, 5.

Here the virtue is hope rather than faith, and the opposite of hope is not doubt, but despair. Again, despair is not the enemy of hope but the dialectical complement of hope, the thing that hope must fight against if it's to attain its reality.
> "Symbolism in the Bible" (1981–82), *Northrop Frye's Notebooks and Lectures on the Bible and Other Religious Texts* (2003), CW, 13.

It's one thing to believe in God, but nobody can believe in Godot. He isn't there. He will never come. I would say that the alternative to this kind of hope is a genuine hope, which I should locate in the present rather than in the future, and which takes a form of realization rather than expectation.
> "Style and Image in the Twentieth Century" (1967), *Interviews with Northrop Frye* (2008), CW, 24.

Hope without love is ineffectual, just as faith without love is intolerant. But hope is what divides those who see the leap in the dark as the end of things from those who see it also as a new beginning.
> "The Leap in the Dark" (1971), *Northrop Frye on Religion* (2000), CW, 4.

HUMANISM

The humanist ideal offered a "liberal" education to those who were economically liberated: for it, the study of the greatest achievements of humanity provided the only genuine vision of freedom that society possessed.
> *The Critical Path: An Essay on the Social Context of Literary Criticism* (1971), *"The Critical Path" and Other Writings on Critical Theory, 1963–1975* (2009), CW, 27.

I referred above to the humanist tradition in education, a form of education based primarily on literature. The strength of humanism lay in its exploitation of a central fact about literature: that the arts do not, like the sciences, evolve and improve, but revolve around classics or models.
> "The Developing Imagination" (1962), *Northrop Frye's Writings on Education* (2001), CW, 7.

As long as man lives in the world, he will need the perspective and attitude of the scientist; but to the extent that he has created the world he lives in, feels responsible for it and has a concern for its destiny, which is also his own destiny, he will need the perspective and attitude of the humanist.
> "Speculation and Concern" (1966), *Northrop Frye's Writings on Education* (2001), CW, 7.

Everything a humanist most values comes out of some loophole or anomaly in the social order.
> "Preface to *On Education*" (1988), *Northrop Frye's Writings on Education* (2001), CW, 7.

The *professional* humanist hardly exists; if I am a humanist, I'm one in virtue of my interests & social attitudes, not my job.
> Entry, Notebook 11f (1969–70), 147, *Northrop Frye's Notebooks and Lectures on the Bible and Other Religious Texts* (2003), CW, 13.

HUMANITIES

In short, the study of literature belongs to the "humanities," and the humanities, as their name indicates, can take only the human view of the superhuman.
> "Second Essay: Ethical Criticism: Theory of Symbols" (1957), *Anatomy of Criticism: Four Essays* (2006), CW, 22.

But authority in the humanities comes from certain great artists who always have been and always will be models of the highest possible achievement in their fields, classics as we call them. Others may come who will equal them, but no one will ever improve on them.

"Education and the Humanities" (1947), *Northrop Frye's Writings on Education* (2001), CW, 7.

The humanities have always to fight for themselves, whatever the economic conditions, but as they are inherently depressed, a boom period in the economy is disastrous for them. When the market expands, many drift into them with no real vocation for or commitment to them; and for teaching the humanities one needs the vocation and the commitment of the twelve disciples.

"Preface to *ADE and ADFL Bulletins*" (1976), *Northrop Frye's Writings on Education* (2001), CW, 7.

HUMANITY

... becoming finite means becoming genuinely human.

"Conclusion to *Literary History of Canada*" (1965), *Northrop Frye on Canada* (2003), CW, 12.

If we realize that human beings quite as intelligent as ourselves have been around for half a million years, we get quite a different slant on things.

Entry, Notebook 12 (1968–70), 366, *The "Third Book" Notebooks of Northrop Frye, 1964–1972: The Critical Comedy* (2002), CW, 9.

Humanity, alone of all organisms, has elected to transform its environment instead of simply adapting to it, and so only human beings have a lifelong commitment to experiment, trial and error, uncertainty, and all the other burdens of continuing knowledge.

"Some Reflections on Life and Habit" (1988), *Northrop Frye's Writings on the Eighteenth and Nineteenth Centuries* (2005), CW, 17.

Anyway, the difference between the merely human & the genuinely human is crucial: it lets the daylight of the infinite & eternal into the closed human situation.

Entry, Notebook 21 (1969–76), 46, *Northrop Frye's Notebooks and Lectures on the Bible and Other Religious Texts* (2003), CW, 13.

I personally don't see why humanity still exists without some power that cares more about it than it does about itself, as history records nothing persistent or continuous except the impulse to self-destruction.

Entry, Notebook 50 (1987–90), 546, *Northrop Frye's Late Notebooks, 1982–1990: Architecture of the Spiritual World* (2000), CW, 5.

But humanity's primary duty is not to be natural but to be human.

The Double Vision (1991), *Northrop Frye on Religion* (2000), CW, 4.

Even if there are no paradises, lost or hidden, no angels, no divine presence and no hell, there is still the range of human mentality, which could be immensely more powerful and efficient than it normally is, or fall far below even its average performance now.

"First Variation: The Mountain," *Words with Power: Being a Second Study of "The Bible and Literature"* (1990), CW, 26.

HUMILITY

Humility is partly a negative virtue, a way of avoiding self-exposure and disarming criticism. But it can be a positive virtue too: a sense of one's own limitations is the basis of all security, even of sanity.

"Sermon in Merton College Chapel" (1970), *Northrop Frye on Religion* (2000), CW, 4.

HUMOUR

All genuine humour in one sense is gallows humour, because humour begins in the accepting of the limits of the human condition.

"Yorick: The Romantic Macabre" (1968), *Northrop Frye's Writings on the Eighteenth and Nineteenth Centuries* (2005), CW, 17.

To say that a person has no sense of humour amounts to saying that that person is deficient in a sense of reality.

Entry, Notebook 44 (1986–91), 504, *Northrop Frye's Late Notebooks, 1982–1990: Architecture of the Spiritual World* (2000), CW, 5.

The humorous vision sees things in proportion because it sees them out of proportion. That means that the customary proportions of things are somehow all wrong. Probably that's

why we have dreams: to remind us every night that we've spent the previous day in a world of petrified nonsense.
"Tribute to Robert Zend" (1985), *Northrop Frye on Canada* (2003), CW, 12.

Humour, innocence, and nakedness go together, as do solemnity, aggressiveness, and fig leaves.
"*Rencontre:* The General Editor's Introduction" (1960s), referring to Adam's fall in Milton's *Paradise Lost*, *Northrop Frye on Literature and Society, 1936–1989: Unpublished Papers* (2002), CW, 10.

HUXLEY, ALDOUS
I've said already that I've never written fiction because Huxley's novels are there to remind me of how bad it would be.
"New Fictional Formulas: Notebook 20" (after 1965), 18, *Northrop Frye's Fiction and Miscellaneous Writings* (2007), CW, 25.

HYMNS
As for the Blake, "Jerusalem" is the greatest hymn in the English language. While I'm not sure that any musical setting is definitive, that's as good a one as I know.
"Music in My Life" (1985), referring to Sir Hubert Parry's setting of Blake's text, *Interviews with Northrop Frye* (2008), CW, 24.

I managed a bit of outrage myself occasionally: in my opinion two of the greatest hymns ever written are Blake's "Jerusalem" and Luther's "Ein Feste Burg," and there were proposals to throw out both. (They stayed in.)
"Stanley Llewellyn Osborne" (1971), referring to advisory work of the United Church of Canada's committee on hymnology, *Northrop Frye on Religion* (2000), CW, 4.

HYPNOTISM
Mediums have the power to animate & make telekinetic their dreams; dictators are the link between mediumism & hypnosis. The hypnotized subject behaves like a figure in a dream.
Entry, Notebook 33 (1946–50), 58, *Northrop Frye's Notebooks on Romance* (2004), CW, 15.

HYPOCRISY
Hypocrisy has been called the tribute that vice pays to virtue, but to know that you're saying one thing and thinking another requires a self-discipline that's practically a virtue in itself. Certainly it's often an essential virtue for a public figure.
"Northrop Frye on Shakespeare: III, *The Bolingbroke Plays: Richard II* and *Henry IV*" (1986), *Northrop Frye's Writings on Shakespeare and the Renaissance* (2010), CW, 28.

HYSTERIA
This social dimension of madness is, to put it mildly, still with us in the century of Fascism, Communism, and the parasites in the democracies who devote themselves to spreading hysteria.
"The Imaginative and the Imaginary" (1962), *"The Educated Imagination" and Other Writings on Critical Theory, 1933–1963* (2006), CW, 21.

Traditionally, the difference between sanity and hysteria, between reality and hallucination, had always been that sanity and reality lasted longer, and were continuous in a way that their opposites could not be.
"The University and Personal Life: Student Anarchism and the Educational Contract" (1968), *Northrop Frye's Writings on Education* (2001), CW, 7.

All I can suggest is that while nothing is more insistent, demanding, and obviously important than this year's hysterias, nothing is more pathetically ludicrous than the hysterias of last year.
"Hart House Rededicated" (1969), *Northrop Frye's Writings on Education* (2001), CW, 7.

I

I

Nothing *really* exists except "I"; all other existences are inferred. Yet we're so constituted that we work into this backwards. We start by accepting an inferred existence, whether God or nature, & work our way towards our own identity of "I" as the *telos* of that.

    Entry, Notebook 21 (1969–76), 399, *Northrop Frye's Notebooks and Lectures on the Bible and Other Religious Texts* (2003), CW, 13.

IDEALS

The actual makes the ideal look helpless and the ideal makes the actual look absurd.

    "Part Two: The Development of the Symbolism," *Fearful Symmetry: A Study of William Blake* (1947, 2004), CW, 14.

All nations have such a buried or uncreated ideal ... and no nation has been more preoccupied with it than Canada.

    The Modern Century (1967), *Northrop Frye on Modern Culture* (2003), CW, 11.

There are no future ideals to be attained: there are only present ones to be realized.

    "Convocation Address, York University" (1969), *Northrop Frye's Writings on Education* (2001), CW, 7.

IDEAS

No idea is anything more than a half-truth unless it contains its own opposite, and is expanded by its own denial or qualification.

    The Modern Century (1967), *Northrop Frye on Modern Culture* (2003), CW, 11.

Some of the best people I know have intuitions of great ideas, and have spent the rest of their lives confusing the understanding of the ideas with their own emotional pleasure at having felt the intuition of them.

    Entry, Notebook 42b: Notes I (1942–44), 24b, *Northrop Frye's Fiction and Miscellaneous Writings* (2007), CW, 25.

It was consistent for the anarchy and hysteria of the late sixties to attack structure. It goes along with the fallacy of the substantial idea: one can't have "ideas" without being able to express them.

    "On Education I" (after 1960s), 24, *Northrop Frye's Fiction and Miscellaneous Writings* (2007), CW, 25.

Hence, really, all ideas are unborn.

    Entry, Notebook 3 (1946–48), *Northrop Frye's Notebooks and Lectures on the Bible and Other Religious Texts* (2003), CW, 13.

There cannot be many academics in any age who are so highly integrated that they can hardly have an idea on any subject whatever that is not, or may not be, or may not produce something, relevant to their scholarly work.

    "Introduction," "A History of Communications," by Harold A. Innis (1982), *Northrop Frye on Canada* (2003), CW, 12.

Maybe some day I'll get to the point of sanctity where the difference between my ideas & other peoples' ideas will cease to exist, but I'm sure as hell not at that stage now, & every *word* of the Frye Encyclopedia is going to be mine, do you hear? mine! mine!! *mine!!!*

    Entry, Notebook 21 (1969–76), 250, touching upon an unrealized compilation of his reflections, perhaps titled "Century of Meditations," *Northrop Frye's Notebooks and Lectures on the Bible and Other Religious Texts* (2003), CW, 13.

IDENTITIES

Narcissus, looking for things to "identify" with in order to fall in love with his own reflection, seems to be a bad model for literary study, at least beyond childhood.
"Book Learning and Barricades" (1968), *Northrop Frye's Writings on Education* (2001), CW, 7.

Literature, like mythology, is largely an art of misleading analogies and mistaken identities.
"Myth, Fiction, and Displacement" (1961), *"The Educated Imagination" and Other Writings on Critical Theory, 1933–1963* (2006), CW, 21.

The literary universe, therefore, is a universe in which everything is potentially identical with everything else.
"Second Essay: Ethical Criticism: Theory of Symbols" (1957), *Anatomy of Criticism: Four Essays* (2006), CW, 22.

I'm not sure what I mean by identity, but one of the things it means is: a state of being where there's nothing to write about. That is, where one *contains* all subjects as potential, instead of being subjected to events.
Entry, Notebook 10 (late 1964–72), 28, *Northrop Frye's Notebooks on Romance* (2004), CW, 15.

Identity is the opposite of similarity or likeness, and total identity is not uniformity, still less monotony, but a unity of various things.
"Second Essay: Ethical Criticism: Theory of Symbols" (1957), *Anatomy of Criticism: Four Essays* (2006), CW, 22.

The recovery of identity is not the feeling that I am myself and not another, but the realization that there is only one man, one mind, and one world, and that all walls of partition have been broken down forever.
"The Return of Eden: Five Essays on Milton's Epics" (1965), *Northrop Frye on Milton and Blake* (2005), CW, 16.

The basis of poetic language is the metaphor, and the metaphor, in its radical form, is a statement of identity: "This is that." In all our ordinary experience the metaphor is non-literal: nobody but a savage or a lunatic can take metaphor literally.

"Towards Defining an Age of Sensibility" (1956), *Northrop Frye's Writings on the Eighteenth and Nineteenth Centuries* (2005), CW, 17.

Every one should be proud of being what he is and of where he is, otherwise something has gone seriously wrong.
"Italy in Canada" (1990), *Northrop Frye on Canada* (2003), CW, 12.

Identity cannot be preserved either by cutting oneself off from others or by dissolving oneself in others, but only by the flexibility of a larger group where there are great variations of character, and sharp differences of opinion and emphasis, yet all contained within the sense of a common heritage and a common destiny.
"Foreword," *The Prospect of Change* (1965), edited by Abraham Rotstein.

To identify something is first of all to put it in the category of things to which it belongs: the first step in identity is the realization *humanus sum*. We belong to something before we are anything, nor does growing in being diminish the link of belonging.
"The Knowledge of Good and Evil" (1966), *Northrop Frye's Writings on Education* (2001), CW, 7.

Identity is local and regional, rooted in the imagination and in works of culture; unity is national in reference, international in perspective, and rooted in political feeling.
Preface, *The Bush Garden* (1971), *Northrop Frye on Canada* (2003), CW, 12.

This story of the loss and regaining of identity is, I think, the framework of all literature. Inside it comes the story of the hero with a thousand faces, as one critic calls him, whose adventures, death, disappearance, and marriage or resurrection are the focal points of what later become romance and tragedy and satire and comedy in fiction, and the emotional moods that take their place in such forms as the lyric, which normally doesn't tell a story.
"The Singing School," *The Educated Imagination* (1963), *"The Educated Imagination" and Other*

Writings on Critical Theory, 1933–1963 (2006), CW, 21.

If the world really does outgrow its vast jungle cities, its strangling international cartels, and the deadlocked hostility of its superpowers, it may break up into smaller units in which the individual can find once more an identity and a function.
"The Authority of Learning" (1984), *Northrop Frye's Writings on Education* (2001), CW, 7.

Alternation of "oceanic" merging with a totality and the individual feeling he's a whole of which the totality is a part corresponds to identity with and identity as.
Entry, Notebook 44 (1986–91), 156, *Northrop Frye's Late Notebooks, 1982–1990: Architecture of the Spiritual World* (2000), CW, 5.

The road to identity runs through a growing awareness of role-playing, of understanding the extent to which one is playing ritual games in society.
"Reviews of Television Programs for the Canadian Radio-Television Commission ... November 1971–March 1972" (1972), *Northrop Frye on Literature and Society, 1936–1989: Unpublished Papers* (2002), CW, 10.

IDEOLOGIES

If I were explaining this situation in my own words, I should say that an ideology expresses secondary and derivative human concerns, and that what ideologies are derived from is mythology, which expresses the primary desires of existence, along with the anxieties attached to their frustration.... I introduce the point because ideology is always nostalgic for the past or expectant of the future, or both, whereas mythology transposes everything into a present directly confronting the reader.
"In the Earth, or in the Air?" (1986), *Northrop Frye's Writings on the Eighteenth and Nineteenth Centuries* (2005), CW, 17.

All ideologies sooner or later get to be circumvented by cynicism and defended by hysteria, and that principle will meet you everywhere you turn in a world driven crazy by ideologies, like ours.

Northrop Frye on Shakespeare (1986), *Northrop Frye's Writings on Shakespeare and the Renaissance* (2010), CW, 28.

As a literary critic, I am interested in the fact that Freud and Marx are the two most influential thinkers in the world today, that both of them developed an encyclopedic programme that they called scientific, and that nine-tenths of the science of both turns out to be applied mythology.
"Speculation and Concern" (1966), *Northrop Frye's Writings on Education* (2001), CW, 7.

It makes no difference what any modern power calls its ideology: its end product will be the same, a bureaucracy of officials who have authority but no freedom.
"Novels on Several Occasions" (1950–51), *Northrop Frye on Twentieth-Century Literature* (2010), CW, 29.

Ideology functions properly in a tolerance that tries to contain the opposite. Dogmas that exclude the opposite are pernicious. The worst are those that back up political dogma with a religious or quasi-religious one.
Entry, Notebook 44 (1986–91), 7, *Northrop Frye's Late Notebooks, 1982–1990: Architecture of the Spiritual World* (2000), CW, 5.

One gets rather weary of the bourgeois masochism that keeps insisting that we should be receptive to all ideologies except our own, and that we should always be uniformly and indiscriminately suspicious of that.
"Unpublished Introduction to *Beyond Communication*" (1989), *Northrop Frye's Writings on Education* (2001), CW, 7.

Once an ideology goes downhill, it becomes too stupid even to understand itself.
Entry, Notebook 44 (1986–91), 602, *Northrop Frye's Late Notebooks, 1982–1990: Architecture of the Spiritual World* (2000), CW, 5.

The myth is the ideology presented as imaginative possibility.
Entry, Notebook 50 (1987–90), 566, *Northrop Frye's Late Notebooks, 1982–1990: Architecture of the Spiritual World* (2000), CW, 5.

An ideology is thus an applied mythology, and its adaptations of myths are the ones that, when we are inside an ideological structure, we must believe, or say we believe.

"Sequence and Mode," *Words with Power: Being a Second Study of "The Bible and Literature"* (1990), CW, 26.

An ideology is most beneficial when it has least power, when its assumptions can be most freely challenged by others, when the terrible claws of ideological authority, inquisitions and secret police and the like, are not simply pared but removed altogether.

"Sequence and Mode," *Words with Power: Being a Second Study of "The Bible and Literature"* (1990), CW, 26.

IDOLATRY

Idolatry is the "literalizing" or objectifying of metaphor.

Entry, Notebook 46 (1980s–90), 61, *Northrop Frye's Late Notebooks, 1982–1990: Architecture of the Spiritual World* (2000), CW, 6.

The dialectical habit of mind produced the conception of the false god, a conception hardly intelligible to an educated pagan. All false gods, in the Christian view, were idols, and all idolatry came ultimately from the belief that there was something numinous in nature.

"Canada: New World Without Revolution" (1975), *Northrop Frye on Canada* (2003), CW, 12.

IGNORANCE

The really dangerous battlefront is not the one against ignorance, because ignorance is to some degree curable. It is the battlefront against prejudice and malice, the attitude of people who cannot stand the thought of a fully realized humanity, of human life without the hysteria and panic that controls every moment of their own lives.

"Language as the Home of Human Life" (1985), *Northrop Frye's Writings on Education* (2001), CW, 7.

ILIAD

With the *Iliad*, once for all, an objective and disinterested element enters into the poet's vision of human life.

"Fourth Essay: Rhetorical Criticism: Theory of Genres" (1957), *Anatomy of Criticism: Four Essays* (2006), CW, 22.

ILLITERACY

Wherever illiteracy is a problem, it's as fundamental a problem as [not] getting enough to eat or a place to sleep.

"The Motive for Metaphor," *The Educated Imagination* (1963), *"The Educated Imagination" and Other Writings on Critical Theory, 1933–1963* (2006), CW, 21.

ILLUMINATION

You can't expect something, or you'll find an oracle in every spiritual breeze that passes over you; you can't expect nothing, or you'll have in yourself no principle of escape.

Entry, 25 Feb. 1949, 223, *The Diaries of Northrop Frye: 1942–1955* (2001), CW, 8.

In the summer of 1951, in Seattle, I had an illumination about the passing from the oracular into the witty: a few years later, on St. Clair Ave., I had another about the passing from poetry through drama into prose. They were essentially the same illumination, perhaps: the movement from the esoteric to kerygma.

Entry, Notes 53 (1989–90), 43, *Northrop Frye's Late Notebooks, 1982–1990: Architecture of the Spiritual World* (2000), CW, 6.

Those who have crucial illuminations in their lives and record them in autobiography are mostly converts who up to their conversion have been largely unaware of the mental processes going on within them.

"Part Three: The Final Synthesis," *Fearful Symmetry: A Study of William Blake* (1947, 2004), CW, 14.

ILLUSION

In the world of illusion that we take for reality, the past is only the no longer and the future only the not yet: one vanishes into nothingness and the other, after proving itself to be much the same, vanishes after it.

"Shakespeare's *The Tempest*" (1979), *Northrop Frye's Writings on Shakespeare and the Renaissance* (2010), CW, 28.

The distinction between an empirical fact and an illusion is not a rational distinction, and cannot be logically proved. It is "proved" only by the practical and emotional necessity of assuming the distinction.

"Second Essay: Ethical Criticism: Theory of Symbols" (1957), *Anatomy of Criticism: Four Essays* (2006), CW, 22.

If the human race were to destroy both itself and the planet it lives on, that would be the final triumph of illusion.

"The Expanding World of Metaphor" (1984), *"The Secular Scripture" and Other Writings on Critical Theory, 1976–1991* (2006), CW, 18.

Nothing except a positive illusion can possibly have a future.

"Spirit and Symbol," *Words with Power: Being a Second Study of "The Bible and Literature"* (2008), CW, 26.

A little story of the working of advertising and propaganda in the modern world, with their magic-lantern techniques of projected images, will show us how successful they are in creating a world of pure illusion.

The Modern Century (1967), *Northrop Frye on Modern Culture* (2003), CW, 11.

We are surrounded by various forms of verbal illusion, and the genuine magic that inheres in the metaphors of poetry and the words of power is sometimes replaced by the degenerate magic of vogue or cliché words. It is the function of literature, as I see it, to recreate the primitive conception of the word of power, the metaphor that unites the subject and the object.

"Criticism as Education" (1979), *Northrop Frye's Writings on Education* (2001), CW, 7.

There are two kinds of illusion, the negative illusion which merely fails to be a reality, and the illusion which exists as a potentiality or model in the mind, as a fiction which does not yet exist but may be brought into existence or realized by a creative mind.

"On the Bible" (1989), *Northrop Frye on Religion* (2000), CW, 4.

Question: Is it possible that what millions of people have believed for thousands of years could still be an illusion? Answer: What else could it be?

Entry, Notes 53 (1989–90), 167, *Northrop Frye's Late Notebooks, 1982–1990: Architecture of the Spiritual World* (2000), CW, 6.

The world of dream and fantasy can be a source of models as well as illusions, and models are the first product of the chaos of hunch and intuition and guesswork and free association out of which the realities of art and science are made.

"The Bridge of Language" (1981), *Northrop Frye on Modern Culture* (2003), CW, 11.

I can never understand why people should think of disillusionment as something that makes one sad and doleful: surely living in an illusion is the greatest of torments, and becoming disillusioned ought to feel like being let out of jail.

"Baccalaureate Sermon" (1967), *Northrop Frye on Religion* (2000), CW, 4.

IMAGERY

Writing is lineal & successive: it answers to our need for a temporal continuum. The function of an image in a poem is to crumple up the continuum, to force us to group our impressions around a configurative centre.

Entry, Notebook 12 (1968–70), 97, *The "Third Book" Notebooks of Northrop Frye, 1964–1972: The Critical Comedy* (2002), CW, 9.

IMAGINATION

The work of imagination presents us with a vision, not of the personal greatness of the poet, but of something impersonal and far greater: the vision of a decisive act of spiritual freedom, the vision of the recreation of man.

"Second Essay: Ethical Criticism: Theory of Symbols" (1957), *Anatomy of Criticism: Four Essays* (2006), CW, 22.

The imagination, the principle of the unreal, breaks up and breaks down the tyranny of what is there by unifying itself with what is not there, and so suggesting the principle of variety in its existence.

"Wallace Stevens and the Variation Form" (1973), *Northrop Frye on Twentieth-Century Literature* (2010), CW, 29.

Imagination is not fantasy; what it produces is really and permanently there, and the creative mind is not the subjective or introverted mind.
"Convocation Address, Franklin and Marshall" (1968), *Northrop Frye's Writings on Education* (2001), CW, 7.

Literary meaning may best be described, perhaps, as hypothetical, and a hypothetical or assumed relation to the external world is part of what is usually meant by the word "imaginative." This word is to be distinguished from "imaginary," which usually refers to an assertive verbal structure that fails to make good its assertions.
"Second Essay: Ethical Criticism: Theory of Symbols" (1957), *Anatomy of Criticism: Four Essays* (2006), CW, 22.

As Shakespeare's Theseus ought to have said, every human being is of imagination all compact.
"Framework and Assumption" (1985), *"The Secular Scripture" and Other Writings on Critical Theory, 1976–1991* (2006), CW, 18.

For better or worse, it is through his literary imagination, such as it is, that modern man participates in society.
"Humanities in a New World" (1958), *Northrop Frye's Writings on Education* (2001), CW, 7.

What seems to reason and experience to be perpetually coming apart at the seams may seem to the imagination sometimes on the point of being put together again.
Preface, *The Bush Garden* (1971), *Northrop Frye on Canada* (2003), CW, 12.

But in the imagination anything goes that can be imagined, and the limit of the imagination is a totally human world. Here we recapture, in full consciousness, that original lost sense of identity with our surroundings, where there is nothing outside the mind of man, or something identical with the mind of man.

"The Motive for Metaphor," *The Educated Imagination* (1963), *"The Educated Imagination" and Other Writings on Critical Theory, 1933–1963* (2006), CW, 21.

The imaginative world is not a world to see but a world to see by.
Entry, Notebook 12 (1968–70), 460, *The "Third Book" Notebooks of Northrop Frye, 1964–1972: The Critical Comedy* (2002), CW, 9.

It is in the imagination that the world becomes more intelligible, and communication proceeds without the obstacles of cultural difference.
"Tradition and Change in the Theory of Criticism" (1969), *Northrop Frye on Literature and Society, 1936–1989: Unpublished Papers* (2002), CW, 10.

We all know how important the reason is in an irrational world, but the imagination, in a society of perverted imagination, is far more essential in making us understand that the phantasmagoria of current events is not real society, but only the appearance of real society.
"Elementary Teaching and Elemental Scholarship" (1963), *Northrop Frye's Writings on Education* (2001), CW, 7.

It is only the language of imagination that can take us beyond imagination.
"History and Myth in the Bible" (1976), *Northrop Frye on Religion* (2000), CW, 4.

Society depends heavily for its well-being on the handful of people who are imaginative in this sense. If the number became a majority, we should be living in a very different world, for it would be the world that we should then have the vision and the power to construct.
"The Developing Imagination" (1962), *Northrop Frye's Writings on Education* (2001), CW, 7.

Yes, because imagination is simply seeing at its most concentrated. Seeing at its least concentrated is simply seeing what is there, what is presented, what is the datum. But seeing at its greatest power of concentration is also creating what you see.

"The Personal Cosmos of William Blake" (1971), *Interviews with Northrop Frye* (2008), CW, 24.

The imaginative cosmos is neither the objective environment studied by natural science nor a subjective inner space to be studied by psychology. It is an intermediate world in which the images of higher and lower, the categories of beauty and ugliness, the feelings of love and hatred, the associations of sense experience, can be expressed only by metaphor and yet cannot be either dismissed or reduced to projections of something else.

"Introduction," *Words with Power: Being a Second Study of "The Bible and Literature"* (1990), CW, 26.

The fundamental job of the imagination in ordinary life, then, is to produce, out of the society we have to live in, a vision of the society we want to live in.

"The Vocation of Eloquence," *The Educated Imagination* (1963), *"The Educated Imagination" and Other Writings on Critical Theory, 1933–1963* (2006), CW, 21.

The writer is neither a watcher nor a dreamer. Literature does not reflect life, but it doesn't escape or withdraw from life either: it swallows it. And the imagination won't stop until it's swallowed everything.

"Giants in Time," *The Educated Imagination* (1963), *"The Educated Imagination" and Other Writings on Critical Theory, 1933–1963* (2006), CW, 21.

... the language of the creative imagination is a language that cannot argue: it is not based on propositions that do battle with their implied opposites. What it does is to create a vision that becomes a focus for a community.

"Culture as Interpenetration" (1982), *Northrop Frye on Canada* (2003), CW, 12.

IMMORTALITY

Consequently, I'm quite prepared to accept the feeling that there's a life that's infinitely larger and more inclusive than the simple cradle-to-grave progression of the individual. The thing I do not believe in is the indefinite survival of the ego in the same categories of time and place, which is more or less the popular conception of heaven.

"Maintaining Freedom in Paradise" (1982), discussing the notion there is experience that the brain "simply can't absorb or assimilate," *Interviews with Northrop Frye* (2008), CW, 24.

Gods are supposed to be immortal in contrast to the mortality of man, but in practice the situation is reversed. After all the temples to Jupiter and Venus had been closed down and their cults abandoned, Jupiter and Venus continued to live a far more intense imaginative life than ever before within literature.

"The *Koiné* of Myth: Myth as a Universally Intelligible Language" (1984), *"The Secular Scripture" and Other Writings on Critical Theory, 1976–1991* (2006), CW, 18.

That man is immortal we suspect; that he is enduring we know; but that he can look forward is his most deeply human quality, and to look forward with acceptance and gladness to experiences that can come only to others is perhaps something even more.

"Hart House Rededicated" (1969), *Northrop Frye's Writings on Education* (2001), CW, 7.

We know of no immortality except a continuing memory in one's own community.

"Foreword to *The Living Name*" (1964), *Northrop Frye's Writings on Education* (2001), CW, 7.

There is, incidentally, no doctrine that I know of in the New Testament like that of Plato, which says that the soul is immortal by nature. I think the Biblical attitude is rather that immortality is something that is created by the power of God, but is not something inborn in man by his nature as a human being.

"Symbolism in the Bible" (1981–82), *Northrop Frye's Notebooks and Lectures on the Bible and Other Religious Texts* (2003), CW, 13.

IMPERFECTION

There are two senses in which the word "imperfect" is used: in one sense it is that which falls short of perfection; in another it is that which is not finished but continuously active, as in the tense system of verbs in most languages.

"Metaphor II," *The Great Code* (1982), *The Great Code: The Bible and Literature* (2006), CW, 19.

INCARNATION

Redemption requires a God, but a God within time is no better off than we are, and a God wholly free of time is of no use to us. Fortunately we have the Incarnation, the descent of something outside time into time, and this creates in time the possibility of a genuine present moment.

"The Rhythms of Time" (1974), *"The Critical Path" and Other Writings on Critical Theory, 1963–1975* (2009), CW, 27.

Time in this world is a horizontal line, and God's timeless presence is a vertical one crossing it at right angles, the crossing point being the Incarnation.

"Fourth Essay: Rhetorical Criticism: Theory of Genres" (1957), *Anatomy of Criticism: Four Essays* (2006), CW, 22.

But God is not God until he becomes man; only the incarnation has any real authority, and the consequence of incarnation or the imposition of order (order without authority, note) is resurrection or liberation.

Entry, Notes 53 (1989–90), 60, *Northrop Frye's Late Notebooks, 1982–1990: Architecture of the Spiritual World* (2000), CW, 6.

But the Incarnation is only the Apollonian or order side of the Word; the Resurrection, the Dionysian expression of the power, completes it. Well, who denies it?

Entry, Notebook 44 (1986–1991), 707, *Northrop Frye's Late Notebooks, 1982–1990: Architecture of the Spiritual World* (2000), CW, 5.

INDIGENOUS PEOPLES

We pay an attention to the indigenous peoples now that we never paid a century ago, because we have a clearer idea of the importance of our culture. And our culture, which is essentially pluralistic, *is* our identity.

Entry, Notebook 50 (1987–90), 763, *Northrop Frye's Late Notebooks, 1982–1990: Architecture of the Spiritual World* (2000), CW, 5.

INDIVIDUALITY

Still, the fact that we have adopted the word "individual," and other words like it, shows how strongly we want to believe in some kind of hidden inner essence that remains stable and consistent, even though we may run through a dozen personal masks in an hour or so.

"The Stage Is All the World" (1985), *Northrop Frye's Writings on Shakespeare and the Renaissance* (2010), CW, 28.

A famine is a social problem, but only the individual starves. So a sustained attempt to express primary concerns can develop only in societies where the sense of individuality has also developed.

"Concern and Myth," *Words with Power: Being a Second Study of "The Bible and Literature"* (2008), CW, 26.

Uniqueness and individuality are elements of experience, not elements of knowledge. We cannot know the unique, or even the individual, as such: knowledge is of likenesses within differences.

"Frye, Literary Critic" (1987), *Interviews with Northrop Frye* (2008), CW, 24.

Individuality, which is the condition of freedom, is never achieved without some genuine form of education.

"On Teaching Literature" (1972), *Northrop Frye's Writings on Education* (2001), CW, 7.

We keep going largely by pretending that we are individuals, and that when we say "I" we are speaking of ourselves as unified conscious beings. Actually we are about as unified as the Parliament in Ottawa.

"On Lent" (1988), *Northrop Frye on Religion* (2000), CW, 4.

INERTIA

I hope that the greatest of all political forces, inertia, will manifest its majestic power here.

"The Cultural Development of Canada" (1990), with respect to separatism, *Northrop Frye on Canada* (2003), CW, 12.

INFLUENCES

The relation of a poet to the ideology he expounds or reflects is the genuine form of the "anxiety of influence," and it affects all writers without exception. The psychological and Freudian aspect of it celebrated by Harold Bloom seems to me mainly a by-product of the law of copyright.

"The Expanding World of Metaphor" (1984), *"The Secular Scripture" and Other Writings on Critical Theory, 1976–1991* (2006), CW, 18.

Canadian poetry may echo Hopkins or Auden today as it echoed Tom Moore a century ago, but in every age Echo is merely the discarded mistress of Narcissus.

"Preface to an Uncollected Anthology" (1956), *Northrop Frye on Canada* (2003), CW, 12.

Immense erudition is needed to understand the variety of influences on contemporary artists, and the work of Picasso, of Stravinsky, of T.S. Eliot, might from one point of view be studied as a mass of quotations and allusions.

"Academy without Walls" (1961), *Northrop Frye on Modern Culture* (2003), CW, 11.

INNIS, HAROLD ADAMS

He saw that every new form or technique generates both a positive impulse to exploit it and a negative impulse, especially strong in universities, to resist it, and that the former of course always outmanoeuvres the latter.

"Across the River and Out of the Trees" (1980), *Northrop Frye on Canada* (2003), CW, 12.

INNOCENCE

The fact that innocence may not have been lost but simply never possessed does not impair the validity of the vision, in fact it strengthens it.

"The Meeting of Past and Future in William Morris" (1982), *Northrop Frye's Writings on the Eighteenth and Nineteenth Centuries* (2005), CW, 17.

Man should learn to think of this pastoral myth as a vision of innocence, not an innocence forever lost under a curse, but an innocence which is present in the mind and is a potentially creative power. Such innocence can, when guided by the poetic imagination, be realized in experience, and can thereby assimilate experience to its own form.

"Endymion: The Romantic Epiphanic" (1968), *Northrop Frye's Writings on the Eighteenth and Nineteenth Centuries* (2005), CW, 17.

INSIGHT

Just as God is no respecter of persons, so literature is no respecter of persons either. Any kind of person may come through as a person of unforgettable insight.

"Literature as a Critique of Pure Reason" (1982), *"The Secular Scripture" and Other Writings on Critical Theory, 1976–1991* (2006), CW, 18.

INSPIRATION

I have no objection to inspiration if it means the written expression of some sense of enlightenment or internal conviction. I have a problem with inspiration when it's taken as an automatic, infallible way of writing.

"Time Fulfilled" (1990), *Interviews with Northrop Frye* (2008), CW, 24.

One has glimpses of the immense foreshortening of time that can take place in the world of the spirit; we may speak of "inspiration," a word that can hardly mean anything except the coming or breaking through of the spirit from a world beyond time.

The Double Vision (1991), *Northrop Frye on Religion* (2000), CW, 4.

One may, as I have done myself, spend the better part of seventy-eight years writing out the implications of insights that have taken up considerably less than an hour of all those years.

The Double Vision (1991), *Northrop Frye on Religion* (2000), CW, 4.

True, the greatest moments of poetic *furor* and *raptus* are involuntary, but they never descend on those who are not ready for them. Could one acquire such an imagination if one didn't have it? No, but one could develop it if one did have it.

"How True a Twain" (1962), *Northrop Frye's Writings on Shakespeare and the Renaissance* (2010), CW, 28.

We learn from the history of the arts and the sciences that a single crystallization of inspiration may change the whole history of literature or of science and consequently of human life generally.

"Education and the Rejection of Reality" (1971), *Northrop Frye's Writings on Education* (2001), CW, 7.

As for "inspiration," if there is one thing that Biblical scholarship has established beyond reasonable doubt, it is that authorship, inspired or not, counts for very little in the Bible."
"The Double Mirror" (1981), *Northrop Frye on Religion* (2000), CW, 4.

INSTITUTIONS
Institutions grow as ideas when they decline in physical strength.
"Regina vs. the World" (1953), *Northrop Frye on Modern Culture* (2003), CW, 11.

Further, we discover in the permanence and continuity of social institutions, such as church and state, something that not only civilizes man, but adds a dimension of significance to his otherwise brief and insignificant life.
"The University and Personal Life: Student Anarchism and the Educational Contract" (1968), *Northrop Frye's Writings on Education* (2001), CW, 7.

INSTRUCTION
We have always been told that the function of literature is to instruct and delight, but only when we try to locate our literary experiences within literature do these two things become one thing.
"The Well-Tempered Critic (II)" (1961), *"The Educated Imagination" and Other Writings on Critical Theory, 1933–1963* (2006), CW, 21.

There is such a thing as a right answer and a wrong answer, and the right answer is usually the one in the book, though by no means invariably.
"The Social Importance of Literature" (1968), *Northrop Frye's Writings on Education* (2001), CW, 7.

In a book published over twenty years ago, I wrote that literature is not a coherent subject at all unless its elementary principles could be explained to any intelligent nineteen-year-old. Since then, Buckminster Fuller has remarked that unless a first principle can be grasped by a six-year-old, it is not really a first principle, and perhaps his statement is more nearly right than mine.
"Criticism as Education" (1979), referring to *Anatomy of Criticism* (1957), *Northrop Frye's Writings on Education* (2001), CW, 7.

INTELLECTUALS
To defend the autonomy of culture in this sense seems to me the social task of the "intellectual" in the modern world: if so, to defend its subordination to a total synthesis of any kind, religious or political, would be the authentic form of the *trahison des clercs*.
"Second Essay: Ethical Criticism: Theory of Symbols" (1957), the betrayal of principles by intellectuals, *Anatomy of Criticism: Four Essays* (2006), CW, 22.

People like myself who teach literature are often referred to as intellectuals because we wear glasses, but actually I think we'd be much more accurately described as emotionals. We are just as much concerned with trying to stimulate a feeling response to literature as a logical one.
"The Only Genuine Revolution" (1969), *Interviews with Northrop Frye* (2008), CW, 24.

I remember the thirties, when so many "intellectuals" were trying to rationalize or ignore the Stalin massacres or whatever such horrors did not fit their categories, and thinking even then that part of their infantilism was in being men of print: they saw only lines of type on a page, not lines of prisoners shuffling off to death camps.
"Conclusion to *Literary History of Canada*" (1965), *Northrop Frye on Canada* (2003), CW, 12.

INTELLIGENCE
Intelligence is a No-Man's Land between intuition & instinct: one perceives & creates as a vehicle of a higher unity....
Entry, Notebook 31 (late 1946–50), 11, *Northrop Frye's Notebooks on Romance* (2004), CW, 15.

INTENSITY
What is furthest in distance is often nearest in intensity.

"Canadian and Colonial Painting" (1941), referring to the absence of evidence of life in Tom Thomson's paintings, *Northrop Frye on Canada* (2003), CW, 12.

Imaginative intensity applied to a wrong or inadequate object can be corrected; a deficiency in intensity never can be.
"Part Three: The Final Synthesis," *Fearful Symmetry: A Study of William Blake* (1947, 2004), CW, 14.

INTERPENETRATION

I speak of interpenetration because it seems to me that one decisive feature of high culture is cross-fertilization, something that's beyond the external influence of a mother country and the internal response to it.
"Notes for 'Culture as Interpenetration'" (1977), 29, *Northrop Frye's Fiction and Miscellaneous Writings* (2007), CW, 25.

The opposite of interpenetration, where everything exists everywhere at once, is an objective centrality, which, it seems to me, is a most tyrannical conception.
"Northrop Frye in Conversation" (1989), *Interviews with Northrop Frye* (2008), CW, 24.

This is where the principle of interpenetration operates: the more intensely Faulkner concentrates on his unpronounceable county in Mississippi, the more intelligible he becomes to readers all over the world.
"Culture as Interpenetration" (1977), *Northrop Frye on Canada* (2003), CW, 12.

Interpenetration of belief is unity with variety, like metaphor: reconciliation, conversion, agreement, are all forms of imperialistic compulsion.
Entry, Notes 53 (1989–90), 214, *Northrop Frye's Late Notebooks, 1982–1990: Architecture of the Spiritual World* (2000), CW, 6.

INTERPRETATION

Now a reconstruction of a poem in abstract nouns is not necessarily a false interpretation of part of its meaning. But it is a translation, which means that it assumes the reader's ignorance of the original language.

"Part One: The Argument," *Fearful Symmetry: A Study of William Blake* (1947, 2004), CW, 14.

I now feel that the word "interpretation" is a red herring: to be given a poem and look around for an interpretation of it is like being given the kernel of a nut and looking round for a shell, which seems to me as perverse an approach to poems as it is to nuts.
"The Double Mirror" (1981), *Northrop Frye on Religion* (2000), CW, 4.

INTROVERSION

This is part of the general growth of introversion during the last fifty years, for nearly all our technological developments — the automobile, the passenger airplane, the high-rise apartment, the television set, even the cocktail party — make for increased introversion, and our traditional communities, the school, the home, the university, the church, the labour temple, the corner store, disintegrate in direct proportion.
"Rear-View Crystal Ball?" (1970), *Northrop Frye on Canada* (2003), CW, 12.

INTUITIONS

"Intuition" as generally understood is a mental short cut employed by the unintelligent, who are no doubt pleased to be told that it's superior to intelligence.
Entry, 24 Aug. 1942, 76, *The Diaries of Northrop Frye: 1942–1955* (2001), CW, 8.

I get intuitions, in odd moments, of what life could be like if the intelligence and the imagination were totally and consistently functional in it. Of how essential it is to human dignity to recognize that making things and learning things are the most important activities of life. Of how powerful authority is in society when it is a purely internal authority, the authority of the rational argument, the repeatable experiment, the imaginative classic.
"An Ideal University Community" (1969), *Northrop Frye's Writings on Education* (2001), CW, 7.

INUIT

... in fact we set so high a value now on such art that we have almost transformed

the Eskimos into a nation of sculptors, at least with one hand, even though we may be destroying the sources of their creativeness with the other.
"Canada: New World Without Revolution" (1975), *Northrop Frye on Canada* (2003), CW, 12.

If you see, for example, the Inuit people on television, they no longer are abstractions wrapped up in seal skins. They are people like ourselves.
"On the Media" (1986), *Interviews with Northrop Frye* (2008), CW, 24.

And, of course, if you look at a simplified culture, like that of the Inuit people, where life is reduced to a few basic needs of survival, poetry and painting and sculpture leap into the foreground as some of those primary necessities of existence.
"The Primary Necessities of Existence" (1985), *Interviews with Northrop Frye* (2008), CW, 24.

Once you abolish alienation you set free the real energies of man. It's easy to dismiss this as fantasy, yet look at the Inuit people.
Entry, Notes 54-13 (1975–82), 15, *Northrop Frye's Notebooks on Romance* (2004), CW, 15.

INVECTIVE

... invective is one of the most readable forms of literary art, just as panegyric is one of the dullest.
"Third Essay: Archetypal Criticism: Theory of Myths" (1957), *Anatomy of Criticism: Four Essays* (2006), CW, 22.

INVENTIONS

All new inventions are apt to come first as social headaches, and it takes a while before their real usefulness is understood.
"Violence and Television" (1975), *Northrop Frye on Modern Culture* (2003), CW, 11.

It has often happened in the sciences that a new discovery, even a new invention, seems to be of no immediate practical use. But fifty years later, it may turn out to be exactly what that science is then looking for. Similarly, it has been noted many times that what poets have seen in any given period becomes what the whole world is doing fifty or a hundred years later.
"The Authority of Learning" (1984), *Northrop Frye's Writings on Education* (2001), CW, 7.

IRISH THEATRE

For the last 250 years practically every great comic dramatist in English literature has been an Irishman.
"William Butler Yeats" (1950), *Northrop Frye on Literature and Society, 1936–1989: Unpublished Papers* (2002), CW, 10.

IRONY

For irony is not simply the small man's way of fighting a bigger one: it is a kind of intellectual tear-gas that breaks the nerves and paralyzes the muscles of everyone in its vicinity, an acid that will corrode healthy as well as decayed tissues.
"The Nature of Satire" (1944), *"The Educated Imagination" and Other Writings on Critical Theory, 1933–1963* (2006), CW, 21.

Irony is consistent both with complete realism of content and with the suppression of attitude on the part of the author.
"Third Essay: Archetypal Criticism: Theory of Myths," *Anatomy of Criticism* (1957).

There are two forms of true equivocal meaning: allegory & irony. We have irony when there is contrast between the meaning-parts; allegory when there is a complementary relationship.
Entry, Notebook 3 (1946–48), 130, *Northrop Frye's Notebooks and Lectures on the Bible and Other Religious Texts* (2003), CW, 13.

But so far the great writers of the twentieth century have been preoccupied with ironic and fatalistic patterns, and have lacked the wisdom or energy to look consistently beyond them. Perhaps this is something we may hope for from the writers of the immediate future.
"*Rencontre*: The General Editor's Introduction" (1960s), *Northrop Frye on Literature and Society, 1936–1989: Unpublished Papers* (2002), CW, 10.

Irony preserves the seriousness of literature by demanding an expanded perspective on the action it presents, but it preserves the integrity of literature by not limiting or prescribing for that perspective.

"The Road of Excess" (1970), *Northrop Frye on Milton and Blake* (2005), CW, 16.

ISLAM

In Moslem countries everything that happened before Mohammed's time is part of the age of ignorance.

"Canada: New World Without Revolution" (1975), *Northrop Frye on Canada* (2003), CW, 12.

Islamic culture, Sufi mysticism, geometrical art, mathematics & the like, descend from the suppressed poet; Islamic fanaticism descends from the paranoid prophet. Yet, human nature being what it is, there would never have been any Islamic culture without the brainwashing paranoia.

Entry, Notebook 11f (1969–70), 82, *Northrop Frye's Notebooks and Lectures on the Bible and Other Religious Texts* (2003), CW, 13.

I know Islamic culture produced distinguished histories (Ibn Khaldun) but its typical products are mystics, mathematicians, and geometrical arts.

Entry, Notebook 12 (1968–70), 352, *The "Third Book" Notebooks of Northrop Frye, 1964–1972: The Critical Comedy* (2002), CW, 9.

… the last of all, the "Revolt of Islam," is still ahead of us.

Entry, Notes 52 (1982–90), 676, *Northrop Frye's Late Notebooks, 1982–1990: Architecture of the Spiritual World* (2000), CW, 6.

The Islamic revelation was a counter-apocalypse, which arose as a part of the Christian failure to separate the two words. They failed because science hadn't developed far enough.

Entry, Notes 53 (1989–90), 102, *Northrop Frye's Late Notebooks, 1982–1990: Architecture of the Spiritual World* (2000), CW, 6.

As Marxist and American imperialisms decline, the Moslem world is emerging as the chief threat to world peace, and the sparkplug of its intransigence, so to speak, is its fundamentalism or false literalism of belief.

The Double Vision (1991), *Northrop Frye on Religion* (2000), CW, 4.

The Moslems, on the other hand, got stuck with a God who's a nut and a crank, and they're led by unscrupulous people who want to make this obscene creature a political fetish. In the sign of a stinker-God shalt thou conquer.

Entry, Notebook 44 (1986–91), 740, *Northrop Frye's Late Notebooks, 1982–1990: Architecture of the Spiritual World* (2000), CW, 5.

ISRAEL

The peculiar prophetic mission entrusted to Israel was not one that brought strength or success; what it brought was suffering and endurance.

"Symbols" (1968), *Northrop Frye on Religion* (2000), CW, 4.

The Christian Bible begins with the beginning of time at the Creation, ends with the end of time at the Last Judgment, and surveys the history of humankind — under the symbolic names of Adam and Israel — in between.

"Bible as Literature" (1985), *"The Secular Scripture" and Other Writings on Critical Theory, 1976–1991* (2006), CW, 18.

A mythology may develop by accretion, as in Greece, or by rigorous codifying and the excluding of unwanted material, as in Israel; but the drive toward a verbal circumference of human experience is clear in both cultures.

"Myth, Fiction, and Displacement" (1961), *"The Educated Imagination" and Other Writings on Critical Theory, 1933–1963* (2006), CW, 21.

The Israelites made their great contribution to history, as is the wont of human nature, through their least amiable characteristic. It was not their belief that their God was the true God but their belief that all other gods were false that proved decisive.

"Typology II," *The Great Code* (1982), *The Great Code: The Bible and Literature* (2006), CW, 19.

ITALIANS

Of all the major ethnical groups in Canada, I think the Italians are the most aware (though the Japanese run them a close second) of the interlocking relevance of everything that we normally call culture.

"Italy in Canada" (1990), *Northrop Frye on Canada* (2003), CW, 12.

The Italians are on the whole honest, and in Rome only sporadically not so: the only place where one gets systematically gypped and rooked and fleeced and hornswoggled is in Venice.

"NF to HK," 28 Apr. 1937, written in Florence, *The Correspondence of Northrop Frye and Helen Kemp, 1932–1939* (1996), CW, 1.

Florence remains the best town in the world.

"NF to HK," 28 Apr. 1937, written in Florence, *The Correspondence of Northrop Frye and Helen Kemp, 1932–1939* (1996), CW, 1.

Favourite Cities: When I was a student in Italy, the first places I saw were Pisa and Siena. Siena has remained in my mind with great vividness as a place full of colour and warmth and life.

"*Chatelaine's* Celebrity I.D." (1982), *Interviews with Northrop Frye* (2008), CW, 24.

IVORY TOWER

The man who reads Tolstoy and Marx will not be able to find refuge in an "ivory tower": he will only be able to see with horrid clarity that most businessmen are living in one.

"A Liberal Education" (1945), *Northrop Frye's Writings on Education* (2001), CW, 7.

Don't speak of the university as an "ivory tower": that's a cant phrase used by people whose only feeling about the university is one of vague resentment.

"Universities and the Deluge of Cant" (1972), *Northrop Frye's Writings on Education* (2001), CW, 7.

J

JACKSON, A.Y.
A.Y. Jackson remarked to me some time before his death that he still had guilt feelings when a picture of his sold for more than thirty-five dollars.

"Across the River and Out of the Trees" (1980), *Northrop Frye on Canada* (2003), CW, 12.

JAPANESE PUPPET THEATRE
It seemed to me that these puppets were quite certain that they themselves were producing all the movements and noises that the audience was hearing, even though the audience could see that they were not.

"The Teacher's Source of Authority" (1978), *Northrop Frye's Writings on Education* (2001), CW, 7.

JARGON
By jargon I mean writing in which words do not express meanings, but are merely thrown in the general direction of their meanings; writing which can always be cut down by two-thirds without loss of whatever sense it has. Jargon always unconsciously reveals a personal attitude.

"Humanities in a New World" (1958), *Northrop Frye's Writings on Education* (2001), CW, 7.

If educators speak jargon, they're not educating; if academics speak jargon, they're not scholars; if revolutionaries speak jargon, they're neo-fascists.

"On Education I" (after 1960s), 26, *Northrop Frye's Fiction and Miscellaneous Writings* (2007), CW, 25.

JEHOVAH
Jehovah seems to have all the characteristics of a false god: he's only true through the act of criticism I call resonance.

Entry, Notes 54.1(May 1990), 11, *Northrop Frye's Late Notebooks, 1982–1990: Architecture of the Spiritual World* (2000), CW, 6.

JEST
I've always had a strong interest in the nature of comedy and the way in which even tragedy seems to fit inside as a kind of episode in a total story which is comic. While I'm not sure that everything in the world is simply a jest, there is a point at which the oracular and the witty do come together.

"Music in My Life" (1985), *Interviews with Northrop Frye* (2008), CW, 24.

JESUS
The suffering man who represents God may be a martyr in the original sense of a witness. That is, he is a man whose vision of a better form of human life and society is so strong that he lives in the light of that vision and acts according to what it suggests.

"Into the Wilderness" (1969), *Interviews with Northrop Frye* (2008), CW, 24.

There is early secular evidence for the rise of Christianity, but there is practically no real evidence for the life of Jesus outside the New Testament, all the evidence for a major historical figure being hermetically sealed within it. But it seems clear also that the writers of the New Testament preferred it that way.

"Myth I," *The Great Code* (1982), *The Great Code: The Bible and Literature* (2006), CW, 19.

It would be interesting to see, if we could, what the original "historical" Jesus was like, before his teachings got involved in the mythical and legendary distortions of his followers. But if we try to do this with any

thoroughness, there will be, quite simply, nothing left of the Gospels at all.
> "Myth I," *The Great Code* (1982), *The Great Code: The Bible and Literature* (2006), CW, 19.

I don't find it convincing, but I suspect that if we found "the" historical Jesus it would be so shattering an anticlimax that very little Christianity would survive it.
> Entry, Notebook 44 (1986–91), 301, *Northrop Frye's Late Notebooks, 1982–1990: Architecture of the Spiritual World* (2000), CW, 5.

Jesus was not the world's only saviour or enlightened or even divine man: his uniqueness has to do only with his being the only-begotten Son of the Father. I don't yet know what I mean by that, but it's important to find out.
> Entry, Notebook 11e (1978), 27, *Northrop Frye's Notebooks and Lectures on the Bible and Other Religious Texts* (2003), CW, 13.

Jesus is the particular or individualizing aspect of God, and as such he individualizes the supra-personal essence, the ground of being, the super-duper whatzit, as the Father. Jesus' own Father was the Spirit.
> Entry, Notebook 50 (1987–90), 72, *Northrop Frye's Late Notebooks, 1982–1990: Architecture of the Spiritual World* (2000), CW, 5.

We are all born inside the belly of the leviathan, which is why there is so much about Jesus as a fisherman in the Gospels.
> "Symbolism in the Bible" (1981–82), *Northrop Frye's Notebooks and Lectures on the Bible and Other Religious Texts* (2003), CW, 13.

I'm not shocked by the suggestion that Jesus had a physical wife & children, but his "blood line" would have got mixed in average humanity pretty damn soon. It's just one more guess about the historical Jesus, derived from Gospels that don't care about the historical Jesus.
> Entry, Notebook 44 (1986–91), 37, *Northrop Frye's Late Notebooks, 1982–1990: Architecture of the Spiritual World* (2000), CW, 5.

Jesus is the apotheosis of *totemism:* the human-animal immortal ancestor whose animal form — the sacrificed lamb's body & blood which is also the bread & wine — sustains the life of his worshippers.
> Entry, Notebook 23 (early 1980s), 20, *Northrop Frye's Notebooks and Lectures on the Bible and Other Religious Texts* (2003), CW, 13.

Jesus is the Logos or Word of God, the totality of creative power, the universal visionary in whose mind we perceive the particular.
> "Part One: The Argument," *Fearful Symmetry: A Study of William Blake* (1947, 2004), CW, 14.

Hence the *essential* life of Jesus must be discontinuous, a series of epiphanic appearances called up, like the presence in the mass, in response to a significant situation.
> Entry, 16 Apr. 1950, 277, *The Diaries of Northrop Frye: 1942–1955* (2001), CW, 8.

JEWISH PEOPLE

It may be only a Christian prejudice, but I think if I were a Jew I'd be strongly tempted to accept Christ as at least a plausible working model of what a Messiah would be like. Which means that on the basis of imaginative literalism there's no real difference.
> Entry, Notes 54.1 (May 1990), 49, *Northrop Frye's Late Notebooks, 1982–1990: Architecture of the Spiritual World* (2000), CW, 6.

Thus the Jew became the scapegoat for the voice inside the Nazi that kept saying "this racism is a lot of crap, and you know it."
> Entry, Notebook 44 (1986–91), 11, *Northrop Frye's Late Notebooks, 1982–1990: Architecture of the Spiritual World* (2000), CW, 5.

For some reason or other the Jews managed to preserve an imaginative tradition which the Greeks and others lost sight of, and possessed only in disguised and allegorical forms.
> "Part One: The Argument," referring to the Bible, *Fearful Symmetry: A Study of William Blake* (1947, 2004), CW, 14.

JOB

The vision of Job is the vision of a man who has seen the essential sanity of the world, in spite of the utter insanity of what has happened to him.

"The Great Teacher" (1988), *Interviews with Northrop Frye* (2008), CW, 24.

The Book of Job is technically a comedy by virtue of its final chapter, which tells us that God restored to Job everything he had lost with interest, including three very beautiful daughters named Jemima, Keziah, and Kerenhappuch.
"A Natural Perspective: The Development of Shakespearean Comedy and Romance; IV, The Return from the Sea" (1963), *Northrop Frye's Writings on Shakespeare and the Renaissance* (2010), CW, 28.

Anyone interested in both the Bible and literature will eventually find himself revolving around the Book of Job like a satellite.
"Fourth Variation: The Furnace," *Words with Power: Being a Second Study of "The Bible and Literature"* (1990), CW, 26.

JOKES

Someone who is about to tell a joke may say, regrettably, "Stop me if you've heard this one," indicating that what follows is addressed primarily to the ear. But if we "see" the joke, the joke is all over, and we are considering the afterimage of its total structure.
"The *Koiné* of Myth: Myth as a Universally Intelligible Language" (1984), *"The Secular Scripture" and Other Writings on Critical Theory, 1976–1991* (2006), CW, 18.

... at any time the chance of a joke may bring something else along with it, a shift of vision, perhaps, that will suddenly turn one into a different person, before the old one has stopped laughing.
"Don Harron" (1987), *Northrop Frye on Canada* (2003), CW, 12.

... the audiences of vaudeville, comic strips, and television programs still laugh at the jokes that were declared to be outworn at the opening of *The Frogs*.
"Third Essay: Archetypal Criticism: Theory of Myths" (1957), *Anatomy of Criticism: Four Essays* (2006), CW, 22.

We hear a joke and then we "see" it.

Entry, Notebook 44 (1986–91), 31, *Northrop Frye's Late Notebooks, 1982–1990: Architecture of the Spiritual World* (2000), CW, 5.

JOUAL

The debates over the use of *joual* are, it seems to me, of immense benefit, whatever the attitude taken towards it, in sharpening the sense of what is going on in language and in the relation of oral to written French.
"Across the River and Out of the Trees" (1980), *Northrop Frye on Canada* (2003), CW, 12.

JOURNALISM

Most people nowadays are accustomed to the double talk of journalism, and it is not the difficulty of poetry that they find baffling, but its simplicity.
"Letters in Canada: Poetry" (1960), *Northrop Frye on Canada* (2003), CW, 12.

I wouldn't, if I were a journalist, want to give up entirely to philosophers the saying of memorable things.
"The Great Test of Maturity" (1986), *Interviews with Northrop Frye* (2008), CW, 24.

JOURNALS

The decline of the journal of opinion is in society what the decline of debating is in the university: the sign of a corresponding decline in the belief in the reality of ideas, in the role of dialectic in shaping history, in the sense of the social function of the disinterested intelligence.
"Foreword to *The Living Name*" (1964), *Northrop Frye's Writings on Education* (2001), CW, 7.

JUDGMENTS

Criticism is not well enough organized as yet to know what the factors of value in a critical judgment are.
"The Function of Criticism at the Present Time" (1949), *"The Educated Imagination" and Other Writings on Critical Theory, 1933–1963* (2006), CW, 21.

Consequently knowledge always has the power of veto over taste.
"Literary Criticism" (1963), *"The Critical Path" and Other Writings on Critical Theory, 1963–1975* (2009), CW, 27.

... the study of literature always has the power of veto over any value judgment.
> "Literature as a Critique of Pure Reason" (1982), *"The Secular Scripture" and Other Writings on Critical Theory, 1976–1991* (2006), CW, 18.

Judgment is therefore the activity of the critic that has to be outgrown before genuine criticism starts.
> Entry, Notes 53 (1989–90), 63, *Northrop Frye's Late Notebooks, 1982–1990: Architecture of the Spiritual World* (2000), CW, 6.

All judgment in which the values are not based on literary experience but are sentimental or derived from religious or political prejudice may be regarded as casual.
> "The Archetypes of Literature" (1951), *"The Educated Imagination" and Other Writings on Critical Theory, 1933–1963* (2006), CW, 21.

JUNG, C.G.

It would be an advantage to critics if Frazer were completely rejected by anthropologists, and Jung by psychologists, as then it could be seen more clearly that their work belongs to literary criticism, but such questions are no concern of ours.
> "The Literary Meaning of 'Archetype'" (1936), *Northrop Frye on Literature and Society, 1936–1989: Unpublished Papers* (2002), CW, 10.

Without belittling Jung's achievements in psychology, it is possible that he too, like Spengler and Frazer, is of greatest significance as a critical and cultural theorist.
> "Expanding Eyes" (1975), *"The Critical Path" and Other Writings on Critical Theory, 1963–1975* (2009), CW, 27.

Jung's archetypes are powers within the soul, and they have very intimate and very fascinating analogies to some of the conventional characters of literature, but Jung's treatment of literature, I think, is barbaric, and most of the Jungians don't seem to be much better.
> "Northrop Frye in Conversation" (1989), *Interviews with Northrop Frye* (2008), CW, 24.

I didn't realize at the time how much Jung had cornered the field with his use of archetype in his own highly idiosyncratic sense. Jung is a psychologist whose private myth is a myth of individuation, where you start out with the ego and you end up with the individual, which is the same thing, only much profounder.
> "Frye's Literary Theory in the Classroom," referring to his early use of the concept of the literary rather than the psychological archetype, *Interviews with Northrop Frye* (2008), CW, 24.

My objections to Jung are not to him but to my being called Jungian: I'm not much interested in alchemy and I don't want *literature* to be turned into a psychological allegory of individuation.
> Entry, Notebook 44 (1986–91), 138, *Northrop Frye's Late Notebooks, 1982–1990: Architecture of the Spiritual World* (2000), CW, 5.

K

KABBALISM

... there was even a Christian form of Kabbalism, which turned mainly on putting the letter *shin* in the middle of the Hebrew YHWH and thereby changing Yahweh to Yeshua.

    The Double Vision (1991), *Northrop Frye on Religion* (2000), CW, 4.

KAFKA, FRANZ

The powerful appeal of Kafka for our age is largely due to the way in which such stories as *The Trial* or *The Castle* manage to suggest at once the atmosphere of an anxiety dream, the theology of the Book of Job, and the police terrorism and bureaucratic anonymity of the society that inspired Freud's term "censor."

    "The Nightmare Life in Death" (1960), *Northrop Frye on Twentieth-Century Literature* (2010), CW, 29.

KARMA

Karma is the real ouroboros, the last enemy to be destroyed.

    Entry, Notebook 21 (1969–76), 271, *Northrop Frye's Notebooks and Lectures on the Bible and Other Religious Texts* (2003), CW, 13.

KERNELS

The four material kernels, commandment, aphorism, oracle & pericope or epiphany, are as stated: they're the basis of law, wisdom, prophecy & theophany respectively.

    Entry, Notebook 21 (1969–76), 292, *Northrop Frye's Notebooks and Lectures on the Bible and Other Religious Texts* (2003), CW, 13.

KERYGMA

Kerygma is a mode of rhetoric, though it is rhetoric of a special kind.... It is the vehicle of what is traditionally called "revelation," a word I use because it is traditional and I can think of no better one.

    "Language I," *The Great Code* (1982), *The Great Code: The Bible and Literature* (2006), CW, 19.

Kerygma is a word I took from Rudolph Bultmann, who has used it in the sense of the proclamation of the gospel. I thought it could be extended to the entire Bible, and I used it as a way of explaining why the Bible is essentially a rhetorical book.

    "Back to the Garden" (1982), *Interviews with Northrop Frye* (2008), CW, 24.

I think it is important to keep the word kerygma, but it has to mean not ordinary rhetoric but a mode of language that takes account of the mythical and literary qualities which cannot be separated from the Biblical texture. In short, a mode of language on the *other side* of the poetic.

    "Spirit and Symbol," *The Great Code, Words with Power: Being a Second Study of "The Bible and Literature"* (1990), CW, 26.

Kerygma is the completion of the personal possession of the written word: it's linked with mantra, but without the "vain repetition" [Matthew 6:7] that often goes with that. It's the actualized form of the "myth to live by," assuming that the real life is a spiritual one, delivered once and for all from all ideologies or rationalizations of power.

    Entry, Notebook 50 (1987–90), 254, *Northrop Frye's Late Notebooks, 1982–1990: Architecture of the Spiritual World* (2000), CW, 5.

Kerygma can never, except in the sacred book, become form, and even there its form is provisional. That's because its habitat is the decentered, or rather omni-centered, universe.

Entry, Notebook 50 (1987–90), 65, *Northrop Frye's Late Notebooks, 1982–1990: Architecture of the Spiritual World* (2000), CW, 5.

When myth becomes form, kerygma becomes the content.
Entry, Notebook 50 (1987–90), 64, *Northrop Frye's Late Notebooks, 1982–1990: Architecture of the Spiritual World* (2000), CW, 5.

We are close to the kergymatic whenever we meet the statement, as we do surprisingly often in contemporary writing, that it seems to be language that uses man rather than man that uses language.
"Spirit and Symbol," *Words with Power: Being a Second Study of "The Bible and Literature"* (1990), CW, 26.

KINGSHIP

The real king is not that man there with a unique authority; the real king is the invisible presence which is the real individuality within a community.
Entry, Notebook 11c (late 1970s), 19, *Northrop Frye's Notebooks and Lectures on the Bible and Other Religious Texts* (2003), CW, 13.

I suppose the king represents individuality without guilt: he can do as he likes, but the ordinary citizen is relieved from the guilt of individuality by the king's existence.
Entry, Notebook 24 (1970–72), 7, *The "Third Book" Notebooks of Northrop Frye, 1964–1972: The Critical Comedy* (2002), CW, 9.

KIRKCONNELL, WATSON

A malicious but admiring legend said that when he became president of Acadia he took to shaking hands with his left hand so as not to interrupt his writing.
"Across the River and Out of the Trees" (1980), *Northrop Frye on Canada* (2003), CW, 12.

KNIGHT, G. WILSON

There were times when I suspected that Knight didn't know a Folio from a Quarto text — certainly he didn't care; he worked entirely with a Globe Shakespeare and a mass of pencilled annotations.
"Autobiographical Notes III: The Critic and the Writer" (1974), 7, referring to the Shakespearian scholar who taught at Trinity College, *Northrop Frye's Fiction and Miscellaneous Writings* (2007), CW, 25.

KNOWLEDGE

The only knowledge that is worth while is the knowledge that leads to wisdom, for knowledge without wisdom is a body without life.
"The Instruments of Mental Production" (1966), *Northrop Frye's Writings on Education* (2001), CW, 7.

The idea of universal knowledge achieved in and through poetry has haunted poets and their students from the beginning.
The Critical Path: An Essay on the Social Context of Literary Criticism (1971), *"The Critical Path" and Other Writings on Critical Theory, 1963–1975* (2009), CW, 27.

Specialized knowledge is possessed knowledge, knowledge which excludes others, and it is thus repressive knowledge. It is for this reason that a pretence of naiveté is valuable, and that we need fools who will come in from outside and trespass on the specialist terrain.
"On *The Great Code* (IV)" (1982), *Interviews with Northrop Frye* (2008), CW, 24.

It's not the trained mind but the dedicated mind that matters most; a mind dedicated to knowledge.
"Love of Learning" (1987), *Interviews with Northrop Frye* (2008), CW, 24.

The knowledge that you can have is inexhaustible, and what is inexhaustible is benevolent. The knowledge that you cannot have is of the riddles of birth and death, of our future destiny and the purposes of God. Here there is no knowledge, but illusions that restrict freedom and limit hope. Accept the mystery behind knowledge: it is not darkness but shadow.
"Baccalaureate Service (III)" (1988), *Northrop Frye on Religion* (2000), CW, 4.

Knowledge is a personal possession, but in itself it is impersonal. History is what happened, not what we think should have happened; science is what is there, not what we'd prefer to see there.

Apparently knowledge in all its varied forms is the path taken by the natural consciousness till it reaches true knowledge. Along this path Soul becomes purified into Spirit.
> Entry, Notes 53 (1989–90), 182 , *Northrop Frye's Late Notebooks, 1982–1990: Architecture of the Spiritual World* (2000), CW, 6.

I suppose there is such a thing as practically and inherently useless knowledge, that is, subjects without content or founded on false assumptions, like palmistry or the racial theories cherished by the Nazis; but the danger of a student's being deflected by them is remote.
> "The Instruments of Mental Production" (1966), *Northrop Frye's Writings on Education* (2001), CW, 7.

There is nothing new under the sun except our knowledge of what is under the sun, but that new knowledge is a constant recreation of old knowledge.
> "Address on Receiving the Royal Bank Award" (1978), *Northrop Frye's Writings on Education* (2001), CW, 7.

It takes a good deal of maturity to see that every field of knowledge is the centre of all knowledge, and that it doesn't matter so much what you learn when you learn it in a structure that can expand into other structures.
> "The Beginning of the Word" (1980), *Northrop Frye's Writings on Education* (2001), CW, 7.

Production in society is the result of technological developments; technological developments are the result of the advance of knowledge. The advance of knowledge is what is *really* happening in the world, and the more we direct our attention to it the more real our lives become.
> "The Quality of Life in the '70s" (1971), *Northrop Frye on Modern Culture* (2003), CW, 11.

The knowledge of most worth, for a genuine student, is that body of knowledge to which he has already made an unconscious commitment.
> "The Instruments of Mental Production" (1966), *Northrop Frye's Writings on Education* (2001), CW, 7.

"Wisdom and Knowledge" (1973), *Northrop Frye on Religion* (2000), CW, 4.

What there is left of the data-world is the sense that there is infinitely more to be known. I am uttering the profound truth that we do not know what we do not know.
> Entry, Notebook 27 (1986), 212, *Northrop Frye's Late Notebooks, 1982–1990: Architecture of the Spiritual World* (2000), CW, 5.

Knowledge is what you have; wisdom is what others may find in you.
> "Wisdom and Knowledge" (1973), *Northrop Frye on Religion* (2000), CW, 4.

KOOK BOOKS

For years I have been collecting and reading pop-science & semi-occult books, merely because I find them interesting. I now wonder if I couldn't collect enough ideas from them for an essay on neo-natural theology. Some are very serious books I haven't the mathematics (or the science) to follow: some are kookbooks with hair-raising insights or suggestions.
> Entry, Notebook 11h (1980s), 8, *Northrop Frye's Late Notebooks, 1982–1990: Architecture of the Spiritual World* (2000), CW, 6.

… yesterday's kook book becomes tomorrow's standard text.
> Entry, Notebook 27 (1986), 90, *Northrop Frye's Late Notebooks, 1982–1990: Architecture of the Spiritual World* (2000), CW, 5.

KORAN

The Koran is one clear historical instance of the beginning of the Western period of the mythical mode in action.
> "First Essay: Historical Criticism: Theory of Modes" (1957), *Anatomy of Criticism: Four Essays* (2006), CW, 22.

Anyway, the Koran is, of course, deadly dull. All sacred books are neurotic in proportion to the amount of yelling they do about the punishments of the unbelievers, and the proportion in the Koran is high. The neurotic impression is increased a hundredfold by the oral pre-literate style, which depends on & demands endless repetition.
> Entry, Notebook 11f (1969–70), 71, *Northrop Frye's Notebooks and Lectures on the Bible and Other Religious Texts* (2003), CW, 13.

The Bible is a work in which authorship counts for very little & editing & redacting & glossing & conflating & expurgating a great deal. Because of this it's also a *translatable* book, in contrast to the Koran, which is so dependent on Arabic that the Arabic language has had to go everywhere Islam does. The Koran seems to me a simple, logical, & totally inadequate conception of a sacred book.

> Entry, Notebook 11f (1969–70), 67, *Northrop Frye's Notebooks and Lectures on the Bible and Other Religious Texts* (2003), CW, 13.

... suras arranged in order of length only means that if the Koran is the Word of God, God doesn't give a damn about narrative sequence.

> Entry, Notebook 11f (1969–70), 69, *Northrop Frye's Notebooks and Lectures on the Bible and Other Religious Texts* (2003), CW, 13.

Just as in the Bible we cannot distinguish the voice of God from the voice of the Deuteronomic redactor, so in the Koran we cannot distinguish the voice of the angel Gabriel from the voice of Mohammed in a bad temper.

> Entry, Notebook 21 (1969–76), 349, *Northrop Frye's Notebooks and Lectures on the Bible and Other Religious Texts* (2003), CW, 13.

The late Ayatollah of Iran, by urging the murder of Rushdie, turned the whole of the Koran into Satanic verses.

> Entry, Notes 53 (1989–90), 190, *Northrop Frye's Late Notebooks, 1982–1990: Architecture of the Spiritual World* (2000), CW, 6.

They think of the Koran as words descending from heaven as rain descends from the sky, all over the place at once, and if you're looking for rain to break a drought, you don't complain that one raindrop is much like another.

> Entry, Notebook 11f (1969–70), 80, *Northrop Frye's Notebooks and Lectures on the Bible and Other Religious Texts* (2003), CW, 13.

The Koran still baffles me: I can't figure out why the hell anybody went for that book. It probably makes a lot more sense in Arabic as a prose-poetry synthesis of the Word in which rhetorical & dialectic aspects are indistinguishable.

> Entry, 17 May 1949, 375, *The Diaries of Northrop Frye: 1942–1955* (2001), CW, 8.

The repetitiousness of the Koran would drive a reader out of his mind if he were reading it as he would read any other book. But for a Mohammedan, brought up from infancy to learn it by heart, to attach the greatest possible reverence & weight to what it says, it does exactly the job it should do. It gives the impression that while man's will bucks & plunges in all directions, God's will is steady & unyielding, incessantly coming back to the same point, until the horse is broken in, so to speak, & has learned to move with a direction and a will that are not his own.

> Entry, Notebook 21 (1969–76), 294, *Northrop Frye's Notebooks and Lectures on the Bible and Other Religious Texts* (2003), CW, 13.

L

LACAN, JACQUES
... I find Lacan a most rewarding writer to "misread"....

"Lacan and the Full Word" (1985), *"The Secular Scripture" and Other Writings on Critical Theory, 1976–1991* (2006), CW, 18.

LADDERS
It seems obvious that the very widespread, almost universal, images of ladders and stairs and mountains and trees owe their existence to the fact that man cannot fly, and cannot think of any way to raise himself, physically and metaphorically, in space except by climbing.

"Repetitions of Jacob's Dream" (1983), *Northrop Frye on Religion* (2000), CW, 4.

LAISSEZ-FAIRE
Laissez-faire by itself is antidemocratic: all progress in the conditions of the working classes has been wrung from it in a kind of cold civil war — not always so cold, as it has included lynchings, sadistic beatings, systematic starvation, and an occasional massacre.

"Trends in Modern Culture" (1952), *Northrop Frye on Modern Culture* (2003), CW, 11.

... for all our political parties are now running away from laissez-faire and they differ among themselves only in their estimate of how fast and how far they can run.

"Preserving Human Values" (1961), *Northrop Frye on Modern Culture* (2003), CW, 11.

LAMBS
Isaiah may imagine a state in which the lion lies down with the lamb [cf. 11:6], but we live in a state in which the lion could not exist without eating lambs, or something dietetically equivalent.

The Double Vision (1991), *Northrop Frye on Religion* (2000), CW, 4.

LAND
I have often thought that Robert Frost's line, "The land was ours before we were the land's," however appropriate to the United States, does not apply to Canada, where the opposite seems to me to be true, even in the free land grant days. Canadians were held by the land before they emerged as a people on it, a land with its sinister aspects....

"Conclusion to *Literary History of Canada*" (1965), *Northrop Frye on Canada* (2003), CW, 12.

LANDSCAPE
If you fly over a city at night in a plane and look down on the geometrical patterns of lights you can see why this is the century of Kandinsky and not the century of Renoir.

"Nature and Civilization" (1989), *Interviews with Northrop Frye* (2008), CW, 24.

If you look at Mr. Jackson's paintings, you will see a most impressive pictorial survey of Canada: pictures of Georgian Bay and Lake Superior, pictures of the Quebec Laurentians, pictures of Great Bear Lake and the Mackenzie River. What you will not see is a typically Canadian landscape: no such place exists.

"Culture and the National Will" (1957), referring to the canvases of A.Y. Jackson, *Northrop Frye on Canada* (2003), CW, 12.

LANGUAGE
The more seriously we try to think and express ourselves, the more clearly we realize that we can think and talk only within the limits of the language we know.

"Shakespeare and the Modern World" (1964), *Northrop Frye's Writings on Shakespeare and the Renaissance* (2010), CW, 28.

Language is the most fragmented of all human activities, and poetic language is the most fragmented aspect of it.
"On Translation" (1979), *"The Secular Scripture" and Other Writings on Critical Theory, 1976–1991* (2006), CW, 18.

Language in a human mind is not a list of words with their customary meanings attached, but a single interlocking structure, one's total power of expressing oneself.
"Levels of Meaning in Literature" (1950), *"The Educated Imagination" and Other Writings on Critical Theory, 1933–1963* (2006), CW, 21.

Hence the language of metaphor is the language of the spirit and the language of the spirit is the language of love and the language of love is the language of God.
Entry, Notes 53 (1989–90), 4, *Northrop Frye's Late Notebooks, 1982–1990: Architecture of the Spiritual World* (2000), CW, 6.

It should be clear by now that there is nothing "natural" about language, except that for a conscious being, the natural and the artificial are the same thing.
"Language as the Home of Human Life" (1985), *Northrop Frye's Writings on Education* (2001), CW, 7.

In the seventeenth century there were Puritans who refused to pronounce the word Christmas because the last syllable was "mass," and there are people today who refuse to pronounce the word chairman for much the same reason.
"The View from Here" (1980), *Northrop Frye's Writings on Education* (2001), CW, 7.

There is only one way to degrade mankind permanently, and that is to destroy language.
"Humanities in a New World" (1958), *Northrop Frye's Writings on Education* (2001), CW, 7.

It is obvious that social change would be reflected in changes of language but what interests me much more is the reverse possibility: that the teaching of language, and the structures of literature in which language is contained, may foster and encourage certain social changes.
"The Authority of Learning" (1984), *Northrop Frye's Writings on Education* (2001), CW, 7.

The awareness of language may begin with the awareness of ordinary consciousness, but it soon becomes clear that language is a means of intensifying consciousness, lifting us into a new dimension of being altogether.
Entry, Notebook 11h (1980s), 31, *Northrop Frye's Late Notebooks, 1982–1990: Architecture of the Spiritual World* (2000), CW, 6.

I wonder what sort of people find languages easy. Any I ever tackled let me in for fearsome complications of paradigms, idioms, irregular verbs, & syntax, followed, if at all, by looking fifty thousand words up in a dictionary.
Entry, 16 Jul. 1942, 18, *The Diaries of Northrop Frye: 1942–1955* (2001), CW, 8.

In reading any poem we have to know at least two languages: the language the poet is writing and the language of poetry itself. The former exists in the words the poet uses, the latter in the images and ideas which those words express.
"Yeats and the Language of Symbolism" (1947), *"The Critical Path" and Other Writings on Critical Theory, 1963–1975* (2009), CW, 27.

… if we do not know another language, we have missed the best and simplest opportunity of getting our ideas disentangled from the swaddling clothes of their native syntax.
"Fourth Essay: Rhetorical Criticism: Theory of Genres" (1957), *Anatomy of Criticism: Four Essays* (2006), CW, 22.

Canadians speak American: apart from one or two private schools, our political connection with Great Britain has had no effect on our language except to confuse our spelling.
"The Well-Tempered Critic (I)" (1961), *"The Educated Imagination" and Other Writings on Critical Theory, 1933–1963* (2006), CW, 21.

Descriptive language is objectified language, and belongs in the world of the cloven

fiction; symbolic language is the language of incarnation.
> Entry, Notebook 12 (1968–70), 239, *The "Third Book" Notebooks of Northrop Frye, 1964–1972: The Critical Comedy* (2002), CW, 9.

Words inform the bodies of knowledge that we call the humanities, as well as most of the social sciences; mathematics informs the sciences, more particularly the physical sciences.
> "The Instruments of Mental Production" (1966), *Northrop Frye's Writings on Education* (2001), CW, 7.

Science and philosophy remind us that language is a total human effort at communication; literature reminds us that language is also one of the most fragmented of human activities, so that it is a life's work to master completely more than one or two.
> "The Bridge of Language" (1981), *Northrop Frye on Modern Culture* (2003), CW, 11.

The language of reason is implicitly aggressive. It is only the language of symbol that can express a faith which is pure, and has no wish to attack or improve on anyone else's faith.
> "Symbols" (1968), *Northrop Frye on Religion* (2000), CW, 4.

LATIN

A little Latin, so the argument ran, is a dangerous thing, for all it can lead to is more Latin, which is practically a fatal thing.
> "The Critical Discipline" (1960), ridiculing an educational fallacy, *Northrop Frye's Writings on Education* (2001), CW, 7.

LAW

What I am really saying, I suppose, is that all respect for the law is a product of the social imagination, and the social imagination is what literature directly addresses.
> "Literature and the Law" (1970), *"The Critical Path" and Other Writings on Critical Theory, 1963–1975* (2009), CW, 27.

Obviously, society could not hold together if an honest man were nothing more than a man who had never been convicted of stealing: where the law ends is where genuinely civilized life begins.
> "Literature and the Law" (1970), *"The Critical Path" and Other Writings on Critical Theory, 1963–1975* (2009), CW, 27.

As it is law is an inorganic study, for it breeds nothing but lawyers, & makes judges come out of an esoteric professional group, which is bad, particularly when they're so close to the police.
> Entry, 4 Jun. 1950, 394, *The Diaries of Northrop Frye: 1942–1955* (2001), CW, 8.

Law is the final cause of social science, and the efficient cause of freedom.
> Entry, 4 Jun. 1950, 394, *The Diaries of Northrop Frye: 1942–1955* (2001), CW, 8.

LAWRENCE, D.H.

God, I wish D.H. Lawrence had some sense of real satire; if he had he'd have been by long odds the greatest fiction writer of the century.
> Entry, Notebook 50 (1987–90), 332, *Northrop Frye's Late Notebooks, 1982–1990: Architecture of the Spiritual World* (2000), CW, 5.

LAYTON, IRVING

The kind of thing that will forever keep Irving Layton a minor poet: the fact that we're never for an instant out of touch with Irving Layton, is at the opposite end of the act of surrender to the genre that marks the major writer.
> "Notes for 'Framework and Assumption'" (1984), 28, *Northrop Frye's Fiction and Miscellaneous Writings* (2007), CW, 25.

One can get as tired of buttocks in Mr. Layton as of buttercups in the *Canadian Poetry Magazine*; and a poet whose imagination is still fettered by a moral conscience, even an anticonventional one, gives the impression of being in the same state of bondage as the society he attacks.
> "Letters in Canada: Poetry" (1952), *Northrop Frye on Canada* (2003), CW, 12.

LEADERSHIP

The leader for whom men will die is not necessarily a kind man, but he is necessarily a man who can suggest that he has no need of his follower, or at any rate that it is an objective duty to follow him.

Entry, Notebook 3 (1946–48), 20, *Northrop Frye's Notebooks and Lectures on the Bible and Other Religious Texts* (2003), CW, 13.

People need political and social leaders who can define policies, articulate problems, and express the aims and ideals of their society for those who cannot express them for themselves, though they may feel them very deeply. But the evidence is overwhelming that voters in a democracy want, and expect, bumble and burble from their leaders, and seem to be disturbed, if not upset, by the impact of articulate speech.
"The Authority of Learning" (1984), *Northrop Frye's Writings on Education* (2001), CW, 7.

The genuine leader of our time is what the United Church calls a "moderator," whether his position in the colour spectrum of personality is at the Khrushchev or at the Eisenhower end. Pope John is the most impressive example of this contemporary type of irenic leader.
"Foreword to *The Prospect of Change*" (1965), *Northrop Frye on Canada* (2003), CW, 12.

The head of a great power, like the President of the U.S., has a considerable potential power of destruction, but relatively little chance for creativity or innovation.
Entry, Notebook 12 (1968–70), 359, *The "Third Book" Notebooks of Northrop Frye, 1964–1972: The Critical Comedy* (2002), CW, 9.

The phrase "leaders of thought" itself begs a large question: leaders imply followers, and few coherent thinkers have had, in society, any follower except those who have followed in the wrong direction.
"The Present Condition of the World" (1943), *Northrop Frye on Literature and Society, 1936–1989: Unpublished Papers* (2002), CW, 10.

On Political Leaders in history: Most of the people who rank as great leaders — say, Lenin — seem to me to be utter creeps.
"*Chatelaine's* Celebrity I.D." (1982), *Interviews with Northrop Frye* (2008), CW 26.

We naturally demand leadership from our leaders, but thugs and gangsters can give us leadership, of a kind: if we demand articulateness as well, we are demanding something that only a genuine vision of human life can provide.
"Humanities in a New World" (1958), *Northrop Frye's Writings on Education* (2001), CW, 7.

Ordinarily we associate authority with leadership, but Canada is the sort of environment in which we can see most clearly that leadership is a conception that modern society is trying to outgrow.
"The View from Here" (1980), *Northrop Frye's Writings on Education* (2001), CW, 7.

You certainly wouldn't turn to contemporary poets for guidance or leadership in the twentieth century world.
The Educated Imagination (1963), *"The Educated Imagination" and Other Writings on Critical Theory, 1933–1963* (2006), CW, 21.

LEARNING

Learning things is linear; growth is a curve, and learning has to be bent into that curve before it's part of a personality. Otherwise the personality is flattened out to fit the inhuman straight line of the intellect.
"NF to HK," 22 May 1935, *The Correspondence of Northrop Frye and Helen Kemp, 1932–1939* (1996), CW, 1.

Once we think of learning as a disentangling & relaxing process, we think of ideas tending toward wisdom, or the growth of a free spirit, instead of to more & more learning.
Entry, Notebook 3 (1946–48), 114, *Northrop Frye's Notebooks and Lectures on the Bible and Other Religious Texts* (2003), CW, 13.

This takes us back to the principle that everything connected with the university, with education, and with knowledge, must be structured and continuous. Until this is grasped, there can be no question of "learning to think for oneself." In education one cannot think at random.
"The University and Personal Life: Student Anarchism and the Educational Contract" (1968), *Northrop Frye's Writings on Education* (2001), CW, 7.

LEAVIS, F.R.

If you open F.R. Leavis anywhere, you will find appreciative references to D.H. Lawrence and sneers at Joyce. Well, what Leavis says about Lawrence is genuine criticism, because he understands Lawrence. What he says about Joyce is rubbish, and we have to wait for somebody else to deal with him.

"Freedom and Concern" (1985), *Interviews with Northrop Frye* (2008), CW, 24.

LECTURING

University lecturing is not teaching but a form of intellectualized preaching.

Entry, 19 Jan. 1949, 100, *The Diaries of Northrop Frye: 1942–1955* (2001), CW, 8.

LEGEND

The legend is halfway between the nomadic folktale and the centralized myth. It is typically a story pattern associated with a particular place.

Entry, Notebook 44 (1986–91), 300, *Northrop Frye's Late Notebooks, 1982–1990: Architecture of the Spiritual World* (2000), CW, 5.

LEISURE

That is, any leisure activity which is not sheer idleness or distraction depends on some acquired skill, and the acquiring and practice of that skill is a mode of education.

The Modern Century (1967), *Northrop Frye on Modern Culture* (2003), CW, 11.

As soon as we realize that leisure is as genuine and important an aspect of everyone's life as remunerative work, leisure becomes something that also demands discipline and responsibility.

The Modern Century (1967), *Northrop Frye on Modern Culture* (2003), CW, 11.

The reading of poetry is a leisurely occupation, and is possible only for that small minority which believes in leisure.

"Letters in Canada: Poetry" (1960), *Northrop Frye on Canada* (2003), CW, 12.

Leisure is the opposite of laziness, & hasn't really any more to do with rest than with work. It's the essential condition of creative life, the relaxation from ritual, the removal of the censorious urgency of routine, in which that free association of ideas which begins the creative process is allowed to function. In short, it's listening to the Word.

Entry, 8 Jan. 1950, 25, *The Diaries of Northrop Frye: 1942–1955* (2001), CW, 8.

Leisure-class people lead complicated lives because they haven't anything else to do but complicate them.

Entry, Notes 58-4 (*c.* 1987), 87, *Northrop Frye's Notebooks on Romance* (2004), CW, 15.

Leisure is not idleness, which is neurotic; and still less is it distraction, which is psychotic. Leisure begins in that moment of consciousness peculiar to a rational being, when we become aware of our own existence and can watch ourselves act, when we have time to think of the worth and purpose of what we are doing, to compare it with what we might or would rather be doing. It is the moment of the birth of human freedom, when we are able to subject what is actual to the standard of what is possible.

"Humanities in a New World" (1958), *Northrop Frye's Writings on Education* (2001), CW, 7.

LEWIS, WYNDHAM

It does not matter that Mozart sounds like Mozart and Lewis's prose like an army tank falling into the Grand Canyon.

"The Diatribes of Wyndham Lewis: A Study in Prose Satire" (1936), *Northrop Frye's Student Essays, 1932–1938* (1997), CW, 3.

It is true that relatively few if any of the world's greatest geniuses have been born in Canada, although a remarkable British painter and writer, Wyndham Lewis, went so far as to get himself born on a strip off Canadian shores, and developed an appropriately seasick view of Canada in later life.

The Modern Century (1967), *Northrop Frye on Modern Culture* (2003), CW, 11.

LIBERALISM

The word "liberal" implies a disinterested pursuit of truth as its own end, in contrast to the attempt to manipulate it or press it into the service of an immediate social aim.

"Trends in Modern Culture" (1952), *Northrop Frye on Modern Culture* (2003), CW, 11.

It seems to follow that the existence of liberalism in any society has a lot to do with the tolerated presence of the religious perspective.
"Trends in Modern Culture" (1952), *Northrop Frye on Modern Culture* (2003), CW, 11.

When we act in this light, we find that we are not members of a social group, but of one body. Without this infinite expansion of the liberal ideal, liberalism cannot avoid the dilemma of either returning to a criterion of immediate usefulness or getting lost in an impossible objectivity.
"Trends in Modern Culture" (1952), *Northrop Frye on Modern Culture* (2003), CW, 11.

I suppose what my bourgeois liberalism really amounts to is the sense of the ultimately demonic nature of all ideological constructs.
Entry, Notebook 44 (1986–91), 702, *Northrop Frye's Late Notebooks, 1982–1990: Architecture of the Spiritual World* (2000), CW, 5.

More and more people are beginning to realize that there is no coherent liberalism nowadays except that which is attached to a socialist theory of economy: to increase freedom, therefore, is also to increase co-operation, and introduce subtler problems of discipline. But the other side of this principle is that there is no coherent socialism except that which is attached to a liberal theory of education, and derives its ideals from that theory.
"A Liberal Education" (1945), *Northrop Frye's Writings on Education* (2001), CW, 7.

The realization that in the great works of culture there is a vision of reality which is completely human and comprehensible, and yet just a bit better than what we can get by ourselves, is the mainspring of all liberal thought.
"A Liberal Education" (1945), *Northrop Frye's Writings on Education* (2001), CW, 7.

LIBERATION

Art is the model of dialectical liberation: what an artist gives through his art is a pattern for understanding what's redeemable in him, & in man generally.
Entry, Notebook 24 (1970–72), 199, *The "Third Book" Notebooks of Northrop Frye, 1964–1972: The Critical Comedy* (2002), CW, 9.

LIBERTY

Liberty is good for man because God wants him to have it, but without grace no man wants it.
"The Survival of Eros in Poetry" (1983), *"The Secular Scripture" and Other Writings on Critical Theory, 1976–1991* (2006), CW, 18.

LIBRARIES

The individual's powers are limited & predictable, or if they aren't he soon passes out of our range. But a big library really has the gift of tongues & vast potencies of telepathic communication.
Entry, Notebook 3 (1946–48), 128, *Northrop Frye's Notebooks and Lectures on the Bible and Other Religious Texts* (2003), CW, 13.

Certainly the absence of a national library is a national disgrace.
"Culture and the Cabinet" (1949), *Northrop Frye on Canada* (2003), CW, 12.

I can never read library books, partly because I work with marginalia in books I own, perhaps because every book out of sight is also out of mind.
Entry, Notebook 12 (1968–70), 318, *The "Third Book" Notebooks of Northrop Frye, 1964–1972: The Critical Comedy* (2002), CW, 9.

LIEUTENANT-GOVERNORS

Not that everyone knows what the office is: an American friend of mine, formerly a lootenant in the American Navy, said to me with a most puzzled expression: "But what *is* a left-handed Governor?"
"Tribute to Don and Pauline McGibbon" (1990), *Northrop Frye on Canada* (2003), CW, 12.

LIFE

Within the limitations of human life, the most highly developed human types are those whose lives have become, as we say, a legend, that is, lives no longer contemplating a vision of objective revelation or imprisoned within a subjective dream.

"The Koiné of Myth: Myth as a Universally Intelligible Language" (1984), *"The Secular Scripture" and Other Writings on Critical Theory, 1976–1991* (2006), CW, 18.

This means that what is important about your life is not that you should achieve something, but that you should manifest something.

"Baccalaureate Sermon" (1967), *Northrop Frye on Religion* (2000), CW, 4.

In other words, real life, in the long run, is either life within the love of God or life under the wrath of God.

"Substance and Evidence" (1974), *Northrop Frye on Religion* (2000), CW, 4.

That means that the important categories of your life are no longer the subject and the object, the watcher and the things being watched: the important categories are what you have to do and what you want to do — in other words, necessity and freedom.

"The Motive for Metaphor," *The Educated Imagination* (1963), *"The Educated Imagination" and Other Writings on Critical Theory, 1933–1963* (2006), CW, 21.

The only features in human life that are genuinely human are creation and criticism.

Entry, Notes 53 (1989–90), 225, *Northrop Frye's Late Notebooks, 1982–1990: Architecture of the Spiritual World* (2000), CW, 6.

LIFE & DEATH

The meaning of death is something bound up in life itself. Life doesn't make sense without the conception of death, but neither does death make any sense without the conception of life. The two awarenesses go hand in hand all the time that we are conscious of living.

"*Imprint* Interview" (1990), *Interviews with Northrop Frye* (2008), CW, 24.

The feeling that death is inevitable comes to us from ordinary experience; the feeling that new life is inevitable comes to us from myth and fable. The latter is both more true and more important.

The Secular Scripture: A Study of the Structure of Romance (1975), *"The Secular Scripture" and Other Writings on Critical Theory, 1976–1991* (2006), CW, 18.

Being is a life-death complex: I don't mean that the dead are still alive: I mean that to have been is a part of being. That which is to be is not part of being, but that which was is. It's the other half, like the world of anti-matter in physics, where entropy goes into reverse. God is dead; therefore God exists.

Entry, Notebook 19 (1964–67), 342, *The "Third Book" Notebooks of Northrop Frye, 1964–1972: The Critical Comedy* (2002), CW, 9.

Christianity says you got born but you don't die; Buddhism says you die but you never got born.

Entry, Notebook 6 (1967–68), 28, *The "Third Book" Notebooks of Northrop Frye, 1964–1972: The Critical Comedy* (2002), CW, 9.

We come from the unknown at birth, and we rejoin it at death with all our questions about it unanswered. Sometimes we wonder whether humanity is capable of living in any world at all where consciousness is really a function of life.

"To Come to Light" (1986), *Northrop Frye on Religion* (2000), CW 4.

The question of life after death, certainly, would have to give place to the question of life before death — not whether you live after death but whether there's any proof you've ever come alive.

"The Voice in the Crowd" (1966), *Interviews with Northrop Frye* (2008), CW, 24.

The business of life is to make a path for the incarnation: the business of death is to make a path for the resurrection.

Entry, Notebook 11b (late 1980), 31, *Northrop Frye's Notebooks and Lectures on the Bible and Other Religious Texts* (2003), CW, 13.

The Spirit that broods on the chaos of our psyches brings to birth a body that is in time and history but not enclosed by them, and

is in death only because it is in the midst of life as well.
> *The Double Vision* (1991), *Northrop Frye on Religion* (2000), CW, 4.

LIFE & LITERATURE

Life has no shape; literature has.
> "The Renaissance of Books" (1973), *Northrop Frye on Modern Culture* (2003), CW, 11.

Real life does not start or stop; it never ties up loose ends; it never manifests meaning or purpose except by blind accident; it is never comic or tragic, ironic or romantic, or anything else that has a shape.
> "Dickens and the Comedy of Humours" (1967), *Northrop Frye's Writings on the Eighteenth and Nineteenth Centuries* (2005), CW, 17.

Literature, we say, neither reflects nor escapes from ordinary life: what it does reflect is the world as human imagination conceives it, in mythical, romantic, heroic, and ironic as well as realistic and fantastic terms.
> "The Well-Tempered Critic (II)" (1961), *"The Educated Imagination" and Other Writings on Critical Theory, 1933–1963* (2006), CW, 21.

To bring anything really to life in literature we can't be lifelike: we have to be literature-like.
> "The Keys to Dreamland," *The Educated Imagination* (1963), *"The Educated Imagination" and Other Writings on Critical Theory, 1933–1963* (2006), CW, 21.

LIFESTYLES

In a more sensible Christian world people would move in and out of Catholic and Protestant lifestyles, instead of all this ideological crap about once-for-all baptism or conversion, always having to be either in or out of the church.
> Entry, Notebook 44 (1986–91), 193, *Northrop Frye's Late Notebooks, 1982–1990: Architecture of the Spiritual World* (2000), CW, 5.

LIGHT

God says "Let there be light," and light appears, unable to protest that it might have been more logical to create first a source of light, such as the sun.
> "Language II," *The Great Code* (1982), *The Great Code: The Bible and Literature* (2006), CW, 19.

And so, whenever we look at the visible things in the world, we should remember that their daylight appearance is not their whole reality.
> "Symbols" (1968), *Northrop Frye on Religion* (2000), CW, 4.

LINCOLN, ABRAHAM

The Republicans owe their existence to the fact that a century ago a long-legged Illinois lawyer put a few words together that made up a social vision for the American people of genuine dignity and power, and so enabled the Republican party to stand for something.
> "Humanities in a New World" (1958), *Northrop Frye's Writings on Education* (2001), CW, 7.

LISTENING

The art of listening to stories is a basic training for the imagination. You don't start arguing with the writer: you accept his postulates, even if he tells you that the cow jumped over the moon, and you don't react until you've taken in all of what he has to say.
> "Verticals of Adam," *The Educated Imagination* (1963), *"The Educated Imagination" and Other Writings on Critical Theory, 1933–1963* (2006), CW, 21.

It seems to me that nobody should be trained to talk unless he is simultaneously trained to listen, because, if he is, then what is called "dialogue" simply becomes a series of solipsistic monologues, and any gathering of people will take on that form of group psychosis which can be studied in almost any conference called in the modern world.
> "The Definition of a University" (1970), *Northrop Frye's Writings on Education* (2001), CW, 7.

LITERACY

I think a literate person is first and foremost an articulate person, one who has the power to say what he means, which sounds simple but is immensely difficult.
> "A Literate Person Is First and Foremost an Articulate Person" (1977), *Interviews with Northrop Frye* (2008), CW, 24.

The simple ability to read, write, and count is essentially a passive acquirement, a means of social adjustment. All genuine teaching starts with this passive literacy and then tries to transform it into an activity, reading with discrimination and writing with articulateness. Without this background, one may be able to read and write and still be functionally illiterate. It is discouraging for a student to find that he has reached university and is still totally unable to say what he thinks.

>   Address, "The Authority of Learning" (1984), *Northrop Frye's Writings on Education* (2001), CW, 7.

If such tendencies had continued to spread unchecked, we should have been assuming by about the year 2000 that a Ph.D. in English literature was a minimum requirement for passing a literacy test.

>   "Convocation Address, Franklin and Marshall" (1968), referring to remedial courses in graduate school, *Northrop Frye's Writings on Education* (2001), CW, 7.

I think that teachers faced with a restless and often inattentive class tend to become magicians.... I have sat in committee meetings in the Department of English at the university where we have discussed for hours whether putting ABCD in the form ADCB wouldn't create a kind of magical response on the part of the student. The magical belief that literacy is going to transform civilization is simply an illusion.

>   "The Only Genuine Revolution" (1969), *Interviews with Northrop Frye* (2008), CW, 24.

LITERALISM

The person who cannot be brought to understand literary convention is often said to be "literal-minded." But as "literal" surely ought to have some connection with letters, it seems curious to use the phrase "literal-minded" for imaginative illiterates.

>   "Second Essay: Ethical Criticism: Theory of Symbols" (1957), *Anatomy of Criticism: Four Essays* (2006), CW, 22.

Such things as creation and the fall of man are not literally events: they are realities symbolically expressed. They are thus neither subjective ideas nor objective facts, but finite modes of perception correlated with something infinite.

>   "Review of Paul Tillich, *Systematic Theology*" (1963), *Northrop Frye's Fiction and Miscellaneous Writings* (2007), CW, 25.

The view I have, I think, consistently advanced is one that can be expressed in the phrase "literary literalism," a jingle so hideous that it may be memorable. The Bible should be read as literally as any fundamentalist could desire, but the real literal meaning is an imaginative and poetic one.

>   "Introduction" (1990), *Words with Power: Being a Second Study of "The Bible and Literature"* (2008), CW, 26.

Demonic literalism seeks conquest by paralysing argument; imaginative literalism seeks what might be called interpenetration, the free flowing of spiritual life into and out of one another that communicates but never violates.

>   *The Double Vision* (1991), *Northrop Frye on Religion* (2000), CW, 4.

LITERATURE

Literature is the total body of stories and symbols that provides hypotheses or models of human behaviour and experience.

>   "On Teaching Literature" (1972), *Northrop Frye's Writings on Education* (2001), CW, 7.

For some reason it has never been consistently understood that the ideas of literature are not real propositions, but verbal formulas which imitate real propositions.

>   "Second Essay: Ethical Criticism: Theory of Symbols" (1957), *Anatomy of Criticism: Four Essays* (2006), CW, 22.

The world of literature is human in shape, a world where the sun rises in the east and sets in the west over the edge of a flat earth in three dimensions, where the primary realities are not atoms or electrons but bodies, and the primary forces not energy or gravitation but love and death and passion and joy.

>   "The Motive for Metaphor," *The Educated Imagination* (1963), *"The Educated Imagination"*

and Other Writings on Critical Theory, 1933–1963 (2006), CW, 21.

Literature is not a subject of study, but an object of study: the fact that it consists of words, as we have seen, makes us confuse it with the talking verbal disciplines.
"Polemical Introduction" (1957), *Anatomy of Criticism: Four Essays* (2006), CW, 22.

As soon as one begins the serious study of English literature, one makes two paradoxical discoveries about it. One is that there is no such thing as English literature, and the other is that there is no such thing as literature.
Entry, Notebook 42a (1942–44), 7, *Northrop Frye's Notebooks on Romance* (2004), CW, 15.

Literature, we said, is conscious mythology: it creates an autonomous world that give us an imaginative perspective on the actual one.
"Conclusion to *Literary History of Canada*" (1965), *Northrop Frye on Canada* (2003), CW, 12.

Literature is an art of words, and the student of it may be interested primarily either in the art or in the words.
"Identity and Metaphor," *Words with Power: Being a Second Study of "The Bible and Literature"* (1990), CW, 26.

At the heart of all literature is what I have called the cycle of *forza* and *froda*, where violence and guile are coiled up within each other like the yin-and-yang emblem of Oriental symbolism.
The Secular Scripture: A Study of the Structure of Romance (1975), *"The Secular Scripture" and Other Writings on Critical Theory, 1976–1991* (2006), CW, 18. This is a reference to Dante's force and fraud.

... the possession of literature is something which at a certain point has to be transformed into a state of mind in which literature possesses you, in which it is a regenerating influence into which you enter, in which you participate, and which at the same time keeps moving you on more and more towards some kind of vision, and the fact that you are moving towards it is the important thing.

"Literature as Possession" (1959), *"The Educated Imagination" and Other Writings on Critical Theory, 1933–1963* (2006), CW, 21.

Literature is at the centre of those because literature is the great laboratory of myths, that is, the statement of reality in terms of man's hopes and desires and fears.
"The Only Genuine Revolution" (1968), referring to "the concerned subjects" or existential ones, *Interviews with Northrop Frye* (2008), CW, 24.

Wherever we have an autonomous verbal structure of this kind, we have literature. Wherever this autonomous structure is lacking, we have language, words used instrumentally to help human consciousness do or understand something else.
"Second Essay: Ethical Criticism: Theory of Symbols" (1957), *Anatomy of Criticism: Four Essays* (2006), CW, 22.

It's a curious law of literature that the greater variety there is, the more cohesion there is. If you've got twenty really good writers, you've got a much more coherent literature than if you had two, even though the twenty may be wildly different from one another.
"Notes of a Maple Leaf" (1971), *Interviews with Northrop Frye* (2008), CW, 24.

Literature is an aspect of the human compulsion to create in the face of chaos.
The Secular Scripture: A Study of the Structure of Romance (1975), *"The Secular Scripture" and Other Writings on Critical Theory, 1976–1991* (2006), CW, 18.

The study of literature takes us toward seeing poetry as the imitation of infinite social action and infinite human thought, the mind of a man who is all men, the universal creative word which is all words.
"Second Essay: Ethical Criticism: Theory of Symbols" (1957), *Anatomy of Criticism: Four Essays* (2006), CW, 22.

In literature the sense of fact is subordinated to an ultimate intention of producing a pattern of words for its own sake.

"Three Meanings of Symbolism" (1952), *"The Educated Imagination" and Other Writings on Critical Theory, 1933–1963* (2006), CW, 21.

Now it seems to me that it is the fundamental function of literature, and more particularly of poetry, to keep recreating in society that first phase of language, that original, metaphorical sense of immediacy, a sense of identity between personality and nature.
"The Meaning of Recreation: Humanism in Society" (1979), *Northrop Frye on Religion* (2000), CW, 4.

The roots of literature are in a specific culture, but its fruits are in a world without boundaries.
"Tradition and Change in the Theory of Criticism" (1969), *Northrop Frye on Literature and Society, 1936–1989: Unpublished Papers* (2002), CW, 10.

At the top of literature are such writers as Dante or Shakespeare or Milton whose works are infinitely great, but they also belong in families. Although these works are infinitely great, the whole of literature is still greater than the sum of even its greatest parts, and even the greatest works of literature gain in impressiveness and in social significance through the resonance of context.
"The Social Uses of Literature" (1972), *Northrop Frye on Literature and Society, 1936–1989: Unpublished Papers* (2002), CW, 10.

I said earlier that there's nothing new in literature that isn't the old reshaped.
"Giants in Time," *The Educated Imagination* (1963), *"The Educated Imagination" and Other Writings on Critical Theory, 1933–1963* (2006), CW, 21.

Literature is founded on the metaphor that arrests logic and the myth that arrests history; its works are objects of contemplation.
Entry, Notebook 27 (1986), 68, *Northrop Frye's Late Notebooks, 1982–1990: Architecture of the Spiritual World* (2000), CW, 5.

It is the illusions of literature that begin to seem real, and ordinary life, pervaded as it is with all the phoney and lying myths that surround us, begins to look like the real hallucination, a parody of the genuine imaginative world.
"The View from Here" (1980), *Northrop Frye's Writings on Education* (2001), CW, 7.

The forms of literature are autonomous: they exist within literature itself, and cannot be derived from any experience outside literature.
"Conclusion to *Literary History of Canada*" (1965), *Northrop Frye on Canada* (2003), CW, 12.

It never speaks unless we take the time to listen in leisure, and it speaks only in a voice too quiet for panic to hear.
"The Vocation of Eloquence," *The Educated Imagination* (1963), *"The Educated Imagination" and Other Writings on Critical Theory, 1933–1963* (2006), CW, 21.

Literature is a world where phoenixes and unicorns are quite as important as horses and dogs — and in literature some of the horses talk, like the ones in *Gulliver's Travels*.
"The Keys to Dreamland," *The Educated Imagination* (1963), *"The Educated Imagination" and Other Writings on Critical Theory, 1933–1963* (2006), CW, 21.

Literature is a human apocalypse, man's revelation to man, and criticism not a body of adjudications, but the awareness of that revelation, the last judgment of mankind.
"The Keys to Dreamland," *The Educated Imagination* (1963), *"The Educated Imagination" and Other Writings on Critical Theory, 1933–1963* (2006), CW, 21.

What makes some literature endure? And if literature endures because it is good, what makes it good? I have never been able to answer that question, although it is the most natural kind of question to ask.
"Freedom and Concern" (1985), *Interviews with Northrop Frye* (2008), CW, 24.

… the study of mediocre works of art, however energetic, obstinately remains a random and peripheral form of critical experience, whereas the profound masterpiece seems to draw us to a point at which we can see an enormous number of converging patterns of significance.

> "The Archetypes of Literature" (1951), *"The Educated Imagination" and Other Writings on Critical Theory, 1933–1963* (2006), CW, 21.

But the writing that got most direct public response tended to be subliterary rhetoric, like the Confederation poetry which was really inspired by a map and not by a country or a people, or the yawny French verse about the *terroir* which seemed to be written out of duty rather than discovery.

> "Across the River and Out of the Trees" (1980), *Northrop Frye on Canada* (2003), CW, 12.

Everything in literature is a reply to something in the Bible.

> Entry, Notebook 50 (1987–90), 116, *Northrop Frye's Late Notebooks, 1982–1990: Architecture of the Spiritual World* (2000), CW, 5.

Literature as a whole is not an aggregate of exhibits with red and blue ribbons attached to them, like a cat-show, but the range of articulate human imagination as it extends from the height of imaginative heaven to the depth of imaginative hell.

> "The Keys to Dreamland," *The Educated Imagination* (1963), *"The Educated Imagination" and Other Writings on Critical Theory, 1933–1963* (2006), CW, 21.

... I wonder if the unfinished or destroyed masterpieces of the past, resentful at being excluded from history, keep trying to come back, or yelling like the martyrs under the altar, & if they are part of the imagination of other works.

> Entry, Notebook 12 (1968–70), 294, *The "Third Book" Notebooks of Northrop Frye, 1964–1972: The Critical Comedy* (2002), CW, 9.

If I had to make a statement about the literature of our own time, I should say that it was mainly a literature of closed perspectives, an ironic literature, concentrating upon the cruelty or absurdity or obscenity of life, strongly moralizing in tone.

> "Shakespeare and the Modern World" (1964), *Northrop Frye's Writings on Shakespeare and the Renaissance* (2010), CW, 28.

I think of literature as a specific field of imaginative activity, but the metaphor of "field" I have in mind is something like a magnetic field, a focus of energy, not a farmer's field with a fence around it.

> "Framework and Assumption" (1985), *"The Secular Scripture" and Other Writings on Critical Theory, 1976–1991* (2006), CW, 18.

The end of the study of literature is not an act of genuflection in front of a masterpiece, but the incorporation into the student's mind of the articulateness which literature represents.

> "Criticism as Education" (1979), *Northrop Frye's Writings on Education* (2001), CW, 7.

LOGIC

Two and two certainly make four, but only because four is another way of saying two and two.

> *The Double Vision* (1991), *Northrop Frye on Religion* (2000), CW, 4.

LOGOS

The word logos doesn't and never did mean word in Greek.

> Entry, Notes 53 (1989–90), 174, *Northrop Frye's Late Notebooks, 1982–1990: Architecture of the Spiritual World* (2000), CW, 6.

Two dragons I want to kill are Bultmann's "demythologize" and Derrida's "logocentric." The Bible is myth from Genesis to Revelation, & to demythologize it is to obliterate it. The climax of the (Christian) Bible is "The Word became flesh, and dwelt among us" [John 1:14], which is the most logocentric sentence ever written.

> Entry, Notebook 44 (1986–91), 253 *Northrop Frye's Late Notebooks, 1982–1990: Architecture of the Spiritual World* (2000), CW, 5.

LONDON

If we visit a great city with a long history, say London, we find it a mere mass of people and buildings sprawled over most of southeast England. But at its heart in the City there are a few traces, and place names ending in "gate," which remind us that it was once a small, clearly defined, walled town. Those who are fond of London or feel identified with it usually build a mental wall around a relatively small part of it.

"Foreword to *The Prospect of Change*" (1965), *Northrop Frye on Canada* (2003), CW, 12.

LOS ANGELES

Every Canadian has some feeling of sparseness when he compares, for example, Canada's fifth largest city, which I believe is Hamilton, with the fifth largest across the line, which I believe is Los Angeles.

"Canada and Its Poetry" (1943), *Northrop Frye on Canada* (2003), CW, 12.

Los Angeles, a city never designed at all, seems to have broken through the control even of the automobile. It was, after all, named after angels, who traditionally do not travel through space but simply manifest themselves elsewhere.

"Canada: New World Without Revolution" (1975), *Northrop Frye on Canada* (2003), CW, 12.

LOUISIANA

The French lost the country primarily because they had very little interest in keeping it, and if they had held it they would doubtless have sold it, as they did Louisiana.

"Haunted by Lack of Ghosts" (1976), *Northrop Frye on Canada* (2003), CW, 12.

LOVE

Love was for the Renaissance poet a kind of creative yoga, an imaginative discipline in which he watched the strongest possible feelings swirling around sexual excitement, jealousy, obsession, melancholy, as he was snubbed, inspired, teased, ennobled, forsaken, or made blissful by his mistress.

"How True a Twain" (1962), *Northrop Frye's Writings on Shakespeare and the Renaissance* (2010), CW, 28.

Love is a specific relation between two people which individualizes them both; lust is an unspecified drive which cares nothing for its object.

"A Natural Perspective: The Development of Shakespearean Comedy and Romance; II, Making Nature Afraid" (1963), *Northrop Frye's Writings on Shakespeare and the Renaissance* (2010), CW, 28.

Although much of our life is rooted in the anxiety of time, in other words the fear of death, the continuity of knowledge and wisdom that has brought us here together is rooted in love, a love that is not only as strong as death, but able to cast out its fear.

"To Come to Light" (1986), *Northrop Frye on Religion* (2000), CW, 4.

The cosmos of love is a cosmos that reminds us of the etymological link with "cosmetic": that is, it contains the categories of beauty and ugliness.

"Second Variation: The Garden," *Words with Power: Being a Second Study of "The Bible and Literature"* (1990), CW, 26.

Love goes with absorption into the whole, or into the loved one's body; beauty goes with the individual, carrying the whole inside him, getting all the fun out of an objective world & none of the uneasiness or oppressiveness.

Entry, Notebook 50 (1987–90), 77, *Northrop Frye's Late Notebooks, 1982–1990: Architecture of the Spiritual World* (2000), CW, 5.

… the state of being in love is the sense of the infinite possibilities of what is to come.

Entry, Notebook 3 (1946–48), 65, *Northrop Frye's Notebooks and Lectures on the Bible and Other Religious Texts* (2003), CW, 13.

The love of God is the revelation, to man, that he can, if he tries, find something at the centre of his life that is not only immortal but invulnerable.

"Substance and Evidence" (1974), *Northrop Frye on Religion* (2000), CW, 4.

Let your approach to your life revolve around love, for love is not a virtue among others but the only virtue there is.

"Baccalaureate Service (IV)" (1989), *Northrop Frye on Religion* (2000), CW, 4.

LOVE LETTERS

Don't you see, darling? I can't write you a sustained love letter, because when I try — and I have tried — the result sounds like a Chopin nocturne scored for brass.

"NF to HK," Jul. 1932, *The Correspondence of Northrop Frye and Helen Kemp, 1932–1939* (1996), CW, 1.

LOVE POETRY

It is not the experience of love but practice in writing love sonnets that releases the floods of poetic emotion.

"Nature and Homer" (1958), *"The Educated Imagination" and Other Writings on Critical Theory, 1933–1963* (2006), CW, 21.

LOVE'S LABOUR'S LOST

Love's Labour's Lost is the only play of Shakespeare which suggests that the original audience may have been enjoying a good deal that we cannot now recapture.

"Shakespeare's Experimental Comedy" (1961), *Northrop Frye's Writings on Shakespeare and the Renaissance* (2010), CW, 28.

LOYALTY

To commit one's final loyalties to an empire in the world is to be guilty of what Israel summed up in the word "idolatry."

"Symbols" (1968), *Northrop Frye on Religion* (2000), CW, 4.

I think a natural human tendency is to be loyal to the smaller unit that makes sense.

"Between Paradise and Apocalypse" (1978), *Interviews with Northrop Frye* (2008), CW, 24.

There must always be a tension of loyalties, not in the sense of opposed forces pulling apart, but in the sense of one feeling of belonging attached to and complemented by another, which is very often the relating of a smaller ethnical [sic] community to a larger one.

"The Cultural Development of Canada" (1990), *Northrop Frye on Canada* (2003), CW, 12.

The end of commitment is the community; and commitment is what used to be called loyalty.

"The Ethics of Change: The Role of the University" (1968), *Northrop Frye's Writings on Education* (2001), CW, 7.

We will need loyalty to something with enough authority to form a community, but it must be a *free authority*, something that fulfils and does not diminish the individual. Such an authority can ultimately only be the kind of authority that education embodies.

"The Ethics of Change: The Role of the University" (1968), *Northrop Frye's Writings on Education* (2001), CW, 7.

LUST

The difference between love & lust is, of course, that the former is personal and particular, & the latter impersonal & general.

Entry, Notebook 3 (1946–48), 65, *Northrop Frye's Notebooks and Lectures on the Bible and Other Religious Texts* (2003), CW, 13.

LYING

The cause of freedom is not quite hopeless as long as someone realizes that the voice of tyranny is misusing words, that is, lying.

"Sequence and Mode," *Words with Power: Being a Second Study of "The Bible and Literature"* (1990), CW, 26.

Probably one has to lie to men — certainly to women — but not to know that one is lying is to lie to God. Honesty with oneself carries off social lies in a private excretion.

Entry, Notebook 3 (1946–48), 161, *Northrop Frye's Notebooks and Lectures on the Bible and Other Religious Texts* (2003), CW, 13.

Does there *have* to be a lie at the centre of *all* myths of concern? I'm getting very close to saying so. Certainly a *closed* myth must lie.

Entry, Notebook 11f (1969–70), 198, *Northrop Frye's Notebooks and Lectures on the Bible and Other Religious Texts* (2003), CW, 13.

A lie is to the intellect what a neurosis is to the emotions, a blocking point which dams up the current; a stone around which it forms whirlpools.

Entry, Notebook 3 (1946–48), 161, *Northrop Frye's Notebooks and Lectures on the Bible and Other Religious Texts* (2003), CW, 13.

LYRICS

If we read a sixteenth-century lyrical poet, we do not look primarily to see what he is going to say. We know what he is going to say: he is going to complain about the cruelty of his mistress.

"A Natural Perspective: The Development of Shakespearean Comedy and Romance: I, Mouldy Tales" (1963), *Northrop Frye's Writings on Shakespeare and the Renaissance* (2010), CW, 28.

MADNESS

I'm thinking of the fact that the first word in European poetry is the word "madness." In the first words of the *Iliad*, Homer says, "I'm going to sing about madness." And the result is one of the most beautifully structured and symmetrical poems that the human imagination has ever completed.

"The Limits of Dialogue" (1969), *Interviews with Northrop Frye* (2008), CW, 24.

But the notion that madness can be a social disease affecting a specific society at a specific time is, I think, not older than the French Revolution.

"The Imaginative and the Imaginary" (1962), *"The Educated Imagination" and Other Writings on Critical Theory, 1933–1963* (2006), CW, 21.

MAGAZINES

The trouble is that the debasing of a paper's standards cannot be prevented by anybody's good intentions, even an owner's: it can only be prevented by good journalists.

"New Liberties for Old" (1952), referring to the purchase by Jack Kent Cooke of *Saturday Night* magazine, *Northrop Frye on Canada* (2003), CW, 12.

MAGIC

Magic postulates the same kind of universe the artist works in: a universe in which like is connected with like. All forms of occultism, where magic impinges on science, are essentially products of artistic thinking and are frequently sources of inspiration for art, although they are bad science.

"The Relation of Religion to the Arts" (1933–34), *Northrop Frye's Student Essays, 1932–1938* (1997), CW, 3.

Belief in magic: certain things inherently "relevant"; certain subjects ought to "do good" if they're taught.

"On Education II" (1972), 28, *Northrop Frye's Fiction and Miscellaneous Writings* (2007), CW, 25.

Magic seems to begin as something of a voluntary effort to recapture a lost rapport with the natural cycle.

"Second Essay: Ethical Criticism: Theory of Symbols" (1957), *Anatomy of Criticism: Four Essays* (2006), CW, 22.

Magic establishes a charmed circle where spirits can be invoked, held, and commanded by words, and in this unity of word and spirit we have perhaps the most genuine form of an altered state of consciousness.

"The Double Mirror" (1981), with special reference to Shakespeare's play *The Tempest*, *Northrop Frye on Religion* (2000), CW, 4.

The fear of representation is closely connected with the fear of magic. Magic is a sympathetic connexion of consciousness & natural forces where the magician temporarily gains power but is eventually taken over by what he has dominated, as in all legends about bargains with the devil. Idolatry is first a temptation, then a demonic possession.

Entry, Notebook 21 (1969–76), 523, *Northrop Frye's Notebooks and Lectures on the Bible and Other Religious Texts* (2003), CW, 13.

If a spirit is being conjured by the seventy-two names of God as set forth in the *Shemhamphoras*, it will not do if the magician can remember only seventy-one of them.

"The Structure of Imagery in *The Faerie Queene*" (1960), *Northrop Frye's Writings on Shakespeare and the Renaissance* (2010), CW, 28.

MAJORITIES
There is no question of one group of people being inherently less violent than another: the principle involved is simply the elementary arithmetic of original sin. More people are always worse than fewer people.

"National Consciousness in Canadian Culture" (1976), *Northrop Frye on Canada* (2003), CW, 12.

MAKING
What can man make? He can make objects of art; he can develop science, and that's it. He can't make a society except some form of hell. Hence we say that only the grace of God can do anything.

Entry, Notes 53 (1989–90), 60, *Northrop Frye's Late Notebooks, 1982–1990: Architecture of the Spiritual World* (2000), CW, 6.

MALAPROPISM
...malapropism is a parody of poetic etymology.

"Fourth Essay: Rhetorical Criticism: Theory of Genres" (1957), *Anatomy of Criticism: Four Essays* (2006), CW, 22.

MALICE
Malice, like other pacts with the devil, certainly gives one preternatural perceptions, up to a point.

Entry, Notebook 46 (1980s–90), 55, *Northrop Frye's Late Notebooks, 1982–1990: Architecture of the Spiritual World* (2000), CW, 6.

MANDALA
In Jung the symbol of the "individual" perception is the mandala, as he calls it (perhaps he should have called it a yantra), a symmetrical diagram recalling the geometrical cosmologies so common in the Middle Ages and the Renaissance.

"Expanding Eyes" (1975), *"The Critical Path" and Other Writings on Critical Theory, 1963–1975* (2009), CW, 27.

A mandala is not, of course, something to look at, except incidentally: it is or should become a projection of the way one sees.

"Expanding Eyes" (1975), *"The Critical Path" and Other Writings on Critical Theory, 1963–1975* (2009), CW, 27.

MANKIND
What a man essentially is is revealed in two ways: by the record of what he has done, and by what he is trying to make of himself at any given moment.

"Myth I," *The Great Code* (1982), *The Great Code: The Bible and Literature* (2006), CW, 19.

A comparative study of dreams and rituals can lead us only to a vague and intuitive sense of the unity of the human mind; a comparative study of works of art should demonstrate it beyond conjecture.

"Part Three: The Final Synthesis," *Fearful Symmetry: A Study of William Blake* (1947, 2004), CW, 14.

Man has always lived in the middle earth. That's not Tolkien's discovery. It's one of the most ancient myths we have.... Just as man lives in the middle world so he lives in a middle time. He lives in a state of exile between the paradise in the past and the apocalypse in the future.

"Between Paradise and Apocalypse" (1978), *Interviews with Northrop Frye* (2008), CW, 24.

God is a spirit: man is a mixture of spirit and shit. Whatever isn't spirit gets shat, including I think his soul — I still feel that soul is something to get lost, not saved.

Entry, Notebook 50 (1987–90), 268, *Northrop Frye's Late Notebooks, 1982–1990: Architecture of the Spiritual World* (2000), CW, 5.

But there is no such thing as human nature in the abstract. Human nature is always to be found in social contacts, and those social contacts can be improved. Man's nature is expressed in man's institutions, and it is not his nature but his destiny that may be good.

"Preserving Human Values" (1961), *Northrop Frye on Modern Culture* (2003), CW, 11.

Man lives in two worlds. There is a world around him, which he tries to understand and know more about, and which is the particular preserve, I suppose, of the physical sciences. There is also the civilization that he is trying to build and live in, and this, because it concerns him to know what kind of a world he is going to live in, is the peculiar province of these interrelated studies which I have been calling "mythology" and of which literature is a central part.

"Research and Graduate Education in the Humanities" (1968), *Northrop Frye's Writings on Education* (2001), CW, 7.

MAP
Surely there must be a middle ground between a map that tells us nothing about a territory and a map that attempts to replace it.

"Maps and Territories" (1987), *"The Secular Scripture" and Other Writings on Critical Theory, 1976–1991* (2006), CW, 18.

MARIA CHAPDELAINE
Only the outsider to a country finds characters or patterns of behaviour that are seriously typical. *Maria Chapdelaine* has something of this typifying quality, but then *Maria Chapdelaine* is a tourist's novel.

"Culture and the National Will" (1957), *Northrop Frye on Canada* (2003), CW, 12.

MARITIMES
A Bluenose is interested about equally in the existence of God, the nature of man, the destiny of nations, and whether the road from Shubenacadie to Musquodoboit should be paved or left in gravel.

"Haliburton: Mask and Ego" (1962), referring to the views of T.C. Haliburton in the 1830s, *Northrop Frye on Canada* (2003), CW, 12.

If I learn that somebody is a New Brunswicker, that tells me nothing except that he lives in New Brunswick. But if I hear words like "Maritimer" or "Acadian," that tells me a great deal more. It gives me a much more rounded sense of what that person is.

"Autobiographical Reflections: Speech at Moncton's Centennial Celebration" (1990), *Northrop Frye's Fiction and Miscellaneous Writings* (2007), CW, 25.

When I was growing up in the Maritime Provinces during the nineteen-twenties, there was a strong political loyalty to Confederation, but an even stronger sense that Boston was our real capital, and that the Maritimes formed the periphery of New England, or what was often called "the Boston states."

"Canadian Culture Today" (1977), *Northrop Frye on Canada* (2003), CW, 12.

MARRIAGE
I certainly wouldn't marry anybody unless she were beautiful and intelligent and accomplished and sensible and virtuous and — what else are you darling?

"NF to HK," 13 Apr. 1939, *The Correspondence of Northrop Frye and Helen Kemp, 1932–1939* (1996), CW, 1.

I suppose when people ask me they want either a personal touch or less religion than they get from professionals.

Entry, 3 Jan. 1949, 27, referring to officiating at the wedding of a friend, *The Diaries of Northrop Frye: 1942–1955* (2001), CW, 8.

MARTYRDOM
Every martyr dies for the same cause: any social vision to which one will commit his life is genuine. And of course a revolutionary's social vision may be quite intense enough for that: the sense of demonic possession is partly superstitious.

Entry, Notebook 24 (1970–72), 95, *The "Third Book" Notebooks of Northrop Frye, 1964–1972: The Critical Comedy* (2002), CW, 9.

Martyrs don't necessarily believe in rewards for martyrdom, but they behave *as* though they were citizens of a bigger multi-dimensional world than their persecutors.

Entry, Notebook 44 (1986–91), 215, *Northrop Frye's Late Notebooks, 1982–1990: Architecture of the Spiritual World* (2000), CW, 5.

MARX, KARL
Marx says that a quantitative increase at a certain point will produce a qualitative change; he forgot to add that ninety-nine times out of a hundred the qualitative change is disastrous.

"Towards an Oral History of the University of Toronto" (1982), *Interviews with Northrop Frye* (2008), CW, 24.

I'm trying to arrive at a conception of faith which will permit one to say: "Karl Marx believed in the myth of Prometheus."

Entry, Notebook 21 (1969–76), 594, *Northrop Frye's Notebooks and Lectures on the Bible and Other Religious Texts* (2003), CW, 13.

Marx himself was undoubtedly a great writer in the anatomic tradition: he had the satirist's truculence, excremental imagery, & inability to finish books.

Entry, Notebook 19 (1964–67), 348, *The "Third Book" Notebooks of Northrop Frye, 1964–1972: The Critical Comedy* (2002), CW, 9.

The two greatest modern achievements in this field are represented by Marx and Spengler, one a Communist and the other more or less a Nazi.

"Toynbee and Spengler" (1947), referring to "the synthesis of modern thought," *Northrop Frye on Modern Culture* (2003), CW, 11.

MARXISM

Marxism and Freudianism are two of the most powerful intellectual forces in the world today: I think it is quite intelligible to say that Marxism grew out of the myth of Prometheus, as Freudianism did out of the myth of Eros.

"The Mythical Approach to Creation" (1985), *Northrop Frye on Religion* (2000), CW, 4.

The United States never got sold on Marxism apart from the intellectuals, because they had their mattress to sleep on, the American way of life, with all its anti-intellectual cosiness.

Entry, Notes 53 (1989–90), 155, *Northrop Frye's Late Notebooks, 1982–1990: Architecture of the Spiritual World* (2000), CW, 6.

It's natural that Marxism should find a rest home in the humanities now that it's on the skids everywhere else.

Entry, Notebook 46 (1980s–1990), 56, *Northrop Frye's Late Notebooks, 1982–1990: Architecture of the Spiritual World* (2000), CW, 6.

Marxism is a vision of life, with its roots in the social imagination, and it will endure, at least as a vision, until another of greater intensity grows up in its place.

"Humanities in a New World" (1958), *Northrop Frye's Writings on Education* (2001), CW, 7.

It's ironic that Marxism, which tried to define ideology as the rationalizings of non-Marxists, should have turned into the one movement of our day that absolutizes ideology.

Entry, Notebook 44 (1986–91), 28, *Northrop Frye's Late Notebooks, 1982–1990: Architecture of the Spiritual World* (2000), CW, 5.

… I wouldn't call Marxism a pseudoreligion. I would call it a quite genuine religion.

"Into the Wilderness" (1969), *Interviews with Northrop Frye* (2008), CW, 24.

Marxism is a very remarkable intellectual achievement as well as the dominant moral force in the contemporary world, but, at least wherever it has come to power, it cannot really cope with the humanities or with the place of the arts in modern society.

"Conclusion to *Literary History of Canada*" (1965), *Northrop Frye on Canada* (2003), CW, 12.

MASQUE

The most dramatic aspect of the masque is its transitory quality: like a World's Fair, which erects a whole city and then tears it down, an enormously costly, elaborate, and variegated performance is put on and then disappears.

Entry, Notes 58-7 (c. 1975), *Northrop Frye's Notebooks on Renaissance Literature* (2006), CW, 20.

MASSEY REPORT

The Massey Report, published in 1951, was a landmark in the history of Canadian culture, not merely because it recommended a Canada Council, but because it signified the end of cultural laissez-faire and assumed that the country itself had a responsibility for fostering its own culture.

"Across the River and Out of the Trees" (1980), referring to the Royal Commission on the National Development in the Arts, Letters and Sciences, usually referred to as the Massey Commission, which was chaired by Vincent Massey, *Northrop Frye on Canada* (2003), CW, 12.

MATERIALISM

Speaking with contempt of the merely material world seems to be one of the privileges of having a middle-class income.

"Substance and Evidence" (1974), *Northrop Frye on Religion* (2000), CW, 4.

Our physical bodies are part of a world usually described as material, but if matter is simply energy cooled down to the point at which our physical bodies can live with it, perhaps spirit can enter a world of higher energies where the separate things spread around objective heres and theres are no longer things to keep bumping into.
The Double Vision (1991), *Northrop Frye on Religion* (2000), CW, 4.

MATHEMATICS
The arts might be more clearly understood if they were thought of as forming a circle, stretching from music through literature, painting, and sculpture to architecture, with mathematics, the missing part, occupying the vacant space between architecture and music.
"Notes" (1957), *Anatomy of Criticism: Four Essays* (2006), CW, 22.

I know nothing about this, but it seems to me that contemplative mysticism is akin to mathematics, not to existential concern. Also that mathematics affords the only clue to what's left of the order & purpose that's out there.
Entry, Notebook 19 (1964–67), 326, *The "Third Book" Notebooks of Northrop Frye, 1964–1972: The Critical Comedy* (2002), CW, 9.

The sciences deal with facts and truths, but mathematics sets one free from the particular case: it leads us from three apples to three, and from a square field to a square.
"Humanities in a New World" (1958), *Northrop Frye's Writings on Education* (2001), CW, 7.

For a time, I thought that the exclamation marks in the equations of the mathematicians represented some enthusiasm for the beauty of their subject, and that there was at least that much communication possible; but I was undeceived on this point.
"The Changing Pace in Canadian Education" (1963), *Northrop Frye's Writings on Education* (2001), CW, 7.

MATURITY
We have to conclude, it seems to me, that there are no mature people. Maturity is not a thing you find in people; it's a thing that you find only in certain mental processes.
"The Definition of a University" (1970), *Northrop Frye's Writings on Education* (2001), CW, 7.

McLUHAN, MARSHALL
His relation to the public was the opposite of Innis's: he was caught up in the manic-depressive roller-coaster of the news media, so that he was hysterically celebrated in the 1960s and unreasonably neglected thereafter.
"Across the River and Out of the Trees" (1980), *Northrop Frye on Canada* (2003), CW, 12.

When Trudeau became prime minister and adopted Marshall McLuhan as one of his advisors, Canada reverted to tribalism.
"Culture as Interpenetration" (1977), *Northrop Frye on Canada* (2003), CW, 12.

McLuhan defines a specialist as the man who never makes a minor mistake on his way to a major fallacy.
"Across the River and Out of the Trees" (1980), *Northrop Frye on Canada* (2003), CW, 12.

But metaphor was made for man and not man for metaphor; or, as my late and much beloved colleague Marshall McLuhan used to say, man's reach should exceed his grasp, or what's a metaphor.
"The Double Mirror" (1981), *Northrop Frye on Religion* (2000), CW, 4.

Not long ago I was asked to speak to a group of alumni in a neighbouring city, and a reporter on a paper in that city phoned my secretary and asked if this was to be a "hot" item. My secretary explained that Professor Frye was what his late colleague Marshall McLuhan would have called a cool medium of low definition, and that he could well skip the occasion, which he did with obvious relief. The incident was trivial, but it started me thinking about the curiously topsy-turvy world of "news" as reported today.
Address, "The Authority of Learning" (1984), *Northrop Frye's Writings on Education* (2007), CW, 7.

Marshall McLuhan's phrase "the medium is the message" has been quoted so often, even at this conference, that it has lost all its meaning, if it ever had any. But another phrase of McLuhan's is much more concrete: he speaks of the need for civil defence against media fallout, which exactly describes what I mean here.

"Violence and Television" (1975), speaking at a Symposium on Television Violence at Queen's University, Kingston, *Northrop Frye on Modern Culture* (2003), CW, 11.

Marshall McLuhan is a typical example: a reputation as a great thinker based on the fact that he doesn't think at all.

Entry, Notebook 12 (1968–70), 66, suggesting that "greatness *ended* around 1940," *The "Third Book" Notebooks of Northrop Frye, 1964–1972: The Critical Comedy* (2002), CW, 9.

A scholar who is a serious and original thinker has a good deal of the charismatic leader about him.

"A Meeting of Minds" (1967), with special reference to Marshall McLuhan and the Centre for Culture and Technology, *Northrop Frye's Writings on Education* (2001), CW, 7.

MEANING

The principle of manifold or "polysemous" meaning, as Dante calls it, is not a theory any more, still less an exploded superstition, but an established fact.

"Second Essay: Ethical Criticism: Theory of Symbols" (1957), *Anatomy of Criticism: Four Essays* (2006), CW, 22.

There is no "real" meaning in literature, nothing to be "got out of it" or abstracted from the total experience; yet all criticism seems to be concerned with approaching such a meaning.

"Criticism, Visible and Invisible" (1964), *"The Critical Path" and Other Writings on Critical Theory, 1963–1975* (2009), CW, 27.

What Jesus meant may not be so easy to say, but everyone is united on what he did not mean.

"Metaphor I," *The Great Code* (1982), *The Great Code: The Bible and Literature* (2006), CW, 19.

The ultimate significance of a work of art is simply a dimension added to its literal meaning, which can no more be separated from it than the depth of a pool of water can be separated from its surface.

"Part One: The Argument," *Fearful Symmetry: A Study of William Blake* (1947, 2004), CW, 14.

Perhaps a good mental exercise would be to take a sentence at random & ponder it until it becomes utterly meaningless, as I should think the proposition "there is a God" would be to a really religious man.

Entry, Notebook 3 (1946–48), 64, *Northrop Frye's Notebooks and Lectures on the Bible and Other Religious Texts* (2003), CW, 13.

The meaning of a work of art is independent of its creator, because a universal imagination is involved in it.

"Part Three: The Final Synthesis," *Fearful Symmetry: A Study of William Blake* (1947, 2004), CW, 14.

Every work of literature meant something in its own day and now means something rather different to us.

"Teaching the Humanities Today" (1977), *Northrop Frye's Writings on Education* (2001), CW, 7.

The assertion that the critic should not look for more in a poem than the poet may safely be assumed to have been conscious of putting there is a common form of what may be called the fallacy of premature teleology. It corresponds to the assertion that a natural phenomenon is as it is because Providence in its inscrutable wisdom made it so.

"The Archetypes of Literature" (1951), *"The Educated Imagination" and Other Writings on Critical Theory, 1933–1963* (2006), CW, 21.

MECHANISMS

The difference between a mechanism and an organism is in will, not in capacity.

Entry, Notes 52 (1982–90), 189, *Northrop Frye's Late Notebooks, 1982–1990: Architecture of the Spiritual World* (2000), CW, 6.

Marginal elements in the mind express themselves as automatisms. They are threatening as such, because any mechanism brings along with it the shock troops of alienation. Are these automatisms the devils cast out in the Gospels?
> Entry, Notebook 21 (1969–76), 520, *Northrop Frye's Notebooks and Lectures on the Bible and Other Religious Texts* (2003), CW, 13.

I note that the Robot aspect of man is easiest to see across a gap of generations: the young see it in the old, the old in the young.
> Entry, 16 Jan. 1952, 37, *The Diaries of Northrop Frye: 1942–1955* (2001), CW, 8.

I regard all machines as malignant demons: The best thing they can do is come apart in my hands.
> Remark quoted by Gillian Cosgrove, *Toronto Star*, 7 Aug. 1980.

MEDIA

New media of communication are not causes of social change: they are only the conditions of change, and we cannot discover the *direction* of social change from them; it is society itself that will determine the direction of change.
> "Literature and Society" (1968), *"The Critical Path" and Other Writings on Critical Theory, 1963–1975* (2009), CW, 27.

All the mass media have a close connection with the centres of social authority, and reflect their anxieties. In socialist countries they reflect the anxiety of the political Establishment to retain power; in the United States they reflect the anxiety of the economic Establishment to keep production running. In either case communication is a one-way street.
> "Communications" (1970), *Northrop Frye on Modern Culture* (2003), CW, 11.

This is why I think students should be encouraged to become aware of the extent to which they are being conditioned by the mass media, as a central part of their literary training.
> "On Teaching Literature" (1972), *Northrop Frye's Writings on Education* (2001), CW, 7.

One would hope to see the present notion disappear that mass media must be controlled either by propaganda or by advertising, that the former means totalitarianism and slavery and the latter democracy and freedom. The confusion of the liberal and the *laissez-faire* is still very much with us.
> "The Instruments of Mental Production" (1966), *Northrop Frye's Writings on Education* (2001), CW, 7.

The television set is so much more introverted than even the movie, and the movie in turn more introverted than the concert hall or the stage.
> "Northrop Frye in Conversation" (1989), *Interviews with Northrop Frye* (2008), CW, 24.

Democracy and book culture are interdependent, and the rise of oral and visual media represents, not a new order to adjust to, but a subordinate order to be contained.
> *The Critical Path: An Essay on the Social Context of Literary Criticism* (1971), *"The Critical Path" and Other Writings on Critical Theory, 1963–1975* (2009), CW, 27.

It is all very well to say that the medium is the message, but as we seem to get much the same message from all the media, it follows that all media, within a given social environment like that of the Soviet Union or the United States, are much the same medium.
> *The Critical Path: An Essay on the Social Context of Literary Criticism* (1971), *"The Critical Path" and Other Writings on Critical Theory, 1963–1975* (2009), CW, 27.

In our day the electronic media of film, radio, and television have brought about a revival of the oral culture that we had before writing, and many of the social characteristics of a preliterate society are reappearing in ours.
> "Communications" (1970), *Northrop Frye on Modern Culture* (2003), CW, 11.

Television, newspapers, films, are all educational agencies, though what they do mostly is more like dope peddling than like serious education.
> "Leisure and Boredom" (1963), *Northrop Frye on Literature and Society, 1936–1989: Unpublished Papers* (2002), CW, 10.

Thus the primary determining quality of the medium comes from the social motive for using it and not from the medium itself.
> *The Modern Century* (1967), *Northrop Frye on Modern Culture* (2003), CW, 11.

It is not just the voice we hear that haunts us, but the voice that goes on echoing in our minds, forming our habits of speech, our processes of thought.
> "Communications" (1970), *Northrop Frye on Modern Culture* (2003), CW, 11.

Media may be hot or cool, but societies do not turn hot or cool in consequence of adopting them. Canada is a cool country with cool people in it, hence all its media are cool.
> "Across the River and Out of the Trees" (1980), *Northrop Frye on Canada* (2003), CW, 12.

The difference between the linear and the simultaneous is not a difference between two kinds of media, but a difference between two mental operations within all media. There is always a linear response followed by a simultaneous one, whatever the medium.
> "Communications" (1970), *Northrop Frye on Modern Culture* (2003), CW, 11.

I see the media age as *reshaping* the old myths — there aren't any new ones. No matter what the mechanical devices employed, mythologies are transmitting words and pictures, which is what the human race has transmitted since Palaeolithic times.
> "On the Media" (1986), *Interviews with Northrop Frye* (2008), CW, 24.

I remember that the old silent movies tended strongly to be grotesque in comedy and fantastic in more serious themes. This was a deaf man's art, at the opposite extreme from the blind man's art of radio, where the hysterical and the hypnotic are always just around the corner.
> "Icons and Iconoclasm" (1970), *Northrop Frye on Literature and Society, 1936–1989: Unpublished Papers* (2002), CW, 10.

MEDICINE
Some demon took advantage of my enfeebled state this morning to whisper into my ear that the two greatest medicines of antiquity were poppy and mummy.
> Entry, Notebook 42b (1942–44), 9, *Northrop Frye's Fiction and Miscellaneous Writings* (2007), CW, 25.

The professor in our day is in the same position as the modern doctor who has to try to cure *Weltschmerz* as well as bellyaches. The doctor may long for the simple old days when hysteria and hypochondria were specific disturbances of the womb or the abdomen, but he is not living in those days, and must struggle as best he can with the intangible.
> "The University and Personal Life: Student Anarchism and the Educational Contract" (1968), *Northrop Frye's Writings on Education* (2001), CW, 7.

MEDITATION
Even granting the human tendency to look in every direction except the obviously right one, it seems strange to overlook the possibility that the arts, including literature, might just conceivably be what they have always been taken to be, possible techniques of meditation, in the strictest sense of the word, ways of cultivating, focussing, and ordering one's mental processes, on a basis of symbol rather than concept.
> "Expanding Eyes" (1975), *"The Critical Path" and Other Writings on Critical Theory, 1963–1975* (2009), CW, 27.

Why are there no pictures or statues of Christ in meditation, as there are of the Buddha?
> Entry, Notebook 12 (1968–70), 198, *The "Third Book" Notebooks of Northrop Frye, 1964–1972: The Critical Comedy* (2002), CW, 9.

And whenever I turn in pursuit of my verbal interests, I come up against the fact that our ordinary experience rests on unreal and fuzzy experiences of time and space, and that myth and metaphor are among other things techniques of meditation, designed to focus our minds on a more real view of both.
> "The Mythical Approach to Creation" (1985), *Northrop Frye on Religion* (2000), CW, 4.

Practically all techniques of meditation, for example, work with symbols, verbal or

pictorial, that expand toward an identity, however defined, with what they symbolize.
> "Spirit and Symbol," *Words with Power: Being a Second Study of "The Bible and Literature"* (1990), CW, 26.

As a technique of focussing the mind, literature is a medium of meditation.
> Entry, Notes 52 (1982–90), 641, *Northrop Frye's Late Notebooks, 1982–1990: Architecture of the Spiritual World* (2000), CW, 6.

MEDIUM
The principle that the medium is the message, for any form of *interested* communication, lasts only so long as we remain relatively unconscious of the form: as soon as we become conscious of it the content separates from it.
> Entry, Notebook 12 (1968–70), 491, *The "Third Book" Notebooks of Northrop Frye, 1964–1972: The Critical Comedy* (2002), CW, 9.

I have never understood why that blithering nonsense "the medium is the message" caught on so. Apparently the terms "medium" and "message" are being aligned with "form" and "content" respectively. And while it would make sense to say that form and content are inseparable, a medium is just that, a medium.
> Entry, Notebook 44 (1986–91), 651, *Northrop Frye's Late Notebooks, 1982–1990: Architecture of the Spiritual World* (2000), CW, 5.

If the medium is the message, & newspapers & magazines & radio & television all carry the same message, it follows that they're all pretty much the same medium.
> Entry, Notebook 11f (1969–70), 112, *Northrop Frye's Notebooks and Lectures on the Bible and Other Religious Texts* (2003), CW, 13.

MEECH LAKE ACCORD
For the last few weeks we've been watching that curious one-sided football game that Canadians seem to be preoccupied with — eleven men kicking around a compromise.
> "Tribute to Don and Pauline McGibbon" (1990), *Northrop Frye on Canada* (2003), referring to the failed accord for constitutional renewal, CW, 12.

MELODRAMA
Melodrama leans to the moral and conceptual, and tries to identify us with a heroism we admire and separate us from a villainy we detest. Melodrama thus tends to find its emotional tragic focus in the punishment of the villain, and our reaction to that is primarily: "Oh, the difference from me!"
> "*Fools of Time*: III, Little World of Man: The Tragedy of Isolation" (1966), *Northrop Frye's Writings on Shakespeare and the Renaissance* (2010), CW, 28.

MEMORIAL SERVICE
The impulse to speak nothing but good of the dead is not superstition: it is one of the deepest and most accurate feelings about life that we have.
> "Baccalaureate Sermon" (1967), *Northrop Frye on Religion* (2000), CW, 4.

MEMORIZATION
Many a boy who cannot remember what countries are in South America can tell the year and make of an automobile a hundred yards away, a feat mainly achieved within what literary critics call the oral tradition.
> "Introduction to *Design for Learning*" (1962), *Northrop Frye's Writings on Education* (2001), CW, 7.

MEMORY
The pianist cannot consciously remember all the notes he played, but there is a data bank inside him which is vastly more efficient than his conscious memory.
> "Some Reflections on Life and Habit" (1988), *Northrop Frye's Writings on the Eighteenth and Nineteenth Centuries* (2005), CW, 17.

Only when conscious memory is treated as an end in itself does education become a treadmill of repetition.
> "Some Reflections on Life and Habit" (1988), *Northrop Frye's Writings on the Eighteenth and Nineteenth Centuries* (2005), CW, 17.

My happiest & most intense moments are *remembered* moments associated with specific places like the streets of Toronto. The tearing down of houses & other familiar landmarks I find emotionally disturbing, yet of course at the same time I understand how phony this feeling is.

> Entry, Notebook 21 (1969–76), 26, *Northrop Frye's Notebooks and Lectures on the Bible and Other Religious Texts* (2003), CW, 13.

And yet, there is a personal test which every critic applies to poetry, the test of involuntary memorizing. If one remembers a poem, or part of a poem, without making a conscious effort to do so, one is probably dealing with a genuine poet.

> "Letters in Canada: Poetry" (1955), *Northrop Frye on Canada* (2003), CW, 12.

Je me souviens is an ambiguous motto: everything depends on what one is expected to remember.

> "The Cultural Development of Canada" (1990), referring to the official motto of the Province of Quebec, *Northrop Frye on Canada* (2003), CW, 12.

I've always said that when a person loses his memory, he's senile. A nation that loses its sense of history goes senile. That's why I think the memory should be kept active in the educational process; because of the continuity.

> "Love of Learning" (1987), *Interviews with Northrop Frye* (2008), CW, 24.

The memory selects, rejects, rearranges, condenses and displaces. In short, it *mythicizes* our history.

> Entry, Notebook 27 (1986), 211, *Northrop Frye's Late Notebooks, 1982–1990: Architecture of the Spiritual World* (2000), CW, 5.

A man with a large stock of facts is not always a student, any more than a miser is always an economist.

> "By Liberal Things" (1959), *Northrop Frye's Writings on Education* (2001), CW, 7.

MERCHANT OF VENICE, THE

Someone asked me a while ago whether *The Merchant of Venice* was anti-Semitic. You might as well say that *Dracula* is anti-Hungarian. You have to take these things in the context in which they appeared.

> "Love of Learning" (1987), *Interviews with Northrop Frye* (2008), CW, 24.

MESSIAH

If a Jew tells me he can't accept Jesus as the Messiah, there isn't, in these days, any question of conversion on either side, merely a realization that we both see the same things from different points of view: in short, interpenetration.

> Entry, Notes 53 (1989–90), 191, *Northrop Frye's Late Notebooks, 1982–1990: Architecture of the Spiritual World* (2000), CW, 6.

METAHISTORY

We notice that metahistory, though it usually tends to very long and erudite books, is far more popular than regular history: in fact metahistory is really the form in which most history reaches the general public. It is only the metahistorian, whether Spengler or Toynbee or H.G. Wells or a religious writer using history as his source of *exempla*, who has much chance of becoming a bestseller.

> "New Directions from Old" (1960), *"The Educated Imagination" and Other Writings on Critical Theory, 1933–1963* (2006), CW, 21.

METAPHOR

It is a primitive form of awareness, established long before the distinction of subject and object became normal, but when we try to outgrow it we find that all we can really do is rehabilitate it.

> "Introduction" (1990), *Words with Power: Being a Second Study of "The Bible and Literature"* (2008), CW, 26.

The basis of poetic expression is the metaphor, and the basis of naive allegory is the mixed metaphor.

> "Second Essay: Ethical Criticism: Theory of Symbols" (1957), *Anatomy of Criticism: Four Essays* (2006), CW, 22.

The Bible expands metaphor into what might be called existential metaphor, the actual identifying of a conscious subject with something objective to itself.

> "Framework and Assumption" (1985), *"The Secular Scripture" and Other Writings on Critical Theory, 1976–1991* (2006), CW, 18.

Nobody can deal with a metaphor except by something like Saint Patrick's shamrock expounding the doctrine of the Trinity. The actual statement is a metaphor, and the function of the metaphor is to release the imagination by paralysing the discursive reason. It's like the koan in Zen Buddhism.
> "Symbolism in the Bible" (1981–82), *Northrop Frye's Notebooks and Lectures on the Bible and Other Religious Texts* (2003), CW, 13.

Every one of the standard figures of speech, except the metaphor, draws attention to the fact that it's "just" a figure. The simile has its reassuring "like," the oxymoron draws attention to its self-contradiction; the hyperbole to its excess; the synecdoche to its deficiency; the metonym to its "signified." Only the metaphor says "This is [not]." Juxtaposition of two images suggests identity, whether asserted by "is" or not; the fact that there are two images to be juxtaposed suggests the "is not" counterpoint.
> Entry, Notebook 44 (1986–91), 320, *Northrop Frye's Late Notebooks, 1982–1990: Architecture of the Spiritual World* (2000), CW, 5.

... there are no courses in remedial metaphor.
> "Elementary Teaching and Elemental Scholarship" (1963), *Northrop Frye's Writings on Education* (2001), CW, 7.

Our visions of what our society is, what it could be, and what it should be, are all structures of metaphor, because the metaphor is the unit of all imagination. Logical thinking in this field seldom does more than rationalize these metaphoric visions.
> "The Authority of Learning" (1984), *Northrop Frye's Writings on Education* (2001), CW, 7.

... but I think metaphor provides an identity beyond difference, a construction beyond deconstruction.
> Entry, Notes 52 (1982–90), 450, *Northrop Frye's Late Notebooks, 1982–1990: Architecture of the Spiritual World* (2000), CW, 6.

What you are dealing with when you are thinking in metaphors is not a world of solid blocks or obstacles, not a world of nouns that can be kicked around by verbs: it's a world of metaphors, and metaphorical imagery is a world of forces and energies which often modulate into one another.
> "Symbolism in the Bible" (1981–82), *Northrop Frye's Notebooks and Lectures on the Bible and Other Religious Texts* (2003), CW, 13.

METAPHYSICS

And I think that new philosophical developments are beginning to see at least metaphysics, if not in fact logic, as an outgrowth of verbalism.
> Entry, Notebook 30n (1946–50), 1, *Northrop Frye's Notebooks on Romance* (2004), CW, 15.

MIDDLE CLASS

Those who accept and are loyal to the social contract are known consistently, throughout the whole period, as the bourgeoisie or middle class, otherwise known, in different contexts, as Philistines or squares.
> *The Modern Century* (1967), *Northrop Frye on Modern Culture* (2003), CW, 11.

I love the propertied middle class, though not for being that, & never walk along residential streets in Toronto without thinking that it really is a very great civilization. I see it now somewhat as our envious great-grandchildren will.
> Entry, 12 Feb. 1950, 109, occasioned by a Sunday evening walk at dusk through the Deer Park area of the city, *The Diaries of Northrop Frye: 1942–1955* (2001), CW, 8.

People feel ashamed to adopt the principle, which I think they might very well adopt, that bourgeois equals human being and anything else is strictly out of the trees.
> "A Literate Pearson Is First and Foremost an Articulate Person" (1977), *Interviews with Northrop Frye* (2008), CW, 24.

I'm also a bourgeois liberal. I feel that anybody who isn't one, or at least doesn't want to be one, is still in the trees.
> "Northrop Frye in Conversation" (1992), *Interviews with Northrop Frye* (2008), CW, 24.

MILL, JOHN STUART

J.S. Mill could write of civilization, but not of culture: he had too much of the deracinated protestant animal and too little of the rank catholic vegetable.

> Entry, Notebook 30c: John Stuart Mill (after 1965), 2, *Northrop Frye's Fiction and Miscellaneous Writings* (2007), CW, 25.

MILNE, DAVID

Milne's whole aim is apparently to present a pure visual experience, detached from all the feelings which belong to the sense of separation from the object, feelings which are mainly tactile in origin.

> "David Milne: An Appreciation" (1948), *Northrop Frye on Canada* (2003), CW, 12.

Few if any contemporary painters, in or outside Canada, convey better than he does the sense of painting as an emancipation of visual experience, as a training of the intelligence to see the world in a spirit of leisure and urbanity.

> "David Milne: An Appreciation" (1948), *Northrop Frye on Canada* (2003), CW, 12.

MILTON, JOHN

If you teach Milton, you find that those tremendous lines in *Paradise Lost* begin to separate from their context and take on an individual life and start chasing themselves around your skull. Any poet who does that to you is obviously somebody you have to reckon with.

> "Northrop Frye in Conversation" (1989), *Interviews with Northrop Frye* (2008), CW, 24.

In an enlightened age like ours, a politically active poet could not possibly survive four revolutions. And there are many today who would admire Milton more if he had been executed in 1660.

> "Introduction to '*Paradise Lost*' and Selected Poetry and Prose" (June 1950), *Northrop Frye on Milton and Blake* (2005), CW, 16.

MIND

We have long since weathered the Newtonian crisis of separating mythological from natural space, and the Darwinian crisis of separating mythological from natural time. A third crisis, more difficult and subtle, is succeeding it: the distinguishing of the ordinary waking consciousness of external reality from the creative and transforming aspects of the mind.

> "Expanding Eyes" (1975), *"The Critical Path" and Other Writings on Critical Theory, 1963–1975* (2009), CW, 27.

The mind seems to want to expand, to move from the closed fortress of believer and sceptic to the community of vision.

> "Language II," *The Great Code* (1982), *The Great Code: The Bible and Literature* (2006), CW, 19.

The mind best fitted for survival in any world is the mind that has discovered how knowledge can be joyful, leading to the friendship with wisdom that is pure delight, and is ready to tackle any kind of knowledge with clarity of perception and intentness of will. I should call such a mind not a trained but a dedicated mind, and any business or profession would be lucky to have one.

> "To Come to Light" (1988), *Northrop Frye on Religion* (1999), CW, 4.

The discovery that all men are the same man is the point of Nous, the symposium disappearing into the wise man's mind and seeing there the pattern of the just state.

> Entry, Notebook 12 (1968–70), 570, employing the Greek word for "mind," *The "Third Book" Notebooks of Northrop Frye, 1964–1972: The Critical Comedy* (2002), CW, 9.

The sources of creative power in the human mind are inexhaustible. If we could realize that they are infinite and eternal as well, and that the human mind is therefore linked in its nature and destiny with a divine mind, that would be the final motive for learning and the final guarantee of its value.

> "By Liberal Things" (1959), *Northrop Frye's Writings on Education* (2001), CW, 7.

MIRACLES

A miracle in the sense of a simply incredible or impossible event is, doubtless, not an event at all but a symbol.

> Entry, Notebook 21 (1969–76), 369, *Northrop Frye's Notebooks and Lectures on the Bible and Other Religious Texts* (2003), CW, 13.

God works within human life and under "fallen" human conditions. That's why the Gospel, not the Book of Genesis, is the Christian centre. But then why do the Gospels feature miracles? I know the symbolic answers: the only real miracle is not a "sign" but the transformation of the believer, but I'm groping for other kinds of answers.
> Entry, Notebook 18 (1956–62), 147, *Notebooks for "Anatomy of Criticism"* (2007), CW, 23.

And of course it's all wrong to pray for miracles, in the sense of interruptions into the order of nature. Miracles are epiphanies, not primarily favours. (Mustard seed?)
> Entry, Notebook 44 (1986–91), 169, *Northrop Frye's Late Notebooks, 1982–1990: Architecture of the Spiritual World* (2000), CW, 5.

The miraculous element in the Gospels can't be assimilated to history or it becomes accusation: once we could have and see miracles, but now, you poor jerks, etc. There never were any miracles, but there can be miracles: miracles represent present potentials, not past actuals.
> Entry, Notes 53 (1989–90), 241, *Northrop Frye's Late Notebooks, 1982–1990: Architecture of the Spiritual World* (2000), CW, 6.

… they are a crude form of scientific experiment. The miracles of Jesus depended on the belief of the recipient. A real miracle is an imaginative effort which meets with an imaginative response.
> "Part One: The Argument," *Fearful Symmetry: A Study of William Blake* (1947, 2004), CW, 14.

Miracles reveal what the imagination can do. The opposite of revelation is mystery, and a miracle which remains mysterious is a fraud, especially if it is an authentic miracle.…
> "Part One: The Argument," considering Blake's view, *Fearful Symmetry: A Study of William Blake* (1947, 2004), CW, 14.

MISERY

The more one says he is happy, the more quickly we get out of his way to prevent him from making us miserable.
> "On Value Judgments" (1968), *"The Critical Path" and Other Writings on Critical Theory, 1963–1975* (2009), CW, 27.

MITHRAISM

Mithraism went everywhere with the Roman Empire: a Nazi bomb falling in London exposed a Mithraic temple during the war, and if you go to Rome, one place that you should definitely not miss is the church of San Clemente, where there is a series of four or five churches of different periods, and a Mithraic temple lying at the very bottom of the whole structure.
> "Symbolism in the Bible" (1981–82), *Northrop Frye's Notebooks and Lectures on the Bible and Other Religious Texts* (2003), CW, 13.

MOB

An aggregate of egos is a mob.
> *The Well-tempered Critic* (1963), *"The Educated Imagination" and Other Writings on Critical Theory, 1933–1963* (2006), CW, 21.

… a mob is a society without any individuals.
> "Into the Wilderness" (1969), *Interviews with Northrop Frye* (2008), CW, 24.

Yet the only really permanent way to turn society into a mob is to debase the arts: to turn literature into slanted news, painting into billboard advertising, music into caterwauling transistor sets, architecture into mean streets.
> "Academy without Walls" (1961), *Northrop Frye on Modern Culture* (2003), CW, 11.

A mob always has a leader, but a people is a larger human body in which there are no leaders or followers, but only individuals acting as functions of the group.
> "Trends in Modern Culture" (1952), *Northrop Frye on Modern Culture* (2003), CW, 11.

MODELS

One feels of the wax mannequins in a modern shop window that any girl who succeeded in being as haughty and aloof as they look would be in an advanced state of narcissism, and ought to see a psychiatrist before going out of business entirely.

"Design as a Creative Principle in the Arts" (1966), *"The Critical Path" and Other Writings on Critical Theory, 1963–1975* (2009), CW, 27.

MODERN
"Modern," in itself, means simply recent: in Shakespeare's day it meant mediocre, and it still sometimes carries that meaning as an emotional overtone.
> *The Modern Century* (1967), *Northrop Frye on Modern Culture* (2003), CW, 11.

It is true that many aspects of modern culture, especially popular culture, are of American origin, like jazz, but America is a province conquered by the international modern much more than it is a source of it.
> *The Modern Century* (1967), *Northrop Frye on Modern Culture* (2003), CW, 11.

MODERN LANGUAGE ASSOCIATION
A hundred years is not a long time, geologically speaking: I have been teaching for nearly half that time myself, and for well over a third of it I have belonged to the MLA and watched its letters come increasingly to stand for Miscellaneous Linguistic Activities.
> "Literary and Linguistic Scholarship in a Postliterate World" (1983), address, MLA Centennial Convention, *"The Secular Scripture" and Other Writings on Critical Theory, 1976–1991* (2006), CW, 18.

MODESTY
It is a natural human tendency, said to be abnormally developed among Canadians, to undervalue whatever one has oneself.
> "Introduction to Charles T. Currelly, *I Brought the Ages Home*" (1956), *Northrop Frye on Canada* (2003), CW, 12.

MOHAMMED THE PROPHET
Mohammed was a very great inspired poet, but he found that this quality was precisely what made him distrusted. So he insisted that he wasn't a poet but a prophet, & started brainwashing his followers with interminable repetitions of the you-just-wait type.
> Entry, Notebook 11f (1969–70), 82, *Northrop Frye's Notebooks and Lectures on the Bible and Other Religious Texts* (2003), CW, 13.

MONA LISA
If I am looking at *Mona Lisa*, I can no more get away from the gum-chewing tourist beside me than I can get away from Walter Pater, except by responding to a meaning in the picture essentially "evocative" and "spell-bearing."
> "The Diatribes of Wyndham Lewis: A Study in Prose Satire" (1936), *Northrop Frye's Student Essays, 1932–1938* (1997), CW, 3.

MONARCHY
The real point about a monarchy is that it puts the cult of personality where it belongs, in the area of ceremonial symbolism.
> "Speech at the New Canadian Embassy, Washington" (1989), *Northrop Frye on Canada* (2003), CW, 12.

The monarch today has become the exact opposite of the dictator, who stands for personality alone. Respect paid to a monarch is paid to a symbol of society; respect paid to a dictator is the narcissism of the mob.
> "Regina versus the World" (1953), *Northrop Frye on Modern Culture* (2003), CW, 11.

MONCTON, N.B.
I grew up in two towns, Sherbrooke and Moncton, where the population was half English and half French, divided by language, education, and religion, and living in a state of more or less amiable Apartheid.
> Preface, *The Bush Garden* (1971), *Northrop Frye on Canada* (2003), CW, 12.

Amiable apartheid, not a word I'd use for anything I approved of, but there are degrees.
> "Autobiographical Notes III: First Memories" (1980s), 4, *Northrop Frye's Fiction and Miscellaneous Writings* (2007), CW, 25.

Everybody in Moncton who was adult simply regarded Moncton as a kind of remote suburb of Boston.
> "Music in My Life" (1985), *Interviews with Northrop Frye* (2008), CW, 24.

I think I should rather starve in Toronto than feed in luxury here.

"NF to HK," 25 Aug. 1932, written in Moncton, N.B., *The Correspondence of Northrop Frye and Helen Kemp, 1932–1939* (1996), CW, 1.

Some of my most vivid dream settings have been on Moncton streets. Streets are, of course, a labyrinth symbol, full of Eros: they recapture not past reality but *my* reality, reality for me.

Entry, Notebook 12 (1968–70), 148, *The "Third Book" Notebooks of Northrop Frye, 1964–1972: The Critical Comedy* (2002), CW, 9.

MONOTHEISM

A god, as distinct from gods, suggests, as above, oneness and unity: this oneness is what we continually try to make out of the world, despite the fact that there is obviously an infinite number of things in it.

Entry, Notes 52 (1982–90), 293, *Northrop Frye's Late Notebooks, 1982–1990: Architecture of the Spiritual World* (2000), CW, 6.

God is, among other things, unity: monotheism is a lot more than just economy of hypothesis.

Entry, Notebook 21 (1969–76), 433, *Northrop Frye's Notebooks and Lectures on the Bible and Other Religious Texts* (2003), CW, 13.

The conception of monotheism comes with the world-state, and all through history both the One God and the supreme ruler of an empire have been associated with the sun.

"Icons and Iconoclasm" (1970), *Northrop Frye on Literature and Society, 1936–1989: Unpublished Papers* (2002), CW, 10.

MONSTER

The walls of the labyrinth are the walls that wall you off from yourself. The Minotaur has to be something you created yourself. The Monster is externalization.

Remark made at St-Jovite, Que., 12 May 1964, influencing the myth of the Minotaur for the NFB's Labyrinth pavilion at Expo 67, as recorded by Tom Daly and quoted by D.B. Jones in *The Best Butler in the Business* (1996).

MONTREAL

... one reason why Montreal has been so lively a cultural centre is that there are a good many Montreals, each one with its own complexities and inner conflicts.

"Canadian Culture Today" (1977), *Northrop Frye on Canada* (2003), CW, 12.

MONUMENTS

In general, the kind of artefact that posterity usually finds the most expendable culturally is also the hardest to remove physically.

"Canada: New World Without Revolution" (1975), *Northrop Frye on Canada* (2003), CW, 12.

The vitality of words written on papyrus, as compared with the hugest monuments of perennial brass, has perhaps some analogy to the fact that life, precarious and easily snuffed out as it is, is still at least as strong a force as death.

"The Renaissance of Books" (1973), *Northrop Frye on Modern Culture* (2003), CW, 11.

MOON

It is a well-known fact that whatever is lost on earth is collected in the moon, that being what the moon is for.

"The Myth of Deliverance: III, The Reversal of Reality" (1981), adopting an idea in Ariosto's *Orlando Furioso*, *Northrop Frye's Writings on Shakespeare and the Renaissance* (2010), CW, 28.

MOON LANDING

This last was a ritual in the sense that it was a planned social action where nothing unpredictable could have happened except disaster.

"Reviews of Television Programs for the Canadian Radio-Television Commission: Reflections on Television ... November 1971–March 1972" (1972), referring to television presentations of "the ritual element in social life," *Northrop Frye on Literature and Society, 1936–1989: Unpublished Papers* (2002), CW, 10.

When I was watching the moon expeditions of 1969, it seemed to me that the greatest moment was not the actual landing on the moon, but previously, two expeditions before that, when the crew went round to the dark side of the moon, and what they called the "good earth" disappeared from view. At that point they began reciting the

Christian hymn with which the book of Genesis opens. They were the first men who were unable to see the earth from which they had sprung, and in reciting this hymn they established the principle that the real giant step for mankind must be taken on that earth. The really significant events of human life are hidden from view when they occur.

"The Leap in the Dark" (1971), *Northrop Frye on Religion* (2000), CW, 4.

MORAL MAJORITY

I think there is such a thing as a moral majority, even if the people who call themselves that aren't it.

"Criticism in Society" (1985), *Interviews with Northrop Frye* (2008), CW, 24.

MORALITY

The great writers, like Shakespeare, are writers who are extremely moral — morally coherent — but they never moralize.

"The Scholar in Society" (1983), *Interviews with Northrop Frye* (2008), CW, 24.

Civilization tends to try to make the desirable and the moral coincide.

"Third Essay: Archetypal Criticism: Theory of Myths" (1957), *Anatomy of Criticism: Four Essays* (2006), CW, 22.

There is no reason why a great poet should be a wise and good man, or even a tolerable human being, but there is every reason why his reader should be improved in his humanity as a result of reading him.

"Tentative Conclusion" (1957), *Anatomy of Criticism: Four Essays* (2006), CW, 22.

All "good" men by any standards may be "bad" by other standards, just as an egg that is bad to eat may be good to throw at someone.

"Part Two: The Development of the Symbolism," *Fearful Symmetry: A Study of William Blake* (1947, 2004), CW, 14.

There's no such thing as a morally bad novel: its moral effect depends entirely on the moral quality of its reader, and nobody can predict what that will be. And if literature isn't morally bad it isn't morally good either.

"The Keys to Dreamland," *The Educated Imagination* (1963), *"The Educated Imagination" and Other Writings on Critical Theory, 1933–1963* (2006), CW, 21.

That is, all religions say that if you're good you'll stop being bad.

"Between Paradise and Apocalypse" (1978), *Interviews with Northrop Frye* (2008), CW, 24.

I don't think that the arts work by magic, and I don't think they can make anyone a better person. If the person wants to be a better person, the arts can certainly help.

"The Scholar in Society" (1983), *Interviews with Northrop Frye* (2008), CW, 24.

The corresponding illusion of our own time is the belief in the possibility of achieving a moral superiority to society by withdrawing from it and its values, contemplating it from without as something alien, or, in the fashionable metaphor, "sick."

"The Ethics of Change: The Role of the University" (1968), *Northrop Frye's Writings on Education* (2001), CW, 7.

Tragedy is pre-moral, as comedy & romance are post-moral; morality begins in and depends on the ironic vision.

Entry, Notebook 19 (1964–67), 249, *The "Third Book" Notebooks of Northrop Frye, 1964–1972: The Critical Comedy* (2002), CW, 9.

We don't really lack the moral feelings; what we lack is a social structure in which to embody them.

Entry, Notebook 24 (1970–72), 193, *The "Third Book" Notebooks of Northrop Frye, 1964–1972: The Critical Comedy* (2002), CW, 9.

MORMONISM

If Blake had told us that he had copied a vision of an ancient Atlantic Continent from golden plates given him by an angel, we should know what he meant. When Joseph Smith tells us the same thing about the Mormon Bible we are not sure what he means.

"Part Three: The Final Synthesis," *Fearful Symmetry: A Study of William Blake* (1947, 2004), CW, 14.

I suppose the Mormon Bible is a parody of the lost histories of the great civilizations that came pouring over the Bering Straits into the New World.
> Entry, Notebook 44 (1986–91), 479, *Northrop Frye's Late Notebooks, 1982–1990: Architecture of the Spiritual World* (2000), CW, 5.

MOSES

It has not been sufficiently remarked, I think, that Moses was the only man in history ever to see the Promised Land. Those who went further merely entered Canaan, and started another cycle of history.
> "The Journey as Metaphor" (1985), *"The Secular Scripture" and Other Writings on Critical Theory, 1976–1991* (2006), CW, 18.

Perhaps Moses was really the only person to see the Promised Land: perhaps the mountain outside it he climbed in his last hours was the only place from which it could be seen.
> "Fourth Variation: The Furnace," *Words with Power: Being a Second Study of "The Bible and Literature"* (1990).

MOVEMENTS

Political and economic movements tend to expand and centralize; cultural ones tend to decentralize, to bring to articulateness smaller and smaller communities. One has to keep the contrast steadily in mind: if we hitch a political development to a cultural one, as in separatism, we get a kind of neo-fascism; if we hitch a cultural development to a political one, we get a pompous, bureaucratic pseudo-culture.
> "The Authority of Learning" (1984), *Northrop Frye's Writings on Education* (2001), CW, 7.

MOZART, W.A.

More and more I find myself turning to Bach & Haydn, which means more & more away from Mozart. Mozart's a skeptic & Haydn's a Christian. Haydn has everything.
> Entry, Notebook 5 (1935–42), 15, *Northrop Frye's Fiction and Miscellaneous Writings* (2007), CW, 25.

Akin to this is the fact that there *is* a cultural hierarchy: I am not satisfied to say that Mozart is greater than Victor Herbert only in my own mind and taste. He *is* objectively greater, and anyone who says the opposite is objectively *wrong*.
> Entry, Notebook 30b: "Matthew Arnold" (after 1965), 38, *Northrop Frye's Fiction and Miscellaneous Writings* (2007), CW, 25.

There again is the difference between the complexity of the meanings and the tremendous simplicity of what is actually being portrayed. *The Magic Flute* is a fairy tale and is comprehensible to anybody who'll listen to a fairy tale.
> "Frye's Literary Theory in the Classroom," *Interviews with Northrop Frye* (2008), CW, 24.

MULTICULTURALISM

As a conflict of pressure groups, multiculturalism is ridiculous: as an expression of the variety of culture that a healthy society ought to have, it's fundamental.
> "Notes for 'Levels of Cultural Identity'" (1989), 15, *Northrop Frye's Fiction and Miscellaneous Writings* (2007), CW, 25.

It has always seemed to me that this very relaxed absorption of minorities, where there is no concerted effort at a "melting pot," has something to do with what the Queen symbolizes, the separation of the head of state from the head of government.
> "Canadian Culture Today" (1977), referring to Toronto's new ethnic diversity the late 1950s, *Northrop Frye on Canada* (2003), CW, 12.

MURDER

Murder is doubtless a serious crime, but if private murder really were a major threat to our civilization it would not be relaxing to read about it.
> "First Essay: Historical Criticism: Theory of Modes" (1957), *Anatomy of Criticism: Four Essays* (2006), CW, 22.

MUSES

In Greek myth the muses bore the names of literary genres and were in the aggregate daughters of memory, that is, of literary convention. In our day they bear names like Anxiety, Absurdity, and Alienation, and they are the daughters of Frustration; but their

power is as great as ever, and their cultural achievements could be as impressive as ever.
> "The Survival of Eros in Poetry" (1983), *"The Secular Scripture" and Other Writings on Critical Theory, 1976–1991* (2006), CW, 18.

And I would certainly not want to leave the impression that all Muses are soft cuddly nudes: some of them are ravening harpies who swoop and snatch and carry off, who destroy a poet's peace of mind, his position in society, even his sanity.
> "Framework and Assumption" (1985), *"The Secular Scripture" and Other Writings on Critical Theory, 1976–1991* (2006), CW, 18.

The true gods are the Muses, except that there are six of them: literature, painting, sculpture, architecture, mathematics and music. There is a seventh God who combines all these and creates us, rather than being the means of our own creation.
> Entry, Notes 54.1 (May 1990), 30, *Northrop Frye's Late Notebooks, 1982–1990: Architecture of the Spiritual World* (2000), CW, 6.

MUSIC

I don't see why music should depend so completely on performance; if there were a decent level of musical education in the country we could read music just as we read books.
> "Autobiographical Reflections" (1942–44), 13, *Northrop Frye's Fiction and Miscellaneous Writings* (2007), CW, 25.

Music is a sequence of discords ending in a harmony.
> "Music in Poetry" (1942), *"The Educated Imagination" and Other Writings on Critical Theory, 1933–1963* (2006), CW, 21.

No external God can be adored with music He did not compose.
> Entry, 19 Apr. 1950, 283, reflection on hearing Bach's B-minor Mass, *The Diaries of Northrop Frye: 1942–1955* (2001), CW, 8.

The young people one sees on streets with headsets clamped over their ears are acting out what was a science fiction nightmare a few years ago.
> "Introduction to *Art and Reality*" (1986), *Northrop Frye on Modern Culture* (2003), CW, 11.

What the museums did for the visual arts modern recordings have done for music.
> *The Modern Century* (1967), *Northrop Frye on Modern Culture* (2003), CW, 11.

Just as any freshman in a conservatory may learn from records more about pre-Mozartian music than Mozart himself ever knew, so any student in a small college may have access, potentially, to a range of materials formerly available only in the biggest libraries.
> "The Renaissance of Books" (1973), *Northrop Frye on Modern Culture* (2003), CW, 11.

If I believed in reincarnation I should want to be reborn as a perfectly educated man, i.e. able to distribute rhythms properly, social, intellectual, spiritual, physical. I suppose that's why music is the ideal art.
> Entry, Notebook 21 (1969–76), 14, *Northrop Frye's Notebooks and Lectures on the Bible and Other Religious Texts* (2003), CW, 13.

It is nothing against popular music to say that it has a savage ancestry; so has everything else.
> "Music and the Savage Breast" (1938), *Northrop Frye on Modern Culture* (2003), CW, 11.

But I have always thought of music, and to lesser extent of literature, as a rich and glowing paradise of variegated genius, and it is with the greatest unwillingness that I have recognized the presence of stupidity, dullness and ineptitude in it.
> Entry, 19 Mar. 1952, 190, *The Diaries of Northrop Frye: 1942–1955* (2001), CW, 8.

MUSIC OF THE SPHERES

When men ceased to believe that the sun went around the earth, they gave up the music of the spheres.
> "Music and the Savage Breast" (1938), *Northrop Frye on Modern Culture* (2003), CW, 11.

MYSTERIES

Once upon a time there was a school of wise men who concealed all mysteries in fables, and our existing myths are all distortions of these. This version, originally developed to explain the resemblances between Biblical and extra-Biblical myths, keeps turning up in various occult forms, the school of wise men being located in Atlantis or India or ancient Egypt, whence their doctrines and symbols were diffused around the world like the trade winds.

"Literature and Myth" (1967), *"The Critical Path" and Other Writings on Critical Theory, 1963–1975* (2009), CW, 27.

The mystery of the unknown or unknowable essence is an extrinsic mystery, which involves art only when art is also made illustrative of something else, as religious art is to the person concerned primarily with worship. But the intrinsic mystery is that which remains a mystery in itself no matter how fully known it is, and hence is not a mystery separated from what is known.

"Second Essay: Ethical Criticism: Theory of Symbols" (1957), *Anatomy of Criticism: Four Essays* (2006), CW, 22.

Let your approach to knowledge be without fear, for God wills to reveal himself, and his revelation is mysterious only because it is infinite.

"Baccalaureate Service (III)" (1988), *Northrop Frye on Religion* (2000), CW, 4.

The sublime, the *mysterium tremendum*, is, as is generally accepted now, propaedeutic to the sense of God.

Entry, Notes 53 (1989–90), 68, *Northrop Frye's Late Notebooks, 1982–1990: Architecture of the Spiritual World* (2000), CW, 6.

MYSTICISM

Once you start thinking about religion as a specialized activity, or as a retreat from ordinary living, you immediately think of it as mysterious, ghostly, esoteric and so forth. Hence all the sham mysticism. Perhaps all mysticism is sham — I don't know; I sometimes think so, probably because I don't know anything about it.

"NF to HK," 24 Jul. 1935, *The Correspondence of Northrop Frye and Helen Kemp, 1932–1939* (1996), CW, 1.

The nearest I have come to such experiences are glimpses of my own creative powers — Spengler in Edmonton and two nights with Blake — and these are moments or intervals of inspiration rather than vision.

Entry, Notebook 19 (1964–67), 265, *The "Third Book" Notebooks of Northrop Frye, 1964–1972: The Critical Comedy* (2002), CW, 9.

The mystic finds, at the heart of the illusion of time, a real present, and, at the heart of the illusion of space, a real presence.

"T.S. Eliot" (1963), *Northrop Frye on Twentieth-Century Literature* (2010), CW, 29.

MYTH

Myth: A narrative in which some characters are superhuman beings who do things that "happen only in stories"; hence, a conventionalized or stylized narrative not fully adapted to plausibility or "realism."

"Glossary," *Anatomy of Criticism: Four Essays* (1957, 2006), CW, 22.

The things that happen in myths are things that happen only in stories; they are in a self-contained literary world.

"Myth, Fiction, and Displacement" (1961), *"The Educated Imagination" and Other Writings on Critical Theory, 1933–1963* (2006), CW, 21.

Myth is the only language of the present tense and it is also the language of poetry. As Aristotle said long ago, history tells us what happened; poetry tells us what happens. The myth confronts the reader directly with something which is set over against him, and which he has to come to terms with at the moment of reading.

"Literature and Society" (1968), *"The Critical Path" and Other Writings on Critical Theory, 1963–1975* (2009), CW, 27.

The closed myth, in short, defines the enemy, and the open myth defines the friend or the neighbour.

"Style and Image in the Twentieth Century" (1967), *Interviews with Northrop Frye* (2008), CW, 24.

Myths are like human beings: every one is unique. And yet there's a very small number of conventions which apply to all of them.
"Family Stories" (1990), *Interviews with Northrop Frye* (2008), CW, 24.

Pastoral myths are mostly illusions projected from the experience of growing older.
"Address on Receiving the Royal Bank Award" (1978), *Northrop Frye's Writings on Education* (2001), CW, 7.

The myth is a story which is neither true nor not true.
"The Limits of Dialogue" (1969), *Interviews with Northrop Frye* (2008), CW, 24.

Myths tell us about the actions of gods. There are no gods, so myths are verbal narratives only. But the stories of gods recapture (a) the concrete (b) the disinterested (c) the bodily.
Entry, Notebook 50 (1987–90), 72, *Northrop Frye's Late Notebooks, 1982–1990: Architecture of the Spiritual World* (2000), CW, 5.

More accurately a myth is a microcosm of mythology, and a mythology is a metaphorical vision of the cosmos.
Entry, Notebook 27 (1986), 330, *Northrop Frye's Late Notebooks, 1982–1990: Architecture of the Spiritual World* (2000), CW, 5.

The union of ritual and dream in a form of verbal communication is myth.
"Second Essay: Ethical Criticism: Theory of Symbols" (1957), *Anatomy of Criticism: Four Essays* (2006), CW, 22.

MYTH & HISTORY

Why does myth always falsify history? Because myth is about what overturns history: it's the opposite of history, the dream spiral working against the waking one.
Entry, Notebook 21 (1969–76), 450, *Northrop Frye's Notebooks and Lectures on the Bible and Other Religious Texts* (2003), CW, 13.

The myth, in short, dehistoricizes; that is a barbarous word, but no more so than other words beginning with "de."

Entry, Notebook 44 (1986–91), 291, *Northrop Frye's Late Notebooks, 1982–1990: Architecture of the Spiritual World* (2000), CW, 5.

Myth is neither historical nor antihistorical: it is counterhistorical.
The Double Vision (1991), *Northrop Frye on Religion* (2000), CW, 4.

MYTH & LITERATURE

At the centre of literature is myth, which doesn't exist: around it are poetic, fictional, dramatic, and rhetorical displacements of myth.
Entry, Notebook 19 (1964–67), 295, *The "Third Book" Notebooks of Northrop Frye, 1964–1972: The Critical Comedy* (2002), CW, 9.

Myth is the language of religion *and* the structural principle of literature. No discussion of mythology can leave out literature.
Entry, Notebook 10 (late 1964–72), 76, *Northrop Frye's Notebooks on Romance* (2004), CW, 15.

My own interest in myth begins with its literary development: to me a literary myth is not a contaminated myth but a matured one.
Creation and Recreation (1980), *Northrop Frye on Religion* (2000), CW, 4.

Mythology is a form of imaginative thinking, and its direct descendant in culture is literature, more particularly fiction, works of literature that tell stories.
"The Times of the Signs" (1973), *"The Critical Path" and Other Writings on Critical Theory, 1963–1975* (2009), CW, 27.

The reason for studying mythology is that mythology as a whole provides a kind of diagram or blueprint of what literature as a whole is all about, an imaginative survey of the human situation from the beginning to the end, from the height to the depth, of what is imaginatively conceivable.
"Elementary Teaching and Elemental Scholarship" (1963), *Northrop Frye's Writings on Education* (2001), CW, 7.

… recognizing that 99% of mythology is literature….

Entry, Notebook 12 (1968–70), 70, parenthetical remark about "an introduction to mythology," *The "Third Book" Notebooks of Northrop Frye, 1964–1972: The Critical Comedy* (2002), CW, 9.

Literature is conscious mythology: as society develops, its mythical stories become structural principles of story-telling, its mythical concepts, sun-gods and the like, become habits of metaphoric thought. In a fully mature literary creation the writer enters into a structure of traditional stories and images.

"Conclusion to *Literary History of Canada*" (1965), *Northrop Frye on Canada* (2003), CW, 12.

The informing structures of literature are myths, that is, fictions and metaphors that identify aspects of human personality with the natural environment, such as stories about sun-gods and tree-gods.

"A Study of English Romanticism" (1968), *Northrop Frye's Writings on the Eighteenth and Nineteenth Centuries* (2005), CW, 17.

To summarize briefly my central thesis on this point: every human society possesses a mythology which is inherited, transmitted and diversified by literature.

"Introduction," *Words with Power: Being a Second Study of "The Bible and Literature"* (1990), CW, 26.

MYTH & MEANING

Myth moves from the past to the present. That's one reason why the profoundest treatments of myth are the latest ones.

Entry, Notebook 27 (1986), 288, *Northrop Frye's Late Notebooks, 1982–1990: Architecture of the Spiritual World* (2000), CW, 5.

Its proclamation is not so much "This is true" as "This is what you must know."

"Concern and Myth," referring to the power of myth to define "a shared possession of knowledge," *Words with Power: Being a Second Study of "The Bible and Literature"* (1990), CW, 26.

To me myth is not simply an effect of a historical process, but a social vision that looks toward a transcending of history, which explains how it is able to hold two periods of history together, the author's and ours, in direct communication. It is very difficult, perhaps impossible, to suggest a social vision of this kind, even within an ideology, without invoking some kind of pastoral myth, past or future.

"Concern and Myth," *Words with Power: Being a Second Study of "The Bible and Literature"* (2008), CW, 26.

In any case what a myth means is what it has been made to mean over the centuries, and some of its profoundest recreations are very recent.

"Concern and Myth," *Words with Power: Being a Second Study of "The Bible and Literature"* (2008), CW, 26.

Here's the germ of an important critical principle: that the "real meaning" of a myth is often best grasped not by tracing it back to some hypothetical original, but by following its successive treatments by various writers.

"Notes for 'The World as Music and Idea in Wagner's *Parsifal*'" (1982), 6, *Northrop Frye's Fiction and Miscellaneous Writings* (2007), CW, 25.

A myth is designed not to describe a specific situation but to contain it in a way that does not restrict its significance to that one situation. Its truth is inside its structure, not outside.

"Myth I," *The Great Code* (1982), *The Great Code: The Bible and Literature* (2006), CW, 19.

This reversal is what stops us from the genetic fallacy, and enables us to see that myths mean everything they've effectively been made to mean.

Entry, Notes 54-5 (1976), 72, *Northrop Frye's Notebooks and Lectures on the Bible and Other Religious Texts* (2003), CW, 13.

A myth, in this sense, is an expression of man's concern about himself, about his place in the scheme of things, about his relation to society and God, about the ultimate origin and ultimate fate, either of himself or of the human species generally.

The Modern Century (1967), *Northrop Frye on Modern Culture* (2003), CW, 11.

In primitive verbal cultures myths are distinguished from folk tales or legends, not by their structure, but by a specific social function. Myths are the *serious* stories: they are the ones that really happened or explain what is of primary importance to their society.

"*Pistis* and *Mythos*" (1972), *Northrop Frye on Religion* (2000), CW, 4.

As such, mythology belongs to the world of art, not nature: that is, it is a cultural construct expressing the model world that man wants to live in or the demonic world that he wants to avoid living in, or else it explains to him why his life is ordered in the way that it is, with reference to the history and traditions underlying that life.

"*Rencontre:* The General Editor's Introduction" (1960s), discussing mythology as "a framework of metaphors and allusions for the poets," *Northrop Frye on Literature and Society, 1936–1989: Unpublished Papers* (2002), CW, 10.

MYTH & METAPHOR

Myth and metaphor express what language is primarily equipped to express, and only myth and metaphor can evoke the deeper world of identity in which different things are one thing, and all men the same man.

"*Pistis* and *Mythos*" (1972), *Northrop Frye on Religion* (2000), CW, 4.

The word myth refers to its unity; the word metaphor to its units.

"Literature and Language" (1974), referring to "a structure of myth and metaphor," *Northrop Frye on Literature and Society, 1936–1989: Unpublished Papers* (2002), CW, 10.

Myth is counter-historical, metaphor counter-logical.

Entry, Notes 52 (1982–90), 805, *Northrop Frye's Late Notebooks, 1982–1990: Architecture of the Spiritual World* (2000), CW, 6.

Metaphor is the language of immanence; metonymy of transcendence.

Entry, Notebook 11c (1980), 21, *Northrop Frye's Notebooks and Lectures on the Bible and Other Religious Texts* (2003), CW, 13.

So metaphor is the *arrest* of magic and of logic; myth is the arrest of history and dialectic.

Entry, Notebook 27 (1986), 59, *Northrop Frye's Late Notebooks, 1982–1990: Architecture of the Spiritual World* (2000), CW, 5.

What the metaphor does to space the myth does to time.

"The Mythical Approach to Criticism" (1985), *Northrop Frye on Religion* (2000), CW, 4.

Myth says two things to us at once: "this happened" and "this cannot have happened in precisely this way." Similarly, metaphor says to us "A is B," two things are the same thing, and at the same time conveys the meaning "A is clearly not B, and no one could be fool enough to think it was."

"Maps and Territories" (1987), *"The Secular Scripture" and Other Writings on Critical Theory, 1976–1991* (2006), CW, 18.

MYTHOGRAPHERS

Point in the humanism essay: a large part of humanism consists in comparative mythology. And all good mythographers have two characteristics: one, they sound like cranks or nuts (not typical of the humanist pose, of course); two, they show a great respect for the "wisdom of the ancients."

Entry, Notebook 11f (1969–70), 177, *Northrop Frye's Notebooks and Lectures on the Bible and Other Religious Texts* (2003), CW, 13.

MYTHOLOGY

For mythology is not primarily an attempt to picture reality: it is not a primitive form of science or philosophy, however crude. It is rather an attempt to articulate what is of greatest human concern to the society that produces it.

"The Times of the Signs" (1973), *"The Critical Path" and Other Writings on Critical Theory, 1963–1975* (2009), CW, 27.

An open mythology is one where there is an atmosphere of criticism and where there is room for the imagination to have free play and all the other things we associate with cultural freedom.

"Northrop Frye in Conversation" (1989), as contrasted with a closed mythology which says "this is what you must believe," *Interviews with Northrop Frye* (2008), CW, 24.

Yet the end of mythology is the conceivable, not the real, or, as Aristotle said, the impossible made probable.
"The Times of the Signs" (1973), *"The Critical Path" and Other Writings on Critical Theory, 1963–1975* (2009), CW, 27.

I think that there exists only one social mythology which results from the co-existence of many contradictory mythologies.
"The New American Dreams over the Great Lakes" (1979), *Interviews with Northrop Frye* (2008), CW, 24.

I mean by a mythology a body of informing ideas or conceptions or images which hold a society together and unify its social vision.
"Criticism and Society" (1966–76), *Northrop Frye on Literature and Society, 1936–1989: Unpublished Papers* (2002), CW, 10.

A mythology emerges when the mental landscapes of a group of writers begin to fuse with their physical environment.
"Culture and Society in Ontario, 1784–1984" (1984), *Northrop Frye on Canada* (2003), CW, 12.

In every age there is a structure of ideas, images, beliefs, assumptions, anxieties, and hopes which express the view of man's situation and destiny generally held at that time. I call this structure a mythology, and its units myths.
The Modern Century (1967), *Northrop Frye on Modern Culture* (2003), CW, 11.

Mythology does not expand and progress in the way that science does, but it keeps constantly transforming itself, as though there were a power of renewal within it as infinite as the galaxies.
"The Times of the Signs" (1973), *"The Critical Path" and Other Writings on Critical Theory, 1963–1975* (2009), CW, 27.

Mythology is curiously like technology in its development: the more man invents of it, the more strongly tempted he is to project it into something that controls him.

"Reflections in a Mirror" (1966), *"The Critical Path" and Other Writings on Critical Theory, 1963–1975* (2009), CW, 27.

I think all mythologies are religious in nature, and I think that every new mythology is a modification of an old one.
"Into the Wilderness" (1969), *Interviews with Northrop Frye* (2008), CW, 24.

Mythology is not a *datum* but a *factum* of human existence: it belongs to the world of culture and civilization that man has made and still inhabits.
"Myth I," *The Great Code* (1982), *The Great Code: The Bible and Literature* (2006), CW, 19.

Anyway, mythology is the simplest, most direct, and hieroglyphic way of expressing the fact that we see things out of a conceptual universe.
Entry, Notes 54-5 (1976), 41, *Northrop Frye's Notebooks and Lectures on the Bible and Other Religious Texts* (2003), CW, 13.

The mythological universe has the kind of reality which is made, not there.
Entry, Notebook 54-8 (late 1972–77), 47, *Northrop Frye's Notebooks on Romance* (2004), CW, 15.

We have no choice about teaching mythology; we have only the choice between teaching genuine and perverted kinds of it.
"On Teaching Literature" (1972), *Northrop Frye's Writings on Education* (2001), CW, 7.

I have spent most of my professional life studying one aspect of the way man constructs the world he lives in; the aspect I call a mythology, the building of worlds out of words.
"Address on Receiving the Royal Bank Award" (1978), *Northrop Frye's Writings on Education* (2001), CW, 7.

The world of mythology, which stretches from creation to last judgment and from heaven to hell, belongs not so much to the waking world, the world of fact which is explored by science; it belongs rather to the dream world, not so much to the world after death as to the world after dark.

"The Social Uses of Literature" (1972), *Northrop Frye on Literature and Society, 1936–1989: Unpublished Papers* (2002), CW, 10.

MYTHOPOEIA

The immense pressure toward conformity in thought and imagination is society's anxious response to mythopoeia, creating institutional religion in one age and total political alignments in another.

"Reflections in a Mirror" (1966), *"The Critical Path" and Other Writings on Critical Theory, 1963–1975* (2009), CW, 27.

Mythology projects itself as theology: that is, a mythopoeic poet usually accepts some myths as "true" and shapes his poetic structure accordingly.

"First Essay: Historical Criticism: Theory of Modes" (1957), *Anatomy of Criticism: Four Essays* (2006), CW, 22.

The age that has produced the hell of Rimbaud and the angels of Rilke, Kafka's castle and James's ivory tower, the spirals of Yeats and the hermaphrodites of Proust, the intricate dying-god symbolism attached to Christ in Eliot and the exhaustive treatment of Old Testament myths in Mann's study of Joseph, is once again a great mythopoeic age.

"Part Three: The Final Synthesis," *Fearful Symmetry: A Study of William Blake* (1947, 2004), CW, 14.

MYTHOS

Myth to me, then, means first of all *mythos* or narrative, words arranged in a sequential order.

Creation and Recreation (1980), *Northrop Frye on Religion* (2000), CW, 4.

To me a myth means fundamentally what it means in Greek, *mythos*, meaning a narrative or a sequential arrangement of words. I think that anything which can be read sequentially, that is any book except possibly a telephone book, does have a narrative and therefore a *mythos*.

"The Meaning of Recreation" (1979), *Northrop Frye on Religion* (2000), CW, 4.

The *mythos* is the *dianoia* in movement; the *dianoia* is the *mythos* in stasis.

"Second Essay: Ethical Criticism: Theory of Symbols" (1957), *Anatomy of Criticism: Four Essays* (2006), CW, 22.

N

NAME
A thing's name is its numen, its imaginative reality in the eternal world of the human mind.
> "Part One: The Argument," *Fearful Symmetry: A Study of William Blake* (1947, 2004), CW, 14.

NARCISSUS
Narcissus at least had a beautiful face to look at, but the face of humanity that would look out of such a mirror is that of a psychotic ape.
> *Creation and Recreation* (1980), *Northrop Frye on Religion* (2000), CW, 4.

NARRATIVES
We may speak of these two types of narrative as the "hence" narrative and the "and then" narrative.
> *The Secular Scripture: A Study of the Structure of Romance* (1975), *"The Secular Scripture" and Other Writings on Critical Theory, 1976–1991* (2006), CW, 18.

History emerges from chronicle as soon as we have a writer who can see chronicles as material for some other kind of form, an organizing form which is not simply sequence but a *mythos* or narrative.
> "History and Myth in the Bible" (1975), *Northrop Frye on Religion* (2000), CW, 4.

NATIONAL FILM BOARD
I remember a *Spring Thaw* skit which was a takeoff of an NFB film, ending with the line "on view in your local Sunday-School basement."
> "Across the River and Out of the Trees" (1980), *Northrop Frye on Canada* (2003), CW, 12.

NATIONALISM
Nationalism, as the term is generally understood, is simply a psychotic state of mind. But there *is* such a thing as cultural consciousness, which I'm glad to see Canada developing.
> "*Chatelaine's* Celebrity I.D." (1982), asked to comment on Canadian nationalism, *Interviews with Northrop Frye* (2008), CW, 24.

Perhaps we ask more from our culture than it can well give. Canadian intellectuals, whether French or English, are apt to be fierce cultural nationalists. Yet it is the destiny of man to unite rather than to divide, and our real loyalties are to unities much larger than Canada, or North America, or even to Western civilization.
> "Governor General's Awards (I)" (1963), *Northrop Frye on Canada* (2003), CW, 12.

Canadian intellectuals have always been, for the most part, cultural nationalists, fostering a Messianic hope that something of major importance is just about to happen to Canada, but they never have been more so than at present.
> "English Canadian Literature, 1929–1954" (1955), *Northrop Frye on Canada* (2003), CW, 12.

… Canada seems to have moved from a prenational to a postnational phase of existence without ever having been a nation.
> "A Summary of the 'Options' Conference" (1977), *Northrop Frye on Canada* (2003), CW, 12.

As third-world nations began to emerge in Africa and Asia, Canada's much more low-keyed nationalism became increasingly inaudible, like a lute in a brass band.
> "Culture as Interpenetration" (1977), *Northrop Frye on Canada* (2003), CW, 12.

NATIONS
The nation is rapidly ceasing to be the real defining unit of society.

The Modern Century (1967), *Northrop Frye on Modern Culture* (2003), CW, 11.

I have said that culture seems to flourish best in national units, which implies that the empire is too big and the province too small for major literature.
"Canada and Its Poetry" (1943), *Northrop Frye on Canada* (2003), CW, 12.

If even a united Canada failed to become a distinctive nation, a fragmented one would have about the rating of a banana republic, even if Canada's exports seem more basic than bananas.
"A Summary of the 'Options' Conference" (1977), *Northrop Frye on Canada* (2003), CW, 12.

I do not remember any other time in history when a nation disintegrated merely through a lack of will to survive, nor do I think ours will.
"A Summary of the 'Options' Conference" (1977), *Northrop Frye on Canada* (2003), CW, 12.

NATIVE PEOPLES
It seems clear that for Canadian culture the old imperialist phrase "going native" has come home to roost. We are no longer an army of occupation, and the natives are ourselves.
"Canadian Culture Today" (1977), *Northrop Frye on Canada* (2003), CW, 12.

The primary principle of white settlement in this country, in practice if not always in theory, was that the indigenous cultures should be destroyed, not preserved or continued or even set apart.
"Canada: New World Without Revolution" (1975), *Northrop Frye on Canada* (2003), CW, 12.

NATIVITY
It would have been strange if Christ had been born into a world whose temporal master was a protégé of Hercules, ruling the world probably from Egypt.
"Northrop Frye on Shakespeare: VI, *Antony and Cleopatra*" (1986), *Northrop Frye's Writings on Shakespeare and the Renaissance* (2010), CW, 28.

NATURE
Everything in nature is submoral, subintellectual, and subhuman, and man gets nothing from that at all in the way of inspiration.
"Into the Wilderness" (1969), *Interviews with Northrop Frye* (2008), CW, 24.

What we see in nature is our own body turned inside out.
"Part Three: The Final Synthesis," interpreting Blake's view, *Fearful Symmetry: A Study of William Blake* (1947, 2004), CW, 14.

Everywhere we look today, we see the conquest of nature by an intelligence that does not love it, that feels no part of it, that splits its own consciousness off from it and looks at it as an object.
"Canada: New World Without Revolution" (1975), *Northrop Frye on Canada* (2003), CW, 12.

Exploring nature leads to a search for concealed power in or behind nature; liberal humanism explores history. So we get a humanized power in nature & a deified love or sense of community in history.
Entry, 15 Mar. 1949, 269, *The Diaries of Northrop Frye: 1942–1955* (2001), CW, 8.

Man never lives directly in nature: he lives inside the construct of culture or civilization, of which the verbal aspect is a mythology.
"Criticism and Environment" (1981), *Northrop Frye on Canada* (2003), CW, 12.

Nature doesn't care how I feel. Close them.
"Moncton, Mentors, and Memories" (1986), asking his assistant Jane Widdicombe to pull the curtains on the view of mountains, following the death of his wife Helen in Australia, *Interviews with Northrop Frye* (2008), CW, 24.

Nature is traditionally a second Word of God, a book of things to read.
Entry, Notes 52 (1982–90), 28, *Northrop Frye's Late Notebooks, 1982–1990: Architecture of the Spiritual World* (2000), CW, 6.

Art does not reflect nature; it contains nature, for the essence of content is to be contained.

"Nature and Homer" (1958), *"The Educated Imagination" and Other Writings on Critical Theory, 1933–1963* (2006), CW, 21.

In nature the lighting comes first & the thunder follows, but in revelation God speaks & the light comes after.
Entry, Notebook 21 (1969–76), 295, *Northrop Frye's Notebooks and Lectures on the Bible and Other Religious Texts* (2003), CW, 13.

The vision of nature is an *alienating* vision, a vision of what is *not* human.
Entry, Notebook 24 (1970–72), 5, *The "Third Book" Notebooks of Northrop Frye, 1964–1972: The Critical Comedy* (2002), CW, 9.

Not much interest in reviving gods or nature-spirits today: rather a feeling of a common consciousness engaged with total nature.
Entry, Notes 52 (1982–90), 625, *Northrop Frye's Late Notebooks, 1982–1990: Architecture of the Spiritual World* (2000), CW, 6.

The human mind has nothing but human and moral values to cling to if it is to preserve its integrity or even its sanity, yet the vast unconsciousness of nature in front of it seems an unanswerable denial of those values.
"Conclusion to *Literary History of Canada*" (1965), *Northrop Frye on Canada* (2003), CW, 12.

It seems to me that the capitalist-socialist controversy is out of date, and that a détente with an outraged nature is what is important now. Canada is still a place of considerable natural resources, but it is no longer simply a place to be looted, either by Canadians or by non-Canadians.
"Canadian Culture Today" (1977), *Northrop Frye on Canada* (2003), CW, 12.

There is nothing that you can define as inherently unnatural.
"Symbolism in the Bible" (1981–82), *Northrop Frye's Notebooks and Lectures on the Bible and Other Religious Texts* (2003), CW, 13.

NAUSEA

Everything that nauseates us is a memento mori, an aspect of our own dead bodies.

Entry, Notebook 19 (1964–67), 263, *The "Third Book" Notebooks of Northrop Frye, 1964–1972: The Critical Comedy* (2002), CW, 9.

NAZISM

The rise of Nazi Germany suggested the possibility of a social hysteria indefinitely prolonged by the control of communications.
"The University and Personal Life: Student Anarchism and the Educational Contract" (1968), *Northrop Frye's Writings on Education* (2001), CW, 7.

This essay is worth the price of admission in itself. Reading it, one can see how tragically complicated the whole problem of Nazism is, and how obvious it is that when the Germans talk about the Jews they mean themselves. For their relation to our time is exactly that of the Jews to the Roman world: the same superstitions of racial purity, the same alternation of scholarship and fanatical rebellion, the same legalizing of culture, the same longing for a conquering Messiah, the same tendency to believe that every crackpot who comes along may be one.
"Review of *New Writing and Daylight* (I)" (1943), *Northrop Frye on Twentieth-Century Literature* (2010), CW, 29. The essay in the Winter 1942–43 issue of that publication was written by Demetrios Capetanakis about the German poet Stefan George.

NECESSITY

Just as reason is the circumference of energy, so necessity is the circumference of freedom: *noblesse oblige*.
"Part One: The Argument," *Fearful Symmetry: A Study of William Blake* (1947, 2004), CW, 14.

NEUROSIS

Every psychiatrist knows the neurotic whose request is not to remove his neurosis, but to make it more comfortable to live with. However opposed at first, innovators in ideology become immensely influential; it's innovators in mythology who are lunatics or criminals.
Entry, Notebook 11h (1980s), 36, *Northrop Frye's Late Notebooks, 1982–1990: Architecture of the Spiritual World* (2000), CW, 6.

The only real cure for a neurotic is to recapture his neurosis.

> Entry, Notebook 31 (late 1946–50), 80, *Northrop Frye's Notebooks on Romance* (2004), CW, 15.

NEW CRITICISM

The reaction of what was called the "new criticism" (which is called "new" because it cannot be traced much further back than Plato, who is full of it) insisted on the central critical problems, beginning with the explicatory reading of the text and going on from there.

> "Research and Graduate Education in the Humanities" (1968), *Northrop Frye's Writings on Education* (2001), CW, 7.

The New Criticism simply approached a work without any reference to its structure or its genre or its convention, and studied what Ransom called its "texture." Well, I could see that the texture was important, but I could also see that words like "convention" and "genre" were pretty important too.

> "Back to the Garden" (1982), *Interviews with Northrop Frye* (2008), CW, 24.

NEW YEAR'S DAY

New Year's is a dull holiday: Christmas provides a definite ritual of things to do, but New Year's is just a day to dither & dawdle through, overeating & underthinking.

> Entry, 1 Jan. 1949, *The Diaries of Northrop Frye: 1942–1955* (2001), CW, 8.

Every year I think with some awe that my lines have fallen to me in pleasant places, and that if one's luck depended on one's merit, the burden of responsibility would be too great to bear.

> Memorandum from 1951, 1 Jan. 1952, *The Diaries of Northrop Frye: 1942–1955* (2001), CW, 8.

NEWFOUNDLAND

A Newfoundlander told me once that he thought his people had most in common with the Poles, and like them tended to celebrate defeats rather than victories.

> "National Consciousness in Canadian Culture" (1976), *Northrop Frye on Canada* (2003), CW, 12.

NEWS

The experience of life is a continuity, and news is essentially what breaks into that continuity. That is why so much news consists of disaster, and why all disaster is news.

> "Violence and Television" (1975), *Northrop Frye on Modern Culture* (2003), CW, 11.

I suppose the advantage that television has over the newspaper is that it can get to the personalities that newspaper readers think of as being "behind" the news. But even so, this type of talking newspaper format seems to me a bit more impoverished than the newspaper itself.

> "Reviews of Television Programs for the Canadian Radio-Television Commission: Reflections on Television ... November 1971–March 1972" (1972), *Northrop Frye on Literature and Society, 1936–1989: Unpublished Papers* (2002), CW, 10.

NEWSPAPERS

Many newspapers are called the Star or the Sun; but you never hear of one called the Moon. Something in our symbolic subconsciousness never thinks of the moon as a watcher.

> Entry, Notebook 1 (late 1930s), 73, *Northrop Frye's Fiction and Miscellaneous Writings* (2007), CW, 25.

Newspapers are, or should be, addressed to those who have already heard the newscast, & are prepared for a more participatory role.

> Entry, Notebook 11f (1969–70), 110, *Northrop Frye's Notebooks and Lectures on the Bible and Other Religious Texts* (2003), CW, 13.

NEWTON, ISAAC

That God was a good Anglican could be taken for granted, but that Newton was a good Anglican, if a somewhat heterodox one, was much more profoundly reassuring.

> "The Times of the Signs" (1973), *"The Critical Path" and Other Writings on Critical Theory, 1963–1975* (2009), CW, 27.

NIAGARA FALLS

It is often said that if it hadn't been for Niagara Falls, Ontario would have been a most idyllic and pastoral community.

> "Culture and Society in Ontario, 1784–1984" (1984), an allusion to its hydroelectric-power

generators, *Northrop Frye on Canada* (2003), CW, 12.

NIETZSCHE, FRIEDRICH
Given ever so slight a list to port, the history of the future might have gone through Nietzsche instead of through Marx. By the future I mean his future, our present.
> Entry, 4 Mar. 1953, 143, *The Diaries of Northrop Frye: 1942–1955* (2001), CW, 8.

NIGHTMARES
Nightmare is to dreaming what vomiting is to digestion — it's the violent rejection of hostile increment — and practically all that we remember of dreams is excreta: Freud actually uses that metaphor.
> Entry, Notebook 3 (1946–48), 142, *Northrop Frye's Notebooks and Lectures on the Bible and Other Religious Texts* (2003), CW, 13.

NINETEEN FIFTIES
There was a time, back in the 1950s — it seems an eternity ago now — when everybody was complaining about the apathy of students, and I can remember a girl saying to me then, with exasperation in her voice, "But what do they want us to get excited about?"
> "The Social Importance of Literature" (1968), *Northrop Frye's Writings on Education* (2001), CW, 7.

NINETEENTH CENTURY
We shall never fully understand the nineteenth century until we realize how hampered its poets were by the lack of a coherent tradition of criticism which would have organized the language of poetic symbolism for them.
> "Yeats and the Language of Symbolism" (1947), *"The Critical Path" and Other Writings on Critical Theory, 1963–1975* (2009), CW, 27.

NOISE
A noise in the middle of a concert, or the sound of a violin in a city street, is an interruption from another order of things.
> "Interior Monologue of M. Teste" (1959), *"The Educated Imagination" and Other Writings on Critical Theory, 1933–1963* (2006), CW, 21.

NORTH, THE
There is an immense difference in feeling between north and south Canada, but as north Canada is practically uninhabited, it exists in Canadian painting only through southern eyes. In those eyes it is a "solemn land" as frightening and fantastic as the moon.
> "Canadian Scene: Explorers and Observers" (1973), *Northrop Frye on Canada* (2003), CW, 12.

NORTH STAR
I suppose the North Star could be a symbol of the focussed consciousness, as it never falls beneath the waters.
> Entry, Notebook 43 (1949–50), referring to a reference in Book 1, Canto 2, of *The Faerie Queene*, *Northrop Frye's Notebooks on Renaissance Literature* (2006), CW, 20.

NOTHINGNESS
Nothingness is that which cannot be transformed into negation.
> Entry, Notebook 11b (late 1980), 74, *Northrop Frye's Notebooks and Lectures on the Bible and Other Religious Texts* (2003), CW, 13.

NOVEL
Each age has its own inevitable forms of expression: what ours are, God only knows, but I do not think they include the novel.
> "Dr. Edgar's Book" (1933), *"The Educated Imagination" and Other Writings on Critical Theory, 1933–1963* (2006), CW, 21.

In our day the born storyteller is even rather peripheral to fiction, at best a borderline case like Somerset Maugham, and the serious novelist is as a rule the novelist who writes not because he has a story to tell but because he has a theme to illustrate.
> "The Road of Excess" (1970), *Northrop Frye on Milton and Blake* (2005), CW, 16.

NOVELTY
Only when we realize that nothing is new can we live with an intensity in which everything becomes new.
> "Typology II," *The Great Code* (1982), *The Great Code: The Bible and Literature* (2006), CW, 19.

I'm not saying that there's nothing new in literature: I'm saying that everything is new, and yet recognizably the same kind of thing as the old, just as a new baby is a genuinely new individual, although it's also an example of something very common, which is human beings, and also it's lineally descended from the first human beings there ever were.

"The Singing School," *The Educated Imagination* (1963), *"The Educated Imagination" and Other Writings on Critical Theory, 1933–1963* (2006), CW, 21.

NUDITY

Re the Greek cult of the body: I think the point about the nude is that it's a powerful visual focus, the pride of the eyes. The *naked* body of a god or goddess is also a centre of authority.

Entry, Notebook 21 (1969–76), 390, *Northrop Frye's Notebooks and Lectures on the Bible and Other Religious Texts* (2003), CW, 13.

NUMBERS

Recurrent numbers, seven & twelve & the like, are elements of design only: they represent no hidden mystery or numinousness in things. Not even the trinitarian three or the Jungian four. There are twelve signs in the zodiac, but it would be equally easy to see nine or eleven or fourteen and a half. Only fractions seem so *vulgar*.

Entry, Notebook 44 (1986–91), 255, *Northrop Frye's Late Notebooks, 1982–1990: Architecture of the Spiritual World* (2000), CW, 5.

The two great instruments that man has devised for understanding and transforming the world are words and numbers. The humanities are primarily the *verbal* disciplines; the natural sciences are the numerical ones.

"Humanities in a New World" (1958), *Northrop Frye's Writings on Education* (2001), CW, 7.

NURSERY RHYMES

Nursery rhymes are not only the best possible introduction to poetry; they represent almost the only genuine poetic experience that many people ever get.

"The Oxford Dictionary of Nursery Rhymes" (1952), *"The Educated Imagination" and Other Writings on Critical Theory, 1933–1963* (2006), CW, 21.

Right now they're the only really popular poetry we have, and millions of people know "Hi diddle diddle" and "Jack and Jill" who have never read a line of Shakespeare or Milton.

"Laurence Hyde, 'Southern Cross,' and 'The Oxford Dictionary of Nursery Rhymes'" (1952), *Northrop Frye on Literature and Society, 1936–1989: Unpublished Papers* (2002), CW, 10.

O

OBJECTIVITY
We all tend to like what is like ourselves: if we try to be objective, we may eventually come to like what is like our best self.

"Douglas Duncan" (1974), *Northrop Frye on Canada* (2003), CW, 12.

One must continually create reality, whether as artist or as saint, to produce or build up in oneself the kind of egoless objectivity which will enable one to recognize the oracular given when it comes.

Entry, Notebook 19 (1964–67), 9, *The "Third Book" Notebooks of Northrop Frye, 1964–1972: The Critical Comedy* (2002), CW, 9.

OBSCENITY
There is, of course, such a thing as genuine obscenity: there are words that no self-respecting person would seriously use. But those are not the celebrated four-letter words: they are words that express hatred or contempt for people of different religion or nationality or skin colour.

"Literature and the Law" (1970), *"The Critical Path" and Other Writings on Critical Theory, 1963–1975* (2009), CW, 27.

One indication that laws against obscene literature have no real legal basis is the impossibility of framing a legal definition of obscenity. One hopeful American court in the 1890s said that it was anything which would give offence to a modest woman. Then all it had to do was to define a modest woman.

"Literature and the Law" (1970), *"The Critical Path" and Other Writings on Critical Theory, 1963–1975* (2009), CW, 27.

Comedy is moral insofar as it expands the range of response: obscenity, for instance, is profoundly moral.

Entry, Notebook 8 (1946–58), *Northrop Frye's Notebooks on Renaissance Literature* (2006), CW, 20.

But it's impossible to give legal definitions of such terms as obscenity in relation to works of literature. What happens to the book depends mainly on the intelligence of the judge. If he's a sensible man we get a sensible decision; if he's an ass we get that sort of decision, but what we don't get is a legal decision, because the basis for one doesn't exist.

"The Keys to Dreamland," *The Educated Imagination* (1963), *"The Educated Imagination" and Other Writings on Critical Theory, 1933–1963* (2006), CW, 21.

OCCULTISM
I dropped into a second-hand bookshop which sells books on occultism near the British Museum. Bloomsbury is a great centre of occultism — you see Theosophy, Swedenborg, Rudolf Steiner and all the rest of the Cosmic Consciousness and Third Eye apparatus every time you turn around. Even over London as a whole it's one of the three largest groups of advertised books of non-fiction — the other two being Marxist political and economic treatises and books relating to sexual intercourse.

"NF to HK," 24 Sep. 1936, *The Correspondence of Northrop Frye and Helen Kemp, 1932–1939* (1996), CW, 2.

As science moves beyond the schematic stage, the poet does not move with it, but is driven into the intellectual underground of occultists and theosophists, like Swedenborg or

Madame Blavatsky, in the search for structures that are still naively symmetrical. Poetry has a limited tolerance for conceptual or technical language in any field: it is compelled to design, not to describe.
"Tradition and Change in the Theory of Criticism" (1969), *Northrop Frye on Literature and Society, 1936–1989: Unpublished Papers* (2002), CW, 10.

In occult writing there normally is, or is assumed to be, a long oral tradition preceding, which does not commit itself to writing until the tradition has begun to break down.
"Language II," *The Great Code* (1982), *The Great Code: The Bible and Literature* (2006), CW, 19.

Poets find it much easier to live in the Ptolemaic universe than in ours, because it is more associative; modern poets turn from science to occultism because the latter still features associative patterns.
"Speculation and Concern" (1966), *Northrop Frye's Writings on Education* (2001), CW, 7.

The occult tradition, stemming as it did partly from Swedenborg and St. Martin in the West and partly from an increasing flow of information about Hindu and Buddhist philosophies, was especially attractive because it seemed to hint more clearly at a universal language of symbolism. This tradition comes to its climax near the end of the century with Madame Blavatsky's huge *The Secret Doctrine*, after which the growth of the scientific study of comparative religion and psychoanalysis took the whole question out of the palsied hands of literary critics.
"Yeats and the Language of Symbolism" (1947), *"The Critical Path" and Other Writings on Critical Theory, 1963–1975* (2009), CW, 27.

The point is that there are four branches of occultism, alchemy, astrology, magic & cabbalism, & out of them chemistry, astronomy, physics (in both senses) & philology have evolved. This hasn't destroyed, or shouldn't have done, the occult sciences: it has merely shifted their sphere of value from the scientific to the poetic.
Entry, Notebook 33 (1946–50), 15, *Northrop Frye's Notebooks on Romance* (2004), CW, 15.

Most of the critics of Blake up to that point told me that Blake's prophecies were related primarily to a mystical or to an occult tradition, and this constituted a difficulty for me, because Blake's poems interested me a great deal and most of the occultism I had read did not interest me at all. But I eventually saw that I would have to follow Blake's own instructions and read him within the tradition of English literature.
"The Critic and the Writer" (1972), *Northrop Frye's Writings on Education* (2001), CW, 7.

OLD TESTAMENT
For Christianity the Old Testament was primarily a book of prophecy, foretelling the future event of the Incarnation and thereby pointing to the transcendence of the law.
"Typology I," *The Great Code* (1982), *The Great Code: The Bible and Literature* (2006), CW, 19.

ONTARIO
Ontario is a place to stand, we are told: the cultural complications begin with sitting down.
"Culture and Society in Ontario, 1784–1984" (1984), referring to Ontario's theme song "A Place to Stand" introduced at Expo 67, *Northrop Frye on Canada* (2003), CW, 12.

... he has succeeded, as I think no poet has so succeeded before, in bringing southern Ontario, surely one of the most inarticulate communities in human culture, into a brilliant imaginative focus.
"Letters in Canada: Poetry" (1959), reviewing James Reaney's *A Suit of Nettles*, *Northrop Frye on Canada* (2003), CW, 12.

OPERA
Part of the trouble is the absurdity of the opera convention itself: it's hard enough in a verbal drama to get actors properly cast, but to find the right actors who can sing as well is just beyond human capacity.
"Notes for 'The World as Music and Idea in Wagner's *Parsifal*'" (1982), 2, *Northrop Frye's Fiction and Miscellaneous Writings* (2007), CW, 25.

As long as we have Mozart or Verdi or Sullivan to listen to, we can tolerate identical twins and lost heirs and love potions and folktales:

we can even stand a fairy queen if she is under two hundred pounds.

"Comic Myth in Shakespeare" (1952), *Northrop Frye's Writings on Shakespeare and the Renaissance* (2010), CW, 28.

All that is left is the theatre, and the theatre for the moment is the real presence of a real world, timeless and spaceless, intelligent and organized, and full of an inexhaustible joy.

"Shakespeare's Comedy of Humours" (1950), referring to the use of music in opera, *Northrop Frye on Literature and Society, 1936–1989: Unpublished Papers* (2002), CW, 10.

OPINION

One's "definite position" is one's weakness, the source of one's liability to error and prejudice, and to gain adherents to a definite position is only to multiply one's weakness like an infection.

"Polemical Introduction" (1957), *Anatomy of Criticism: Four Essays* (2006), CW, 22.

OPPORTUNITY

All thoughtful democrats agree that the main threat to democracy from within arises, not from disparities of wealth, but from disparities of opportunity.

"Trends in Modern Culture" (1952), *Northrop Frye on Modern Culture* (2003), CW, 11.

OPTIMISM

In interviews I am almost invariably asked at some point whether I feel optimistic or pessimistic about some contemporary situation. The answer is that these imbecile words are euphemisms for manic-depressive highs and lows, and that anyone who struggles for sanity avoids both.

The Double Vision (1991), *Northrop Frye on Religion* (2000), CW, 4.

We have manic people talking about the Age of Aquarius, where everything is just going to be wonderful, and then we have depressive people talking about atomic bombs and the destruction of civilization.

"Between Paradise and Apocalypse" (1978), *Interviews with Northrop Frye* (2008), CW, 24.

ORACLES

The oracle develops a number of subsidiary forms, notably the commandment, the parable, the aphorism, and the prophecy. Out of these, whether strung loosely together as they are in the Koran or carefully edited and arranged as they are in the Bible, the scripture or sacred book takes shape.

"First Essay: Historical Criticism: Theory of Modes" (1957), *Anatomy of Criticism: Four Essays* (2006), CW, 22.

All minds are passive to impressions 90% of the time, and probably people are more affected by oracles than they admit.

Entry, 13 Jul. 1942, 7, *The Diaries of Northrop Frye: 1942–1955* (2001), CW, 8.

ORAL CULTURE

In an oral culture prose tends to be detached into isolated proverbs, epigrams or oracles; a writing culture brings in the conception of prose as a continuous form of verbal expression.

"Tradition and Change in the Theory of Criticism" (1969), *Northrop Frye on Literature and Society, 1936–1989: Unpublished Papers* (2002), CW, 10.

In our day the electronic media of film, radio, and television have brought about a revival of the oral culture that we had before writing, and many of the social characteristics of a pre-literate society are reappearing in ours.

"Communications" (1970), *Northrop Frye on Modern Culture* (2003), CW, 11.

In general, it may be said that oral verbal culture expresses itself in continuous verse and discontinuous prose.

The Critical Path: An Essay on the Social Context of Literary Criticism (1971), *"The Critical Path" and Other Writings on Critical Theory, 1963–1975* (2009), CW, 27.

ORATORY

Once you have heard words used with genuine power and intensity, you can never again for the rest of your life pretend that you've not heard them used in that way. That's the voice of authority, and that's the kind of authority that never detracts from the dignity of anyone who assents to it.

"Frye's Literary Theory in the Classroom: A Panel Discussion" (1978), *Interviews with Northrop Frye* (2008), CW, 24.

ORDER

... order is not a matter of morality but of morale.

"Part One: The Argument," *Fearful Symmetry: A Study of William Blake* (1947, 2004), CW, 14.

Every ordered structure, in art or scholarship, represents an ethical victory over the anxieties of ego, which express themselves in digressions.

Entry, Notebook 12 (1968–70), 477, *The "Third Book" Notebooks of Northrop Frye, 1964–1972: The Critical Comedy* (2002), CW, 9.

ORDER OF CANADA

It seems to me very characteristic of Canada that its highest Order should have for its motto: "Looking for a better country." The quotation is from the New Testament, where the better country really is the City of God, but the feeling it expresses has more mundane contexts.

"Conclusion to *Literary History of Canada*" (1965), *Northrop Frye on Canada* (2003), CW, 12. The Latin motto of the Order of Canada, established 1 July 1967, is taken from the Epistle to the Hebrews (11:16) and reads *Desiderantes meliorem patriam*.

ORDER OF WORDS

In literature, whatever has a shape has a mythical shape, and leads us towards the centre of the order of words.

"Myth, Fiction, and Displacement" (1961), *"The Educated Imagination" and Other Writings on Critical Theory, 1933–1963* (2006), CW, 21.

It is obvious, for instance, that one major source of order in society is an established pattern of words.

"Tentative Conclusion" (1957), *Anatomy of Criticism: Four Essays* (1957, 2006), CW, 22.

We find it hard to conceive of literature as an order of words, as a unified imaginative system that can be studied as a whole by criticism. If we had such a conception, we could readily see that literature as a whole provides a framework or context for every work of literature, just as a fully developed mythology provides a framework or context for each of its myths.

"Myth, Fiction, and Displacement" (1961), *"The Educated Imagination" and Other Writings on Critical Theory, 1933–1963* (2006), CW, 21.

In the greatest moments of Dante and Shakespeare, in, say *The Tempest* or the climax of the *Purgatorio*, we have a feeling of converging significance, the feeling that here we are close to seeing what our whole literary experience has been about, the feeling that we have moved into the still centre of the order of words. Criticism as knowledge, the criticism which is compelled to keep on talking about the subject, recognizes the fact that there *is* a centre of the order of words.

"Second Essay: Ethical Criticism: Theory of Symbols" (1957), *Anatomy of Criticism: Four Essays* (2006), CW, 22.

It is clear that criticism cannot be systematic unless there is a quality in literature which enables it to be so, an order of words corresponding to the order of nature in the natural sciences.

"The Archetypes of Literature" (1951), *"The Educated Imagination" and Other Writings on Critical Theory, 1933–1963* (2006), CW, 21.

... literature, considered as a whole, is not the aggregate of all the works of literature that have got written, but an order of words, a coherent field of study which trains the imagination quite as systematically and efficiently as the sciences train the reason.

"Elementary Teaching and Elemental Scholarship" (1963), *Northrop Frye's Writings on Education* (2001), CW, 7.

ORIGINALITY

A serious study of literature soon shows that the real difference between the original and the imitative poet is that the former is more profoundly imitative. Originality returns to the origins of literature; radicalism returns to its roots.

"The Language of Poetry" (1955), *"The Educated Imagination" and Other Writings on Critical Theory, 1933–1963* (2006), CW, 21.

The possession of originality cannot make an artist unconventional; it drives him further into convention, obeying the law of the art itself, which seeks constantly to reshape itself from its own depths, and which works through its geniuses for metamorphosis, as it works through minor talents for mutation.

"Third Essay: Archetypal Criticism: Theory of Myths" (1957), *Anatomy of Criticism: Four Essays* (2006), CW, 22.

American even more than Canadian poetry has been deeply affected by the clash between two irreconcilable views of literature: the view that poets should be original and the view that they should be aboriginal.

"Canada and Its Poetry" (1943), *Northrop Frye on Canada* (2003), CW, 12.

I do not deny the reality of the sense of the unexpected, the shocking or radically novel, about the original writer, but the difference between the original and the derivative writer does need restating, on the basis of the fact that the original writer is derivative at a deeper level.

"Nature and Homer" (1958), *"The Educated Imagination" and Other Writings on Critical Theory, 1933–1963* (2006), CW, 21.

You can't be original unless you work with hunches and treat them exactly as a paranoiac would do.

Entry, Notes 52 (1982–90), 10, *Northrop Frye's Late Notebooks, 1982–1990: Architecture of the Spiritual World* (2000), CW, 6.

ORIGINS

An English friend once remarked to me that a Canadian's conversational opening gambit seemed to be invariably, "Where you from?"

"Culture and Society in Ontario, 1784–1984" (1984), *Northrop Frye on Canada* (2003), CW, 12.

ORWELL, GEORGE

He wrote the novel that so many of us have wanted to write or see written, simply because he had the courage to look the present world straight in the face and the ability to set down what he saw there without panic or any desire to moralize. He had written the *Inferno* of the twentieth century, and however inferior he may be to Dante in all literary respects, he excels him in one point: his hell is a real hell, a dreadful state of torment that could last forever and yet is potentially here now.

"George Orwell" (1950), *Northrop Frye on Twentieth-Century Literature* (2010), CW, 29. Frye is discussing Orwell's dystopian satire *1984*.

OTTAWA

Each man carries inside him an entire Ottawa of politicians jockeying for power, civil servants struggling with routine, mass demonstrators organizing temper tantrums, secretaries trying to transcribe the inner turmoil into some kind of self-justifying narrative.

"The Stage Is All the World" (1985), *Northrop Frye's Writings on Shakespeare and the Renaissance* (2010), CW, 28.

OVID

... as is obvious, the plays of Shakespeare were really written by Ovid. Honest Ovid among the Goths, that is.

Entry, Notebook 24 (1970–72), 208, alluding to Shakespeare's *As You Like It, The "Third Book" Notebooks of Northrop Frye, 1964–1972: The Critical Comedy* (2002), CW, 9.

OWL

As for the owl, proverbial both for wisdom and for dullness, its kinship with the academic profession has never been doubted.

"By Liberal Things" (1959), *Northrop Frye's Writings on Education* (2001), CW, 7.

OXFORD UNIVERSITY

That, of course, throws a flood of light on a number of other Oxford geniuses, such as Pater and Hopkins. And when I read in Newman's *Apologia* that so-and-so taught him the doctrine of the apostolic succession in the course of a walk around the Christ Church meadows, I mean no disrespect to the doctrine of apostolic succession when I say that this seems to be in exactly the key of slightly nutty fantasy which has been the characteristics of Oxford from time immemorial, and which was still going on when I was there as a student in the kind of work associated with C.S. Lewis, Charles Williams, and Tolkien.

> "The Critic and the Writer" (1972), referring to the production of "hyperlogical fantasy" at Oxford University, *Northrop Frye's Writings on Education* (2001), CW, 7.

I'm simply going mad in this place. Dismally cold, wet, clammy, muggy, damp and moist, like a morgue. The room is always as cold as a barn — I can't play the piano because the keys are too cold. The mice are all over everything — they've eaten all my food, and shit all over my dishes. I've got a cold, and I feel like hell. It rains all the time.

> "NF to HK," 8 Dec. 1936, regarding his time in Oxford, *The Correspondence of Northrop Frye and Helen Kemp, 1932–1939* (1996), CW, 2.

P

PACIFISM

I'm not a pacifist because that would still mean that war was taking up too much of my thoughts and actions.

    Entry, 26 Jun. 1950, 444, *The Diaries of Northrop Frye: 1942–1955* (2001), CW, 8.

PAGEANT

The defeat of Sedition and Discord by Sound Government and Encouragement of Trade would be the right sort of theme for a pageant designed only to entertain a visiting monarch.

    "Second Essay: Ethical Criticism: Theory of Symbols" (1957), *Anatomy of Criticism: Four Essays* (2006), CW, 22.

PAINTERS & PAINTING

What painter has done the most to reeducate our visual associations? Picasso gets the publicity, but maybe Braque did the essential job.

    Entry, 26 Jan. 1950, 69, *The Diaries of Northrop Frye: 1942–1955* (2001), CW, 8.

There have been painters since the last ice age, and I hope there'll be painters until the next one: they show every conceivable variety of vision, and of originality in setting it out.

    "The Singing School," *The Educated Imagination* (1963), *"The Educated Imagination" and Other Writings on Critical Theory, 1933–1963* (2006), CW, 21.

The phrase "non-representational painting" seems to me illogical, a painting being itself a representation.

    "Third Essay: Archetypal Criticism: Theory of Myths" (1957), *Anatomy of Criticism: Four Essays* (2006), CW, 22.

Where we see a landscape, a painter also sees the possibility of a picture. He sees more than we see, and the picture itself is proof that he really does see it.

    "The Imaginative and the Imaginary" (1962), *"The Educated Imagination" and Other Writings on Critical Theory, 1933–1963* (2006), CW, 21.

A picture has to suggest three dimensions before it can suggest four, before the object can become a higher reality by becoming also an event, a moment suspended in time.

    "Lawren Harris" (1969), *Northrop Frye on Canada* (2003), CW, 12.

A painter of cows in a field is bound to be addressing some people who want to be reminded of cows more than they want to see pictures.

    Creation and Recreation (1980), *Northrop Frye on Religion* (2000), CW, 4.

… it is hard not to feel that painting completely detached from any form of representation becomes merely a piece of interior decorating, and belongs with streamlined pipe-chairs, indirect lighting, and oppressively chaste and sterile colours, just as the cows in the field go with velvet curtains, cut glass, gloom, and mangled mahogany.

    "Gordon Webber and Canadian Abstract Art" (1941), *Northrop Frye on Canada* (2003), CW, 12.

… painting, the art that began in the deep caves of palaeolithic times, has always had something of an unborn world about it, the projecting on nature of colours in the dark, this last phrase being the title of a Canadian play by James Reaney. Painting is in the front line of imaginative efforts to humanize a nonhuman world, to fight back, in a sparsely settled country, against a silent otherness that refuses to assimilate to anything human.

"Canadian Culture Today" (1977), *Northrop Frye on Canada* (2003), CW, 12.

PALAEOLITHIC ART

When one considers the skill and precision of these works, and the almost impossible difficulties of positioning and lighting surrounding their creation, we begin to grasp something of the intensity behind them to unite human consciousness with its own perceptions, an intensity we can hardly imagine now.

"Third Variation: The Cave," *Words with Power: Being a Second Study of "The Bible and Literature"* (1990), CW, 26.

PANDORA

Pandora is a baggage: that is, she's identical with her box.

Entry, Notebook 50 (1987–90), 441, *Northrop Frye's Late Notebooks, 1982–1990: Architecture of the Spiritual World* (2000), CW, 5.

PARADISE

In the histories we notice the working of a principle that we might call Proust's law. The only paradises are the paradises we have lost, and every period of history seems to create a pastoral myth out of something in a previous age.

"Nature and Nothing" (1964), referring specifically to Shakespeare's history plays, *Northrop Frye's Writings on Shakespeare and the Renaissance* (2010), CW, 28.

The earthly paradise is a vision in which all four concerns merge. Food is abundant; sex is accessible; shelter needs no construct; play is there from the start, not reached after work. It's therefore primarily a vision of regenerated nature.

Entry, Notebook 44 (1986–91), 18, *Northrop Frye's Late Notebooks, 1982–1990: Architecture of the Spiritual World* (2000), CW, 5.

The only Paradises are those we have lost or are about to gain: no jam today.

Entry, Notebook 19 (1964–67), 23, *The "Third Book" Notebooks of Northrop Frye, 1964–1972: The Critical Comedy* (2002), CW, 9.

Myths of an original paradise and of man's having lost the gift of immortality — those are worldwide. Frazer has made tremendous collections of them. They're just everywhere.

"Between Paradise and Apocalypse" (1978), *Interviews with Northrop Frye* (2008), CW, 24.

PARANOIA

One of the most remarkable works of fiction in our time, Thomas Pynchon's *Gravity's Rainbow*, suggests that the human instinct to see humanly intelligible pattern and design in nature is a form of paranoia. That is, man cannot endure the thought of an environment that was not made primarily for his benefit, or, at any rate, made without reference to his own need to see order in it.

"Culture as Interpenetration" (1977), *Northrop Frye on Canada* (2003), CW, 12.

PARENTING

Parental deficiency is permissiveness; parental excess is possessiveness.

Entry, Notebook 21 (1969–76), 607, *Northrop Frye's Notebooks and Lectures on the Bible and Other Religious Texts* (2003), CW, 13.

PARTI QUÉBÉCOIS

There are some very unpleasant things, of course, under the surface of the Parti Québécois. It's a very nasty neo-fascist movement, and if they got their head then that would be quite literally a case of hell breaking loose.

"An Eminent Victorian" (1978), *Interviews with Northrop Frye* (2008), CW, 24.

PAST

... the past is functional in our lives only when we neither forget it nor try to return to it. This is, of course, the principle on which the study of the humanities is also founded.

"Teaching the Humanities Today" (1977), *Northrop Frye's Writings on Education* (2001), CW, 7.

Man cannot attain his true dignity until he exists in time, in a historical dimension as well as in his spatial surroundings, until some of the gates of the past have been opened, and he can see something of the relativeness of his own standards and values.

"The Beginning of the Word" (1980), *Northrop Frye's Writings on Education* (2001), CW, 7.

Those who reject the past have no defence against the future, for the future is nothing but the analogy of the past.
"Rear-View Crystal Ball" (1970), *Northrop Frye on Canada* (2003), CW, 12.

Our attitude to the past needs more of the impartiality of the archaeologist who excavates all layers and cultural periods of his site with equal care.
"Canada: New World Without Revolution" (1975), *Northrop Frye on Canada* (2003), CW, 12.

The artefacts of a vanished civilization were produced in the normal climate of human cruelty and folly, but they themselves are in an unchanging state of innocence.
"Repetitions of Jacob's Dream" (1983), *Northrop Frye on Religion* (2000), CW, 4.

PATHETIC FALLACY
The pathetic fallacy is pathetic because it is a fallacy.
"Part Two: The Development of the Symbolism," *Fearful Symmetry: A Study of William Blake* (1947, 2004), CW, 14.

PATTERNS
Pattern-making extends over philosophy from Pythagoras to the Renaissance as a kind of intermediate stage between magic and science.
"Part One: The Argument," *Fearful Symmetry: A Study of William Blake* (1947, 2004), CW, 14.

PEACE
So much talk about pacifism is too vaguely moral. Peace is an economic system functioning. War is an economic system breaking down. States are healthy in war and degenerate in peace because of original sin and because anarchy is the best form of government.
Entry, Notebook 4 (1939), 89, *Northrop Frye's Fiction and Miscellaneous Writings* (2007), CW, 25.

Those of us who remember living through the Second World War will remember also how often we were told that we had to win the peace as well as the war. The assumption was that a new and greatly expanded life would await us as soon as the war was over. This was an illusion of considerable importance in sustaining democratic morale, and when the war ended it disappeared, having performed its function. But the myth of deliverance is not always a deliberately summoned up mirage of this kind. On the contrary, it seems to be at the core of every major myth of concern.
"The Myth of Deliverance: I, The Reversal of Action" (1981), *Northrop Frye's Writings on Shakespeare and the Renaissance* (2010), CW, 28.

…but surely a world in which the lion is said to lie down with the lamb is a world of stuffed lions.
"Part One: The Argument," reflecting Blake's ideas, *Fearful Symmetry: A Study of William Blake* (1947, 2004), CW, 14.

The intelligent and critical reader has two main interests: the war of civilization and the peace of civilization. By the peace of civilization is meant the enjoyment of the best available cultural interests: books, movies, records, and the current trend of ideas. A Canadian reader will naturally have an additional interest in what is being done in Canada.
"Editorial Statement" (1948), *Northrop Frye on Canada* (2003), CW, 12.

PEARSON, LESTER B.
I do not think of Mr. Pearson as a great man: I think of him as one of the best products of a society which is gradually outgrowing the conception of the great man. He was a good man, trying to do a good job; a man of exceptional abilities who used those abilities for public service and not for private profit. If I read the Gospels correctly, this is a more impressive achievement than what is usually meant by greatness.
"Lester Bowles Pearson, 1897–1972" (1973), *Northrop Frye on Canada* (2003), CW, 12.

PENSÉES
I've always wanted to write "my own" book of *pensées*, not like Pascal's but more like Anatole France's *Jardin d'Epicure* or (I've just discovered) Connolly's *The Unquiet Grave*.

Entry, Notebook 50 (1987–90), 568, *Northrop Frye's Late Notebooks, 1982–1990: Architecture of the Spiritual World* (2000), CW, 5. Frye noted, "The disadvantage of this project is that it can't be planned." Denham, editor of *Northrop Frye Unbuttoned* (2004), added, "Frye never got around to writing his book of *pensées*.... "

PERCEPTION

An object impregnated, so to speak, by a perceiver is transformed into a presence.

"Identity and Metaphor," *Words with Power: Being a Second Study of "The Bible and Literature"* (1990), CW, 26.

PERICLES, SHAKESPEARE'S

If archaeologists ever discover a flourishing drama in Mayan or Minoan culture, it may not have plays like *Lear* or *Oedipus*, but it will assuredly have plays like *Pericles*.

"Comic Myth in Shakespeare" (1952), *Northrop Frye's Writings on Shakespeare and the Renaissance* (2010), CW, 28.

PERSONA

Our own experience tells us that we spend our lives acting out roles and assuming one persona after another. There are pathetic illusions about encounter groups, which are supposed to get underneath a persona to the real person, but there is never anything under a persona except another persona; there is no core to that onion.

"The Teacher's Source of Authority" (1978), *Northrop Frye's Writings on Education* (2001), CW, 7.

The attitude I take is phenomenological: for me there is never any persona except another persona. As *Hamlet* proves in its soliloquies, we dramatize ourselves to ourselves even when alone.

"Reviews of Television Programs for the Canadian Radio-Television Commission: Reflections on November 5th" (1970), *Northrop Frye on Literature and Society, 1936–1989: Unpublished Papers* (2002), CW, 10.

Persona or mask: nothing under it except another persona, but still important to know that we are playing roles.

"On Education II" (1972), 27, *Northrop Frye's Fiction and Miscellaneous Writings* (2007), CW, 25.

PERSPECTIVE

One cannot combine the convex and concave to get a new perspective.

"The Diatribes of Wyndham Lewis: A Study in Prose Satire" (1936), *Northrop Frye's Student Essays, 1932–1938* (1997), CW, 3.

PH.D.

A young humanist compelled to write a pseudo-book, and rewrite it as a real book while teaching surveys and marking freshman exercises or essays, often feels that he is getting a crash course in schizophrenia.

"Preface to *ADE and ADFL Bulletins*" (1976), referring to the doctoral dissertation, *Northrop Frye's Writings on Education* (2001), CW, 7.

The Ph.D. is as dead as the dodo, but it keeps on ticking automatically because we haven't found the machinery to replace it.

Entry, Notebook 42b: Notes I (1942–44), 48, *Northrop Frye's Fiction and Miscellaneous Writings* (2007), CW, 25.

PHILOLOGY

This association is, of course, subject to the first law of philology, which is that every association of words that looks in the least interesting has been shown by scholars to be a mere coincidence.

Entry, Notebook 11b (late 1980), 23, *Northrop Frye's Notebooks and Lectures on the Bible and Other Religious Texts* (2003), CW, 13.

PHILOSOPHY

The philosopher has to be banished from the poet's republic: perhaps the *Symposium* says so.

Entry, Notebook 3 (1946–48), *Northrop Frye Newsletter*, Fall 2000.

For a philosopher, isolation is the first act of consciousness. I am myself alone, he says, and the rest of the world then becomes objective to him.

"*Fools of Time*: III, Little World of Man: The Tragedy of Isolation" (1966), *Northrop Frye's Writings on Shakespeare and the Renaissance* (2010), CW, 28.

All religions are one, not alike: a metaphorical unity of different things, not a bundle of similarities. In that sense there is no "perennial

philosophy": that's a collection, at best, of denatured techniques of concentration. As doctrine, it's platitude: moral maxims that have no application. What there is, luckily, is a perennial struggle.
> Entry, Notebook 44 (1986–91), 48, *Northrop Frye's Late Notebooks, 1982–1990: Architecture of the Spiritual World* (2000), CW, 5.

Philosophy is a love of wisdom, and we do not love what we possess, except as self-love.
> "Josef Pieper, 'Leisure: The Basis of Culture'" (1950s), *Northrop Frye on Literature and Society, 1936–1989: Unpublished Papers* (2002), CW, 10.

Literature itself is not a field of conflicting arguments but of interpenetrating visions. I suspect that this is true even of philosophy, where the place of argument seems more functional. The irrefutable philosopher is not the one who cannot be refuted, but the one who is still there after he has been refuted.
> "Letter to the English Institute, 1965" (1965), *"The Critical Path" and Other Writings on Critical Theory, 1963–1975* (2009), CW, 27.

The problems of philosophy are not solved, but we do succeed in losing interest in them.
> Entry, Notebook 3 (1946–48), 64, *Northrop Frye's Notebooks and Lectures on the Bible and Other Religious Texts* (2003), CW, 13.

PHOENIX

There is no way out of these ambiguities: criticism is a phoenix preoccupied with constructing its own funeral pyre, without any guarantee that a bigger and better phoenix will manifest itself as a result.
> "Criticism, Visible and Invisible" (1964), *"The Critical Path" and Other Writings on Critical Theory, 1963–1975* (2009), CW, 27.

The phoenix, the bird born of its own sacrifice, could well stand for a church made possible by the consenting of dissenters.
> "By Liberal Things" (1959), *Northrop Frye's Writings on Education* (2001), CW, 7.

The phoenix appears on the coat of arms of Victoria College. It ought to represent the Faculty of Theology, but again the original designers were more cautious and put it there as a symbol of medicine: they knew that *that* at least might do you some good.
> "Symbolism in the Bible" (1981–82), *Northrop Frye's Notebooks and Lectures on the Bible and Other Religious Texts* (2003), CW, 13.

PHOTOGRAPHY

A real & artistic passion for observation in itself with no attempt at a creative follow-through is rare, but it exists. And there's a riddling, gnomic quality in the photograph absent from the painting.
> Entry, 20 Aug. 1942, 69, discussing Samuel Pepys, *The Diaries of Northrop Frye: 1942–1955* (2001), CW, 8.

PHYSICS

No one can know the whole of physics at once, but physics would not be a coherent subject unless this were theoretically possible.
> "Levels of Meaning in Literature" (1950), *"The Educated Imagination" and Other Writings on Critical Theory, 1933–1963* (2006), CW, 21.

The encounter of God and man in creation seems to be rather like what some of the great poets of nuclear physics have described as the encounter of matter with anti-matter: each annihilates the other. What seems one of the few admirable forms of human achievement, the creation of the arts, turns out to be a kind of decreation....
> *Creation and Recreation* (1980), *Northrop Frye on Religion* (2000), CW, 4.

Niels Bohr is said to have advised Einstein to stop telling God what to do: the advice would be relevant to a lot of people besides Einstein.
> Entry, Notes 53 (1989–90), 129, *Northrop Frye's Late Notebooks, 1982–1990: Architecture of the Spiritual World* (2000), CW, 6.

PIANISTS

A first-rate pianist may play thousands of notes in a few minutes, attending to every rest, dynamic shading, and predominance of one voice over another. He does not consciously attend to each of these details, but there must have been a time when he did.

"Some Reflections on Life and Habit" (1988), *Northrop Frye's Writings on the Eighteenth and Nineteenth Centuries* (2005), CW, 17.

To practice the piano is to set oneself free to play it.
"Fourth Variation: The Furnace," *Words with Power: Being a Second Study of "The Bible and Literature"* (1990), CW, 26.

The two forms of touch don't seem to have clashed a great deal, although many people said that I played the piano as though it were a typewriter.
"Music in My Life" (1985), referring to his prowess as a typist and his talent as a pianist, *Interviews with Northrop Frye* (2008), CW, 24.

PICTURESQUENESS

Taking such accidents to be primary instead of occasional gives us, in painting, the heresy of the picturesque, which is only one of the many forms of ready-made subject. The picturesque, whether found in the quack doctor Rosa or not, is a type of art which takes wonder, or the contemplating of the quizzical, to be an end as well as a beginning of imagination, and hence implies that the found object or random vision is of oracular significance.
"Part One: The Argument," *Fearful Symmetry: A Study of William Blake* (1947, 2004), CW, 14.

PITY

Pity without an object has never to my knowledge been given a name, but it expresses itself as an imaginative animism, or treating everything in nature as though it had human feelings or qualities.
"Towards Defining an Age of Sensibility" (1956), *Northrop Frye's Writings on the Eighteenth and Nineteenth Centuries* (2005), CW, 17.

PLAGIARISM

To demonstrate the debt of A to B may get C his doctorate if A is dead, but may land him in a libel suit if A is alive.
"The Language of Poetry" (1955), *"The Educated Imagination" and Other Writings on Critical Theory, 1933–1963* (2006), CW, 21.

PLATITUDES

The difference between the platitude and the aphorism, hinted at earlier, is that the platitude involves no disturbance of a commonplace standard of values. A platitude may be true, even universally true; but it would not occur to us to call it profoundly true. We do not call a statement profound unless we are pleased with its wit.
"Part One: The Argument," *Fearful Symmetry: A Study of William Blake* (1947, 2004), CW, 14.

I suppose everyone knows this, but one of the major activities of art consists in sharpening the edge of platitudes to make them enter the soul as realities. A simple change in vowel-quantity may (I don't say it does) make the whole difference.
Entry, Notebook 3 (1946–48), 12, *Northrop Frye's Notebooks and Lectures on the Bible and Other Religious Texts* (2003), CW, 13.

It is always safe to begin with platitudes. In the history of European culture....
"A Reconsideration of Chaucer" (1938), *Northrop Frye's Student Essays, 1932–1938* (1997), CW, 3.

PLATO

Plato made the most heroic effort in human history to construct a one-man scripture.
Entry, Notebook 54-8 (late 1972–77), 53, *Northrop Frye's Notebooks on Romance* (2004), CW, 15.

But the supremely suggestive and fertilizing quality of Plato's philosophy lies in the fact that he was the only philosopher who was artist enough to master a visionary form, and hence *par excellence* the philosopher who suggests an infinity of responses instead of compelling a single one.
"Part One: The Argument," *Fearful Symmetry: A Study of William Blake* (1947, 2004), CW, 14.

PLAY

In ordinary speech we distinguish work and play, work being energy expended for a further end in view, play being energy expended for its own sake.
"Some Reflections on Life and Habit" (1988), *Northrop Frye's Writings on the Eighteenth and Nineteenth Centuries* (2005), CW, 17.

The turning of literal act into play is a fundamental form of the liberalizing of life which appears in more intellectual levels as liberal education.
"Third Essay: Archetypal Criticism: Theory of Myths" (1957), *Anatomy of Criticism: Four Essays* (2006), CW, 22.

Whenever a thing exists for its own end, rather than as a means to a further end, that thing is associable with play rather than with work.
"Symbolism in the Bible" (1981–82), *Northrop Frye's Notebooks and Lectures on the Bible and Other Religious Texts* (2003), CW, 13.

The interpenetration of work and play is also the interpenetration of necessity and freedom. If we define genuine work as creative act (vs. Drudgery or exploited & alienated work), what we have to do and what we want to do are the same thing.
Entry, Notebook 44 (1986–91), 147, *Northrop Frye's Late Notebooks, 1982–1990: Architecture of the Spiritual World* (2000), CW, 5.

Play is that for the sake of which work is done, the climactic Sabbath vision of mankind.
"Conclusion to *Literary History of Canada*" (1965), *Northrop Frye on Canada* (2003), CW, 12.

This world of play or spontaneous energy is the deliverance to which all religious and political ideals point, and some glimpse of it is accessible to any artist or scientist at any moment.
"The Bridge of Language" (1981), *Northrop Frye on Modern Culture* (2003), CW, 11.

... the principle that work was energy directed toward an end, and that play was the end, energy for its own sake.
Entry, Notebook 55 (1987–90), 6, *Northrop Frye's Late Notebooks, 1982–1990: Architecture of the Spiritual World* (2000), CW, 5.

I have a hunch that what I call work is directed to a goal of return or revival; what I call play is an expression of belief in resurrection.
Entry, Notes 52 (1982–90), 980, *Northrop Frye's Late Notebooks, 1982–1990: Architecture of the Spiritual World* (2000), CW, 6.

If you distinguish work and play, I think you may see that work is energy expanded for a further aim in view; whereas play is the expression of energy for its own sake, or the manifestation of what the end in view is.
"Symbolism in the Bible" (1981–82), *Northrop Frye's Notebooks and Lectures on the Bible and Other Religious Texts* (2003), CW, 13.

The ordinary division of our lives into work and play makes work the endless pursuit of a donkey's carrot into the future, and play a relaxation from this that reminds us of the carefree days of our childhood. But the genuine human energy of the arts and sciences converges on a world where work and play have become the same thing.
"The Bridge of Language" (1981), *Northrop Frye on Modern Culture* (2003), CW, 11.

PLOT

The plot, then, is like the trees and houses that we focus our eyes on through a train window: the narrative is more like the weeds and stones that rush by in the foreground.
"Myth, Fiction, and Displacement" (1961), *"The Educated Imagination" and Other Writings on Critical Theory, 1933–1963* (2006), CW, 21.

What begins to emerge from the chaos of literature are certain recurring principles of verbal design, embodied in such conventions and genres as comedy, romance, and tragedy, which link Shakespeare with Kalidasa, Melville with the Old Testament, Proust with Lady Murasaki.
"Design as a Creative Principle in the Arts" (1966), *"The Critical Path" and Other Writings on Critical Theory, 1963–1975* (2009), CW, 27.

Just as the pun is the lowest form of wit, so it is generally agreed, among knowledgeable people like ourselves, that summarizing a plot is the lowest form of criticism.
"The Road of Excess" (1970), *Northrop Frye on Milton and Blake* (2005), CW, 16.

PLURALISM

Whether the universe is pluralistic or not, there is no doubt that the world of the intellect is.

"The Changing Pace in Canadian Education" (1963), *Northrop Frye's Writings on Education* (2001), CW, 7.

POE, EDGAR ALLAN

The greatest literary genius this side of Blake is Edgar Allan Poe — that's why he's regarded as fit only for adolescents, or French poets who don't really know English.

Entry, Notebook 44 (1986–91), 290, *Northrop Frye's Late Notebooks, 1982–1990: Architecture of the Spiritual World* (2000), CW, 5.

POETRY

Thus the centre of the literary universe is whatever poem we happen to be reading. One step further, and the poem appears as a microcosm of all literature, an individual manifestation of the total order of words.

"Second Essay: Ethical Criticism: Theory of Symbols" (1957), *Anatomy of Criticism: Four Essays* (2006), CW, 22.

But the poem is also a power of speech to be possessed in his own way by the reader, and some death and rebirth process has to be gone through before the poem revives within him, as something now uniquely his, though still also itself.

"Expanding Eyes" (1975), *"The Critical Path" and Other Writings on Critical Theory, 1963–1975* (2009), CW, 27.

The personal poet has to be represented by somebody, however remote from the poet or however silent. But, of course, the poem is not a direct address, but broadcast like a radio program.

Entry, Notes 52 (1982–90), 570, *Northrop Frye's Late Notebooks, 1982–1990: Architecture of the Spiritual World* (2000), CW, 6.

Reading poetry is a technique of meditation; we must keep reading and rereading the same poem for quite a while before its real intensity will emerge.

"Extracts from *The Practical Imagination: Stories, Poems, Plays*" (1980), *"The Secular Scripture" and Other Writings on Critical Theory, 1976–1991* (2006), CW, 18.

Poetry, which is at the heart of all mythology, finds its function in providing verbal imaginative models for human civilization, and seeing reality in terms of human desires and emotions.

"The Times of the Signs" (1973), *"The Critical Path" and Other Writings on Critical Theory, 1963–1975* (2009), CW, 27.

Poetry is a *disinterested* use of words: it does not address a reader directly.

"Polemical Introduction" (1957), *Anatomy of Criticism: Four Essays* (2006), CW, 22.

Poetry, then, does not state historical truth, but contains it: it sets forth what we may call the *myth* of history, the kind of thing that happens.

"The Road of Excess" (1970), *Northrop Frye on Milton and Blake* (2005), CW, 16.

The inference is that there may be something potentially unlimited or infinite in the response to poetry, something that turns on a light in the psyche, so that instead of the darkness of the unknown we see something of the shadows of other kinds of emerging being.

"Identity and Metaphor," *Words with Power: Being a Second Study of "The Bible and Literature"* (2008), CW, 26.

Whatever science may say, the poet's world continues to be built out of a flat earth with a rising and setting sun, with four elements and an animate nature, the concrete world of emotions and sensations and fancies and transforming memories and dreams.

The Critical Path: An Essay on the Social Context of Literary Criticism (1971), *"The Critical Path" and Other Writings on Critical Theory, 1963–1975* (2009), CW, 27.

Poetry organizes the content of the world as it passes before the poet, but the forms in which that content is organized come out of the structure of poetry itself.

"Second Essay: Ethical Criticism: Theory of Symbols" (1957), *Anatomy of Criticism: Four Essays* (2006), CW, 22.

Poetry has a limited tolerance for conceptual or technical language in any field: it is compelled to design, not to describe.

"Tradition and Change in the Theory of Criticism" (1969), *Northrop Frye on Literature and Society, 1936–1989: Unpublished Papers* (2002), CW, 10.

The representational tendency in poetry is sophisticated and civilized: the formal tendency is primitive, oracular, close to the riddle and the spell.
"Letters in Canada: Poetry" (1956), *Northrop Frye on Canada* (2003), CW, 12.

Poetry is concerned with the ambiguities, the unconscious diagrams, the metaphors and the images out of which actual ideas grow.
"The Realistic Oriole: A Study of Wallace Stevens" (1957), *Northrop Frye on Twentieth-Century Literature* (2010), CW, 19.

But one of the functions of poetry, as I see it, is to keep alive the metaphoric habit of mind and to make sure that its significance remains obvious to all receptive people.
"Freedom and Concern" (1985), *Interviews with Northrop Frye* (2008), CW, 24.

Poetry is the most direct and simple means of expressing oneself in words: the most primitive nations have poetry, but only quite well developed civilizations can produce good prose. So don't think of poetry as a perverse and unnatural way of distorting ordinary prose statements: prose is a much less natural way of speaking than poetry is.
"Verticals of Adam," *The Educated Imagination* (1963), *"The Educated Imagination" and Other Writings on Critical Theory, 1933–1963* (2006), CW, 21.

… a growing sense that the whole point of poetry is that God and man meet in a Logos.
"The Church and Modern Culture" (1950), *Northrop Frye on Modern Culture* (2003), CW, 11.

It's the function of poetry to recreate the hieroglyphic or mythical form of knowledge in each generation, and the function of metaphysics to recreate the hieratic form in our generation.
Entry, Notes 54-5 (1976), 28, *Northrop Frye's Notebooks and Lectures on the Bible and Other Religious Texts* (2003), CW, 13.

Every major poet is the apex of a pyramid of minor ones, and a contempt for minor poetry is more vulgar and more dangerous than the merely ignorant avoidance of all poetry.
"Canadian Chapbooks" (1941), *Northrop Frye on Canada* (2003), CW, 12.

Poetry expresses the central imaginative needs of society: it is, both historically and psychologically, primitive: it does not improve when social conditions do.
"*Rencontre*: The General Editor's Introduction" (1960s), *Northrop Frye on Literature and Society, 1936–1989: Unpublished Papers* (2002), CW, 10.

POETRY, CANADIAN

The appearance of a fine new book of poems in Canada is a historical event, and its readers should be aware that they are participating in history.
"Letters in Canada: Poetry" (1960), *Northrop Frye on Canada* (2003), CW, 12.

I suppose there are about thirty or forty poets in Canada whom I find interesting to read. There is a reflective quality in the Canadian consciousness that is a good breeding ground for poetic expression.
"Sacred and Secular Scriptures" (1975), *Interviews with Northrop Frye* (2008), CW, 24.

… in what Canadian poets have tried to do there is an interest for Canadian readers much deeper than what the achievement in itself justifies.
"Canada and Its Poetry" (1943), *Northrop Frye on Canada* (2003), CW, 12.

I see constantly in Canadian culture, more particularly in its poetry, a sense of meditative shock produced by the intrusion of the natural world into the imagination. I say intrusion, because it so often looms up with a greater urgency than the poet's social, political, or religious outlook is prepared to allow for.
"National Consciousness in Canadian Culture" (1976), *Northrop Frye on Canada* (2003), CW, 12.

There has on the whole been little Tarzanism in Canadian poetry. One is surprised to find

how few really good Canadian poets have thought that getting out of cities into God's great outdoors really brings one closer to the sources of inspiration.
"Canada and Its Poetry" (1943), *Northrop Frye on Canada* (2003), CW, 12.

Canadian poetry is at its best a poetry of incubus and *cauchemar*, the source of which is the unusually exposed contact of the poet with nature which Canada provides.
"Canada and Its Poetry" (1943), *Northrop Frye on Canada* (2003), CW, 12.

The two central themes in Canadian poetry: one a primarily comic theme of satire and exuberance, the other a primarily tragic theme of loneliness and terror.
"Preface to an Uncollected Anthology" (1956), *Northrop Frye on Canada* (2003), CW, 12.

In Canada poets are conditioned to utter a good deal of anti-academic patter as part of their own sales pitch, even when they are struggling for tenure appointments in universities themselves.
"The Search for Acceptable Words" (1973), *"The Critical Path" and Other Writings on Critical Theory, 1963–1975* (2009), CW, 27.

POETS

It is a law of poetic creation that the poet who is willing to lose his personality in his work finds it again.
"Preface and Introduction to Pratt's Poetry" (1958), *Northrop Frye on Canada* (20030, CW, 12.

What a poet *says* is not what makes him a poet.
"Introduction" (1990), *Words with Power: Being a Second Study of "The Bible and Literature"* (2008), CW, 26.

… we see that the poet cannot become the focus of a myth of freedom. Poets have always been the children of concern: they still show a liking for being converted to dogmatic creeds of all kinds, sometimes with the greatest contempt for the toleration they receive; they are a competitive and traditionally an irritable group; their genius is one of intensity rather than wisdom or serenity.
The Critical Path: An Essay on the Social Context of Literary Criticism (1971), *"The Critical Path" and Other Writings on Critical Theory, 1963–1975* (2009), CW, 27.

The poet constructs wholes or configurations; these become in their turn part of the one great poem that all the poets in history have helped to construct, that is, the mythological universe which is the model for the world man wants to live in, as distinct from the world that is there.
"The Rhythms of Time" (1974), *"The Critical Path" and Other Writings on Critical Theory, 1963–1975* (2009), CW, 27.

One of my guiding principles is that a poet can be any kind of damn fool and still be a poet.
"Northrop Frye in Conversation" (1989), *Interviews with Northrop Frye* (2008), CW, 24.

Personal sincerity in the poet is like virtue in Machiavelli's prince: the reality of it is of no consequence; the appearance of it may be.
"Nature and Homer" (1958), *"The Educated Imagination" and Other Writings on Critical Theory, 1933–1963* (2006), CW, 21.

The poet does not think of himself as making his poems. He thinks of himself as a place where poems happen.
"Reconsidering Levels of Meaning" (1979), *Northrop Frye's Fiction and Miscellaneous Writings* (2007), CW, 25.

It is always dangerous to assume that any poet writes with one eye on his own time and the other confidentially winking at ours.
"Part One: The Argument," *Fearful Symmetry: A Study of William Blake* (1947, 2004), CW, 14.

To encourage a genuine poet is impertinence, and to encourage a mediocre one is condescension.
"Letters in Canada: Poetry" (1960), *Northrop Frye on Canada* (2003), CW, 12.

A poet able to rank with the great names of English literature today is one in ten million, whereas in Shakespeare's day he was one in ten thousand.

"William Butler Yeats" (1950), *Northrop Frye on Literature and Society, 1936–1989: Unpublished Papers* (2002), CW, 10.

But one may always recognize the integrity of a poet who sees poetry steadily as an expression of whatever is humane in a creature who behaves so much of the time like a psychotic ape.
"Cold Green Element" (1974), *Northrop Frye on Canada* (2003), CW, 12.

I think that the poet is part of the creative imagination of the country, and the creative imagination tells you things about an environment which nothing else can tell you. That's always the function of the creative imagination in a society.
"Canadian Energies: Dialogues on Creativity" (1980), *Interviews with Northrop Frye* (2008), CW, 24.

A few novelists, most of them bad ones, may eke out a small living by writing, or even hit a best-seller jackpot; but a poet would have to be spectacularly bad before he could live on his poetry.
"Culture and the National Will" (1957), *Northrop Frye on Canada* (2003), CW, 12.

The poet who records the world as it is is by turns prophet, madman, outcast, clown, for genuine dignity is inseparable from the ridiculous, just as genuine seriousness is from humour.
"Cold Green Element" (1974), *Northrop Frye on Canada* (2003), CW, 12.

The poet's job is not to tell you what happened, but what happens: not what did take place, but the kind of thing that always does take place.
"Giants in Time," referring to Aristotle's view of poetry, *The Educated Imagination* (1963), *"The Educated Imagination" and Other Writings on Critical Theory, 1933–1963* (2006), CW, 21.

It doesn't matter if the poet doesn't exist. Our greatest poets never existed: Homer, for example, and Moses.
Entry, Notes 52 (1982–90), 639, *Northrop Frye's Late Notebooks, 1982–1990: Architecture of the Spiritual World* (2000), CW, 6.

The fact that revision is possible, that the poet makes changes not because he likes them better but because they are better, means that poems, like poets, are born and not made.
"The Archetypes of Literature" (1951), *"The Educated Imagination" and Other Writings on Critical Theory, 1933–1963* (2006), CW, 21.

Practically everybody who habitually reads poetry habitually writes it as well. That is as it should be: there are many things wrong with the position of the poet in modern society, but this is not one of the wrong things.
"Letters in Canada: Poetry" (1956), *Northrop Frye on Canada* (2003), CW, 12.

I think that in the twentieth century particularly, you have to deal with a kind of duality within some of the greatest writers. That is, you have, in the great poets of the twentieth century, an imagination which has made them great poets and, at the same time, a kind of ego which makes them rather repugnant to some people at any rate as personalities.
"Aldous Huxley" (1973), *Northrop Frye on Twentieth-Century Literature* (2010), CW, 29.

POLICE

In a totalitarian state it is obviously necessary to keep the police as stupid and brutal as possible. In democracies a reactionary government, if secure and at peace, generally prefers to have its police slightly confused.
"Two Books on Christianity and History" (1949), *Northrop Frye on Modern Culture* (2003), CW, 11.

POLITICS

But one of the worst mental diseases in our society is panpoliticism, the doctrine, especially favoured among "radicals," that there's no activity in society except politics. That's because the people who hold this doctrine don't want to do anything except agitate.
"Notes for 'Levels of Canadian Identity'" (1989), 15, *Northrop Frye's Fiction and Miscellaneous Writings* (2007), CW, 25.

The normal political instinct is to rule by dividing; the cultural instinct is to unite by

reflecting. It has often been pointed out that one may oppose or attack an argument, but not a song or a story.
    "Governor General's Awards (II)" (1963), *Northrop Frye on Canada* (2003), CW, 12.

Thus the word "Christian" in the name of a political party usually means "Roman Catholic Fascist"; and those who are afraid of Christianity in any form are only too pleased to draw what seems to them an obvious inference.
    "The Present Condition of the World" (1943), *Northrop Frye on Literature and Society, 1936–1989: Unpublished Papers* (2002), CW, 10.

Everywhere I look in Canada, I get an impression of immense energies trying to find their proper regional outlets, continually thwarted by unreal political abstractions.
    "A Summary of the 'Options' Conference" (1977), *Northrop Frye on Canada* (2003), CW, 12.

POLYTHEISM

Polytheism is impossible without a strong visual focus. In ancient cultures the gods are visualized on the analogy of social structures.
    "Icons and Iconoclasm" (1970), *Northrop Frye on Literature and Society, 1936–1989: Unpublished Papers* (2002), CW, 10.

Man is sectarian. That's why he's instinctively a polytheist.
    Entry, Notebook 21 (1969–76), 433, *Northrop Frye's Notebooks and Lectures on the Bible and Other Religious Texts* (2003), CW, 13.

POPULARITY

By popular literature I mean roughly the imaginative verbal experience of those with no specifically literary training or interest. The popular in this sense is the contemporary primitive, and it tends to become primitive with the passing of time.
    "Nature and Homer" (1958), *"The Educated Imagination" and Other Writings on Critical Theory, 1933–1963* (2006), CW, 21.

Popular art is normally decried as vulgar for a century or two, then it merges into the softer lighting of "quaint," and after another couple of centuries it takes on the archaic dignity of the primitive.
    "The Literary Meaning of 'Archetype'" (1936), *Northrop Frye on Literature and Society, 1936–1989: Unpublished Papers* (2002), CW, 10.

What is popular in one generation often becomes ridiculous in the next one, quaint in the third, and is finally regarded as primitive in the fourth.
    "A Natural Perspective: The Development of Shakespearean Comedy and Romance; II, Making Nature Afraid" (1963), *Northrop Frye's Writings on Shakespeare and the Renaissance* (2010), CW, 28.

The good popular poet is usually one who does well what a great many have tried to do with less success.
    "Emily Dickinson" (1962), *Northrop Frye's Writings on the Eighteenth and Nineteenth Centuries* (2005), CW, 17.

Clearly, if Blake can be popular we need a new definition of popularity.
    "Blake after Two Centuries" (1957), *Northrop Frye on Milton and Blake* (2005), CW, 16.

PORNOGRAPHY

Most denunciations of popular romance on such grounds, we notice, assume that the pornographic and the erotic are the same thing: this overlooks the important principle that it is the function of pornography to stun and numb the reader, and the function of erotic writing to wake him up.
    The Secular Scripture: A Study of the Structure of Romance (1975), *"The Secular Scripture" and Other Writings on Critical Theory, 1976–1991* (2006), CW, 18.

Sex books in a bookshop are not there to tell you anything you don't know; they're there to keep your mind on the subject. Similarly with devotional literature, Christian & Marxist.
    Entry, Notebook 21 (1969–76), 310, *Northrop Frye's Notebooks and Lectures on the Bible and Other Religious Texts* (2003), CW, 13.

POSTNATIONALISM

For, of course, this postnational trend is a worldwide one, and if Canada works out its

POUND, EZRA

Ezra Pound was a great poet and a nut: perhaps some great poets have to be nuts, but great poetry and nuttiness will always be different things, and it's part of a critic's job to see them as different.

"Schools of Criticism (I)" (1987), *Interviews with Northrop Frye* (2008), CW, 24.

POVERTY

It's a polite social fiction to speak of oneself as poor — everyone does it — but it is insolent cowardice for a privileged, well fed & well provided for middle class to claim for themselves the sympathy that belongs to the genuine victims of social inequality.

Entry, Notebook 42b: Autobiographical Notes I (1942–44), 15, *Northrop Frye's Fiction and Miscellaneous Writings* (2007), CW, 25.

POWER

... if I am right in saying that literature is a power to be possessed, and not a body of objects to be studied, then the difference between good and bad is not something inherent in literary works themselves, but the difference between two ways of using literary experience.

"Criticism, Visible and Invisible" (1964), *"The Critical Path" and Other Writings on Critical Theory, 1963–1975* (2009), CW, 27.

The word with power is the metaphor.

Entry, Notebook 44 (1986–91), 420, *Northrop Frye's Late Notebooks, 1982–1990: Architecture of the Spiritual World* (2000), CW, 5.

If we could transcend the level of professed belief, and reach the level of a worldwide community of action and charity, we should discover a new creative power in man altogether. Except that it would not be new, but the power of the genuine Word and Spirit, the power that has created all our works of culture and imagination, and is still ready to recreate both our society and ourselves.

Creation and Recreation (1980), *Northrop Frye on Religion* (2000), CW, 4.

However, it is gradually becoming clearer that the real principle of democracy is not "faith in human nature," but the limitation of human power.

"Trends in Modern Culture" (1952), *Northrop Frye on Modern Culture* (2003), CW, 11.

The will to power is evil if it's work, because, unless it's practice work, the end in view is bound to be destructive.

Entry, Notebook 50 (1987–90), 31, *Northrop Frye's Late Notebooks, 1982–1990: Architecture of the Spiritual World* (2000), CW, 5.

PRAIRIES

Fiction of the prairies has manifested a number of lively and readable variations on what used to be profanely called the "no fun on the farm" formula.

"English Canadian Literature, 1929–1954" (1955), *Northrop Frye on Canada* (2003), CW, 12.

PRATT, E.J.

He worked unperturbed while the bright young men of the 1920s, the scolding young men of the '30, the funky young men of the '40s, and the angry young men of the '50s, were, like Leacock's famous hero, riding off rapidly in all directions.

"Preface and Introduction to Pratt's Poetry" (1958), *Northrop Frye on Canada* (2003), CW, 12.

The real hero of the poem is a society's will to take intelligible form; the real quest is for physical and spiritual communication within that society. I have a notion that the technical problems involved in *Towards the Last Spike* are going to be central problems in the poetry of the future.

"Letters in Canada: Poetry" (1953), *Northrop Frye on Canada* (2003), CW, 12.

He had the typical mark of originality: the power to make something poetic out of what everybody had just decided could no longer be poetic material.

"Preface and Introduction to Pratt's Poetry" (1958), *Northrop Frye on Canada* (2003), CW, 12.

Ned Pratt is the only figure in Canadian literature, so far, great enough to establish a personal legend. And the legend was unique, because it had the poet behind it.

"A Poet and a Legend" (1965), *Northrop Frye on Canada* (2003), CW, 12.

Under Notes on Contributors it said, "E.J. Pratt is the best poet and the kindest man in Canada." It is difficult to improve on the economy of that statement, and few men can have left behind them a more uniform impression of good will.

"Silence upon the Earth" (1964), *Northrop Frye on Canada* (2003), CW, 12.

The Truant, to my mind, is not only the greatest of Canadian poems, but one of the most definitive poetic statements of our time, and its theme is the confrontation of the force of nature with the force of humanity.

"Opening Ceremonies of the E.J. Pratt Memorial Room" (1964), *Northrop Frye on Canada* (2003), CW, 12.

… and I have much sympathy for the student who informed me in the examinations last May that Pratt had written a poem called Beowulf and his Brothers.

"Preface to an Uncollected Anthology" (1956), referring to E.J. Pratt's narrative *Brébeuf and His Brethren*, *Northrop Frye on Canada* (2003), CW, 12.

PRAYER

The most obvious result of this is prayer, and prayer seems to require a rhetoric of parataxis, short phrases strung together in a rhythm close to free verse.

"Fourth Essay: Rhetorical Criticism: Theory of Genres" (1957), *Anatomy of Criticism: Four Essays* (2006), CW, 22.

Sanctify our talents that our minds may re-echo thy praise which resounds from the beauty of nature and the great works of love and intellect.

"Undated Prayers" (1992), *Northrop Frye on Religion* (2000), CW, 4.

Prayer is not directly addressed to anyone in this world, though others may overhear it, and though it is in part a talking to oneself, a way of achieving self-awareness with introversion.

"Fourth Variation: The Furnace," *Words with Power: Being a Second Study of "The Bible and Literature"* (1990), CW, 26.

And if I'm right in saying that prayer is self-knowledge not gained through introspection, then revelation, or counter-prayer, gives knowledge of what is not oneself through introspection, the word in the heart.

Entry, Notebook 21 (1969–76), 578, *Northrop Frye's Notebooks and Lectures on the Bible and Other Religious Texts* (2003), CW, 13.

All thought is talking to oneself. All prayer is talking to God. The difference between thought & prayer thus depends on one's conception of where God is.

Entry, 5 Mar. 1949, 242, *The Diaries of Northrop Frye: 1942–1955* (2001), CW, 8.

Harold Bloom asked me what prayer was: I told him I thought it was an effort at self-knowledge that doesn't come from introspection.

Entry, Notebook 11f (1969–70), 171, referring to the American literary academic, *Northrop Frye's Notebooks and Lectures on the Bible and Other Religious Texts* (2003), CW, 13.

PREACHING

Only preachers believe that they ought to believe that they believe every word they say, and look at what happens to them.

Entry, Notebook 33 (1946–50), 62, *Northrop Frye's Notebooks on Romance* (2004), CW, 15.

Is there only one Bible? Is it possible not only to preach Christ to the heathen, but to find Christ there?

Entry, Notebook 3 (1946–48), 125, *Northrop Frye's Notebooks and Lectures on the Bible and Other Religious Texts* (2003), CW, 13.

PRECAMBRIAN SHIELD

The metamorphic stratum is too old: the mind cannot contemplate the azoic without turning it into the monstrous.

"Canadian and Colonial Painting" (1941), referring to the absence of evidence of life in Tom Thomson's paintings, *Northrop Frye on Canada* (2003), CW, 12.

PREDESTINATION

When the Westerner tries to absorb the idea of unbornness, he tumbles into the "predestination" pitfall; when the Easterner tries to get clear about deathlessness, he gets into the "reincarnation" one.

Entry, Notebook 3 (1946–48), 119, *Northrop Frye's Notebooks and Lectures on the Bible and Other Religious Texts* (2003), CW, 13.

PREDICTION

The realm of eternal possibility belongs to art; the realm of future probability to science. One of the major functions of science is prophetic, predicting the future.

Entry, 30 Jan. 1949, 138, *The Diaries of Northrop Frye: 1942–1955* (2001), CW, 8.

PREJUDICES

For prejudice is simply inadequate deduction, as a prejudice in the mind can never be anything but a major premise which is mostly submerged, like an iceberg.

"Polemical Introduction" (1957), *Anatomy of Criticism: Four Essays* (2006), CW, 22.

Prejudices one doesn't share always impress one as absurd, deeply sinful, and very easily removable.

Entry, Notebook 42b: Notes I (1942–44), 29, *Northrop Frye's Fiction and Miscellaneous Writings* (2007), CW, 25.

The only things that people say spontaneously are prejudices, that is, ready-made rhetorical formulas.

"Reviews of Television Programs for the Canadian Radio-Television Commission: Reflections on November 5th" (1970), *Northrop Frye on Literature and Society, 1936–1989: Unpublished Papers* (2002), CW, 10.

PRESENCE

What proclamation proclaims is *presence*, and the presence of presence busts the universe.

Entry, Notebook 50 (1987–90), 65, *Northrop Frye's Late Notebooks, 1982–1990: Architecture of the Spiritual World* (2000), CW, 5.

And perhaps, as we struggle to apply our education and practical wisdom to society, we may occasionally feel a sense of a Presence which is ourselves yet infinitely bigger than ourselves, which lives with us but will not disappear into death when we do.

"Baccalaureate Sermon" (1967), *Northrop Frye on Religion* (2000), CW, 4.

PRESENT, THE

What education does is to increase the significance of the present moment. It brings us into contact with the powers of the human imagination, as it embodies itself in science, philosophy, religion, the arts. These powers transcend our own egos, and they need no drugs to help them.

"Convocation Address, Franklin and Marshall" (1968), *Northrop Frye's Writings on Education* (2001), CW, 7.

The present is the expanded moment of awareness that is as long as recorded human history; the presence is the love that moves the sun and the other stars.

"Fourth Variation: The Furnace," discussing the end of Dante's *Paradiso*, *Words with Power: Being a Second Study of "The Bible and Literature"* (1990), CW, 26.

This present is a resurrection which is not the reviving of a corpse, and a rebirth which is not an emerging of a new life from a dying older body to die in its turn. It is rather a transfiguration into a world we keep making even when we deny it, as though a coral insect were suddenly endowed with enough consciousness and vision to be able to see the island it has been helping to create.

Creation and Recreation (1980), *Northrop Frye on Religion* (2000), CW, 4.

PRESERVATION

However strongly we may condemn Henry VIII's dissolution of the monasteries, it might have been a crushing burden for the National Trust if all those abbeys had survived.

"Canada: New World Without Revolution" (1975), *Northrop Frye on Canada* (2003), CW, 12.

Our sense of the need for preservation has in it a certain distrust in the integrity of our own cultural tradition: once things are gone, we have little confidence in our ability to replace them with new things equally good.... The rudder, so to speak, that guides our philosophy of preservation ultimately has to be the continuing vitality of our cultural tradition. Without that, the task of preserving our heritage will have in it a quality of desperation unhealthy both for it and for us.

"Canada: New World Without Revolution" (1975), *Northrop Frye on Canada* (2003), CW, 12.

PRIMITIVE

The primitive is simply the popular in a temporal dimension. There is still the same thing going on.

"Reconsidering Levels of Meaning" (1979), *Northrop Frye's Fiction and Miscellaneous Writings* (2007), CW, 25.

By primitive and popular I mean here the ability to communicate in time and space respectively. Otherwise they mean much the same thing.

"The Literary Meaning of 'Archetype'" (1936), *Northrop Frye on Literature and Society, 1936–1989: Unpublished Papers* (2002), CW, 10.

Yet greater experience with literature soon shows that it is metaphor which is direct and primitive, and conceptual thought which is sophisticated.

"Blake after Two Centuries" (1957), *Northrop Frye on Milton and Blake* (2005), CW, 16.

Poetry which is not primitive is of no use to anybody: every genuine work of the imagination comes out of the most primitive depths of human concern.

"The Social Context of Literary Criticism" (1968), *Northrop Frye on Literature and Society, 1936–1989: Unpublished Papers* (2002), CW, 10.

Once we accept the fact that human beings at least as intelligent as ourselves have been around for half a million years or so, our perspective on the "primitive" mind changes somewhat.

Entry, Notebook 11f (1969–70), 177, *Northrop Frye's Notebooks and Lectures on the Bible and Other Religious Texts* (2003), CW, 13.

PRISONS

Prisons exist because Selfhoods do: they are the real things the Selfhood produces, and symbols of it only in that sense.

"Part One: The Argument," *Fearful Symmetry: A Study of William Blake* (1947, 2004), CW, 14.

PRIVACY

If certain tendencies within our civilization were to proceed unchecked, they would rapidly take us towards a society which, like that of a prison, would be both completely introverted and completely without privacy.

The Modern Century (1967), *Northrop Frye on Modern Culture* (2003), CW, 11.

PROBLEMS

A genuine problem is a specific formulation of experience that can be adequately stated in other terms: to use a common analogy, it is like a knot in a rope that can be untied or retied without affecting the identity of the rope.

"Speculation and Concern" (1966), *Northrop Frye's Writings on Education* (2001), CW, 7.

PROCLAMATION

So the Bible uses the language of symbolism and imagery because the language of symbolism and imagery, which bypasses argument and aggressiveness and at the same time clearly defines the difference between life and death, between freedom and slavery, between happiness and misery, is in short the language of love, and to St. Paul, that is likely to last longer than most other forms of human communication.

"Symbolism in the Bible" (1981–82), *Northrop Frye's Notebooks and Lectures on the Bible and Other Religious Texts* (2003), CW, 13.

PRODUCTION

The natural drive of a producing society is not democratic but oligarchic or managerial: it increases inequalities of privilege instead of

reducing them, and in itself is no longer capable of leading us to the vision of the just state.
"The Instruments of Mental Production" (1966), *Northrop Frye's Writings on Education* (2001), CW, 7.

PROFESSIONS
Nobody can enter a profession unless he makes at least a gesture recognizing the ideal existence of a world beyond his own interests: a world of health for the doctor, of justice for the lawyer, of peace for the social worker, a redeemed world for the clergyman, and so on.
"The Vocation of Eloquence," *The Educated Imagination* (1963), *"The Educated Imagination" and Other Writings on Critical Theory, 1933–1963* (2006), CW, 21.

PROFUNDITY
We never call a thing profound unless we are pleased with its wit. Or conciseness. Therefore "profundity" is not a matter of breadth but of depth, & depth is a matter of illustration, a ray into a cave.
"Autobiographical Reflections" (1942–44), 37, *Northrop Frye's Fiction and Miscellaneous Writings* (2007), CW, 25.

Every great work of art is profound, profundity being an essential part of the conception of greatness.
Entry, Notebook 19 (1964–67), 267, *The "Third Book" Notebooks of Northrop Frye, 1964–1972: The Critical Comedy* (2002), CW, 9.

PROGRESS
The arts do not evolve or improve, partly because vision, being pure wish, can reach its conceivable limits at once.
"The Imaginative and the Imaginary" (1962), *"The Educated Imagination" and Other Writings on Critical Theory, 1933–1963* (2006), CW, 21.

The Christian sense that there is meaning in history beyond just an endless series of cycles gave birth to the modern theory of progress.
"Two Books on Christianity and History" (1949), *Northrop Frye on Modern Culture* (2003), CW, 11.

Works of literature, music, and the other arts do not, apparently, improve or progress with time, but the understanding of their meaning, their importance, and their function in history can and to some extent does improve.
The Double Vision (1991), *Northrop Frye on Religion* (2000), CW, 4.

There is genuine progress only in education, and the progress in that is a continual rediscovery of ignorance.
"Education — Protection against Futility" (1964), *Northrop Frye's Writings on Education* (2001), CW, 7.

Science and technology progress and develop, and so help to create the sense of a rational order that is just about to become clear. Such a feeling has of course nothing to do with either science or technology, but is a social mirage, like flying saucers.
"Appendix: The Social Context of Literary Criticism" (1968), *Northrop Frye on Literature and Society, 1936–1989: Unpublished Papers* (2002), CW, 10.

For most thoughtful people progress has lost most of its original sense of a favourable value judgment and has become simply progression, towards a goal more likely to be a disaster than an improvement.
The Modern Century (1967), *Northrop Frye on Modern Culture* (2003), CW, 11.

The element of continuity in progress suggests that the only practicable action is continuous with what we are already doing: if, for instance, we are engaged in a war, it is practicable to go on with the war, and only visionary to stop it.
The Modern Century (1967), *Northrop Frye on Modern Culture* (2003), CW, 11.

... I am saying that no improvement in the human situation can take place independently of the human will to improve, and that confidence in automatic or impersonal improvement is always misplaced.
The Modern Century (1967), *Northrop Frye on Modern Culture* (2003), CW, 11.

There is no reason to feel complacent about Stalin's Russia, however: many Canadians defend the destruction of their country by such phrases as "you can't stop progress,"

unaware that "progress" in such contexts is an idol on the same level as the legendary Hindu Juggernaut or the Old Testament Moloch.
 The Double Vision (1991), *Northrop Frye on Religion* (2000), CW, 4.

A more serious consequence is that under a theory of progress present means have constantly to be sacrificed to future ends, and we do not know the future well enough to know whether those ends will be achieved or not. All we actually know is that we are damaging the present.
 The Modern Century (1967), *Northrop Frye on Modern Culture* (2003), CW, 11.

PROHIBITION
That is, after a generation of Prohibition North American society has become as boozy a society as the world has ever seen, and after a century or so of the most frantic prudery about sex, it has become — well, you can finish that sentence for yourselves.
 "Violence and Television" (1975), *Northrop Frye on Modern Culture* (2003), CW, 11.

PROJECTION
The first thing man does is *project*: reality for him is at first the shadows on the wall of his cave. Mythology makes sense to the degree that he recovers his projections.
 Entry, Notebook 24 (1970–72), 151, *The "Third Book" Notebooks of Northrop Frye, 1964–1972: The Critical Comedy* (2002), CW, 9.

PROLETARIAT
There are only two branches of the human race: those who belong to the bourgeoisie and those who wish they did. There is no such thing as a proletarian consciousness.
 Entry, Notebook 44 (1986–91), 533, *Northrop Frye's Late Notebooks, 1982–1990: Architecture of the Spiritual World* (2000), CW, 5.

A proletariat, in the Marxist sense, is a group of people excluded from the benefits of society to which their efforts entitle them. We were showering students with privileges, and yet, at the same time, carefully excluding them from the general process of adult society.
 "The Social Importance of Literature" (1968), referring to student unrest at the time, *Northrop Frye's Writings on Education* (2001), CW, 7.

PRONUNCIATION
If a man says he will pay you what he owes you next Toisday, it is useful to know whether he means Tuesday or Thursday: if there were no accepted forms there could be no communication.
 "Humanities in a New World" (1958), *Northrop Frye's Writings on Education* (2001), CW, 7.

PROPAGANDA
There is no reason, in a state which controls both history and the news media, why Big Brother should ever die.
 "Foreword to *1984*" (1967), *Northrop Frye on Twentieth-Century Literature* (2010), CW, 29.

In our world the control of communications is connected with what is called advertising in some contexts and propaganda in others, depending on the economic context involved.
 "Criticism and Environment" (1981), *Northrop Frye on Canada* (2003), CW, 12.

PROPHECY
What happens in literature is very likely to happen in life as a whole a century or so later.
 "The University and Personal Life: Student Anarchism and the Educational Contract" (1968), *Northrop Frye's Writings on Education* (2001), CW, 7.

The great achievement of the Bible was to show that prophecy, though it may be fragmentary in expression, springs from a coherent & unified imaginative world. The articulating of that world, however, is post-Biblical.
 Entry, Notebook 11b (late 1980), 18, *Northrop Frye's Notebooks and Lectures on the Bible and Other Religious Texts* (2003), CW, 13.

And just as wisdom is conservative, continuous, and linked to the past, so prophecy is discontinuous, radical, and linked to the future.
 "Teaching the Humanities Today" (1977), *Northrop Frye's Writings on Education* (2001), CW, 7.

The prophetic utterance in the Bible is assumed to be one that is magical in the sense of having the greatest possible penetrating power.

"Spirit and Symbol," *Words with Power: Being a Second Study of "The Bible and Literature"* (1990), CW, 26.

PROPHETS

The function of the prophet is not to point out what is inevitable, but to show what can be built up out of an inevitable development.

"Part Three: The Final Synthesis," *Fearful Symmetry: A Study of William Blake* (1947, 2004), CW, 14.

… the prophet with the authentic message is the man with the unpopular message.

"Typology II," *The Great Code* (1982), *The Great Code: The Bible and Literature* (2006), CW, 19.

The fear of being thought a prig will do far more to weaken the prophet than the fear of social hatred.

"Part Three: The Final Synthesis," *Fearful Symmetry: A Study of William Blake* (1947, 2004), CW, 14.

One thing I do have in common with most of the prophets is a profound unwillingness to be a prophet.

Entry, 22 Jan. 1952, 55, *The Diaries of Northrop Frye: 1942–1955* (2001), CW, 8.

The significance of what the prophets say is in what the people did to them for saying it. Anyway, it begins there.

Entry, Notebook 21 (1969–76), 493, *Northrop Frye's Notebooks and Lectures on the Bible and Other Religious Texts* (2003), CW, 13.

PROPORTION

Because it's scaled to the body, a great cathedral like York Minster represents the absolute maximum of vast soaring grandeur, and would even if a ninety-story skyscraper were erected beside it.

Entry, Notebook 19 (1964–67), 118, *The "Third Book" Notebooks of Northrop Frye, 1964–1972: The Critical Comedy* (2002), CW, 9.

PROSE

Prose, therefore, is not ordinary speech, but ordinary speech on its best behaviour, in its Sunday clothes, aware of an audience and with its relation to that audience prepared beforehand.

"The Well-Tempered Critic (I)" (1961), *"The Educated Imagination" and Other Writings on Critical Theory, 1933–1963* (2006), CW, 21.

We grow up with the superstition like that of Molière's Jourdain, who says he's been speaking prose all his life. Well, prose is actually very difficult to speak. Yet students come to university convinced that prose is the language of ordinary speech, when they can't speak it and they certainly can't write it.

"The Scholar in Society" (1983), *Interviews with Northrop Frye* (2008), CW, 24.

As far as literature is concerned, all prose is prose fiction, that is, prose looked at in terms of its form.

Entry, Notebook 33 (1946–50), 6, *Northrop Frye's Notebooks on Romance* (2004), CW, 15.

For poetry develops out of ritual & prose out of myth.…

Entry, Notebook 33 (1946–50), 37, *Northrop Frye's Notebooks on Romance* (2004), CW, 15.

Continuous or expository prose assumes an equality between writer and reader: the writer is putting all he has in front of us. Discontinuous prose, with gaps in the sense that only intuition can cross, assumes an aloofness on the writer's part, a sense of reserves of connection that we must make special efforts to reach.

"Emily Dickinson" (1962), *Northrop Frye's Writings on the Eighteenth and Nineteenth Centuries* (2005), CW, 17.

Prose, which is organized by syntax and sentence structure, is more difficult to write than verse, which is one reason why it normally develops so much later than verse in the history of literature. Continuous prose is a by-product of writing: oral prose is discontinuous, just as oral verse is continuous.

"*Rencontre*: The General Editor's Introduction" (1960s), *Northrop Frye on Literature and Society, 1936–1989: Unpublished Papers* (2002), CW, 10.

PROTEST

... many of the assumptions under which protest in the universities appears to be operating seem to me to take the form of a misapplied religious reformation, based on a view of the ideal university as a bastard church, resembling the Congregationalists in government, the Catholics in outlook, the Quakers in doctrine, and the Jehovah's Witnesses in tactics.

"The Ethics of Change: The Role of the University" (1968), *Northrop Frye's Writings on Education* (2001), CW, 7.

The university is, of course, a good place in which to carry out social protest, because it is a flexible and tolerant place, and occupationally disposed to argument. As the private said when he saluted the sergeant-major, "You'll do to practise on."

"The Social Importance of Literature" (1968), *Northrop Frye's Writings on Education* (2001), CW, 7.

It has often been noted during student demonstrations that hundreds of students suddenly discover that they have political convictions as soon as the television cameras arrive. They express their aggressiveness, in other words, by putting themselves on the other side of the tube.

Entry, Notebook 11f (1969–70), 113, *Northrop Frye's Notebooks and Lectures on the Bible and Other Religious Texts* (2003), CW, 13.

PROTESTANTISM

I'm just beginning to wonder if Protestantism & Zen — not as churches but as approaches to God-Man — aren't the same thing, possessed by the same Saviour.

Entry, Notebook 3 (1946–48), 110, *Northrop Frye's Notebooks and Lectures on the Bible and Other Religious Texts* (2003), CW, 13.

PROVERBS

The proverb is a secular or purely human oracle....

"Fourth Essay: Rhetorical Criticism: Theory of Genres" (1957), *Anatomy of Criticism: Four Essays* (2006), CW, 22.

There seems to be something about the proverb that stirs the collector's instinct — which is natural if one accepts its usefulness as a key to success in life.

"Typology II," *The Great Code* (1982), *The Great Code: The Bible and Literature* (2006), CW, 19.

PROVINCIALISM

The general principle appears to be that a painter or writer who is self-conscious about his immediate context will be likely to sound provincial, whereas a painter or writer who accepts a provincial milieu, in, say, Newfoundland or southern British Columbia, will be much less likely to do so.

"Culture as Interpenetration" (1977), *Northrop Frye on Canada* (2003), CW, 12.

PRUDERY

Even so, prudery in Ontario at its worst is mild enough compared to what one would find in Islamic or most Communist countries today.

"Culture and Society in Ontario, 1784–1984" (1984), *Northrop Frye on Canada* (2003), CW, 12.

PSYCHEDELICS

There were psychedelic clothes before anybody had heard of Timothy Leary.

"Canadian Literature and Culture" (after 1967), 9, *Northrop Frye's Fiction and Miscellaneous Writings* (2007), CW, 25.

PSYCHOANALYSIS

Psychoanalysis is just the old purging & bleeding routine anyway, and a certain amount of purging can be done by the healthy organism itself.

Entry, 26 Feb. 1950, 148, reflecting on uncensored dreams, *The Diaries of Northrop Frye: 1942–1955* (2001), CW, 8.

The psychoanalyst's couch is Promethean, & perhaps Procrustean.

Entry, Notebook 3 (1946–48), 75, *Northrop Frye's Notebooks and Lectures on the Bible and Other Religious Texts* (2003), CW, 13.

PSYCHOLOGY

Psychology, to pick one such science at random, does not tell us how people behave;

PUBLIC RELATIONS

It seems curious that hardly anybody rejects the values of contemporary civilization to the point of disbelieving in the necessity or effectiveness of public relations. Yet the invariable tendency of public relations, whatever they are working for, is to destroy the critical intelligence and its sense of the gap between appearance and reality.

> The Critical Path: An Essay on the Social Context of Literary Criticism (1971), "The Critical Path" and Other Writings on Critical Theory, 1963–1975 (2009), CW, 27.

The words "advertising" and "propaganda" come closest to suggesting a communication deliberately imposed and passively received. They represent respectively the communicating interests of the two major areas of society, the economic and the political. Recently these two conceptions have begun to merge into the single category of "public relations."

> The Modern Century (1967), Northrop Frye on Modern Culture (2003), CW, 11.

PUBLISHING

I suppose that writing a book is an intellectual achievement, or at any rate publishing one may be.

> "The Question of 'Success'" (1967), Northrop Frye's Writings on Education (2001), CW, 7.

In our day every publisher of books and learned journals employs functionaries whose duty it is to see that every twentieth-century text shall be corrupted at its source.

> "Welcoming Remarks to Conference on Editorial Problems, 1967" (1967), "The Critical Path" and Other Writings on Critical Theory, 1963–1975 (2009), CW, 27.

Good new books are rare enough at any time, but they will always appear somehow or other: it is the keeping of good old books in print that is important.... It is probably harder to buy Shakespeare in England right now than Sir Oswald Mosley's new book on the futility of democracy.

> "James, Le Fanu, and Morris" (1948), commenting on the paper shortage in Britain, Northrop Frye's Writings on the Eighteenth and Nineteenth Centuries (2005), CW, 17.

A publishing house I am connected with myself in New York is now attached to a zoo in Florida: what effect this will have on its interest in books I have yet to discover.

> "Language as the Home of Human Life" (1985), Northrop Frye's Writings on Education (2001), CW, 7.

Why should putting out books in brightly coloured soft covers, with the pages glued instead of sewn, be an important cultural change?

> "The Renaissance of Books" (1973), Northrop Frye on Modern Culture (2003), CW, 11.

PUNISHMENT

The battle of Peterloo was won on the flogging-blocks of Eton.

> Entry, Notebook 3 (1946–48), 170, Northrop Frye's Notebooks and Lectures on the Bible and Other Religious Texts (2003), CW, 13.

PUNS

Speaking of buttocks (I remember that I once described a well-upholstered young woman as asymmetrical), I wonder why nudists are considered cranks when every point they have has long ago been socially accepted.

> "Autobiographical Reflections" (1942–44), 7, Northrop Frye's Fiction and Miscellaneous Writings (2007), CW, 25.

Puns are absolutely essential to poetic thinking, because the poet is establishing the powers of words rather than defining things.

> "On The Great Code (I)" (1982), Interviews with Northrop Frye (2008), CW, 24.

Paronomasia is one of the essential elements of verbal creation, but a pun introduced into a conversation turns its back on the sense of the conversation and sets up a self-contained verbal sound-sense pattern in its place.

"Fourth Essay: Rhetorical Criticism: Theory of Genres" (1957), *Anatomy of Criticism: Four Essays* (2006), CW, 22.

PURGATORY

Perhaps the purgatorial & paradisal visions keep working together in this life, whether in another or not.

Entry, Notebook 50 (1987–90), 690, *Northrop Frye's Late Notebooks, 1982–1990: Architecture of the Spiritual World* (2000), CW, 5.

The only conception of an after-life that doesn't identify God with Satan is that of purgatory, a realizing of one's true nature in a process which is still temporal but leads out of time.

Entry, Notebook 21 (1969–76), 612, *Northrop Frye's Notebooks and Lectures on the Bible and Other Religious Texts* (2003), CW, 13.

Q

QUEBEC

I've always said that cultural developments decentralize, and political and economic ones centralize, so I think that separatism in Quebec in the cultural area is a very genuine development, but as a political and economic development, it seems to me to be nonsense.

"On *The Great Code* (II)" (1982), *Interviews with Northrop Frye* (2008), CW, 24.

A political entity, in any case, is not a cultural one. French-speaking Canada is a cultural reality of the highest importance: "Quebec" is a province like other provinces, and always will be: the more separatist its policies, the more inevitably provincial their characteristics.... Quebec had been an architect of Confederation in 1867, and it has no higher destiny now than to become an architect of Reconfederation on a renewed cultural basis.

"The Cultural Development of Canada" (1990), *Northrop Frye on Canada* (2003), CW, 12.

The conception "Québécois," for example, belongs culturally to the area of political leverage, not to anything genuinely creative.

"Speech at the New Canadian Embassy, Washington" (1989), *Northrop Frye on Canada* (2003), CW, 12.

QUEBEC ACT

The two factors to be taken into account were: (a) the British have conquered the French (b) the British have done nothing of the kind. The only way out of this was a settlement that guaranteed some rights to both parties.

"Conclusion to *Literary History of Canada*" (1965), *Northrop Frye on Canada* (2003), CW, 12.

QUEEN

Royalty has always had a unique power to fascinate, but it is only with the last two British monarchs that pathos has become an essential part of the fascination. Very few people envy the Queen for being a queen: nearly everyone pities her for being also a human being.

"Regina versus the World" (1953), *Northrop Frye on Modern Culture* (2003), CW, 11.

In an age of neurotic egotism, the Queen is a centripetal social focus who can still remind us that in some dim and mysterious way we are all members of one body. In an age of barbaric rapaciousness and ambition, the Queen stands above all attainable power, as the honour of wearing the crown is too great to be deserved or won; it can only be gained by accident.

"Regina versus the World" (1953), *Northrop Frye on Modern Culture* (2003), CW, 11.

The character of Elizabeth II is a function of her royalty: she dramatizes the idea of royalty, and belongs in the class of things represented by the Unknown Soldier, not in the class of things represented by presidents or premiers.

"Regina versus the World" (1953), *Northrop Frye on Modern Culture* (2003), CW, 11.

QUEST

In myths of ascent, descent or quest, we *go* only in dream, with the soul leaving the body. The goal of the quest is to integrate what we're getting with what we've got, and the only way to reach the goal is to wake up & find ourselves in the same place. Jacob's ladder.

Entry, Notebook 12 (1968–70), 454, *The "Third Book" Notebooks of Northrop Frye, 1964–1972: The Critical Comedy* (2002), CW, 9.

The quest as question is of course future-oriented, & its ultimate answer, which goes beyond any origin or first-cause answer (as in Job), is resurrection in the present.

Entry, Notebook 12 (1968–70), 373, *The "Third Book" Notebooks of Northrop Frye, 1964–1972: The Critical Comedy* (2002), CW, 9.

QUESTIONS

The teacher who refuses to answer a question has to have tremendous authority given him by his students if he is to get away with it.

"The Teacher's Source of Authority" (1978), *Northrop Frye's Writings on Education* (2001), CW, 7.

To answer a question (a point we shall return to later in the book) is to consolidate the mental level on which the question is asked. Unless something is kept in reserve, suggesting the possibility of better and fuller questions, the student's mental advance is blocked.

"Introduction," *The Great Code* (1982), *The Great Code: The Bible and Literature* (2006), CW, 19.

Real questions are stages in formulating better questions; answers cheat us out of the right to do this.

"Myth II," *The Great Code* (1982), *The Great Code: The Bible and Literature* (2006), CW, 19.

The questions I find it impossible to answer are the questions which are personal questions: what do you personally believe? Because my answer is always, "Well, what you're really asking me is do I believe things in the same way that you do," and the answer is probably no.

"Getting the Order Right" (1978), referring specifically to questions of students about Symbolism in the Bible, *Interviews with Northrop Frye* (2008), CW, 24.

It brings into the focus of a practical problem my own point that the teacher doesn't answer a question so much as try to raise the questioner's mental level to where he can outgrow the question.

Entry, 14 Mar. 1952, 177, *The Diaries of Northrop Frye: 1942–1955* (2001), CW, 8.

It's always difficult for me to think of possible questions not asked. I don't have much initiative thinking of them myself, and I'm very much dependent on questions that are asked.

"Moncton, Mentors, and Memories" (1986), *Interviews with Northrop Frye* (2008), CW, 24.

The teacher's function is to help create the structure of the subject in the student's mind. That is why it is the teacher who asks most of the questions and not the student.

"The Beginning of the Word" (1980), *Northrop Frye's Writings on Education* (2001), CW, 7.

The point that I want to return to when we come to the Book of Job is that no serious religion ever tries to answer anybody's questions, because in any serious or existential matter the progress in understanding is a progress through a sequence of formulating better questions.

"Symbolism in the Bible" (1981–82), *Northrop Frye's Notebooks and Lectures on the Bible and Other Religious Texts* (2003), CW, 13.

It is a well-known principle in science and philosophy that the simplest questions are those that only great genius can answer, because it takes great genius to become aware of them as questions.

"Introduction to *Blake: A Collection of Critical Essays*" (1966), *Northrop Frye on Milton and Blake* (2005), CW, 16.

I'm also particularly good, or used to be, at answering questions: my ability to translate a dumb question into a searching one has often been commented on. This should be leading to something useful, but it hasn't yet. The central thing is that my "creative" faculty is the power of *personalizing* occasions.

Entry, Notebook 44 (1986–91), 719, *Northrop Frye's Late Notebooks, 1982–1990: Architecture of the Spiritual World* (2000), CW, 5.

QUIET REVOLUTION

For the Quiet Revolution was as impressive an achievement of imaginative freedom as the contemporary world can show: freedom not so much from clerical domination or corrupt politics as from the burden of tradition.

"Conclusion to *Literary History of Canada*" (1965), *Northrop Frye on Canada* (2003), CW, 12.

QUOTATION

"In the beginning was the Word," and the beginning is consciousness. Not necessarily a chronological beginning, but every beginning that matters is verbal and conscious.

"The Darkening Mirror: Reflections on the Bomb and Language" (1985), *Interviews with Northrop Frye* (2008), CW, 24.

All those tremendous stone monuments disappeared under the sand, and the little papyrus scrolls are still in reasonably good shape.

"The Great Teacher" (1988), contrasting the ruined structures of Ozymandias with the survival of words in passages on scrolls, *Interviews with Northrop Frye* (2008), CW, 24.

What distinguishes, not simply the epigram, but profundity itself from platitude is very frequently rhetorical wit. In fact it may be doubted whether we ever really call an idea profound unless we are pleased with the wit of its expression.

"Fourth Essay: Rhetorical Criticism: Theory of Genres" (1957), *Anatomy of Criticism: Four Essays* (2006), CW, 22.

In the twentieth century it was succeeded in favour by another phrase of "the adjective noun of noun" type, in which the first noun is usually concrete and the second abstract. Thus: "the pale dawn of longing," "the broken collar-bone of silence," "the massive eyelids of time," "the crimson tree of love." I have made these up myself, and they are free to any poet who wants them, but on examining a volume of twentieth-century lyrics I find, counting all the variants, thirty-eight phrases of this type in the first five poems.

"Fourth Essay: Rhetorical Criticism: Theory of Genres" (1957), *Anatomy of Criticism: Four Essays* (2006), CW, 22.

The discontinuity of the educated man, which is shown by his power to quote from or allude to what he has read, indicates that at that point literature is disappearing from a systematic course of study into somebody's personal life.

"Literature as Possession" (1959), *"The Educated Imagination" and Other Writings on Critical Theory, 1933–1963* (2006), CW, 21.

R

RADICALISM

Thus the university is precisely in the position of radical groups in modern society, belonging to society yet striving to become aware of its conditioning, trying to throw off whatever is illegitimate in that conditioning, and therefore ethically bound to help carry out a long-term transformation of society.

"The Ethics of Change: The Role of the University" (1968), *Northrop Frye's Writings on Education* (2001), CW, 7.

It seems to me that some recognition of the role of religion in society is essential in clarifying today's radical protest, which is religious to a degree that it can hardly comprehend itself.

"The Ethics of Change: The Role of the University" (1968), *Northrop Frye's Writings on Education* (2001), CW, 7.

The strongly negative mood in today's radicalism, the tendency to be against rather than for, is consistent with this: whatever is defined is hampering, and only the undefined is free.

"The University and Personal Life: Student Anarchism and the Educational Contract" (1968), *Northrop Frye's Writings on Education* (2001), CW, 7.

The most ferocious of radicals can only keep going as long as he can live in a relatively stable society created by his radicalism: the society of those who agree with him and support his views. Whatever else he wants to change, he never wants to change *that*.

"The Quality of Life in the '70s" (1971), *Northrop Frye on Modern Culture* (2003), CW, 11.

But radical concern also has its rituals, and the rituals of demonstration, protest, terrorism, confrontation, sit-in, love-in, and folk festival are still new. In another two or three years they will become as conventionalized as an Empire Club lunch, but right now they attract more attention. With the newspapers full of rituals of burning brassieres and bombing libraries, a convocation seems as genteel and uninvolved as an actress with her clothes on.

"A Revolution Betrayed: Freedom and Necessity in Education" (1970), *Northrop Frye's Writings on Education* (2001), CW, 7.

RADIO

Machines get more closely related to the human body as they get less cumbersome: the radio by now is palpably just a hearing aid.

"New Fictional Formulas: Notebook 20" (after 1965), 16, *Northrop Frye's Fiction and Miscellaneous Writings* (2007), CW, 25.

A country in which a housewife with a radio can lighten her washday by listening to Mozart is by no means a total cultural loss.

"Have We a National Education?" (1952), *Northrop Frye's Writings on Education* (2001), CW, 7.

The radio is the subtlest attack on human peace of mind yet made, and constitutes a major obstacle, perhaps in many cases an insuperable one, to it.... I suppose radios incarnate the semiconsciousness of others, and of course increase the mental disturbance they're turned on to soothe.

Entry, Notebook 3 (1946–48), 16, *Northrop Frye's Notebooks and Lectures on the Bible and Other Religious Texts* (2003), CW, 13.

The man who can appreciate Bach and Dante will be bored to death by most movies, nauseated by most radio programmes, stupefied by most sermons, and sickened by most politicians.

"A Liberal Education" (1945), *Northrop Frye's Writings on Education* (2001), CW, 7.

RAILWAYS
In the United States, exploration and the building of railways have naturally been of central importance in the imagination of the country. In Canada they have been obsessive.
"Canadian Culture Today" (1977), *Northrop Frye on Canada* (2003), CW, 12.

To make a nation out of the stops on the Intercolonial and Canadian Pacific lines seemed as chimerical a notion as building an African civilization on a Cape-to-Cairo railway.
"The Cultural Development of Canada" (1990), *Northrop Frye on Canada* (2003), CW, 12.

RATIONALIZATION
It isn't easy to distinguish the rational from the rationalized, but one sure sign of rationalization is offering inconsistent arguments, on the any-stick-is-good-enough principle.
Entry, Notebook 11f (1969–70), 234, *Northrop Frye's Notebooks and Lectures on the Bible and Other Religious Texts* (2003), CW, 13.

In ordinary life we do not reason, we rationalize. There is nothing that cannot be rationalized: terrorists can rationalize blowing up a plane as political idealism; homicidal maniacs can rationalize murder as an indictment of an evil society; indecisive leaders can rationalize doing nothing as prudence or wisdom.
"A Revolution Betrayed: Freedom and Necessity in Education" (1970), *Northrop Frye's Writings on Education* (2001), CW, 7.

READER
Every work of literature has to die and to be reborn in the individual studying it. It doesn't just stay out there; it becomes part of him or her. Without that death and resurrection, there is no genuine possession of literature.
"Literature as a Critique of Pure Reason" (1982), *"The Secular Scripture" and Other Writings on Critical Theory, 1976–1991* (2006), CW, 18.

It is an established datum of literature that we like hearing people cursed and are bored with hearing them praised, and almost any denunciation, if vigorous enough, is followed by a reader with the kind of pleasure that soon breaks into a smile.
"Third Essay: Archetypal Criticism: Theory of Myths" (1957), *Anatomy of Criticism: Four Essays* (2006), CW, 22.

The consumer of literature is the cultivated man, the man of liberal education and disciplined taste, for whose benefit the poet has worked, suffered, despaired, or even wrecked his life.
"Humanities in a New World" (1958), *Northrop Frye's Writings on Education* (2001), CW, 7.

There's been a considerable shift in the centre of gravity away from the writer and towards the reader. Now the reader is the hero of what he reads. Culturally, for anyone interested in the verbal arts, it's quite an exciting time to live in.
"Canadian Energies: Dialogues on Creativity" (1980), *Interviews with Northrop Frye* (2008), CW, 24.

A reader interested in Canadian literature may feel in the position of one who has bought a box of candy and discovered from the fine print on the box that he has acquired a melange of twenty-three food, chemical, and additive substances. But he still expects some unity of taste in the final product, not a mere recognition of the subtle contributions made by invertase or lecithin.
"Speech at the New Canadian Embassy, Washington" (1989), *Northrop Frye on Canada* (2003), CW, 12.

Note to cheer myself up with: I'm not a great 17th c. poet like Milton, or a great 18th-19th c. visionary like Blake, but I am a great 20th c. reader, and this is the age of the reader.
Entry, Notebook 44 (1986–91), 461, *Northrop Frye's Late Notebooks, 1982–1990: Architecture of the Spiritual World* (2000), CW, 5.

One end of this process is creation, and the other end is recreation.
Creation and Recreation (1980), *Northrop Frye on Religion* (2000), CW, 4.

There are no dead ideas in literature; there are only tired readers.
> *The Critical Path: An Essay on the Social Context of Literary Criticism* (1971), *"The Critical Path" and Other Writings on Critical Theory, 1963–1975* (2009), CW, 27.

Wherever there is a literature, there is a community of shared imaginative experience; and yet, wherever there are books, there is the opposite tendency of individualizing the audience.
> "The Renaissance of Books" (1973), *Northrop Frye on Modern Culture* (2003), CW, 11.

I had innocently thought that people read the *Reader's Digest* because they believed it to be an abridgment of contemporary magazine articles, not because they found it a comic-book monthly version of a school reader.
> "Report on the 'Adventures' Readers" (1965), *Northrop Frye's Writings on Education* (2001), CW, 7.

The chief deficiency in today's literature, for example, is not the lack of good writers, but the lack of a reading public sufficiently large, informed, and articulate to establish the real social importance of the good writer.
> "The Instruments of Mental Production" (1966), *Northrop Frye's Writings on Education* (2001), CW, 7.

READING

We *listen to* the poem as it moves from beginning to end, but as soon as the whole of it is in our minds at once we "see" what it means.
> "Second Essay: Ethical Criticism: Theory of Symbols" (1957), *Anatomy of Criticism: Four Essays* (2006), CW, 22.

One of the most familiar facts of literary experience is that one's understanding deepens as well as expands. We not only learn more by reading new poems; we increase the *kind* of understanding we have of poems we have already read.
> Entry, Notebook 30e (1952), 1, *Notebooks for "Anatomy of Criticism"* (2007), CW, 23.

There is one consciousness that subjects itself to the text and understands, and another that, so to speak, overstands. It is only the possession of the latter that makes the operation of reading worthwhile: without it a reader is a pedant who understands but does not comprehend.
> "Identity and Metaphor," *Words with Power: Being a Second Study of "The Bible and Literature"* (2008), CW, 26.

It seems that one becomes the ultimate hero of the great quest of man, not so much by virtue of what one does, as by virtue of what and how one reads.
> *The Secular Scripture: A Study of the Structure of Romance* (1975), *"The Secular Scripture" and Other Writings on Critical Theory, 1976–1991* (2006), CW, 18.

... it is only the preliminary process of reading that is really linear: once read, the book becomes a focus of a community, and may come to mean, simultaneously, any number of things to any number of people.
> "The View from Here" (1980), *Northrop Frye's Writings on Education* (2001), CW, 7.

All reading begins in the revolt against narcissism: when a book stops reflecting your own prejudices, whether for or against what you think you "see in it," & begins to say something closer to what it does say, the core of the reality in the "objective" aspect of it takes shape & you start wrestling with an angel.
> Entry, Notebook 44 (1946–48), *Northrop Frye's Late Notebooks, 1982–1990: Architecture of the Spiritual World* (2000), CW, 5.

I can't remember a time when I couldn't read.
> "Beginnings" (1981), *Northrop Frye on Canada* (2003), CW, 12.

The act of reading as a continuous act of judgment is the key to equality, and the key to freedom. Its purpose is the maintaining of the consistent consciousness which is the basis of human freedom and of human dignity. The end of the process is perhaps the occasional moments of heightened consciousness which are for those who have experienced them the centres around which all one's life appears to revolve.

"Education and the Rejection of Reality" (1971), *Northrop Frye's Writings on Education* (2001), CW, 7.

There are some people who assume that "reading for enjoyment" is a different activity from criticism, but, speaking as a critic, I am glad that I am not of their company.
"Appendix: The Social Context of Literary Criticism" (1968), *Northrop Frye on Literature and Society, 1936–1989: Unpublished Papers* (2002), CW, 10.

REAGAN, RONALD
Reagan may be a cipher as President, but as an actor acting the role of a decisive President in a Grade B movie he's I suppose acceptable to people who think life is a Grade B movie.
Entry, Notebook 27 (1986), 282, *Northrop Frye's Late Notebooks, 1982–1990: Architecture of the Spiritual World* (2000), CW, 5.

REALITY
The sense of reality is, for instance, far higher in tragedy than in comedy, as in comedy the logic of events normally gives way to the audience's desire for a happy ending.
"Second Essay: Ethical Criticism: Theory of Symbols" (1957), *Anatomy of Criticism: Four Essays* (2006), CW, 22.

Reality's what's there; illusion is what's not there. Except that most reality is something we've put there and could take away again; most illusions are creations, and have that sort of reality.
Entry, Notes 54-13 (1980–81), *Northrop Frye's Notebooks on Renaissance Literature* (2006), CW, 20.

Human kind, as Eliot says, cannot bear very much reality: what it can bear, if it is skilfully enough prepared for it, is an instant of illusion which is the gateway to reality.
"Romance as Masque" (1975), *"The Secular Scripture" and Other Writings on Critical Theory, 1976–1991* (2006), CW, 18.

The last enemy to be destroyed is the metaphor of "within." Reality is not subjective, of course; but neither is it a subject grown objective to itself.

Entry, Notes 54-13 (1980–81), *Northrop Frye's Notebooks on Renaissance Literature* (2006), CW, 20.

… because our civilization is tied up in words, we are apt to think that whatever we can't verbalize is unreal.
"Canadian Culture Today" (1977), *Northrop Frye on Canada* (2003), CW, 12.

Ubi bene, ubi patria: the centre of reality is wherever one happens to be, and its circumference is whatever one's imagination can make sense of.
"Letters in Canada: Poetry" (1960), *Northrop Frye on Canada* (2003), CW, 12.

We think of reality as out there and of illusion as mostly in here, but if we go into a theatre the illusion is what's out there and the reality is what's generated in the mind of the audience. There's no reality behind, in the wings or the dressing rooms
Entry, Notes 54-6 (1981), 14, *Northrop Frye's Notebooks and Lectures on the Bible and Other Religious Texts* (2003), CW, 13.

Nine-tenths of what we call reality is not some ineluctably existing group of objects or conditions "out there": it is rather the rubbish left over from previous human constructs.
"Introduction to *Art and Reality*" (1986), *Northrop Frye on Modern Culture* (2003), CW, 11.

But that's the way we do grasp reality: we grasp it with a category which is totally nonexistent.
"Symbolism in the Bible" (1981–82), referring to the experience of the passing of time, *Northrop Frye's Notebooks and Lectures on the Bible and Other Religious Texts* (2003), CW, 13.

What keeps us apart is our own illusion; what unites us is reality, but there is no reality except in thy presence, which is now and forever.
"Undated Prayers (4)" (1992), *Northrop Frye on Religion* (2000), CW, 4.

A society in which the presidency of the United States can be changed by one psychotic with a rifle is not sufficiently real for any thoughtful person to want to live wholly within it.

"The Instruments of Mental Production" (1966), *Northrop Frye's Writings on Education* (2001), CW, 7.

Maybe the "greatest" artists are also the greatest realists: they discover, like the scientists, patterns & constructs actually latent in nature.

Entry, Notebook 12 (1968–70), 467, *The "Third Book" Notebooks of Northrop Frye, 1964–1972: The Critical Comedy* (2002), CW, 9.

REAR-VIEW MIRRORS

I began by saying that the rear-view mirror is our only crystal ball: there is no guide to the future except the analogy of the past.

"Address on Receiving the Royal Bank Award" (1978), *Northrop Frye's Writings on Education* (2001), CW, 7.

REASON

The reasonable is the opposite of the rational.

Entry, Notebook 44 (1986–91), 742, *Northrop Frye's Late Notebooks, 1982–1990: Architecture of the Spiritual World* (2000), CW, 5.

REBELLION

To rise above one's state is rebellion; to fall from it is delinquency.

"Repetitions of Jacob's Dream" (1983), *Northrop Frye on Religion* (2000), CW, 4.

RECOGNITION

… in any case, in reading fiction there are two kinds of recognition. One is the continuous recognition of credibility, fidelity to experience, and of what is not so much lifelikeness as life-liveliness. The other is the recognition of the identity of the total design, into which we are initiated by the technical recognition in the plot.

"Myth, Fiction, and Displacement" (1961), *"The Educated Imagination" and Other Writings on Critical Theory, 1933–1963* (2006), CW, 21.

Whether that's true or not, it certainly is true that what you know is what other people have known, and it is a recognition for us in that sense.

"The Meaning of Recreation: Humanism in Society" (1979), *Northrop Frye on Religion* (2000), CW, 4.

That is, we expect a certain point near the end at which linear suspense is resolved and the unifying shape of the whole design becomes conceptually visible. This point was called *anagnorisis* by Aristotle, a term for which "recognition" is a better rendering than "discovery."

"Myth, Fiction, and Displacement" (1961), *"The Educated Imagination" and Other Writings on Critical Theory, 1933–1963* (2006), CW, 21.

RECREATION

The process itself contains the greatest possible mystery in the study of literature: why is it that somebody as remote in time and space and language and cultural assumptions from us as Homer or the writers of the Old Testament can still speak across all those barriers of time and space and hit us where we live.

"Reconsidering Levels of Meaning" (1979), *Northrop Frye's Fiction and Miscellaneous Writings* (2007), CW, 25.

Clearly there is something essential about the place of creation in the total Biblical vision, but our ways of comprehending it seem to be grossly inadequate. When we turn to human creative power, we see that there is a quality in it better called recreation, a transforming of the chaos within our ordinary experience of nature.

"Typology II," *The Great Code* (1982), *The Great Code: The Bible and Literature* (2006), CW, 19.

The real form of God's creation is man's recreation, which is God in man destroying the cycles of empire.

Entry, Notebook 21 (1969–76), 391, *Northrop Frye's Notebooks and Lectures on the Bible and Other Religious Texts* (2003), CW, 13.

REGIONALISM

There is a paradoxical and mysterious law regarding culture and in particular literature: the more intensely local and provincial a work is, the more universal is its message.

"Identity and Myth" (1979), *Interviews with Northrop Frye* (2008), CW, 24.

What I am saying is that the cultural and imaginative situation of French Canada in Quebec ought to be a norm for Canada generally, that the primary feeling should be regional and local, and that programming by the radio and television media should keep this in mind.

"Canadian Identity and Cultural Regionalism" (1970), *Northrop Frye on Literature and Society, 1936–1989: Unpublished Papers* (2002), CW, 10.

REINCARNATION

Eternal recurrence: in the mind of God everything happens once only. That's the Biblical view: no reincarnation is *necessary*, just as no fall is necessary in yoga.

Entry, Notebook 46 (1980s–90), 26, *Northrop Frye's Late Notebooks, 1982–1990: Architecture of the Spiritual World* (2000), CW, 6.

Reincarnation is not a doctrine, whether true or false: it's experience, a kind of self-guided fantasy. The conception of interpenetration makes it easy to see how one can enter various personalities.

Entry, Notebook 50 (1987–90), 143, *Northrop Frye's Late Notebooks, 1982–1990: Architecture of the Spiritual World* (2000), CW, 5.

When the Westerner tries to absorb the idea of unbornness, he tumbles into the "predestination" pitfall; when the Easterner tries to get clear about deathlessness, he gets into the "reincarnation" one.

Entry, Notebook 3 (1946–48), 119, *Northrop Frye's Notebooks and Lectures on the Bible and Other Religious Texts* (2003), CW, 13.

I was born in 1912 but will live forever: that sounds silly. The Buddhist complement, that I am an unborn spirit incarnated in 1912 who will soon return to that unborn world, is badly needed here.

Entry, Notes 54.1 (May 1990), 36, *Northrop Frye's Late Notebooks, 1982–1990: Architecture of the Spiritual World* (2000), CW, 6.

I don't think much of reincarnation, the prolonging of individual identity, though it may happen sometimes with dying children.

Entry, Notebook 27 (1986), 494, *Northrop Frye's Late Notebooks, 1982–1990: Architecture of the Spiritual World* (2000), CW, 5.

RELATIVITY

Nowadays many people feel that there is something about "relativity" or the "principle of indeterminacy" that gives them the best of both worlds: an up-to-date scientific doctrine which enables them to preserve their moral and religious intuitions. But this is tame compared to the kind of excitement that Newton aroused with his mathematical genius and his deep religious convictions, his irrefutable laws of motion and his suggestion that space was the sensorium of God.

"Nature Methodized " (1960), *Northrop Frye's Writings on the Eighteenth and Nineteenth Centuries* (2005), CW, 17.

RELEVANCE

I think that relevance is something which the student has to establish for himself, whatever he studies. If he can't do that he isn't worthy of the very impressive and dignified title of student.

"Impressions" (1973), *Interviews with Northrop Frye* (2008), CW, 24.

There is no such thing as inherent or built-in relevance; no subject is relevant in itself, because every field of knowledge is equally the centre of all knowledge.

"On Teaching Literature" (1972), *Northrop Frye's Writings on Education* (2001), CW, 7.

What is relevant to the student is not what is related to what or where he is at the moment, but to what he may become or where he may arrive as the result of being a student.

"Unpublished Introduction to *Beyond Communication*" (1989), *Northrop Frye's Writings on Education* (2001), CW, 7.

RELIGION

It seems to me that the first thing that any religion does anywhere is to create a community, that what it sets up is a focus for a community, and that as soon as it stops being a community it stops being anything. It may

be a philosophy, it may be a theology, it may be all kinds of things, but unless it is something with its roots in the society around it, it is no longer a religion.
"Into the Wilderness" (1969), *Interviews with Northrop Frye* (2008), CW, 24.

Religion is a matter of finding one's identity. I think you could almost define a man's religion as that with which he is trying to identify himself.
"Into the Wilderness" (1969), *Interviews with Northrop Frye* (2008), CW, 24.

Religion, to me, means the achieving and the holding of a social vision which comes from inside and yet includes others as well.
"Into the Wilderness" (1969), *Interviews with Northrop Frye* (2008), CW, 24.

I think all religions are really concerned with the expanding of human consciousness.
"On *The Great Code* (I)" (1982), *Interviews with Northrop Frye* (2008), CW, 24.

I have occasionally felt that there was no such subject as comparative religion, as I'm not sure just what gets compared.
Entry, Notebook 37 (1949–55), 11, *Notebooks for "Anatomy of Criticism"* (2007), CW, 23.

Between the secularists and the churches are those who regard religion as a kind of palladium that it might be unlucky to throw away, or feel that religion has a place as a loyal conservative opposition, checking the overconfidence of human progress with reminders that all is not yet well.
"Trends in Modern Culture" (1952), *Northrop Frye on Modern Culture* (2003), CW, 11.

Religion is still where medicine was in, say, 1750: its practitioners are sincere, but it can't really cure.
Entry, 8 Jan. 1950, 25, *The Diaries of Northrop Frye: 1942–1955* (2001), CW, 8.

Everything in religion has its secular aspect, and everything in secular life has religious implications, however ignored or undefined they may be.
"To Come to Light" (1988), *Northrop Frye on Religion* (1999), CW, 4.

The only place I can think of where religion still influences the common law are the obstacles placed on divorce and the law against attempting suicide. Obstacles to birth control perhaps too. Whatever they are, they're invariably nonsense.
Entry, 4 Jan. 1952, 11, *The Diaries of Northrop Frye: 1942–1955* (2001), CW, 8.

Religion tends increasingly to make its primary impact, not as a system of taught and learned belief, but as an imaginative structure which, whether "true" or not, has imaginative consistency and imaginative informing power.
The Modern Century (1967), *Northrop Frye on Modern Culture* (2003), CW, 11.

Truth in religion is increasingly felt to be something that conforms to scientific and scholarly conceptions of truth, instead of being thought to reside primarily in the miraculous, or in the transcendence of other conventions of truth.
"The Knowledge of Good and Evil" (1966), *Northrop Frye's Writings on Education* (2001), CW, 7.

When I was a student, each college had its own variety of religious instruction, although in University College it had to be called Oriental Languages or Ancient Near Eastern Literature, in order to preserve the decencies of secularism.
"Installation Address as Chancellor" (1978), referring to the University of Toronto's "secular college," *Northrop Frye's Writings on Education* (2001), CW, 7.

The fact that the world is always trying to kill God is what, it seems to me, is distinctive of the Biblical religions.
"Northrop Frye in Conversation" (1989), *Interviews with Northrop Frye* (2008), CW, 24.

All religions constitute an intellectual handicap; the *worth* of a religion depends on the intellectual honesty it permits.
Entry, Notebook 18 (1956–62), 133, *Notebooks for "Anatomy of Criticism"* (2007), CW, 23.

The world's great religious teachers tend to avoid writing and keep to direct discourse, leaving the writing down of their teachings to secretaries.

"Introduction," "A History of Communications" by Harold A. Innis (1982), *Northrop Frye on Canada* (2003), CW, 12.

RELIGION & ART

Once again we come back to the point that religion is raw imaginative material clarified by art.

"Part One: The Argument," *Fearful Symmetry: A Study of William Blake* (1947, 2004), CW, 14.

Art is essentially esoteric; religion open to all.

"The Relation of Religion to the Arts" (1933–34), *Northrop Frye's Student Essays, 1932–1938* (1997), CW, 3.

Now religion and art are the two most important phenomena in the world; or rather the most important phenomenon, for they are basically the same thing. They constitute, in fact, the only reality of existence.

"NF to HK," 23 Apr. 1935, *The Correspondence of Northrop Frye and Helen Kemp, 1932–1939* (1996), CW, 1.

Between religion's "this is" and poetry's "but suppose *this* is," there must always be some kind of tension, until the possible and the actual meet at infinity.

"Second Essay: Ethical Criticism: Theory of Symbols" (1957), *Anatomy of Criticism: Four Essays* (2006), CW, 22.

To the extent that *a* religion separated itself from the rest of culture, it started heading for sectarianism. To the extent that it rejoins the total body of culture, it improves itself as well as the culture.

Entry, Notebook 27 (1986), 401, *Northrop Frye's Late Notebooks, 1982–1990: Architecture of the Spiritual World* (2000), CW, 5.

The disinterested imaginative core of mythology is what develops into literature, science, philosophy. Religion is applied mythology.

Entry, Notebook 21 (1969–76), 101, *Northrop Frye's Notebooks and Lectures on the Bible and Other Religious Texts* (2003), CW, 13.

REMORSE & REPENTANCE

Remorse is the comparison of one's actual self with an idealized self, of what one actually is with what one naturally might have been. Hence it is a reaction of wounded pride. Repentance is, first, the same dissatisfaction with the actual natural self, but from then on it seeks reality instead of regrets.

Entry, 9 Jul. 1950, 472, *The Diaries of Northrop Frye: 1942–1955* (2001), CW, 8.

I suppose that repentance or metanoia consists first of all in determining the conditions under which your life must henceforth operate. The irrelevant emotion of regret thereby built up is remorse.

Entry, 9 Jul. 1950, 470, *The Diaries of Northrop Frye: 1942–1955* (2001), CW, 8.

REPETITION

Perhaps, of course, repetitiveness is merely the result — the flip side, so to speak — of getting it right the first time.

"Introduction" (1990), *Words with Power: Being a Second Study of "The Bible and Literature"* (2008), CW, 26.

On the other hand, whatever I repeat I believe to be substantially true.

"Canadian Culture Today" (1977), referring to reiterations in his addresses on subjects of Canadian interest, *Northrop Frye on Canada* (2003), CW, 12.

REPUTATION

The literary chit-chat which makes the reputations of poets boom and crash in an imaginary stock exchange is pseudo-criticism. The wealthy investor Mr. Eliot, after dumping Milton on the market, is now buying him again; Donne has probably reached his peak and will begin to taper off; Tennyson may be in for a slight flutter but the Shelley stocks are still bearish.

"The Archetypes of Literature" (1951), *"The Educated Imagination" and Other Writings on Critical Theory, 1933–1963* (2006), CW, 21.

It seems to be difficult for some to understand that a contemporary writer cannot be "great," whatever his merits or his future reputation, because greatness includes the dimension of having been dead for a long time.

"The Beginning of the Word" (1980), *Northrop Frye's Writings on Education* (2001), CW, 7.

RESEARCH

If research is subordinated to teaching, the instructor soon falls behind in his subject, and his teaching suffers accordingly. If teaching is subordinated to research, the instructor, unless he leaves the university and attaches himself to a research institute, loses touch with the social context of his research.

"The Search for Acceptable Words" (1973), *"The Critical Path" and Other Writings on Critical Theory, 1963–1975* (2009), CW, 27.

RESOURCES

The archaeologists who explore royal tombs in Egypt and Mesopotamia find that they are almost always anticipated by grave robbers, people who got there first because they had better reasons for doing so than the acquisition of knowledge. We are the grave robbers of our own resources, and posterity will not be grateful to us.

"Canada: New World Without Revolution" (1975), *Northrop Frye on Canada* (2003), CW, 12.

A society valued mainly for its beaver pelts, its softwood forests, and the soldiers it can supply for other countries' wars, is unlikely to develop any cultural phenomena beyond a problem of identity, a general state of wondering why it exists.

"The Cultural Development of Canada" (1990), *Northrop Frye on Canada* (2003), CW, 12.

RESPONSIBILITY

The more free you are, the more responsibility you have to take on.

"The Scholar in Society" (1983), *Interviews with Northrop Frye* (2008), CW, 24.

RESTORATION

Restoration is an often disastrous solution: tourists in English cathedrals hear a good deal about the vandalism of Cromwell's soldiers, but the devastation wrought by Victorian restorers has been often far worse, however much better the motive.

"Canada: New World Without Revolution" (1975), *Northrop Frye on Canada* (2003), CW, 12.

RESTRAINT

A man may specialize in self-restraint or in restraint of others. The former produces the vices which spring from fear; the latter those which spring from cruelty.

"Part One: The Argument," *Fearful Symmetry: A Study of William Blake* (1947, 2004), CW, 14.

RESURRECTION

As far as I can read it, the centre of Christianity is not the salvation of the soul, but the Resurrection of the body.

"Symbolism in the Bible" (1981–82), *Northrop Frye's Notebooks and Lectures on the Bible and Other Religious Texts* (2003), CW, 13.

Rebirth normally means loss of memory; resurrection, based on the analogy of waking up from sleep, means restoring its current.

Entry, Notebook 54-4 (late 1970s), 126, *Northrop Frye's Notebooks on Romance* (2004), CW, 15.

What is immortal is not the life we are going to live after death, but the life we have lived. The Resurrection must be *retrospective*.

Entry, Notebook 11f (1969–70), 98, *Northrop Frye's Notebooks and Lectures on the Bible and Other Religious Texts* (2003), CW, 13.

Revolution in the Lenin sense is a vulgarization of the revolutionary principle that finds its focus in resurrection. But resurrection is not now a historical event to be believed but a fact of spiritual existence to be lived or made use of.

Entry, Notebook 21 (1969–76), 551, *Northrop Frye's Notebooks and Lectures on the Bible and Other Religious Texts* (2003), CW, 13.

REVELATION

The language of revelation is not invented by man to express his thoughts about God: it is used by God to accommodate himself to man.

"Review of Paul Tillich" (1964), 6, *Northrop Frye's Fiction and Miscellaneous Writings* (2007), CW, 25.

There is thus a natural alliance between the language of the imagination and the teachings of most of the higher religions. The poet may follow closely the canons of divine revelation as they are accepted in whatever religion is contemporary with him, or he may ignore these canons and concentrate on some other aspect of human experience, real or imagined. In either case, whatever he reveals, he reveals in human terms.

"Religion and Modern Poetry" (1959), *Northrop Frye on Twentieth-Century Literature* (2010), CW, 29.

There are mysteries in the life brought forth by thy Spirit that we cannot know, for we know only what it is within the form of our natures to know. But thou art not a God of mystery; thou art a God of revelation, through whom we may see visions and dream dreams. We may not see thee, but it is through thee that we see, and it is as thy instruments that we may understand the world above our world.

"Prayers: Wednesday" (1992), *Northrop Frye's Fiction and Miscellaneous Writings* (2007), CW, 25.

A revelation from an infinite mind may transcend the reason of a finite one, but does not contradict or humiliate it.

"The Problem of Spiritual Authority in the Nineteenth Century" (1964), *Northrop Frye's Writings on the Eighteenth and Nineteenth Centuries* (2005), CW, 17.

To the corporeal understanding, in short, the Bible's final "Revelation" is an utter mystery: that is, it bears the same name as the Great Whore whose destruction it foretells.

"Part One: The Argument," *Fearful Symmetry: A Study of William Blake* (1947, 2004), CW, 14.

Myth is a human language, so it isn't revelation. So what is revelation? What comes through human language the other way.

Entry, Notebook 21 (1969–76), 76, *Northrop Frye's Notebooks and Lectures on the Bible and Other Religious Texts* (2003), CW, 13.

It is, I am convinced, through the criticism of mythology, which unravels the implications of a myth from within and studies its context with other myths outside it, that we arrive most closely to what we can learn through words, or the contact with words that has traditionally been called revelation.

"The Mythical Approach to Creation" (1985), *Northrop Frye on Religion* (2000), CW, 4.

I suppose the moral is that all religions are one and that revelation can only come through an individual.

Entry, Notebook 12 (1968–70), 499, *The "Third Book" Notebooks of Northrop Frye, 1964–1972: The Critical Comedy* (2002), CW, 9.

Revelation itself *is* kerygma: beyond it is the word of words as seen by the Word.

Entry, Notebook 50 (1987–90), 430, *Northrop Frye's Late Notebooks, 1982–1990: Architecture of the Spiritual World* (2000), CW, 5.

If prayer is the attempt of the creature to direct words to his creator, revelation is not merely an answer to prayer but a *counter-prayer*. If the revelation is thought of as definitive, it is the answer to all possible prayers.

Entry, Notebook 21 (1969–76), 578, *Northrop Frye's Notebooks and Lectures on the Bible and Other Religious Texts* (2003), CW, 13.

Myth is the form of human language appropriate to the revelation of religion. Revelation is mythical in form & content, but its *direction* is reversed.

Entry, Notebook 21 (1969–76), 153, *Northrop Frye's Notebooks and Lectures on the Bible and Other Religious Texts* (2003), CW, 13.

REVIEWING

Book reviewers are among the shock troops of culture. They are the first victims of the fact that far too many people can read and write.

"On Book Reviewing" (1949), *Northrop Frye on Modern Culture* (2003), CW, 11.

The end of book reviewing is the beginning of criticism proper.

Remark quoted in *Here and Now* (University College), June 1949; quoted by Robert D. Denham, editor of *Northrop Frye: On Culture and Literature* (1979).

Aristotle was a great critic, but I should guess that he would have been a rather poor book reviewer.

"On Book Reviewing" (1949), *Northrop Frye on Modern Culture* (2003), CW, 11.

REVOLUTION

We have revolutionary thought whenever the feeling "life is a dream" becomes geared to an impulse to awaken from it.

"Typology I," *The Great Code* (1982), *The Great Code: The Bible and Literature* (2006), CW, 19.

It is possible that social, political, or religious revolution always, and necessarily, betrays a revolutionary ideal of which the imagination alone preserves the secret.

The Secular Scripture: A Study of the Structure of Romance (1975), *"The Secular Scripture" and Other Writings on Critical Theory, 1976–1991* (2006), CW, 18.

I think the real longing is not for a mass movement sweeping up individual concerns, but for an individualized movement reaching out to social concerns.

The Double Vision (1991), *Northrop Frye on Religion* (2000), CW, 4.

I would think of education as the only genuine revolution that society is ever likely to accomplish.

"The Only Genuine Revolution" (1969), *Interviews with Northrop Frye* (2008), CW, 24.

... the revolutionary element is built into contemporary society everywhere. A technological revolution makes the world more uniform: one cannot take off in a jet plane and expect a radically different way of life in the place where the plane lands.

"The Meeting of Past and Future in William Morris" (1982), *Northrop Frye's Writings on the Eighteenth and Nineteenth Centuries* (2005), CW, 17.

The primary revolutionary categories tend to be psychological rather than economic, closer in many respects to Freud than to Marx.

"The Ethics of Change: The Role of the University" (1968), *Northrop Frye's Writings on Education* (2001), CW, 7.

The revolutionary thinks dialectically and understands what he wants by defining its opposite. The humanist thinks in a process of expansion & containment.

Entry, Notebook 11f (1969–70), 147, *Northrop Frye's Notebooks and Lectures on the Bible and Other Religious Texts* (2003), CW, 13.

The real meaning of tradition is learning from the past how to live in the present. And the real meaning of revolutionary action is learning from what could be to see more clearly what is there.

"Convocation Address, Franklin and Marshall" (1968), *Northrop Frye's Writings on Education* (2001), CW, 7.

Revolutions are started, though they are seldom finished, by people of conviction. Nothing is more tedious than other people's convictions, and the most natural response to tedium is apathy.

"Convocation Address: Acadia University" (1969), *Northrop Frye on Literature and Society, 1936–1989: Unpublished Papers* (2002), CW, 10.

REVOLUTION, AMERICAN

Yet there is, I think, a more distinctive attitude in Canadian poetry than in Canadian life, a more withdrawn and detached view of that life which may go back to the central fact of Canadian history: the rejection of the American Revolution.

"Preface to an Uncollected Anthology" (1956), *Northrop Frye on Canada* (2003), CW, 12.

Who is a Canadian? Well, the political answer is that he is an American who avoided revolution.

"View of Canada" (1976), *Northrop Frye on Canada* (2003), CW, 12.

RHETORIC

It is the language of rhetoric and the language of ideology that are the spark plugs of history.

"Literature as Therapy" (1989), *"The Secular Scripture" and Other Writings on Critical Theory, 1976–1991* (2006), CW, 18.

In poetry there is no direct address: in rhetoric there is nothing else.

Entry, Notebook 44 (1986–91), 615, *Northrop Frye's Late Notebooks, 1982–1990: Architecture of the Spiritual World* (2000), CW, 5.

It seems to me that the study of literature should be accompanied, as early as possible, by the study of the rhetorical devices of advertising, propaganda, official releases, news media, and everything else in a citizen's verbal experience that he is compelled to confront but is not (so far in our society) compelled to believe, or say he believes.

"On Teaching Literature" (1972), *Northrop Frye's Writings on Education* (2001), CW, 7.

We distinguish two forms of rhetoric which, if not always debased, are certainly suspect: propaganda and advertising.

"Sequence and Mode," *Words with Power: Being a Second Study of "The Bible and Literature"* (1990), CW, 26.

Rhetoric lies about history; kerygma overrides it.

Entry, Notes 53 (1989–90), 168, *Northrop Frye's Late Notebooks, 1982–1990: Architecture of the Spiritual World* (2000), CW, 6.

The social vision of rhetoric is that of society dressed up in its Sunday clothes, people parading in front of each other, and keeping up the polite, necessary and not always true assumption that they are what they appear to be.

"The Vocation of Eloquence," *The Educated Imagination* (1963), *"The Educated Imagination" and Other Writings on Critical Theory, 1933–1963* (2006), CW, 21.

Rhetoric is figured language like poetry, and shades off imperceptibly into the mythical and poetic. Because it makes assertions, it "answers" to dialectic.

Entry, Notebook 50 (1987–90), 25, *Northrop Frye's Late Notebooks, 1982–1990: Architecture of the Spiritual World* (2000), CW, 5.

RHYTHM

My own teacher, Pelham Edgar, once told me that if the rhythm of a sentence was right, its sense could look after itself.

"Verticals of Adam," *The Educated Imagination* (1963), *"The Educated Imagination" and Other Writings on Critical Theory, 1933–1963* (2006), CW, 21.

I am not saying that the "real" rhythm is the four-stress one: I am saying that the real rhythm is contrapuntal, a tension between four stresses and five feet.

"*Rencontre*: The General Editor's Introduction" (1960s), *Northrop Frye on Literature and Society, 1936–1989: Unpublished Papers* (2002), CW, 10.

RIDDLES

Similarly, the riddle is essentially a charm in reverse: it represents the revolt of the intelligence against the hypnotic power of commanding words.

"Charms and Riddles" (1975), *"The Critical Path" and Other Writings on Critical Theory, 1963–1975* (2009), CW, 27.

The idea of the riddle is descriptive containment: the subject is not described but circumscribed, a circle of words drawn around it.

"Fourth Essay: Rhetorical Criticism: Theory of Genres" (1957), *Anatomy of Criticism: Four Essays* (2006), CW, 22.

I read riddles; I don't "solve" or destroy them. But what's riddling about them, in this sense, is their egocentricity, their isolation from the rest of literary experience.

Entry, Notebook 24 (1970–72), 212, *The "Third Book" Notebooks of Northrop Frye, 1964–1972: The Critical Comedy* (2002), CW, 9.

RIGHTS

There can hardly be a society that does not at least pretend to provide some legal rights for its citizens, and when a totalitarian state resorts to arbitrary violence it is still breaking its own laws.

"Introduction,"*"A History of Communications"* by Harold A. Innis (1982), *Northrop Frye on Canada* (2003), CW, 12.

To put the question in another way, what gives a minority a right? Criminals are a minority, but clearly have no right to be criminals.

"The Problem of Spiritual Authority in the Nineteenth Century" (1964), *Northrop Frye's*

Writings on the Eighteenth and Nineteenth Centuries (2005), CW, 17.

RILKE, RAINER MARIA
I think the current interest in such writers as Rimbaud & Rilke is also caused by a desire to study, not the "great" artists, but those who have made most obviously a yoga out of art, who have employed art as a discipline of the spirit that takes one all the way. Rimbaud is the great denier & Rilke the great affirmer of this aspect of art.

Entry, Notebook 3 (1946–48), 50, *Northrop Frye's Notebooks and Lectures on the Bible and Other Religious Texts* (2003), CW, 13.

RITUAL
The pull of ritual is toward pure cyclical narrative, which, if there could be such a thing, would be automatic and unconscious repetition.

"Second Essay: Ethical Criticism: Theory of Symbols" (1957), *Anatomy of Criticism: Four Essays* (2006), CW, 22.

Ritual is primarily the dramatization of myth....

Entry, Notebook 27 (1986), 501, *Northrop Frye's Late Notebooks, 1982–1990: Architecture of the Spiritual World* (2000), CW, 5.

A ritual relates our life in time to those two primary moments of birth and death, the moment of entering the world and the moment of leaving it, and it makes us realize how every moment in between is the death of the past and the birth of the future.

"Convocation Address: McGill University" (1983), *Northrop Frye on Literature and Society, 1936–1989: Unpublished Papers* (2002), CW, 10.

But rituals don't *do* anything: you can no more bring about permanent social change by demonstrating than you can bring about the end of the world by attending church.

"Universities and the Deluge of Cant" (1972), *Northrop Frye's Writings on Education* (2001), CW, 7.

RIVIÈRE DU LOUP, QUE.
Rivière du Loup, a hideous little pigsty full of ignorance, superstition, dirt, the quaint charm of old Quebec and the devout unspoiled piety of the habitant, is not a black hole I should care to be stuck in with half a dollar.

"NF to HK," 1 Sep. 1933, *The Correspondence of Northrop Frye and Helen Kemp, 1932–1939* (1996), CW, 1.

ROBOT
What, psychologically, is the connection in eeriness between the robot & the ghost?

Entry, 11 Mar. 1949, 259, *The Diaries of Northrop Frye: 1942–1955* (2001), CW, 8.

Here's a science fiction story with a man & a female robot: it's assumed that no man could ever love a robot. I imagine I could: no robot could be more completely programmed & conditioned than some people I've known & been quite fond of. The robot is simply the idea of the slave realized.

Entry, Notebook 48 (1993), 17, *Northrop Frye's Late Notebooks, 1982–1990: Architecture of the Spiritual World* (2000), CW, 6.

ROCKY MOUNTAINS
Flying over the Rockies recently I thought how human civilization cuts into the continuum of nature, which is really doing something else, with another rhythm & dimension from another world.

Entry, Notebook 12 (1968–70), 240, *The "Third Book" Notebooks of Northrop Frye, 1964–1972: The Critical Comedy* (2002), CW, 9.

ROMANCE
Romance in its totality is the record of the journey of the human imagination around its own cosmos.

Entry, Notebook 54-8 (late 1972–77), 50, *Northrop Frye's Notebooks on Romance* (2004), CW, 15.

It looks as though the romance is actually the primitive and popular basis of dramatic entertainment, all other forms being specialized varieties of it.

"Comic Myth in Shakespeare" (1952), *Northrop Frye's Writings on Shakespeare and the Renaissance* (2010), CW, 28.

The perennially child-like quality of romance is marked by its extraordinarily persistent

nostalgia, its search for some kind of imaginative golden age in time or space.
"Third Essay: Archetypal Criticism: Theory of Myths" (1957), *Anatomy of Criticism: Four Essays* (2006), CW, 22.

Romance is older than the novel, a fact which has developed the historical illusion that it is something to be outgrown, a juvenile and underdeveloped form.
"Fourth Essay: Rhetorical Criticism: Theory of Genres" (1957), *Anatomy of Criticism: Four Essays* (2006), CW, 22.

The difference between romance & comedy is that comedy attains, romance contains: one drives toward a telos, the other revolves around it in the circular quest shape.
Entry, Notebook 19 (1964–67), 128, *The "Third Book" Notebooks of Northrop Frye, 1964–1972: The Critical Comedy* (2002), CW, 9.

Romance, fantasy, and mythopoeia are the inescapable forms for a society which no longer believes in its own permanence or continuity.
"The Renaissance of Books" (1973), *Northrop Frye on Modern Culture* (2003), CW, 11.

ROMANTICISM
The Romantic movement has only been around for about 160 years, and it will perhaps be another couple of centuries before the educational theory catches up with it.
"The Only Genuine Revolution" (1968), *Interviews with Northrop Frye* (2008), CW, 24.

Any such conception as "Romanticism" is at one or more removes from actual literary experience, in an inner world, where ten thousand different things flash upon the inward eye with all the bliss of oversimplification.
"The Drunken Boat: The Revolutionary Element in Romanticism" (1963), *Northrop Frye's Writings on the Eighteenth and Nineteenth Centuries* (2005), CW, 17.

The effect of the romantic revival on English literature was so powerful and widespread that no subsequent poet can be considered without some reference to it, so that all the poetry of the last century or so is to that extent postromantic.
"Robert Browning: An Abstract Study" (1932–33), *Northrop Frye's Student Essays, 1932–1938* (1997), CW, 3.

ROME
What Prussia is to Germany, what Scotland is to Britain, that Rome is to Italy — sterile as an egg and proud of it.
"NF to HK," 5 Apr. 1937, written in Rome, *The Correspondence of Northrop Frye and Helen Kemp, 1932–1939* (1996), CW, 1.

ROUSSEAU, JEAN-JACQUES
Rousseau became the first modern revolutionary thinker because he was the first thinker to emphasize the primacy of primary concern.
Entry, Notebook 50 (1987–90), 239, *Northrop Frye's Late Notebooks, 1982–1990: Architecture of the Spiritual World* (2000), CW, 5.

ROWSE, A.L.
Literary criticism ought to be profoundly grateful to Professor Rowse for writing so bad a book: it practically proves that writing a good book on Shakespeare is a task for a mere critic.
"Criticism, Visible and Invisible" (1964), characterizing Rowse's *Shakespeare's Sonnets* (1964), *"The Critical Path" and Other Writings on Critical Theory, 1963–1975* (2009), CW, 27.

ROYAL CANADIAN MOUNTED POLICE
A satirical revue in Toronto some years ago known as *Spring Thaw* depicted a hero going in quest of a Canadian identity and emerging with a mounted policeman and a bottle of rye. If he had been Australian, one realizes, he would have emerged with a kangaroo and a boomerang. One needs to go deeper than ridicule, however, if one is to understand the subtlety of the self-deceptions involved.
"Criticism and Environment" (1981), *Northrop Frye on Canada* (2003), CW, 12.

ROYAL COMMISSIONS
To establish a Royal Commission to look into the possibility of doing something that should have been done fifty years ago is, perhaps, timely. There is nothing to show, however,

that this will not be merely one more vast expenditure of brains and time and money and organization which will then gather dust in the Department of Procrastination.

"Culture and the Cabinet" (1949), *Northrop Frye on Canada* (2003), CW, 12.

ROYAL ONTARIO MUSEUM

It is part of the greatness of such an achievement that so much of Crete and Mexico and China should now be "ours," not in the sense of possession, but in the sense of shared experience.

"Introduction to Charles T. Currelly, *I Brought the Ages Home*" (1956), referring to ROM and its founder C.T. Currelly, *Northrop Frye on Canada* (2003), CW, 12.

RUSSIA

Soviet Russia is very proud of its production of tractors, but it will be some time before the tractor replaces the sickle on the Soviet flag.

"The Language of Poetry" (1955), *"The Educated Imagination" and Other Writings on Critical Theory, 1933–1963* (2006), CW, 21.

Unfortunately, the Sputnik affair had not put the fear of God into America, only a fear of Russian technology, and by the time American astronauts had reached the moon, a good deal of the anti-intellectualism was back in charge.

"Preface to *On Education*" (1988), *Northrop Frye's Writings on Education* (2001), CW, 7.

S

SABBATH
Remembering the Sabbath is dubious legalism: it's really a matter of experiencing creation as an end instead of as a beginning.
> Entry, Notes 54-5 (1976), 59, *Northrop Frye's Notebooks and Lectures on the Bible and Other Religious Texts* (2003), CW, 13.

Sabbath means among other things that god withdraws from his creation, becomes objective to it.
> Entry, Notes 52 (1982–90), 26, *Northrop Frye's Late Notebooks, 1982–1990: Architecture of the Spiritual World* (2000), CW, 6.

Time is the endless Sabbath when God rests and we work.
> Entry, Notebook 44 (1986–91), 411, *Northrop Frye's Late Notebooks, 1982–1990: Architecture of the Spiritual World* (2000), CW, 5.

As I say, all culture originates in remembering the Sabbath.
> Entry, Notebook 3 (1946–48), 153, *Northrop Frye's Notebooks and Lectures on the Bible and Other Religious Texts* (2003), CW, 13.

SACRAMENT
As a student said: sacrament is the occasion but not the cause of grace. If it were the cause, it would be a magical system, not religious at all.
> Entry, Notebook 21 (1969–76), 515, *Northrop Frye's Notebooks and Lectures on the Bible and Other Religious Texts* (2003), CW, 13.

SACREDNESS
It is not merely that science has destroyed the sense of sacredness in time and space, but that poetry has recovered it for the world to which it really belongs.
> "World Enough Without Time" (1959), *"The Educated Imagination" and Other Writings on Critical Theory, 1933–1963* (2006), CW, 21.

SACRIFICES
A sacrificial ritual requires one murderer; a moral ritual requires two, the Mosaic life for life.
> Entry, Notebook 34 (1946–50), 14, *Northrop Frye's Notebooks on Romance* (2004), CW, 15.

SAINTS
It may seem self-evident to say that a saint is a better man than a sinner, otherwise the word "better" would have no meaning, but the saint himself is very unlikely to hold such a view.
> "Preserving Human Values" (1961), *Northrop Frye on Modern Culture* (2003), CW, 11.

The same tendencies continue after a monotheistic religion has been established: in Christianity the saints play a prominent role in absorbing local gods, and Notre Dame de Chartres is the same person as Notre Dame de Crabtree Mills, Quebec.
> "Literature and Myth" (1967), *"The Critical Path" and Other Writings on Critical Theory, 1963–1975* (2009), CW, 27.

Is Michael the only saint who is also an angel? If so, why? If not, who are the others?
> Entry, Notebook 44 (1986–91), 157, *Northrop Frye's Late Notebooks, 1982–1990: Architecture of the Spiritual World* (2000), CW, 5.

SALVATION
I would find the search for salvation to have something to do with a kind of awareness of freedom which is also an awareness that one has somehow or other come alive, moved

from ordinary life into the same life repeated more intensely.
"The Voice in the Crowd" (1966), *Interviews with Northrop Frye* (2008), CW, 24.

SASKATCHEWAN
I think most Canadians realize that Saskatchewan is not a province like other provinces. It has been, at least since the Regina manifesto of the CCF, a kind of experimental station in Canadian life.
"The University and the Heroic Vision" (1968), *Northrop Frye's Writings on Education* (2001), CW, 7.

SATAN
Satan could not have fallen at all without convincing himself that God was not God but *a* god, and he himself therefore another god.
"Introduction to 'Paradise Lost' and Selected Poetry and Prose" (1950), *Northrop Frye on Milton and Blake* (2005), CW, 16.

God has hope and a few successes; Satan most of the facts and the balance of probabilities.
Entry, 1 Jan. 1952, 5, *The Diaries of Northrop Frye: 1942–1955* (2001), CW, 8.

SATIRE
I should define satire, then, as poetry assuming a special function of analysis, that is, of breaking up the lumber of stereotypes, fossilized beliefs, superstitious terrors, crank theories, pedantic dogmatisms, oppressive fashions, and all the other things that impede the free movement of society.
"The Nature of Satire" (1944), *"The Educated Imagination" and Other Writings on Critical Theory, 1933–1963* (2006), CW, 21.

The chief distinction between irony and satire is that satire is militant irony: its moral norms are relatively clear, and it assumes standards against which the grotesque and absurd are measured.
"Third Essay: Archetypal Criticism: Theory of Myths" (1957), *Anatomy of Criticism: Four Essays* (2006), CW, 22.

SCANDINAVIA
In Scandinavia the divergence in culture and imagination, with Norway turned outwards towards the west and Sweden eastward towards the Baltic, enabled the countries to separate politically on equal terms, with mutual respect, while still co-operating economically.
"Canadian Identity and Cultural Regionalism" (1970), *Northrop Frye on Literature and Society, 1936–1989: Unpublished Papers* (2002), CW, 10.

SCEPTICISM
Scepticism itself may be or become a dogmatic attitude, a comic humour of doubting plain evidence.
"Third Essay: Archetypal Criticism: Theory of Myths" (1957), *Anatomy of Criticism: Four Essays* (2006), CW, 22.

SCHOLARS
Of course a scholar who attempts anything but scholarship is rather in the position of a man who has volunteered to amuse a children's party: he is not sure that his really solid virtues will count for much.
"By Liberal Things" (1959), *Northrop Frye's Writings on Education* (2001), CW, 7.

A teacher who is not a scholar is soon going to be out of touch with his own subject, and a scholar who is not a teacher is soon going to be out of touch with the world.
"The Definition of a University" (1970), *Northrop Frye's Writings on Education* (2001), CW, 7.

If he has no idea what scholarship is, he has no idea what a university is either.
"The Social Importance of Literature" (1968), referring to the appointment of scholars as administrators, *Northrop Frye's Writings on Education* (2001), CW, 7.

Every scholar develops something analogous to a sense of smell, and if a book has declared itself intellectually bankrupt on page 2 the experienced scholar, left to himself, will not read on to page 302.
"Literary Criticism" (1963), *"The Critical Path" and Other Writings on Critical Theory, 1963–1975* (2009), CW, 27.

There could be no more impressive tribute to the fact that a first-rate scholar, simply by being what he is and by what he does, creates and fosters a community around him, a community not of discipleship but of a high morale sustained by the awareness that he is there.
"Foreword to *Unfolded Tales*" (1989), contributing to the *Festschrift* in honour of the scholar A.C. Hamilton, *Northrop Frye's Writings on Shakespeare and the Renaissance* (2010), CW, 28.

The whole notion of "productive" is an assembly-line notion that is now being outgrown. A scholar should take a *creative* interest in his subject, and what will make the "productive" compulsion less universal will be the rise in adult education.
Entry, Notebook 50 (1987–90), 575, *Northrop Frye's Late Notebooks, 1982–1990: Architecture of the Spiritual World* (2000), CW, 5.

Nevertheless, scholars are the public on whom the artist must make his first impression, and from his point of view he could hardly do better.
"Academy without Walls" (1961), *Northrop Frye on Modern Culture* (2003), CW, 11.

SCHOLARSHIP
Actual scholarship is esoteric, almost conspiratorial, and the principles of academic freedom require that it should be left that way.
"The Instruments of Mental Production" (1966), *Northrop Frye's Writings on Education* (2001), CW, 7.

So in a sense you can't miss in the humanities. If your book is any good, it's a contribution to scholarship; if it's no good, it's a document in the history of taste, and has its importance there.
"Research and Graduate Education in the Humanities" (1968), *Northrop Frye's Writings on Education* (2001), CW, 7.

Academics of course are a conservative breed, and they still try to keep explaining to one another that scholarship knows no boundaries. Scholarship may not but culture does: and the only reason for having scholarship is that it is necessary to culture.
"Conclusion to *Literary History of Canada*" (1965), *Northrop Frye on Canada* (2003), CW, 12.

We find in our own experience that the feeling of progressive advance is very rare, and that scholarship is mostly a matter of continuous fumbling for a light switch in a dark room.
"Teaching the Humanities Today" (1977), *Northrop Frye's Writings on Education* (2001), CW, 7.

But literary scholarship was beginning to resemble the well-known caterpillar, staring at a butterfly and saying, "You'll never catch me going up in one of those things."
"Across the River and Out of the Trees" (1980), referring to scholarly writing in Toronto in the 1930s, *Northrop Frye on Canada* (2003), CW, 12.

To subordinate teaching to scholarship is the only way of guaranteeing the independence of the teacher within the university, and of encouraging his independence outside of it.
"The Critical Discipline" (1960), *Northrop Frye's Writings on Education* (2001), CW, 7.

Although one may plunge into impersonal scholarship for a while, one has finally to come out on the other side with some kind of personal absorption of what one has learned.
"Criticism as Education" (1979), *Northrop Frye's Writings on Education* (2001), CW, 7.

SCHOOLING
For sooner or later Canada must come to grips with a problem which, as yet, lies far over the horizon of practical politics. This is the problem of federal policy on education, of some means of getting educational standards emancipated from the poverty, the disorganization, and the well-meaning ignorance of parochial school boards and provincial governments. If this happens in our time, it will be as important an event in the twentieth century as Confederation was in the nineteenth.
"Culture and the Cabinet" (1949), *Northrop Frye on Canada* (2003), CW, 12.

We must learn to read in order to read traffic signs and advertising; we must learn to write and cipher to make out our income tax.

"Language as the Home of Human Life" (1985), *Northrop Frye's Writings on Education* (2001), CW, 7.

In the verbal arts, the student of eighteen is about where he should be at fourteen, apart from what he does on his own with the help of a sympathetic teacher or librarian. To say this is not to reflect on the schools, but on the social conditions that cripple them.

"Humanities in a New World" (1958), *Northrop Frye's Writings on Education* (2001), CW, 7.

SCIENCE

It is one of the primary functions of science to remind us of how much we still do not know, to present to us a universe of infinite scope and infinite possibilities of further discovery.

"The Times of the Signs" (1973), *"The Critical Path" and Other Writings on Critical Theory, 1963–1975* (2009), CW, 27.

However, if there are any readers for whom the word "scientific" conveys emotional overtones of unimaginative barbarism, they may substitute "systematic" or "progressive" instead.

"Polemical Introduction" (1957), *Anatomy of Criticism: Four Essays* (2006), CW, 22.

Myth, in short, is the only possible language of *concern*, just as science, with its appeal to evidence, accurate measurement, and rational deduction, is the only possible language of detachment.

"Literature and Myth" (1967), *"The Critical Path" and Other Writings on Critical Theory, 1963–1975* (2009), CW, 27.

Science is a vision of nature which perceives the elements in nature that correspond to the reason and the sense of structure in the scientist's mind.

The Modern Century (1967), *Northrop Frye on Modern Culture* (2003), CW, 11.

A new law or conception in, say, physics describes what has always been there waiting to be identified and described (objectively), and represents a scientist making up an arrangement of phenomena out of his head (subjectively). Both aspects have to be there, and have to correspond.

Entry, Notes 52 (1982–90), 499, *Northrop Frye's Late Notebooks, 1982–1990: Architecture of the Spiritual World* (2000), CW, 6.

Astrology develops into astronomy and alchemy into chemistry, but the poet remains on a flat earth where the sun rises in the east and sets in the west, an earth made up of four elements, earth, air, fire, and water. The situation in poetry is unlikely to change until that remote time in the distant future when chemistry, or whatever the relevant science will then be, will have discovered that as a matter of fact there are really four elements, and that their names are earth, air, fire and water.

"Tradition and Change in the Theory of Criticism" (1969), *Northrop Frye on Literature and Society, 1936–1989: Unpublished Papers* (2002), CW, 10.

Nothing has improved in this century except science and scholarship, which have improved because they have no boundaries. If they do have boundaries, in other words if they are politically controlled, they soon become sinister and dangerous.

"The Cultural Development of Canada" (1990), *Northrop Frye on Canada* (2003), CW, 12.

The world of art is human in perspective, a world in which the sun continues to rise and set long after science has explained that its rising and setting are illusions.

"Myth, Fiction, and Displacement" (1961), *"The Educated Imagination" and Other Writings on Critical Theory, 1933–1963* (2006), CW, 21.

Every science is the queen of sciences, or, if it is a new science, a pawn that may become a queen.

"The Changing Pace in Canadian Education" (1963), *Northrop Frye's Writings on Education* (2001), CW, 7.

If science were to explain every fact in the universe except one, that one fact would clamour for admission until it had shattered the whole explanatory structure.

"By Liberal Things" (1959), *Northrop Frye's Writings on Education* (2001), CW, 7.

Science is based on a withdrawal of consciousness from existence, a capacity to turn around and look at one's environment, which is perhaps the most distinctively human of all acts.
"The Knowledge of Good and Evil" (1966), *Northrop Frye's Writings on Education* (2001), CW, 7.

I wonder if "science" is really the criticism of mathematics?
Entry, Notebook 19 (1964–67), 283, *The "Third Book" Notebooks of Northrop Frye, 1964–1972: The Critical Comedy* (2002), CW, 9.

Perhaps that's the whole point about science: that it's a universal structure of knowledge that will help mankind to break out of culture-group barriers, and get rid of war by moving into a higher area of conflict.
"Oswald Spengler" (1955), *Northrop Frye on Modern Culture* (2003), CW, 11.

The notion that science, left to itself, is bound to evolve more and more of the truth about the world is another illusion, for science can never exist outside a society, and that society, whether deliberately or unconsciously, directs its course.
The Modern Century (1967), *Northrop Frye on Modern Culture* (2003), CW, 11.

Science cannot destroy mythology: science cannot destroy anything except an earlier version of the same science.
Entry, Notebook 21 (1969–76), 137, *Northrop Frye's Notebooks and Lectures on the Bible and Other Religious Texts* (2003), CW, 13.

Just as the sciences show us the physical world of nature, so the arts show us the human world that man is trying to build out of nature.
"Academy without Walls" (1961), *Northrop Frye on Modern Culture* (2003), CW, 11.

SCIENCE & SCIENTISTS

The scientist cannot think as a scientist until he has immersed himself in the structure of his science, and until whatever he thinks becomes an organic extension and development of the science, so that in a sense the science itself is thinking through him.

"Sign and Significance" (1969), *"The Critical Path" and Other Writings on Critical Theory, 1963–1975* (2009), CW, 27.

The scientist can appeal to an authority beyond controversy, the authority of repeatable experiments, accurate measurements, prediction, and verified observations. The humanities can never escape from controversy, because they are in the world of ethical choice. For verified experiment and observation, students need to face in the same direction; for ethical choice, they need to face one another.
"Installation Address as Chancellor" (1978), *Northrop Frye's Writings on Education* (2001), CW, 7.

I have observed that all students of science who are any good are proud of the impersonal authority of their subject: they deeply appreciate the fact that the truth of science has nothing to do with feelings or emotions.
"A Liberal Education" (1945), *Northrop Frye's Writings on Education* (2001), CW, 7.

SCIENCE FICTION

When I wrote the *Anatomy*, science fiction was not yet in the centre of popular literature, but I knew that it would be very soon, because it would revive romantic and eventually mythical formulas.
"Northrop Frye in Conversation" (1989), *Interviews with Northrop Frye* (2008), CW, 24.

Even popular literature appears to be slowly shifting its centre of gravity from murder stories to science fiction — or at any rate a rapid growth of science fiction is certainly a fact about contemporary popular literature.
"First Essay: Historical Criticism: Theory of Modes" (1957), *Anatomy of Criticism: Four Essays* (2006), CW, 22.

Science fiction is almost entirely based on the theme of the dream of flight, so that there is, without question, a link to the desiring self.
"Four Questions for Northrop Frye" (1979), *Interviews with Northrop Frye* (2008), CW, 24.

The imaginary society is a central theme in our century of what is so inaccurately called science fiction. There are two main forms of science fiction: a software philosophical fantasy descending from More's *Utopia*, and a hardware technological one of which the ancestor is Bacon's *New Atlantis*.

"Natural and Revealed Communities" (1987), *Northrop Frye's Writings on Shakespeare and the Renaissance* (2010), CW, 28.

Science fiction frequently tries to imagine what life would be like on a plane as far above us as we are above savagery; its setting is often of a kind that appears to us as technologically miraculous. It is thus a mode of romance with a strong inherent tendency to myth.

"First Essay: Historical Criticism: Theory of Modes" (1957), *Anatomy of Criticism: Four Essays* (2006), CW, 22.

This night side of the map runs out in Rider Haggard — with jet planes it's no use talking about mysterious cities buried in Africa — you have to go to outer space.

Entry, Notebook 56a (late 1972–75), 70, *Northrop Frye's Notebooks on Romance* (2004), CW, 15.

Science fiction isn't seriously concerned with science — it's a form of philosophical romance, and is forced into outer space by technology, its relation to which is negative.

Entry, Notebook 56a (late 1972–75), 70, *Northrop Frye's Notebooks on Romance* (2004), CW, 15.

In science fiction it's the world within that's really existing, & the world without is only a projection of it. At least, when the within isn't interesting the without isn't either.

Entry, Notebook 24 (1970–72), 226, *The "Third Book" Notebooks of Northrop Frye, 1964–1972: The Critical Comedy* (2002), CW, 9.

Science fiction may conceivably be a primitive beginning of a new form of heroic epic; Beckett and similar types of literary nihilism the primitive beginnings of a new antithetical pessimism.

Entry, Notebook 56a (late 1972–75), 3, *Northrop Frye's Notebooks on Romance* (2004), CW, 15.

Fiction seems to be shifting its ground to a more explicit use of mythology and symbolism: in science fiction especially it is exploring new areas of experience, and the more romantic writing of the previous century is becoming more central in its tradition.

"*Rencontre:* The General Editor's Introduction" (1960s), *Northrop Frye on Literature and Society, 1936–1989: Unpublished Papers* (2002), CW, 10.

What the hero of a science fiction story finds on a planet of Arcturus, however elaborate and plausible the hardware that got him there, is still essentially what heroes of earlier romances found in lost civilizations buried in Africa or Asia.

"The Bridge of Language" (1981), *Northrop Frye on Modern Culture* (2003), CW, 11.

SCOTCH

I knew an old man once who settled for drinking straight Scotch, and he said, "I find it agrees with me." I find the same thing.

"*Chatelaine's* Celebrity I.D." (1982), asked to identify his favourite drink, *Interviews with Northrop Frye* (2008), CW, 24.

SCOTT, DUNCAN CAMPBELL

And whatever a Canadian writer may be, there is no doubt that Scott had as varied and comprehensive a knowledge of Canada as any writer we have produced.

"Duncan Campbell Scott" (1948), *Northrop Frye on Canada* (2003), CW, 12.

SCRIPTURE

It seemed to me that there was an epic form that tended to expand into a kind of imaginative encyclopedia, and that the limit of this encyclopedic form was the sacred book, the kind of scriptural myth that we find in the Bible, the *Prose Edda*, and in Hindu literature.

"Cycle and Apocalypse in *Finnegans Wake*" (1987), *Northrop Frye on Twentieth-Century Literature* (2010), CW, 29.

The relation in bulk between commentary and a sacred book, such as the Bible or the Vedic hymns, is even more striking, and indicates that when a poetic structure attains a certain degree of concentration or social recognition, the amount of commentary it will carry is infinite.

"Second Essay: Ethical Criticism: Theory of Symbols" (1957), *Anatomy of Criticism: Four Essays* (2006), CW, 22.

My search for literary grounds for criticism took me in the direction of the sacred book, which was as far as I could get. The sacred book both is and is not a work of literature....
"Critical Views" (1980s), 18, *Northrop Frye's Fiction and Miscellaneous Writings* (2007), CW, 25.

Finally, the tendency of both ritual and epiphany to become encyclopedic is realized in the definitive body of myth which constitutes the sacred scriptures of religions.
"The Archetypes of Literature" (1951), *"The Educated Imagination" and Other Writings on Critical Theory, 1933–1963* (2006), CW, 21.

SECORD, LAURA
No genuine portrait of English Canada's best known heroine, Laura Secord, exists, and the deficiency is made up for by a grisly reproduction of a male elder statesman, with the beard removed and a shawl put over the head, purporting to represent her in old age.
"Haunted by Lack of Ghosts" (1976), *Northrop Frye on Canada* (2003), CW, 12.

SECULARISM
Whether the community is nominally Catholic or Protestant or Jewish or Moslem or Hindu, every secular state guided by religious principles seems to turn them into a form of devil worship.
Creation and Recreation (1980), *Northrop Frye on Religion* (2000), CW, 4.

SEER
The "seer" has insight, not second sight: he is not a charlatan but the contrary of one, an honest man with a sharper perception and a clearer perspective than other honest men possess.
"Part One: The Argument," reflecting the thought of William Blake, *Fearful Symmetry: A Study of William Blake* (1947, 2004), CW, 14.

SELF-EXPRESSION
The general principle involved is that there is really no such thing as self-expression in literature.

The Educated Imagination (1963), *"The Educated Imagination" and Other Writings on Critical Theory, 1933–1963* (2006), CW, 21.

SELF-HELP
Books on the power of positive thinking and on winning friends and influencing people have been popular since the days of ancient Egypt: an eighteenth-century example was called *The Way to Be Rich and Respectable*, which is as good a title as any.
"Culture and the National Will" (1957), *Northrop Frye on Canada* (2003), CW, 12.

SELF-KNOWLEDGE
The motto of Delphi was "Know thyself," which suggests that the self intended was a conscience far below the ego with its anxieties of self-interest, far below all social and cultural conditioning, in short the spiritual self.
"Third Variation: The Cave," *Words with Power: Being a Second Study of "The Bible and Literature"* (1990), CW, 26.

SELFHOOD
A person's real self is perhaps more clearly evoked by what other people think of him than by his own analysis of himself. The "real me" may be a layer of personae, the relationships with other people.
"Sacred and Secular Scriptures" (1975), *Interviews with Northrop Frye* (2008), CW, 24.

Selfhood contemplates Selfhood with irritation & the imagination with resentment; imagination contemplates Selfhood with wrath and imagination with love.
Entry, 31 Dec. 1949, 12, *The Diaries of Northrop Frye: 1942–1955* (2001), CW, 8.

SENSIBILITY, AGE OF
Our students are thus graduated with a vague notion that the age of sensibility was the time when poetry moved from a reptilian Classicism, all cold and dry reason, to a mammalian Romanticism, all warm and wet feeling.
"Towards Defining an Age of Sensibility" (1956), *Northrop Frye's Writings on the Eighteenth and Nineteenth Centuries* (2005), CW, 17.

SENTIMENTALITY

The word sentimental is one of many euphemisms for the infantilism that is, as noted, the besetting sin of an uncritical attachment to an ideology of any kind — in fact, it is the most dangerous form of original sin.

"Prefatory Note," *Words with Power: Being a Second Study of "The Bible and Literature"* (1990), CW, 26.

SEPARATISM

Separatism is a very healthy movement within culture. It's a disastrous movement within politics and economics.

"Canadian Energies: Dialogues on Creativity" (1980), *Interviews with Northrop Frye* (2008), CW, 24.

And I think that separatism is a very unattractive combination of a progressive cultural movement and a regressive political one — and that the cultural side is the *genuine* part of it.

"From Nationalism to Regionalism: The Maturing of Canadian Culture" (1980), *Interviews with Northrop Frye* (2008), CW, 24.

As for external relations, not all the dangers in this country come from separatism: the bureaucratic obsession with centralizing may prove in the long run to be even more disastrous.

"Address at the Installation of Gordon Keyes as Principal of Victoria College" (1976), *Northrop Frye's Writings on Education* (2001), CW, 7.

Separation, except when it is a genuine effort to escape from tyranny, is in most respects a mean, squalid & neurotic philosophy, but it is the strongest force yet thrown up by any age of total communication.

Entry, Notebook 11f (1969–70), 116, *Northrop Frye's Notebooks and Lectures on the Bible and Other Religious Texts* (2003), CW, 13.

Here there certainly has been tension, but even in the worst days of separatist terrorism a dozen years ago I never saw in Canada anything like the *mort aux flamands* graffiti that I have seen in Belgium.

"The View from Here" (1980), *Northrop Frye's Writings on Education* (2001), CW, 7.

SEPARATISM & CANADA

Of course, in Canadian history, the entire country is separatist.

"Introduction to Canadian Literature: Moscow Talk" (1988), 17, *Northrop Frye's Fiction and Miscellaneous Writings* (2007), CW, 25.

Hence one is not inconsistent if one sympathizes warmly with French Canadian cultural aspirations and still opposes separatism, which is, in my view, a quite mistaken yoking of a progressive cultural movement to a regressive political one.

"Across the River and Out of the Trees" (1980), *Northrop Frye on Canada* (2003), CW, 12.

But everywhere in Canada we find solitudes touching other solitudes: every part of Canada has strong separatist feelings, because every part of it is in fact a separation.

"Canadian Culture Today" (1977), *Northrop Frye on Canada* (2003), CW, 12.

The political, and still more the economic, picture is one of deep gloom, lightened by an occasional gleam of neurosis.

"A Summary of the 'Options' Conference" (1977), *Northrop Frye on Canada* (2003), CW, 12.

In every part of Canada there are strong separatist feelings, and separatism can lead only to increased American penetration, especially economic and ideological. This is not to say that such penetration must be sinister, merely that it is the opposite of what separatism aims at.

"Speech at the New Canadian Embassy, Washington" (1989), *Northrop Frye on Canada* (2003), CW, 12.

In spirit I agree with the optimists: it is the destiny of man to unite rather than divide, and as a Canadian I have little sympathy with separatism, which seems to me a mean and squalid philosophy. But I can hardly ignore the fact that separatism is the strongest political force yet thrown up by the age of television.

"Communications" (1970), *Northrop Frye on Modern Culture* (2003), CW, 11.

Separatism in Quebec is an intellectuals' movement, a *trahison des clercs*: it has dominated the communications media for some years, and bypasses economic issues with a simple emotional construct in which Confederation equals bondage and separation freedom. As an intellectuals' movement, even a revolutionary one, it may settle for a purely symbolic separation: if it goes beyond that, whatever is distinctive in the culture of Quebec will be its first casualty.
> "Canadian Culture Today" (1977), *Northrop Frye on Canada* (2003), CW, 12.

Whatever political or economic deals could conceivably be arranged between Canada and Quebec, the overriding economic conditions are those of an American-dominated continent, and there is no greater will to resist this domination in French than in English Canada.
> "A Summary of the 'Options' Conference" (1977), *Northrop Frye on Canada* (2003), CW, 12.

SERMONS

But the advantage of speaking from the pulpit of a "sectarian college" is that I do not have to pretend, out of politeness, to be ignorant of a number of things that I know perfectly well.
> "Baccalaureate Sermon" (1967), *Northrop Frye on Religion* (2000), CW, 4.

Because no society in the world can afford to be complacent about such dangers, there is no more useful literary genre than the hellfire sermon, as long as the hell is the real one that we make for ourselves, and as long as our response is genuinely concerned and not hysterical or counter-hysterical.
> "Fourth Variation: The Furnace," *Words with Power: Being a Second Study of "The Bible and Literature"* (2008), CW, 26.

SEVEN

The Apocalypse in the Bible is an imaginative and visionary work of art, but it is not the less so for making a symbolic use of the number seven. The recurrence of this number is part of its unity as a poem, not an attempt to indicate a sevenfold aspect of things in general.
> "Part One: The Argument," *Fearful Symmetry: A Study of William Blake* (1947, 2004), CW, 14.

SEX

Similarly, the story of *Measure for Measure* deals with a law prescribing death for extramarital sexual relations: a law so absurd that its only other appearance in English literature is in Gilbert and Sullivan's *Mikado*.
> "Literature and the Law" (1970), *"The Critical Path" and Other Writings on Critical Theory, 1963–1975* (2009), CW, 27.

And it is clear that the middle-class feeling that there is something obscene about the sexual side of life is connected with the realization that sex is something equally available to the working class.
> "Literature and the Law" (1970), *"The Critical Path" and Other Writings on Critical Theory, 1963–1975* (2009), CW, 27.

I noted too that two things which were rigidly excluded from all our reading material were the themes of sex and violence. I began to understand why sex and violence are the most genuinely popular elements of popular culture.
> "The Definition of a University" (1970), referring to the school curriculum, *Northrop Frye's Writings on Education* (2001), CW, 7.

With ideology, all sex becomes sex in the head.
> Entry, Notebook 27 (1986), 522, *Northrop Frye's Late Notebooks, 1982–1990: Architecture of the Spiritual World* (2000), CW, 5.

In a more relaxed society sex would be as well under control as hunger, & birth control would be within the organism, not a mechanical brake on an organism assumed to be out of control.
> Entry, 9 Mar. 1952, 167, *The Diaries of Northrop Frye: 1942–1955* (2001), CW, 8.

The sedentary are the most sex-ridden of all men, despite a popular superstition to the contrary largely invented by them.
> Entry, 12 Sep. 1942, 105, *The Diaries of Northrop Frye: 1942–1955* (2001), CW, 8.

I have never myself felt any physical basis to my affectionate feelings for other men, but there must be one, and it seems to me as pointless to speak of all male love as buggery as it would be to speak of all marriage as legalized whoring.

Entry, 2 Jan. 1952, 8, *The Diaries of Northrop Frye: 1942–1955* (2001), CW, 8.

SHAKESPEARE, WILLIAM

One of the greatest benefits of studying Shakespeare is that he makes us more aware of our assumptions and so less confined by them.

"Northrop Frye on Shakespeare: Introduction" (1986), *Northrop Frye's Writings on Shakespeare and the Renaissance* (2010), CW, 28.

And there is, of course, no greater writer than Shakespeare. So, whenever we open our mouths to speak, the rhythms and cadences of Shakespeare are helping to form what we say. Whenever we think, or think we think, Shakespeare's metaphors and images are entering into the sanctuary of our thought. Whenever we attain any understanding or love of one another beyond the range of our immediate experience, Shakespeare's insight into humanity is helping to make our insight possible.

"Toast to the Memory of Shakespeare" (1961), *Northrop Frye's Writings on Shakespeare and the Renaissance* (2010), CW, 28.

I think it's fair to say he's the world's greatest poet, but I think of him as a dramatist who used poetry rather than as a poet who used the drama.

"The Great Teacher" (1988), *Interviews with Northrop Frye* (2008), CW, 24.

We can hardly conceive of an imagination so concrete that for it the structure is prior to the attitude, and prescribes the attitude. Shakespeare's impartiality is a totally involved and committed impartiality: it expresses itself in bringing everything equally to life.

"*A Natural Perspective: The Development of Shakespearean Comedy and Romance*; II, Making Nature Afraid" (1963), *Northrop Frye's Writings on Shakespeare and the Renaissance* (2010), CW, 28.

In every play Shakespeare wrote, the hero or central character is the theatre itself.

"Northrop Frye on Shakespeare: Introduction" (1986), *Northrop Frye's Writings on Shakespeare and the Renaissance* (2010), CW, 28.

We may get writers in the future as good as Shakespeare, though they'd be very different writers, but he's one of the writers who represent the limits of imaginative expression. The arts don't improve in the way that the sciences do.

"*Morningside* Interview on Shakespeare" (1987), *Interviews with Northrop Frye* (2008), CW, 24.

His chief motive in writing, apparently, was to make money, which is the best motive for writing yet discovered, as it creates exactly the right blend of detachment and concern.

"*A Natural Perspective*: The Development of Shakespearean Comedy and Romance: II, Making Nature Afraid" (1963), *Northrop Frye's Writings on Shakespeare and the Renaissance* (2010), CW, 28.

First, Shakespeare's plays were not so much written as written out. What the hell was the greatest creative mind of modern times doing with the first 20-odd years of his life? If he'd been a saint instead of a genius we'd have had all sorts of stories about how he refused his mother's breast the day he was born and sucked a bottle of ink instead. He was obviously thinking of what he would write.

Entry, Notebook 8 (1946–58), *Northrop Frye's Notebooks on Renaissance Literature* (2006), CW, 20.

The purpose of reading a Shakespeare play in high school is not to know more about Shakespeare, but to drop a seed of great vision into the mind in the hope of stimulating the growth of that mind as a whole.

"Education and the Humanities" (1947), *Northrop Frye's Writings on Education* (2001), CW, 7.

I think Shakespeare dreamed his plays: I find no evidence that he did anything but hold the nozzle of the hose, so to speak. I picture him as vaguely bewildered & irritated by his own genius, perhaps frightened by it into comporting his conscious life in a deliberately trivial manner.

Entry, 3 Jan. 1949, 26, *The Diaries of Northrop Frye: 1942–1955* (2001), CW, 8.

Our twentieth-century understanding of Shakespeare is quite different from the Elizabethan understanding of Shakespeare, and if

there is one thing certain about the body of Shakespearean criticism in the twentieth century, it is that Shakespeare himself would have found it unintelligible.
> "The Teacher's Source of Authority" (1978), *Northrop Frye's Writings on Education* (2001), CW, 7.

As for Shakespeare, he clearly understood everything, even if he doesn't say everything.
> Entry, Notebook 12 (1968–70), 45, *The "Third Book" Notebooks of Northrop Frye, 1964–1972: The Critical Comedy* (2002), CW, 9.

I once heard a speaker recommending Shakespeare as a poet who said profound things about life, but this was the kind of poetry he liked, and I couldn't help noticing that all his quotations were from Polonius and Iago.
> "Culture and the National Will" (1957), *Northrop Frye on Canada* (2003), CW, 12.

The place where the greatest fusions of words have occurred in English was in the mind of Shakespeare, and Shakespeare, as a personality, was so self-effacing that he has irritated some people into a frenzy of trying to prove that he never existed.
> "Humanities in a New World" (1958), *Northrop Frye's Writings on Education* (2001), CW, 7.

Shakespeare survives not as a man, but as a book of plays.
> "Education and the Humanities" (1947), *Northrop Frye's Writings on Education* (2001), CW, 7.

Identifying the Mr. W.H. connected with Shakespeare's sonnets with Southampton or Pembroke or Willie Hughes (Oscar Wilde's contribution) or what not is an activity very little, if at all, more culturally productive than identifying Shakespeare himself with Bacon or Oxford.
> "Tradition and Change in the Theory of Criticism" (1969), *Northrop Frye on Literature and Society, 1936–1989: Unpublished Papers* (2002), CW, 10.

The Winter's Tale has got to be the profoundest stage play ever written.
> Entry, Notes 54-5 (1976), 62, *Northrop Frye's Notebooks and Lectures on the Bible and Other Religious Texts* (2003), CW, 13.

About all that one can get out of the sonnets, considered as transcripts of experience, is the reflection that pederastic infatuations with beautiful and stupid boys are probably very bad for practising dramatists.
> "How True a Twain" (1962), *Northrop Frye's Writings on Shakespeare and the Renaissance* (2010), CW, 28.

Any critic of Shakespeare's sonnets will, to some extent, tell the world more about his own critical limitations than about his subject; and if he starts out with very marked limitations, the clear surface of the sonnets will faithfully reflect them.
> "How True a Twain" (1962), *Northrop Frye's Writings on Shakespeare and the Renaissance* (2010), CW, 28.

SHAW, GEORGE BERNARD

I read all of Shaw at fifteen and he turned me from a precocious child into an adolescent fool. Therefore he has had far more influence on me than any other writer.
> "NF to HK," 28 May 1933, *The Correspondence of Northrop Frye and Helen Kemp, 1932–1939* (1996), CW, 1.

The Fabian Society, when Bernard Shaw first joined it, was a group esoteric enough to satisfy Yeats himself: after Fabian socialism became a mass movement, Shaw turned into what became at length unmistakably a frustrated royalist.
> "First Essay: Historical Criticism: Theory of Modes" (1957), *Anatomy of Criticism: Four Essays* (2006), CW, 22.

SHE

Whereas *She* is a very serious book: it has to be read with great concentration, noting all the archetypes, the images, the aphorisms, the plot devices, in their different contexts.
> Entry, "Work in Progress" (1972), 20, contrasting H. Rider Haggard's novel *She* with Wyndham Lewis' *Apes of God*, *The "Third Book" Notebooks of Northrop Frye, 1964–1972: The Critical Comedy* (2002), CW, 9.

SHEEP

Perhaps the use of this particular convention is due to the fact that, being stupid, affectionate, gregarious, and easily stampeded, the societies formed by sheep are most like human ones.

"Third Essay: Archetypal Criticism: Theory of Myths" (1957), *Anatomy of Criticism: Four Essays* (2006), CW, 22.

SHERBROOKE, QUE.

I got all my own archetypes in the city of Sherbrooke, where I spent the first five years of my life, and heaven, for example, is still the other side of the St. Francis River, which goes up on a hill.

"Science Policy and the Quality of Life" (1972), *Interviews with Northrop Frye* (2008), CW, 24.

SILENCE

In a world given over to obsessive utterance, a world of television and radio and shouting dictators and tape recorders and beeping space ships, to restore silence is the role of serious writing.

"The Nightmare Life in Death" (1960), *Northrop Frye on Twentieth-Century Literature* (2010), CW, 29.

The silence of the eternal spaces remained at the bottom of the Canadian psyche for a long time, and in many respects is still there.

"Speech at the New Canadian Embassy, Washington" (1989), *Northrop Frye on Canada* (2003), CW, 12.

In all my life I've never known an instant of real silence. That, of course, is because I've never gone through the years of discipline and practice in meditation.

Entry, Notebook 44 (1986–91), 448, *Northrop Frye's Late Notebooks, 1982–1990: Architecture of the Spiritual World* (2000), CW, 5.

SIMILE

The teacher needs to have the principle clearly in his mind that it is the function of literature to assimilate the natural world to the human world, chiefly through the associations of analogy and identity, the two modes of thought that reappear in literature as simile and metaphor.

"Elementary Teaching and Elemental Scholarship" (1963), *Northrop Frye's Writings on Education* (2001), CW, 7.

A world of total simile, where everything was like everything else, would be a world of total monotony; a world of total metaphor, where everything is identified as itself and with everything else, would be a world where subject and object, reality and mental organization of reality, are one.

"The Realistic Oriole: A Study of Wallace Stevens" (1957), *Northrop Frye on Twentieth-Century Literature* (2010), CW, 29.

SIN

The word sin has no meaning outside a religious context, of course; but it's a long time before the word crime has any meaning at all apart from sin.

"Notes for 'Crime and Sin in the Bible'" (1986), 4, *Northrop Frye's Fiction and Miscellaneous Writings* (2007), CW, 25.

Original sin is not being born with the capacity to murder and rape. Original sin is essentially inertia, the feeling of helplessness — that beyond a certain point we can't go.

"The Survival of Eros in Poetry" (1983), *"The Secular Scripture" and Other Writings on Critical Theory, 1976–1991* (2006), CW, 18.

I manage to keep my pride, wrath, envy, avarice, gluttony and lechery within moral bounds to some extent: the great enemy is inertia.

Entry, 1 Jan. 1952, 3, *The Diaries of Northrop Frye: 1942–1955* (2001), CW, 8.

SLAVERY

One sometimes gets the impression that the audience of Plautus and Terence would have guffawed uproariously all through the Passion. We may ascribe this to the brutality of a slave society....

"Third Essay: Archetypal Criticism: Theory of Myths" (1957), *Anatomy of Criticism: Four Essays* (2006), CW, 22.

When a master owns a slave he gets taken over by the psychology of slavery & becomes the slave of his slaves. Whatever you have sooner or later has you.

> Entry, Notebook 21 (1969–76), 524, *Northrop Frye's Notebooks and Lectures on the Bible and Other Religious Texts* (2003), CW, 13.

SLEEP

... every sleep is a harrowing of hell. It buries some memories and rearranges others, in the interest of one's picture of oneself. The creative person is the one who has some power to resurrect suppressed memories.

> Entry, Notes 54-5 (1976), 20, *Northrop Frye's Notebooks and Lectures on the Bible and Other Religious Texts* (2003), CW, 13.

It is good to sleep deeply, for obvious reasons; but I think it is good to sleep lightly too, so that the suggestions of the unconscious can come more readily into the consciousness, and be held there by the memory.

> Entry, Notebook 3 (1946–48), 96, *Northrop Frye's Notebooks and Lectures on the Bible and Other Religious Texts* (2003), CW, 13.

Nothing vital rests, not even the brain — least of all the brain. Animals sleep lightly because they never really wake up. No, I think sleep is the key to memory, the continuity of consciousness. If I can't sleep, thoughts race through my head in a stream or else circle around one point — often an anxiety point. Sleep digests the stream of impressions & transforms them into a mental circulation of ideas: the myths of dreams are the chyle of sense experience.

> Entry, Notebook 3 (1946–48), 141, *Northrop Frye's Notebooks and Lectures on the Bible and Other Religious Texts* (2003), CW, 13.

I wonder if sleeping should be conceived, not as rest at the end of the day, but as leisure at the beginning of it?

> Entry, 12 Feb. 1950, 110, *The Diaries of Northrop Frye: 1942–1955* (2001), CW, 8.

SLOGANS

A society entirely controlled by their slogans and exhortations would be introverted, because nobody would be saying anything: there would only be echo, and Echo was the mistress of Narcissus.

> *The Modern Century* (1967), *Northrop Frye on Modern Culture* (2003), CW, 11.

SLOVENIA

I thought to myself that this is typical of what a culture is: it is the indestructible core of a human society, so far as it is a human society and not a mere aggregate of atoms in a human mass.

> "The Cultural Development of Canada" (1990), thoughts on speaking in Ljubljana, *Northrop Frye on Canada* (2003), CW, 12.

SNOW

The philosopher who said that dirt is matter in the wrong place did not make a very exhaustive analysis: the snow that falls on one's sidewalk in winter is matter in the wrong place, but the difference between clean and dirty snow is something else again.

> "Third Variation: The Cave," *Words with Power: Being a Second Study of "The Bible and Literature"* (2008), CW, 26.

There is no reason why we should feel that a snowflake has an exquisite and subtle design: we just do, and there is a feeling of wonder and mystery about this that mathematical explanations of the forming of crystals do not affect: they are made in a different area.

> "Literature as a Critique of Pure Reason" (1982), *"The Secular Scripture" and Other Writings on Critical Theory, 1976–1991* (2006), CW, 18.

We say that a snowflake has a symmetrical design, not because the snowflake has consciously produced it, but because we can see the design. We see that the snowflake has achieved something of which we alone can see the form, and the form of the snowflake is therefore a human form.

> "Part One: The Argument," *Fearful Symmetry: A Study of William Blake* (1947, 2004), CW, 14.

SOCIAL CONTRACT

We are all born under a social contract; we belong to something before we are anything, and that is the source of all the "de facto" authority which exists in a context of subordination.

> "The Teacher's Source of Authority" (1978), *Northrop Frye's Writings on Education* (2001), CW, 7.

The social contract, which from a distance seems a reasonable effort of cooperation, looks closer up like an armed truce founded on passion, in which the real purpose of law is to defend by force what has been snatched in self-will.
> "Blake's Treatment of the Archetype" (1950), *Northrop Frye on Milton and Blake* (2005), CW, 16.

I mean that genuine society preserves the continuity of the dead, the living, and the unborn, the memory of the past, the reality of the present, and the anticipation of the future which is the one unbreakable social contract.
> "The Instruments of Mental Production" (1966), *Northrop Frye's Writings on Education* (2001), CW, 7.

SOCIAL SCIENCES
The social sciences, which are very largely twentieth-century in origin, are entirely founded on the need to observe the observer. I think of criticism as ultimately a form of social science.
> "Scientist and Artist" (1981), *Interviews with Northrop Frye* (2008), CW, 24.

The social sciences are so new, and so anxious to be sciences, that they are largely unaware of how naive their assumptions are, and of the extent to which they are forming a patristic commentary on the above oracles.
> "Trends in Modern Culture" (1952), referring to the cultural consequences of Deism, *Northrop Frye on Modern Culture* (2003), CW, 11.

SOCIAL VISION
The basis of my approach, as a teacher of the humanities, has always been that we participate in society by means of our imagination or the quality of our social vision, and that training the imagination and clarifying the social vision are the only ways of developing citizens capable of taking part in a society as complicated as ours.
> "The View from Here" (1980), *Northrop Frye's Writings on Education* (2001), CW, 7.

But behind these private possessions lies a social possession, a vision of life that we share with others. This shared vision is the total form of art, man's vision of a human world, to which every individual work of art belongs.
> "Humanities in a New World" (1958), *Northrop Frye's Writings on Education* (2001), CW, 7.

The fundamental job of the imagination in ordinary life, then, is to produce, out of the society we have to live in, a vision of the society we want to live in.
> *The Educated Imagination* (1963), *"The Educated Imagination" and Other Writings on Critical Theory, 1933–1963* (2006), CW, 21.

Beyond any personal convictions, however, there is the vision of society which creates and shapes those convictions. This image is something that literature is meant to express, because social vision is derived from the imagination and the imagination is what is fundamental in literature.
> "The Wisdom of the Reader" (1979), *Interviews with Northrop Frye* (2008), CW, 24.

It is obvious that the basis of the world we want to live in is mythological. That is, the world we construct is built to the model of a common social vision produced by the imagination.
> "The Times of the Signs," (1974), *"The Critical Path" and Other Writings on Critical Theory, 1963–1975* (2009), CW, 27.

SOCIAL WORK
I can't imagine a social worker, for example, devoting herself to such a profession unless she had in her mind, at some level of consciousness, a vision of a better society than the one she's actually engaged with day after day.
> "Back to the Garden" (1982), *Interviews with Northrop Frye* (2008), CW, 24.

SOCIALISM
I think with the liberals that Socialism, as it is bound to develop historically, is an impracticable remedy, not because it is impracticable — it is inevitable — but because it is not a remedy.
> "NF to HK," 4 Sep. 1933, *The Correspondence of Northrop Frye and Helen Kemp, 1932–1939* (1996), CW, 1.

At present we have capitalist and socialist societies, but the old notion of socialism as the fulfilment of capitalism, so sacrosanct in my youth, I don't believe in now. I think socialism as it got established was only the antithesis of capitalism, and the fulfilment is ahead of us. The core of the fulfilment is what we call democracy, which I see, at least at present, as a tension between politico-economic and cultural rhythms.

> Entry, Notes 52 (1982–90), 675, *Northrop Frye's Late Notebooks, 1982–1990: Architecture of the Spiritual World* (2000), CW, 6.

The only possible economic alternative to capitalism, we feel, is socialism, but if capitalism is a destroyer, socialism is even more of one, because more committed to technology.

> "Canada: New World Without Revolution" (1975), *Northrop Frye on Canada* (2003), CW, 12.

SOCIETY

There are three confrontations with society in the West: the confrontation of love, or the crucifixion of Christ; the confrontation of wisdom, or the death of Socrates; the confrontation of power, or the assassination of Caesar.

> Entry, Notebook 2 (after 1968), 12, *Northrop Frye's Fiction and Miscellaneous Writings* (2007), CW, 25.

... it is possible for a myth to take over a whole society, so that that society may act out its life within a continuous mythology.

> "Literature and Society" (1968), *"The Critical Path" and Other Writings on Critical Theory, 1963–1975* (2009), CW, 27.

The imagination, which conceives the forms of human society, is the source of the power to change that society.

> *The Critical Path: An Essay on the Social Context of Literary Criticism* (1971), *"The Critical Path" and Other Writings on Critical Theory, 1963–1975* (2009), CW, 27.

Everything that goes on in a society is also going on inside the individual.

> "The Limits of Dialogue" (1969), *Interviews with Northrop Frye* (2008), CW, 24.

But now we have a society which is not just post-literate but post-electronic, & heading straight for being post-communicative. The entertaining is becoming the boring, because people build up resistance to being treated passively.

> Entry, Notebook 11f (1969–70), 108, *Northrop Frye's Notebooks and Lectures on the Bible and Other Religious Texts* (2003), CW, 13.

The open society thus has an open mythology; the closed society has a controlling myth from which all scholarship is assumed to be logically derived.

> "The Knowledge of Good and Evil" (1966), *Northrop Frye's Writings on Education* (2001), CW, 7.

But as long as we accept, even unconsciously, a vision of society in which the machinery of production assumes an overwhelming and inescapable urgency, our defences of the liberal arts and sciences will continue to have a panic-stricken tone.

> "The Instruments of Mental Production" (1966), *Northrop Frye's Writings on Education* (2001), CW, 7.

The degenerating of society begins with the sacrifice of primary concerns to the secondary concerns of an ideology. Once a society is at this point it finds that it cannot maintain a consistent ideology either, but breaks down into simple brutality and barbarism. The final stage is a genocide that eventually turns on itself.

> "Fourth Variation: The Furnace," *Words with Power: Being a Second Study of "The Bible and Literature"* (1990), CW, 26.

Anybody who's lived as long as I have can't possibly believe that any society is going to do anything sensible for more than the time it takes to break a New Year's resolution.

> Entry, Notes 53 (1989–90), 39, *Northrop Frye's Late Notebooks, 1982–1990: Architecture of the Spiritual World* (2000), CW, 6.

Not too long ago, the King of England was the Emperor of India; Nazi Germany ruled Europe from the Atlantic to the Volga; China was a bourgeois friend, Japan a totalitarian enemy, and so on. The moral that one ought to draw from this is that what appears to be real society is not real society at all, but only the transient appearance of society. The permanent form of human society is the form which can only be studied in the arts and the sciences. These are the genuinely organized structures of human civilization.

"The Definition of a University" (1970), *Northrop Frye's Writings on Education* (2001), CW, 7.

If Canada in 1962 is a different society from the Canada of 1942, it can't be real society, but only a temporary appearance of real society.

"The Vocation of Eloquence," *The Educated Imagination* (1963), *"The Educated Imagination" and Other Writings on Critical Theory, 1933–1963* (2006), CW, 21.

But to improve society we must have a standard for improvement, and the only possible standard is that of the permanent values of civilization, the ideals of freedom, wisdom, reason, equality, and co-operation which are true for all countries and for all ages. The place to find these is in the products of civilization which are of permanent value, that is, the works of the greatest thinkers and artists.

"A Liberal Education" (1945), *Northrop Frye's Writings on Education* (2001), CW, 7.

I think the mob is simply the intensified and the logical form of the adjusted society: the one thing that a mob cannot stand is the individual.

"The Only Genuine Revolution" (1969), *Interviews with Northrop Frye* (2008), CW, 24.

Over a long period, say two centuries or more, no society is respected for anything whatever except the evidences of cultural vitality that it has produced in that time.

"Preface to *On Education*" (1988), *Northrop Frye's Writings on Education* (2001), CW, 7.

Real society, the total body of what humanity has done and can do, is revealed to us only by the arts and sciences; nothing but the imagination can apprehend that reality as a whole, and nothing but literature, in a culture as verbal as ours, can train the imagination to fight for the sanity and the dignity of man.

"Elementary Teaching and Elemental Scholarship" (1963), *Northrop Frye's Writings on Education* (2001), CW, 7.

Painting, music, and architecture, no less than literature, reflect an anonymous and cold-blooded society, a society without much respect for personality and without much tolerance for difference in opinion, a society full of slickness, smugness, and spiritual inanity.

"Academy without Walls" (1961), *Northrop Frye on Modern Culture* (2003), CW, 11.

Behind the transient appearance of society are the permanent realities of the arts and sciences which education leads us to. It is obvious, therefore, that the social contract has to be supplemented by an educational contract.

"The Teacher's Source of Authority" (1978), *Northrop Frye's Writings on Education* (2001), CW, 7.

SOCIOLOGY

You can dither around with silly little courses in sociology, but the minute you start to take it seriously you're involved in evaluating the quality of legislation.

Entry, 4 Jun. 1950, 394, *The Diaries of Northrop Frye: 1942–1955* (2001), CW, 8.

SOCRATES

Socrates remains the archetypal teacher, and the modern teacher finds that Socrates' irony is equally essential to him.

"The Beginning of the Word" (1980), *Northrop Frye's Writings on Education* (2001), CW, 7.

And, however breath-taking the myths and visions that we see on the way, over it all hangs the greater irony of the eventual martyrdom of Socrates, the fact that society as a whole can only absorb his influence by killing him.

"The Ethics of Change: The Role of the University" (1968), *Northrop Frye's Writings on Education* (2001), CW, 7.

SODOM & GOMORRAH

The Bible tell us that ten righteous men would have saved Sodom from destruction [Genesis 18:32]. We need a new slogan for education: how about "Education for Gomorrah"?

> "A Liberal Education" (1945), *Northrop Frye's Writings on Education* (2001), CW, 7.

SOLEMNITY

Being serious, of course, has nothing to do with being solemn: many solemn people are quite superficial.

> "The Writer as Prophet: Milton, Blake, Swift, Shaw" (1950), referring specifically to G.B. Shaw, *Northrop Frye on Literature and Society, 1936–1989: Unpublished Papers* (2002), CW, 10.

SOUL & SPIRIT

The soul goes on adventures; the spirit has work to do.

> Entry, Notebook 11e (1978), 57, *Northrop Frye's Notebooks and Lectures on the Bible and Other Religious Texts* (2003), CW, 13.

SPACE & TIME

Metaphor arrests space, just as myth arrests time.

> Entry, Notebook 27 (1986), 122, *Northrop Frye's Late Notebooks, 1982–1990: Architecture of the Spiritual World* (2000), CW, 5.

SPAIN

Such a question as, Why does everything in Spain look Spanish? is one of those apparently idiotic questions that opens up quite unexpected areas of vision.

> "Spirit and Symbol," *Words with Power: Being a Second Study of "The Bible and Literature"* (2008), CW, 26.

SPANISH ARMADA

In Christian centuries the action of Providence, as a divine force intervening in human affairs, can be seen more clearly when you win: thus the storm that destroyed the Spanish Armada was providential to the English, but a natural event to the Spaniards.

> "History and Myth in the Bible" (1975), *Northrop Frye on Religion* (2000), CW, 4.

SPECULATION

A certain amount of free, in the sense of irresponsible, speculation is a good thing, because it's part of the wise process of letting things come & not forcing or cramping or repressing them. That's what Goethe told Schiller, anyway.

> Entry, Notebook 3 (1946–48), *Northrop Frye Newsletter*, Fall 2000.

SPEECH

There is some shame attached to speaking the language articulately, which is a very deep-rooted social problem.

> "Love of Learning" (1987), *Interviews with Northrop Frye* (2008), CW, 24.

Ordinary speech is concerned mainly with putting into words what is loosely called the stream of consciousness: the daydreaming, remembering, worrying, associating, brooding, and mooning that continually flows through the mind and which we often speak of, even more loosely, as thought.

> "The Well-Tempered Critic (I)" (1961), *"The Educated Imagination" and Other Writings on Critical Theory, 1933–1963* (2006), CW, 21.

And as wisdom and prophecy approach each other, it becomes clear that there is a point where they meet and become the same thing, the point where there is no longer any wise man or any prophet, but simply the word itself, a power of speech articulating itself independently of the speaker's ego.

> "Teaching the Humanities Today" (1977), *Northrop Frye's Writings on Education* (2001), CW, 7.

You can't cultivate speech, beyond a certain point, unless you have something to say, and the basis of what you have to say is your vision of society.

> *The Educated Imagination* (1963), *"The Educated Imagination" and Other Writings on Critical Theory, 1933–1963* (2006), CW, 21.

SPEECH, AMERICAN

In other words, the Americans have already begun to pronounce words like house, cow and about as though they were lyrical poems composed by an amorous tomcat.

"Haliburton: Mask and Ego" (1962), discussing the speech-patterns of T.C. Haliburton's character Sam Slick in the 1830s, *Northrop Frye on Canada* (2003), CW, 12.

SPEECH, CANADIAN

... where Canadians got the monotone honk that you're listening to now I don't know — probably from the Canada goose.
> "Verticals of Adam," referring to his delivery over radio of the Massey Lectures, *The Educated Imagination* (1963), *"The Educated Imagination" and Other Writings on Critical Theory, 1933–1963* (2006), CW, 21.

I can't understand the superstitious & barbaric notion in this country that it's sissified to cultivate an accent. The idea that correct & well-modulated speech is a fundamental cornerstone of culture doesn't occur to my students, many of whom make noises like the cry of the great bronze grackle in the mating season.
> Entry, 6 Sep. 1942, 98, *The Diaries of Northrop Frye: 1942–1955* (2001), CW, 8.

To the average Canadian or American, cultivating an accent means cultivating an English accent, and anyone who does that is a sissy, a snob, and a hypocrite. The fact that it is far better to cultivate an English accent than not to cultivate an accent at all is quite lost on him.
> "Reflections at a Movie" (1942), *Northrop Frye on Modern Culture* (2003), CW, 11.

SPEECH, FREE

The area of ordinary speech, as I see it, is a battleground between two forms of social speech, the speech of a mob and the speech of a free society.... There can be no free speech in a mob: free speech is one thing a mob can't stand.
> "The Vocation of Eloquence," *The Educated Imagination* (1963), *"The Educated Imagination" and Other Writings on Critical Theory, 1933–1963* (2006), CW, 21.

SPEECHES

There is a story, which I understand to be true, of a late colleague of mine, a professor of English who was private secretary to Prime Minister Mackenzie King during the war. In working on King's speeches, he inserted various quotations from Canadian poets, English and French, touched up clichés with a few metaphors, rounded out stock formulas with more concrete and lively language. These were regularly and routinely struck out. Eventually, the Prime Minister said: "Professor, the public memory for a picturesque phrase is very retentive."
> "Authority of Learning" (1984), *Northrop Frye's Writings on Education* (2001), CW, 7.

SPENGLER, OSWALD

But his thesis has bitten deeply into us: we are all Spenglerian to some extent, and if the enemy has any ammunition that we can capture, we should fire it back at the enemy.
> "Toynbee and Spengler" (1947), referring to the organic view expressed in Spengler's opus *The Decline of the West*, *Northrop Frye on Modern Culture* (2003), CW, 11.

The Decline of the West is one of those books that have always been utterly refuted last Tuesday, but somehow won't go away. Spengler's book is a vision rather than a theory or a philosophy, and a vision of haunting imaginative power. Its truth is the truth of poetry or prophecy, not of science.
> "Oswald Spengler" (1955), *Northrop Frye on Modern Culture* (2003), CW, 11.

SPENSER, EDMUND

Spencer got hold of a thoroughly bad idea in this canto, and about the best thing one can say of it is that whatever else one may say of Spenser, he is no quitter.
> Entry, Notebook 43 (1949–50), referring to a passage in Book 4, Canto 3, of *The Faerie Queene*, *Northrop Frye's Notebooks on Renaissance Literature* (2006), CW, 20.

SPHINX

The sphinx would be a good emblem for Canada itself, put together in defiance of all natural law, yet amazingly solid and permanent, with dominionprovincial relations forming its unsolved riddle and its inscrutable smile.

"By Liberal Things" (1959), *Northrop Frye's Writings on Education* (2001), CW, 7.

SPIRIT

But as the subject-object cleavage becomes increasingly unsatisfactory, subject and object merge in an intermediate verbal world, where a Word not our own, though also our own, proclaims and a Spirit not our own, though also our own, responds. We capitalize these terms for the same reason that we capitalize other people's names.

"Spirit and Symbol," *Words with Power: Being a Second Study of "The Bible and Literature"* (2008), CW, 26.

If the world of the Spirit were outside us only, it could not be known; if it were inside us only, it could not be real. Like the air, it keeps continually crossing the middle partition between without and within.

"To Come to Light" (1988), *Northrop Frye on Religion* (1999), CW, 4.

If the spirit of man and the spirit of God inhabit the same world, that fact is more important than the theological relation between them.

The Double Vision (1991), *Northrop Frye on Religion* (2000), CW, 4.

The Spirit of the Bible is to the conscious world what the air is to the physical world. In the physical world, the things we see are visible only because the air is invisible. For the corresponding reason, the Spirit has to be invisible to consciousness, but is none the less a personal presence, personal as we are, present as everything around us is.

"To Come to Light" (1988), *Northrop Frye on Religion* (1999), CW, 4.

SPIRITS

I've been wondering, partly as a result of a dream I had, whether our memories & impressions of other people don't become to some degree autonomous after those people die. Maybe the spirits that turn up at séances are autonomous projections of this sort....

Entry, Notebook 24 (1970–72), 234, *The "Third Book" Notebooks of Northrop Frye, 1964–1972: The Critical Comedy* (2002), CW, 9.

It would be interesting to know if a spirit came to a séance who was the spirit of someone who, unknown to the enquirer, was still alive. If this has never happened, the hypothesis is still possible, but indicates some essential but hidden link with the living person.

Entry, Notebook 24 (1970–72), 234, *The "Third Book" Notebooks of Northrop Frye, 1964–1972: The Critical Comedy* (2002), CW, 9.

Elemental spirits are the internalized images of a visible numinous nature: they are controlled by a magician's aural formulas.

Entry, Notebook 24 (1970–72), 178, *The "Third Book" Notebooks of Northrop Frye, 1964–1972: The Critical Comedy* (2002), CW, 9.

Most of the occult mafia of our time seem to think that getting taken over by another spirit is always good. (Others may think it always bad, but they're out of fashion.)

Entry, Notebook 11b (late 1980), 26, *Northrop Frye's Notebooks and Lectures on the Bible and Other Religious Texts* (2003), CW, 13.

SPIRITUALITY

The beginning of spiritual life is a second birth; it's also a preliminary death, a cutting off of the world in search of one's real source.

Entry, Notes 53 (1989–90), 48, *Northrop Frye's Late Notebooks, 1982–1990: Architecture of the Spiritual World* (2000), CW, 6.

If the word "spiritual" has any function for you — and even Marx uses it — your God is alive, & you don't have to think in such stupid terms as "*a* God."

Entry, Notebook 50 (1987–90), 365, *Northrop Frye's Late Notebooks, 1982–1990: Architecture of the Spiritual World* (2000), CW, 5.

The spiritual world is a *bodily* world, not a metaphysical one. It's most easily seen in the arts, which em*body* the spiritual vision of a people.

Entry, Notebook 24 (1970–72), 232, *The "Third Book" Notebooks of Northrop Frye, 1964–1972: The Critical Comedy* (2002), CW, 9.

It is not hard to understand that spiritual may be used to mean the highest intensity of consciousness.

"Spirit and Symbol," *Words with Power: Being a Second Study of "The Bible and Literature"* (2008), CW, 26.

SPONSORSHIP
The commercial sponsorship of radio programs (partly counteracted in Canada by a publicly owned broadcasting commission) and the complete commercialization of the Hollywood film industry are alike fatal to independent and original creative effort.

"The Church and Modern Culture" (1950), *Northrop Frye on Modern Culture* (2003), CW, 11.

SQUARE
Around 1900 the word "square" was a general term of approval: today it means something we are trying to get away from.

"National Consciousness in Canadian Culture" (1976), *Northrop Frye on Canada* (2003), CW, 12.

STAGE
The stage is all the world, and human life has become what the stage is: a place where illusion is reality, with a procession of actors waiting to be applauded, not for what they have been or done, but for what they have remembered in time to say.

"The Stage Is All the World" (1985), *Northrop Frye's Writings on Shakespeare and the Renaissance* (2010), CW, 28.

STALIN, JOSEPH
Speaking of Marxist dialectic incarnations, the morning paper brought out its second-coming headlines to announce that Stalin was dying. I don't suppose even we expected him to live forever, though whenever we believe someone to be demonic something of the immortality of the devil gets attached to him.

Entry, 3 Mar. 1953, 13, *Diaries of Northrop Frye: 1942–1955* (2001), CW, 8.

STARS
The stars in their courses are all that is now left of the order of nature as God originally designed it: the earthly paradise for man was lost with the fall of Adam.

"The Top of the Tower" (1969), *Northrop Frye on Twentieth-Century Literature* (2010), CW, 29.

STATESMANSHIP
The more important the statesman's position, the more exclusively he is devoted to reconciliation, to containing conflict within and lessening tension without.

"Foreword to *The Prospect of Change*" (1965), *Northrop Frye on Canada* (2003), CW, 12.

STATISTICS
Hence statistical trends can achieve so high a form of predictability: the *mass* tendency approximates the mechanical, whereas each individual is a variant.

Entry, Notebook 48 (1993), 18, *Northrop Frye's Late Notebooks, 1982–1990: Architecture of the Spiritual World* (2000), CW, 6.

STEIN, GERTRUDE
If Stein is anything, she is demotic — the absolute lack of complication in her style, the hypnotic effect of her repetitions, produce a startlingly vivid effect of colloquial vigour, when properly handled (as it is sometimes, more often perhaps by her imitators than by her).

"The Diatribes of Wyndham Lewis: A Study in Prose Satire" (1936), *Northrop Frye's Student Essays, 1932–1938* (1997), CW, 3.

STEVENS, WALLACE
Stevens saw that I was embarrassed, so he put me at ease by asking about various stockbrokers and insurance people in Toronto, whom he had met the last time he had visited Toronto, which was in 1908.

"Making the Revolutionary Act New" (1983), referring to meeting the poet Wallace Stevens after he delivered his paper "Imagination as Value" at the English Institute in New York City in 1948, a paper Frye strained to hear because of extraneous noises, *Interviews with Northrop Frye* (2008), CW, 24.

STONES
They're not continuous but they're contiguous. That is, each person is a stone in himself but he's part of the building.

"Two Heretics: Milton and Melville" (1970), referring to the temple of God in Milton's *Areopagitica*, *Interviews with Northrop Frye* (2008), CW, 24.

STORIES
But this is mostly illusion: what man does is what he has done from the dawn of consciousness: make up stories. All ideologies are derived from stories or story patterns.
"The Stage Is All the World" (1985), distinguishing between mythology and ideology, *Northrop Frye's Writings on Shakespeare and the Renaissance* (2010), CW, 28.

Stories distort events, but every story tells the truth about itself as a story, & some truth about its teller.
Entry, Notebook 10 (before 1977), 109, *Northrop Frye's Notebooks on Romance* (2004), CW, 15.

Writers of stories, however literary, do not invent their stories even when they think they do: they inherit them.
"The Bride from the Strange Land" (1985), *Northrop Frye on Religion* (2000), CW, 4.

The circle of stories (or ocean of story, as it is called in India) is there to keep us continually expanding and reshaping that vision. It exists for us; it exists for itself; perhaps we may even feel, for a few moments in our lives, that it really is ourselves on an infinite plane.
"On Teaching Literature" (1972), *Northrop Frye's Writings on Education* (2001), CW, 7.

All stories begin in the middle, because it's impossible to think of a beginning of time.
Entry, Notes 52 (1982–90), 46, *Northrop Frye's Late Notebooks, 1982–1990: Architecture of the Spiritual World* (2000), CW, 6.

All stories in literature are developments of fundamental fictional shapes which can be studied most clearly in myths and folk tales.
"The Developing Imagination" (1962), *Northrop Frye's Writings on Education* (2001), CW, 7.

There's only one story — the story of your life.
Remark made at St-Jovite, Que., 12 May 1964, influencing the myth of the Minotaur for the NFB's Labyrinth pavilion at Expo 67, as recorded by Tom Daly and quoted by D.B. Jones in *The Best Butler in the Business* (1996).

The central story of all literature is the loss and regaining of *identity*.
"On Teaching Literature" (1972), *Northrop Frye's Writings on Education* (2001), CW, 7.

STRATFORD, ONT.
In 1952 some people in a small town in Ontario, simply because it was called Stratford, decided to put on some Shakespeare, and a Shakespeare festival began there the next year.
"Culture as Interpenetration" (1977), *Northrop Frye on Canada* (2003), CW, 12.

A random example is calling Shakespeare the "swan of Avon" — he was called that by Ben Jonson. The town of Stratford, Ontario, keeps swans in its river partly as a literary allusion.
"The Keys to Dreamland," *The Educated Imagination* (1963), *"The Educated Imagination" and Other Writings on Critical Theory, 1933–1963* (2006), CW, 21.

STRUCTURALISM
It seems to be an occupational disease among the French to add the suffix "ism" to everything they are interested in. I think structure is an essential element of literature; I am well aware that this is really a metaphor from architecture, and I do not for the life of me see why one cannot be interested in structure without becoming a "structuralist." I am interested in my own existence too, but I don't necessarily have to be an existentialist.
"The Critical Path" (1979), *Interviews with Northrop Frye* (2008), CW, 24.

The word "Structuralism" was a word that I was not aware of before I wrote the *Anatomy*. Later, they told me that I had in fact written a work about Structuralism.
"Schools of Criticism (III)" (1990), *Interviews with Northrop Frye* (2008), CW, 24.

STRUCTURE
Yet we have been saying all through this paper that the primary axiom of critical procedure is: Go for the structure, not for the content. This must be the invariable attitude of every genuine critic, whether he is teaching *Paradise Lost* in a church college or on a witness stand testifying to the merits of *Lady Chatterley's Lover*.

"Literary Criticism" (1963), *"The Critical Path" and Other Writings on Critical Theory, 1963–1975* (2009), CW, 27.

I may work hard enough to weld my books into a narrative unity, but it is possible that many of my readers tend to find their way back to the original aphoristic form, finding me more useful for detached insights than for total structures.
"Response to Papers on 'Northrop Frye and Eighteenth-Century Literature'" (1990), *"The Secular Scripture" and Other Writings on Critical Theory, 1976–1991* (2006), CW, 18.

STUDENTS

There is no irony whatever in saying that the memory of one's experience as a student is more real than the experience itself.
"To Come to Light" (1988), *Northrop Frye on Religion* (1999), CW, 4.

Once a student gets on a self-righteous kick, he becomes utterly impervious to argument because he's still too young and insecure to listen to anything except the applause of his own conscience.
"Northrop Frye in Conversation" (1989), *Interviews with Northrop Frye* (2008), CW, 24.

When I see the almost psychotic state that some of these students have got themselves into, I think of a sentence I once read in a cookbook: "Brains are very perishable, and unless frozen or precooked, should be used as soon as possible."
"Convocation Address: Acadia University" (1969), *Northrop Frye on Literature and Society, 1936–1989: Unpublished Papers* (2002), CW, 10.

Yet it does not matter a tinker's curse what a student thinks and feels about literature until he can think and feel, which is not until he passes the stage of stock response.
"Criticism, Visible and Invisible" (1964), *"The Critical Path" and Other Writings on Critical Theory, 1963–1975* (2009), CW, 27.

I have known a good many mature students, who were as undergraduates exactly what they were going to be forty years later, and a most depressing lot they were.

"The Social Importance of Literature" (1968), *Northrop Frye's Writings on Education* (2001), CW, 7.

In any case no teacher thinks of himself as stuffing information into young people who haven't got any. Students have acquired a large body of verbal experience, of which perhaps one per cent has been derived from anything recognizable as literature.
"Teaching the Humanities Today" (1977), *Northrop Frye's Writings on Education* (2001), CW, 7.

There is nothing much wrong with the fact that most students are conformists, including of course the rebellious students, who are bigoted conformists.
"Address on Receiving the Royal Bank Award" (1978), *Northrop Frye's Writings on Education* (2001), CW, 7.

You are physically and socially mature. You are, of course, intellectually immature. So are we, on the staff; so is everybody. In the intellectual world the only mature people are those who are willing to admit their immaturity.
"Speech at a Freshman Welcome" (1966), *Northrop Frye's Writings on Education* (2001), CW, 7.

On the contrary, I think students are a stabilizing and conservative force in university government, who help to balance the recklessness of the junior faculty and the cynical laissez-faire of the senior professors. But they are around for such a short time, shorter even than the teaching staff who are looking for better jobs elsewhere, or the administrators who are looking for any jobs elsewhere.
"Convocation Address, York University" (1969), *Northrop Frye's Writings on Education* (2001), CW, 7.

Our kids are so immature, and their intellectual and cultural adolescence so artificially delayed, that when they're graduated they keep hanging around the graduate school because they don't know how to graduate mentally. And as their social conscience is being outraged and they haven't any vocation for the profession, they get pretty neurotic.

Entry, 14 Mar. 1952, 178 *The Diaries of Northrop Frye: 1942–1955* (2001), CW, 8.

For what the student unrest specifically appears to be is partly what it is: a highly contagious epidemic of hysteria that simply has to be lived through until it stops. My guess is that it will end as suddenly as it began, with nothing much accomplished or permanently changed.

"Convocation Address: Acadia University" (1969), *Northrop Frye on Literature and Society, 1936–1989: Unpublished Papers* (2002), CW, 10.

Whatever you think you think, there's more growing ahead of you; and when you're involved in a process that can never stop, you may begin to wonder what words like "infinite" really mean.

"The Principal's Message" (1963), *Northrop Frye's Writings on Education* (2001), CW, 7.

STYLE

Students of English are often urged, in Romantic fashion, to use as many short words of native origin as possible, on the ground that they make one's vocabulary concrete, but a style founded on simple native words can be the most artificial of all styles.

"Fourth Essay: Rhetorical Criticism: Theory of Genres" (1957), *Anatomy of Criticism: Four Essays* (2006), CW, 22.

Yet the ability to speak in a relaxed, colloquial, associative rhythm, recognizably close to prose, that is, a lucid but articulate speaking style, is the foundation of all good writing: in fact it is the foundation of any cultivated life.

"The Beginning of the Word" (1980), *Northrop Frye's Writings on Education* (2001), CW, 7.

I note a tendency to the overuse of the colon in my writing: I must try more — uh — dashes.

Entry, 13 Mar. 1950, 186, *The Diaries of Northrop Frye: 1942–1955* (2001), CW, 8.

But do please remember that good writing is *not* a product of style. It always has style, but *style is the result of form* and organization. That is why trying to acquire a style is chasing a shadow and waste of time, while trying to organize and arrange material is the chief job of every artist.

"NF to HK," 22 Jun. 1934, *The Correspondence of Northrop Frye and Helen Kemp, 1932–1939* (1996), CW, 1.

What I call the Gertrude Stein style, of hypnotic repetitiveness, is the style of discovery and of teaching. It's the style of the First Epistle of John & of most mystical literature — Boehme, for instance — and of my lecturing at its best.

Entry, 4 Mar. 1952, 154, *The Diaries of Northrop Frye: 1942–1955* (2001), CW, 8.

SUB-LITERARY WORLD

All of us, even the most highbrow, spend much time in the sub-literary world; all of us derive many surreptitious pleasures from it; but this world is, from the point of view of actual literature, mainly a babbling chaos, waiting for the creative word to brood over it and bring it to literary life.

"Nature and Homer" (1958), *"The Educated Imagination" and Other Writings on Critical Theory, 1933–1963* (2006), CW, 21.

SUBJECT

We think of the "sub"ject as being under the objective, including the objective text, but the subject is metaphorically on top.

Entry, Notebook 44 (1986–91), 546, *Northrop Frye's Late Notebooks, 1982–1990: Architecture of the Spiritual World* (2000), CW, 5.

The only authority in the classroom is the authority of the subject taught, not the teacher.

"Northrop Frye in Conversation" (1989), *Interviews with Northrop Frye* (2008), CW, 24.

SUBSIDIES

I hesitate to draw the inference that there is a connection between limited funds and liveliness of intellect, but....

"From Nationalism to Regionalism: The Maturing of Canadian Culture" (1980), *Interviews with Northrop Frye* (2008), CW, 24.

... if such a grant had been made to Keats in the summer of 1819 the whole sensibility of the modern world might have been very different.

"Culture and the National Will" (1957), *Northrop Frye on Canada* (2003), CW, 12.

The cutbacks which threaten our cultural life at the present time are the product of superstitious priorities. In the twenty-third century nobody, except a Ph.D. student desperately looking for a subject in Canadian history, will dig out the names of the people who are promoting cutbacks today. Those amongst us who are producing the literature, the poetry, and other cultural artefacts are the people who will interest mankind in the twenty-third century. They will be the essence of Canada.

"The Primary Necessities of Existence" (1985), *Interviews with Northrop Frye* (2008), CW, 24.

SUCCESS

Similarly, a success is not what anybody is; it is what other people think he is.

"The Question of 'Success'" (1967), *Northrop Frye's Writings on Education* (2001), CW, 7.

Swimming is, in fact, a remarkable example of success through intellectual achievement, because it is an operation in which you are supporting yourself in an alien element by keeping your head in a higher world.

"The Question of 'Success'" (1967), *Northrop Frye's Writings on Education* (2001), CW, 7.

SUFFERING

The articulation of suffering is a central aspect of human awareness.

Entry, Notebook 9 (1963–66), *Northrop Frye's Notebooks on Renaissance Literature* (2006), CW, 20.

I'm saying that the only role that God can have in human life is that of a man who cares enough about society to go even to the extent of a hideous death for man's salvation, and I think it is the conception of God as the power that recreates man rather than God as the creator of the order of nature that is the really valid element in Christianity.

"Into the Wilderness" (1969), *Interviews with Northrop Frye* (2008), CW, 24.

SUN

One can understand the worship of the sun. It seems to me a very natural human tendency. But when the sun is a blast furnace ninety million miles away it's just as impressive as it ever was, though it's not as worshipful as it was.

"Between Paradise and Apocalypse" (1978), *Interviews with Northrop Frye* (2008), CW, 24.

SUNDAY

The Jewish Sabbath was a day of rest at the end of the week: the Christian Sunday is a day of leisure at the beginning of the week.

Entry, 8 Jan. 1950, 25, *The Diaries of Northrop Frye: 1942–1955* (2001), CW, 8.

SUPERMARKET

A supermarket, for instance, is a shoddy symbol of an embryonic paradise: one wanders at will gathering food off the shelves, then departs by the turnstile of birth.

Entry, Notebook 24 (1970–72), 80, *The "Third Book" Notebooks of Northrop Frye, 1964–1972: The Critical Comedy* (2002), CW, 9.

SUPERSTITION

Superstition of this kind is frozen ideology, a pathological social condition that obstructs the developments in the arts and sciences, and so frustrates the central aim of education.

"Some Reflections on Life and Habit" (1988), *Northrop Frye's Writings on the Eighteenth and Nineteenth Centuries* (2005), CW, 17.

Superstition is persisting in a thing out of habit without investigating whether it is worth persisting in or not.

"Symbolism in the Bible" (1981–82), *Northrop Frye's Notebooks and Lectures on the Bible and Other Religious Texts* (2003), CW, 13.

A superstition is something we do without knowing why we do it; if we are faced with the question of why we do it, we must rush in to plaster it over with rationalizations.

Entry, Notebook 27 (1986), 209, *Northrop Frye's Late Notebooks, 1982–1990: Architecture of the Spiritual World* (2000), CW, 5.

SUPREME COURT OF CANADA

I wish Canada had junked this dismal cliché and been the first nation to vest supreme legislative powers in another nation: the kind of super-national conception that the Commonwealth of Nations permits.

> Entry, Notebook 18 (1956–62), 146, *Notebooks for "Anatomy of Criticism"* (2007), CW, 23.

SURREALISM

Idealism obstinately clings to these pictures, the belief that the world exists as it is perceived, and that a renewed imagination would create a better world.

> "Men As Trees Walking" (1938), *Northrop Frye on Modern Culture* (2003), CW, 11.

How far the surrealists can go in their apocalyptic attempt to make the human mind create a new heaven and a new earth, no one can say. But it's worth trying.

> "Men As Trees Walking" (1938), *Northrop Frye on Modern Culture* (2003), CW, 11.

SURVIVAL

The word survival implies living through a series of crises, each one unexpected and different from the others, each one to be met on its own terms. Failure to meet the crisis means that some death principle moves in.

> "Conclusion to *Literary History of Canada*" (1965), *Northrop Frye on Canada* (2003), CW, 12.

But the survival of society as a whole is usually considered a good thing: we may be surviving in a fool's paradise, but perhaps no other paradise is appropriate for human beings.

> "Address on Receiving the Royal Bank Award" (1978), *Northrop Frye's Writings on Education* (2001), CW, 7.

It is quite simply true that the survival of the human race depends on the way that it responds to language over the next few years.

> "Language as the Home of Human Life" (1985), *Northrop Frye's Writings on Education* (2001), CW, 7.

SWITZERLAND

In many ways, Switzerland is a model for a peaceful and co-operating Europe, and Canada, ringed around with the world's great powers, is a kind of global Switzerland. Politically, it is constantly falling apart and being patched together by ad hoc compromises; economically, it has been trampled over by exploiters from three continents. But somewhere in its literature, its universities, its scholarship staggering and limping under budget cuts, there may be buried the model vision of a new world, where nightmare visions of tyranny and destruction have vanished as even the worst dreams do.

> "The Authority of Learning" (1984), *Northrop Frye's Writings on Education* (2001), CW, 7.

SYMBOLS

An archetypal symbol is usually a natural object with a human meaning, and it forms part of the critical view of art as a civilized product, a vision of the goals of human work.

> "Second Essay: Ethical Criticism: Theory of Symbols" (1957), *Anatomy of Criticism: Four Essays* (2006), CW, 22.

...any unit of any literary structure that can be isolated for critical attention.

> "Second Essay: Ethical Criticism: Theory of Symbols" (1957), *Anatomy of Criticism: Four Essays* (2006), CW, 22.

A *symbolon* is something that is not complete in itself, but needs something else, or another half of itself, to make it complete. A *symbolos*, in contrast, links us to something too complex or mysterious to grasp all at once.

> "The Symbol as a Medium of Exchange" (1984), *"The Secular Scripture" and Other Writings on Critical Theory, 1976–1991* (2006), CW, 18.

Any symbol may be used ambivalently, and may be virtuous or demonic according to its context, an obvious example being the symbolism of gold.

> "The Structure of Imagery in *The Faerie Queene*" (1961), *Northrop Frye's Writings on Shakespeare and the Renaissance* (2010), CW, 28.

For the psychologist all dream symbols are private ones, interpreted by the personal life of the dreamer; for the critic there is no such thing as private symbolism, or, if there is, it is his job to make sure that it does not remain so.

> "The Language of Poetry" (1955), *"The Educated Imagination" and Other Writings on Critical Theory, 1933–1963* (2006), CW, 21.

In short, the language of symbols is the language of love, and that, as Paul reminds us, will last longer than any other form of human communication.
> "Symbols" (1968), *Northrop Frye on Religion* (2000), CW, 4.

There is no question about the film, because that is a literary art in itself, and it has a power of expressing symbolism that I think is unmatched by any other form in the history of mankind.
> "Engagement and Detachment" (1968), referring to theatre and especially cinema as adjuncts to courses in literature, during a filmed interview, *Interviews with Northrop Frye* (2008), CW, 24.

Seeing anything with expert knowledge turns an image into a symbol by linking it to a corpus of significance. Perhaps Cassirer is right in suggesting that the ability to see the image as a symbol, a unit to be completed with the understander (in one aspect) and the context (in another) supplying the other half, is what's distinctively human.
> Entry, Notes 52 (1982-90), 959, referring to the philosopher Ernst Cassirer, *Northrop Frye's Late Notebooks, 1982–1990: Architecture of the Spiritual World* (2000), CW, 5.

T

TALK
Why do I set up such a deafening clatter of inner talk in my mind? Probably for the same reason that villagers gossip and urban people intrigue: to keep myself reassured about the reality of the ordinary world. If I'd shut up and listen I might be able to hear other things. It corresponds to the senses' filtering out and giving us the reality we can take.

> Entry, Notebook 50 (1987–90), 52, *Northrop Frye's Late Notebooks, 1982–1990: Architecture of the Spiritual World* (2000), CW, 5.

TALMUD
Judaism still finds the Bible's centre of gravity in the Torah: the Talmud, which in some respects is the Jewish counterpart of the New Testament, takes mainly the form of a commentary on the Torah.

> "Typology I," *The Great Code* (1982), *The Great Code: The Bible and Literature* (2006), CW, 19.

TASTE
Every attempt to exalt taste over knowledge has behind it the feeling that the possessor of taste is certainly a gentleman, while the possessor of knowledge may be only a pedant.

> "On Value Judgments" (1968), *"The Critical Path" and Other Writings on Critical Theory, 1963–1975* (2009), CW, 27.

In my experience, that phrase, "I don't know anything about art but I know what I like," always turns out to be that what you like is pretty dismal.

> "The Great Teacher" (1988), *Interviews with Northrop Frye* (2008), CW, 24.

It is entirely impossible to know nothing of art and yet to know what one likes: what one likes is always a measure of what one knows.

> "Academy without Walls" (1961), *Northrop Frye on Modern Culture* (2003), CW, 11.

Yes, and very often you can understand the taste of an age from the least interesting writers.

> "Canadian and American Values" 1988), *Interviews with Northrop Frye* (2000), CW, 24.

TEACH-INS
Teach-ins, for example, are entertainment of a very high quality but they are not a form of education. We cannot have education without incessant repetition and practice, drill, and going over the same things over and over until they become automatic responses.

> "The Social Importance of Literature" (1968), *Northrop Frye's Writings on Education* (2001), CW, 7.

TEACHERS & TEACHING
The teacher has to try to transform himself into a kind of transparent medium for whatever he is teaching. If he's lucky, there may come a point at which the entire classroom is pervaded by the spirit of the subject — of Blake, or Shakespeare, or romance. And then the relationship between teacher and student, which in itself is a somewhat embarrassing relationship, disappears, and you are all united in the same vision.

> "Freedom and Concern" (1985), *Interviews with Northrop Frye* (2008), CW, 24.

But if Canada ever becomes as famous in cultural history as the Athens of Socrates, it will be largely because, in spite of indifference or Philistinism or even contempt, he has persisted in the immortal task granted only to teachers, the task of corrupting its youth.

"The Beginning of the Word" (1980), *Northrop Frye's Writings on Education* (2001), CW, 7.

Certainly the influence of my teachers on me was not directly through anything they taught me, but the impression they gave that the life of a scholar was worth living.
"The Scholar in Society" (1983), *Interviews with Northrop Frye* (2008), CW, 24.

The distance between pupil and teacher diminishes as the former gets older: by the end of high school the teacher should be a fellow student.
"Speech at a Freshman Welcome" (1966), *Northrop Frye's Writings on Education* (2001), CW, 7.

They have tried to teach you to compare your society's ideas with Plato's, its language with Shakespeare's, its calculations with Newton's, its love with the love of the saints.
"Culture and the National Will" (1957)," *Northrop Frye on Canada* (2003), CW, 12.

You can't be a teacher, or rather, you can't stand in the role of a teacher (in a university you get little chance to do any real teaching) without being something of an exhibitionist.
"Autobiographical Reflections" (1942–44), 25, *Northrop Frye's Fiction and Miscellaneous Writings* (2007), CW, 25.

It's the job of a teacher of the humanities to keep fighting for the liberalizing of the imagination, to encourage students to confront experience, to explore the shadows and the darkness, to distinguish evil from the portrayal of evil, and to meet the unexpected with tolerance.
"Address on Receiving the Royal Bank Award" (1978), *Northrop Frye's Writings on Education* (2001), CW, 7.

But the dedicated teacher realizes that the end of education is to get yourself detached from society without withdrawing from it.
"Canadian and American Values" (1988), *Interviews with Northrop Frye* (2008), CW, 24.

If you're teaching mathematics, you get inspired by mathematics. Nobody gets inspired by some vague notion like teaching as an end in itself.
"There Is Really No Such Thing As Methodology" (1969), *Interviews with Northrop Frye* (2008), CW, 24.

I have always considered that my teaching and my writing are interconnected and that teaching is a sufficiently dramatic performance to be considered an independent literary form.
"Schools of Criticism (II)" (1990), *Interviews with Northrop Frye* (2008), CW, 24.

A good deal of the strategy of teaching is rhetorical strategy, choosing words and images with great care in order to evoke the response: "I never thought of it that way before," or, "Now that you put it that way, I can see it."
"Fourth Essay: Rhetorical Criticism: Theory of Genres" (1957), *Anatomy of Criticism: Four Essays* (2006), CW, 22.

While many things can bring teacher and students together personally, only one thing can ever *equalize* them, and that is the authority of the subject being taught. In relation to the subject being taught the teacher is also a student, and so the difference between teacher and students is at a minimum.
"On Teaching Literature" (1972), *Northrop Frye's Writings on Education* (2001), CW, 7.

I suspect that no teaching is worth doing unless it has a militant quality to it.
"Canadian Energies: Dialogues on Creativity" (1980), *Interviews with Northrop Frye* (2008), CW, 24.

For a teacher, patience has to be a substitute for heroism.
Remark quoted in *Maclean's*, 5 April 1982.

What both teacher and student are trying to do, I think, is to escape from the intolerable burden of being teachers and students.
"The Ethics of Change: The Role of the University" (1968), *Northrop Frye's Writings on Education* (2001), CW, 7.

We hold up to all students, whether casual or committed, the ideal of the scholarly life, a life detached yet not withdrawn from the social environment, working constantly, not to create an élite, but to dissolve all élites into the classless society which is the final embodiment of culture.

"Teaching the Humanities Today" (1977), *Northrop Frye's Writings on Education* (2001), CW, 7.

One can teach only what is teachable, and what the university must teach is the only thing it can teach: the specific disciplines into which genuine knowledge is divided.

The Modern Century (1967), *Northrop Frye on Modern Culture* (2003), CW, 11.

I imagine a dramatist, for example, wouldn't actually believe in the reality of his play until it had been performed. And in a sense I don't believe anything I say until I hear myself saying it.

"Maintaining Freedom in Paradise" (1982), *Interviews with Northrop Frye* (2008), CW, 24.

Again, I have always tended to distrust conceptions of teaching which regarded it as a personal encounter between teacher and taught. It seems to me that the authority of the subject being taught is supreme over both teacher and student.

"The Critic and the Writer" (1972), *Northrop Frye Newsletter*, Winter 1991–92.

TEACHING LITERATURE

People like myself who teach literature are often referred to as intellectuals because we wear glasses, but actually I think we'd be much more accurately defined as emotionals. We are just as much concerned with trying to simulate a feeling response to literature as a logical one.

"The Only Genuine Revolution" (1968), *Interviews with Northrop Frye* (2008), CW, 24.

The English teacher's ideal is the exact opposite of "effective communication," or learning to become audible in the market place. What he has to teach is the verbal expression of truth, beauty, and wisdom: in short, the disinterested use of words.

"The Study of English in Canada" (1957), *Northrop Frye's Writings on Education* (2001), CW, 7.

The teacher who is not dedicated is a mass man, and he gets a mass product. He teaches largely because he has particular certainties that he wants to implant in the minds of his students. But the dedicated teacher realizes that the end of education is to get yourself detached from society without withdrawing from it. If a man is teaching English literature, for example, he's in contact with the entire verbal experience of his students. Now nine tenths of that verbal experience is picked up from prejudice and cliché and things the students hears on street corners, on the playgrounds, and from his family and his home, and so forth.

"Canadian and American Values" (1988), *Interviews with Northrop Frye* (2008), CW, 24.

Teaching literature is impossible; that is why it is difficult.

"Criticism, Visible and Invisible" (1964), *"The Critical Path" and Other Writings on Critical Theory, 1963–1975* (2009), CW, 27.

In a sense one may say that the social ideal of the teacher of literature is a prerevolutionary society, which his teaching helps to recreate. By that I mean a society in which new ideas, new structures of intelligence and imagination, can still have a revolutionary impact.

"The Beginning of the Word" (1980), *Northrop Frye's Writings on Education* (2001), CW, 7.

It is therefore impossible to "learn literature": one learns about it in a certain way, but what one learns, transitively, is the criticism of literature. Similarly, the difficulty often felt in "teaching literature" arises from the fact that it cannot be done: the criticism of literature is all that can be directly taught.

"The Archetypes of Literature" (1951), *"The Educated Imagination" and Other Writings on Critical Theory, 1933–1963* (2006), CW, 21.

It is becoming more obvious that we do not teach or learn literature, in universities or elsewhere, and that only the criticism of literature can be directly taught and learned.

"The Study of English in Canada" (1957), *Northrop Frye's Writings on Education* (2001), CW, 7.

Difficulty is all that a teacher can deal with, & the job of a teacher of literature is the thankless one of showing that what looks easy really is difficult.
> Entry, Notebook 19 (1964–67), 267, *The "Third Book" Notebooks of Northrop Frye, 1964–1972: The Critical Comedy* (2002), CW, 9.

It's clear that the end of literary teaching is not simply the admiration of literature; it's something more like the transfer of imaginative energy from literature to the student.
> "Verticals of Adam," *The Educated Imagination* (1963), *"The Educated Imagination" and Other Writings on Critical Theory, 1933–1963* (2006), CW, 21.

As for our scholarship and research, what sustained me, as it still does, when I first went into the study of literature, was the feeling that I had the best subject-matter in the world, and a job to do with it that literature could not do by itself.
> "Teaching the Humanities Today" (1977), *Northrop Frye's Writings on Education* (2001), CW, 7.

How can you teach Milton to a class in heat?
> Attributed with respect to teaching English to returned servicemen in the late 1940s and early 1950s by Edmund Carpenter, "Remembering Explorations," *Canadian Notes & Queries*, Spring 1993.

TECHNIQUE
Once technique reaches a certain degree of skill, it turns into something that we may darkly suspect to be fun: fun for the writer to display it, fun for the reader to watch it.
> "Conclusion to *Literary History of Canada*" (1965), *Northrop Frye on Canada* (2003), CW, 12.

TECHNOLOGY
I often find that, when I read books about the technology available in the near future, the author's eyes are starry while mine are still glazed.
> "Literary and Mechanical Models" (1989), *"The Secular Scripture" and Other Writings on Critical Theory, 1976–1991* (2006), CW, 18.

Technology is the most dramatic aspect of this development: one cannot take off in a jet plane and expect a radically different way of life in the place where the plane lands.
> "Canadian Culture Today" (1977), *Northrop Frye on Canada* (2003), CW, 12.

The more highly developed the technology, the more introversion it creates in society.
> "Convocation Address: University of Bologna" (1989), *Northrop Frye on Literature and Society, 1936–1989: Unpublished Papers* (2002), CW, 10.

In our world technology has immensely increased the potential strength of both sides; and while the active and creative response to our cultural tradition begins with the power of choice, it must soon move on to develop also some power of resisting its better organized enemies.
> "Convocation Address: University of Bologna" (1989), referring to confronting "a mass hatred for human intellect and imagination," *Northrop Frye on Literature and Society, 1936–1989: Unpublished Papers* (2002), CW, 10.

I mentioned the increasing introversion that technology brings with it: the aeroplane is more introverted than the train; the super-highway, where there is a danger of falling asleep, more introverted than the most unfrequented country road. The international airport, completely insulated even from the country it is in, is probably the most eloquent symbol of this, and is parodied in Stanley Kubrick's movie *2001*, where the hero lands on the moon, dependent on human processing even for the air he breathes, and finds nothing to do there except to phone his wife back on earth, who is out.
> "Canada: New World Without Revolution" (1975), *Northrop Frye on Canada* (2003), CW, 12.

Technology by itself cannot produce the kind of scientist that it needs for its own development: at any rate, that seems to be the general opinion of those who are qualified to have an opinion on the subject.
> "Humanities in a New World" (1958), *Northrop Frye's Writings on Education* (2001), CW, 7.

TELECOMMUNICATIONS

About the time transistors appeared, I read a science fiction story in which, in some future nightmare-world, everyone walked around with their ears covered by machines that totally isolated them from the world outside them. A few years later this grisly fantasy became a matter of common observation on our streets.

"Convocation Address: University of Bologna" (1989), *Northrop Frye on Literature and Society, 1936–1989: Unpublished Papers* (2002), CW, 10.

TELEPATHY

Telepathy and the like, again, may exist in human minds, but it seems to be a poor thing there compared to what the technology of telephones and wireless has been providing for a century.

"Literary and Mechanical Models" (1989), *"The Secular Scripture" and Other Writings on Critical Theory, 1976–1991* (2006), CW, 18.

TELEVISION

People who don't want to read can always stare at television, or they can go down the street with headphones on, living in a different world from the ones they see around them.

"Back to the Garden" (1982), *Interviews with Northrop Frye* (2008), CW, 24.

Television does have a profoundly civilizing aspect in that it compels people to look like people. I think of what an abstract notion I had of Eskimos when I was a student at school, or even college, and how that simply disappeared as soon as one began seeing them on television.

"From Nationalism to Regionalism: The Maturing of Canadian Culture" (1980), *Interviews with Northrop Frye* (2008), CW, 24.

If we speak of Canada being flooded with American programs, we find that the Canadian viewer is a fish, not somebody who wants to get into a Canadian ark, floating on top.

"From Nationalism to Regionalism: The Maturing of Canadian Culture" (1980), *Interviews with Northrop Frye* (2008), CW, 24.

It's television that makes you live in a clock.

"The Scholar in Society" (1983), referring to TV as a linear rather than as a non-linear medium, *Interviews with Northrop Frye* (2008), CW, 24.

Once we get past the talking head in television, we are instantly in a world of drama, whether we are watching a hockey game or a race riot.

"Violence and Television" (1975), *Northrop Frye on Modern Culture* (2003), CW, 11.

I have often spoken of the iconoclastic mood of younger people in our own society, and I think it springs from the same cause: the sense that the present visual foci of American life that television presents, including more especially its commercials, represent a form of idolatry.

"Icons and Iconoclasm" (1970), *Northrop Frye on Literature and Society, 1936–1989: Unpublished Papers* (2002), CW, 10.

Commentaries on a news event like this are generally spoken in a dull, flat associative narrative without a flicker of rhythmical or sound interest in it. With the possible exception of hard-core pornography, I doubt if any arrangement of words is duller than ordinary television commentary.

"Reviews of Television Programs for the Canadian Radio-Television Commission: Reflections on Television ... November 1971–March 1972" (1972), *Northrop Frye on Literature and Society, 1936–1989: Unpublished Papers* (2002), CW, 10.

The television set is a curiously ghostly medium: in our day, if we see ghosts or hear ghostly voices in the air, it means that somebody has left the television on. But the passive viewer's whole world is equally spectral: he cannot distinguish fact from fiction either on the screen or off it.

"Violence and Television" (1975), *Northrop Frye on Modern Culture* (2003), CW, 11.

American civilization has to *de-theatricalize* itself, I think, from the prison of television.

Entry, Notebook 44 (1986–91), 491, *Northrop Frye's Late Notebooks, 1982–1990: Architecture of the Spiritual World* (2000), CW, 5.

What I do know is, first, that television illustrates, more vividly than any other medium, the fact that we participate in society dramatically more than we do conceptually; and, second, that on television the structuring of fact is very similar to the structuring of fiction, both falling into much the same dramatic conventions.

"Violence and Television" (1975), *Northrop Frye on Modern Culture* (2003), CW, 11.

In the age of television it is a common experience to attend a public function and then go home to get on television a more comprehensive and comprehensible view of what one has just been engaged in.

"The Renaissance of Books" (1973), *Northrop Frye on Modern Culture* (2003), CW, 11.

My hair prickles when I hear advertisers talk of a television set simply as a means of reaching their market. It so seldom occurs to them that a television set might be their market's way of looking at them, and that the market might conceivably not like what it sees.

"Communications" (1970), *Northrop Frye on Modern Culture* (2003), CW, 11.

I think the inherent tendency of television, as of film and radio, is to decrease the distinction between highbrow and lowbrow listeners, and within its widening central area of appeal to find more room for a greater variety of tastes.

"Across the River and Out of the Trees" (1980), *Northrop Frye on Canada* (2003), CW, 12.

Television is like a telescope, a new method of perception which tells us more, but also makes what it sees look cold, dead, and inconceivably remote.

Entry, Notebook 11f (1969–70), 115, *Northrop Frye's Notebooks and Lectures on the Bible and Other Religious Texts* (2003), CW, 13.

It seems to me that television is able, as no medium of communication has ever been able to before, to alter the balance between waking and dreaming life by providing what is so close to an objectified dream world.

"Reviews of Television Programs for the Canadian Radio-Television Commission: Reflections on Television … November 1971–March 1972"

(1972), *Northrop Frye on Literature and Society, 1936–1989: Unpublished Papers* (2002), CW, 10.

TEMPEST, THE

In many tales of the *Tempest* type, the island sinks back into the sea when the magician leaves. But we, going out of the theatre, perhaps have it in our pockets like an apple: perhaps our children can sow the seeds in the sea and bring forth again the island that the world has been searching for since the dawn of history, the island that is both nature and human society restored to their original form, where there is no sovereignty and yet where all of us are kings.

"Northrop Frye on Shakespeare: IX, *The Tempest*" (1986), *Northrop Frye's Writings on Shakespeare and the Renaissance* (2010), CW, 28.

However we take it, *The Tempest* is a play not simply to be read or seen or even studied, but possessed.

"Introduction to *Shakespeare's Tempest*" (1959), *Northrop Frye's Writings on Shakespeare and the Renaissance* (2010), CW, 28.

I was asked recently why I could never write anything without mentioning Shakespeare's *Tempest*. The reason is that I know of no other work of literature that illustrates more clearly the interchange of illusion and reality which is what literature is all about.

"Auguries of Experience" (1987), *"The Secular Scripture" and Other Writings on Critical Theory, 1976–1991* (2006), CW, 18.

TEMPLES

The real temple is the tent.

Entry, Notebook 50 (1987–90), 52, *Northrop Frye's Late Notebooks, 1982–1990: Architecture of the Spiritual World* (2000), CW, 5.

People don't realize that I'm building temples to — well, "the gods" will do. There's an outer court for casual tourists, an inner court for those who want to stay for communion (incidentally, the rewards of doing so are very considerable). But I've left a space where neither they nor I belong.

Entry, Notebook 44 (1986–91), 93, *Northrop Frye's Late Notebooks, 1982–1990: Architecture of the Spiritual World* (2000), CW, 5.

TERROR

The real terror comes when the individual feels himself becoming an individual, pulling away from the group, and losing the sense of driving power that the group gives him, aware of a conflict within himself far subtler than the struggle of morality against evil....
> Preface, *The Bush Garden* (1971), *Northrop Frye on Canada* (2003), CW, 12.

The outstanding achievement of Canadian poetry is in the evocation of stark terror. Not a coward's terror, of course; but a controlled vision of the causes of cowardice. The immediate source of this is obviously the frightening loneliness of a huge and thinly-settled country.
> "Canada and Its Poetry" (1943), *Northrop Frye on Canada* (2003), CW, 12.

TERRORISM

There is hardly a corner of modern thought where we do not find some image of a beleaguered custodian of conscious values trying to fend off something unconscious which is too strong to be defeated. It seems the appropriate cultural pattern for a period in which the tiny peninsula of Western Europe was encircling the world.... If this age really does see the decisive struggle of liberty and terrorism for the fate of the world, the pattern of thought will make the necessary change — unless terrorism wins, in which case there will be no pattern at all.
> "Trends in Modern Culture" (1952), *Northrop Frye on Modern Culture* (2003), CW, 11.

TEXTS

The text is the presence. I know this sounds a little like "the medium is the message," but at least it gets over the Derrida hurdle of a written word deferring to an oral word deferring to a pre-verbal situation of events.
> Entry, Notes 52 (1982–90), 23, *Northrop Frye's Late Notebooks, 1982–1990: Architecture of the Spiritual World* (2000), CW, 6.

The ultimate aim of critic, teacher, and editor alike is to become a transparent medium for whatever one criticizes, teaches, or edits.
> "Welcoming Remarks to Conference on Editorial Problems, 1967" (1967), *"The Critical Path" and Other Writings on Critical Theory, 1963–1975* (2009), CW, 27.

THEATRE

We are presented with an illusion which we always have to remember is an illusion. But it is also as close to reality as we are ever going to get.
> "The Art of Bunraku" (1981), *Interviews with Northrop Frye* (2008), CW, 24.

The reality-illusion distinction clearly does not work for plays: the illusion *is* the reality.
> "The Bridge of Language" (1981), *Northrop Frye on Modern Culture* (2003), CW, 11.

If you ask where the reality is, the nearest you come to an answer is that it is the mood generated in the audience by the play. So that the experience of entering a theatre turns your ordinary experience of reality and illusion inside out by presenting you with an objective illusion and a subjective reality.
> "Symbolism in the Bible" (1981–82), *Northrop Frye's Notebooks and Lectures on the Bible and Other Religious Texts* (2003), CW, 13.

THEOLOGY

Theology, to me, meant mostly *The Golden Bough*, just as to Pratt it meant things like Emergent Evolution.
> "Autobiographical Notes III: The Critic and the Writer" (1972), 3, comparing and contrasting his views as a young teacher with those of his older colleague the poet E.J. Pratt, *Northrop Frye's Fiction and Miscellaneous Writings* (2007), CW, 25.

In theology the deductive tendency has completely taken over, as there can hardly be such a thing as empirical theology.
> "New Directions from Old" (1960), *"The Educated Imagination" and Other Writings on Critical Theory, 1933–1963* (2006), CW, 21.

All theology is designed to persuade people to go to church, but I'm rather obstinate about not going to church, even when I do nothing better — and it's very easy for me to do better.
> Entry, 8 Jan. 1950, 25, *The Diaries of Northrop Frye: 1942–1955* (2001), CW, 8.

There is no such thing as academic theology: all theology is part of the strategy of a church, and has the rationalizing of that church's claims as one of its primary interests.

"Josef Pieper, 'Leisure: The Basis of Culture'" (1950s), *Northrop Frye on Literature and Society, 1936–1989: Unpublished Papers* (2002), CW, 10.

THEOLOGY, LIBERATION

They talk about liberation theology. We've spent centuries realizing that order and authority are not as necessary as panic and selfishness thought they were: spiritual authority, which is order without authority, is all we need.

Entry, Notes 53 (1989–90), 40, *Northrop Frye's Late Notebooks, 1982–1990: Architecture of the Spiritual World* (2000), CW, 6.

THEORY

In a book I published 25 years ago, *AC* [*Anatomy of Criticism*], I spoke of it as "pure critical theory." This is one of the sentences I regret having written, in view of what critical theory has come to look like since then.

"Notes for Criticism and Environment (2)," (1981), 14, *Northrop Frye's Fiction and Miscellaneous Writings* (2007), CW, 25.

THINKERS

It's the ability to see what's straight in front of his nose that marks the thinker of first-rate importance.

"Oswald Spengler" (1955), *Northrop Frye on Modern Culture* (2003), CW, 11.

But the thinker who was annihilated on Tuesday has to be annihilated all over again on Wednesday: the fortress of thought is a Valhalla, not an abattoir.

Creation and Recreation (1980), *Northrop Frye on Religion* (2000), CW, 4.

THINKING

But thinking, again, is like piano-playing: how well we do it depends primarily on how much of it we have progressively and systematically done already, and at all times the content of thinking is knowledge.

"Some Reflections on *Life and Habit*" (1988), *Northrop Frye's Writings on the Eighteenth and Nineteenth Centuries* (2005), CW, 17.

We can't use our minds at full capacity unless we have some idea of how much of what we think we're thinking is really thought, and how much is just familiar words running along their own familiar tracks.

"Verticals of Adam," *The Educated Imagination* (1963), *"The Educated Imagination" and Other Writings on Critical Theory, 1933–1963* (2006), CW, 21.

In fact we, as individuals or egos, can hardly be said to think at all: we link our minds to an objective body of thought, follow its facts and processes, and finally, if the links are strong enough, our minds become a place where something new in the body of thought comes to light.

"Humanities in a New World" (1958), *Northrop Frye's Writings on Education* (2001), CW, 7.

It is, admittedly, discouraging for a student to find that he has reached university and is still totally unable to say what he thinks. It is even more discouraging to realize that the real trouble is that he cannot think, thinking being a by-product of the skill developed in the practice of language.

"The View from Here" (1980), *Northrop Frye's Writings on Education* (2001), CW, 7.

It is a university if it trains its students to think freely, but thinking, as distinct from musing or speculating, is a power of decision based on habit.

"The Study of English in Canada" (1957), *Northrop Frye's Writings on Education* (2001), CW, 7.

Intense thinking is a byproduct of an active life: surely it dries up when it becomes an end in itself, like happiness.

Entry, 28 Jun. 1950, 447, *The Diaries of Northrop Frye: 1942–1955* (2001), CW, 8.

Thinking, of course, is not something I do: it's something that happens where I am. It gets done in spite of what I do: everything I "do" is mental automatism, running along prefabricated tracks that look like a map of the London subways.

Entry, Notebook 12 (1968–70), 280, *The "Third Book" Notebooks of Northrop Frye, 1964–1972: The Critical Comedy* (2002), CW, 9.

Thought itself is one of the primary forms of human energy, and in its use is all the exhilaration of power.
> "By Liberal Things" (1959), *Northrop Frye's Writings on Education* (2001), CW, 7.

There are no wordless thoughts.
> *The Well-Tempered Critic* (1963), *The Educated Imagination* (1963), *"The Educated Imagination" and Other Writings on Critical Theory, 1933–1963* (2006), CW, 21.

THOMSON, TOM

Griffins and gorgons have no place in Thomson certainly, but the incubus is there, in the twisted stumps and sprawling rocks, the strident colouring, the scarecrow evergreens. In several pictures one has the feeling of something not quite emerging which is all the more sinister for its concealment.
> "Canadian and Colonial Painting" (1941), *Northrop Frye on Canada* (2003), CW, 12.

When the Canadian sphinx brought her riddle of unvisualized land to Thomson it did not occur to him to hide under the bedclothes, though she did not promise him money, fame, happiness, or even self-confidence, and when she was through with him she scattered his bones in the wilderness.
> "Canadian and Colonial Painting" (1941), *Northrop Frye on Canada* (2003), CW, 12.

THRILLER FICTION

The thriller is quite a suggestive form actually: it's the opposite of the detective story, where we get the smug primitive identification with the group & see the individual marked down by a process of hocus pocus. In the thriller we're identified rather with the fugitive from society. The archetype of all thrillers is *The Pilgrim's Progress*, where the refugee from the city of destruction is hounded on by a nameless fear, & has to do battle with various members of its police force like Apollyon.
> Entry, 8 May 1950, 329, *The Diaries of Northrop Frye: 1942–1955* (2001), CW, 8.

In the melodrama of the brutal thriller we come as close as it is normally possible for art to come to the pure self-righteousness of the lynching mob.
> "First Essay: Historical Criticism: Theory of Modes" (1957), *Anatomy of Criticism: Four Essays* (2006), CW, 22.

TIBET

Perhaps the Chinese conquest of Tibet will diffuse the Tantric light over the world, as the Turkish conquests of the Roman Empire spread Greek over Europe.
> Entry, Notebook 24 (1970–72), 200, *The "Third Book" Notebooks of Northrop Frye, 1964–1972: The Critical Comedy* (2002), CW, 9.

TIME

There is no time to be lost, once one has found it again.
> "Northrop Frye on Shakespeare: VIII, Shakespeare's Romances: *The Winter's Tale*" (1986), *Northrop Frye's Writings on Shakespeare and the Renaissance* (2010), CW, 28.

Gospel and apocalypse speak of a present that no longer finds its meaning in the future, as the New Testament's view of the Old Testament, but is a present moment around which past and future revolve.
> "Language II," *The Great Code* (1982), *The Great Code: The Bible and Literature* (2006), CW, 19.

As I've said before, punctuality is the thief of time.
> Entry, 4 Feb. 1952, 90, *The Diaries of Northrop Frye: 1942–1955* (2001), CW, 8.

Time is the fundamental category by which we perceive everything: we perceive nothing that is real except in time. And yet time as we ordinarily experience it consists of three unrealities, a past that doesn't exist any longer, a future that doesn't exist yet, and a present that never quite exists at all. So we get our fundamental reality out of a threefold illusion.
> "Symbolism in the Bible" (1981–82), *Northrop Frye's Notebooks and Lectures on the Bible and Other Religious Texts* (2003), CW, 13.

As our personal future narrows, we become more aware of another dimension of time entirely, and may even catch glimpses of the powers and forces of a far greater creative design.

> On the subject of time, in 1978, as recalled by Albert C. Hamilton, Memorial Issue, *Vic Report*, Spring 1991.

Every moment is a present continuous with past & future … and a discontinuous instant of potential resurrection.

> Entry, Notebook 21 (1969–76), 422, *Northrop Frye's Notebooks and Lectures on the Bible and Other Religious Texts* (2003), CW, 13.

The past & the future are the two great enemies, of tyranny & mystery respectively, yet so much in them is essential that the problem of breaking off from them is not so easy.

> Entry, Notebook 3 (1946–48), 27, *Northrop Frye's Notebooks and Lectures on the Bible and Other Religious Texts* (2003), CW, 13.

If I ever get a big enough office, I shall have the hundred plates of my *Jerusalem* reproduction framed and hung around the walls, so that the frontispiece will have the second plate on one side and the last plate on the other. This will be *Jerusalem* presented as Blake thought of it, symbolizing the state of mind in which the poet himself could say, "I see the Past, Present & Future existing all at once / Before me."

> "The Road of Excess" (1970), *Northrop Frye on Milton and Blake* (2005), CW, 16.

The world is usually called "timeless," which is a beggary of language: there ought to be some such word as "timeful" to express a present moment that includes immense vistas of past and future.

> Entry, Notes 53 (1989–90), 267, *Northrop Frye's Late Notebooks, 1982–1990: Architecture of the Spiritual World* (2000), CW, 6.

In time we all face the past, and are dragged backwards into the future. Nobody knows the future: it isn't there to be known. The past is what we know, and it is all that we know.

> "The Quality of Life in the '70s" (1971), *Northrop Frye on Modern Culture* (2003), CW, 11.

Similarly, the three dimensions of time are the past, present and future, the no longer, the never quite, and the not yet. None of these dimensions exists. Space is the fourth dimension of time, the dimension in which things manifest themselves or come into existence.

> Entry, Notes 54-5 (1976), 4, *Northrop Frye's Notebooks and Lectures on the Bible and Other Religious Texts* (2003), CW, 13.

In the bath this morning I noticed what play I make with my wristwatch and spectacles, the two fragile machines which link me to time and space.

> Entry, Notebook 42b: Notes I (1942–44), 54, *Northrop Frye's Fiction and Miscellaneous Writings* (2007), CW, 25.

TIPS

Any of you who have handed a tip to a taxi driver have probably felt that you are engaged in a social ritual which is both embarrassing to you and humiliating to the taxi driver. The reason is that what you do when you hand the tip over is to dramatize a social situation, the relationship of a gentleman to a flunky which society is trying to outgrow.

> "Preserving Human Values" (1961), *Northrop Frye on Modern Culture* (2003), CW, 11.

TITANIC

I'm interested in the *Titanic* sinking because it was the first tangible sign that European civilization had lost its grip on reality and was about to throw away its cultural leadership of the world.

> Entry, Notebook 50 (1987–90), 208, *Northrop Frye's Late Notebooks, 1982–1990: Architecture of the Spiritual World* (2000), CW, 5.

TOLERANCE

One applauds the tolerance, except that the public is so seldom tolerant about anything unless it is indifferent to it as well. A world where the arts are totally tolerated might easily become a world in which they were merely decorative, and evoked no sense of challenge to repression at all.

> *Creation and Recreation* (1980), *Northrop Frye on Religion* (2000), CW, 4.

That is, tolerance is fundamentally a matter of deciding how much deviation is consistent with the safety of the myth.
> "Criticism and Society" (1966–76), referring to systems like Christianity and Marxism, *Northrop Frye on Literature and Society, 1936–1989: Unpublished Papers* (2002), CW, 10.

Tolerance means carelessness, & carelessness is not possible outside the Orient — well, it's vanished there too.
> Entry, 30 Apr. 1950, 309, *The Diaries of Northrop Frye: 1942–1955* (2001), CW, 8.

Where art and scholarship are autonomous, tolerance is a positive and creative force, the unity of detachment and concern.
> "The Instruments of Mental Production" (1966), *Northrop Frye's Writings on Education* (2001), CW, 7.

TOLKIEN, J.R.R.

I succumbed to the charm of Tolkien, like everyone else, but one *Lord of the Rings* is enough. I read Fowles' *Magus* with the highest expectations, but finished it thinking he didn't know what the hell he was doing.
> "New Fictional Formulas: Notebook 28" (after 1965), 6, *Northrop Frye's Fiction and Miscellaneous Writings* (2007), CW, 25.

TORAH

Wisdom in the Bible is an outgrowth of Torah, instruction, the completion of the knowledge of good and evil in its genuine form.
> Entry, Notebook 44 (1986–91), 48, *Northrop Frye's Late Notebooks, 1982–1990: Architecture of the Spiritual World* (2000), CW, 5.

TORONTO

Coming to a bigger city was an essential part of one's cultural education, even granting that Toronto was something of a hick town then compared to what is available in it now.
> "The View from Here" (1980), referring to changes in the student population, *Northrop Frye's Writings on Education* (2001), CW, 7.

If Toronto is a world-class city, it is not because it bids for the Olympics or builds follies like the Skydome, but because of the tolerated variety of the people in its streets.
> "The Cultural Development of Canada" (1990), *Northrop Frye on Canada* (2003), CW, 12.

Toronto is an excellent town to mind one's business in.
> Quoted by Pelham Edgar in *Across My Path* (1952).

At that time, Toronto was a very homogeneous town; the names of Victoria students read like a Belfast phone book, and the public food was as bad as it is in most right-thinking Anglo-Saxon communities.
> "The View from Here" (1980), discussing the city in the 1930s, *Northrop Frye's Writings on Education* (2001), CW, 7.

I don't know of another city that deserves being cursed and kicked more than Toronto, nor of any city that is so well worth it.
> "NF to HK," 11 Sep. 1932, *The Correspondence of Northrop Frye and Helen Kemp, 1932–1939* (1996), CW, 1.

TORTURE

This connects with one of my favourite superstitions: that in order to rationalize the utterly pointless & hideous tortures men have inflicted on each other, one has to think, not of reincarnation, but of one man getting the total variety of all possible experiences, of hell as well as of heaven.
> Entry, Notebook 24 (1970–72), 90, *The "Third Book" Notebooks of Northrop Frye, 1964–1972: The Critical Comedy* (2002), CW, 9.

Funny about the Indian: I think it was because he tortured his enemies with such enthusiasm that we didn't torture him. Also he never became a real proletariat, but attempted as far as he could to maintain his aristocratic-nomad position, living in "reservations" like the medieval game forests.
> Entry, Notebook 3 (1946–48), 102, *Northrop Frye's Notebooks and Lectures on the Bible and Other Religious Texts* (2003), CW, 13.

TOTALITARIANISM

To attach culture to the centralizing movements of politics and economics produces a cultural totalitarianism, an empty, pompous, officially certified pseudo-art. To attach

a political or economic movement to a decentralizing cultural one produces a kind of neo-fascist separatism.
> "The Meeting of Past and Future in William Morris" (1982), *Northrop Frye's Writings on the Eighteenth and Nineteenth Centuries* (2005), CW, 17.

For the totalitarian impulse is the primitive impulse, the longing to return to the narcotic peace of society's version of truth and reality, where we no longer have to cope with the conflicts of intellectual freedom and social concern.
> "The Day of Intellectual Battle: Reflections on Student Unrest" (1969), *Northrop Frye's Writings on Education* (2001), CW, 7.

TOYNBEE, ARNOLD J.
A Study of History presents an enormous mass of historical material strung along a thin line of argument often represented only by a single word, generally in Greek.
> "Toynbee and Spengler" (1947), *Northrop Frye on Modern Culture* (2003), CW, 11.

TRADITION
Tradition gives meaning to time, and a localized culture surrounds a part of nature and makes it "here."
> "T.S. Eliot" (1963), *Northrop Frye on Twentieth-Century Literature* (2010), CW, 29.

This suggests that the history inside literature is, for the critic, a force immensely more powerful and important than the history outside literature, and that we have to know the history of literature, which is a real history with its own shape and not merely a string of dates, before we can make any sense out of the relation of literature to nonliterary history.
> "Tradition and Change in the Theory of Criticism" (1969), noting the role of conventions in literature, *Northrop Frye on Literature and Society, 1936–1989: Unpublished Papers* (2002), CW, 10.

I can think of no social movement designed to preserve a tradition which succeeded in actually preserving that tradition, and I can think of no revolutionary movement designed to bring about a different future that has not been entirely mistaken about what that future was to be.
> "Convocation Address, Franklin and Marshall" (1968), *Northrop Frye's Writings on Education* (2001), CW, 7.

Tradition is as important now as it ever was, but it is less exclusive: the vast shadow of a total human consensus in the imagination is beginning to take shape behind it.
> "Elementary Teaching and Elemental Scholarship" (1963), *Northrop Frye's Writings on Education* (2001), CW, 7.

Poetry does not improve or progress with the times; it produces classics and continues to rewrite its classics with the same mental attitudes. The first principle of "tradition and change in the theory of criticism," then, is that in criticism all change takes the form of a recovery of some neglected aspect of tradition.
> "Tradition and Change in the Theory of Criticism" (1969), *Northrop Frye on Literature and Society, 1936–1989: Unpublished Papers* (2002), CW, 10.

Perhaps church and university, like moral principles, should change slowly, should keep something archaic about them, something of a voice from another world.
> "Baccalaureate Sermon" (1967), *Northrop Frye on Religion* (2000), CW, 4.

TRAGEDY
But, of course, tragedy is not perverse: it has its own rightness. It might be described, though, as a kind of comedy turned inside out.
> "Northrop Frye on Shakespeare: I, *Romeo and Juliet*" (1986), *Northrop Frye's Writings on Shakespeare and the Renaissance* (2010), CW, 28.

Tragedy forces on us a response of acceptance: we have to say, "Yes, this kind of thing is human life too." But by making that response we've accepted something much deeper: that what is defined or made finite by words becomes infinite through the power of words.
> "Northrop Frye on Shakespeare: V, *King Lear*" (1986), *Northrop Frye's Writings on Shakespeare and the Renaissance* (2010), CW, 28.

It takes the greatest rhetoric of the greatest poets to bring us a vision of the tragic heroic, and such rhetoric doesn't make us miserable but exhilarated, not crushed but enlarged in spirit.

"Northrop Frye on Shakespeare: I, *Romeo and Juliet*" (1986), *Northrop Frye's Writings on Shakespeare and the Renaissance* (2010), CW, 28.

I don't think it's an accident that the two developments of tragedy coincide roughly with the two great developments of science, Renaissance science and Ionian science.

"On Evil" (1985), *Interviews with Northrop Frye* (2008), CW, 24.

Tragedy is at the heart of Classical civilization, comedy at the heart of the Christian one.

The Secular Scripture: A Study of the Structure of Romance (1975), *"The Secular Scripture" and Other Writings on Critical Theory, 1976–1991* (2006), CW, 18.

Tragedy is a paradoxical combination of a fearful sense of rightness (the hero must fall) and a pitying sense of wrongness (it is too bad that he falls).

"Third Essay: Archetypal Criticism: Theory of Myths" (1957), *Anatomy of Criticism: Four Essays* (2006), CW, 22.

Without tragedy, all literary fictions might be plausibly explained as expressions of emotional attachments, whether of wish-fulfilment or of repugnance: the tragic fiction guarantees, so to speak, a disinterested quality in literary experience.

"Third Essay: Archetypal Criticism: Theory of Myths" (1957), *Anatomy of Criticism: Four Essays* (2006), CW, 22.

I wouldn't say that people can't write tragedy in the twentieth century. I would say merely that it's not a central form of expression.

"On Evil" (1985), *Interviews with Northrop Frye* (2008), CW, 24.

TRAHISON DES CLERCS

The *trahison des clercs* occurs when intellectuals give way to their constant itch to be socially important, to help turn the wheel of history.

Entry, Notes 52 (1982–90), 677, *Northrop Frye's Late Notebooks, 1982–1990: Architecture of the Spiritual World* (2000), CW, 6.

TRANSFIGURATION

The Transfiguration is the real Resurrection, just as the Resurrection is the real Ascension.

Entry, Notebook 23 (early 1980s), 75, *Northrop Frye's Notebooks and Lectures on the Bible and Other Religious Texts* (2003), CW, 13.

TRANSFORMATION

... a transformation of consciousness and a transformation of language can never be separated.

"Language II," *The Great Code* (1982), *The Great Code: The Bible and Literature* (2006), CW, 19.

Literary education seems to assume a kind of definitive response which in practice never occurs. A definitive response to a performance of *King Lear* would blow our minds, effect an unimaginable transformation in our whole sense of reality.

"Criticism as Education" (1979), *Northrop Frye's Writings on Education* (2001), CW, 7.

TRANSLATION

No translation of anything worth reading is of any real value except as a crib to the original, and so translations for the general reader ought to be as literal as possible.

"The Classics and the Man of Letters" (1964), *Northrop Frye's Writings on Education* (2001), CW, 7.

Of course the translation of any poem worth translating should be as literal as the language will allow, but it should be a literal rendering of the real and not of the superficial meaning.

"Dialogue on Translation" (1970), *Northrop Frye on Canada* (2003), CW, 12.

But the fact that it can be translated means that a poem is capable of growth: growth in time, growth in space, growth in culture, growth in language; and criticism is its growth.

"Tradition and Change in the Theory of Criticism" (1969), *Northrop Frye on Literature and Society, 1936–1989: Unpublished Papers* (2002), CW, 10.

TRASH
One can only study verbal trash in a spirit of profound detachment, seeing it not as the latest thing in literary fashion but as part of a continuing process.

"Comment" (1961), *Northrop Frye on Twentieth-Century Literature* (2010), CW, 29.

TRAVEL
A technological revolution makes the world more uniform: one cannot take off in a jet plane and expect a radically different way of life in the place where the plane lands.

"The Meeting of Past and Future in William Morris" (1982), *Northrop Frye's Writings on the Eighteenth and Nineteenth Centuries* (2005), CW, 17.

It seems to me that the notion of "travel" in either time or space, the central assumption of science fiction, is a false metaphor derived from the quest-theme of literature.

Entry, Notes 52 (1982–90), 982, *Northrop Frye's Late Notebooks, 1982–1990: Architecture of the Spiritual World* (2000), CW, 6.

It is a type of irony familiar in the modern world that in most respects it is easier to get from Toronto to Moscow or Tokyo than to get to Moosonee, at the other end of the province.

"Culture and Society in Ontario, 1784–1984" (1984), *Northrop Frye on Canada* (2003), CW, 12.

TREASON
In our day the word "treason," almost without our realizing it, has joined the word "heresy" as a word that could once intimidate, but is now only a Hallowe'en mask.

"The University and Personal Life: Student Anarchism and the Educational Contract" (1968), *Northrop Frye's Writings on Education* (2001), CW, 7.

TRINITY
Power, wisdom and love are three persons in one substance.

Entry, Notes 53 (1989–90), 34, *Northrop Frye's Late Notebooks, 1982–1990: Architecture of the Spiritual World* (2000), CW, 6.

A God who is traditionally three persons in one substance confronts man, who is three substances in one person.

Entry, Notebook 15 (1970s), 6, *Northrop Frye's Notebooks and Lectures on the Bible and Other Religious Texts* (2003), CW, 13.

TRISTRAM SHANDY
Tristram Shandy was my favourite novel at the age of sixteen, though I didn't know why. I know now: it's the story of an author trying to get born.

"Notes for 'Varieties of Eighteenth-Century Sensibility'" (1989), 44, *Northrop Frye's Fiction and Miscellaneous Writings* (2007), CW, 25.

TROJAN WAR
Even if there was a Trojan war, everything Homer says about it is legend, not history.

Entry, Notebook 21 (1969–76), 366, *Northrop Frye's Notebooks and Lectures on the Bible and Other Religious Texts* (2003), CW, 13.

TRUISMS
The truism, the sententious axiom, the proverb, the *topos* or rhetorical commonplace, the irresistibly quotable phrase — such things are the very life-blood of poetry.

"New Directions from Old" (1960), *"The Educated Imagination" and Other Writings on Critical Theory, 1933–1963* (2006), CW, 21.

Truisms are never true: the verbal expression of truth has to be sharply pointed to skewer an experience in the reader; but of course it doesn't directly communicate experience. Nor does it necessarily represent anything more than a potential one.

Entry, Notebook 19 (1964–67), 290, *The "Third Book" Notebooks of Northrop Frye, 1964–1972: The Critical Comedy* (2002), CW, 9.

TRUTH
The negative form of the Greek word for truth, *aletheia*, which means something like "unforgetting," suggests that at a certain point searching for the unknown gives way to trying to remove the impediments to seeing what is already there.

"Introduction" (1990), *Words with Power: Being a Second Study of "The Bible and Literature"* (2008), CW, 26.

The anxiety of society, when it urges the authority of a myth and the necessity of believing it, seems to be less to proclaim its truth than to prevent anyone from questioning it. It aims at consent, including the consent of silence, rather than conviction.
> *The Secular Scripture: A Study of the Structure of Romance* (1975), *"The Secular Scripture" and Other Writings on Critical Theory, 1976–1991* (2006), CW, 18.

Truth, like the classic in literature, is whatever won't go away, and keeps returning to confront us.
> Entry, Notes 53 (1989–90), 213, *Northrop Frye's Late Notebooks, 1982–1990: Architecture of the Spiritual World* (2000), CW, 6.

Truth is always a beginning; it can never be the end of anything in this world, for there is no end it can come to except the mind in which it began.
> "By Liberal Things" (1959), *Northrop Frye's Writings on Education* (2001), CW, 7.

I sometimes think I am looking for the truth, in the sense of tremendous insights or intuitions that will illuminate the meaning of life — and of death. But of course I'm not: all I'm looking for is verbal formulations, to fit somewhere in some damn paper.
> Entry, Notebook 19 (1964–67), 290, *The "Third Book" Notebooks of Northrop Frye, 1964–1972: The Critical Comedy* (2002), CW, 9.

And the more we know, the less inclined we are to use metaphors about seizing or grasping or possessing truth. The truth that makes one free must be shared: it cannot be owned.
> "To Come to Light" (1988), *Northrop Frye on Religion* (1999), CW, 4.

Truth of correspondence is really a technique of measurement, where the standard or criterion of measurement is outside the verbal structure.
> "The Mythical Approach to Creation" (1985), *Northrop Frye on Religion* (2000), CW, 4.

Greek critics distinguished verbal structures as true, false, and plastic, or more accurately plasmatic, the presenting of things as they conceivably could be.
> *The Secular Scripture: A Study of the Structure of Romance* (1975), *"The Secular Scripture" and Other Writings on Critical Theory, 1976–1991* (2006), CW, 18.

TWINS
If twins were really identical they would be the same person.
> "Second Essay: Ethical Criticism: Theory of Symbols" (1957), *Anatomy of Criticism: Four Essays* (2006), CW, 22.

TWO CULTURES
The editor of Shakespeare and the chemist live in different scholarly worlds, and proposals to make the humanist memorize the second law of thermodynamics and the scientist a speech from *Macbeth* will not bring them together. What brings them together is social, not intellectual, the fact that they are both citizens of their society with a common stake in that society.
> "The Instruments of Mental Production" (1966), *Northrop Frye's Writings on Education* (2001), CW, 7.

TYPOLOGY
Typology is a figure of speech that moves in time: the type exists in the past and the antitype in the present, or the type exists in the present and the antitype in the future.
> "Typology I," *The Great Code* (1982), *The Great Code: The Bible and Literature* (2006), CW, 19.

How do you know the Old Testament is true? Because it's fulfilled in the New Testament. How do you know that the New Testament is true? Because it fulfils the prophecies of the Old Testament.
> "Northrop Frye in Conversation" (1989), *Interviews with Northrop Frye* (2008), CW, 24.

... there's hardly a passage in the New Testament — I suspect that there is not a *single* passage in the New Testament — that is not related in this type-antitype manner to something in the Old Testament.

"Symbolism in the Bible" (1981–82), *Northrop Frye's Notebooks and Lectures on the Bible and Other Religious Texts* (2003), CW, 13.

It means that the Biblical religions have a diachronic mythology, to use that term, which moves in time and has an historical dimension, whereas the pagan mythologies are synchronic: they deal with elements in nature that recur cyclically but are the same thing every time.

"The Meaning of Recreation: Humanism in Society" (1979), *Northrop Frye on Religion* (2000), CW, 4.

To use fairly familiar terms in a slightly different context, Biblical mythology is diachronic, pagan mythology synchronic.

Creation and Recreation (1980), *Northrop Frye on Religion* (2000), CW, 4.

The archetype of all that is in the Bible, at least in the Christian Bible, where the [N]ew Testament's conception of the Old is, from the point of view of Judaism, a preposterous and perverse misunderstanding.

"The Meaning of Recreation: Humanism in Society" (1979), *Northrop Frye on Religion* (2000), CW, 4.

TYRANNY

The kernel of everything reactionary and tyrannical in society is the impoverishment of the means of verbal communication.

"The Primary Necessities of Existence" (1985), *Interviews with Northrop Frye* (2008), CW, 24.

The unconditioned will even of a majority could bring about as great a tyranny as the unconditioned will of a single ruler.

"The Ideal of Democracy" (1950), *Northrop Frye on Modern Culture* (2003), CW, 11.

TYRANTS

It is significant that our symbolic term for a tyrant is "dictator": that is, an uninterrupted speaker.

"Communications" (1970), *Northrop Frye on Modern Culture* (2003), CW, 11.

The Kurtz of *Heart of Darkness* is a particularly notable example, as he is the prototype of all the tyrant figures who have made the twentieth century perhaps the ghastliest in history.

"Fourth Variation: The Furnace," discussing the theme of "the placing of evil in a position of supreme social power," *Words with Power: Being a Second Study of "The Bible and Literature"* (1990), CW, 26.

The tyrant is the man who narrows the scope of life, in other words creates a hell out of human life, agent of an anti-resurrection.

Entry, Notebook 44 (1986–91), 217, *Northrop Frye's Late Notebooks, 1982–1990: Architecture of the Spiritual World* (2000), CW, 5.

U

ULYSSES
I read *Ulysses* before most Canadian students did, because another Victoria professor smuggled in a copy for me from the States after the ban was lifted there.
> "Autopsy on an Old Grad's Grievance" (1961), *Northrop Frye's Writings on Education* (2001), CW, 7.

UNCONSCIOUS
The mystique of the unconscious has bedevilled myth critics. If you find fragments of a huge myth in primitive times, the process that put it all together is most likely to be in Shakespeare or Wagner or someone producing a waking dream for conscious minds....
> Entry, Notebook 44 (1986–91), 136, *Northrop Frye's Late Notebooks, 1982–1990: Architecture of the Spiritual World* (2000), CW, 5.

UNDERGRADUATES
Undergraduates are parts of which the university is the whole; after graduation they are individuals again, and their university experiences have become a part of them.
> "To Come to Light" (1988), *Northrop Frye on Religion* (1999), CW, 4.

UNDERSTANDING
We project things we don't understand on God, and hope that he does.
> Entry, Notebook 30c: T.S. Eliot's *Four Quartets* (after 1979), 4, *Northrop Frye's Fiction and Miscellaneous Writings* (2007), CW, 25.

... all understanding is in a sense metaphorical understanding.
> "The Transferability of Literary Concepts" (1955), *"The Educated Imagination" and Other Writings on Critical Theory, 1933–1963* (2006), CW, 21.

UNEMPLOYMENT
Perhaps we could develop social services to the point where all the people thrown out of work by automation could be made into a new aristocracy, with nothing to do except go on luxury cruises.
> "Leisure and Boredom" (1963), *Northrop Frye on Literature and Society, 1936–1989: Unpublished Papers* (2002), CW, 10.

UNIDENTIFIED FLYING OBJECTS
Just as you have movies like *Star Wars* that talk about distant galaxies as being united by beings that look remarkably like Hollywood actors, so you have myths about unidentified flying objects that, again, tend to indicate that there is something way out there which is like ourselves.
> "Between Paradise and Apocalypse" (1978), *Interviews with Northrop Frye* (2008), CW, 24.

UNIQUENESS
First, uniqueness is not in itself worth studying, the world's worst poem being as unique as the best; second, uniqueness is unknowable. We cannot know the literary work except in terms of what is typical.
> Entry, Notebook 11f (1969–70), 236, *Northrop Frye's Notebooks and Lectures on the Bible and Other Religious Texts* (2003), CW, 13.

UNITED CHURCH
Protestantism is done for here, unless it listens to a few prophets. I don't want a Church of any kind, but if, say, a student of mine were quavering over conversion to Catholicism, I'd like to be able to point to something better than a committee of temperance cranks, which is about all the United Church is now.
> Entry, 3 Jan. 1949, 27, *The Diaries of Northrop Frye: 1942–1955* (2001), CW, 8.

Personally, I rather like the United Church because it contains a sort of church-destroying principle within itself, having already destroyed three.
> Entry, 29 Jan. 1949, 133, *The Diaries of Northrop Frye: 1942–1955* (2001), CW, 8.

This is an inevitable product of Canadianism — its counterpart would be inconceivable in the U.S.A. — and it is representative of all that Canada means in history — in its good-nature, in its tolerance, in its conscientiousness, in its vague and sentimental combination of Socialism, Imperialism and Nationalism all at once — a very appealing mixture, unpalatable though each individual constituent may be — above all in its determination to apply old traditions to new surroundings which makes Canada sturdier than England and more coherent in its perspective than the United States.
> "NF to HK," 25 Aug. 1932, *The Correspondence of Northrop Frye and Helen Kemp, 1932–1939* (1996), CW, 1.

UNITED NATIONS

The conception of United Civilizations, like the conception of United Nations, is pretty, but it isn't the real thing.
> "Toynbee and Spengler" (1947), *Northrop Frye on Modern Culture* (2003), CW, 11.

UNITED STATES OF AMERICA

In the beginning the Americans created America, and America is the beginning of the world. That is, it is the oldest country in the world: no other nation's history goes back so far with less social metamorphosis. Through all the anxieties and doubts of recent years one can still hear the confident tones of its Book of Genesis: "We hold these truths to be self-evident."
> "Conclusion to *Literary History of Canada*" (1965), *Northrop Frye on Canada* (2003), CW, 12.

Washington, Franklin, Jefferson, with their imperturbable common sense, are thought of, in the popular consciousness, more as deceased contemporaries than as ancestors living among different cultural referents. The past is thus assimilated to the present....
> "Conclusion to *Literary History of Canada*" (1965), *Northrop Frye on Canada* (2003), CW, 12.

The thirteen colonies revolted in the eighteenth century, but they fought a Civil War a century later over the issue of whether there should be any further revolutions or separations.
> "Symbolism in the Bible" (1981–82), *Northrop Frye's Notebooks and Lectures on the Bible and Other Religious Texts* (2003), CW, 13.

If we are looking for imaginative exuberance in American life, we shall find it not in its fiction but in its advertising; not in Broadway drama but in Broadway skyscrapers; not in the good movies but in the vista-visioned and technicoloured silly ones.
> "Preface to an Uncollected Anthology" (1956), *Northrop Frye on Canada* (2003), CW, 12.

I do not see how America can find its identity, much less avoid chaos, unless a massive citizens' resistance develops which is opposed to exploitation and imperialism on the one hand, and to jack-booted radicalism on the other. It would not be a new movement, but simply the will of the people, the people as a genuine society strong enough to contain and dissolve all mobs.
> "America: True or False?" (1969), *Northrop Frye on Canada* (2003), CW, 12.

UNITED STATES & CANADA

The United States became articulate in the eighteenth century, the Age of Reason, and it's had a fixation on the eighteenth century ever since. The Constitution begins by saying, "We hold these facts to be self-evident." Canada is a country where nothing has ever been self-evident and it didn't have an eighteenth century at all. The English and the French spent the eighteen century battering down each other's forts. Canada took shape in the Baroque, aggressive seventeenth century and took new shape in the Romantic, aggressive nineteenth.
> "Canadian Voices" (1975), *Interviews with Northrop Frye* (2008), CW, 24.

Perhaps it is not too presumptuous to say, although few non-Canadians would under-

stand what was meant, that the American way of life is slowly becoming Canadianized.
"Conclusion to *Literary History of Canada*" (1965), *Northrop Frye on Canada* (2003), CW, 12.

UNITY
The need to unify, we suggested, is an indication of the finiteness of the human mind, unity and the finite being aspects of the same thing.
"Language II," *The Great Code* (1982), *The Great Code: The Bible and Literature* (2006), CW, 19.

Unity means something which can comprise a great variety of opinions and views. Unity means something which can include dissension, conflicting ideas and opposition. Uniformity means everybody thinking alike or saying that they think alike.
"Education and the Rejection of Reality" (1971), *Northrop Frye's Writings on Education* (2001), CW, 7.

UNIVERSALS
The universal we reach ought to include within it the individuality with which we started: it should be a supreme Self which gives each self its identity.
"T.S. Eliot" (1963), *Northrop Frye on Twentieth-Century Literature* (2010), CW, 29.

UNIVERSE
To the imagination, the universe has always presented the appearance of a middle world, with a second world above it and a third one below it.
"First Variation: The Mountain," *Words with Power: Being a Second Study of "The Bible and Literature"* (2008), CW, 26.

I have spoken of a vision of literature, because I think that there is a literary universe, which, like every other universe, is unbounded and finite. The variety of individual literary works may be infinite; the total body of what can be produced as literature is not.
"Auguries of Experience" (1987), *"The Secular Scripture" and Other Writings on Critical Theory, 1976–1991* (2006), CW, 18.

Man lives, not directly or nakedly in nature like the animals, but within a mythological universe, a body of assumptions and beliefs developed from his existential concerns.
"Introduction," *The Great Code* (1982), *The Great Code: The Bible and Literature* (2006), CW, 19.

The mythological universe is not an ordered hierarchy but an interpenetrating world, where every unit of verbal experience is a monad reflecting all the others.
The Secular Scripture: A Study of the Structure of Romance (1975), *"The Secular Scripture" and Other Writings on Critical Theory, 1976–1991* (2006), CW, 18.

The etymology of "universe" suggests that everything turns around a centre, that centre being the personal centre that calls it a universe.
Entry, Notebook 50 (1987–90), 86, *Northrop Frye's Late Notebooks, 1982–1990: Architecture of the Spiritual World* (2000), CW, 5.

In the universe of nature, there is no such thing as up or down; in the mythological universe, there is nothing else.
"Symbolism in the Bible" (1981–82), *Northrop Frye's Notebooks and Lectures on the Bible and Other Religious Texts* (2003), CW, 13.

UNIVERSITIES
The universities alone preserve the secret of what is really happening.
"On Education III" (mid-1970s), 17, *Northrop Frye's Fiction and Miscellaneous Writings* (2007), CW, 25.

The hub of the university has always been, and must remain, a community where life can be experienced with greater intensity than anywhere else. The everyday world which comes to us through newspapers and television is not real life but a dissolving phantasmagoria.
"The Primary Necessities of Existence" (1985), *Interviews with Northrop Frye* (2008), CW, 24.

One of the things the university stands for is to give its students some sense of historical imagination, and to convince them that a culture without a memory is senile, just as an individual without a memory is.
"Back to the Garden" (1982), *Interviews with Northrop Frye* (2008), CW, 24.

The university is where you go to learn about an authority that is not externally applied. It doesn't tell you to do this or that.
"Northrop Frye in Conversation" (1989), *Interviews with Northrop Frye* (2008), CW, 24.

In particular, the university seems to me to come closer than any other human institution to defining the community of spiritual authority.
"The Problem of Spiritual Authority in the Nineteenth Century" (1964), *Northrop Frye's Writings on the Eighteenth and Nineteenth Centuries* (2005), CW, 17.

Well, I think that the university stands for a certain attitude to society, which is an attitude of detachment without withdrawal.
"The Scholar in Society" (1983), *Interviews with Northrop Frye* (2008), CW, 24.

The university, then, is the source of free authority in society, not as an institution, but as a place where the appeal to reason, experiment, evidence, and imagination is continuously going on.
"The University and Personal Life: Student Anarchism and the Educational Contract" (1968), *Northrop Frye's Writings on Education* (2001), CW, 7.

The university informs the world, and is not informed by it.
"The Study of English in Canada" (1957), *Northrop Frye's Writings on Education* (2001), CW, 7.

It is logical to link the university and culture: in fact it could almost be said that the university today is to culture what the church is to religion: the social institution that makes it possible. It teaches the culture of the past, and it tries to build up an educated public for the culture of the present.
"Culture and the National Will" (1957), *Northrop Frye on Canada* (2003), CW, 12.

The university is thus a kind of social laboratory in which the most revolutionary conceptions may be valuable, not necessarily as programmes for action, but as insights into the structure of society, nature, or the human mind.
"The Critical Discipline" (1960), *Northrop Frye's Writings on Education* (2001), CW, 7.

I have never lost the sense that the university is very near the centre of the idea of human community, and that our society stands or falls with it.
"Reminiscences" (1977), *Northrop Frye's Writings on Education* (2001), CW, 7.

The university is a community in which the intellect and the imagination have a continuously functional place, and so gives us a sense of what human life could be like if these qualities were always functional in it.
"The View from Here" (1980), *Northrop Frye's Writings on Education* (2001), CW, 7.

A big modern university could almost be defined as whatever group of professional schools in one town happens to be held together by a faculty of arts.
"Humanities in a New World" (1958), *Northrop Frye's Writings on Education* (2001), CW, 7.

The university is the powerhouse of civilization, and the centre of the university has to correspond to the actual centres of human knowledge.
"Humanities in a New World" (1958), *Northrop Frye's Writings on Education* (2001), CW, 7.

The university preserves the memory of mankind, of mature man as distinct from the childishness immersed in the dissolving present or the senility immersed in the past.
"By Liberal Things" (1959), *Northrop Frye's Writings on Education* (2001), CW, 7.

The university can best fulfil its revolutionary function by digging in its heels and doing its traditional job in its traditionally retrograde, obscurantist, and reactionary way.
"The Critical Discipline" (1960), *Northrop Frye's Writings on Education* (2001), CW, 7.

The university is perhaps the most coherent institution that I can think of in society, partly because it, in a sense, pretends to less than either religion or law.
"The Scholar in Society" (1983), *Interviews with Northrop Frye* (2008), CW, 24.

Wherever there is respect for the artist's vision, the scientist's detachment, the teacher's

learning and patience, the child's questioning, there the university is at work in the world.
"By Liberal Things" (1959), *Northrop Frye's Writings on Education* (2001), CW, 7.

The university is the other pole of society: it represents the freedom which is the only genuine product of social concern.
"Convocation Address, York University" (1969), *Northrop Frye's Writings on Education* (2001), CW, 7.

One doesn't realize the immense social prestige of the university until one gets a little outside it.
Entry, 5 Sep. 1942, 97, *The Diaries of Northrop Frye: 1942–1955* (2001), CW, 8.

UNIVERSITIES & STUDENTS

Society consists largely of adolescents and arrested adolescents, and departments of education who have to arrange high-school curricula are well aware of the fact. As a rule a student has to get to university before he can make contact with the culture of his own time.
"Culture and the National Will" (1957), *Northrop Frye on Canada* (2003), CW, 12.

In moments of depression one feels that the majority of university students have already been conditioned beyond the point at which the university can affect them at all.
"The Critical Discipline" (1960), *Northrop Frye's Writings on Education* (2001), CW, 7.

I think the university will never do its job in society until a great mass of people of all ages, from thirty to ninety, feel they can come and get their lives revitalized. The process is somewhat like a religious retreat, except that it would be a much more permanent thing because being involved in some form of cultural activity is what really makes one a human being.
"The Primary Necessities of Existence" (1985), *Interviews with Northrop Frye* (2008), CW, 24.

Undergraduates usually speak of the university as "school," and expect to be taught, but it is part of the function of a university to disappoint them, to insist on treating them as adults.
"The Study of English in Canada" (1957), *Northrop Frye's Writings on Education* (2001), CW, 7.

In such a society it would be appropriate that universities should no longer be almost wholly concerned, as teaching institutions, with young people in the few lucid intervals that occur during four years of the mating season, but would make a place also for adults who could keep dropping into the university at various periods of their lives as an intellectual retreat.
"The Instruments of Mental Production" (1966), *Northrop Frye's Writings on Education* (2001), CW, 7.

The powers of the awakened mind are not children's toys, and the university cannot guarantee that anything it offers will be harmless.
"By Liberal Things" (1959), *Northrop Frye's Writings on Education* (2001), CW, 7.

A university cannot be first-rate unless intellect, passion for ideas, long hours of work, and devotion to one's course are socially acceptable to the student body. If the vulgar attitudes to the longhair or the bookworm are repeated there, we have no university, but only a fresh air camp for the overprivileged.
Principal's Installation Address" (1959), "By Liberal Things" (1959), *Northrop Frye's Writings on Education* (2001), CW, 7.

I've always been impressed by the loyalty and affection of so large a proportion of the alumni to the place where they took their first degree.
"The Scholar in Society" (1983), *Interviews with Northrop Frye* (2008), CW, 24.

The larger university is one you can never leave.
"To the Class of '62 at Queen's" (1962), *Northrop Frye's Writings on Education* (2001), CW, 7.

The student entering the university is the one who is embarking on an encounter with real life. He is descending into the engine room of society, seeing the machinery of the human intellect and the human imagination driving all the great power structures around him. In studying the liberal arts, he studies the permanent form of human society and begins to understand where the causes are that make society change so rapidly and seem so unpredictable.

"The Primary Necessities of Existence" (1985), *Interviews with Northrop Frye* (2008), CW, 24.

Life is lived here in a way which makes such words as culture and civilization mean something. So it's easier to see what human life could be like if intelligence and awareness were constantly being used.

"The Chancellor's Message" (1979), *Northrop Frye's Writings on Education* (2001), CW, 7.

The life of an undergraduate student is a very difficult one, because university students are socially and physically adults, while intellectually they are children. It is because they are willing to admit the immaturity of their minds that they come to college.

"Education — Protection against Futility" (1964), *Northrop Frye's Writings on Education* (2001), CW, 7.

As you leave the University of British Columbia, what you are being invited to join is the lower-case university, the university of the world, as I should call it, which represents the social values that this institution exists for.

"Convocation Address, University of British Columbia" (1963), *Northrop Frye's Writings on Education* (2001), CW, 7.

UNIVERSITIES, CANADIAN

Without the universities, Canada would simply become again what it was at first: the hewer of wood and drawer of water for Americans.

"Making the Revolutionary Act Now" (1983), *Interviews with Northrop Frye* (2008), CW, 24.

If Canadian universities are underfunded so badly that they can no longer function effectively, Canada would disappear overnight from modern history and become again what it was at first, a blank area of natural resources to be exploited by more advanced countries. This is not empty rhetoric: it is a verifiable fact, though I should not care to become known as the person who verified it.

"The Authority of Learning" (1984), *Northrop Frye's Writings on Education* (2001), CW, 7.

And just as Canadians discovered, long before our neighbours did, that it was possible to elect a Roman Catholic to the highest office without becoming annexed to the Vatican, so we have discovered that it is possible for universities to receive federal aid without having to teach their courses from government directives.

"John George Diefenbaker" (1961), *Northrop Frye on Canada* (2003), CW, 12.

UNIVERSITY OF TORONTO

And when I was inaugurated as Chancellor of Victoria I said there were two things that made Toronto a world-class university: one was the Honour Course and the other was the federated college system, and we've destroyed both. But that speech was never reprinted anywhere.

"Towards an Oral History of the University of Toronto" (1982), referring to four-year rather than three-year courses, etc., *Interviews with Northrop Frye* (2008), CW, 24.

When the Honour Course was scrapped in a fit of hysteria in the 1960s it was an irrevocable disaster, and Toronto will never be in the foreseeable future as distinguished a university in its arts and science teaching as it was then.

"A Fearful Symmetry" (1981), *Interviews with Northrop Frye* (2008), CW, 24.

I remain obstinately of the opinion that the Honour Course, with all its rigidity and built-in administrative absurdities, gave the best undergraduate training available on the North American continent, and the best teacher training for the instructor as well.

"The Beginning of the Word" (1980), *Northrop Frye's Writings on Education* (2001), CW, 7.

The university belongs to its society, and the notion of autonomy of the university is an illusion. It is an illusion which it would be hard to maintain on the campus of the University of Toronto, situated as it is between the

Parliament Buildings on one side and the educational Pentagon on the other, like Samson between the pillars of a Philistine temple.
> "The Definition of a University" (1970), *Northrop Frye's Writings on Education* (2001), CW, 7.

URANIUM

The people who make fortunes out of uranium stocks owe their wealth and social prestige to an absent-minded professor, badly in need of a haircut, who scribbled down $e=mc^2$ on a piece of paper fifty years ago.
> "Humanities in a New World" (1958), *Northrop Frye's Writings on Education* (2001), CW, 7.

UTOPIA

In a world like ours a limited Utopia in a restricted or enclosed space is an empty fantasy: Utopia must be a world-wide transformation of the whole social order or it is nothing.
> *The Critical Path: An Essay on the Social Context of Literary Criticism* (1971), *"The Critical Path" and Other Writings on Critical Theory, 1963–1975* (2009), CW, 27.

I asked the two stock questions about the book and got the two stock answers. How many would rather live in Utopia than in Henry VIII's England? Every one. How many would rather live in Utopia than in twentieth-century Canada? Not one. That established the essential points about the book, first, that Utopias present a more coherent form of social life than history does, and second, that no normal human being wants to live in anyone else's Utopia.
> "Natural and Revealed Communities" (1987), teaching Thomas More's work *Utopia* in the 1930s, *Northrop Frye's Writings on Shakespeare and the Renaissance* (2010), CW, 28.

The Utopia, the effort at social imagination, is an area in which specialized disciplines can meet and interpenetrate with a mutual respect for each other, concerned with clarifying their common social context.
> "Varieties of Literary Utopias" (1965), *"The Critical Path" and Other Writings on Critical Theory, 1963–1975* (2009), CW, 27.

The real Utopia is an individual goal, of which the disciplined society is an allegory. The end of commitment and engagement is the community: the logical end of detachment is the individual.
> *The Critical Path: An Essay on the Social Context of Literary Criticism* (1971), *"The Critical Path" and Other Writings on Critical Theory, 1963–1975* (2009), CW, 27.

The question, "Where is Utopia?" is the same as the question, "Where is nowhere?" and the only answer to that question is "Here."
> "Varieties of Literary Utopias" (1965), *"The Critical Path" and Other Writings on Critical Theory, 1963–1975* (2009), CW, 27.

… probably it's the germ of Utopia: nowhere becoming everywhere.
> Entry, Notebook 46 (1980s–90), 37, *Northrop Frye's Late Notebooks, 1982–1990: Architecture of the Spiritual World* (2000), CW, 6.

The Utopia is a vision of the rational form of society, & it is best seen, not as an end, but as an informing principle. It's the objective aspect of what in subjective terms is ideal education.
> Entry, Notebook 19 (1964–67), 88, *The "Third Book" Notebooks of Northrop Frye, 1964–1972: The Critical Comedy* (2002), CW, 9.

V

VAGINA

It's also, of course, the most elaborately concealed part of the body: even "nature" conceals it when the body is stark naked.
>Entry, Notebook 12 (1968–70), 331, *The "Third Book" Notebooks of Northrop Frye, 1964–1972: The Critical Comedy* (2002), CW, 9.

VALUE JUDGMENTS

I think that genuine value judgments are always assumptions; that is, they are working assumptions, heuristic assumptions, and they are consequently subject to later scholarship, which means that scholarship always has the power of veto over value judgments.
>"Back to the Garden" (1982), *Interviews with Northrop Frye* (2008), CW, 24.

I have never said that there were no literary values or that critics should never make value judgments: what I have said is that literary values are not *established* by critical value judgments. Every work of literature establishes its own value; in the past much critical energy has been wasted in trying to reject or minimize these values.
>"Letter to the English Institute, 1965" (1965), *"The Critical Path" and Other Writings on Critical Theory, 1963–1975* (2009), CW, 27.

Value judgments are working assumptions, but nothing can be built on them. They buttress experience but not knowledge, & lead to no discoveries.
>Entry, Notebook 11e (1978), 14, *Northrop Frye's Notebooks and Lectures on the Bible and Other Religious Texts* (2003), CW, 13.

It seemed to me clear that the new knowledge had, as I put it later, a power of veto over the value judgment.
>"Reflections in a Mirror" (1966), referring to the nature of Blake's Prophecies, *"The Critical Path" and Other Writings on Critical Theory, 1963–1975* (2009), CW, 27.

This fact needs explanation, as the value-judgment is often, and perhaps rightly for all I know, regarded as the distinguishing feature of the humanistic and liberal pursuit.
>"Polemical Introduction" (1957), *Anatomy of Criticism: Four Essays* (2006), CW, 22.

Value judgments are founded on the study of literature; the study of literature can never be founded on value judgments.
>"Polemical Introduction" (1957), *Anatomy of Criticism: Four Essays* (2006), CW, 22.

Everyone accepts the value judgment that Shakespeare was a great poet; everyone finds this value judgment confirmed in practice; but no Shakespearean scholarship whatever is founded on that value judgment.
>"The Critical Path" (1979), *Interviews with Northrop Frye* (2008), CW, 24.

In knowledge the context of the work of literature is literature; in value judgment, the context of the work of literature is the reader's experience.
>"On Value Judgments" (1968), *"The Critical Path" and Other Writings on Critical Theory, 1963–1975* (2009), CW, 27.

"Wrong" value judgments are not errors in taste: they are expressions of inadequate knowledge about literature.
>"Frye, Literary Critic" (1987), *Interviews with Northrop Frye* (2008), CW, 24.

Values can be assumed, they can be argued about, but they cannot be demonstrated.
>"Sacred and Secular Scriptures" (1975), *Interviews with Northrop Frye* (2008), CW, 24.

The only value-judgment which is consistently and invariably useful to the scholarly critic is the judgment that his own writings, like the morals of a whore, are no better than they should be.
> "On Value Judgments" (1968), *"The Critical Path" and Other Writings on Critical Theory, 1963–1975* (2009), CW, 27.

My point that knowledge has the power of veto over value in criticism has a lot of implications, including theological ones. More knowledge (or wisdom as potential knowledge) has the power of veto over everything founded on present knowledge.
> Entry, Notebook 21 (1969–76), 468, *Northrop Frye's Notebooks and Lectures on the Bible and Other Religious Texts* (2003), CW, 13.

VALUES

Every deliberately constructed hierarchy of values in literature known to me is based on a concealed social, moral, or intellectual analogy.
> "Polemical Introduction" (1957), *Anatomy of Criticism: Four Essays* (2006), CW, 22.

Values, like god, come first as creative assumptions, not last as judges.
> Entry, Notebook 50 (1987–90), 627, *Northrop Frye's Late Notebooks, 1982–1990: Architecture of the Spiritual World* (2000), CW, 5.

There are so surprisingly few things that really matter. Music matters, and babies matter — so do poetry, sunsets over marshes, plain food, and people's flea-bitten souls. But that's about all. So why bother about anything else?
> "NF to HK," 2 Sep. 1932, *The Correspondence of Northrop Frye and Helen Kemp, 1932–1939* (1996), CW, 1.

The silly things are just as acceptable socially as the shrewd or penetrating thing.
> "The Limits of Dialogue" (1969), *Interviews with Northrop Frye* (2008), CW, 24.

The pursuit of values in criticism is like the pursuit of happiness in the American Constitution: one may have some sympathy with the stated aim, but one deplores the grammar.
> "On Value Judgments" (1968), *"The Critical Path" and Other Writings on Critical Theory, 1963–1975* (2009), CW, 27.

There is such a thing as value in literature, certainly, but a work of literature establishes its own value. What we really mean by such terms as "classic" and "masterpiece" are fundamentally works of literature that insist on their value, and refuse to go away.
> "Criticism as Education" (1979), *Northrop Frye's Writings on Education* (2001), CW, 7.

The goal of ethical criticism is transvaluation, the ability to look at contemporary social values with the detachment of one who is able to compare them in some degree with the infinite vision of possibilities presented by culture. One who possesses such a standard of transvaluation is in a state of intellectual freedom.
> "Tentative Conclusion" (1957), *Anatomy of Criticism: Four Essays* (2006), CW, 22.

When I joined the university I believed in the values it stood for: after thirty years of working in it I am convinced of them. And there are not many other things I am convinced of in this world.
> "The ideal University Community" (1969), *Northrop Frye's Writings on Education* (2001), CW, 7.

VELIKOVSKY, IMMANUEL

Naturally he's deterministic: myth is an effect for him, following a natural event as its cause. He perhaps underrates the absorptive power of mythical language. It's another aspect of my point that there's no such thing as a constellation.
> Entry, Notebook 24 (1970–72), 84, after reading Velikovsky's *Worlds in Collision*, *The "Third Book" Notebooks of Northrop Frye, 1964–1972: The Critical Comedy* (2002), CW, 9.

In our day a writer who has had a considerable vogue, especially among students, Immanuel Velikovsky, has written books to show that two of the most unlikely events recorded in the Bible, the sun standing still during a battle of Joshua's and the shadow of the dial going backward during the illness of Hezekiah, did take place in the way that they are described. What is significant here is that the Bible itself does not appear to record confirming evidence from outside itself as really strengthening its case.

"History and Myth in the Bible" (1976), *Northrop Frye on Religion* (2000), CW, 4.

VERSE

You can have verse in the most primitive societies; you cannot have prose except in developed and sophisticated ones.

"Literature as Possession" (1959), *"The Educated Imagination" and Other Writings on Critical Theory, 1933–1963* (2006), CW, 21.

Blank verse is the easiest metre in English to write accurately and the most difficult to write well.

"Literature as Possession" (1959), *"The Educated Imagination" and Other Writings on Critical Theory, 1933–1963* (2006), CW, 21.

Light verse is more elaborately contrived than serious verse, just as detective and adventure stories are more elaborately contrived than "serious" novels.

"Rencontre: The General Editor's Introduction" (1960s), *Northrop Frye on Literature and Society, 1936–1989: Unpublished Papers* (2002), CW, 10.

VICO, GIAMBATTISTA

I know of no other thinker who is as close to thinking of the entire structure of concern as a poetic myth.

Entry, Notebook 19 (1964–67), 343, *The "Third Book" Notebooks of Northrop Frye, 1964–1972: The Critical Comedy* (2002), CW, 9.

VICTIMS

The focusing of interest on the victim is a common civilizing element in all our major cultural traditions.

"Violence and Television" (1975), *Northrop Frye on Modern Culture* (2003), CW, 11.

Other people are the same: hence the hatred of Jews & negroes, whom even the most ignorant know perfectly well are not the real enemy. It's because they're not the real enemy that they're chosen as victims. Of course the real enemy is inside....

Entry, Notebook 3 (1946–48), 99, *Northrop Frye's Notebooks and Lectures on the Bible and Other Religious Texts* (2003), CW, 13.

VICTORIA COLLEGE

The university is an enormously continuous institution. While Victoria fifty years ago was, I suppose, a small Methodist college and now it's a big cosmopolitan university, nevertheless people who have been around it for half a century, like myself, don't feel any violent discontinuity in what has taken place in that time.

"Music in My Life" (1985), *Interviews with Northrop Frye* (2008), CW, 24.

For you are not leaving Victoria College for the world: you are taking Victoria College with you into the world. From now on, Victoria College will be also wherever you are, and its reputation will depend on you as well as on us.

"Senior Dinner Address" (1960), addressing new graduates, *Northrop Frye's Writings on Education* (2001), CW, 7.

As I've remarked before, playing goal for the girls' hockey team is about the only job I *haven't* been assigned around this place yet.

Entry, 27 Feb. 1952, 143, *The Diaries of Northrop Frye: 1942–1955* (2001), CW, 8.

The advantage of a small college is that everybody feels as though they belonged to it, and the process of education is personal, as education always should be. The disadvantage of a small college is that it's not a great university.

"The Principal's Message" (1963), referring to the origin of Victoria University as a small liberal-arts college in Cobourg, Ont., *Northrop Frye's Writings on Education* (2001), CW, 7.

The principle of federation was that the sciences, on the whole, are best taught when they are centralized, and the humanities when they are decentralized.

"Installation Address as Chancellor" (1978), *Northrop Frye's Writings on Education* (2001), CW, 7.

Victoria College is a church-related arts college ... and such a college in my view permits more and not less academic freedom than a college that has to adopt a prudish and self-censoring avoidance of religious issues.
"Preface" (1987), *No Uncertain Sounds* (1988).

Yet Victoria has kept its church connection, where so many Protestant colleges have cut themselves away from their founding church, leaving behind only a vague religious atmosphere, like a nostalgic smell of mildew in the basement. Victoria, in short, has always taken the practical view that the only really secure way of having one's cake is to eat it.
"By Liberal Things" (1959), *Northrop Frye's Writings on Education* (2001), CW, 7.

I am deeply grateful for the good will, the friendliness, and the courtesy shown me tonight, and expect to remember them as long as I live. Apart from that, however, I am a little startled to find myself being installed: I should have thought that an honour reserved for more massive pieces of equipment, like presidents and refrigerators.
"By Liberal Things" (1959), an address on the occasion of his installation as Principal of Victoria College, *Northrop Frye's Writings on Education* (2001), CW, 7.

VIOLENCE
Controlling violence means, first of all, raising the level of society. The people who produce and sell socially irresponsible programs are thinking of their viewers as a mob rather than a community.
"Violence and Television" (1975), *Northrop Frye on Modern Culture* (2003), CW, 11.

Violence, however long it lasts, can only go around in the circles of lost direction. There is a vaguely Freudian notion that there is something therapeutic in releasing inhibitions; but it is clear that releasing inhibitions is just as compulsive, repetitive, and hysterical an operation as the repressing of them.
"Communications" (1970), *Northrop Frye on Modern Culture* (2003), CW, 11.

Violence is often the only means of emotional release from a sense of unreality, in which even wantonly destructive or sadistic acts help to create a sense of identity in their perpetrators.
"The Ethics of Change: The Role of the University" (1968), *Northrop Frye's Writings on Education* (2001), CW, 7.

In all scenes of violence there is the choice of identifying either with the agent or with the victim of violence. Consequently, it is a very important step in emotional education whether we identify with the agent or with the victim of violence.
"Violence and Television" (1975), *Northrop Frye on Modern Culture* (2003), CW, 11.

The only real justification for violence is self-defence, and of course society has a right to self-defence as well as the individual.
"Violence and Television" (1975), *Northrop Frye on Modern Culture* (2003), CW, 11.

VIRGIL
... for instance, Virgil is a vastly greater name in English literature than the *Beowulf* poet.
Entry, Notebook 42a (1942–44), 7, *Northrop Frye's Notebooks on Romance* (2004), CW, 15.

VIRGIN BIRTH
Hence, though the Virgin Birth is scriptural, there is another sense in which it is apocryphal, & so, while Protestantism accepts it, it tends, in striking contrast to the Catholic doctrine, to become unfunctional.
Entry, 12 Mar. 1949, 263, *The Diaries of Northrop Frye: 1942–1955* (2001), CW, 8.

... I don't "believe in" the Virgin Birth as a historical fact, but I "believe in" it as a poetic myth. That could mean (though it doesn't) that I don't take historical facts seriously. It certainly does mean that I take myth (and literature) very seriously indeed. That doesn't mean (once again) that I take seriously what they *say*: what I take seriously is the structure of what they present.
Entry, Notebook 50 (1987–90), 495, *Northrop Frye's Late Notebooks, 1982–1990: Architecture of the Spiritual World* (2000), CW, 5.

VIRGIN MARY

The Virgin Mary represents the expansion from sex into spiritual love: she's the mother of the Word but the bride of the Spirit.

> Entry, Notebook 50 (1987–90), 617, *Northrop Frye's Late Notebooks, 1982–1990: Architecture of the Spiritual World* (2000), CW, 5.

VIRTUES

Hope is the virtue of the past, the eternal sense that maybe next time we'll do better. The projection of this into the future is faith, the substance of things hoped for. Love belongs to the present, & is the only force able to cast out fear.

> Entry, Notebook 3 (1946–48), 146, *Northrop Frye's Notebooks and Lectures on the Bible and Other Religious Texts* (2003), CW, 13.

VISION

The quest for unmediated vision, then, is really a quest for the recovery of myth, the word hoard guarded by the dragons of ideology.

> "Framework and Assumption" (1985), *"The Secular Scripture" and Other Writings on Critical Theory, 1976–1991* (2006), CW, 18.

Once again, my interest is not in doctrines of faith as such but in the expanding of vision through language.

> "Metaphor II," *The Great Code* (1982), *The Great Code: The Bible and Literature* (2006), CW, 19.

Well, the habit of vision is creative: the habit of seeing what's there is repetitive.

> Entry, Notebook 32 (late 1946–51), 101, *Northrop Frye's Notebooks on Romance* (2004), CW, 15.

The glimpses I have had of the imaginative world have kept me fascinated for nearly half a century, and no one life can begin to exhaust the fascination.

> "The View from Here" (1980), *Northrop Frye's Writings on Education* (2001), CW, 7.

I'm really building everything around a highly personal vision, a vision that I think I've had since I was a child. Consciousness of it came in various stages. I suppose it began to take its present form in my undergraduate years at university.

> "Canadian Energies: Dialogues on Creativity" (1980), *Interviews with Northrop Frye* (2008), CW, 24.

Doubtless the world we see and the world we create meet somewhere at some point of identity, but keeping the two eyes of knowledge focused on that point seems better than a Cyclopean single vision.

> "The Instruments of Mental Production" (1966), *Northrop Frye's Writings on Education* (2001), CW, 7.

This effort of vision, so called, is to be conceived neither as a human attempt to reach God nor a divine attempt to reach man, but as the realization in total experience of the identity of God and Man in which both the human creature and the superhuman Creator disappear.

> "General Note: Blake's Mysticism," *Fearful Symmetry: A Study of William Blake* (1947, 2004), CW, 14.

In the double vision of a spiritual and a physical world simultaneously present, every moment we have lived through we have also died out of into another order. Our life in the resurrection, then, is already here, and waiting to be recognized.

> *The Double Vision* (1991), *Northrop Frye on Religion* (2000), CW, 4.

Vision is relative to the choice of a point of view: this has always been true, of course, but never before so obviously true.

> "Academy without Walls" (1961), *Northrop Frye on Modern Culture* (2003), CW, 11.

Just as a new country cannot become a civilization without explorers and pioneers going out into the loneliness of a deserted land, so no social imagination can develop except through those who have followed their own vision beyond its inevitable loneliness to its final resting place in the tradition of art.

> "Lawren Harris" (1969), *Northrop Frye on Canada* (2003), CW, 12.

Your time here was a mixed experience, but at the centre of it were those brief flashes of insight, often not reaching full consciousness, when you felt, not perhaps that you had got it all together, but that there was something

there that was all together, and that you were part of it.
> "Convocation Address: McGill University" (1983), *Northrop Frye on Literature and Society, 1936–1989: Unpublished Papers* (2002), CW, 10.

May our vision be thy vision in us.
> "Undated Prayers (13)" (1992), *Northrop Frye on Religion* (2000), CW, 4.

... the end of vision is the living form of humanity, not the mathematical form of nature. But how does one get from one to the other? What relation has the physical appearance of nature to the real mental form or body of Man?
> "Part Three: The Final Synthesis," *Fearful Symmetry: A Study of William Blake* (1947, 2004), CW, 14.

Art, the spiritual vision of a culture, harrows the hell of human misery.
> Entry, Notebook 24 (1970–72), 235, *The "Third Book" Notebooks of Northrop Frye, 1964–1972: The Critical Comedy* (2002), CW, 9.

A visionary creates, or dwells in, a higher spiritual world in which the objects of perception in this one have become transfigured and charged with a new intensity of symbolism.
> "Part One: The Argument," *Fearful Symmetry: A Study of William Blake* (1947, 2004), CW, 14.

VOCABULARY

Where should we be today if we had been offered blood, toil, tears, and perspiration?
> "Reflections at a Movie" (1942), *Northrop Frye on Modern Culture* (2003), CW, 11.

VOICE

After that, perhaps, the terrifying and welcome voice may begin, annihilating everything we thought we knew, and restoring everything we have never lost.
> "Fourth Variation: The Furnace," *Words with Power: Being a Second Study of "The Bible and Literature"* (2008), CW, 26. The book concludes with this sentence.

Traditionally, the Bible speaks with the voice of God and through the voice of man.
> "Language II," *The Great Code* (1982), *The Great Code: The Bible and Literature* (2006), CW, 19.

WAGNER, RICHARD

Loathed his music to the point of physical nausea during the war, when I accepted the Nazi identification with him and assumed that certain paranoid things in him like his anti-Semitism were central. Gradually got things into focus, but the preposterous Victorian melodrama of the spectacular effects still put me off.
> "Notes for 'The World of Music and Idea in Wagner's Parsifal'" (1982), 2, *Northrop Frye's Fiction and Miscellaneous Writings* (2007), CW, 25.

One almost dares to hope that neither Wagner nor his godson Hitler have yet bludgeoned all the music out of the German soul.
> "The Jooss Ballet" (1936), *Northrop Frye on Modern Culture* (2003), CW, 11.

I feel similarly helpless with all the Wagner I have heard — that's one reason why I think Wagner a tonic for lazy minds.
> "NF to HK," 18 Apr. 1934, attending a performance of Beethoven and Wagner, *The Correspondence of Northrop Frye and Helen Kemp, 1932–1939* (1996), CW, 1.

For Wagner's bitterest enemies, among whom I include myself, cannot deny that in sheer ability to write music he gets top ranking. But in Wagner's musical dramas we begin to see where the reactionary circus of today comes from.
> "Music and the Savage Breast" (1938), *Northrop Frye on Modern Culture* (2003), CW, 11.

WAR

… Canada, a country that has never found much virtue in war and has certainly never started one, has in its military history a long list of ferocious conflicts against desperate odds.
> "Preface to an Uncollected Anthology" (1956), *Northrop Frye on Canada* (2003), CW, 12.

By the war of civilization is meant in particular all the public activities which spring from the axiom that the price of liberty is eternal vigilance.
> "Editorial Statement" (1948), *Northrop Frye on Canada* (2003), CW, 12.

I suspect that war, along with violence and terror, is perhaps the only really evil form of sexual perversion. That's partly because it's the one socially approved form.
> "On Evil" (1985), *Interviews with Northrop Frye* (2008), CW, 24.

There may be just wars, but no holy wars, because the "good" side is never holy and the "bad" side is still human.
> *The Double Vision* (1991), *Northrop Frye on Religion* (2000), CW, 4.

The Canadian public didn't realize how important universities were until it was clear that we couldn't win a war without them.
> "Culture and the National Will" (1957), *Northrop Frye on Canada* (2003), CW, 12.

I haven't any feeling about war except that I wish it would go away and leave me alone to do my work. I don't care if people have wars if they wouldn't bother me. The last war didn't bother me except when it killed my friends. And I utterly refuse to sanction the notion that the war is something bigger & more important than my concerns. The war is not important unless it makes too much damage to leave a surviving public interested in the work I'm doing, in which case it's important because it's Antichrist. What other

attitude any sane man with real work to do can take towards a war I can't even conceive.
> Entry, 26 Jun. 1950, 444, *The Diaries of Northrop Frye: 1942–1955* (2001), CW, 8.

WAR, SECOND WORLD
War has begun its second farewell tour, Sept. 3, 1939.
> Entry, Notebook 4 (1939), 33, *Northrop Frye's Fiction and Miscellaneous Writings* (2007), CW, 25.

Our moral superiority to our enemies is the moral superiority of a war of defence over a war of conquest. And the aims of the former are to some extent negative.
> "The Present Condition of the World" (1943), *Northrop Frye on Literature and Society, 1936–1989: Unpublished Papers* (2002), CW, 10.

But if war comes, will it be a Marxist or a Spenglerian one? Will it lead at once to socialist revolutions all over Europe and help destroy capitalism, or will it start brutalizing people to the level at which they accept indefinite series of annihilation wars as part of the scheme of things? Both points of view have so much truth in them.
> "NF to HK," 29 Sep. 1938, *The Correspondence of Northrop Frye and Helen Kemp, 1932–1939* (1996), CW, 1.

The Russians call the 1939–45 war the "Great Patriotic War": that's what I mean by a mythical title. But it's more comprehensive, more involving for the Russian people, and in every way that makes sense more true, than a simply historical or descriptive title would be.
> Entry, Notebook 50 (1987–90), 712, *Northrop Frye's Late Notebooks, 1982–1990: Architecture of the Spiritual World* (2000), CW, 5.

After the last war and the atomic bomb, a lot of people began to realize that the express train to Utopia might be derailed, but were unable to turn from a frivolous optimism to anything but an equally frivolous despair.
> "Two Books on Christianity and History" (1949), *Northrop Frye on Modern Culture* (2003), CW, 11.

WAR DEAD
In civilized situations man is seldom ready to die fighting for himself, but he'll die by the millions for a community.
> Entry, Notes 52 (1982–90), 67, *Northrop Frye's Late Notebooks, 1982–1990: Architecture of the Spiritual World* (2000), CW, 6.

A holocaust is not less a holocaust for being a voluntary one.
> "Culture and Society in Ontario, 1784–1984" (1984), a specific reference to the dead of World War II, *Northrop Frye on Canada* (2003), CW, 12.

I keep having a vision of a guide or preacher or some professional haranguer standing in front of a war cemetery in Flanders with a million crosses behind him and explaining how human aggressiveness has such essential survival value.
> Entry, Notes 54.1(May 1990), 64, *Northrop Frye's Late Notebooks, 1982–1990: Architecture of the Spiritual World* (2000), CW, 6.

WAR OF 1812
Queenston Heights. So far as that incredible bungle of the War of 1812 had any meaning at all for Canada, it was Canada's War of Independence and this was where it began.
> "View of Canada" (1976), *Northrop Frye on Canada* (2003), CW, 12.

In time, the United States had a revolutionary war first, a struggle against European domination, and a civil war afterwards, a purely domestic affair. Canada had its civil war first, a struggle of two European powers on its soil, and a war of independence afterwards, which curtailed a thrust of aggression coming from this continent. At least, that was the point of the War of 1812 for Canada, so far as that incredibly bungling and inept collision in the dark had any point.
> "Canadian Scene: Explorers and Observers" (1973), *Northrop Frye on Canada* (2003), CW, 12.

WARNINGS
Once when somebody took me for a ride in British Columbia, I saw on the highway a sign saying "Watch for falling rocks" and then we turned the corner and saw another sign saying "Prepare to meet thy God." I realized

then that the impulse to warn is very deeply imbedded in human nature.

"Literature as a Critique of Pure Reason" (1982), *"The Secular Scripture" and Other Writings on Critical Theory, 1976–1991* (2006), CW, 18.

WASHINGTON, D.C.
Washington was a city designed for automobiles rather than pedestrians long before there were any automobiles....

"Canada: New World Without Revolution" (1975), *Northrop Frye on Canada* (2003), CW, 12.

WATERCOLOURS
And it is here that watercolour painting takes on a peculiar significance, for I think a strong case could be made out for saying that one of the chief functions of watercolour is to keep painters interested in untried possibilities, whether in subject matter or in technique.

"Water-Colour Annual" (1944), *Northrop Frye on Canada* (2003), CW, 12.

WAY, THE
The thing found isn't really communicable: it's the process of finding that is, & no one ever stops finding.

Entry, Notebook 30r: Autobiographical Notes V (1991), 6, *Northrop Frye's Fiction and Miscellaneous Writings* (2007), CW, 25.

Once we form part of a body which is both ourselves and infinitely larger than ourselves, the distinction between movement and rest vanishes: there is no need for a way when the conception "away" is no longer functional.

"Identity and Metaphor," *Words with Power: Being a Second Study of "The Bible and Literature"* (1990), CW, 26.

WEATHER
I remember being at a "church supper" in a rural area of Saskatchewan, and hearing one woman say to another: "You know, this last rain wasn't necessary, in the least." It nearly split my own Canadian psyche to hear, in so middle-class a gathering, the murmur of a timeless peasantry scolding its household gods. But such sudden atavisms are almost a commonplace in Canadian literature, whether the setting is rural or urban.

"National Consciousness in Canadian Culture" (1976), *Northrop Frye on Canada* (2003), CW, 12.

WELLS, H.G.
Wells's writing in general illustrates the common principle that the belief that man is by nature good does not lead to a very good-natured view of man.

"Varieties of Literary Utopias" (1970), *"The Critical Path" and Other Writings on Critical Theory, 1963–1975* (2009), CW, 27.

The pull toward the anatomy has influenced even those temperamentally unsuited to the form. H.G. Wells is a good blackboard example of a growth from first-rate tale to second-rate novel, and from second-rate novel to third-rate anatomy.

"An Enquiry into the Art Forms of Prose Fiction" (1935–39), *Northrop Frye's Student Essays, 1932–1938* (1997), CW, 3.

WESTERN STORIES
... the pastoral of popular modern literature is the Western story....

"First Essay: Historical Criticism: Theory of Modes" (1957), *Anatomy of Criticism: Four Essays* (2006), CW, 22.

WHITMAN, WALT
This was also the "democratic" voice that Whitman attempted to reproduce, and Whitman is the godfather of all the folk singing and other oral developments of our time which cover so large an area of contemporary popular culture.

The Modern Century (1967), *Northrop Frye on Modern Culture* (2003), CW, 11.

WHOLENESS
How do we understand the wholeness of a work of art? By studying the parts. But how do we understand the significance of the parts? By studying the whole.

Entry, Notebook 44 (1986–91), 547, *Northrop Frye's Late Notebooks, 1982–1990: Architecture of the Spiritual World* (2000), CW, 5.

WILDE, OSCAR
He is one of our few genuinely prophetic writers, and, as with other prophets, every-

thing he writes seems either to lead up to his tragic confrontation with society or reflect back on it.
> Creation and Recreation (1980), Northrop Frye on Religion (2000), CW, 4.

WILL

Not only is the popular will wrong as often as right, but when it doesn't have a liberal goal it's *always* wrong.
> Entry, Notebook 50 (1987–90), 763, Northrop Frye's Late Notebooks, 1982–1990: Architecture of the Spiritual World (2000), CW, 5.

I am saying that no improvement in the human situation can take place independently of the human will to improve, and that confidence in automatic or impersonal improvement is always misplaced.
> The Modern Century (1967), Northrop Frye on Modern Culture (2003), CW, 11.

I have always held that when will is informed by a vision the antithesis between free will & compulsion of the will disappears.
> Entry, Notebook 24 (1970–72), 55, The "Third Book" Notebooks of Northrop Frye, 1964–1972: The Critical Comedy (2002), CW, 9.

As I've said so often, living things are animated by a continuous will, and the continuity of the will accounts for the sense of identity between infancy and old age of the "same" person.
> Entry, Notes 54.1 (May 1990), 72, Northrop Frye's Late Notebooks, 1982–1990: Architecture of the Spiritual World (2000), CW, 6.

WINNIPEG

Also that Winnipeg now, as probably 1000 years ago, is a centre of Icelandic culture.
> Entry, Notebook 34 (1946–50), 20, Northrop Frye's Notebooks on Romance (2004), CW, 15.

I feel a close sympathy with a man I met in England who was moving out to a job at Port Credit, which is a dozen miles southwest of Toronto. He was particularly pleased because he had heard that Port Credit was west of Toronto, so he assumed that it would be near Winnipeg, and he would get the best of both worlds.

"Education — Protection against Futility" (1964), Northrop Frye's Writings on Education (2001), CW, 7.

WINTER, CANADIAN

When all the intelligence, morality, reverence, and simian cunning of man confronts a sphinx-like riddle of the indefinite like the Canadian winter, the man seems as helpless as a trapped mink and as lonely as a loon. His thrifty little heaps of civilized values look pitiful beside nature's apparently meaningless power to waste and destroy on a superhuman scale, and such a nature suggests an equally ruthless and subconscious God, or else no God.
> "Canada and Its Poetry" (1943), Northrop Frye on Canada (2003), CW, 12.

WISDOM

The myth of ancestral wisdom goes with the authority of seniors, the anxiety of continuity, the sense of the need for preserving the tried and tested way, the supreme virtues of prudence and precedent.
> "The Beginning of the Word" (1980), Northrop Frye's Writings on Education (2001), CW, 7.

The wise man is not necessarily the man who knows the answer, but the kind of person who knows potential situations, who knows the way to deal with the kind of thing that may happen.
> "Symbolism in the Bible" (1981–82), Northrop Frye's Notebooks and Lectures on the Bible and Other Religious Texts (2003), CW, 13.

The wise person is the person who we feel could meet any number of potential situations in a roughly consistent and yet flexible way.
> "Education and the Rejection of Reality" (1971), Northrop Frye's Writings on Education (2001), CW, 7.

Wisdom is the human capacity to apply knowledge, and hence if knowledge is progressive wisdom must be progressive too, so that the wisdom of the past derives its vitality from its relevance to the present.
> "Trends in Modern Culture" (1952), Northrop Frye on Modern Culture (2003), CW, 11.

Knowledge is knowledge *of* something: wisdom is a sense of the potential rather than the actual, a practical knowledge ready to meet whatever eventualities may occur, rather than a specific knowledge of this or that subject.
"The University and Personal Life: Student Anarchism and the Educational Contract" (1968), *Northrop Frye's Writings on Education* (2001), CW, 7.

Wise and good are words that cannot possibly end any sentence starting with "I am."
"To Come to Light" (1988), *Northrop Frye on Religion* (1999), CW, 4.

There has always been a different conception of wisdom, the conception preserved in the popular proverbs and fables which from ancient times have been among the few really democratic literary genres. This wisdom consists in the possession, by the community as a whole, of the essential axioms for sanity and survival.
"Teaching the Humanities Today" (1977), *Northrop Frye's Writings on Education* (2001), CW, 7.

If we do what has always been done, our actions have the dignity of tradition behind them; if we do what is done around us, our actions have the authority of the community behind them. The wise man is thus a representative of a larger human body, and ultimately the whole human race comes to a focus in him.
"Wisdom and Knowledge" (1973), *Northrop Frye on Religion* (2000), CW, 4.

Wisdom is thus the individual's growth out of tradition. The bee's flight is wisdom; his load of pollen knowledge.
Entry, Notebook 27 (1986), 12, *Northrop Frye's Late Notebooks, 1982–1990: Architecture of the Spiritual World* (2000), CW, 5.

The elders are wiser because they have had more experience in that wisdom of prudence that maintains their stability from one day to the next.
"Symbolism in the Bible" (1981–82), *Northrop Frye's Notebooks and Lectures on the Bible and Other Religious Texts* (2003), CW, 13.

One conception I stumbled over by accident was that of the *apocryphon*, the book hidden or sealed up in a bad time to be released at the right time.
Entry, Notebook 12 (1968–70), 296, *The "Third Book" Notebooks of Northrop Frye, 1964–1972: The Critical Comedy* (2002), CW, 9.

Wisdom is the application of the imaginative vision taught us by art.
"Part One: The Argument," *Fearful Symmetry: A Study of William Blake* (1947, 2004), CW, 14.

There is no group wisdom, though the wise must recognize each other: there is no church except in the mutual recognition of those who respond to prophecy.
Entry, Notebook 44 (1986–91), 524, *Northrop Frye's Late Notebooks, 1982–1990: Architecture of the Spiritual World* (2000), CW, 5.

Knowledge is of the actual: wisdom is rather a sense of the potential, a sense, rather, of the *kind* of thing that one should know.
"Symbolism in the Bible" (1981–82), *Northrop Frye's Notebooks and Lectures on the Bible and Other Religious Texts* (2003), CW, 13.

WISHING

But clearly anything that men have made can be unmade by other men, and in the last few years there has been a dramatic development of the sense that wishing can be a concrete and revolutionary force: that we don't have to live with the mistakes of the past if we don't want to.
"On Teaching Literature" (1972), *Northrop Frye's Writings on Education* (2001), CW, 7.

WIT

Wit detaches the reader; the oracle absorbs him.
"Fourth Essay: Rhetorical Criticism: Theory of Genres" (1957), *Anatomy of Criticism: Four Essays* (2006), CW, 22.

But perhaps wit is the epiphany of oracular mystery — hence the recovery of the power of laughter in the cave of Trophonius.
Entry, Notebook 12 (1968–70), 192, *The "Third Book" Notebooks of Northrop Frye, 1964–1972: The Critical Comedy* (2002), CW, 9.

What distinguishes, not simply the epigram, but profundity itself from platitude is not frequently rhetorical wit. In fact it may be doubted whether we ever really call an idea profound unless we are pleased with the wit of its expression.

The Well-Tempered Critic (1963).

WODEHOUSE, P.G.

If he has a special fondness for P.G. Wodehouse, he may discover not only that Wodehouse is the most conventionalized of modern comic writers, but that the conventions used are identical with those of Plautus.

"Nature and Homer" (1958), *"The Educated Imagination" and Other Writings on Critical Theory, 1933–1936* (2006), CW, 21.

WOMEN

Eve initiates the fall, i.e. man falls as sexual being: hence man must be redeemed by woman (the Virgin in Catholic thought).

Entry, Notebook 44 (1986–91), 18, *Northrop Frye's Late Notebooks, 1982–1990: Architecture of the Spiritual World* (2000), CW, 5.

... even into an era in which the word "ladies" has become simply the vocative case of "females."

"Stanley Llewellyn Osborne" (1971), *Northrop Frye on Religion* (2000), CW, 4.

I suppose that in any society the fact that women bear children will condition some of their behaviour, but beyond that I doubt that it's possible to risk a single generalization about what men or women are like that doesn't amount merely to an observation of a certain kind of society.

Entry, 7 Apr. 1952, 232, *The Diaries of Northrop Frye: 1942–1955* (2001), CW, 8.

I suppose the notion of carrying around an embryonic male is so natural to a woman that it's at a depth he can't reach.

Entry, Notebook 50 (1987–90), 12, *Northrop Frye's Late Notebooks, 1982–1990: Architecture of the Spiritual World* (2000), CW, 5.

All the awards this year are won by men, and in front of the successful male writer there is usually a wife, keeping, if not the wolf from the door, at any rate the magazine salesman, the milkman, the census taker, the questionnaire filler, the Girl Guide cookies, the cancer society subscriptions, and other interruptions of the flowing rhythms of verse and prose. So the wives are to be honoured too.

"Governor General's Awards (II)" (1964), *Northrop Frye on Canada* (2003), CW, 12.

The attention they put on clothes & physical appearance indicates that it is impossible really to fool them about the relation of mind to body, & this close relationship extends to the fact that their range of interests is very closely proportional to their eyesight: their bodies first, then their homes & families, then their acquaintances, & business, politics & abstract ideas a background haze.

Entry, Notebook 3 (1946–48), 17, *Northrop Frye's Notebooks and Lectures on the Bible and Other Religious Texts* (2003), CW, 13.

WOODSTOCK FESTIVAL

There isn't really all that much difference between a revival and a rally. Woodstock, I think, was a rather pathetic illusion that somehow or other you could, again, break through the crust of history and get into a different way of existence altogether by a kind of emotional release. Then of course you had that horrible business afterwards with the motorcycle people.

"Between Paradise and Apocalypse" (1978), referring to the Woodstock and Altamont music festivals, which were accompanied by acts of violence, *Interviews with Northrop Frye* (2008), CW, 24.

WOOLF, VIRGINIA

She was a great novelist, with a conscience about form and structure more Continental than English.

"Virginia Woolf" (1948), *Northrop Frye on Twentieth-Century Literature* (2010), CW, 29.

WORD, THE

The opening words of the Gospel of John, "In the beginning was the Word," are regarded as the most sacred utterance in Christianity, and it is very largely because of

that that churches still have lecterns in the shape of an eagle.
> "Symbolism in the Bible" (1981–82), the eagle being the symbol of John, *Northrop Frye's Notebooks and Lectures on the Bible and Other Religious Texts* (2003), CW, 13.

In this world the Word of God is the aggregate of works of inspired art, the Scripture written by the Holy Spirit which spoke by the prophets.
> "Part One: The Argument," *Fearful Symmetry: A Study of William Blake* (1947, 2004), CW, 14.

Why does the Word have to become flesh? Presumably so that mythically it can accomplish a quest, and metaphorically identify all the categories of being.
> Entry, Notebook 44 (1986–91), 168, *Northrop Frye's Late Notebooks, 1982–1990: Architecture of the Spiritual World* (2000), CW, 5.

In English there is one l of a difference between the Creator & the Creature, the Word & the World.
> Entry, Notebook 30n (1946–50), 2, *Northrop Frye's Notebooks on Romance* (2004), CW, 15.

... you can never get rid of God as long as you continue to use words, because all words are part of the Word.
> "The Great Teacher" (1989), *Interviews with Northrop Frye* (2008), CW, 24.

The Spirit deconstructs the Word.
> Entry, Notebook 27 (1986), 116, *Northrop Frye's Late Notebooks, 1982–1990: Architecture of the Spiritual World* (2000), CW, 5.

WORDS

We use words in two ways: to make statements and arguments and convey information, or what passes as such, and to appeal to the imagination. The former is the province of history, philosophy, and the social sciences; the latter is the province of literature. There is also a large intermediate area of what is called rhetoric, the art of verbal persuasion, where both means are employed.
> "Humanities in a New World" (1958), *Northrop Frye's Writings on Education* (2001), CW, 7.

The poet, in the ancient phrase, unlocks the word hoard, but the word hoard is not a cupboard: it is something more like a world that our senses have filtered out, and that only poets can bring to awareness.
> "Approaching the Lyric" (1982), *"The Secular Scripture" and Other Writings on Critical Theory, 1976–1991* (2006), CW, 18.

What makes a word a word is its difference from all other words, but what makes verbal arrangement, or syntax, possible is the opposite: a prehensile quality that words have of linking up with one another.
> "The Symbol as a Medium of Exchange" (1984), *"The Secular Scripture" and Other Writings on Critical Theory, 1976–1991* (2006), CW, 18.

What words do most powerfully and most accurately and most persuasively is to hang together.
> "Symbolism in the Bible" (1981–82), *Northrop Frye's Notebooks and Lectures on the Bible and Other Religious Texts* (2003), CW, 13.

What words primarily exist to do is to express metaphors and build up myths. Those are the things that are true because they are impossible to understand.
> "Easter" (1973), *Interviews with Northrop Frye* (2008), CW, 24.

My whole life is words: nothing is of value in life except finding verbal formulations that make sense. Yet the great secret in reserve is something you can't read unless you shut up. That's what Zen has to communicate. And how does it communicate? By flooding the world with books about silence. Words are to us what water is to fish: dwelling-house of being....
> Entry, Notebook 50 (1987–90), 52, *Northrop Frye's Late Notebooks, 1982–1990: Architecture of the Spiritual World* (2000), CW, 5.

The thing which is to me so important about the other religions, particularly Christianity, is that they keep the words "eternal" and "infinite" right in the middle of experience, and as long as they are there you don't get claustrophobia.

"Into the Wilderness" (1969), *Interviews with Northrop Frye* (2008), CW, 24.

The verbal universe transcends history, & so it presents all writers as contemporaneous. It transcends philosophy, & so far as I can see at present it is only in the verbal universe that all religions are one.
> Entry, Notebook 38 (1952–55), 16, *Notebooks for "Anatomy of Criticism"* (2007), CW, 23.

If you are carefully taught to put words together at eight, you stand a chance of being able to put ideas together — for ideas *are* words — at eighteen. No words, no ideas. No ideas, no thought. No thought, no free society.
> "For Whom the Dunce Cap Fits" (1952), *Northrop Frye's Writings on Education* (2001), CW, 7.

The agility of language in chasing red herrings has caused some religious traditions to make a cult of the wordless, even to the point of writing books by the score about the utter inadequacy of words to convey genuine experience.
> "Language II," *The Great Code* (1982), *The Great Code: The Bible and Literature* (2006), CW, 19.

What you believe in, in the age of belief, is ultimately in the sequaciousness of words. That's where I get my principle that if you just write enough sentences you can "reconcile" anything with anything else.
> Entry, Notes 54-5 (1976), 98, *Northrop Frye's Notebooks and Lectures on the Bible and Other Religious Texts* (2003), CW, 13.

The first & last epiphanies of God, creation and apocalypse, correspond to the first & last appearance of the human being, birth & death. I'd like to know how far words can go in exploring the silences and mysteries surrounding these events.
> Entry, Notebook 44 (1986–91), 730, *Northrop Frye's Late Notebooks, 1982–1990: Architecture of the Spiritual World* (2000), CW, 5.

WORDS OF POWER

It is the function of literature, as I see it, to recreate the primitive conception of the word of power, the metaphor that unites the subject and the object.
> "Criticism as Education" (1979), *Northrop Frye's Writings on Education* (2001), CW, 7.

All myths are speculative — that means they're in a mirror. Science is popularly supposed to reverse mythology, but it's something else. Reversed, & out of the mirror, mythology is the word with power.
> Entry, Notebook 23 (early 1980s), 52, *Northrop Frye's Notebooks and Lectures on the Bible and Other Religious Texts* (2003), CW, 13.

Words without power don't matter: power without words inevitably turn into genocide, and then to self-genocide.
> Entry, Notebook 44 (1986–91), 518, *Northrop Frye's Late Notebooks, 1982–1990: Architecture of the Spiritual World* (2000), CW, 5.

WORK

Work and leisure are different aspects of the same person (according to the Bible they are even different aspects of the activity of God, in a ratio of six to one).
> "Criticism as Education" (1979), *Northrop Frye's Writings on Education* (2001), CW, 7.

Orare est laborare. Working at what one can do is a sacrament.
> Entry, Notebook 44 (1986–90), 1, *Northrop Frye's Late Notebooks, 1982–1990: Architecture of the Spiritual World* (2000), CW, 5.

But from Biblical times there has been a tendency to regard work as partial reparation for what the soul in a poem of Yeats calls "the crime of birth."
> "The Definition of a University" (1970), *Northrop Frye's Writings on Education* (2001), CW, 7.

A job that permits one to spend an hour in the line of duty talking to an attractive young girl with a quick mind is a pleasant job.
> Entry, 17 Mar. 1952, 184, *The Diaries of Northrop Frye: 1942–1955* (2001), CW, 8.

I'm a Methodist; I hate taking time from the Lord's work. The Lord's work for me is sitting still in a comfortable chair thinking beautiful thoughts, & occasionally writing them down. This also happens to be what I like to do, which just shows you how wise the Lord is.

Entry, 12 Feb. 1949, 183, *The Diaries of Northrop Frye: 1942–1955* (2001), CW, 8.

The really privileged person is not the man who has no work to do, but the man who works freely, and has voluntarily assumed his duties in the light of his conception of himself and his social function.

"Humanities in a New World" (1958), *Northrop Frye's Writings on Education* (2001), CW, 7.

What I am saying is that if you look forward to the future, with the expectation of identifying your lives with a definite body of work achieved, you are doomed to the bitterest disappointment.

"Baccalaureate Sermon" (1967), *Northrop Frye on Religion* (2000), CW, 4.

WORKS, GOOD

I am inclined to think that faith and what I am calling vision are the parents, and works are their offspring.

"Notes for 'The Dialectic of Belief and Vision'" (1983), 33, *Northrop Frye's Fiction and Miscellaneous Writings* (2007), CW, 25.

WORLDS

The New Testament tells us that there is another world that makes considerably more sense, and that this other world is not up in the sky or waiting for us after death, but is directly in front of us. It is in fact, the same world as the newspaper and television world, and we are living in it when we open our eyes and stop holding our breath.

"A Breath of Fresh Air" (1980), *Northrop Frye on Religion* (2000), CW, 4.

Not only is the world we live in a phantasmagoria, it is also a world which seems to be dominated by an almost continuous hysteria.

"Education and the Rejection of Reality" (1971), *Northrop Frye's Writings on Education* (2001), CW, 7.

We live in a world that got along without us for billions of years, and could still get along without us, in fact still may.

"Criticism as Education" (1979), *Northrop Frye's Writings on Education* (2001), CW, 7.

I think that man lives in two worlds. There's the world of external nature, which I assume it's the function of the physical sciences to study. Then there's the world of man's own culture and civilization, and he understands this world verbally by a mythological structure.

"A Literate Person Is First and Foremost an Articulate Person" (1977), *Interviews with Northrop Frye* (2008), CW, 24.

What fun if one could get just a peep at what some of the other worlds are that a new humanity could create — no, live in.

Entry, Notebook 24 (1970–72), 72, *The "Third Book" Notebooks of Northrop Frye, 1964–1972: The Critical Comedy* (2002), CW, 9.

WRATH

When we speak of the death of Christ as appeasing or atoning for the wrath of the Father, we mean that the death of Christ on the cross makes it possible for man to see a few other things besides hell.

"The Leap in the Dark" (1971), *Northrop Frye on Religion* (2000), CW, 4.

The wrath of God is not some senile ghost throwing a tantrum in the sky: the wrath of God is the revelation to man of the hell that man has made of his life on this earth.

"The Leap in the Dark" (1971), *Northrop Frye on Religion* (2000), CW, 4.

WRITERS

In every age there is a large group of writers who seem to be more or less all the same size. Those who eventually turn out to be the greatest writers are seldom wholly ignored in their own day; but even more seldom are they regarded as greatly superior to their contemporaries.

"Nature Methodized " (1960), *Northrop Frye's Writings on the Eighteenth and Nineteenth Centuries* (2005), CW, 17.

If people are morally smug, they will think their writers blasphemous; if they are sodden with integration and adjustment, they will

think their writers neurotic; if they accept a way of life, they will think their writers subversive. Sometimes, of course, they will be right....
> "Culture and the National Will" (1957), *Northrop Frye on Canada* (2003), CW, 12.

You don't find a twenty-thousand-foot mountain on a flat plain: you find it in a mountain range, where it's surrounded with a lot of others like it.
> "Language as the Home of Human Life" (1985), referring to contemporary writers, *Northrop Frye's Writings on Education* (2001), CW, 7.

It is possible that a substantial proportion of our genuinely "creative" writers may work in such peripheral genres as journalism, popular science, criticism, comic strips, or biography. If so, they will not be turning from literature to life, but exploring different literary conventions.
> "Nature and Homer" (1958), *"The Educated Imagination" and Other Writings on Critical Theory, 1933–1963* (2006), CW, 21.

Whatever people do, most of their best writers will be doing the opposite.
> "Culture and the National Will" (1957), *Northrop Frye on Canada* (2003), CW, 12.

Writers don't interpret national characters; they create them.
> "Culture and the National Will" (1957), *Northrop Frye on Canada* (2003), CW, 12.

WRITERS, CANADIAN
There are no Canadian writers, but there are southern Ontario writers, British Columbian writers, Maritime writers, and Quebec writers. When you add them all together, you get a Canadian culture with a distinctive feeling of its own.
> "Northrop Frye in Conversation" (1989), *Interviews with Northrop Frye* (2008), CW, 24.

There is no Canadian writer of whom we can say what we can say of the world's major writers, that their readers can grow up inside their work without ever being aware of a circumference.
> "Conclusion to *Literary History of Canada*" (1965), *Northrop Frye on Canada* (2003), CW, 12.

Today there are about a dozen Canadian writers who are world figures, and at least another dozen who should be.
> "Preface to *On Education*" (1988), *Northrop Frye's Writings on Education* (2001), CW, 7.

WRITING
Nobody's *work* is inherently revolutionary or reactionary, whatever the writer's own views in his lifetime: it is the use made of the work which determines what it is, and any writer may be potentially useful to anybody, in any way.
> *The Critical Path: An Essay on the Social Context of Literary Criticism* (1971), *"The Critical Path" and Other Writings on Critical Theory, 1963–1975* (2009), CW, 27.

The pen is not mightier than the sword, or even the plumb line or chisel; it just lasts longer.
> "Harold Innis" (1982), 12, *Northrop Frye's Fiction and Miscellaneous Writings* (2007), CW, 25.

In fact the attempts to bring words as near as possible to the more repetitive and emphatic rhythm of music or the more concentrated stasis of painting make up the main body of what is usually called experimental writing.
> "Fourth Essay: Rhetorical Criticism: Theory of Genres" (1957), *Anatomy of Criticism: Four Essays* (2006), CW, 22.

Live while you write, and then your writing will be vital accordingly.
> "NF to HK," 9 Jul. 1934, *The Correspondence of Northrop Frye and Helen Kemp, 1932–1939* (1996), CW, 1.

The conviction that written language is normally prose, that its unit is the sentence, and that a period goes at the end of it is one that twelve years of concentrated teaching often fails to evoke.
> "The Developing Imagination" (1962), *Northrop Frye's Writings on Education* (2001), CW, 7.

Writing is an exciting, precise, subtle, difficult business, like a piano recital. It's no job for a weakling....

"NF to HK," 9 Jul. 1934, *The Correspondence of Northrop Frye and Helen Kemp, 1932–1939* (1996), CW, 1.

I think the extent to which one's reading has an influence on one's writing is very hard to verbalize. We're tied up in words the wrong way, and we often assume that whatever we can't put into words is unreal; but there's no question that one's reading puts fuel on the fire and keeps it burning.

"A Literate Person Is First and Foremost an Articulate Person" (1977), *Interviews with Northrop Frye* (2008), CW, 24.

I do not trust any way of teaching writing except composition from models, feeling one's way into the idiom of cultivated prose.

"The Beginning of the Word" (1980), *Northrop Frye's Writings on Education* (2001), CW, 7.

I remember very vividly writing an article for *Canadian Forum*. The introduction grew and grew until I felt I'd have to publish the article in two sections. But after the introduction had itself grown to the length of a full-sized article, a little voice in my ear said I should keep only one sentence of it. After a good deal of resistance, I cut the project down to a single article and kept the one sentence.

"Maintaining Freedom in Paradise" (1982), *Interviews with Northrop Frye* (2008), CW, 24.

X, Y, Z

Y2K

Everything has been predicted for the year 2000, ranging from the total annihilation of the human race to the coming of the millennium. I imagine that what will actually happen will fall somewhere between these two things.

"On *The Great Code* (II)" (1982), *Interviews with Northrop Frye* (2008), CW, 24.

YIPPIE MOVEMENT

In some of the protests of "yippies" and other groups today I detect a note of some desperation. Society does not hate them enough: they have not the prophetic authority to strike at our deeper fears, and are themselves involved in the panic they create.

"The Ethics of Change: The Role of the University" (1968), *Northrop Frye's Writings on Education* (2001), CW, 7.

YOGA

There doesn't seem to be a recognized yoga of art, not that it matters, for there is one anyway, and I don't have to pretend to myself, as I should to students, that I know what it means. Suppose I call it Sutra-Yoga. Sutra, like strophe & verse, means the turn, the vortical twist of the mind in the imagined form.

Entry, Notebook 3 (1946–48), 47, *Northrop Frye's Notebooks and Lectures on the Bible and Other Religious Texts* (2003), CW, 13.

The "yoga" intuition is founded on the notion of transforming the body, & I don't know if there's any Christian alternative answer to it. Our present body is almost wholly unknown to the consciousness which inhabits it. Yoga creates an imaginative body in its place, & goes to work on that.

Entry, Notebook 24 (1970–72), 233, *The "Third Book" Notebooks of Northrop Frye, 1964–1972: The Critical Comedy* (2002), CW, 9.

Yoga is the voluntary suppression of the involuntary actions of the mind. We're all born with a natural yoga: we're freed by objective energy and our consciousness freezes it into matter. Matter is mater, the mother. Materialism, dogmatism, the authority of elders and impotent kings, all assist the freezing process. A higher discipline that would freeze the mind could liberate the spirit.

Entry, Notebook 11h (1980s), 24, *Northrop Frye's Late Notebooks, 1982–1990: Architecture of the Spiritual World* (2000), CW, 6.

YOUTH

I say that I was impressed, because, at the age of seventeen, I was not easy to impress. I knew the answers to a great many more questions than I know now.

"Opening Ceremonies of the E.J. Pratt Memorial Room" (1964), referring to his senior colleagues Pelham Edgar, E.J. Pratt, and John Robins, *Northrop Frye on Canada* (2003), CW, 12.

Perhaps it is as dangerous to eliminate the adolescent in us as it is to eliminate the child.

"Lord Byron" (1959), *Northrop Frye's Writings on the Eighteenth and Nineteenth Centuries* (2005), CW, 17.

ZEN BUDDHISM

I can't make any sense out of these infernal Sutras: they seem designed for people who really can't read.

Entry, Notes 53 (1989–90), 17, referring to the Avatamska Sutra, *Northrop Frye's Late Notebooks, 1982–1990: Architecture of the Spiritual World* (2000), CW, 6.

I think I'll look up the Zen Buddhists, who decided that the best way to follow Buddha was to tell him to go to hell.

> Entry, Notebook 3 (1946–48), 59, *Northrop Frye's Notebooks and Lectures on the Bible and Other Religious Texts* (2003), CW, 13.

What it does is to try to present the world in the form in which you habitually see it, as absurd, so that you break it down through absurdity. And then what you see is what's really there, which has been hidden from you by your previous conditioning.

> "Between Paradise and Apocalypse" (1978), *Interviews with Northrop Frye* (2008), CW, 24.

Empty space is something, namely space; the act of perceiving it is an event in time. No matter. I suppose all Zen "koans" are really about that.

> Entry, Notebook 11f (1969–70), 164, *Northrop Frye's Notebooks and Lectures on the Bible and Other Religious Texts* (2003), CW, 13.

ZEND, ROBERT

He was a notably free and unfettered spirit who was among us for a while, and who, now that he is gone, is irreplaceable. All we can do is read and admire what he has left us.

> "Tribute to Robert Zend" (1985), *Northrop Frye on Canada* (2003), CW, 12.

ZODIAC

The twelvefold Zodiac thus represents, as it does in *Europe*, idolatry in the aggregate: that is, as the twelve sons of Jacob stand for the whole human race, so the Zodiac stands for all the false gods invented by man and suggested by an external nature, specifically the stars.

> "Part Three: "The City of God," referring to Blake's long poem, *Fearful Symmetry: A Study of William Blake* (2004), CW, 14.

Acknowledgements

The foremost acknowledgement is owed to the late Northrop Frye ... *fons et origo* ... without whom there would be no book in the first place. He once explained, "I've always wanted to write "my own" book of *pensées*. The disadvantage of this project is that it can't be planned." Here is his own book, planned.

I am pleased to recognize the contributions of many other men and women. A number of years ago, Roseann Runte, in her capacity as president of Victoria University in the University of Toronto and as representative of the estate of the late author, agreed that the present project was a worthy one. President Paul Gooch and executive assistant Gillian Pearson agreed with her. Work proceeded at the Northrop Frye Centre at Victoria University while the editing and indexing of the series of thirty volumes in the series *The Collected Works of Northrop Frye* were underway, and where I was welcomed as a Fellow of the Northrop Frye Centre.

I am indebted to Alvin A. Lee, general editor of the series, for his enthusiasm and dedication, and to Associate Editor Jean O'Grady, for professional assistance and personal courtesies. Dr. O'Grady served in two capacities: as a Paladium of knowledge and as an ever-helpful Virgil. In point of fact, she cast her editorial eye over the entire text and made innumerable suggestions for corrections and improvements. Her biographical appreciation, included here, is based on addresses that she has delivered in Canada and is a revised version of the essay that appears on her website. Work on the *Collected Works* was assisted by scores of other scholars — editors, researchers, redactors, annotators, interpreters, et cetera. Special note must be made of the contributions of Robert D. Denham, a most knowledgeable scholar; he compiled *Northrop Frye Unbuttoned* (2004), an amusing glance at Frye's lighter moments taken from the notebooks and diaries unpublished at the time. Unfailingly helpful were the librarians and staff members of the E.J. Pratt Library, Victoria University.

I am grateful to Kirk Howard, the publisher of Dundurn Press, for his interest in this undertaking, and also to Beth Bruder, vice-president, for her enthusiasm and expertise. I would like to note, too, the advice and assistance that I received from all of the staff at Dundurn. In particular, I wish to thank Dominic Farrell, who supplied editorial advice; Jesse Hooper, for his work designing the cover and interior of the book; Sheila Douglas, for her help on the contracts; and Jim Hatch, for coordinating the publicity for the book.

With past publications I have acknowledged the contributions made by friends and associates. I will do so again with respect to the present publication. Among the colleagues are Philip Singer, special librarian, Toronto Public Libraries; my long-time researcher, the late Mary Alice Neal; Felice and Frank Spitzer, who supplied computer support; researcher Nicholas Graham; colleagues Ted Davy, Cyril Greenland, and David Gotlib.

Finally, I would be seriously remiss if I failed to note with affection the companionship of my wife, Ruth.

Bibliography

Collected Works of Northrop Frye

The project of producing a scholarly, uniform edition of the *Collected Works of Northrop Frye* (1912–91) grew from modest beginnings in 1993 to the full flowering of the final index volume in 2012. The project was funded by grants from the Michael G. DeGroote family through McMaster University; from the Social Sciences & Humanities Research Council of Canada; from Victoria University, University of Toronto; from the Lilly Endowment; and from the Gelber Foundation. The project proceeded in the Northrop Frye Centre, Victoria University, under the general editorship of Alvin A. Lee, with day-to-day operations supervised by associate editor Jean O'Grady, aided by editorial assistants Margaret Burgess, Ward McBurney, and Erin Reynolds, student helpers, and scholars, researchers, and editors in Canada and abroad. What follows is a list of the thirty volumes, arranged in order of volume number, published by the University of Toronto Press.

The Correspondence of Northrop Frye and Helen Kemp, 1932–1939. Ed. Robert D. Denham. CW, 1-2, 1996.
Northrop Frye's Student Essays, 1932–1938. Ed. Robert D. Denham. CW, 3, 1997.
Northrop Frye on Religion: Excluding "The Great Code" and "Words with Power." Ed. Alvin A. Lee and Jean O'Grady. CW, 4, 1999.
Northrop Frye's Late Notebooks, 1982–1990: Architecture of the Spiritual World. Ed. Robert D. Denham. CW, 5-6, 2002.
Northrop Frye's Writings on Education. Ed. Jean O'Grady and Goldwin French. CW, 7, 2001.
The Diaries of Northrop Frye, 1942–1955. Ed. Robert D. Denham. CW, 8, 2001.
The "Third Book" Notebooks of Northrop Frye: The Critical Comedy, 1964–1972. Ed. Michael Dolzani. CW, 9, 2002.
Northrop Frye on Literature and Society, 1936–1989: Unpublished Papers. Ed. Robert D. Denham. CW, 10, 2002.

Northrop Frye on Modern Culture. Ed. Jan Gorak. CW, 11, 2003.

Northrop Frye on Canada. Ed. Jean O'Grady and David Staines. CW, 12, 2003.

Northrop Frye's Notebooks and Lectures on the Bible and Other Religious Texts. Ed. Robert D. Denham. CW, 13, 2003.

Fearful Symmetry: A Study of William Blake. Ed. Nicholas Halmi. CW, 14, 2004.

Northrop Frye's Notebooks on Romance. Ed. Michael Dolzani. CW, 15, 2004.

Northrop Frye on Milton and Blake. Ed. Angela Esterhammer. CW, 16, 2005.

Northrop Frye's Writings on the Eighteenth and Nineteenth Centuries. Ed. Imre Salusinskzy. CW, 17, 2005.

"The Secular Scripture" and Other Writings on Critical Theory, 1976–1991. Ed. Joseph Adamson and Jean Wilson. CW, 18, 2006.

The Great Code: The Bible and Literature. Ed. Alvin A. Lee. CW, 19, 2006.

Northrop Frye's Notebooks on Renaissance Literature. Ed. Michael Dolzani. CW, 20, 2006.

"The Educated Imagination" and Other Writings on Critical Theory, 1933–1963. Ed. Germaine Warkentin. CW, 21, 2006.

Anatomy of Criticism: Four Essays. Ed. Robert D. Denham. CW, 22, 2007.

Northrop Frye's Notebooks for "Anatomy of Criticism." Ed. Robert D. Denham. CW, 23, 2007.

Interviews with Northrop Frye. Ed. Jean O'Grady. CW, 24, 2008.

Northrop Frye's Fiction and Miscellaneous Writings. Ed. Robert D. Denham and Michael Dolzani. CW, 25, 2007.

Words with Power: Being a Second Study of "The Bible and Literature." Ed. Michael Dolzani. CW, 26, 2008.

"The Critical Path" and Other Writings on Critical Theory, 1963–1975. Ed. Jean O'Grady and Eva Kushner. CW, 27, 2009.

Northrop Frye's Writings on Shakespeare and the Renaissance. Ed. Troni Grande and Garry Sherbert. CW, 28, 2010.

Northrop Frye on Twentieth-Century Literature. Ed. Glen Robert Gill. CW, 29, 2010.

Index to the Collected Works of Northrop Frye. Jean O'Grady. CW, 30, 2012.

www.ingramcontent.com/pod-product-compliance
Lightning Source LLC
Chambersburg PA
CBHW030333240426
43661CB00052B/1614